Feil/Lippert/Lozac'h/Palazzini
Atlas of Surgical Stapling

Atlas of Surgical Stapling

Edited by W. Feil, H. Lippert, P. Lozac'h, G. Palazzini

With Contributions by

B. Descottes, W. Feil, G.B. Grassi, H. Lippert, A. Longo, P. Lozac'h, M. Martelli, G. Palazzini, J. Sökeland

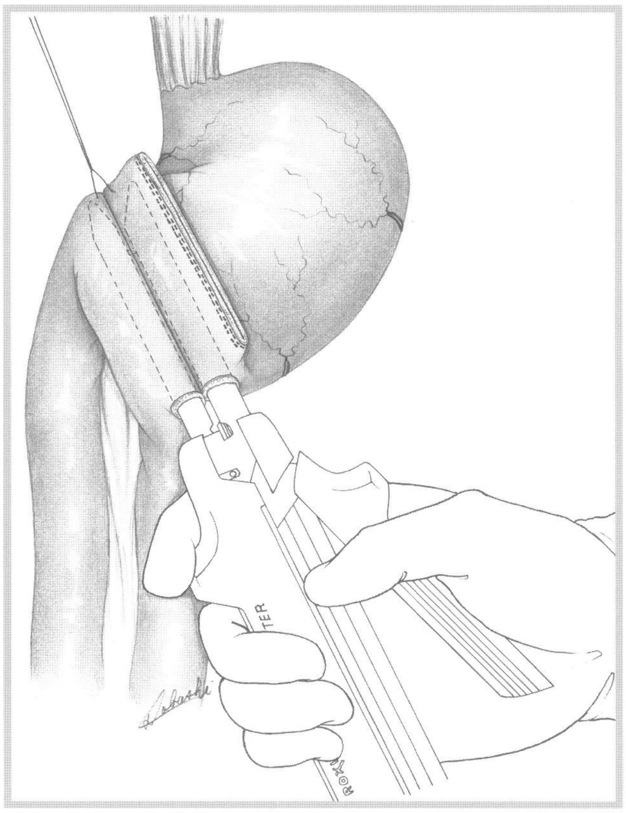

Johann Ambrosius Barth · Heidelberg

Contributors

Italy:	Prof. Dr. G.B. Grassi (Rome) Dr. A. Longo (Palermo) Prof. Dr. M. Martelli (Rome) Prof. Dr. G. Palazzini (Rome)
France:	Prof. Dr. B. Descottes (Limoges) Prof. Dr. P. Lozac'h (Brest)
Germany:	Prof. Dr. H. Lippert (Magdeburg) Prof. Dr. J. Sökeland (Dortmund)
Austria:	Prof. Dr. W. Feil (Vienna)

Die Deutsche Bibliothek – CIP-Einheitsaufnahme

Atlas of Surgical Stapling / ed. by W. Feil... With contributions by B. Descottes... -
Heidelberg : Barth, 2000
ISBN 3-8304-5064-8

The French, Greek, Italian, Spanish, Turkish and US edition of this Atlas can be obtained at Ethicon Endosurgery Europe GmbH, Hummelsbütteler Steindamm 71, 22851 Norderstedt, Germany

Typesetting: Ch. Molter, Heidelberg, Germany
Cover Design: Wachter Design, Schwetzingen, Germany
Printing and Binding: Kösel GmbH & Co. KG, Kempten, Germany

ISBN 3-8304-5064-8
ISBN 0-86577-906-6

Preface

Aims of the Atlas of Surgical Stapling

The main objective of this book is to serve as guide to the application of mechanical staplers and other surgical devices in different surgical procedures.

In the first part of the book, the history of stapling, the description of the various staplers and other technological aids, as well as the basic stapling techniques are dealt with in order to provide the reader with a broad understanding of the principles of surgical stapling.

In the second part of the book, each of the authors describes the application of mechanical staplers and other surgical devices, according to his surgical expertise and school of thought, which may differ from the opinions of other, equally valid schools or surgical practices.

The ultimate aim of this book is to provide the surgeon with a better understanding of, and insight into, the use of mechanical staplers and other devices in his daily surgical practice, enhancing surgery and thus improving patient care.

Contents

II Surgical Procedures

1 Thoracic Surgery

2 Oesophageal Surgery

3 Gastric Surgery

4 Pancreatic Surgery

5 Small Bowel Surgery

6 Large Bowel Surgery

7 Colorectal Surgery

8 Gynaecological Surgery

9 Urological Surgery

III References

I

Mechanical Stapling and other Surgical Devices

1 History of Mechanical Stapling

For centuries, surgeons have been aware of the importance of providing leak-proof and hemostatic wound closures. It was observed that a further key factor for success was to invert the tissue while performing closure or anastomosis. This has typically been achieved through the careful application of sutures. However, surgeons have more recently looked for better ways to close or anastomose tissues.

In 1826, Henroz, a surgeon from Belgium, presented a device made from two rings which allowed the surgeon to approximate everting tissues from two bowel segments, successfully using this device on dogs. Others started to work on devices or studies (Travers, Lembert, Denans) but without paying too much attention to the inversion or eversion of tissue.

In 1892, John B. Murphy from Chicago developed an anastomotic ring (Fig. 1a, b) which was intended to be used on cholecystoduodenostomies. This device became very popular and was then used for bowel and gastric anastomosis. Murphy proved that it was possible to create a mechanical device to perform an anastomosis; however, manual sutures were becoming more and more reliable and were often preferred to this kind of device. Adalbert Ramaugé, a South American surgeon, presented an anastomotic ring at about the same time, but this never became as popular.

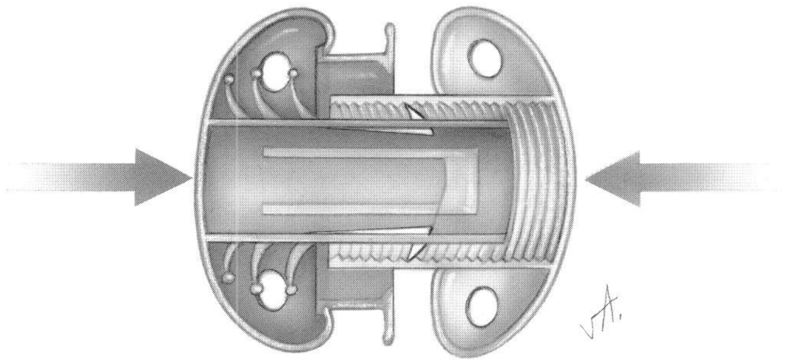

Fig. 1a Murphy ring: technical aspect

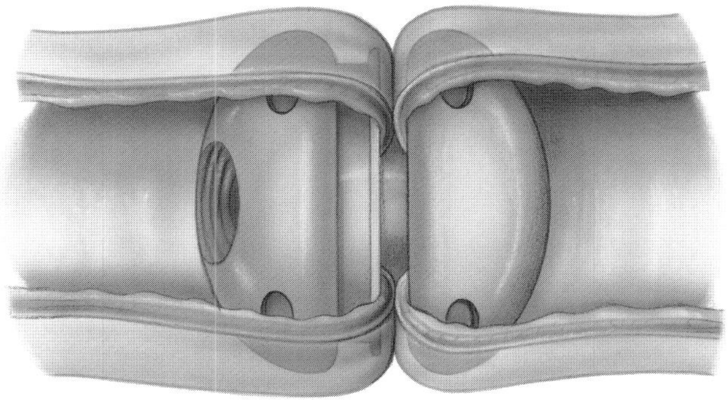

Fig. 1b Murphy ring in place

Many of the principles of mechanical stapling in surgery were defined by Humer Hültl from Budapest in 1909. The most important principles he focused on were:

1) tissue compression;
2) tissue stapling while using a metallic wire to form B-shaped staples;
3) configuration of the closed staple in B-shape form;
4) staggered positioning of two staple lines to perform the suture.

With the help of Victor Fischer, Hültl created an instrument used to close the stomach during gastrectomies (Fig. 2). The limitations of this instrument lay in its weight and bulk, and in 1921 Aladar von Petz, another Hungarian surgeon, created a light and easy-to-use instrument based on the same principles as Hültl's. This instrument was more readily adopted in the surgical field, even though it did not have a double-staggered staple line (Fig. 3).

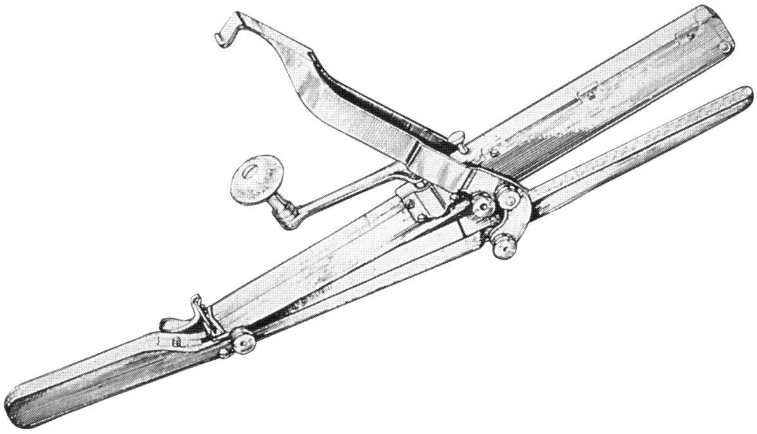

Fig. 2 Hültl stapler

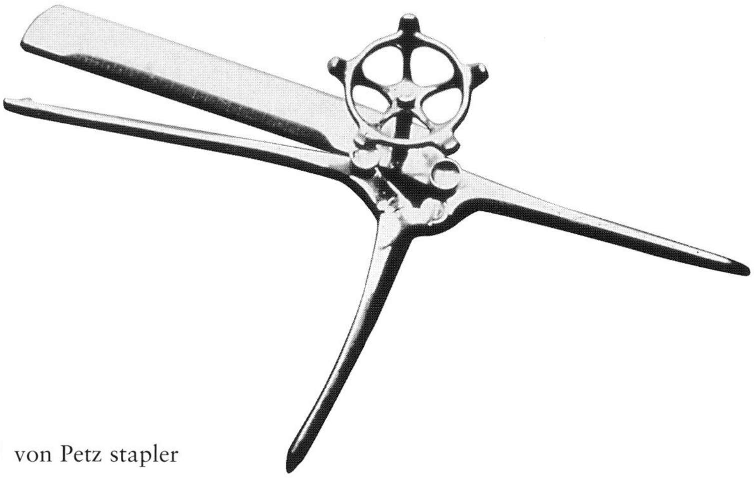

Fig. 3 von Petz stapler

Subsequently, this instrument was improved by H. Friedrich (Fig. 4) and Neuffer from Germany. The two main changes were: simultaneous tissue compression and staple firing, and the creation of cartridges which allowed the instrument to be used several times during the same operation. But still the staples were not placed in a staggered fashion. N. Nakayama from Japan further improved von Petz' instrument, but again without changing the staple position.

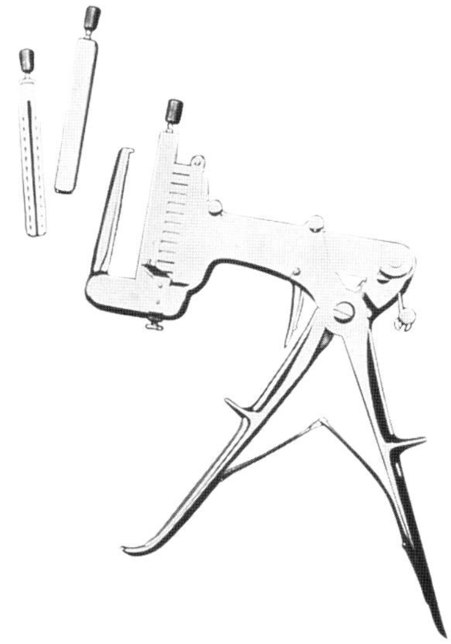

Fig. 4 Friedrich stapler

Many other instruments were developed but they were never used as often as that of von Petz. This was basically the first step in the development of mechanical sutures, where the principles of stapling were established. These instruments were good but not yet ideal.

The second step in the development of mechanical stapling in surgery started at the end of World War II in Moscow, USSR. Due to the size of the country and the disastrous effect the war had on the population, there was a general lack of surgeons, resulting in thousands of deaths.

There was a need for instruments which would allow inadequately trained surgeons to carry out standardised surgical treatments quickly in emergencies, because hospitals and care centres were few and far between. This was the reason for the foundation of the Scientific Institute for Surgical Devices and Instruments. During the Fifties many mechanical stapling devices were developed in this institute and began to be used widely throughout the country. Several instruments were created:

- Instruments for linear stapling, with reloadable cartridges using stainless steel staples. Many different models were built, but the principle remained of placing a double linear line of staples in order to close anatomical structures.

- Instruments to create side-by-side anastomosis with two bowel lumens. This type of instrument allowed the placement of two double lines of staples whilst simultaneously cutting between these lines.
- Instruments to create end-to-end or end-to-side circular anastomosis by approximating two segments of bowel in a circular way to create a new lumen, both segments being sealed with a single line of staples.

These instruments often needed a manually placed suture to complete the staple lines. They required a great deal of preparation before firing and considerable maintenance. They were, however, reliable, and were in use in the entire country.

The third step in the development of mechanical stapling started with the visit of the American surgeon Mark Ravitch to Kiev, where he saw a Russian surgeon using a mechanical stapler on a bronchus. Ravitch then worked in his laboratory in Baltimore on the whole range of Russian products to evaluate their performance. He then developed a totally new range of American instruments, founding a new company focused on surgical staplers. These products were quite different from the Russian ones:

- The staplers remained reusable, but the cartridges to be used with them were made of plastic containing staples already in place (pre-loaded). The cartridge was sterilised and placed in a single package and intended for single-patient use.
- The instruments were lighter and easier to use. They could deliver different lengths of staple lines.
- All the instruments delivered a double-staggered staple line, even the circular stapler, which was not the case with the first generation of Russian instruments.

Linear staplers, linear cutters, and circular staplers, still the main line of instruments, became widespread among American hospitals and all around the world during the Seventies.

The fourth and latest step in the development of mechanical staplers was the development of materials for single-patient use. At the end of the Seventies, surgeons became more and more aware of the risk of cross contamination and cost per procedure, and with the first complete single-use mechanical stapler launched by Ethicon in 1976 (a skin stapler) (Fig. 5), mechanical stapling manufacturers changed the way they manufactured their products by using more and more disposable parts.

Some manufacturers retained a number of reusable products in their product range. Ethicon aimed at an «exclusively single-patient use» option to ensure reliability, lower maintenance, and sterility of the staplers.

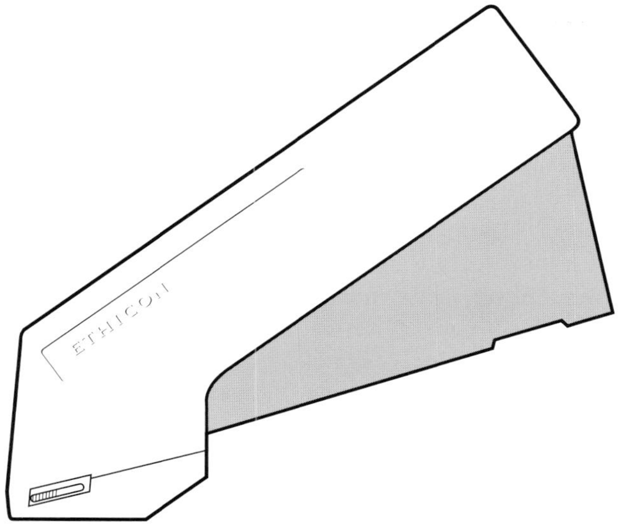

Fig. 5 Single patient use skin stapler

Variations of the standard instruments appeared, such as articulated linear staplers and automatic clip appliers.

In 1989, stainless steel staples and clips were replaced by titanium, this being better for the patient. It has been demonstrated that titanium is more bio-compatible, allowing less distorted magnetic, radiological, and nuclear clinical examinations. Another important improvement was to use absorbable materials for clips, making them radio transparent. These are the last great changes in the world of mechanical sutures, which are now in use in all operating rooms in the world.

Recently, new assisting technologies have been developed and introduced to facilitate and complement the use of the mechanical stapler, the most important one being ultrasonic energy as the means to cut, dissect, and coagulate tissue and structures without the risks of electrosurgery.

2 Product Description of Mechanical Staplers and Other Surgical Devices

Principles of Surgical Stapling

The basic principles for a good suture/anastomosis are:
- creation of an adequate lumen
- provision of proper tissue vascularisation
- avoidance of leakage and fistulas
- avoidance of tissue tension
- provision of good haemostasis

These principles have been established and maintained for years, as determining the conditions of a good anastomosis or closure with a stapler.

Staple Formation

The staples currently used in the majority of devices today have a rectangular shape that alters into a B-shaped form after compression against the anvil of the stapler. This principle is shown in the figures below. The staple height refers to the distance remaining within the staple, in millimetres, when the staple is closed.

Because the tissues to be sutured have different thickness the staples to suture them need to come in different dimensions to accommodate to the tissue and adhere to the principles of surgical stapling mentioned above. There are two technologies available today: one delivers a predetermined staple height and another allows different staple heights (variable staple height) formations within the same instrument.

Fixed Staple Height

The instruments using this technology will deliver a closed staple with the following staple heights:

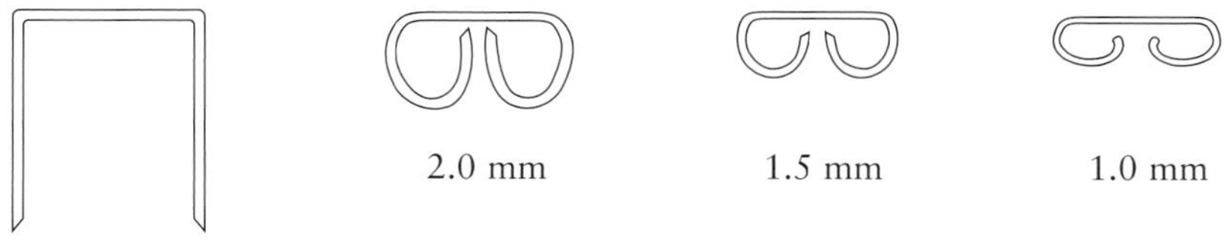

Variable Staple Height

In this case the surgeon can adapt the staple height to the thickness of the tissue to be sutured with the same instrument. The instruments using this technology will deliver staple heights ranging from 2.5 mm to 1.0 mm. The application of the staple line is performed by using different stapling instruments:

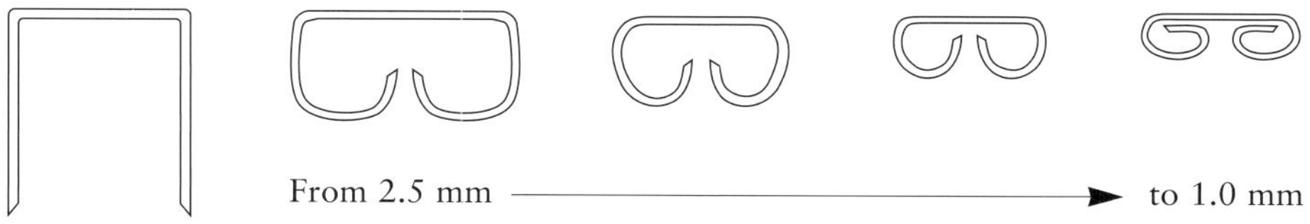

Linear Stapler

These staplers apply double staggered lines of staples. They are available with fixed or variable staple heights. Examples of applications are:

- Creating end-to-end anastomoses (in triangular technique)
- Making terminal closures

Variable staple height:

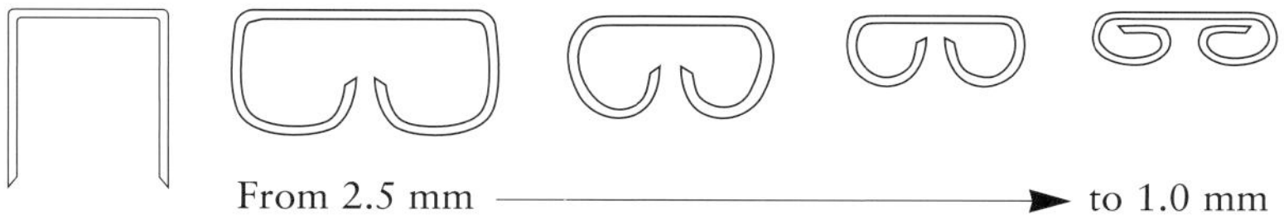

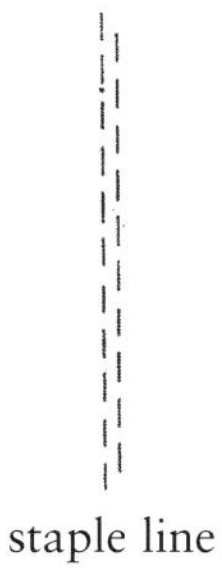

Fixed staple height:

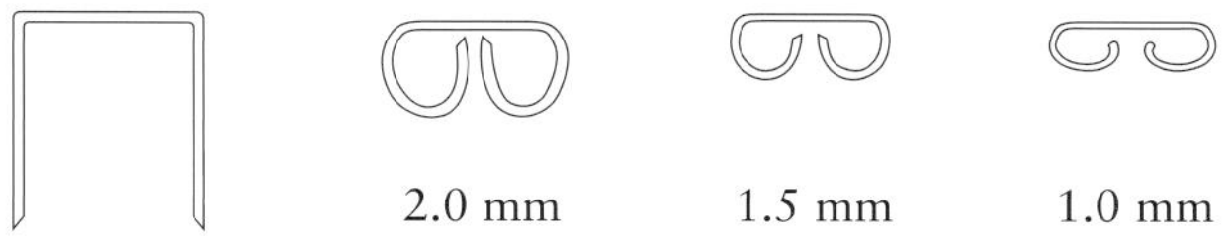

Linear Cutter

These staplers apply a double-staggered line of staples whilst simultaneously transecting the tissue between the lines. They are only available with fixed height staples. Examples of their applications are:

– Creating side-to-side anastomoses

– Making terminal closures

Fixed staple height:

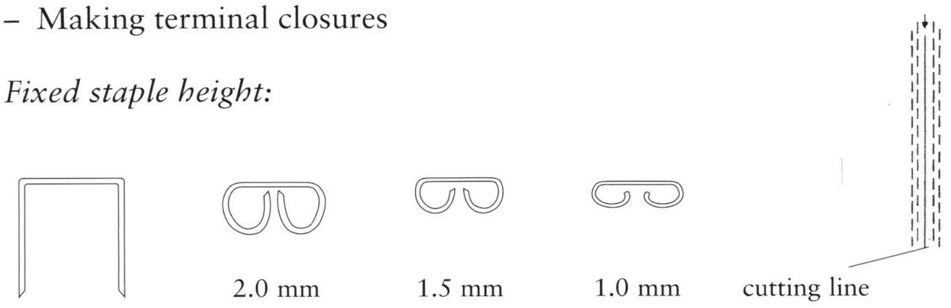

Circular Stapler

These staplers apply a double-staggered circular line of staples whilst simultaneously transecting the tissue within the circle. Examples of their applications are:

– Creating end-to-end anastomoses

– Creating end-to-side anastomoses

Variable staple height:

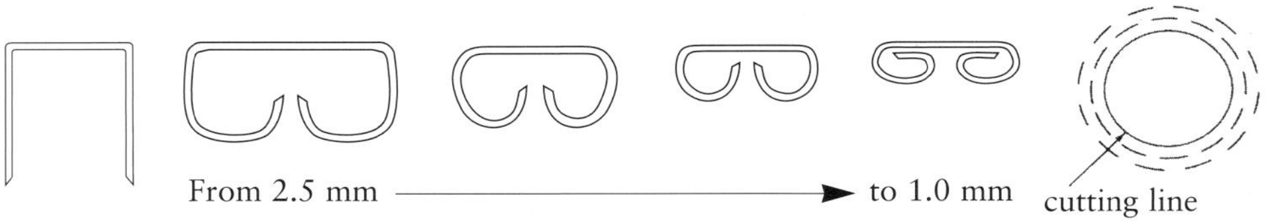

Technical Aspects of Staples

Depending on the kind of instruments and the procedure, the stapling instruments create inverted or everted suture edges. Further development of the surgical staplers led to material changes from silver to surgical steel up to titanium, which is used today. Compared with materials formerly used, titanium offers considerable advantages.

- Titanium is the most bio-compatible material.
- Artefacts caused by titanium staples during X-ray examinations are minimal and can be ignored.

The characteristics of titanium with regard to imaging guidance, such as MRI and CT are more favourable:

- Titanium is not affected by static magnetic fields.
- The rise in temperature in the titanium staple incurred by use of MRI or CT comes to a maximum of 0.1 °C and can therefore be ignored with regard to possible tissue damage.

In the course of the improvement of the staple, the method of application has been further developed, too. While the early stapling instruments compressed the tissue up to traumatisation and the staples were formed under this extreme pressure, present generation stapling instruments offer controlled tissue compression by means of variable staple heights, allowing the surgeon to adjust the staple height to the corresponding tissue.

Owing in particular to the variable staple height adjustment, a very atraumatic application of staples could be achieved. The result is that intramural vessels and therefore also capillary circulation in the area of the staple line seam can be maintained, which leads to improved wound healing. With fixed staple heights instruments this will be achieved by selecting the appropriate stapler according to the tissue.

During this period of development the wire thickness of the staple has been reduced considerably, too. Today the wire thickness is between 0.2 mm and 0.3 mm depending on the stapling instrument. This corresponds to a suture thickness of 2-0 to 3-0.

The height of the open staple legs will vary and create a variation of staple closure, usually from 1.0 mm to 2.5 mm. Some devices may permit adjusting the staple closure to the exact thickness of the tissue, in order to adhere to the principles outlined above.
In some cases, however, fixed staple closure suffices to provide a good suture/anastomosis and may allow the design of more easily handled instruments.

There are different staple closures currently in use, identified with different colour codes.

Colour Code	Fixed Staple Height	Type of Tissue
White Blue Green	 2.0 mm 1.5 mm 1.0 mm	Vascular/Thin Standard Thick
	Variable Staple Height	
Grey Yellow	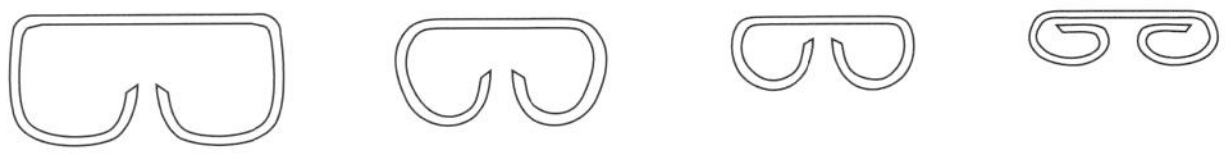 From 2.5 mm → to 1.0 mm	Standard Thick

Generally, these principles for surgical stapling are also valid for mechanical ligating clips. For mechanical ligation, however, it is very important that the selected clip size corresponds with the vessel calibre to be ligated (refer to clip picture page 25, 27).

When using surgical stapling instruments it is important to realise that, as with manual surgical sutures, a learning process must take place.

Mechanical Staplers
Staple Dimensions and Applications

Vascular/Thin
(white)

Staple Dimensions (open):

3.0 × 2.5 mm

Staple Dimensions (closed):

1.0 mm

Applications

- Thin tissues
- Vascularized tissues (omentum, mesentery…)
- Arteries and Veins

Standard
(blue/grey)

Staple Dimensions (open):

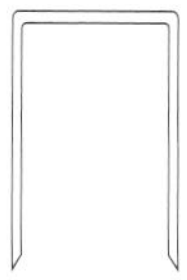

3.0 × 3.5–3.85 mm

Staple Dimensions (closed):

1.5 mm

2.5 – 1.0 mm*

Applications

- Standard tissues
- Gastrointestinal tract (small bowel, oesophagus…)
- Lung

Thick
(green/yellow)

Staple Dimensions (open):

4.0 × 3.5–5.5 mm

Staple Dimensions (closed):

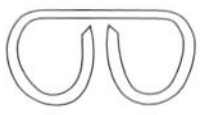

2.0 mm

2.5 –1.0 mm*

Applications

- Thick tissues
- Gastrointestinal tract (stomach…)
- Bronchus/Rectum

*variable staple closure

Linear Staplers

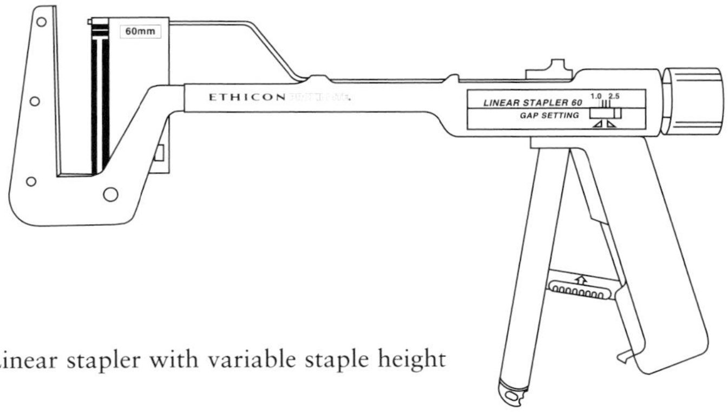

Linear stapler with variable staple height

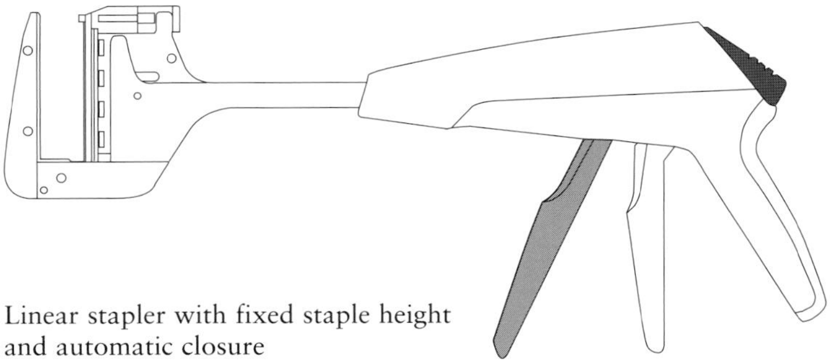

Linear stapler with fixed staple height
and automatic closure

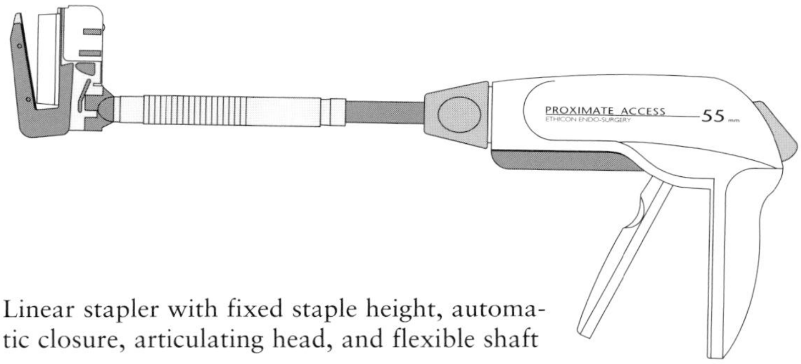

Linear stapler with fixed staple height, automatic closure, articulating head, and flexible shaft

As with all stapling instruments, linear staplers have applications in nearly all surgical procedures, especially for terminal closure of hollow organs, closure of incisions, ligation of large vessels, and, in rare cases, for end-to-end anastomoses.

The instruments are available in different staple sizes and different staple line lengths. They create staple lines of 30 mm, 55 mm, 60 mm, or 90 mm to accommodate different tissues. One type of instrument allows staple formation to a pre-defined height, the other instrument type enables variable adjustment of the staple height to the specific organ according to the tissue thickness. Furthermore there are various wire diameters to enable stapling of different types of tissue, i.e. vessels, bronchus, or bowel.

Linear staplers apply a double-staggered line of staples.

The linear stapler vascular is intended especially for vascular use to ligate large calibre vessels.

Do not use linear staplers on ischaemic or necrotic tissue.

Linear staplers may be reloaded during a single procedure.

Staple Lines

30 mm Linear Stapler Vascular

three staggered lines of staples

30 mm Linear Stapler

two staggered lines of staples

55 mm Linear Stapler

two staggered lines of staples

60 mm Linear Stapler

two staggered lines of staples

90 mm Linear Stapler

two staggered lines of staples

Articulated Linear Staplers

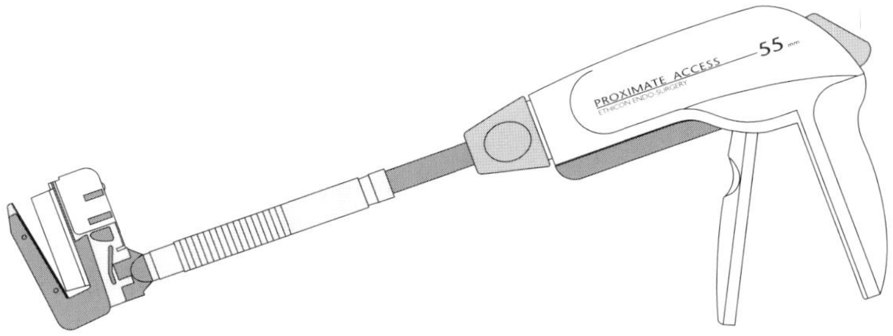

Articulated linear staplers have been designed especially to facilitate access in narrowed areas. Therefore the working end of the instrument can be adjusted to the site.

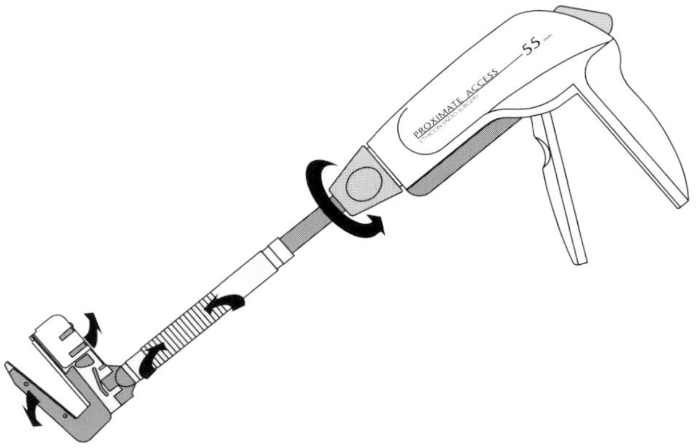

The articulated linear stapler has a 55 mm staple line and is available for standard or thick tissue. It should be noted that articulated linear staplers are not reloadable.

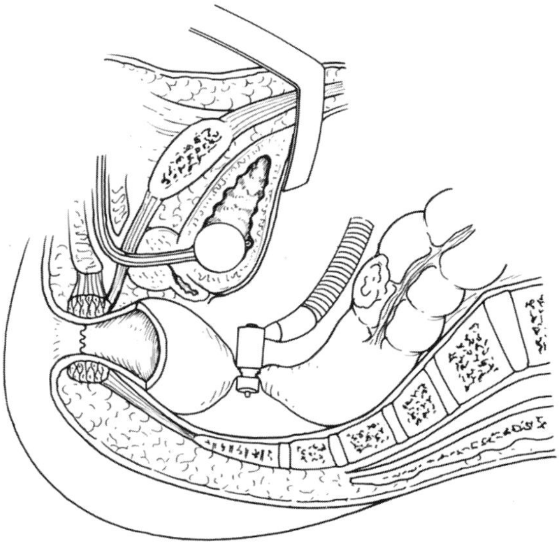

The instrument head is designed to articulate completely on the shaft, which also rotates and flexes. In the case of a low anterior resection this favours a staple line perpendicular to the rectum.

Linear Cutters

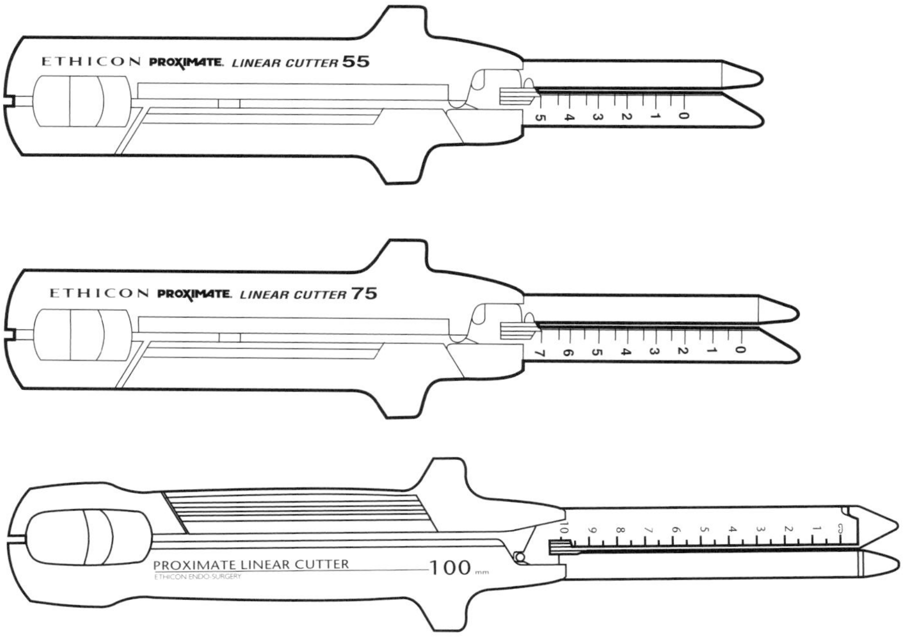

Linear cutters are applied in gastrointestinal, gynaecologic, thoracic, and paediatric surgery for transection of vascular structures, resection of organs and parts of an organ, and creation of inverted side-to-side anastomoses.

The instruments are available in different lengths, staple sizes, and wire diameters, for vascular/thin, standard, and thick tissue suturing, depending on the indication. The staple line lengths are 55 mm, 75 mm, or 100 mm. The 55 mm stapler is also available without a knife (no-knife stapler). Every type of cartridge available in the same length is interchangeable on the same instrument.

Do not use linear cutters on ischaemic or necrotic tissue.

Linear cutters may be reloaded during a single procedure.

Staple Lines

55 mm Linear Cutter

75 mm Linear Cutter

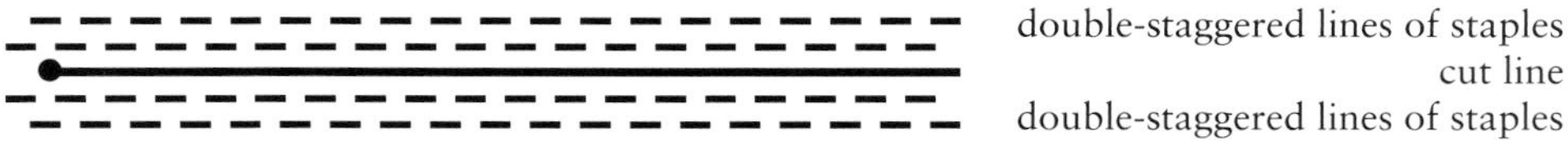

100 mm Linear Cutter

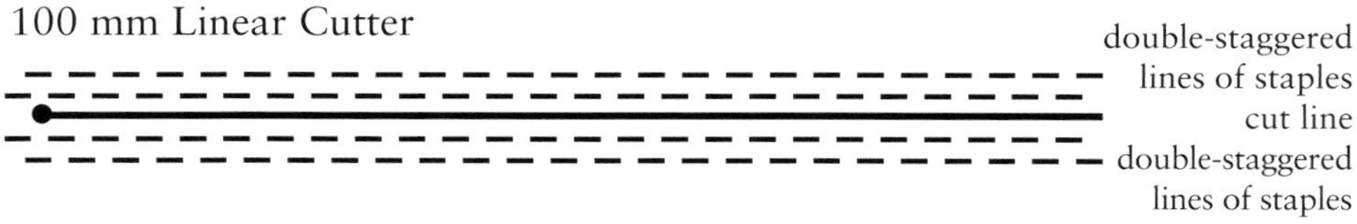

The dot on the cut line of the illustrations indicates the end of the line of incision.

Linear cutters deliver two double-staggered lines of staples while simultaneously dividing the tissue between the lines.

The staple line is four staples longer than the cut line. This ensures good haemostasis at the distal end of the staple line.

The stapling and cutting mechanisms are also synchronised, so that staple formation, which causes tissue adaptation and haemostasis in the wound area, has been finished by compression before the tissue is actually cut and stapled.

The process is shown in Figs. 1–4.

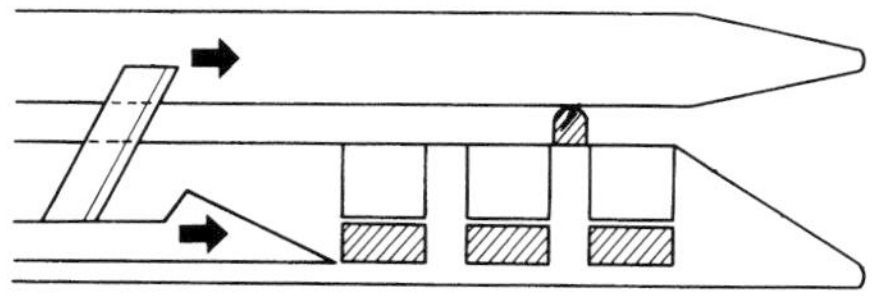

Fig. 1

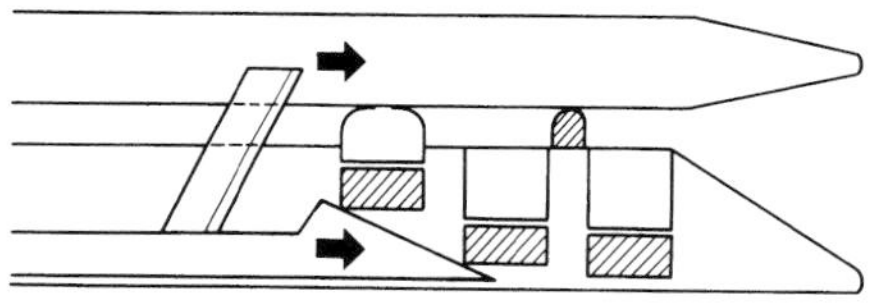

Fig. 2

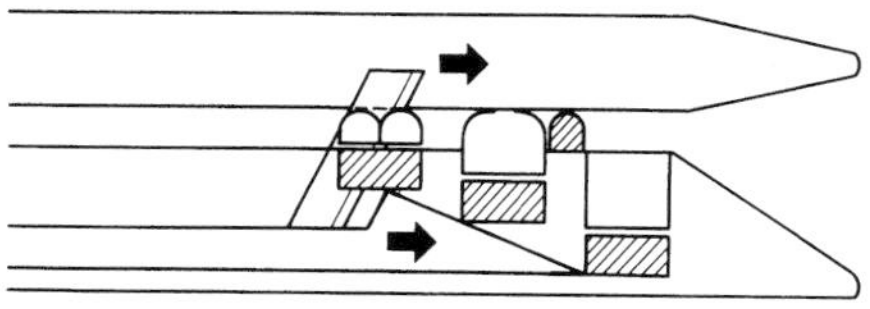

Fig. 3

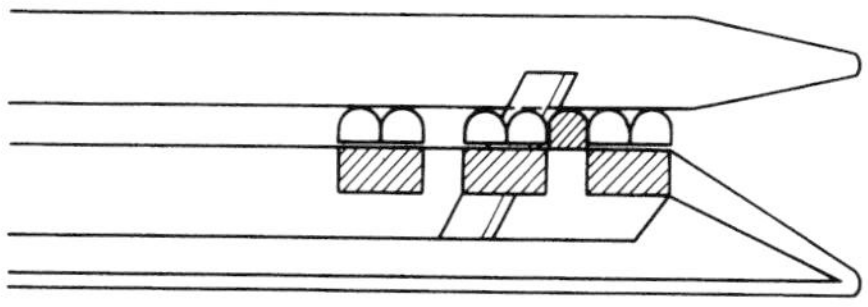

Fig. 4

The tissue is stapled prior to knife activation (Fig. 1). The staple has been completely formed before the tissue is cut by the knife (Fig. 2–3). The knife incision ends before the last four staples (Fig. 4).

Circular Staplers

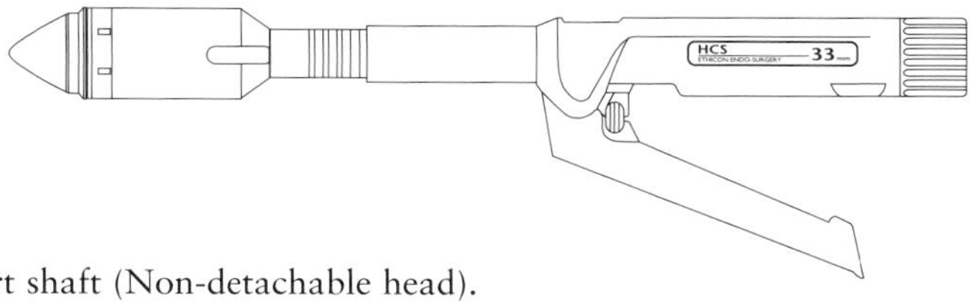

Straight Circular Stapler with short shaft (Non-detachable head).

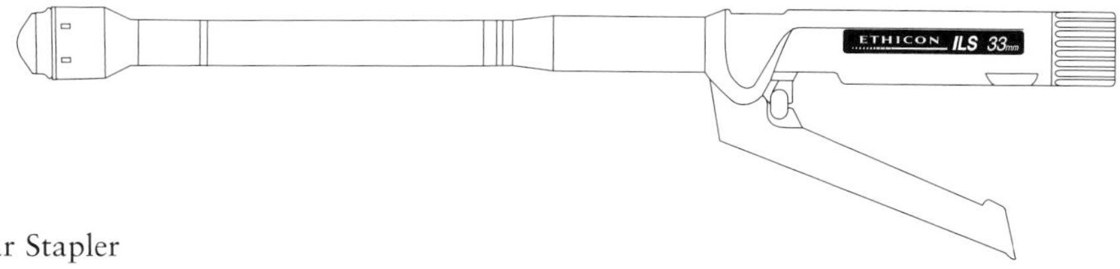

Straight Circular Stapler

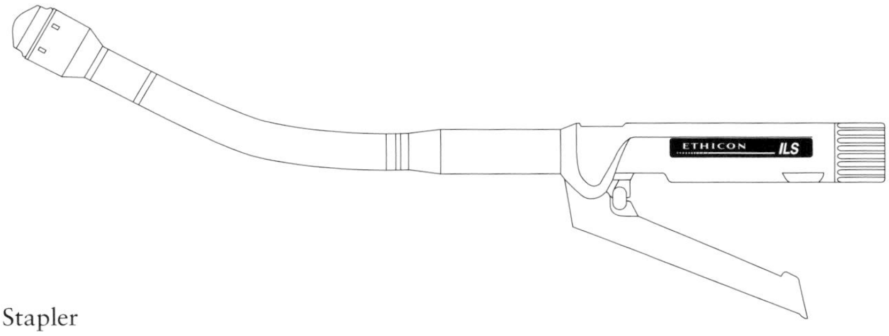

Curved Circular Stapler

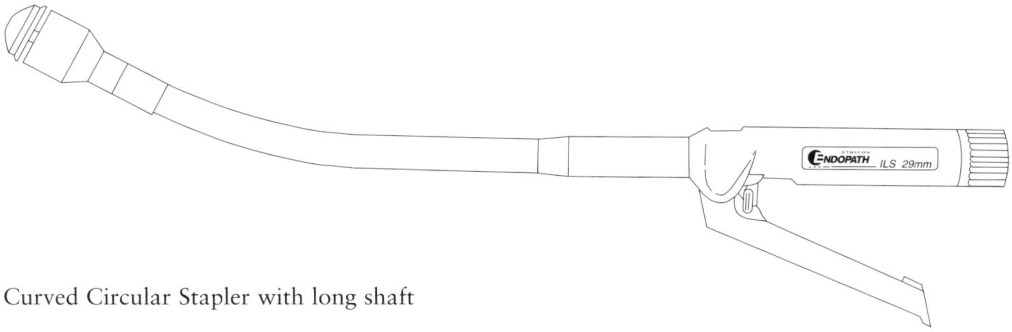

Curved Circular Stapler with long shaft

Circular staplers are applied in gastrointestinal surgery to facilitate inverted end-to-end, end-to-side, and side-to-side anastomoses. The straight circular stapler with short shaft (non-detachable head) is mainly indicated in performing mucosal prolapsectomies.

The instruments, with the exception of the straight circular stapler with short shaft, are available in four different head diameters, which are selected depending on the lumen of the organ. Furthermore, the height of the staple closure can be varied intraoperatively from 1.0 mm to 2.5 mm, depending on the thickness of the structures to be anastomosed.

The curved circular stapler with long shaft can also be used in minimally invasive surgical procedures because of the sealed shaft.

Do not use circular staplers on ischaemic or necrotic tissue. Furthermore, the instruments should not be used to create an anastomosis on structures where the combined tissue thickness is less than 1.0 mm or greater than 2.5 mm.

Circular staplers are not reloadable.

Circular staplers deliver two circular staggered lines of staples, while cutting the tissue.

The stapling and cutting mechanisms are also synchronised, so that staple formation, which causes tissue adaptation and haemostasis in the wound area, has been finished by compression before the tissue in between has been transected by a circular knife.

Staple Lines

21 mm Circular Stapler
two staggered lines of staples
Variable staple height 1.0–2.5 mm

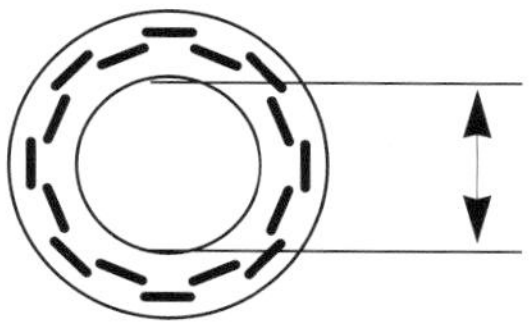

Internal lumen
Circular cut line
12.4 mm diameter

25 mm Circular Stapler
two staggered lines of staples
Variable staple height 1.0–2.5 mm

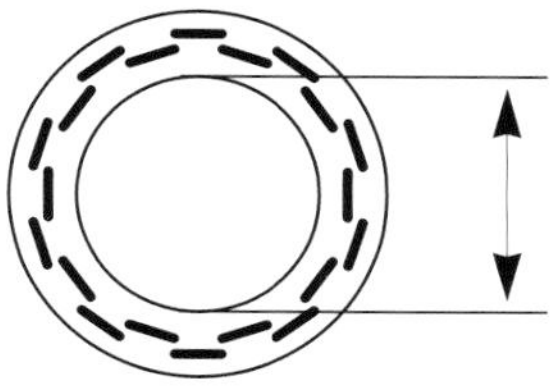

Internal lumen
Circular cut line
16.4 mm diameter

29 mm Circular Stapler
two staggered lines of staples
Variable staple height 1.0–2.5 mm

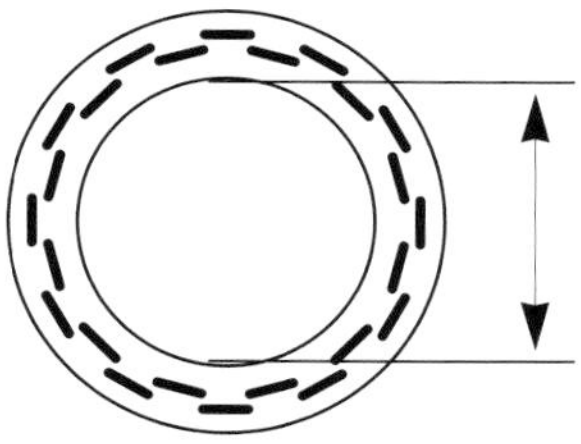

Internal lumen
Circular cut line
20.4 mm diameter

33 mm Circular Stapler
two staggered lines of staples
Variable staple height 1.0–2.5 mm

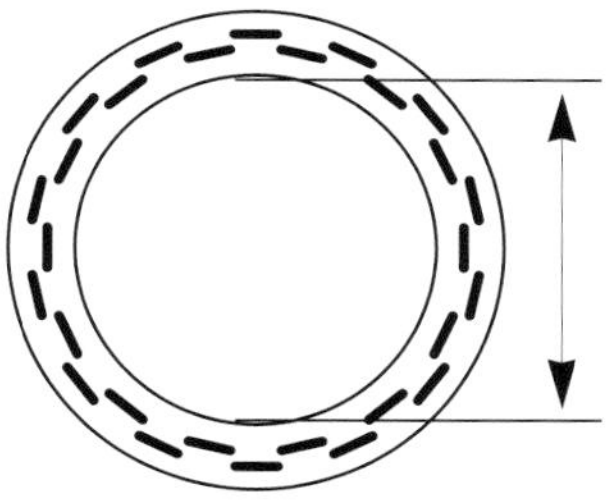

Internal lumen
Circular cut line
24.4 mm diameter

In accordance with the principles of surgical stapling the main aim is to obtain an anastomosis with the largest possible lumen in order to avoid later stenosis. Therefore, when selecting a circular stapler, the surgeon should select the one with the largest internal lumen.

Sizers

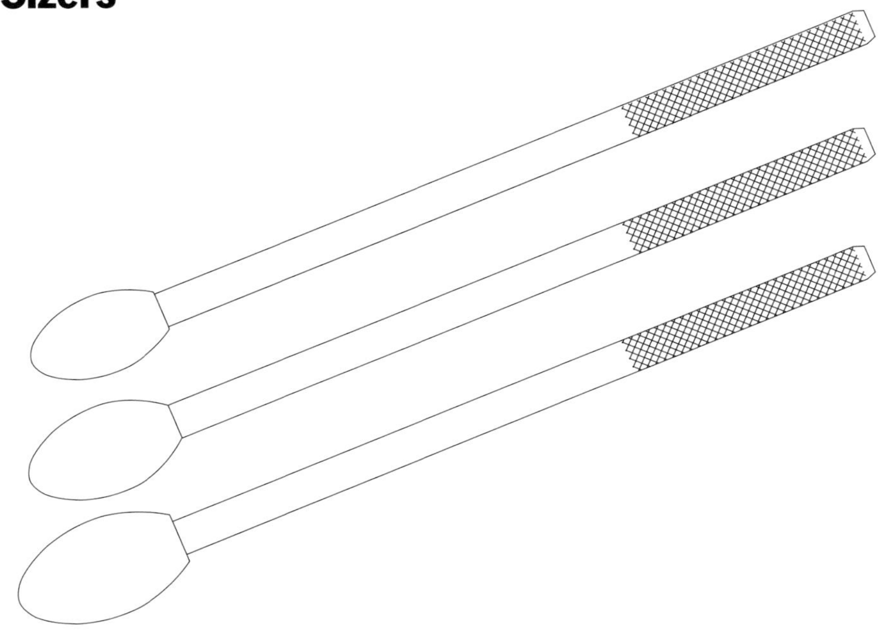

The circular sizers are intended to aid in selecting the appropriate size of circular stapler. In principle, a lumen of as large a size as possible is desired. After transecting the bowel, the contracted lumen can be dilated with the circular sizers atraumatically. Care should be taken, however, that none of the wall layers tear.

The circular sizers are available in 21 mm, 25 mm, 29 mm, and 33 mm diameters, corresponding with the head sizes of the circular staplers. Begin sizing the bowel using the smallest circular sizer, i.e. the 21 mm, and then continue with successively larger ones until the appropriate circular stapler fits in the lumen.

Purse-string Suture Clamp

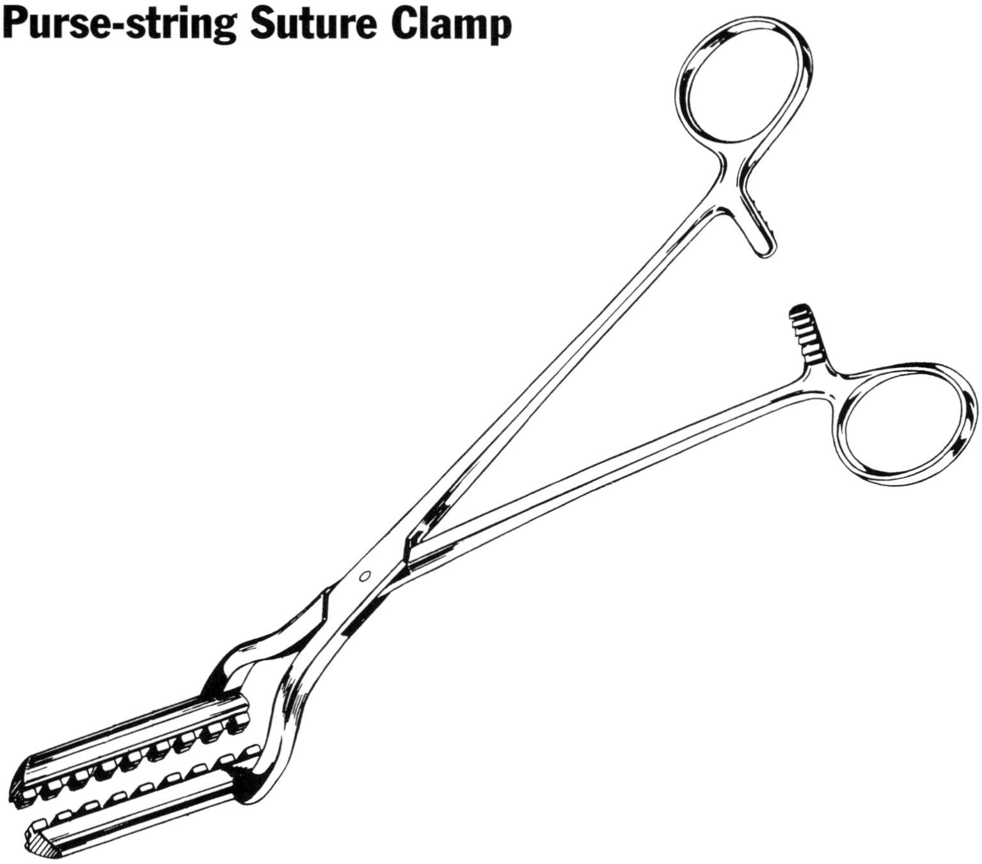

The purse-string-suture clamp is used for the prompt placement of purse-string sutures.

After having closed the clamp, any corrections will only be possible if the bowel segment damaged by the teeth of the clamp is resected. Correct closure of the instrument must be ensured prior to insertion of the needles into the canal.

Resection has to be done along the knife guide to achieve optimal distance between purse-string suture and cutting edge. The clamp must be removed carefully to avoid damage to the purse-string suture.

Inspect the purse-string suture for completeness.

For detailed information refer to the chapter on purse-string suture techniques.

Do not use this instrument on ischaemic or necrotic tissues.

Synthetically Absorbable Clips

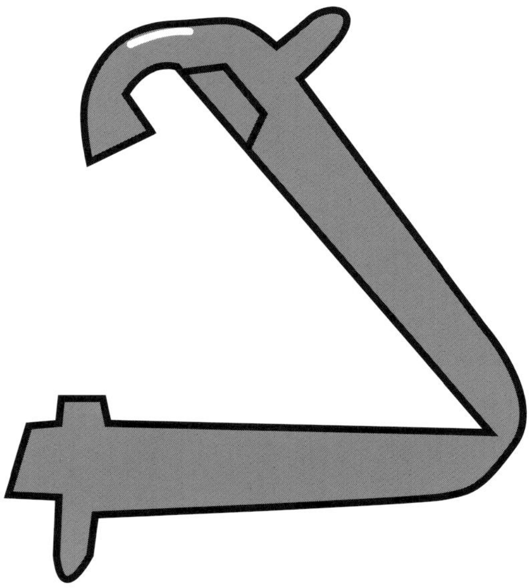

Synthetically absorbable ABSOLOK Clips are made of polydioxanone polymer. During the absorption period the clip causes only an insignificant tissue reaction. The violet polydioxanone polymer reacts neither antigenically nor pyrogenically.

Breakdown occurs through hydrolysis, where H_2O and CO_2 are excreted, mainly via the urine. In the first 90 postoperative days there is minimal absorption and loss of resistance; and after 210 days the polydioxanone polymer will be completely absorbed.

Synthetically absorbable clips are used for the ligation of vessels and tubular structures. The absorbable clip does not conduct heat or electricity. There is no interference with interpretations of radiological, CT, or MRI scans.

When using a ligating clip, it is important that the tissue being ligated be consistent with the size of the clip. Therefore synthetically absorbable clips are available in four different sizes.

Before using a clip, the vessel to be ligated has to be completely dissected from its circumference to ensure proper placement of the clip around the structure. The Absolok Clip has a self-locking mechanism that ligates the structure 360° around its whole circumference. After clip application, inspect the site for haemostasis and ensure that each clip has been securely and completely positioned around the tissue being ligated.

There is a wide range of clip appliers with different sizes and lengths for open and minimally invasive surgery.

Clip	Vessel Diameter
Small **AP 100** Clip Opening 2.4 mm  2.75 mm 5.2 mm	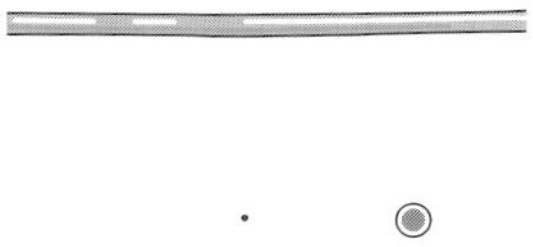 Ø 1.3 mm 0.5 – 2.0 mm
Medium **AP 200** Clip Opening 3.8 mm 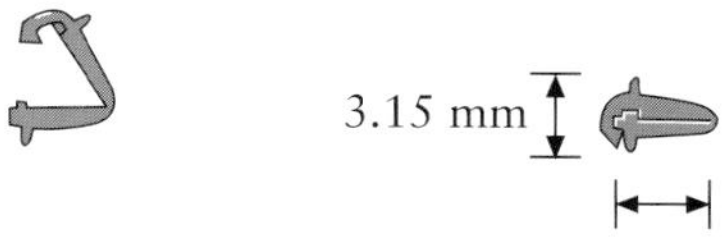 3.15 mm 7.7 mm	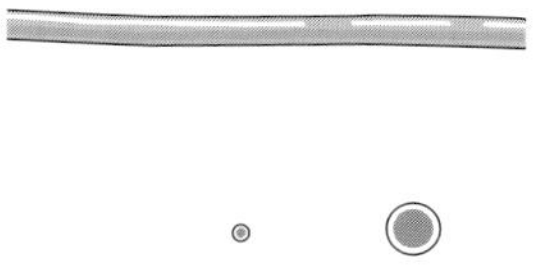 Ø 2.0 mm 1.0 – 3.0 mm
Medium Large **AP 300** Clip Opening 5.3 mm 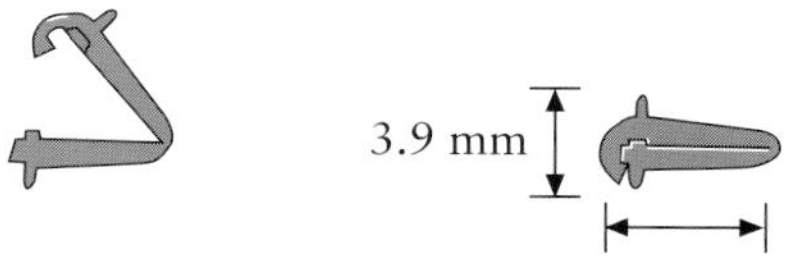 3.9 mm 10.4 mm	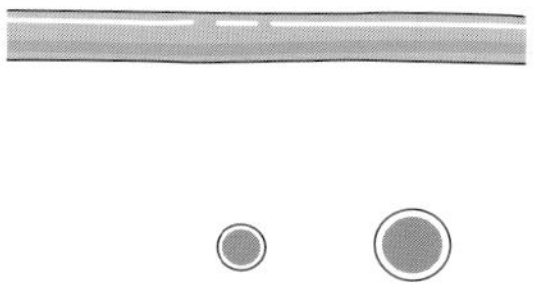 Ø 3.5 mm 2.5 – 4.5 mm
Large **AP 400** Clip Opening 7.5 mm 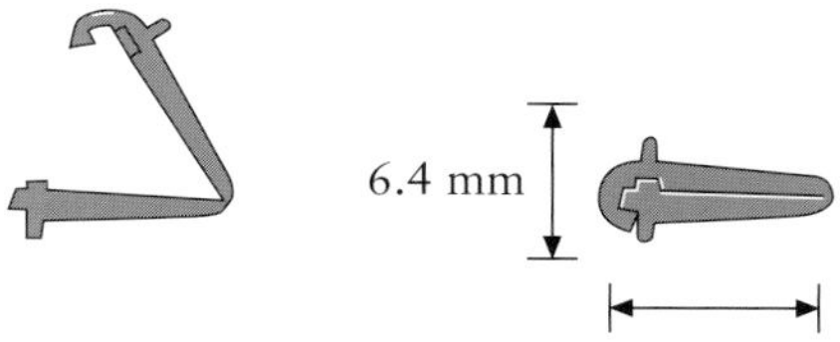 6.4 mm 13.7 mm	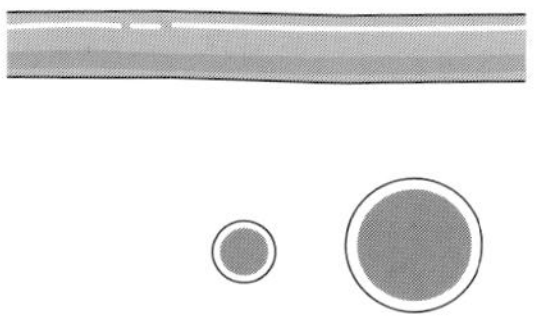 Ø 5.0 mm 3.5 – 7.5 mm

Metal Clips

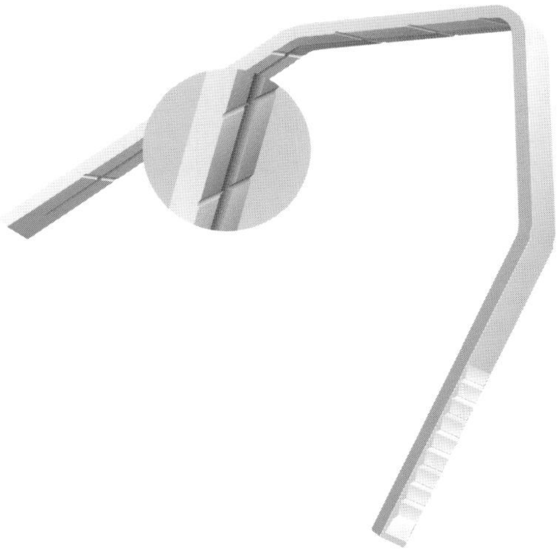

Non-absorbable ligating clips are used for the ligation of tubular structures in all surgical procedures. Furthermore the ligating clips, especially the clips made of titanium, can be used to mark internal structures, as they can be clearly identified on X-rays.

When using ligating clips, the tissue being ligated must be consistent with the size of the clip.

Generally the ligating clips are produced from either 316L stainless steel or titanium. Prior to the procedure it is important to select the appropriate clip material. Clips made of stainless steel will interfere with interpretations of postoperative X-rays, CT, or MRI scans, and therefore interfere with a clear identification of surrounding structures.

Both clips made of stainless steel and those made of titanium cause minimal tissue reaction.

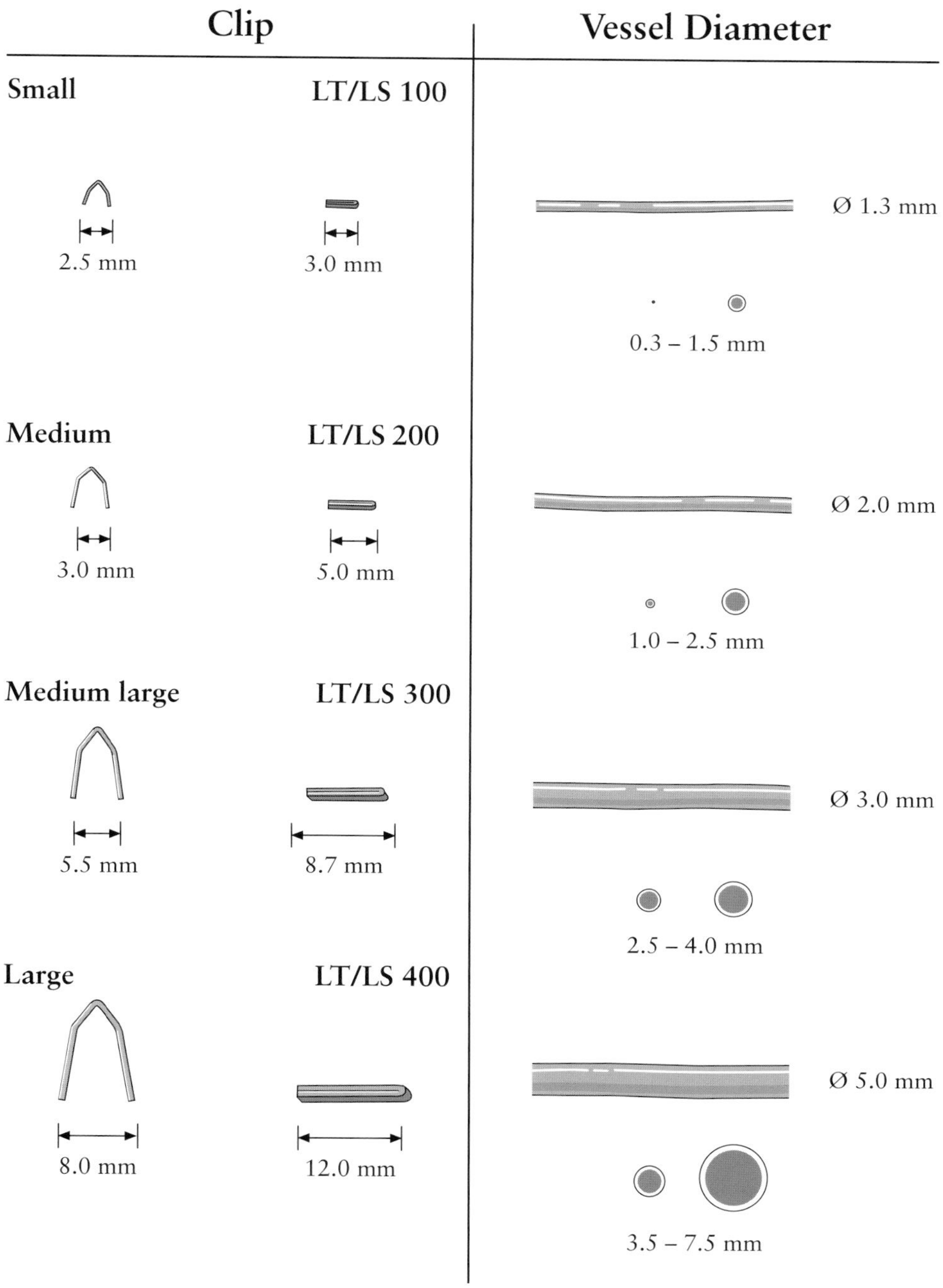

To avoid clip migration, a specially designed profile has been provided on the inner side, as shown in the above picture. However, after clip application, inspect the site for haemostasis and ensure that each clip has been securely and completely positioned around the structure being ligated. Metal clips conduct heat and electricity. Therefore special caution should be exercised when practising electrosurgery.

There is a wide range of clip appliers with different sizes and lengths for open and minimally invasive surgery.

Multiple Clip Appliers

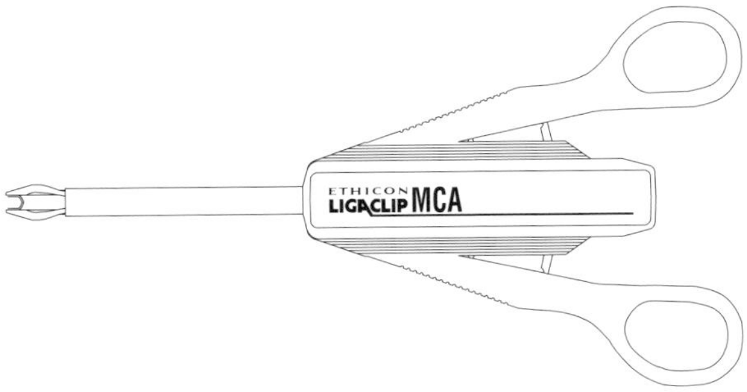

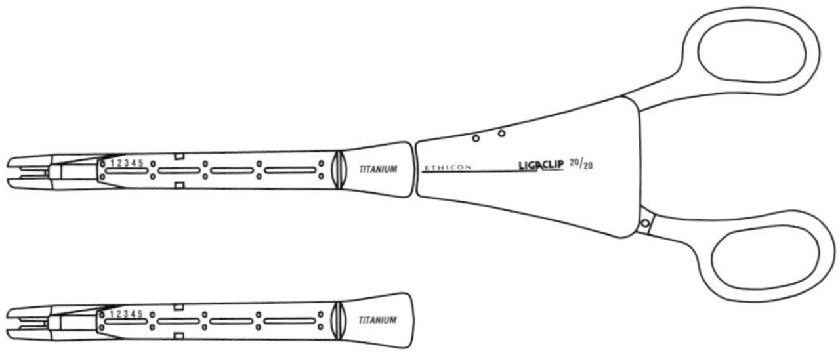

Multiple clip appliers are designed to offer a fast, efficient means of ligation by means of an integrated mechanism that reloads the instrument. Multiple clip appliers have a ratchet mechanism to prevent the accidental fall of the clip from the jaws.

Multiple clip appliers are available in different clip sizes and working lengths, enabling comfortable use even in sites where access could be difficult. For detailed information refer to the table below.

When using multiple clip appliers the same principles must be adhered to as with single clips.

Product Code	Applier Length	No. of Clips	Clip Size	Clip Open	Clip Distal Closure	Clip Closed
MCS20	23.8 cm	20	small	2.1 mm		3.8 mm
MSM20	23.8 cm	20	medium	4.3 mm		6.0 mm
MCM20	29.2 cm	20	medium	4.3 mm		6.0 mm
MCM30	29.2 cm	30	medium	4.3 mm		6.0 mm
MCL20	33.7 cm	20	large	6.3 mm		10.8 mm
TIM20	29.4 cm	20	medium	4.4 mm		4.8 mm
TIR20 (Reload of TIM20)	–	20	medium	4.4 mm		4.8 mm

Skin Staplers

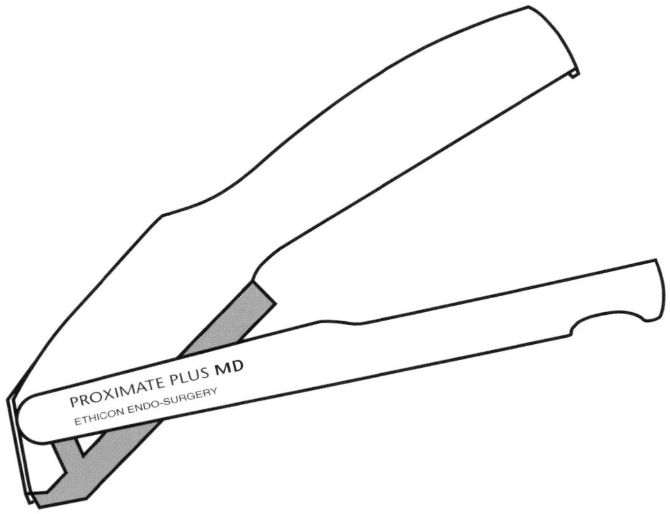

The skin staplers are designed for fast skin closure with excellent cosmetic results. When using the stapler, ensure that the staples are at least 5 mm from underlying structures such as bones, vessels, or other organs.

The instrument delivers staples one by one. The distance between the applied staples should be approx. 8 mm. If the distance is more than 8 mm between the single staples, the cosmetic result will be reduced considerably.

The wound edges must be everted during approximation.

For staple removal a specially designed staple extractor should be used.

unformed skin staple

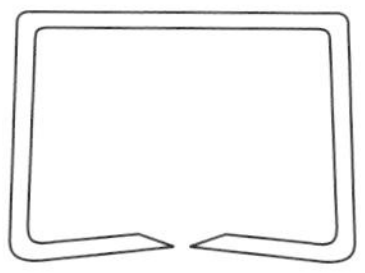

formed skin staple

3 Basic Stapling Techniques

Over the years, various surgical techniques have been developed and consolidated in using mechanical staplers. Below we describe the most widespread and basic uses of mechanical staplers to perform transections, ligations, and anastomoses of anatomical structures.

Examples for the use of Linear Staplers:

Terminal Closure of Hollow Organs

Linear Staplers allow suturing and closing of hollow organs along the resection line with two staggered lines of staples. Basically, the tissue to be stapled has to be evenly positioned into the open jaws of the stapler. Neither clips nor mass ligations or similar foreign bodies may be present in the area of the instrument jaws. Also, intraluminal foreign bodies such as probes or catheters inserted into the hollow organ have to be removed from the staple area.

After verifying that the tissue is correctly positioned in the jaws, the instrument is closed and fired. Before the instrument is opened, excess tissue is cut away, using a scalpel or scissors along the cutting guide of the instrument. A clamp can be used to avoid possible leakages from the side of the specimen that has not been stapled. After stapling the organ, examine the wound edges for haemostasis.

In isolated cases, especially at heavily vascularised structures, eventual bleeding will have to be controlled with a suture stitch.
When using electrosurgery to achieve haemostasis, any contact between staple and electrode must be avoided as this may result in necrosis in the area of the staple line. Therefore haemostasis should preferably be attained by means of a suture stitch or Ultracision. For more details on Ultracision, refer to the chapter concerning this.

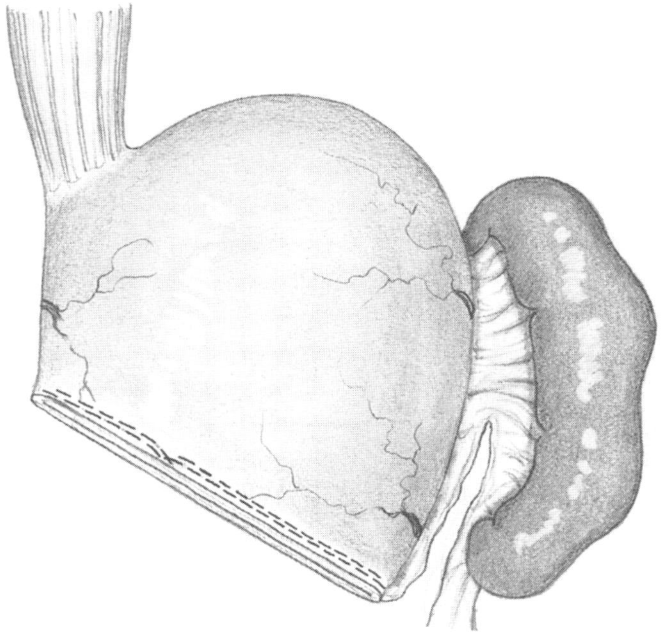

When ligating large vessels or very thin tissue, the linear stapler vascular must be used. As a precaution, when transecting the vessel at the staple line it is advisable to have a clamp around it in case there is a rupture of the thin vessel wall.

Closure of Incisions

The terminal closure of hollow organs using linear staplers can be done lengthwise or crosswise.

Intraluminal haemostasis of the hollow organ must be controlled in the eventual case of bleeding prior to closing the incisions. As shown in the illustration, placement of fixating sutures contributes to proper adaptation of the wound edges to facilitate their introduction into the jaws of the linear stapler.
After closing and firing the stapler and with the instrument jaws still closed, the overlapping tissue must be resected along the cutting guide or parallel to the cartridge by using a scalpel or scissors.

When a linear stapler is used to perform a lateral closure of an otomy on an organ, e.g. small bowel, care must be taken to include as little tissue as possible in the instrument jaws to avoid risks of future stenosis of the lumen of the organ.

After removal of the linear stapler, examine the staple line for haemostasis. Isolated haemorrhages will have to be controlled by manual suturing or Ultracision.

In all mechanical stapling a minimal distance of 3 cm should be left between two staple lines to avoid risk of necrosis of the tissue edges due to poor vascularisation.

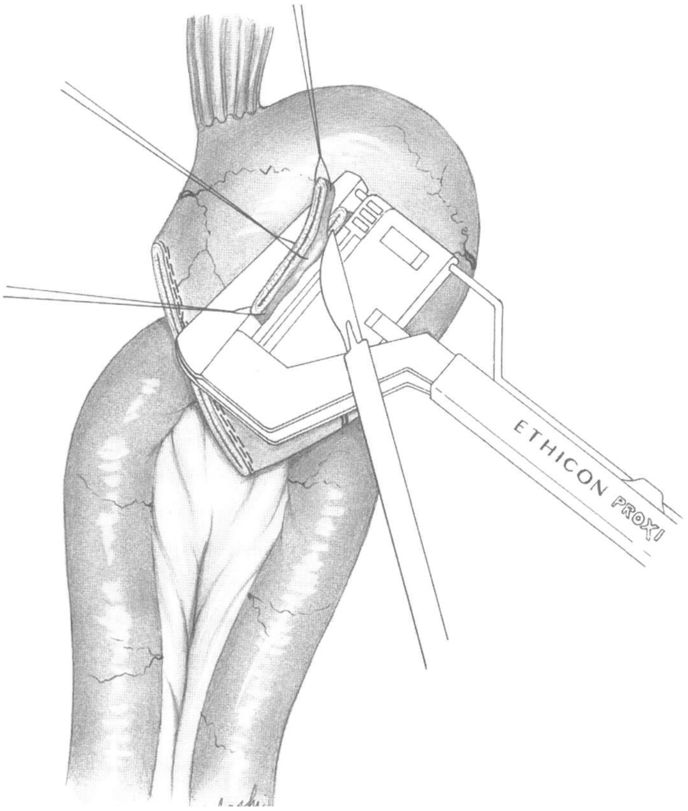

End-to-end Anastomosis: Triangulation Technique

An end-to-end anastomosis can be performed with the linear stapler. The instrument has to be applied three times, in accordance with the principle of triangulation.

The mesenteric and anti-mesenteric borders of the two organs to be anastomosed have to be properly aligned. The application of the instrument around the circumference of the two organs to be anastomosed is prepared by shaping three segments of the same size with fixating sutures.

The first segment stapled is the one in the posterior aspect of the bowels to be anastomosed, creating an inverted staple line. After closing and firing the instrument, but with its jaws still closed, the overlapping tissue can be resected along the cutting guide or parallel to the cartridge by using a scalpel or scissors.
After stapling, examine the site for haemostasis. Light bleeding at the staple lines will have to be controlled with Ultracision or manual suturing.

The other two applications of the stapler on the remaining segments will create two everted staple lines. To achieve an effective anastomosis it is very important that the staple lines cross at their corners. Also, in order to avoid future stenosis, it is important to achieve the largest possible lumen.

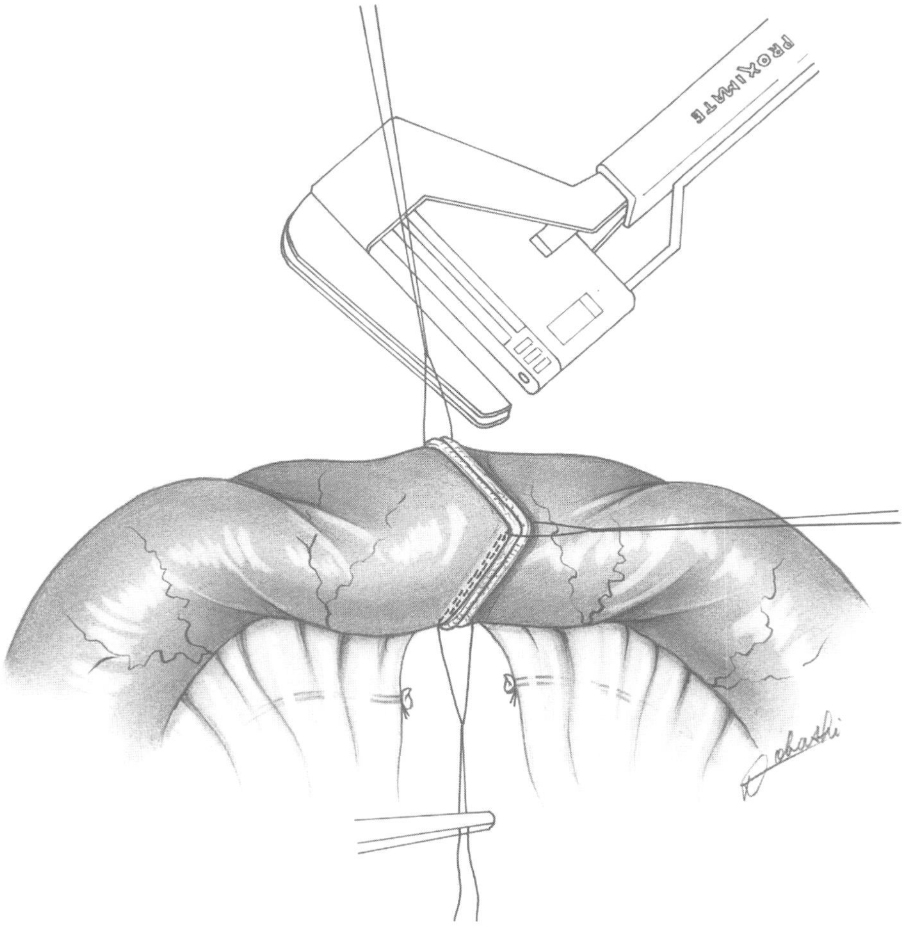

Examples for the use of the Linear Cutter

Transection of Tubular Structures and Hollow Organs

When performing a transection of tubular structures with a linear cutter, both the proximal and the distal wound edges are sutured with two double-staggered lines of staples, while the tissue between them is transected. To favour optimal staple formation, the tissue to be transected must be evenly distributed between the jaws of the instrument. To facilitate this manoeuvre, the surgeon can use the intermediate locking position provided in some linear cutters.

During the application of the linear cutter, neither clips nor mass ligations or similar foreign bodies may be present in the area of the instrument jaws. Intraluminal foreign bodies such as probes or catheters have to be removed from the area, too.

After transecting the tissue, the wound edges must be examined for haemostasis. In isolated cases, especially at heavily vascularised structures, bleeding will have to be controlled with suture stitches or Ultracision.

When using electrosurgery to achieve haemostasis, any contact between staple and electrode must be avoided, as this may result in necrosis in the area of the staple line.

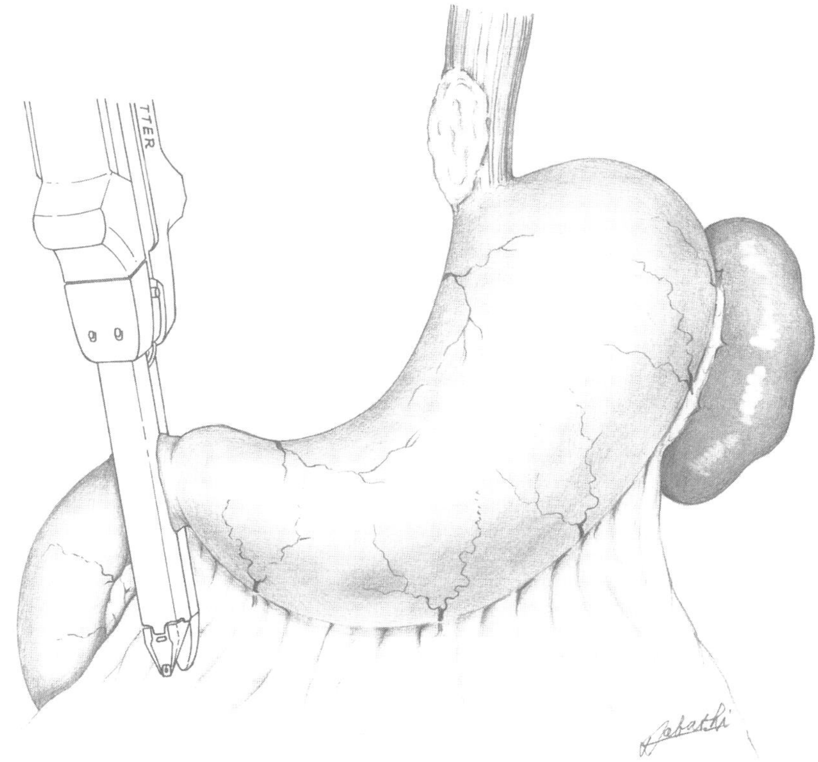

Creation of a Side-to-side (Enterocolostomy) Anastomosis

Let us describe an example of a side-to-side (enterocolostomy) anastomosis with linear cutters. Using stay sutures, the intestinal segments to be anastomosed are drawn together latero-laterally, carefully aligning the anti-mesenteric edges. Small incisions are made on both intestinal segments in relation to the anti-mesenteric edges, using a scalpel or Ultracision. The jaws of the linear cutter are inserted into the incisions.
To facilitate the alignment of the edges of the tissue around the jaws, the instrument is placed into the intermediate locking position. The stapler is closed and fired.

The two segments are anastomosed together with two double-staggered lines of staples. At the same time, the knife divides the walls of the intestine between the two lines of staples, creating the anastomosis.

The common enterostomy is closed by applying a linear stapler or sutures. Before withdrawing the stapler, remove any superfluous tissue protruding from the jaws, using scissors or a scalpel.
To avoid tension at the distal end of the new anastomosis, a single safety stitch should be applied.

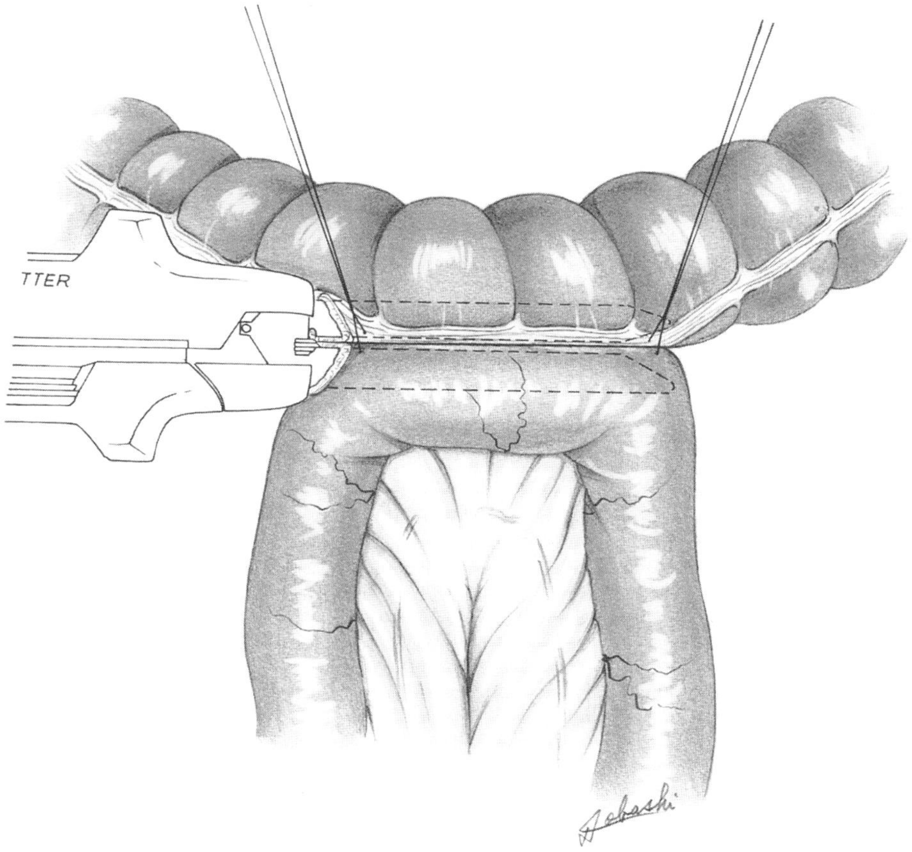

Functional End-to-end Anastomosis – Closing Technique with Linear Cutters

This procedure is carried out by a transection of the pathological tract of the small or large intestine to be resected, applying a linear cutter twice. Later, anastomosis is obtained by applying a linear cutter and the common incision is closed using a linear stapler.

A linear cutter is used proximally and distally to the pathological tract. Using this technique, both the proximal and distal intestinal segments are sutured and closed before the anastomosis, thus avoiding possible leakages that may increase the risk of intra-peritoneal infection.

The anastomosis is obtained by applying a linear cutter as follows. The anti-mesenteric edges of the bowel stumps to be anastomosed are aligned. Supporting sutures can be used to make this step easier. Two enterotomies on the antimesenteric borders are created to allow the insertion of the jaws of the linear cutter. The linear cutter is inserted, closed, and fired, creating the anastomosis. The common intestinal opening is closed by applying a linear stapler or using manual sutures. In order to avoid tension in the distal end of the new anastomosis, a single safety stitch should be applied.

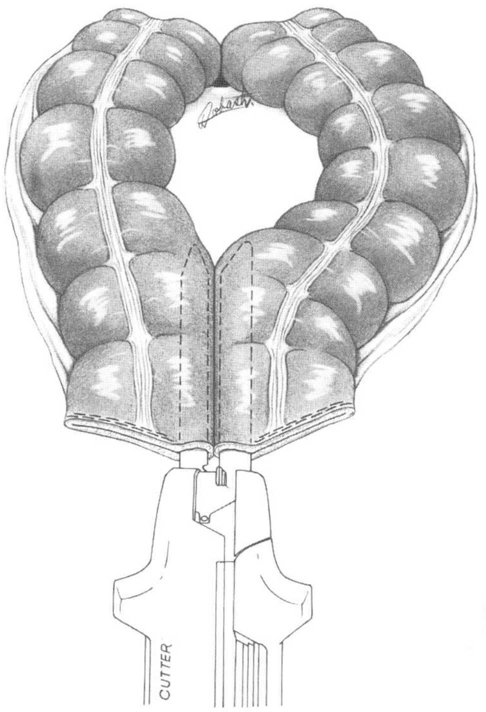

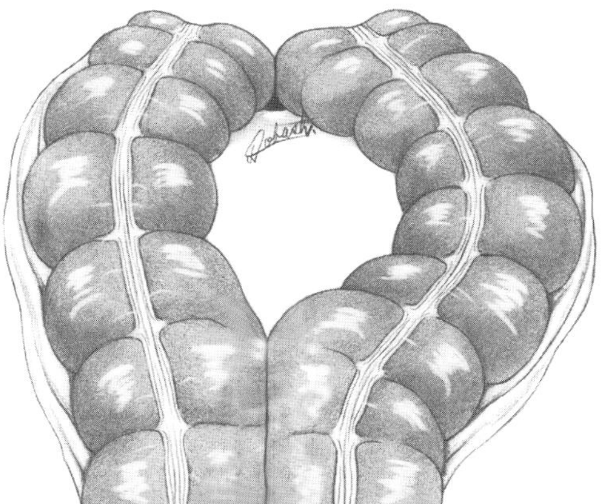

Pulmonary Wedge Resections with Linear Cutters: Atypical Resection

The atypical resection is performed by using the linear cutter twice. When placing the second staple line, both staple lines must intersect in order to achieve sufficient haemostasis and pneumostasis in this area. After application of the linear cutter, examine the staple lines for haemostasis and pneumostasis. If necessary, air leaks can be identified by filling the thoracic cavity with sterile saline solution.

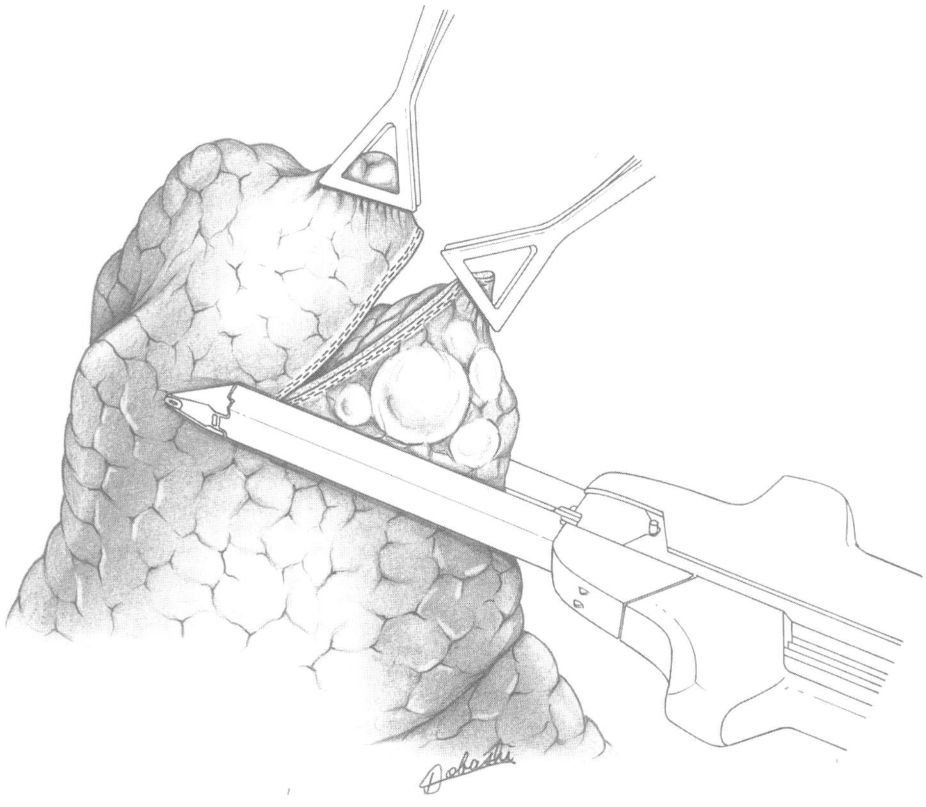

Examples of use of circular staplers

Circular staplers are primarily intended to create anastomosis between hollow and tubular organs. In the following the end-to-end and end-to-side anastomoses are described.

End-to-end Anastomosis via Colotomy with Circular Stapler

The anastomosis is created by the application of a circular stapler via a colotomy. Later, the colotomy is closed with a linear stapler.

The procedure commences with the mobilisation and resection of the pathological tract of the colon by using the linear cutter twice (as described before) or scalpel transection of the bowel with prior application of clamps to avoid any bowel leakages. Two purse-string sutures are placed at the distal and proximal stumps.

Using a scalpel or Ultracision, a colotomy is carried out on the anti-mesenteric side at about 6–8 cm from the edge of the transection. The colotomy, which must be sufficiently large to allow the entrance of the circular stapler, may be carried out on either the proximal or distal stump of the intestine.

The circular stapler with an adequate diameter (selected on the basis of the surgeon's experience or use of sizers) is opened. The stapler head is removed and the integral trocar withdrawn into its body. The circular stapler is inserted into the intestine via the colotomy until it comes out of the open stump. At this point, by turning the adjusting knob, the trocar emerges from the instrument and the purse-string suture is closed around the trocar base.

The head of the circular stapler is inserted into the other intestinal stump and the purse-string is closed around it. The insertion of the head may be facilitated by the application of stay sutures to the intestinal walls. Whilst the purse-string suture is being tied around the anvil's rod, care must be taken not to damage the suture, and to eliminate any excess ligature.

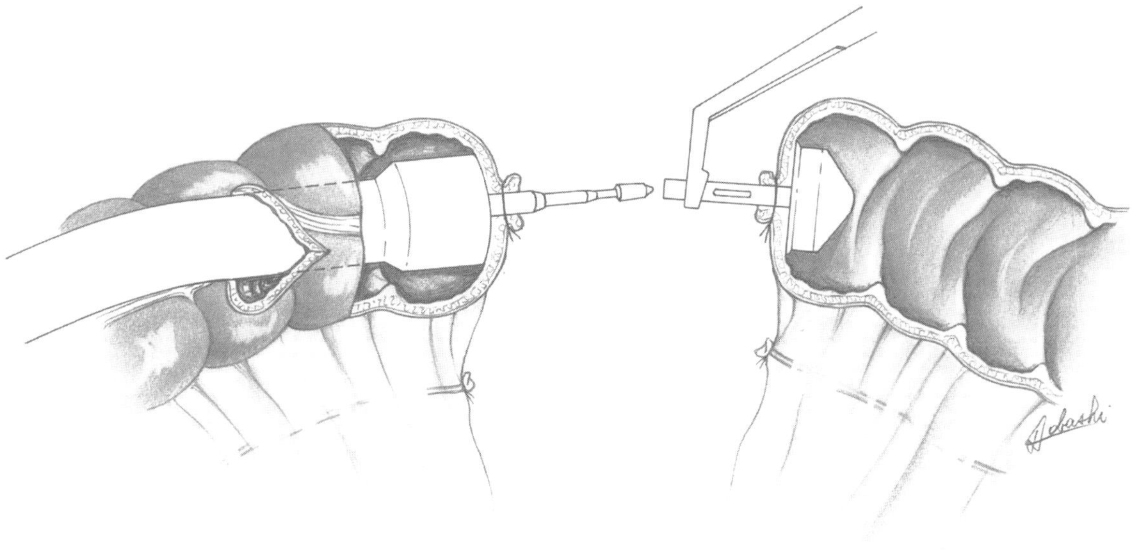

Having ensured that the head and stapler are assembled, and having aligned the two sections of intestine, the stapler is closed and fired.
Before proceeding to remove the circular stapler, the adjusting knob should be slightly opened to facilitate the extraction of the stapler. The colotomy is closed through application of a linear stapler.

Following extraction, the resected tissue inside the stapler should be checked. An incomplete "doughnut" may indicate an imperfect anastomosis.

The colotomy is closed by applying a linear stapler.

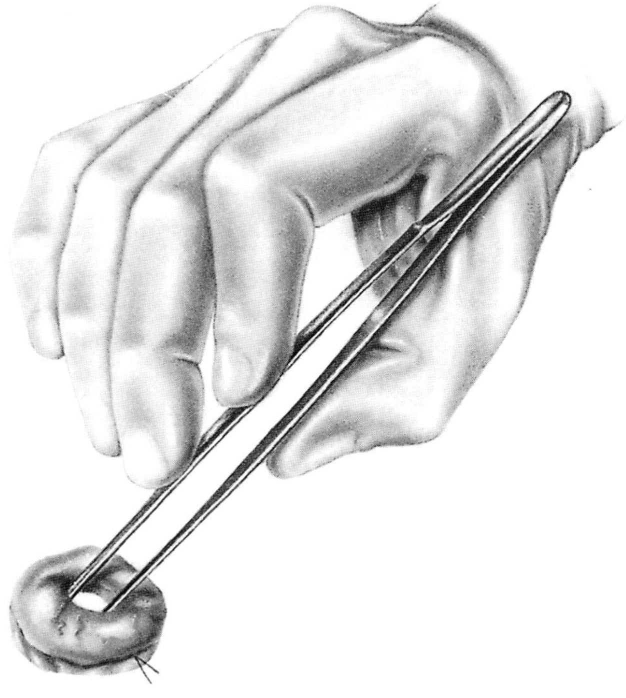

End-to-side Anastomosis with Circular Stapler and Linear Stapler

Using this technique, the anastomosis is performed under application of a circular stapler and closure of the intestine with a linear stapler. The illustration depicts a right hemicolectomy.

Mobilisation, transection, and resection of the right colon and ileum take place by using a linear cutter twice or scalpel transection of the bowel, with prior application of clamps to avoid any bowel leakages.

The circular stapler with an adequate diameter (selected at the surgeon's discretion or by sizers) is opened. The stapler head is removed and the staple body with the integral trocar retreated is inserted 6 to 8 cm into the lumen of the colon. The tip of the instrument's trocar should be gently pressed against the anti-mesenteric aspect of the colon, where the anastomosis will take place, until it perforates the bowel wall.

A purse-string suture is placed at the terminal segment of the ileum. The circular stapler head is inserted so that the purse-string suture is closed around the anvil. In doing this, care must be taken not to damage the suture, and to eliminate any excess ligature.

Having ensured that the head and the instrument are assembled and having aligned the two sections of the intestine, the circular stapler is closed and fired.

Once the circular stapler has been removed and the completeness and haemostasis of the anastomosis has been checked, the colon is closed using a linear stapler.

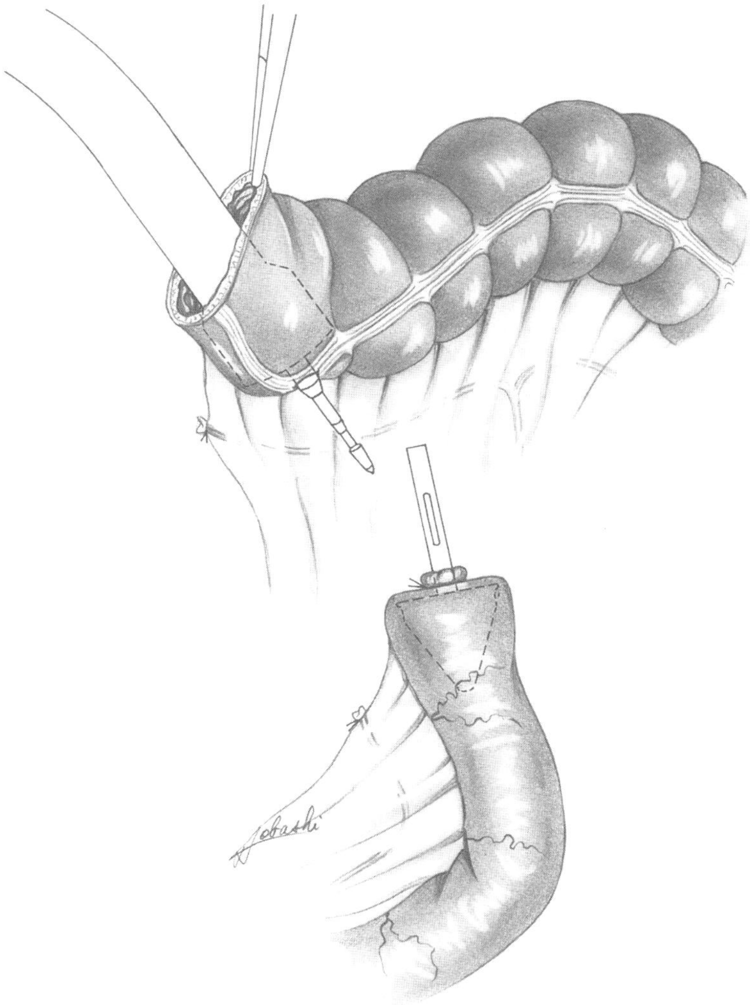

4 Purse-string

In performing an anastomosis one of the critical factors for success is the correct creation of a purse-string suture. Clinical evidence has demonstrated that one of the main reasons anastomoses fail is an incorrect purse-string. This is especially true in the deep pelvis. Therefore, it is essential to have a good understanding of the principles involved in creating a correct purse-string, as well as the different techniques used.

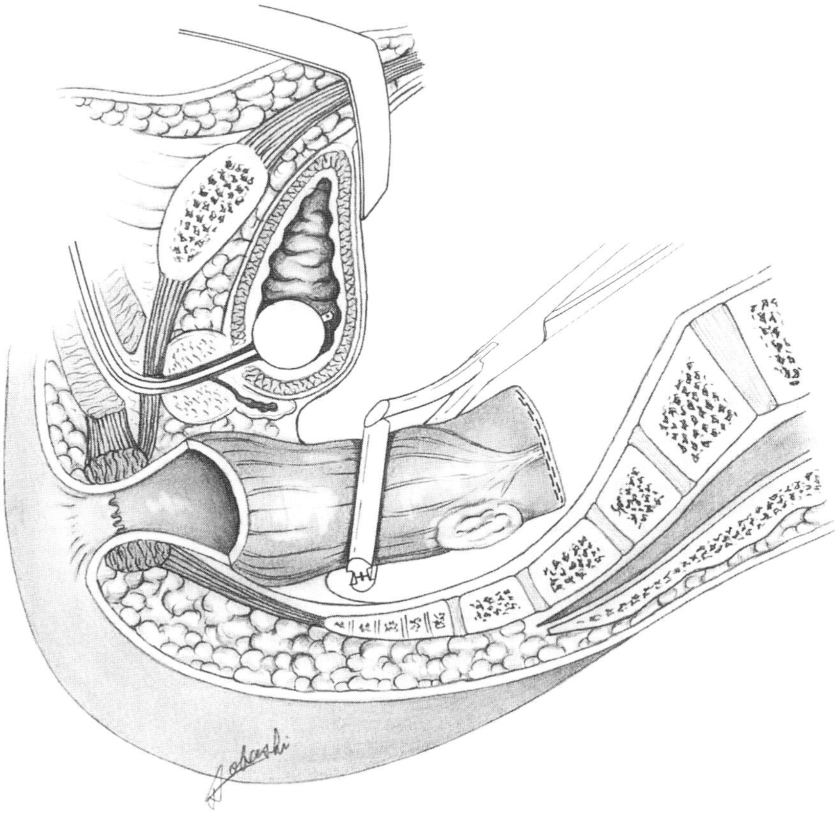

Principles of Creating a Purse-string

A purse-string can be carried out manually or with the aid of a purse-string clamp. In both approaches the suture material of choice is monofilament. This will ensure that the suture will slide easily while the purse-string is being tied, as well as minimising cutting of the tissue in the process. It is important not to damage the suture with needle holders to avoid future suture breakage.

A manually placed purse-string suture should ideally start at the anti-mesenteric bowel side. This will later facilitate purse-string closure under direct visualisation. The maximum distance of the needle stitches (which should include all tissue layers) should be 4 mm from the cutting edge and 6 mm from puncture to puncture.

Hand-sewn Purse-string Suturing Techniques

Standard "Through-and-through"

The suturing will include all tissue layers and is performed by initially running the needle from the external to the internal wall, and ending with the needle passing from the internal to the external wall. This technique has the advantage of easier pull-down while minimising tissue cuff and suture breakage.

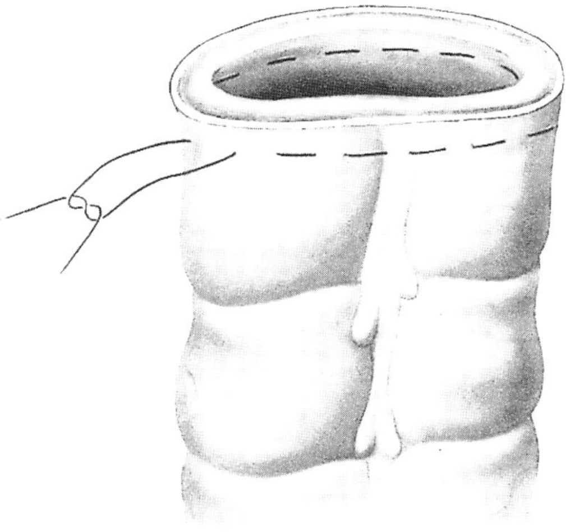

"Baseball" or Whip Stitch Purse-string Suturing

The suturing will include all tissue layers and is performed by running the needle always from the external to the internal wall, including the tissue edges, except for the last stitch. In this technique only monofilament suture material should be used. This technique is sometimes useful with a smaller diameter lumen.

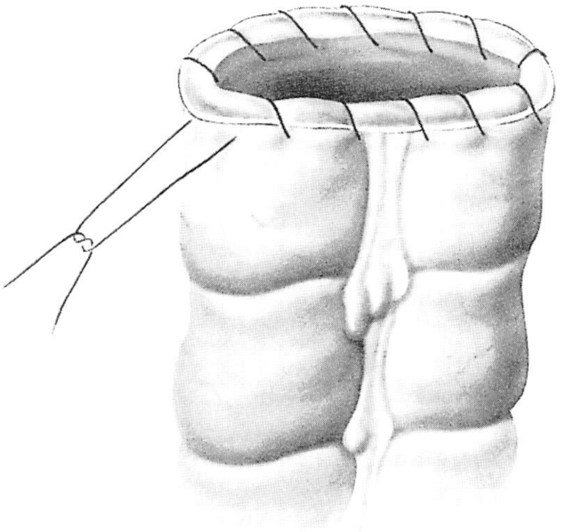

Whip Stitch with Loop

This technique is a variation of the previous one and is used in bowels with a large lumen. A long loop should be left after half of the circumference has been sutured, so as to provide a second pulling point to aid in the closure of the lumen.

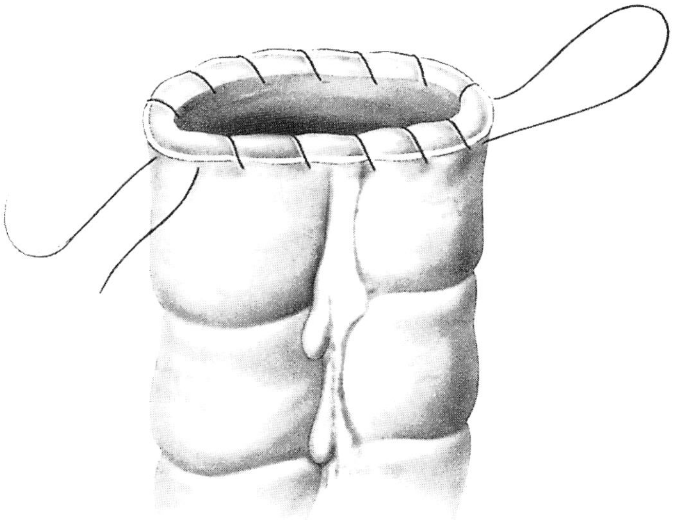

Whip Stitch with Two Sutures

This technique is a variation of the previous one, in that two separate sutures are used to create two pulling points.

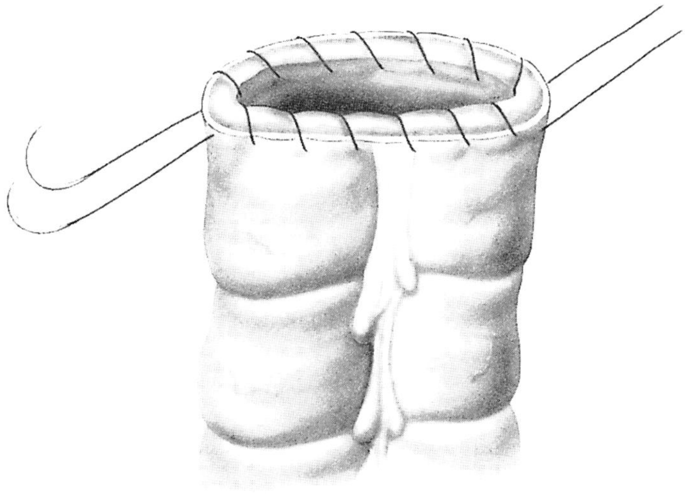

Thorlakson Clamp as an Aid

The Thorlakson clamp facilitates purse-string suturing by keeping the lumen of the bowel open.

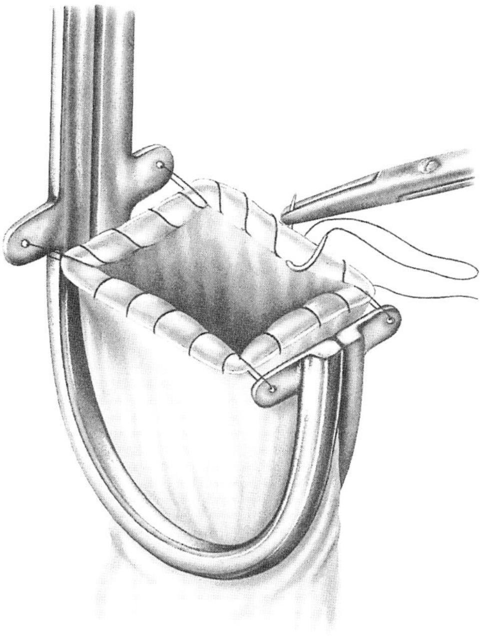

Techniques for Added Security in Creating a Purse-string

After the purse-string has been tied around the axis of the stapler, additional security can be attained by wrapping suture around it.

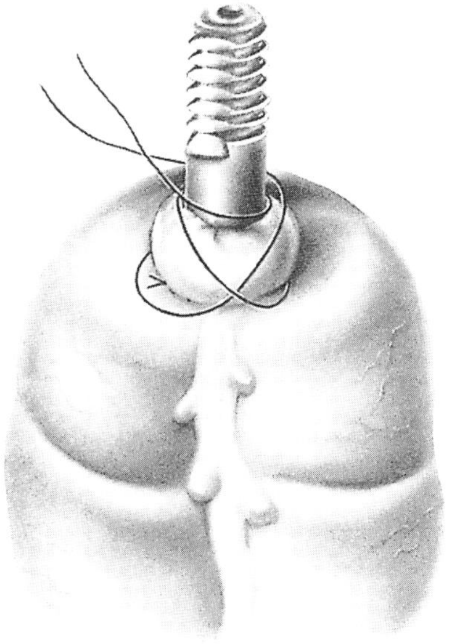

When the distance between the stitches is not uniform, an additional stitch needs to be placed in the gap to maintain the integrity of the purse-string.

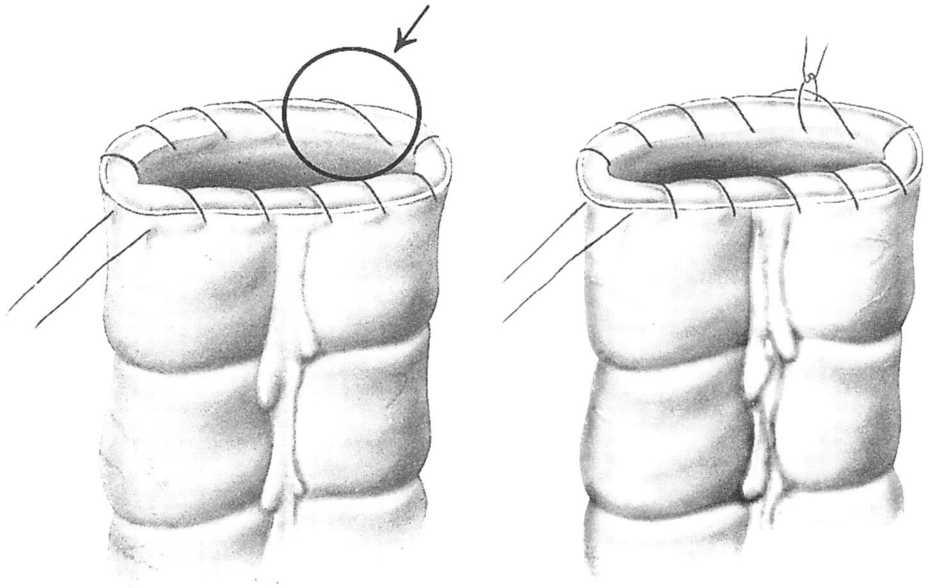

Clamp-Aided Purse-string Suture

In order to apply the purse-string suture clamp, the bowel is dissected from mesentery and fat in the area of the intended anastomosis (1.5–2.0 cm). The clamp must be applied at a right angle, not obliquely, to avoid too much bowel tissue on one side being present in the circular stapler after tying the purse-string. After having applied the clamp any corrections will only be possible if the bowel segment damaged by the teeth of the clamp is resected; if this is not carried out, postoperative complications owing to ischaemia and necrosis could occur.

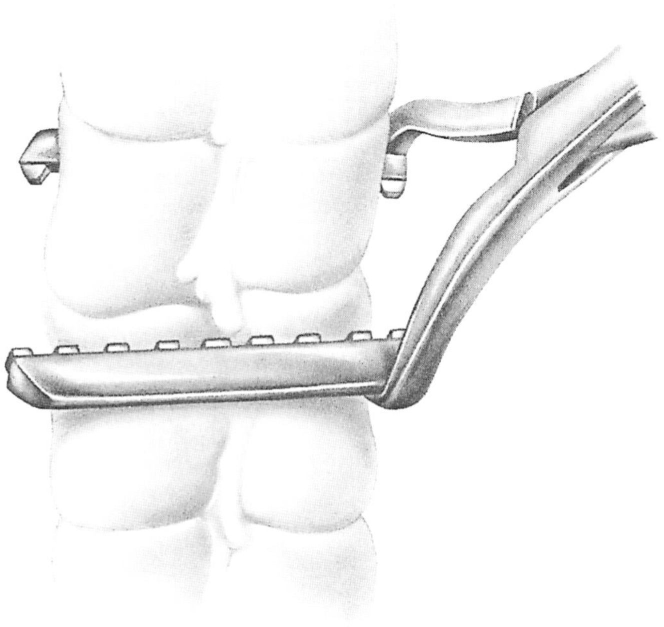

For the placement of a purse-string suture, the ATRALOC Staw-Needle, a 75 cm monofilament suture with two soft 60 mm needles, is recommended. To avoid the needle stitching twice into the same needle canal, it is recommended that both needles be inserted into their respective needle canals. In narrow areas the needle can be bent immediately after it comes out of the needle canal, so that the needle can be adjusted to the corresponding space.

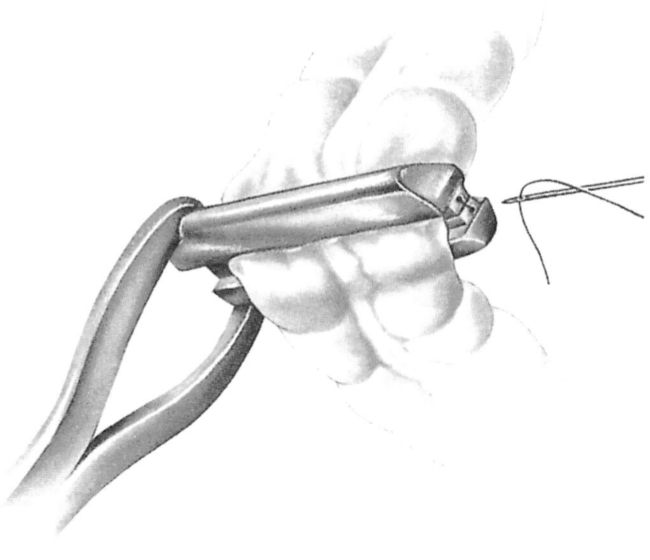

The bowel must be resected with a scalpel along the cutting edge of the purse-string suture clamp. This maintains an optimal distance between purse-string suture and cutting edge to avoid having too much tissue within the instrument head. When opening the clamp, ensure that the suture comes loose from the needle canals and that the purse-string suture is complete.

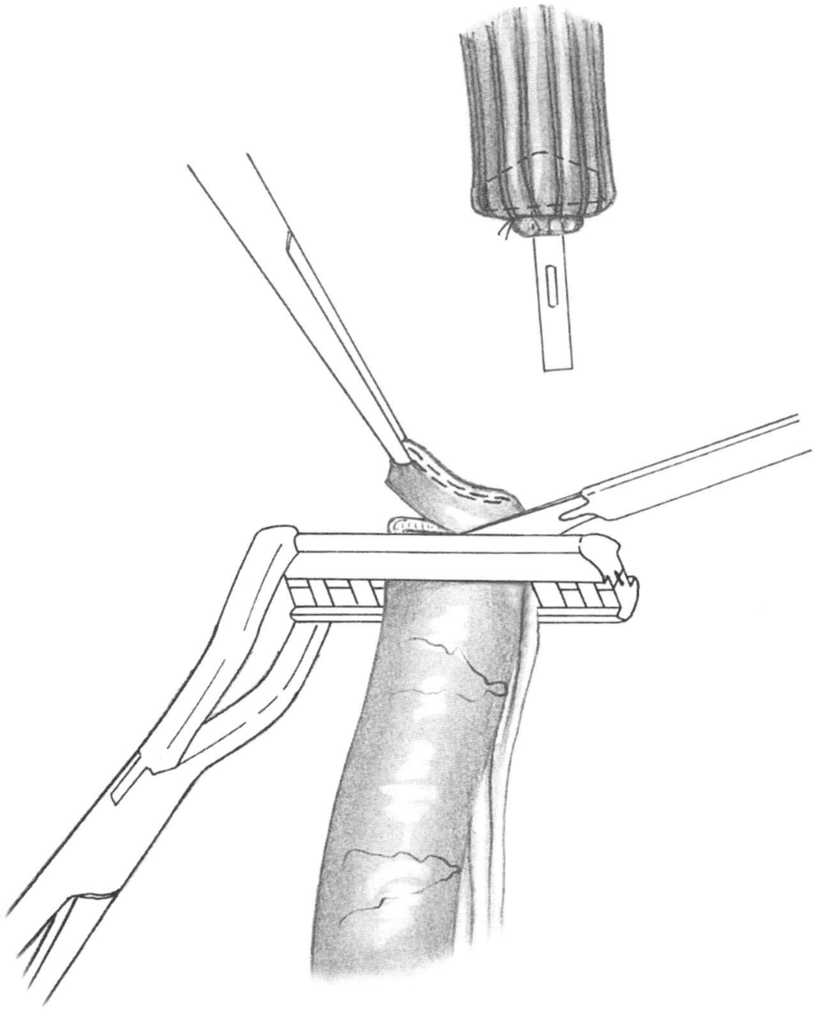

If desired, the purse-string suture clamp can be left in place for a prolonged period. There is no risk of necrosis because the tissue segment traumatised by the clamp is resected by the circular stapler.

5 Ultracision – The Harmonic Scalpel

In surgery, the technique of dissecting without blood loss is of paramount importance. The range of possible indications is significantly influenced by the reliability of the technology employed for dividing tissues while securing haemostasis. Thick and/or adipose structures with numerous blood vessels (greater omentum, mesentery of the large and small intestine, regional lymph drainage areas) are particularly poorly accessible for video-endoscopic haemostasis. Safe video-endoscopic division of these anatomical structures usually exceeds the capacity of both high frequency current techniques and video-endoscopic suturing. Ultrasound dissection technology (Ultracision - the "harmonic scalpel") was developed as an alternative technology.

The harmonic scalpel was conceived primarily for minimally invasive surgery (MIS) in order to dispense with the considerable disadvantages and risks associated with HF (high frequency) current technology. Ultracision also facilitates new methods of extremely gentle surgical dissection without blood loss.

The rationale of the harmonic scalpel is atraumatic surgical dissection and haemostasis, which is gentle to the tissues, using direct application of ultrasound.

Electrical energy is converted into mechanical energy by the generator in the handpiece through a piezoelectric crystal system. The blade or tip of the instrument being used vibrates axially with a constant frequency of 55,500 Hertz. The longitudinal extension of the vibration can be varied between 25 and 100 μm in 5 levels. The energy liberated as an ultrasound wave is directly applied to the tissue.

The harmonic scalpel yields 3 possible effects: cavitation, coaptation/coagulation, and cutting. These effects can be applied to the tissue singly or in synergetic combination. The synergetic expression of these 3 effects depends on the type of tissue (water content), level selection on the generator (extension of longitudinal vibration), application time of energy, type and handling of the active instrument, and tension, pressure, or both to the tissue.

Premises for the Development of Ultracision

In surgery, it is possible to divide small and larger blood vessels between ligatures during dissection or to control them by suturing them in the event of active bleeding. In addition, high frequency electrical coagulation (HF cautery) has been used in all branches of surgery for decades to deal with even the smallest sources of bleeding. HF cautery is used for cutting tissue as well as for haemostasis.

The techniques of tissue division and haemostasis familiar from open surgery cannot be used in the usual way in video-endoscopic surgery. This cir-

cumstance has led to various compromise solutions and has hitherto appreciably narrowed the range of indications of MIS.
The "cautery hook", used mainly for laparoscopic cholecystectomy, is suitable for dissection and division of anatomically distinct planes (non-infected cholecystectomy). The "hook", however, rapidly proves to be an inadequate instrument when local operating conditions are difficult, or when the range of indications of one's own video-endoscopic repertoire is being extended, especially as regards haemostasis.

Classical surgical dissection technique (forceps, scissors) can be used in MIS up to the point at which clamps have to be applied and ligatures or transfixation placed under "open" conditions because of bleeding or for preliminary haemostasis. This situation can occur in a comparable manner in MIS but is then more difficult. Placing clips, suture loops, or transfixion sutures, or the use of stapling devices, even when the surgeon possesses appropriate technical expertise, is often tedious, time-consuming, cost-intensive, and surgically unsatisfactory.

The limited technical possibilities have hitherto prevented an extension of the range of indications of video-endoscopic surgery but, on the other hand, they have stimulated the development of new technology, such as that of the harmonic scalpel.

Ultracision will replace high frequency electrosurgery which is associated with many disadvantages and risks, both in open and minimally invasive surgery.

The concept of ultrasound dissection was first developed for videoscopic surgery. General acceptance of this new technology favoured the practical use of the harmonic scalpel in all fields of surgical activity very rapidly, thus launching a variety of new instruments.

High Frequency Electrosurgery

Principle of High Frequency Surgery

High frequency electrical coagulation (HF cautery) in monopolar and bipolar form has been used in all branches of surgery for decades to deal with even the smallest sources of bleeding and for dividing tissue.

In HF surgery, high frequency electrical alternating current (500 to 1000 kHz; 100 to 20,000 volts) is used directly on the patient. The patient is thus connected directly to the electric circuit (Fig. 1).

The principle of HF surgery is based on an electrically-induced localised development of heat which leads to denaturing of protein compounds, destruction of cells and tissues, and burning or carbonisation.

When cutting with HF cautery, the great localised development of heat at the tip of the instrument causes cells to burst with a release of water vapour. As a result of the extremely high temperature, there is immediate

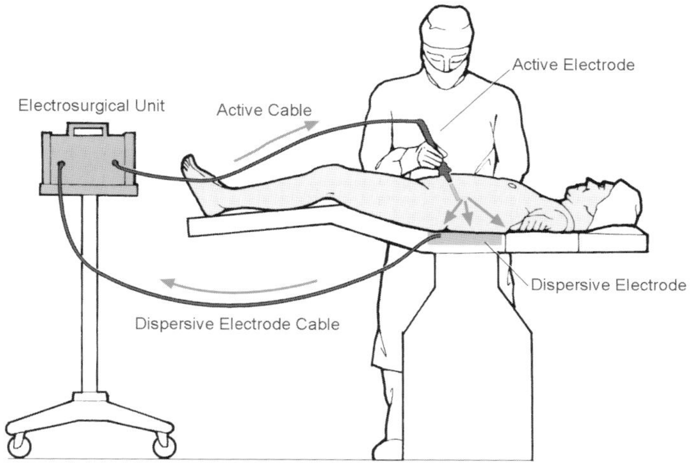

Fig. 1 Flow of electrosurgical current in a complete monopolar unit.

drying of the tissue and burning and carbonisation of the structures in the area affected by the instrument.

With the monopolar method (Fig. 2) which is used predominantly, the electric current is sent through the patient. At the active instrument tip, the current density is bundled towards a large-surface neutral electrode which is applied to the patient. The current density, which is high at the point, causes the liberation of heat energy and leads to coagulation and encrustation of the tissue.

With the bipolar method (Fig. 3) of HF surgery, there is a flow of current between the limbs of a special forceps. In this case, the major part of the electrical current flows between the limbs of the instrument.

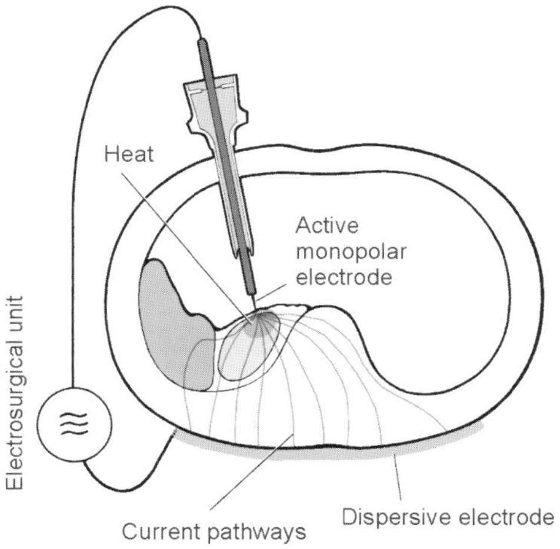

Fig. 2 Monopolar electrosurgery: current passes through tissue to ground pad in videoscopic surgery.

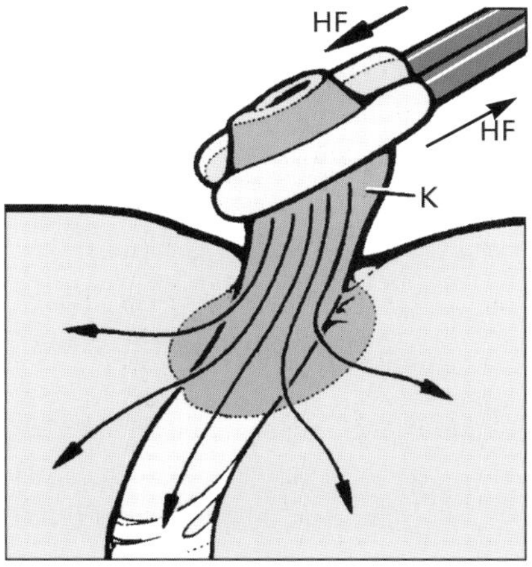

Fig. 3 Bipolar electrosurgery: most current confined between 2 electrodes.

Disadvantages of HF Surgery

A fundamental disadvantage of HF cautery consists of the fact that electrical current is sent through the body of a usually anaesthetised patient. As a result, all of the risks of using an electrical current are present. The international literature reports numerous cases in open surgery of severe burns to patients due to current leakage, and also of explosions during the use of HF cautery on the bowel.

Disadvantages of HF surgery
- direct electrical current flow through the patient
- electric shock and burns or both (patient/surgeon)
- extensive, deep tissue damage (carbonisation)
- unnoticed distant tissue damage due to current leakage

In the event of the slightest damage to the surgical gloves, electrical shocks and unpleasant burns also occur on the surgeon's hands when HF surgery is used.

MIS operations are particularly burdened by complications associated with the use of electrosurgical methods. Numerous cases were reported in the literature in which tissue damage occurred distant from the actual operation area, resulting in very major postoperative complications. For laparoscopic cholecystectomy alone, there have been more than 30 different documented situations of electrosurgically-induced injuries.

Causes of complications of HF surgery
- steel ports, hybrid ports, or both
- absent or defective insulation of the instrument
- contact with metal clips or other instruments
- current flow through fluids and current leakages.

In monopolar HF surgery, the electric current can arc unnoticed to the tissue far beyond the videoscopic field of vision and cause injury. Such "current marks" in the intestinal tract can lead after a delay of up to a week to perforation and life-threatening peritonitis.

Unnoticed bilateral duodenal perforations are reported repeatedly in the literature. The mortality of duodenal perforation is about 50%, as the secondary perforations are often diagnosed and treated adequately only very late after discharge to home care, owing to the short postoperative period in hospital after cholecystectomy.

Defective insulation occurs in conventional cautery hooks mainly because of repeated cleaning procedures with sharp instruments, or with e.g. the Ti polisher, when an attempt is made to get burnt-on and carbonised tissue remnants off the instrument. Insulation defects also arise from scrubbing sharp-edged steel ports.

Due to short circuiting, injuries occur outside the videoscopic field of vision in the hollow organs of the intestinal tract or in the common bile duct.

Modern HF cautery often includes a so-called "cutting aid"; with this, a peak current is applied immediately after pressing the foot pedal. This uncontrollably high energy use leads rapidly to injuries of the gall bladder when the hook is used. Leakage of bile makes the further course of the operation difficult, involves a possible risk of contamination, and causes the awkward and time-consuming loss of the stone in the abdomen.

A systemic problem with the HF hook is the adhesive effect. When haemostasis is attempted, burnt tissue often remains stuck to the forceps after coagulation is complete, and tears small vessels open again when the instrument is removed. This phenomenon also occurs in laparoscopic surgery (e.g. haemostasis in the liver bed) and is highly disagreeable. The cause is the electrical conductivity of the desiccated, scorched tissue, which is in fact reduced to zero.

Current leakages owing to uncontrolled and unpredictable conduction of the electric current in liquids are particularly dangerous (Fig. 4). In MIS, when bleeding occurs, it is seldom possible to stop the injury adequately and to coagulate it, because of the number of available ports limiting the number of instruments.

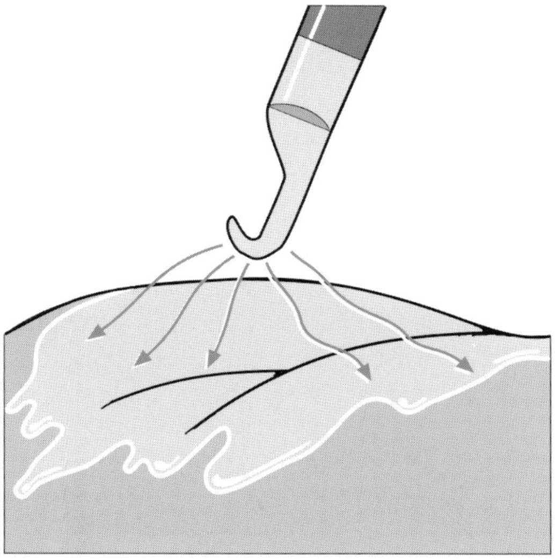

Fig. 4 Electrode is not fully embedded in the tissue so that high voltage sparking occurs from coagulation setting.

A particularly troublesome disadvantage of HF cautery in MIS is the frequently considerable smoke production. The impairment of vision by the smoke often makes repeated deflation of the pneumoperitoneum necessary, causing considerable time delays and possible contamination of surgical personnel.
A further disadvantage is the additional delay of the progress of a MIS operation through the frequently required changes of instruments.

The development of Ultracision, the harmonic scalpel, eliminates the disadvantages of high frequency current technology for surgery, and establishes a new technology for tissue dissection, tissue division, and haemostasis.

Cavitation, Coaptation and Coagulation, Cutting

The new technology of the harmonic scalpel avoids all of the disadvantages of conventional HF surgery. The application of ultrasound to the tissues allows 3 effects which act synergetically at all times: cavitation, coaptation/coagulation, cutting.

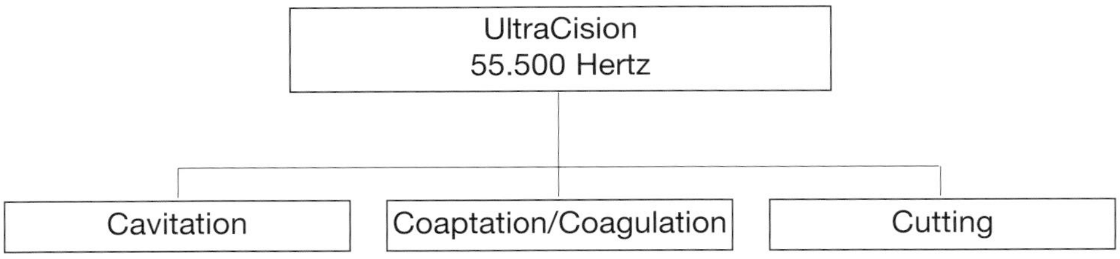

Cavitation

Cavitation describes the formation and disappearance of vapour bubbles in flowing liquids when the velocity is altered (Fig. 5). If the pressure falls below the vapour pressure of the liquid under acceleration in a flowing liquid, vapour bubbles form in the liquid; with subsequent slowing, the pressure rises again, causing condensation. The large alterations of volume give rise to vigorous surges of pressure, which lead to sound radiation and damage to solid bodies. This phenomenon occurs in connection with turbines, valves, and propellers, for example.

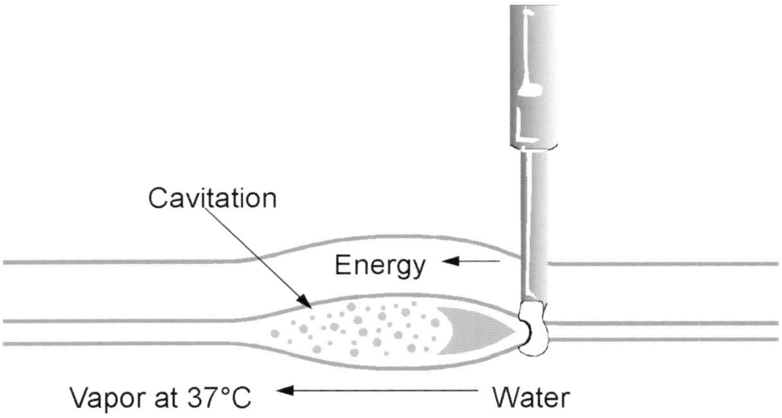

Fig. 5 Cavitation by application of ultrasound to the tissue causes dissection of tissue planes by water vaporisation at body temperature.

When the harmonic scalpel is used, the cavitation occurs the other way around: by means of high-frequency vibration of a solid body. The vibration is transmitted to the tissues and there leads to rapid volume changes of the tissue and cell fluid. This in turn leads to the formation of vapour bubbles at body temperature. In the parenchyma, cells explode while in connective tissue, the bubble formation leads to the dissection of tissue planes.

Cavitation to dissect tissue planes is of benefit especially in anatomically inaccessible regions or in the vicinity of vulnerable structures. In preparation for laparoscopic fundoplication, exposure of the oesophagus with the Ultracision scissors takes place exactly under vision and without any bleeding.

Coaptation and Coagulation

Coaptation (Latin aptare = stick) means the adherence or welding together of tissues. When ultrasound and pressure are used on tissue at the same time, there is disruption of the tertiary hydrogen bonds in proteins. This fragmentation of protein compounds leads to the adherence of collagen molecules at low temperatures (from body temperature up to max. 63 °C). When the locally applied energy acts for longer periods, there is also a rise in temperature leading to the thermally-induced release of water vapour (63 °C to 100 °C) and later to coagulation (denaturing of protein) at a maximum temperature of 150 °C.

Coaptation is used for preliminary haemostasis in laparoscopic cholecystectomy. Application of ultrasound energy to the tissue and exertion of pressure at the same time leads to sealing of superficial vessels, which can then be divided without bleeding.

In coagulation, the ultrasound energy is applied to the tissue together with pressure for longer periods (a few seconds). The additional thermal effect causes coagulation (denaturing) of proteins as well as coaptation (fragmentation).

Cutting

By using tension, pressure, or both, the tissue is rapidly stretched beyond its elastic limit by the high-frequency vibration and is cut smoothly by a sharp blade or instrument tip. In cholecystectomy, for instance, a dissecting blade is used which is similar to the cautery hook familiar from HF surgery.

The effect of cutting can be explained by the "rubber band phenomenon": if the blade of a scalpel is applied to an unstretched rubber band, the band will retreat because of its elasticity. However, if the rubber band is stretched, a light touch of the blade suffices to cut through it.

Local Tissue Temperature

When the harmonic scalpel is used, no electric current is sent through the patient, in contrast to HF cautery. All of the risks associated with the direct use of electric current are thus avoided.

The various effects of the harmonic scalpel in the tissues are achieved at temperatures of up to a maximum of 150 °C. Coaptation leads to fragmentation of proteins and coagulation to denaturing of protein compounds (Fig. 6).

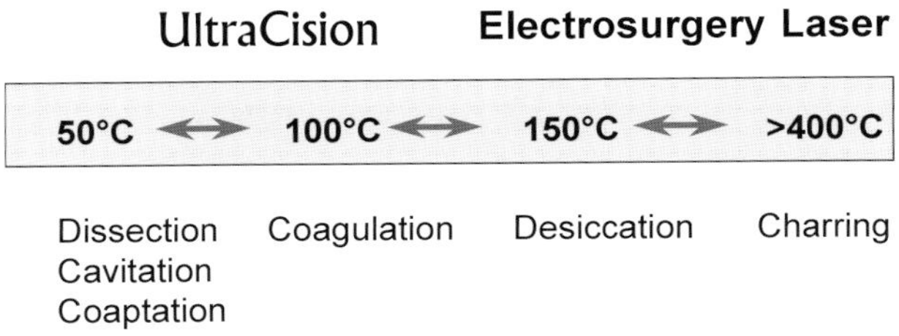

Fig. 6 Local tissue temperature with Ultracision, electrosurgery and Laser.

Cavitation occurs at body temperature, coaptation in the range between body temperature and below 100 °C, and coagulation at a temperature of up to 150 °C. In this way there is no burning, carbonisation, or smoke formation, as is the case with cautery or the laser when temperatures of up to 400 °C are reached (Fig. 7).

UltraCision

Electrosurgery / Laser

Temp. (°C)	Visual Change	Biological Change
37 - 50	Swelling	Heating, Retraction, Reduced Enzyme Activity
50 - 65	Blanching	Coagulation
65 - 90	white/gray	Protein Denaturation
90 - 100	Puckering	Drying of Tissue
> 100	Drying	H_2O boils, Cell Explosion
> 150	Charring	Carbonisation
300 - 400	Blackening	Smoke Generation

Fig. 7 Macroscopic and microscopic tissue changes with Ultracision, electrosurgery, and laser at various local tissue temperatures.

Depth of Energy Penetration

When HF cautery is used, the maximum depth of penetration (Fig. 8) of the thermal electrical effect is reached soon after application of the HF current. When Ultracision, the harmonic scalpel, is used, the depth of penetration of the flow of energy (measured in mm) has a linear correlation with time (measured in seconds). The possibility of deeper penetration of tissue can be controlled more precisely when using the harmonic scalpel using the "application time" factor.

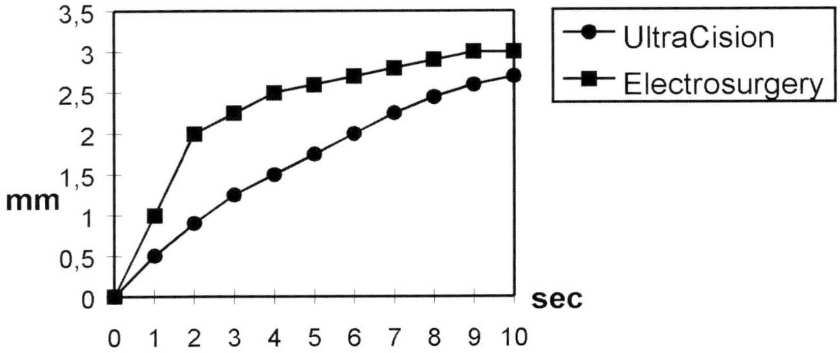

Fig. 8 Depth of energy penetration (liver) using Ultracision or electrocautery.

After an application time of about 5 seconds, which may not be exceeded during practical use of the harmonic scalpel, the depth of penetration is less than half of that in HF cautery. In practice, this is demonstrated by the fact that coagulation using Ultracision, the harmonic scalpel, to achieve an effect equivalent to HF cautery always takes longer, but the effect on tissues is more readily controllable.

Apart from the depth of penetration of the energy, the temperature in the tissues and therefore the risk of unwanted thermal injury is considerably lower.

Lateral Energy Spread

Lateral spread of the energy flow and the effect that can be achieved with it reaches submaximum values after 3 seconds when HF cautery is used (Fig. 9). When the harmonic scalpel is used, there is a linear correlation between the time of application and the lateral spread of the effective energy flow.

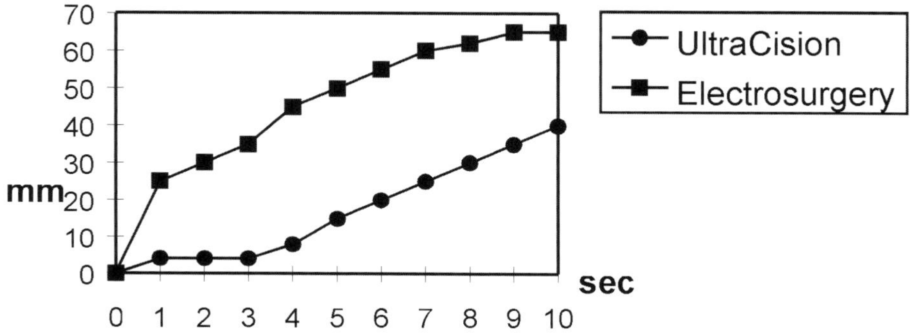

Fig. 9 Lateral spread of energy (liver) using Ultracision or electrocautery.

The risk of distant tissue damage is lower than in HF cautery, because of the lower lateral spread of the coagulation zone per se, and because of the effect being controllable through the time factor.

Safe use of Ultracision, the harmonic scalpel, allows low-risk dissection even close to vulnerable structures (e.g. bowel, ureter, blood vessels) where the use of HF cautery is ruled out or carries a high potential for risk.

Technological advantages of Ultracision

- no electrical current flow through the patient
- no risk of burns to the patient
- no distant tissue damage due to unnoticed current leakages
- no carbonisation of tissue
- no smoke formation
- no depth effect, minimal lateral propagation of the energy flow
- no neuromuscular stimulation
- no neutral electrode
- no risk of electric shocks or burns for the surgeon

Synergy – The Principle of Practical Use

The possible effects of Ultracision, the harmonic scalpel, - cavitation, coaptation/coagulation, and cutting - can always be used both as single functions and in any chosen modified synergetic combination (Fig. 10).

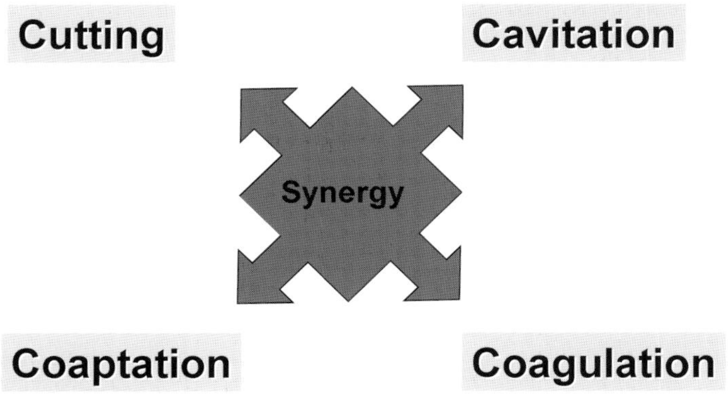

Fig. 10 Synergy of 4 Ultracision qualities: Cavitation, Cutting, Coaptation, Coagulation

The effect of the applied ultrasound energy on the tissue is dependent on the following parameters:

- type of tissue (parenchyma, connective tissue)
- water content of the tissue
- setting of the device (variation of amplitude at 5 levels)
- type of instrument blade used
- exertion of tension, pressure, or both on the tissue
- duration of energy effect on the tissue

The amplitude of the axial vibration of the tip of the instrument can be set on the generator at 5 levels from level 1 to level 5. At level 1 the axial amplitude of vibration (deflection of tip of instrument in its longitudinal axis) is 25 µm. The frequency of the ultrasound energy (55,500 Hertz) is not affected by this setting. At level 5 the amplitude of the vibration of the tip of the instrument is 100 µm. The vibration frequency is 55,500 Hertz. Apart from the type of instrument used (sharp, blunt, pointed, flat), operation of the instrument being used is of importance.

The desired effect of ultrasound energy on the tissue depends on the synergistically combined application of ultrasound energy and mechanical force (tension and/or pressure on the tissue). When shears are used, the side of the instrument blade selected (sharp, blunt, flat) is pressed against the teflon-coated tissue pad with a variable degree of force (Fig. 11). In addition, variable tension on the tissue can be exerted overall with the closed instrument. The "strength" of the ultrasound energy is selected by choosing the amplitude of the axial vibration of the blade (level 1–5), and the amount of applied ultrasound energy is determined by the "application time" factor.

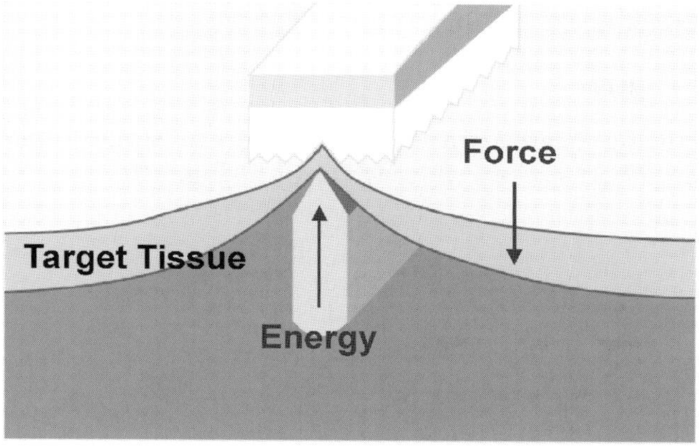

Fig. 11 Shears: the direction of energy is parallel to the applied force.

Cavitation is associated with the presence of water and is therefore employed predominantly in tissues with a high water content (Fig. 12). On the other hand, cutting is preferred in tissues with an extremely low water content (e.g. fascia).

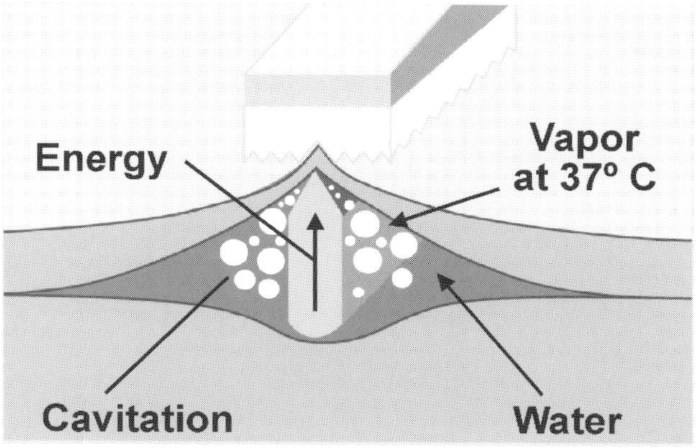

Fig. 12 Low pressure at the blade tip causes fluid to vaporise at low temperature. Cavitation causes separation of tissue planes.

Sharp blades, exertion of tension, pressure, or both on the tissues, and high amplitude (level 5) lead to rapid tissue dissection/transection. Blunt blades or instrument tips, low tension or pressure in the tissues, and low amplitude (level 1–3) lead to coaptation and also to coagulation, depending on the time of effect of the energy.

Practical Use

The practical use of Ultracision entails a considerable change of the individual surgical technique for the surgeon who is used to high frequency electrosurgery. A basic requirement for a successful changeover is precise knowledge and understanding of the technical basis and characteristics of the harmonic scalpel, and the necessary patience. Experience has shown that there are 3 periods in the course of implementation of Ultracision:

The learning phase is limited to the first 2 weeks; during this time, the basic functions of Ultracision are experienced, step by step, in practical use, and can be converted for one's own area of use.

The learning phase can be shortened by attending appropriate theoretical and practical courses.

Although Ultracision was developed primarily for use in laparoscopic surgery, it seems reasonable to first try out the harmonic scalpel only in open surgery, in selected operations, during the initial learning phase.

Attempting to use Ultracision blades as cauterisers results in mainly negative experiences at first. Putting into practice the theoretical knowledge of the significance of tension and pressure, and of the need for a counterpressure for haemostasis, leads rapidly to acceptance and understanding of the functions of Ultracision.

After the first practical experiences in open surgery, use of the dissecting blades for laparoscopic surgery entails no problems. Lysis of adhesions, cholecystectomy, and hernia repair are recommended as being suitable operations initially. The absence of the otherwise very intrusive smoke and the possibility of risk-free dissection close to hilar structures in comparison to cautery rapidly make themselves obvious as particular advantages in laparoscopic cholecystectomy.

Ultracision is employed for general use in the entire personal operating repertoire in a habituation phase of a further 2 weeks, building on the knowledge of basic functions and uses.

After a habituation period of 2–4 weeks, the surgeon will have adapted the advantages of the new technology to his individual surgical technique. In the utilisation phase, Ultracision can be used in all open and minimally invasive (elective and acute) operations. HF cautery is replaced completely by the harmonic scalpel; thus, attachment of a neutral electrode ("for safety") can be omitted.

6 Ultracision – System Components

The system components of Ultracision consist of the generator and transport cart, the foot switch, the handpiece, and the instruments which are connected to it (Fig. 13).

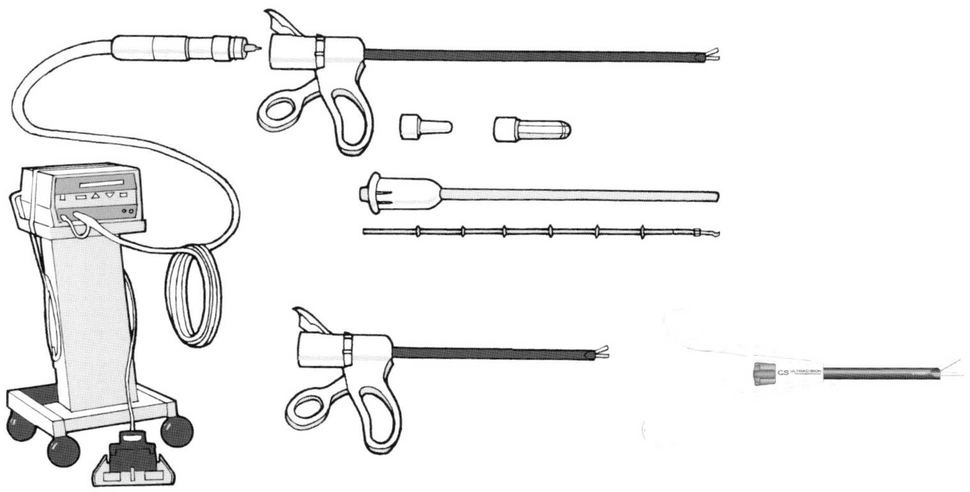

Fig. 13 Ultracision: System components, shears, and blades to be connected to the handpiece.

Generator, Footswitch, and Handpiece

The generator is connected to a regular power supply. The footswitch is used to activate the output of the generator. It has two pedals: from the left one ultrasound energy level can be selected from 5 levels (25 to 100 µm of longitudinal extension of vibration). On the right pedal the level is fixed at 5 (100 µm).

The handpiece contains the ultrasonic transducer and the ultrasonic amplifier (Fig. 14). The generator provides the electrical energy to be converted to ultrasonic energy at the piezoelectric ceramic pieces in the handpiece. The generator also allows continuous monitoring of the ultrasonic function. Irregularities of ultrasonic vibrations in any part of the system result in a continuous acoustic signal and the immediate shutdown of the system.

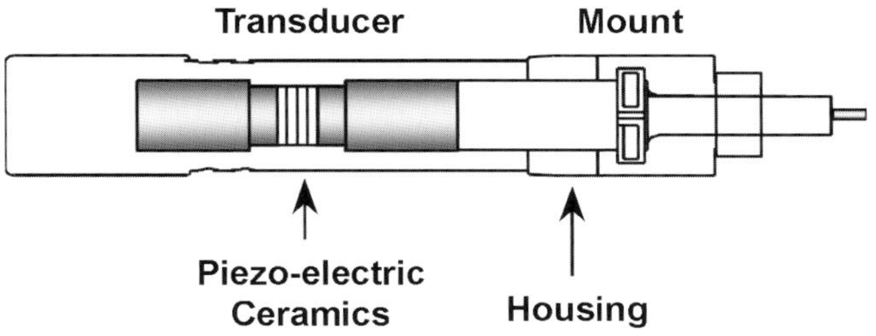

Fig. 14 Handpiece with ultrasonic transducer. Electrical energy is converted into ultrasonic vibration in a piezo-electric ceramic system. Energy is transferred to the blade systems by an acoustic mount coupled to the housing of the handpiece.

Instruments

Ultracision offers a wide range of blades and shears which, when connected to the handpiece, allow surgeons to perform cutting, coagulation, dissection, and grasping of tissue in both open, conventional surgery and in minimally invasive surgery. All of the blades and shears are securely attached to the handpiece with a torque wrench.

Ultracision Blades

According to their diameter there are two type of blades: the 10 mm blades and the 5 mm blades.

The 10 mm blades come in two different lengths, depending on whether they are to be used in open or conventional surgery (short blades: 10cms), or in minimally invasive surgery (long blades: 30cms).

The long 10 mm blades have three different tips according to the desired surgical action (Fig. 15):

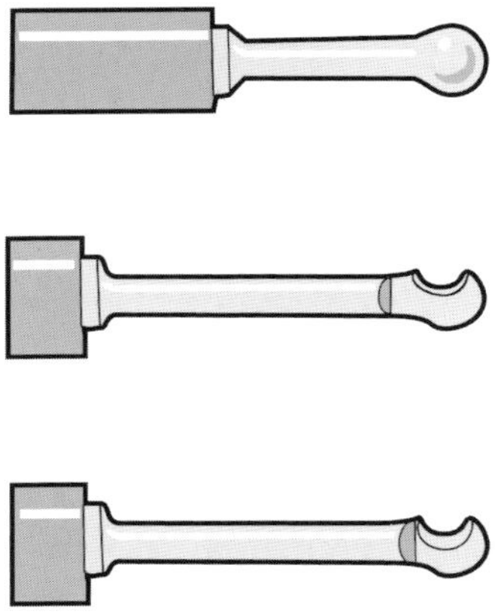

Fig. 15 10mm instruments. The blade tips are configurated as ball coagulator, blunt dissecting blade, and sharp pointed hook.

- *Dissecting hook:* this is a pointed, curved (60° radius of curvature) blade with a blunt outer edge, a sharp inner edge, and a sharp tip.
- *Sharp hook:* this is a pointed, curved (40° radius of curvature) blade with a blunt outer edge, an even sharper inner edge, and a sharp tip.
- *Ball coagulator:* this is a spherical-tip blade.

The blunt outer edge in both the dissecting and sharp blades is used especially for cavitation, point haemostasis, and, to a certain extent, cutting. It corresponds in handling to a poker-like dissecting hook used in HF electrosurgery, and is therefore recommended as a primary instrument during training.

The pointed, sharp, curved blade, on the other hand, is specially designed for cutting. It is more precise in the application of ultrasonic energy. With these sharp edges less tension and pressure is needed for cutting (more so in the sharp than in the dissecting blade). However, the possibility of bleeding while using the sharp edge, if coaptation has not been adequate, is higher than when using the blunt edge.

The flat side of the blade on both the sharp and dissecting hooks can be used for haemostasis just like the blunt outer edge. It should be borne in mind that pressure must be exerted on the tissue, in contrast to HF cautery.

The ball coagulator is used to coagulate broad and diffuse areas of bleeding, e.g. bleeding from the liver bed after cholecystectomy.

The short 10 mm blade has only one tip configuration corresponding to that of the sharp hook (Fig. 16).

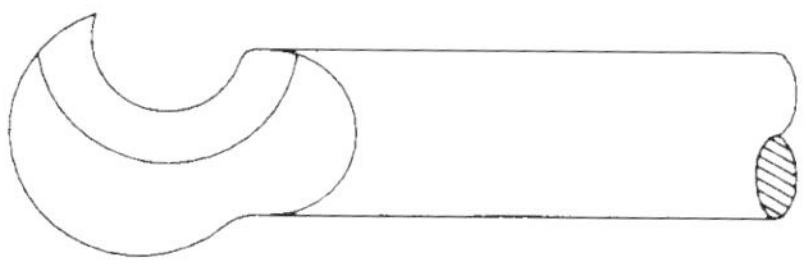

Fig. 16 Design of the 10 mm short blade: blunt outer edge, sharp inner edge, sharp tip.

The 5 mm blades come in three different lengths.

The short 5 mm blades, to be used in open/conventional surgery, have two lengths: 10 and 14 cm, depending on the surgeon's preference and the procedures that he will perform.

The short 5 mm blades have three tip configurations:

- **Dissecting hook:** this is a pointed, curved (60° radius of curvature) blade with a blunt outer edge, a sharp inner edge, and a sharp tip.
- **Sharp hook:** this is a pointed, curved (40° radius of curvature) blade with a blunt outer edge, an even sharper inner edge, and a sharp tip.
- **Curved tip:** This blade has sharp edges on both sides to permit easy cutting in both directions. The concave and convex sides of the blade allow for coagulation, cavitation, and coaptation of tissue. The blunt tip will also facilitate spot coagulation for bleeding points. Due to its curvature, the surgeon will have better visibility and easier access to areas otherwise difficult to reach (Figs. 17–19).

Fig. 17 5 mm sharp blade.

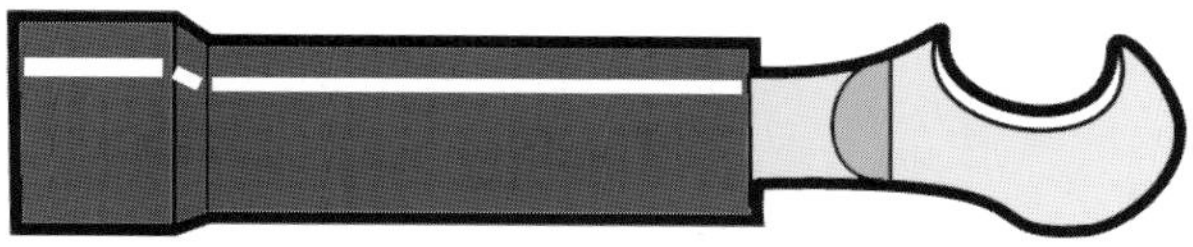

Fig. 18 5 mm dissecting blade.

Fig. 19 5 mm curved blade.

The long 5 mm blades (32 cm) have applications in minimally invasive surgery. They come in four tip configurations:

- **Dissecting hook:** same as in the short 5 mm blade.
- **Sharp hook:** same as in the short 5 mm blade.
- **Curved tip:** same as in the short 5 mm blade.
- **Ball coagulator:** this is a spherical tip blade.

Ultracision Shears

According to the diameter there are two type of shears: the 10 mm shears and the 5 mm shears.

The 10 mm shears come in two lengths:

The short 10 mm shears (20 cm in length), to be used in open/conventional surgery.

The long 10 mm shears (34 cm in length), to be used in minimally invasive surgery.

Both shears consist of a grip housing and a multifunctional blade lodged inside the grip housing. In addition, both shears have two types of handgrip configuration, pistol grip and scissors grip (Fig. 20).

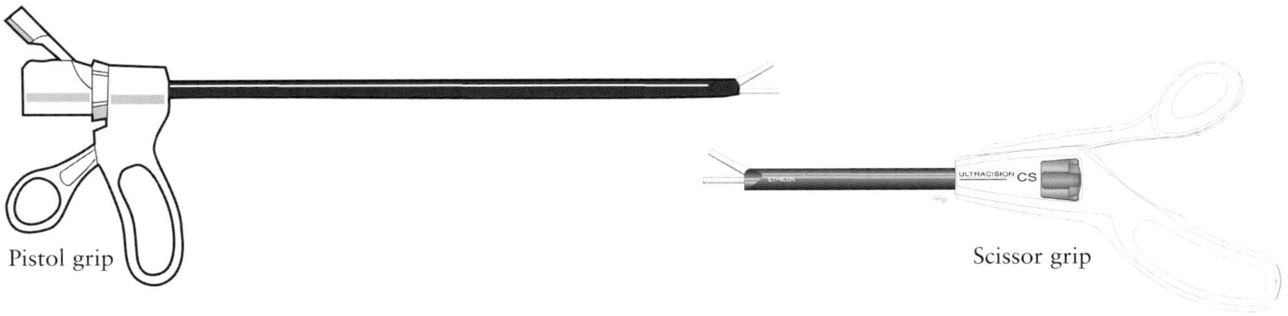

Fig. 20 Ultracision shears with pistol and scissor grip.

The tip of the shears has a mobile non-active branch (Teflon-coated) that allows grasping and blunt dissection of tissue as well as its compression towards the ultrasonic non-mobile active blade.

The multifunctional active blade has 3 sides (sharp, blunt, and flat) that can be adjusted against the tissue pad (Fig. 21).

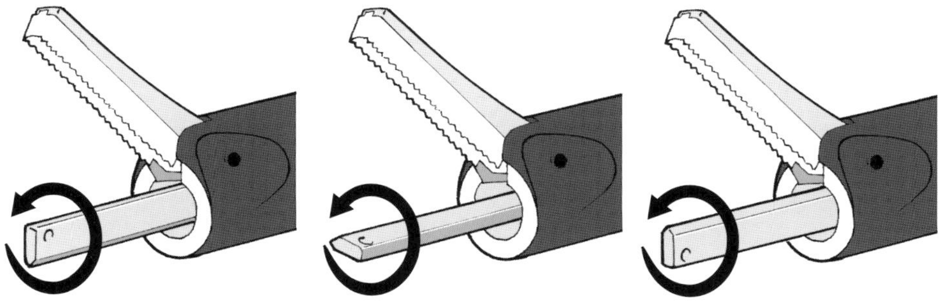

Fig. 21 Ultracision LCS – shears. 3 modes of blade configuration.: blunt, flat, and sharp side.

The sharp edge is designed for cutting tissue. Haemostasis occurs only to a very limited extent with this setting, and is adequate only in the smallest blood vessels (Fig. 22).

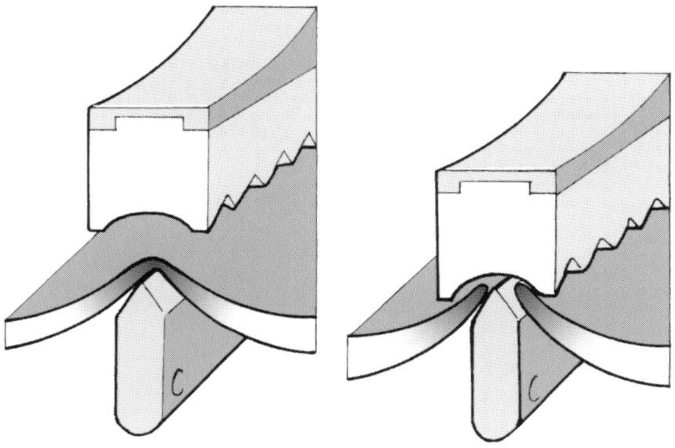

Fig. 22 When cutting tissue with the sharp blade of the shears, the lateral coagulation zone is 0.25 mm to 1 mm.

The blunt edge enables both coaptation/coagulation and, if desired, simultaneous cutting of tissue. Bigger diameter blood vessels can be coagulated with this side of the blade (Fig. 23).

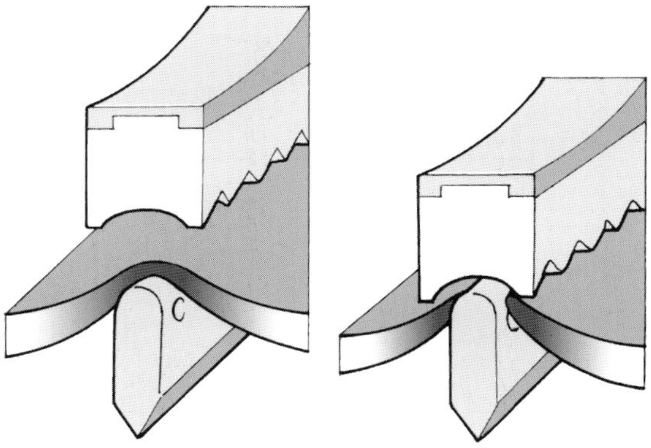

Fig. 23 When cutting tissue with the blunt blade of the shears, the lateral coagulation zone is 0.75 mm to 1.5 mm.

The flat edge is suitable for haemostasis by means of coagulation. It can coagulate vessels of up to 3 mm in diameter (Fig. 24).

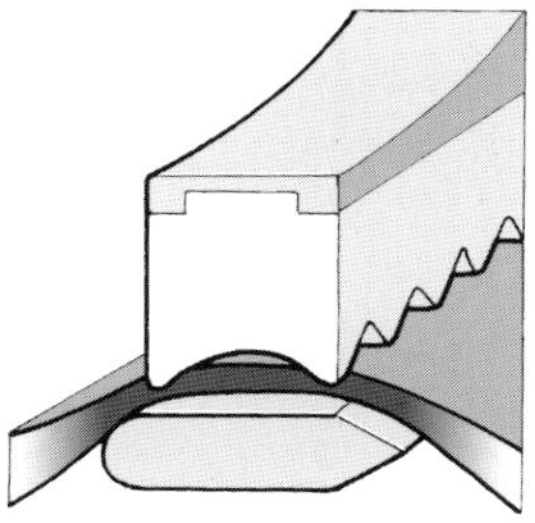

Fig. 24 During coagulation with the flat side, the zone of coagulation corresponds to the width of the tissue pad (2 mm) of the shears.

The cutting and coagulation ability of all of the edges of the blade can be enhanced or decreased by:

- **The power level of the generator:** The higher the level the more cutting and the less coagulation, and vice versa.
- **The grip force on the shears:** The stronger the force the more cutting and the less coagulation, and vice versa.
- **The tension to the tissue:** The stronger the tension the more cutting and the less coagulation, and vice versa.

The 5 mm shears come only in one length (35 cm) adequate for minimally invasive surgery with the pistol grip configuration (Fig. 25).

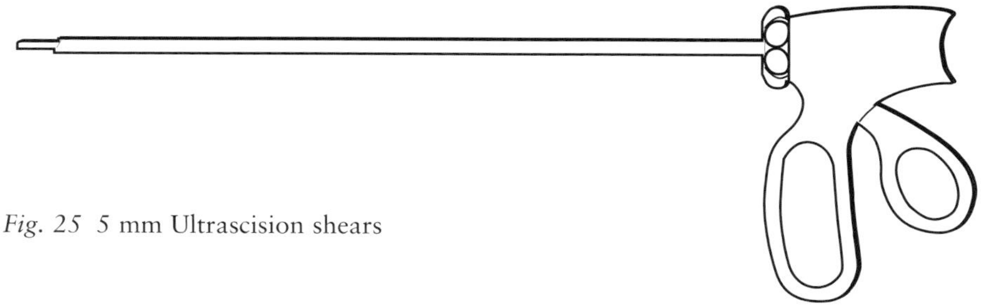

Fig. 25 5 mm Ultrascision shears

As opposed to the 10-mm shears, the blade of the 5-mm shears is fixed with a blunt conical top edge facing the tissue pad. The bottom edge of the blade comes in two configurations, blunt and sharp, in order to enhance tissue back cutting.

The smaller diameter of the 5-mm shears enhances visibility and accessibility to the anatomical structures while allowing surgeons access to the abdominal cavity through a smaller port.

II

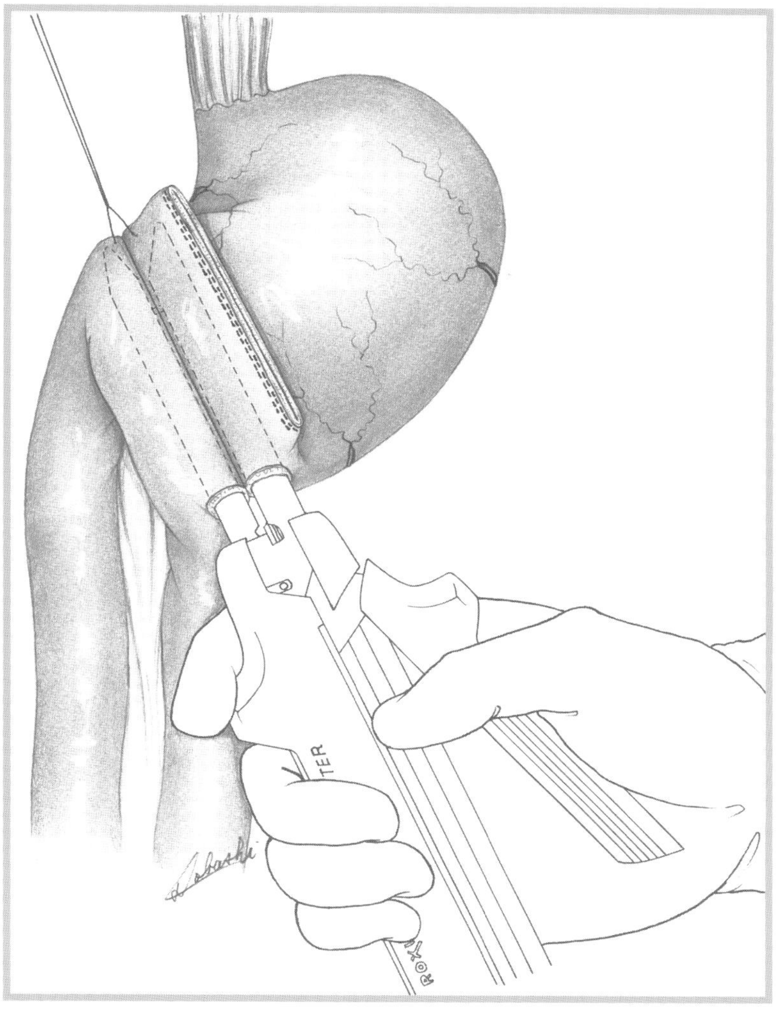

II

Surgical Procedures

1 Thoracic Surgery

2 Oesophageal Surgery

3 Gastric Surgery

4 Pancreatic Surgery

5 Small Bowel Surgery

6 Large Bowel Surgery

7 Colorectal Surgery

8 Gynaecological Surgery

9 Urological Surgery

1 Thoracic Surgery
Pneumonectomy

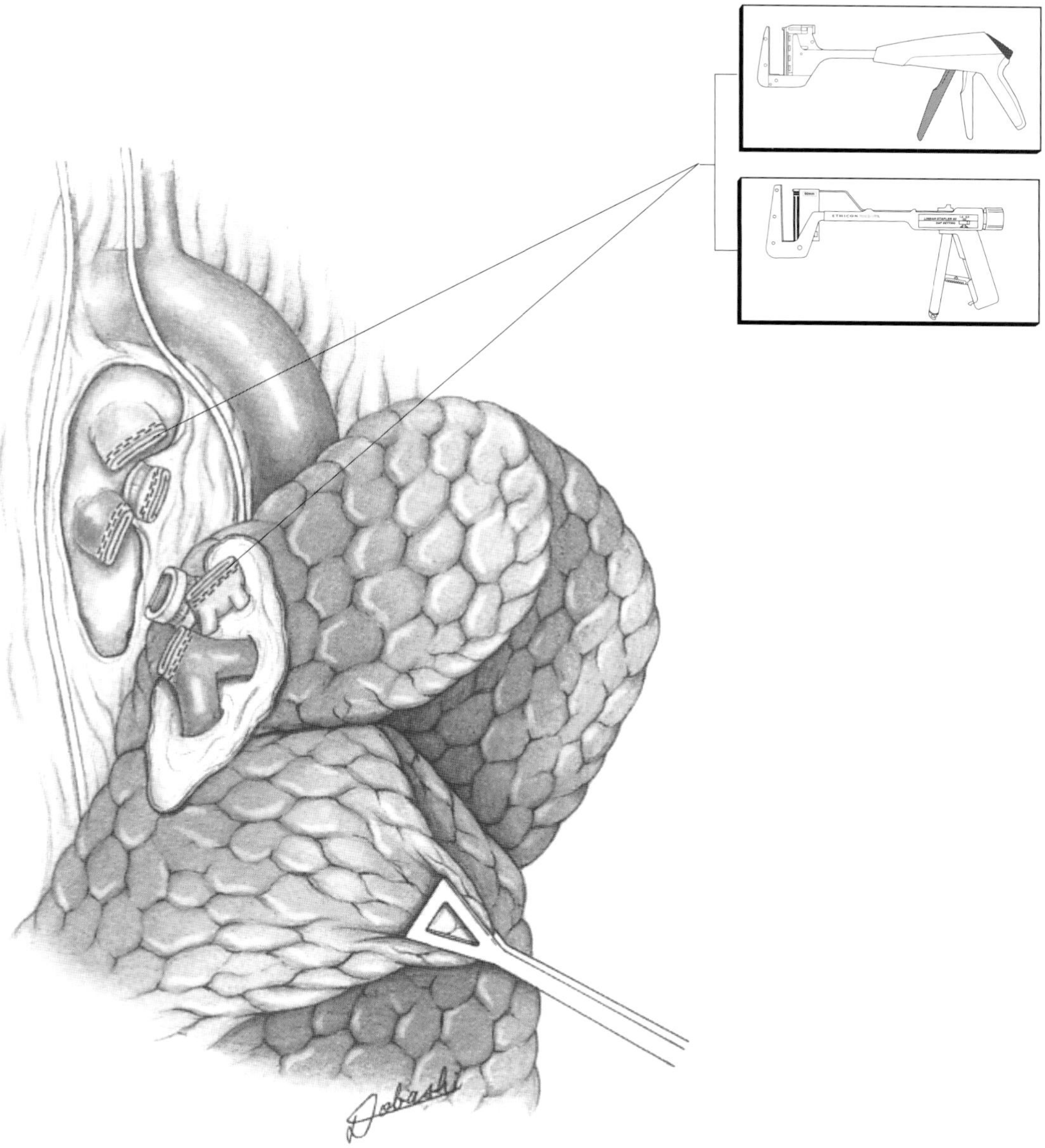

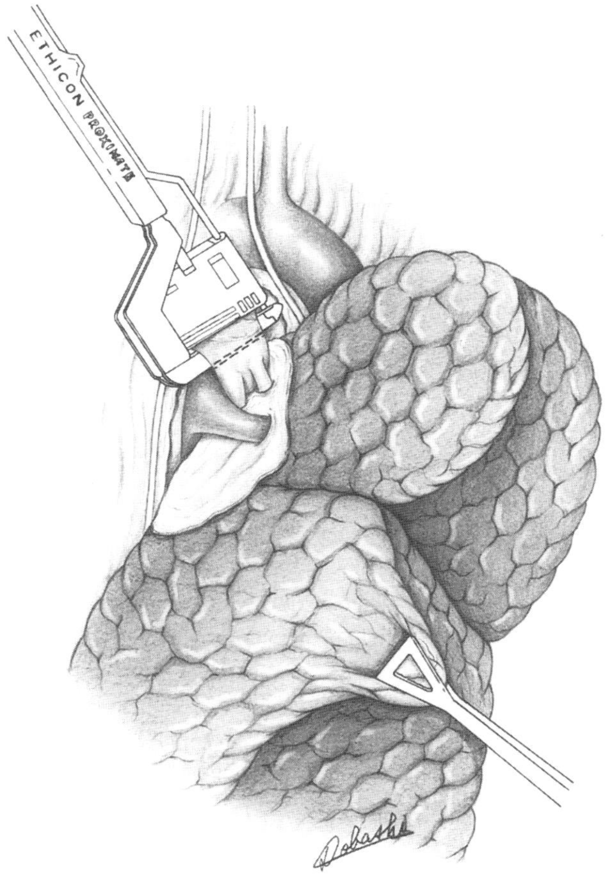

Once prepared and isolated so that they may be completely encircled, the pulmonary veins are stapled using two firings of a linear stapler vascular placed at a distance of approximately 0.5 cm apart.

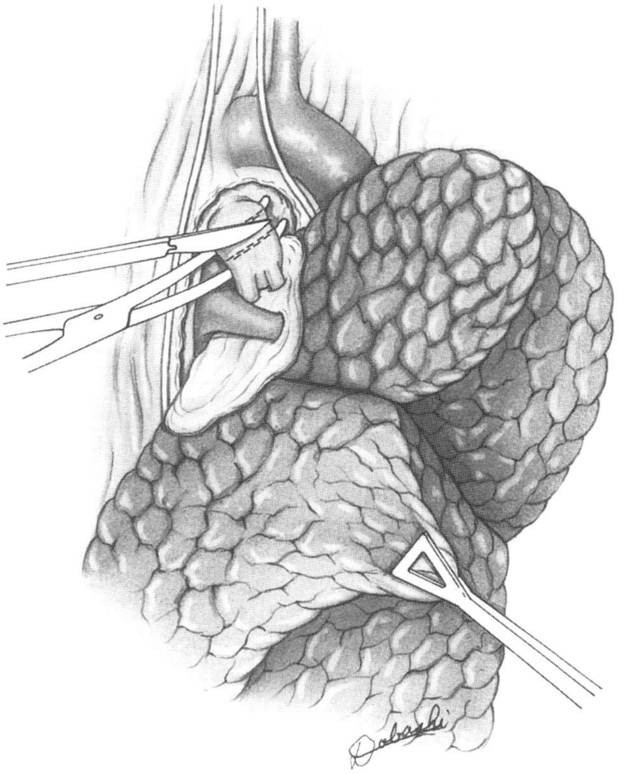

After the integrity of the staple lines has been checked, the veins are transected between the two lines of staples.

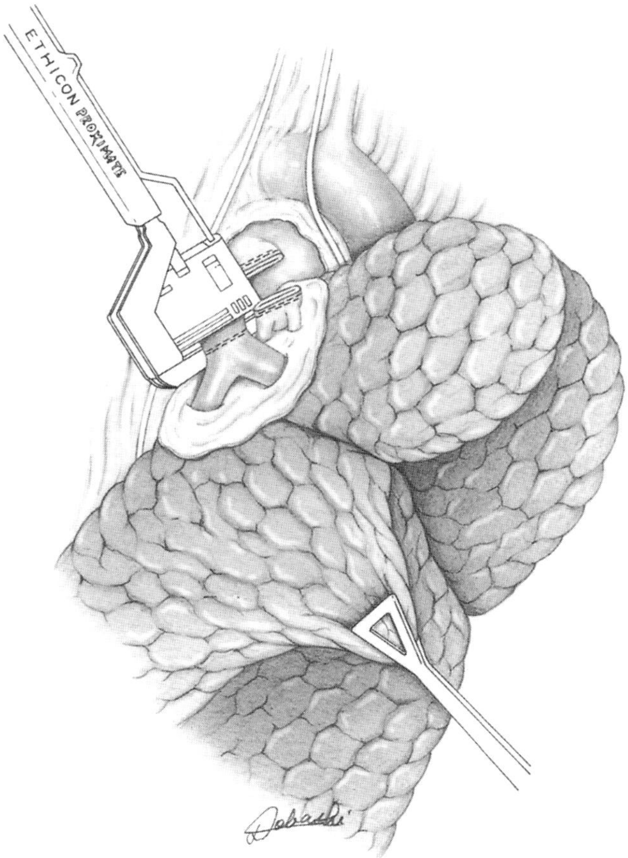

Using the same procedure, the main pulmonary artery is then stapled and transected between the two lines of staples.

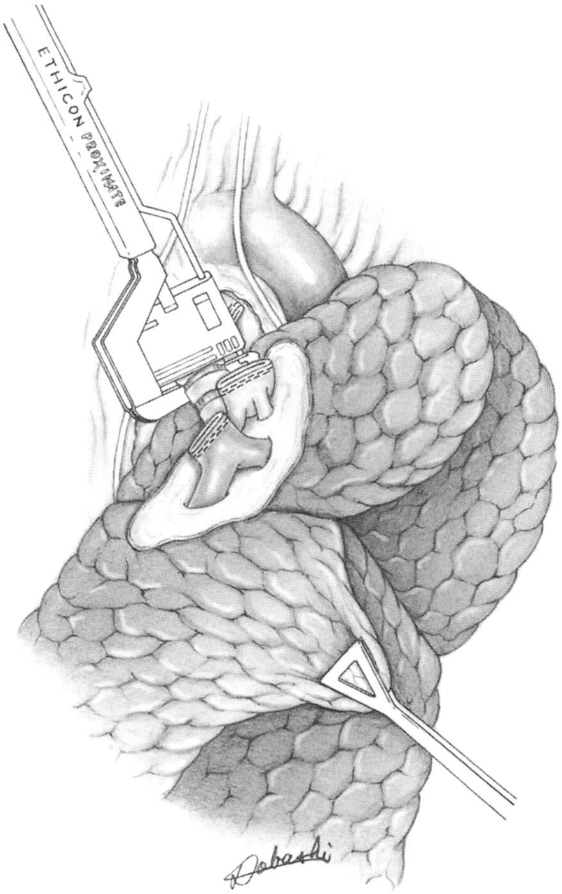

Once the main bronchus has been prepared and isolated, the linear stapler thick is positioned with the staples as close as possible to the tracheal carina, parallel to the cartaliginous rings. The bronchus is then transected distally from the lines of staples.

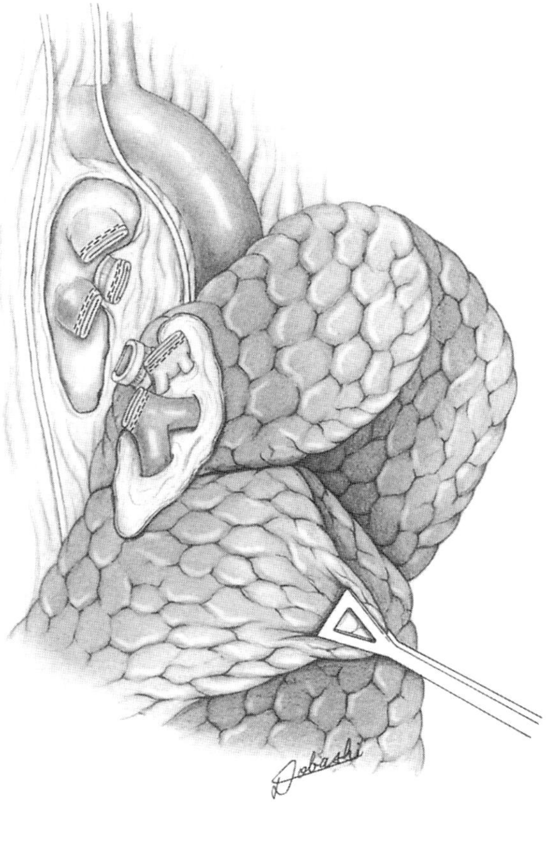

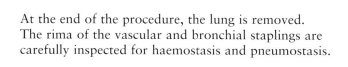

At the end of the procedure, the lung is removed. The rima of the vascular and bronchial staplings are carefully inspected for haemostasis and pneumostasis.

Lobectomy

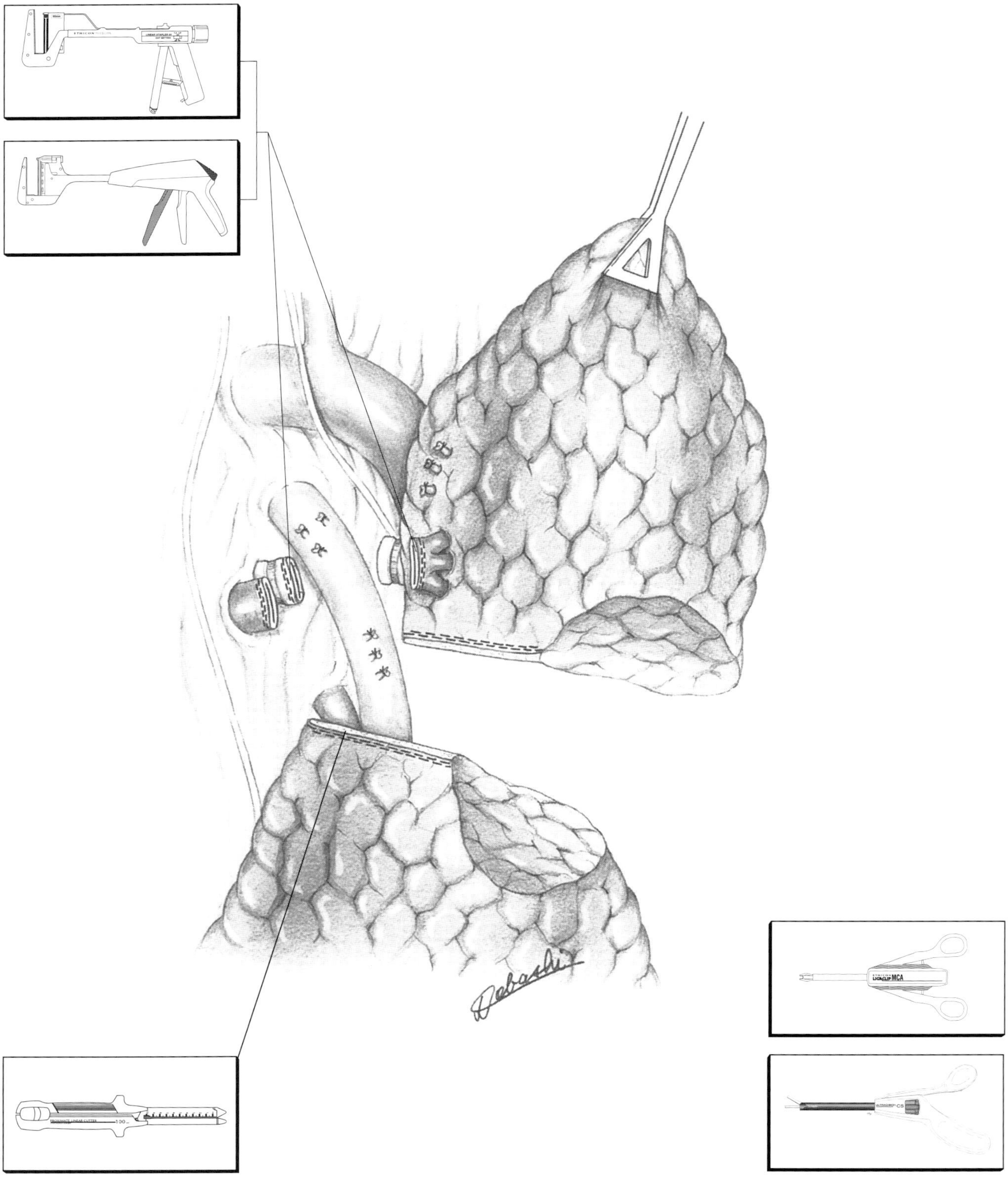

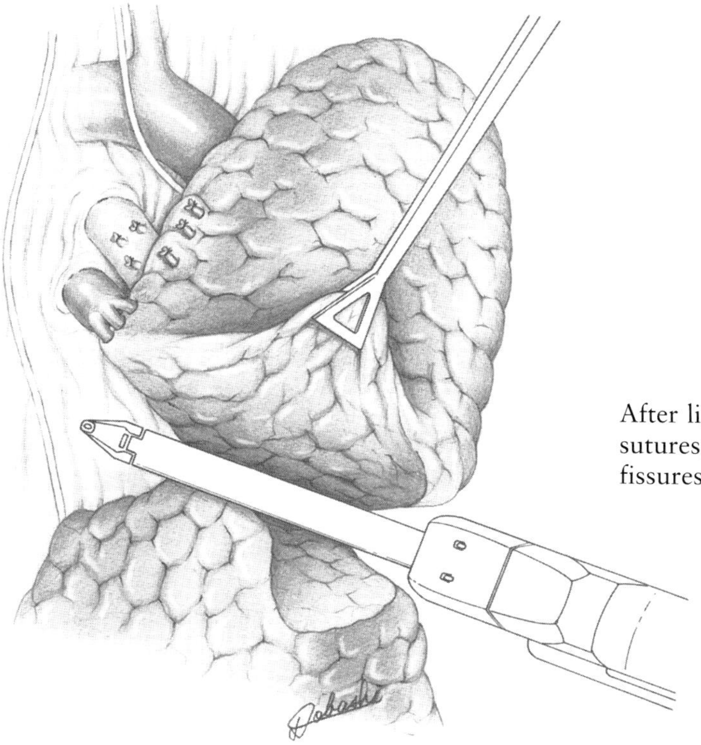

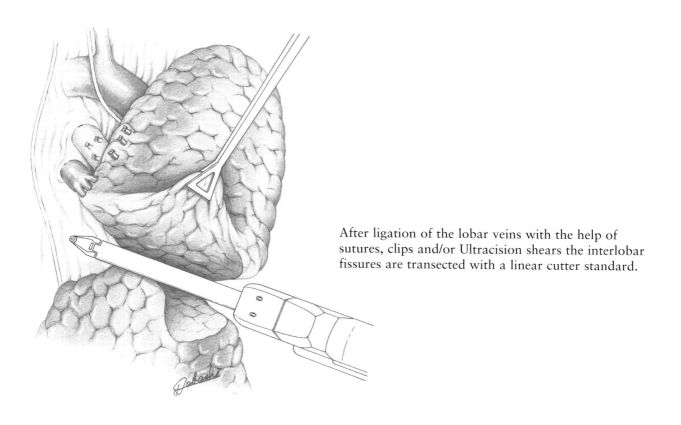

After ligation of the lobar veins with the help of sutures, clips and/or Ultracision shears the interlobar fissures are transected with a linear cutter standard.

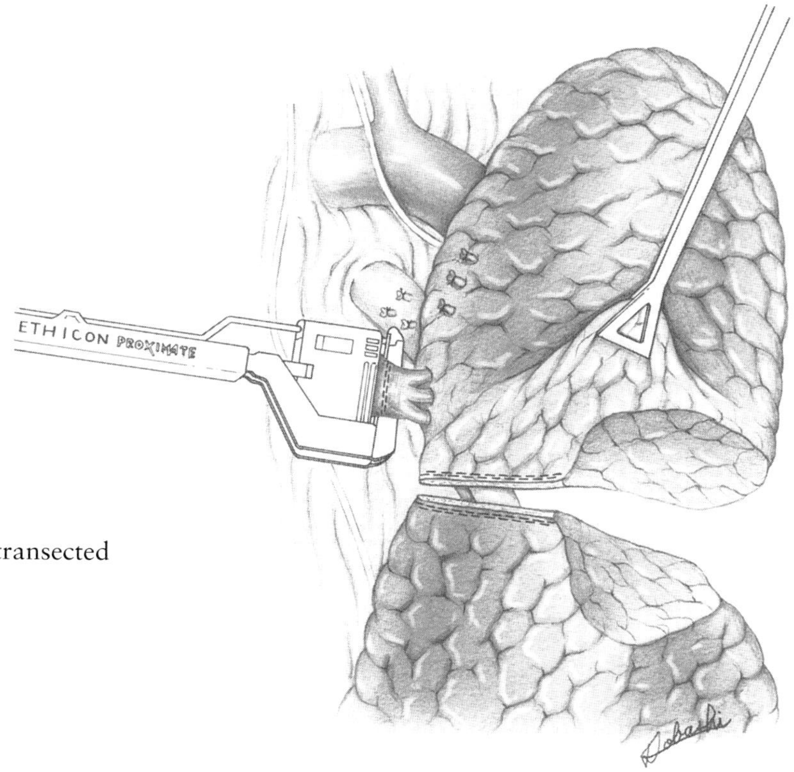

The arterial lobar branches are stapled and transected using a linear stapler vascular.

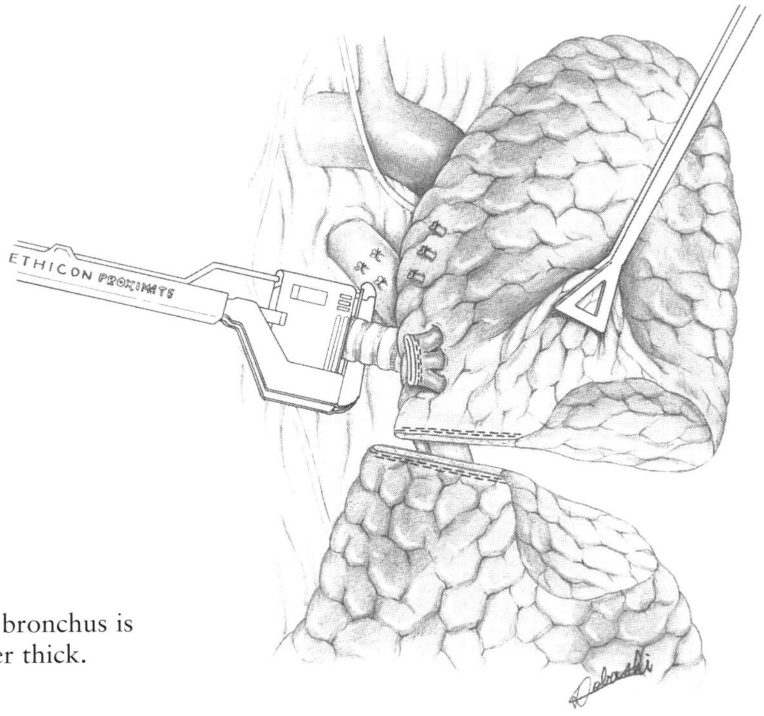

Once prepared and isolated the lobar bronchus is stapled at its root using a linear stapler thick.

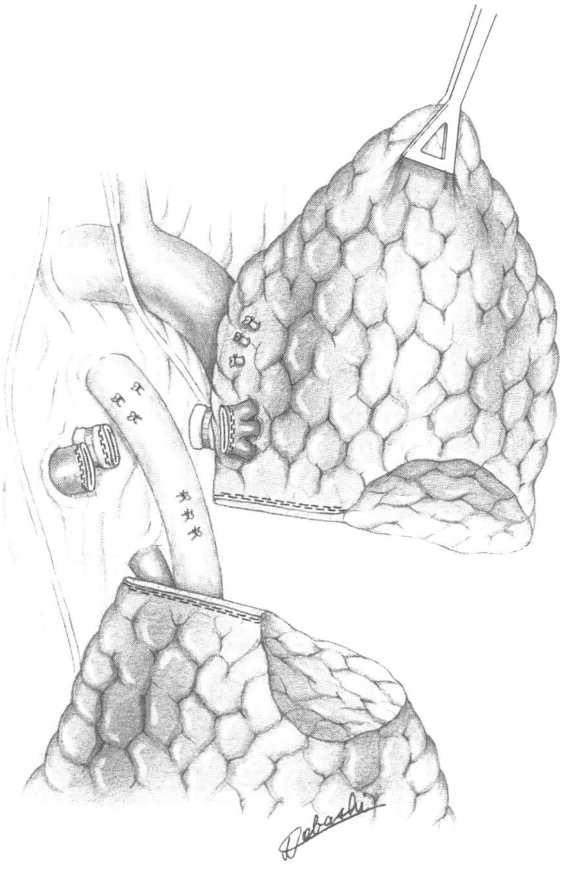

The lobar bronchus is transected distally from the line of metal staples and then removed. The rima of the vascular and bronchial staplings are carefully inspected for haemostasis and pneumostasis.

Atypical Resections (Apical Resection)

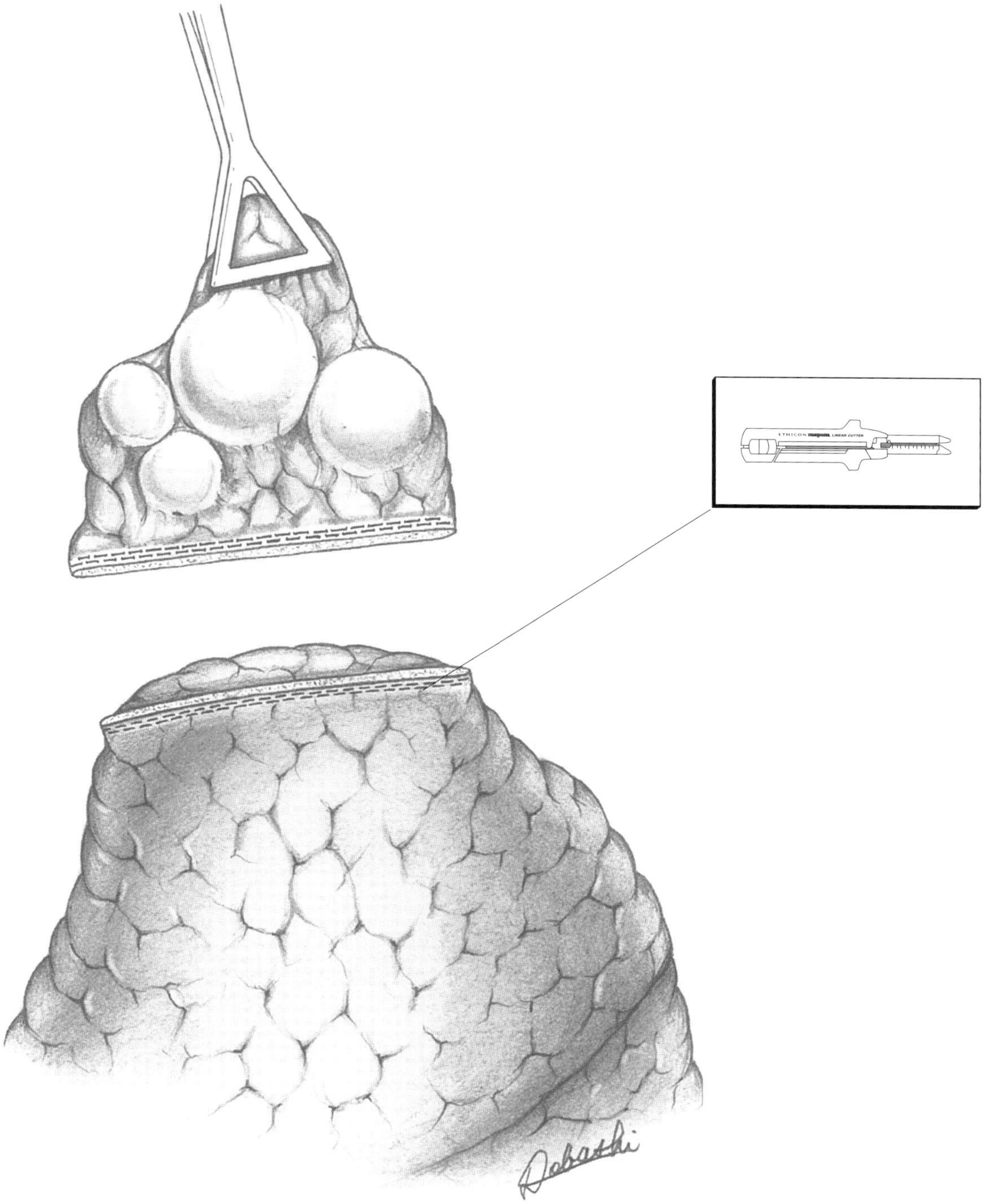

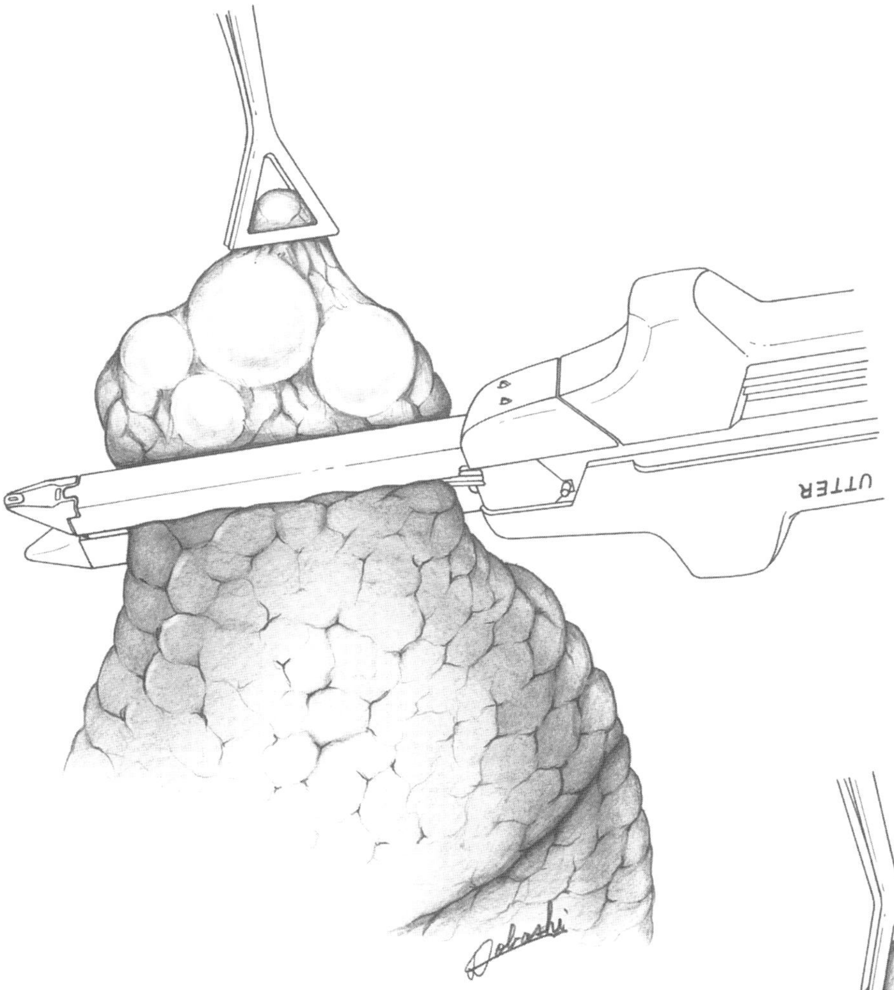

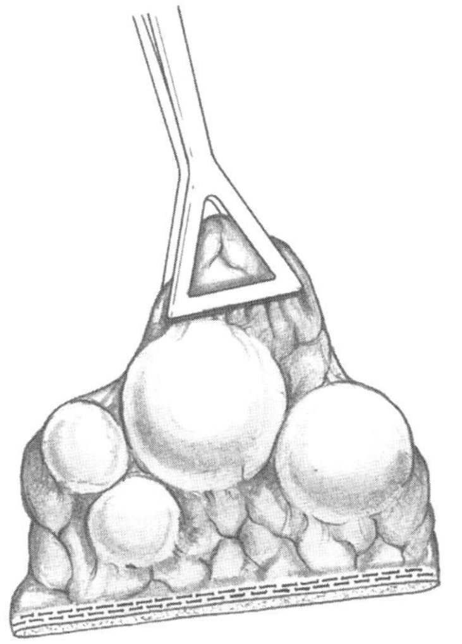

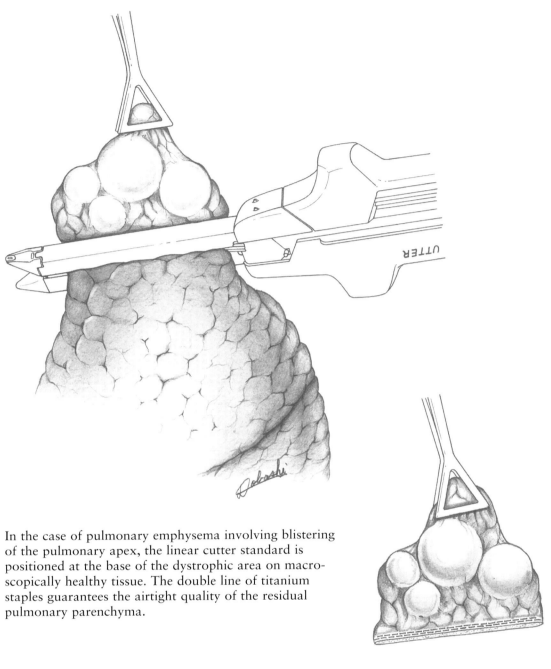

In the case of pulmonary emphysema involving blistering of the pulmonary apex, the linear cutter standard is positioned at the base of the dystrophic area on macroscopically healthy tissue. The double line of titanium staples guarantees the airtight quality of the residual pulmonary parenchyma.

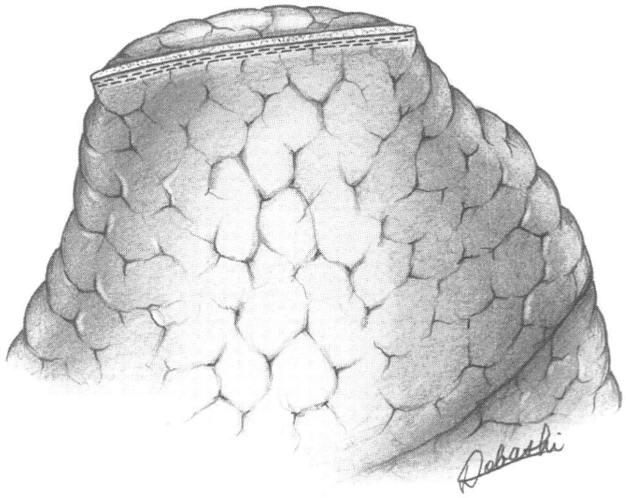

At the end of the procedure the staple lines are carefully inspected for haemostasis and pneumostasis.

Atypical Resections (Wedge resection)

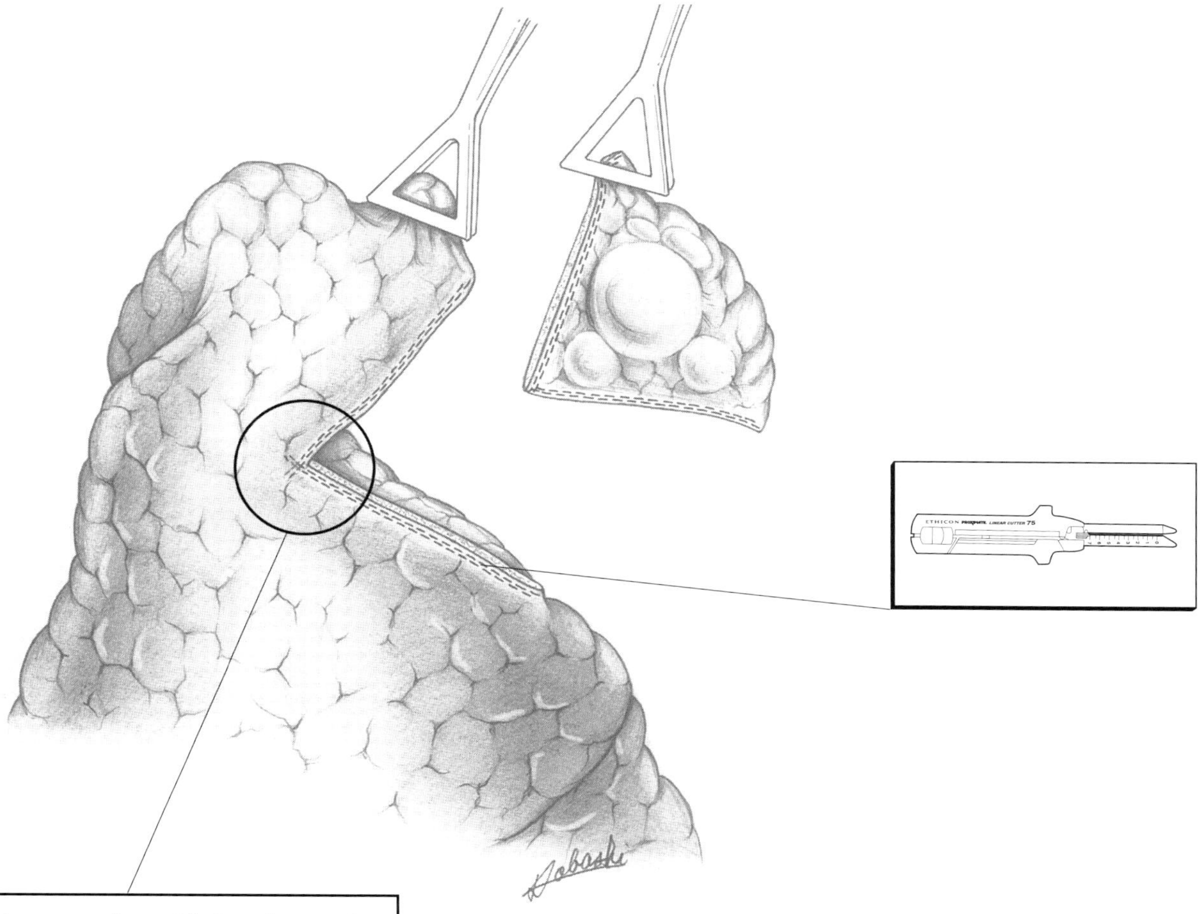

Attention must be paid that the staple lines at this point cross only 3 mm.

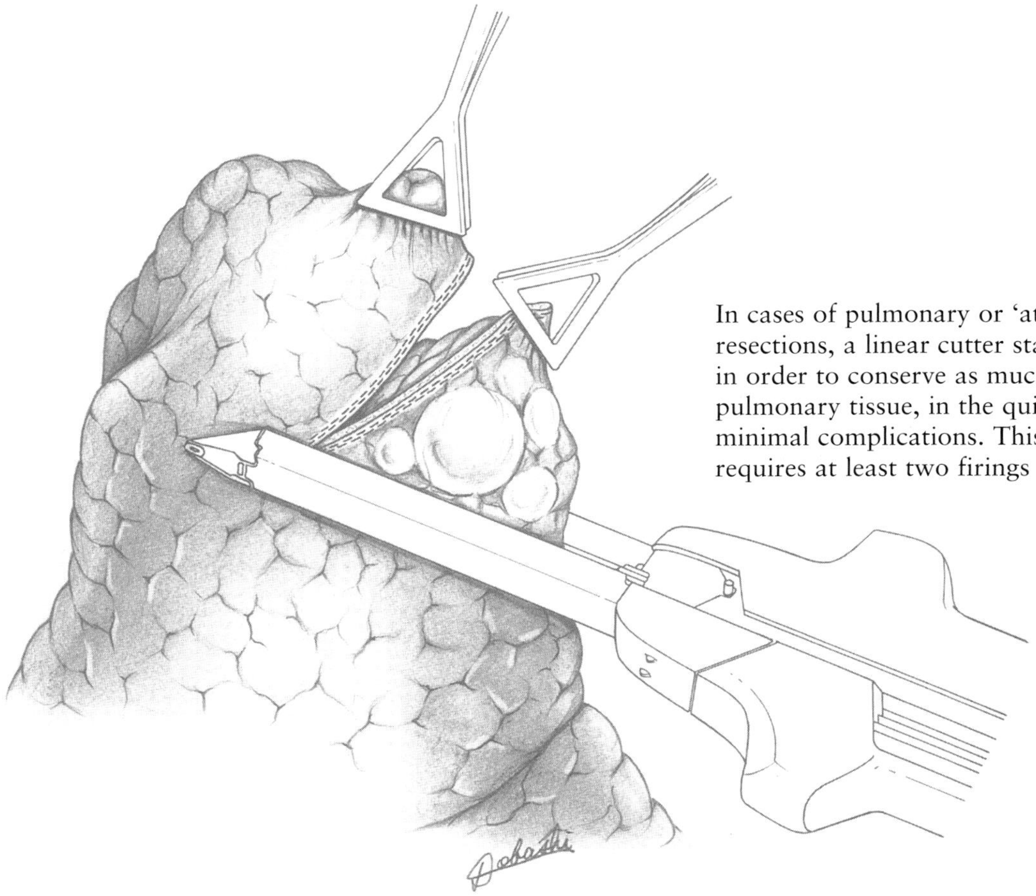

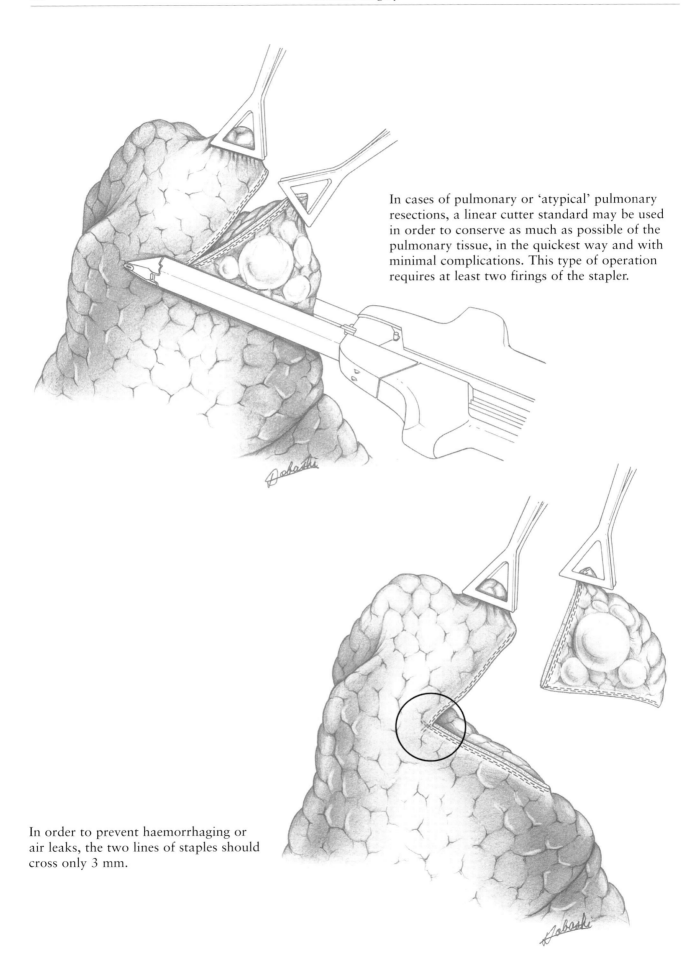

In cases of pulmonary or 'atypical' pulmonary resections, a linear cutter standard may be used in order to conserve as much as possible of the pulmonary tissue, in the quickest way and with minimal complications. This type of operation requires at least two firings of the stapler.

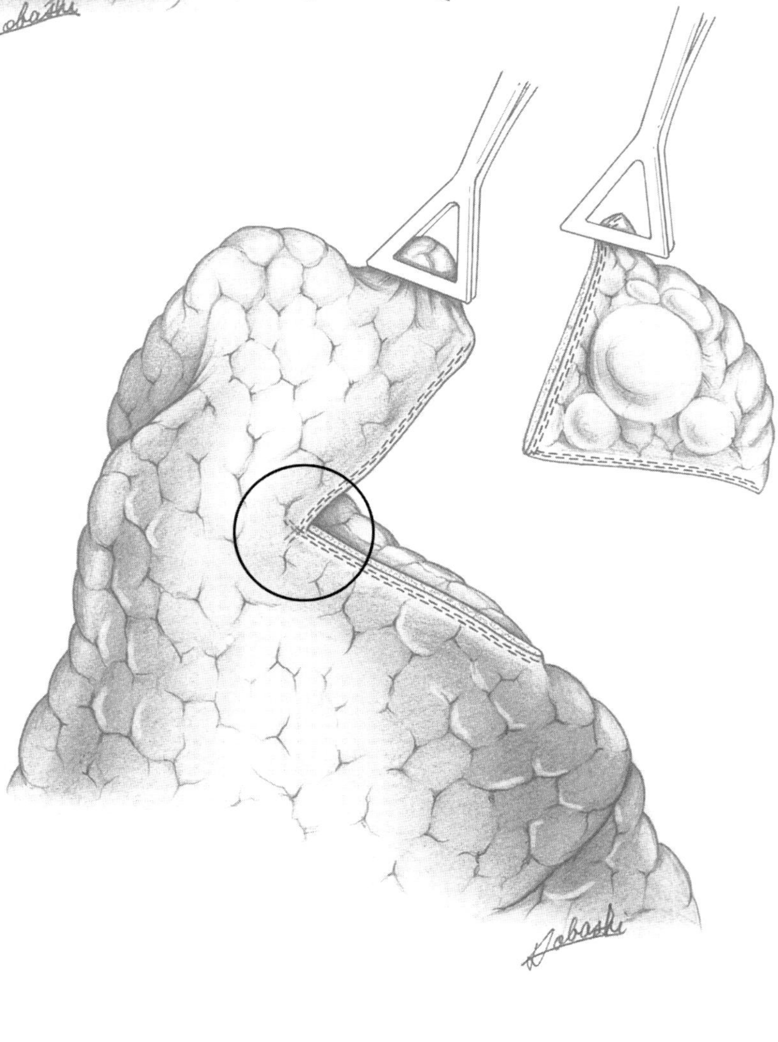

In order to prevent haemorrhaging or air leaks, the two lines of staples should cross only 3 mm.

2 Oesophageal Surgery

Zenker's Diverticulum

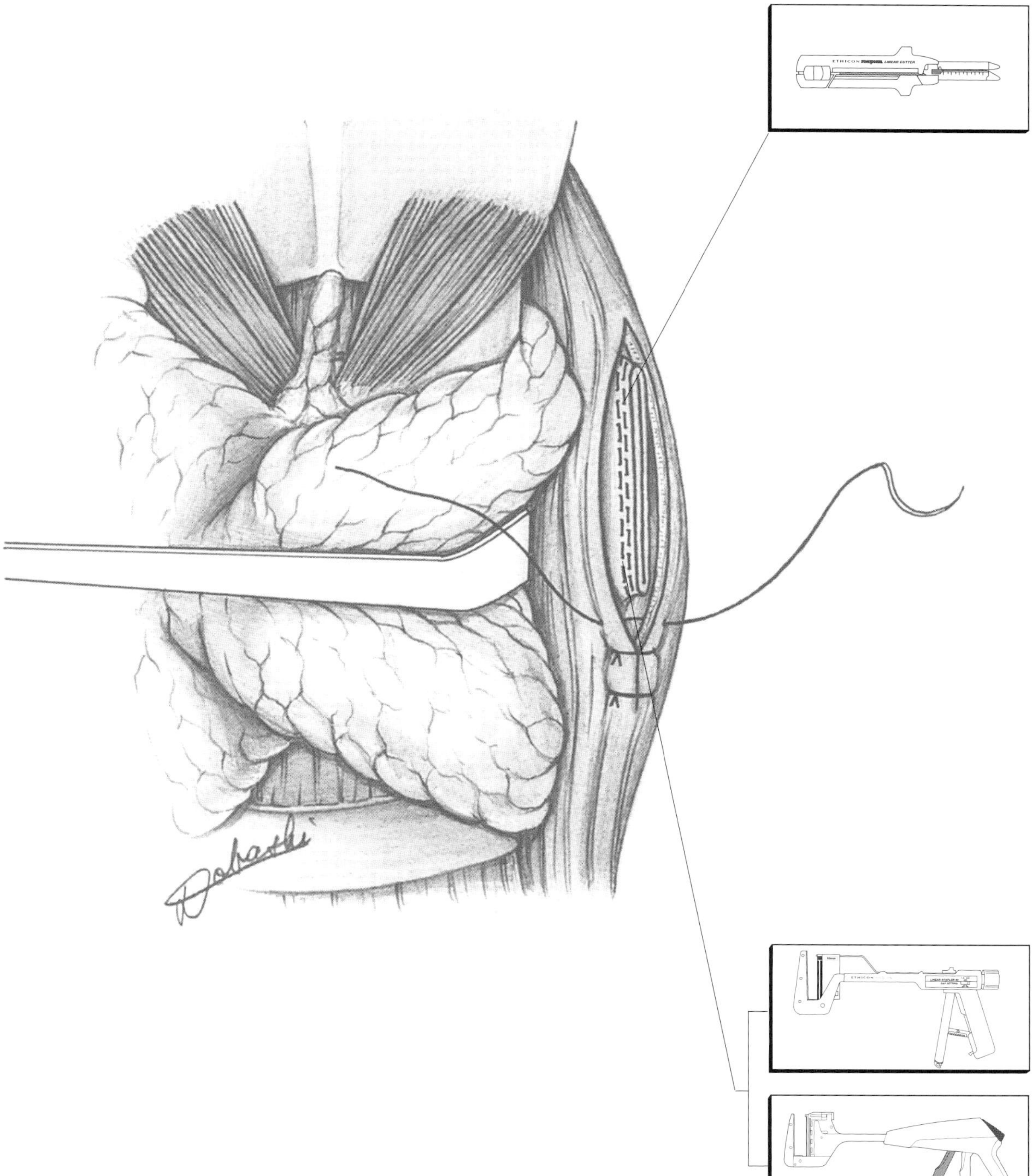

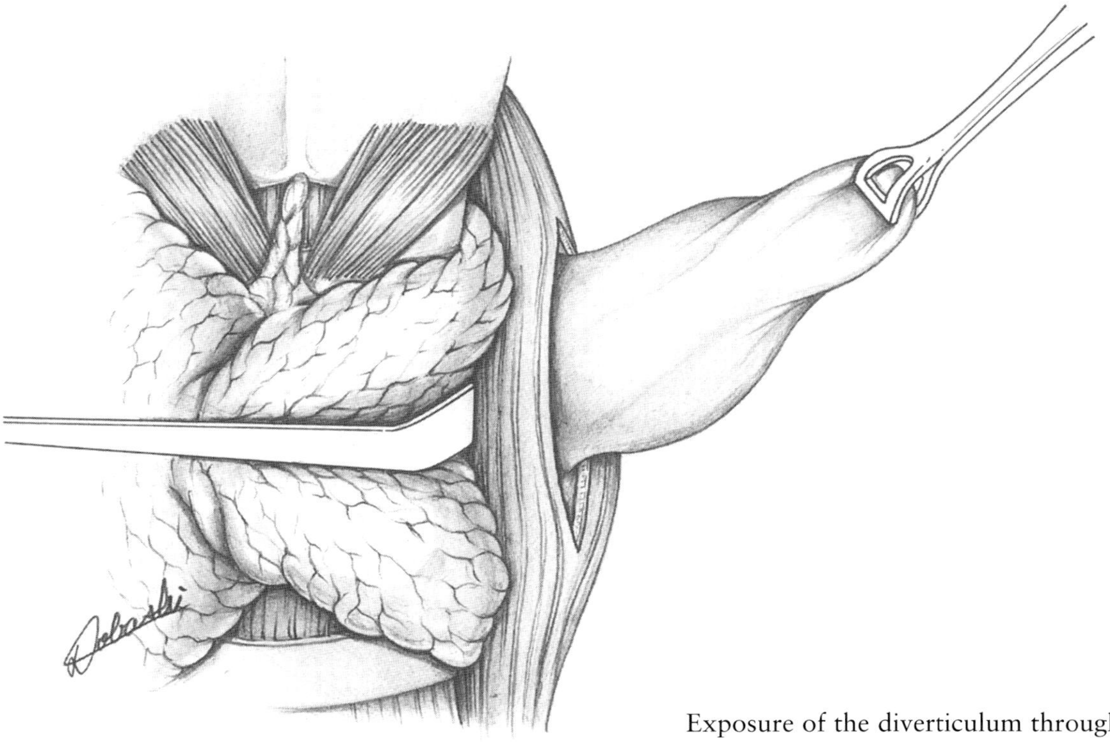

Exposure of the diverticulum through a myotomy.

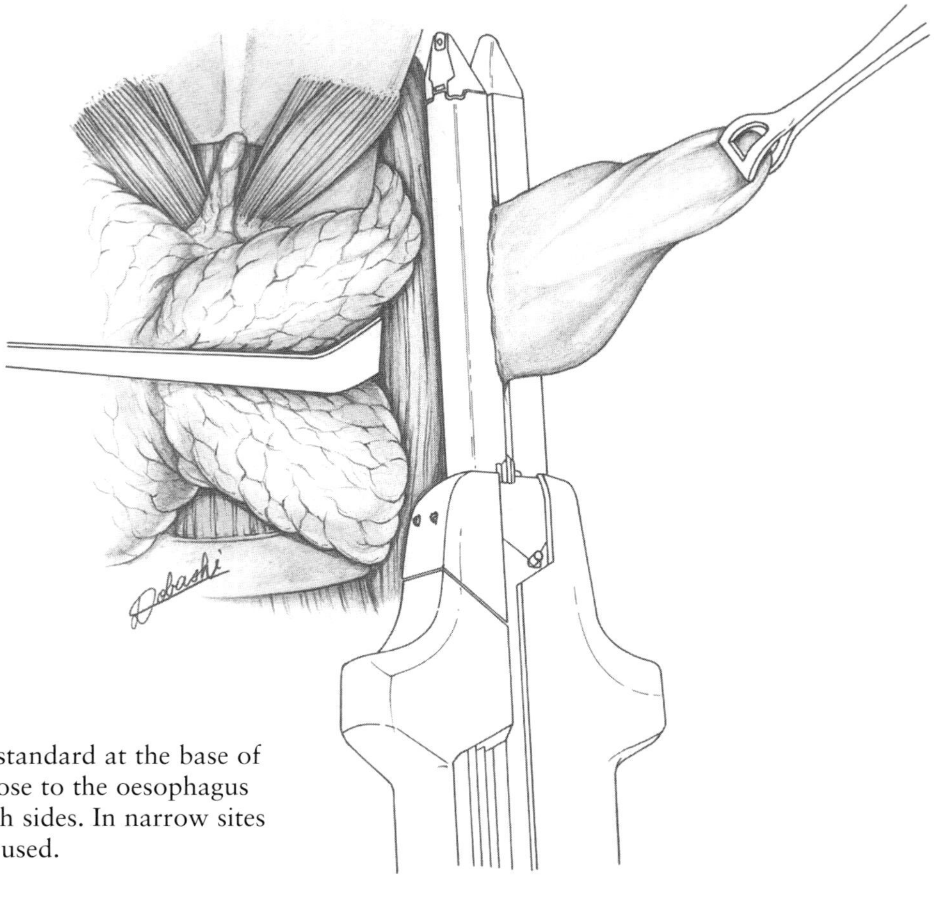

Application of the linear cutter standard at the base of the diverticulum. Transection close to the oesophagus and simultaneous closure of both sides. In narrow sites a linear stapler standard can be used.

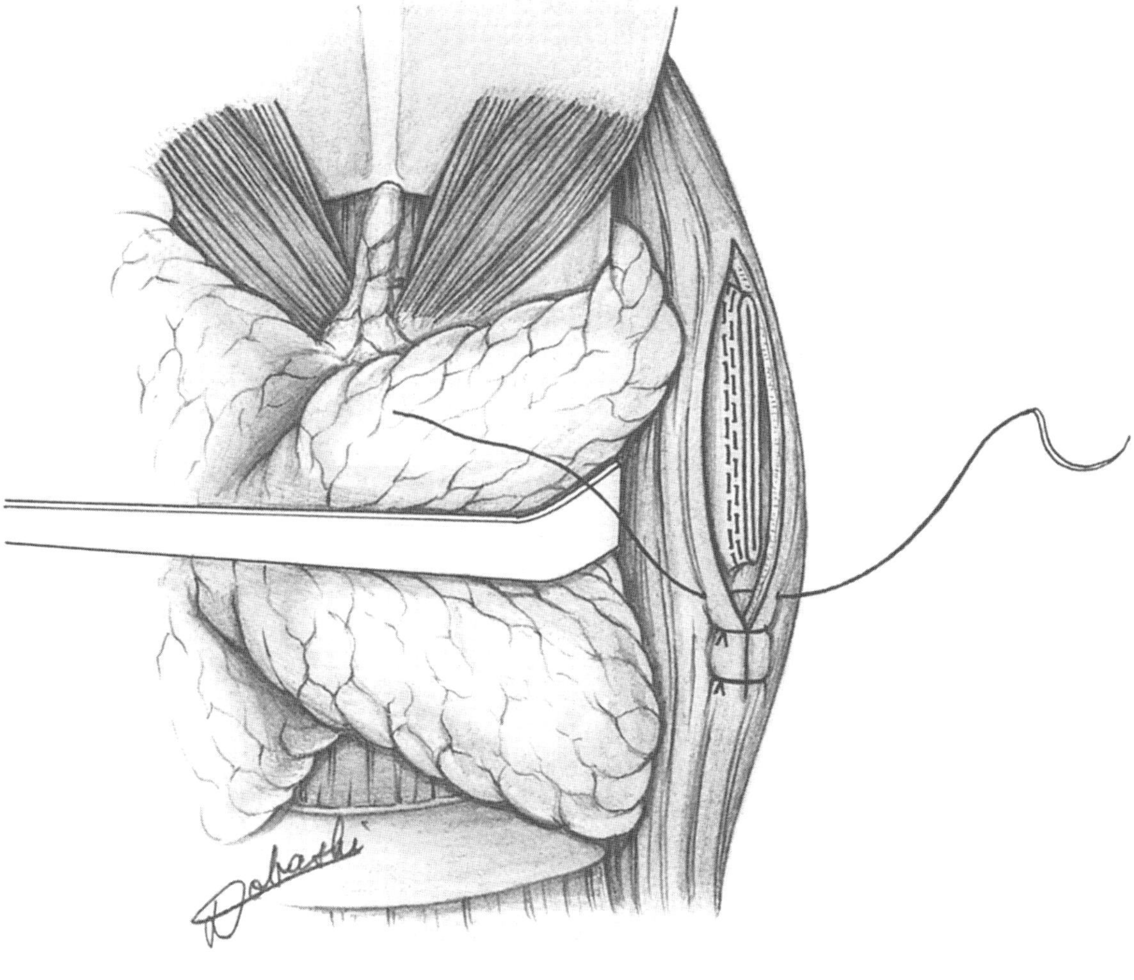

Closure of the myotomy by manual suturing.

Reconstruction of the Thoracic Oesophagus

Oesophagectomy, Gastric Tube and Cervical Anastomosis

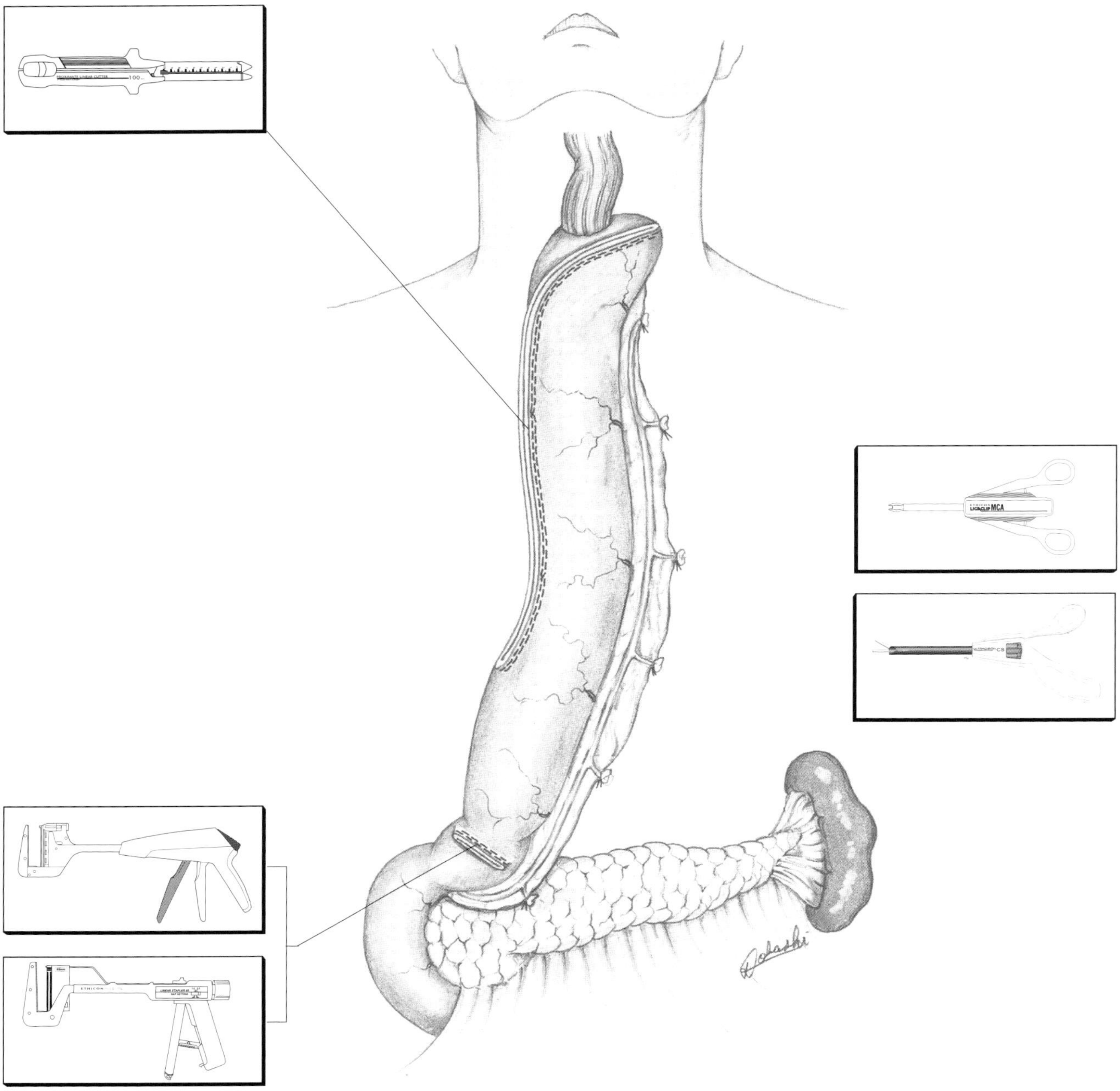

Reconstruction of the thoracic oesophagus with a gastric tube and a cervical anastomosis. The operation can be performed through a right thoracotomy and an abdominal and cervical incision, or through a transhiatal oesophagectomy, avoiding thoracotomy.

The thoracic part and also the abdominal part can be dissected with a thoracoscopic and laparoscopic technique respectively, and the anastomosis performed through a separate cervical incision.

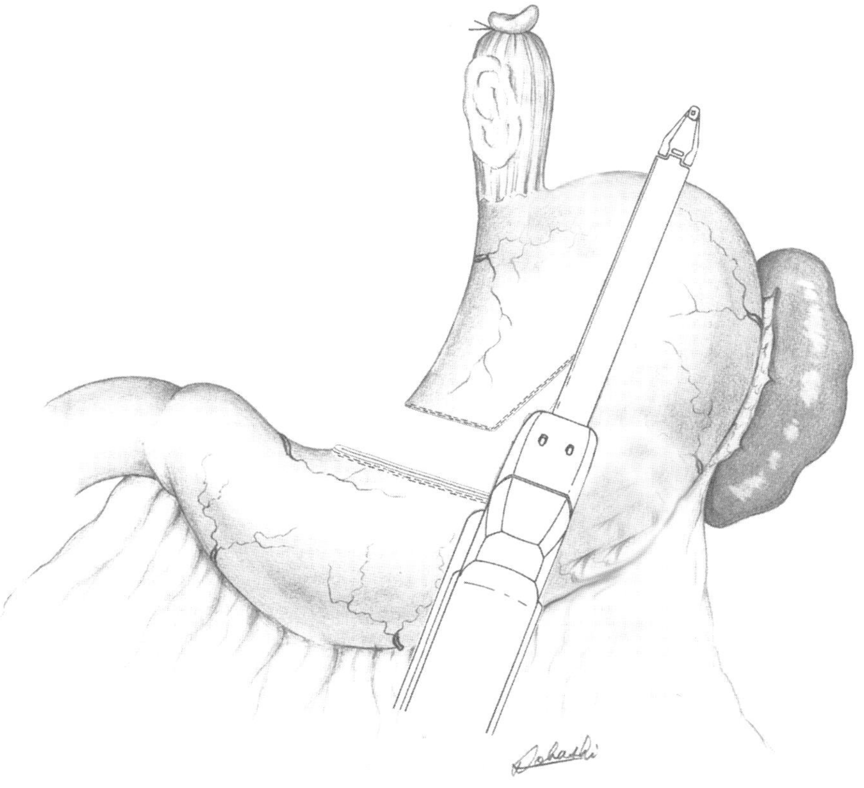

After finishing the thoracic part of the operation, whether performed openly or with a thoracoscope, the abdominal part is performed with the patient in supine position. The stomach is mobilised and vascularised at the right gastroepiploic artery. The gastric tube is done with several applications of the linear cutter thick, starting from the level of the fifth branch of the right gastric artery.

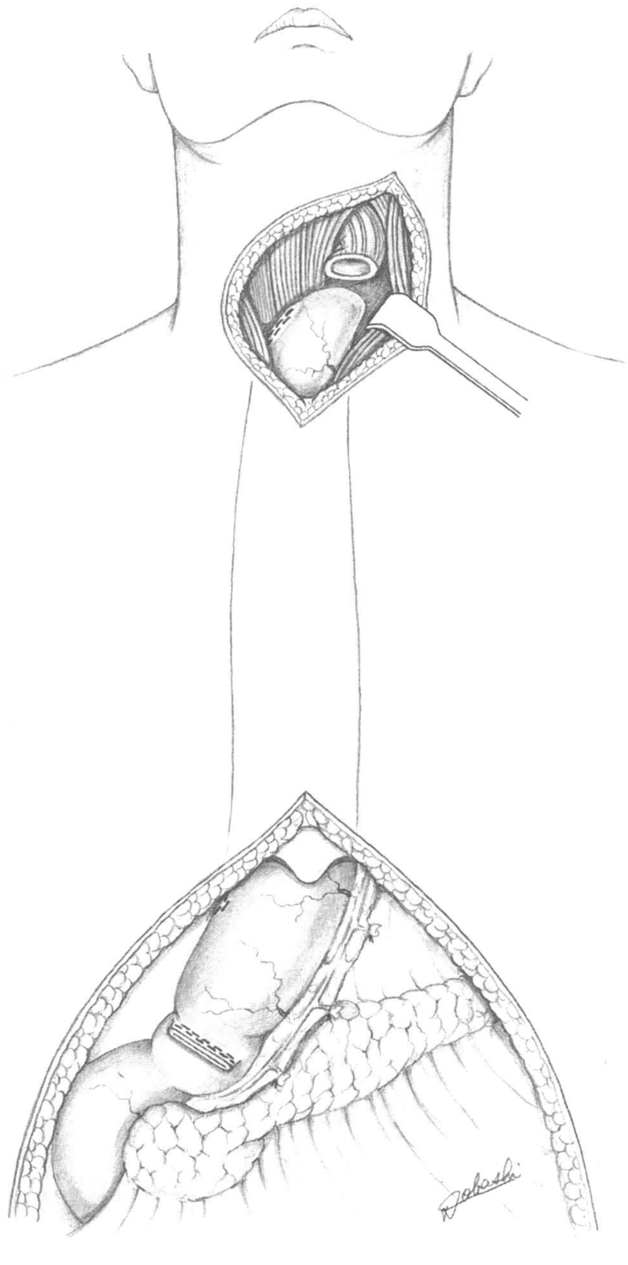

A pyloroplasty is performed by application of a linear stapler standard or manual sutures. The gastric tube is delivered to the neck by gentle traction on the specimen from the cervical incision and pushing from below. The pylorus will be located 2 cm below the hiatus. The cervical part of the operation is carried out by performing an oesophagogastrostomy manually. After ensuring that the anastomosis has been adequately performed, the incisions are closed.

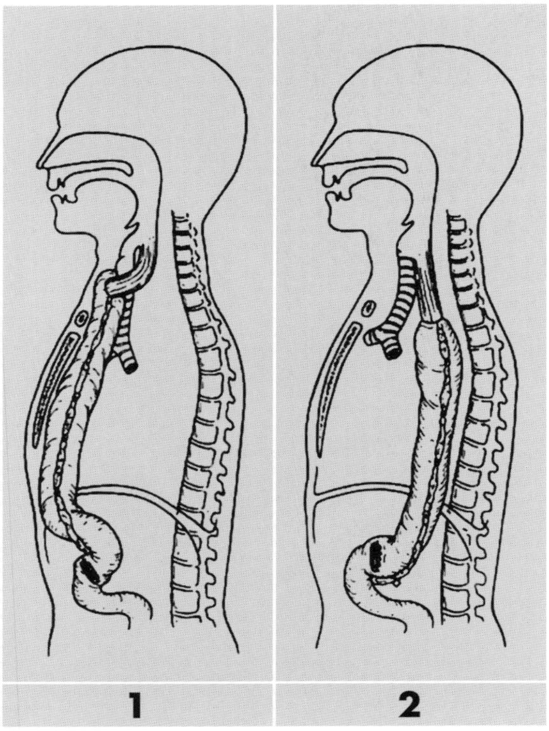

The substitute can be positioned substernally (1) or anatomically (2), of which the latter is the most common practice. The abdominal part of the operation is completed.

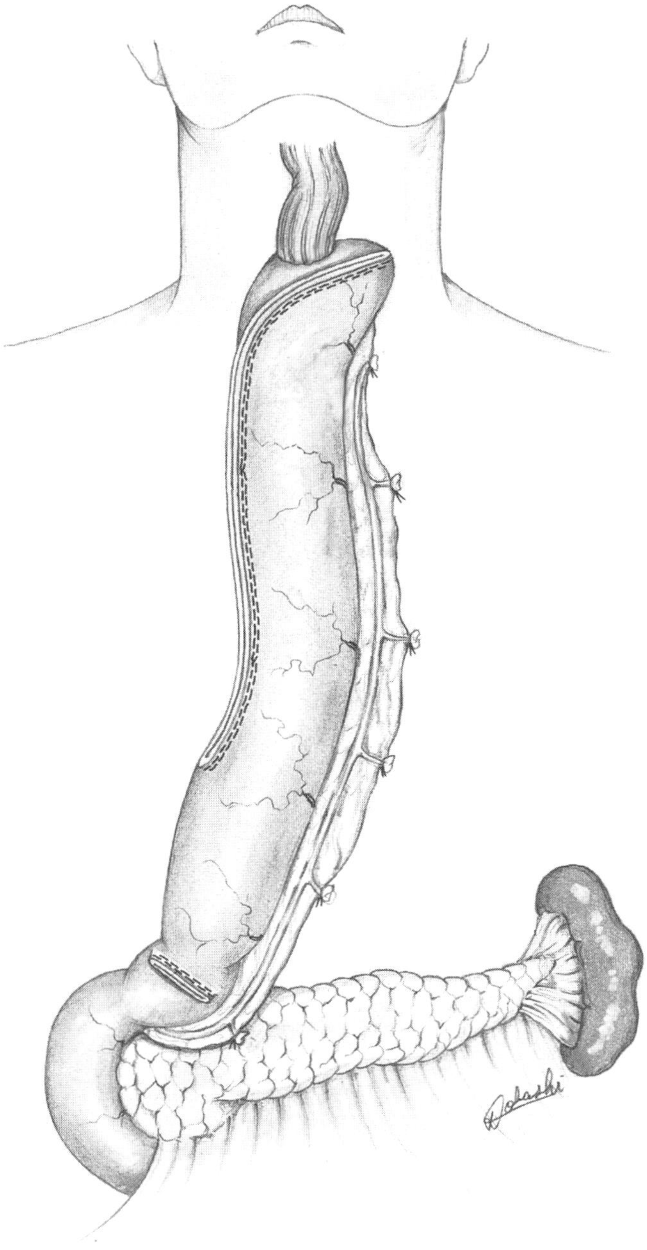

Complete oesophageal reconstruction by end-to-side oesophagogastric anastomosis.

Reconstruction of Thoracic Oesophagus

Oesophagectomy, Colon Replacement, and Cervical Anastomosis

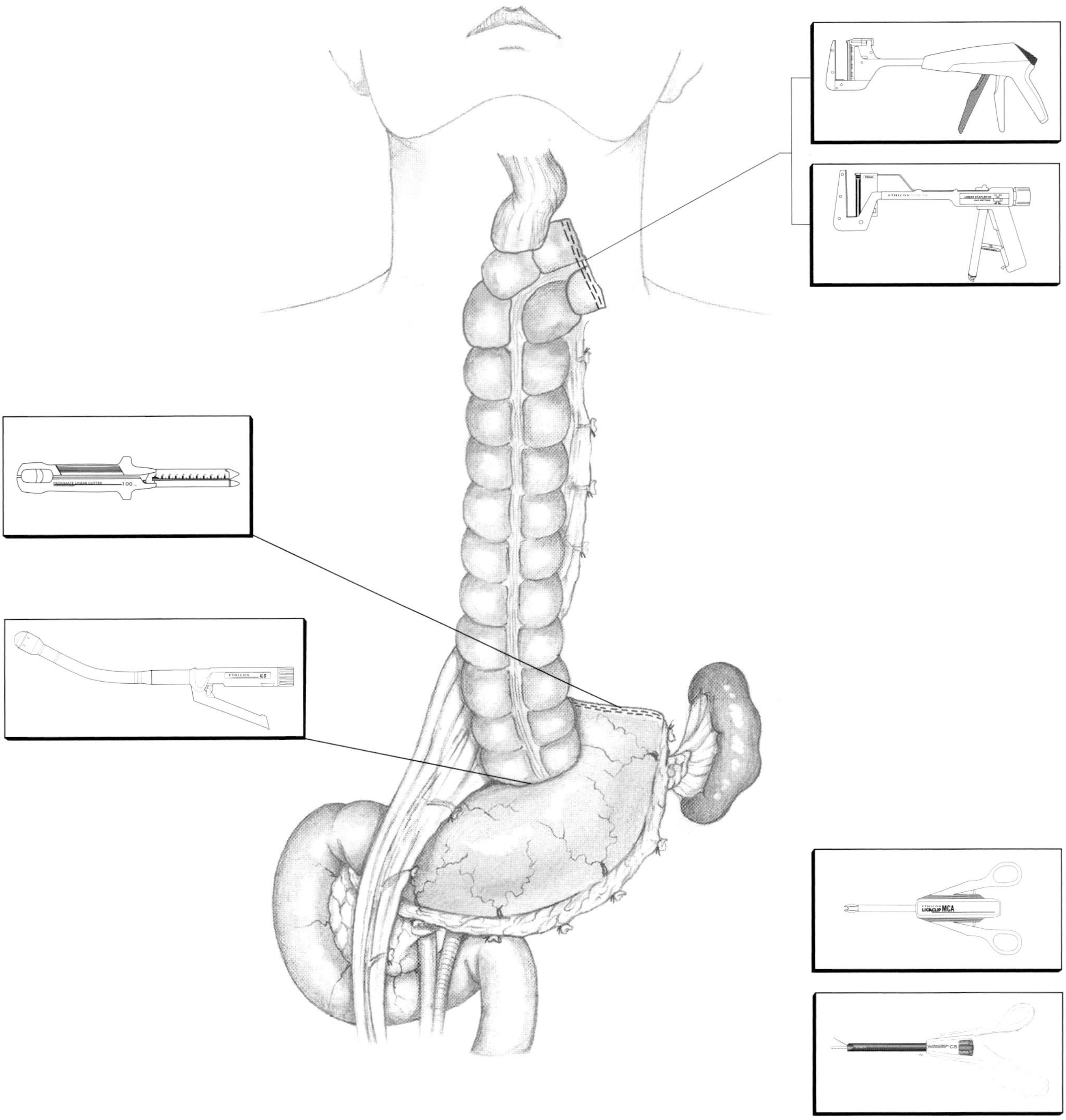

Reconstruction of the thoracic oesophagus with transverse colon.

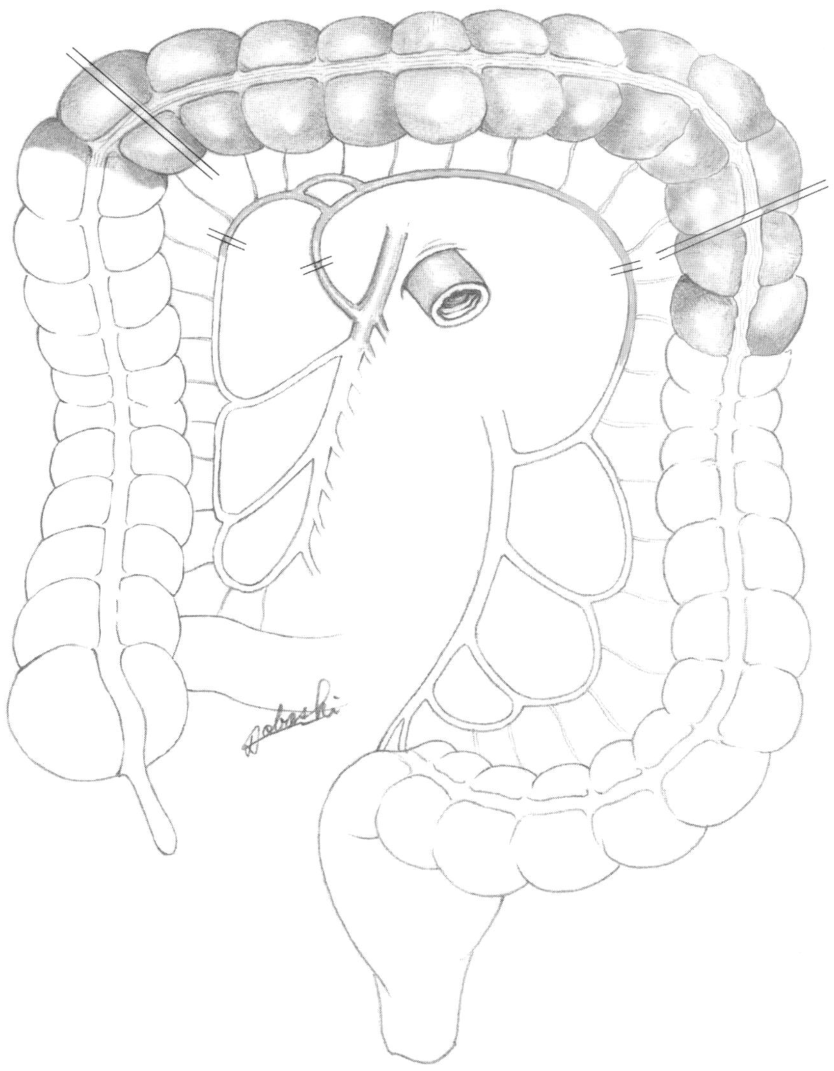

The transverse colon is used in the majority of cases. The use of the right colon is possible, but the volume of the caecum may be too great for the retroesternal space. A linear cutter standard is used at the point of transections shown above.

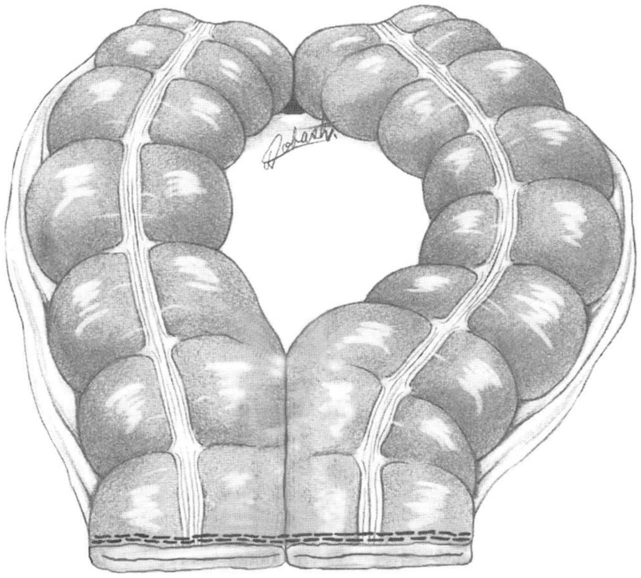

A functional side-to-side anastomosis is performed between the right and left colon with a linear cutter standard in order to re-establish intestinal continuity.

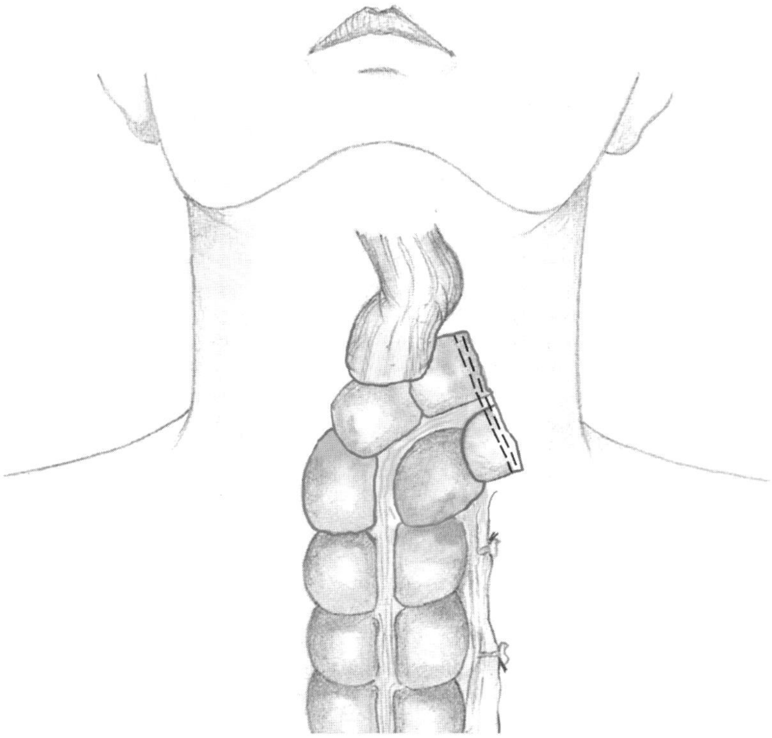

A cervical end-to-side anastomosis is performed with hand sutures.

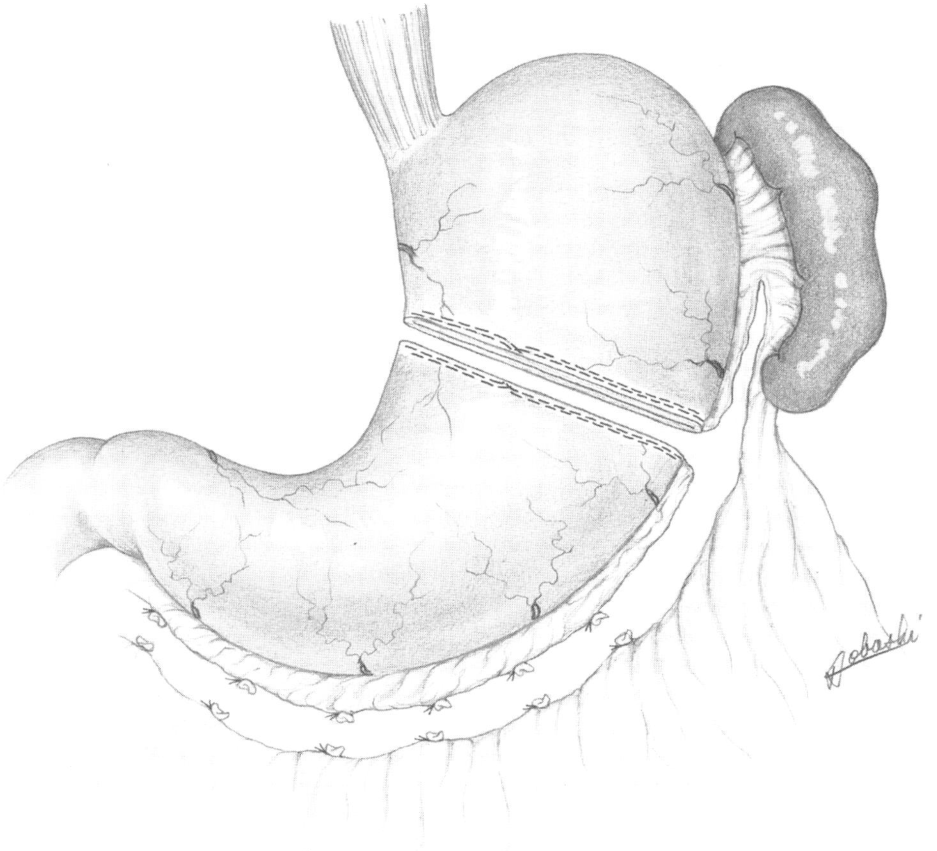

After having mobilised the lower portion of the stomach with multiple clip appliers or Ultracision, a subtotal gastrectomy is performed using a linear cutter thick. In doing this, the spleen is routinely preserved.

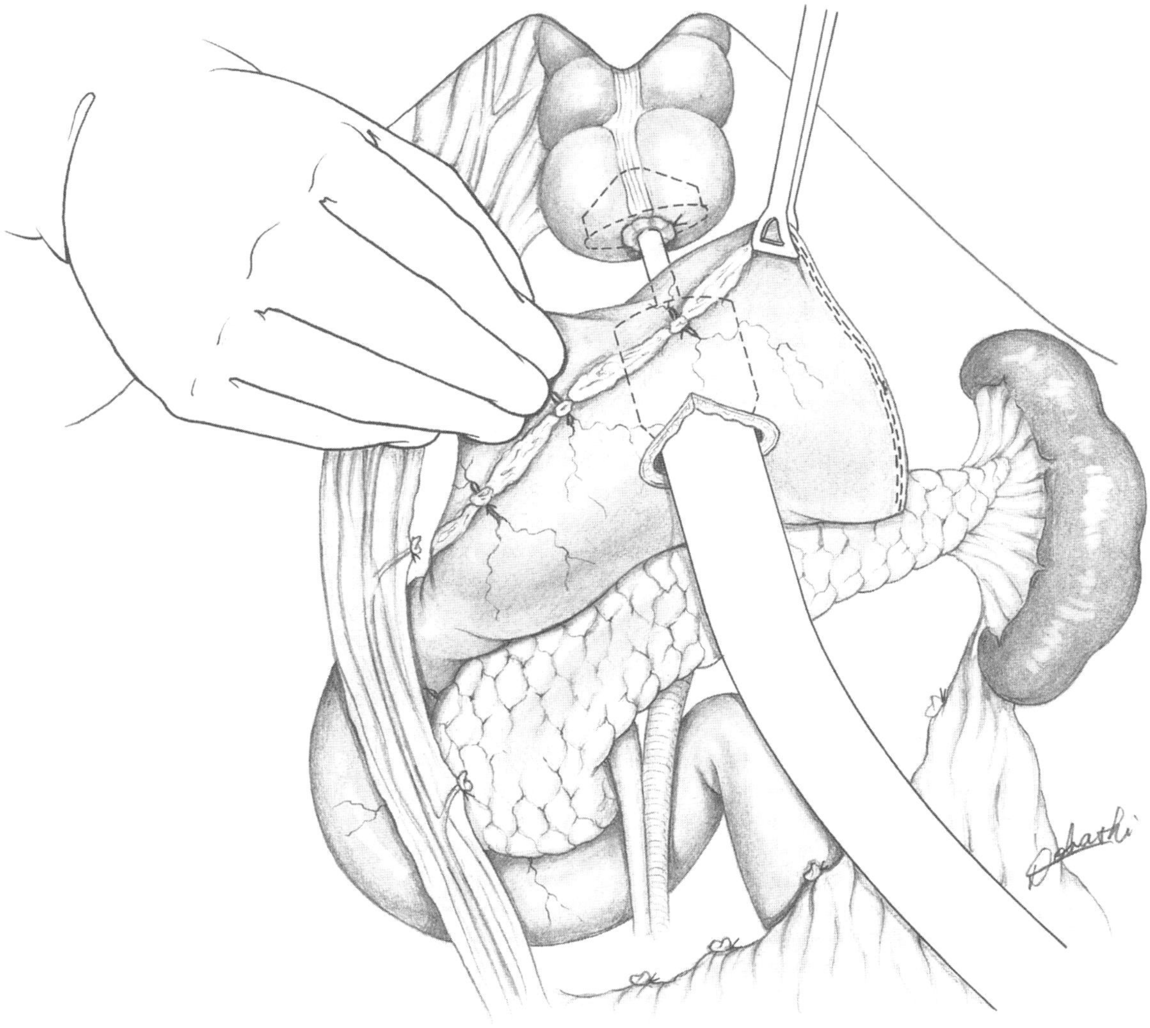

The cologastric anastomosis is made approximately one-third of the way down from the gastric fundus. Here the anastomosis is performed on the front wall, leaving a rim of at least 3 cm between the linear and the circular staple lines. The common technique is to advance the colon and vascular pedicle behind the stomach.

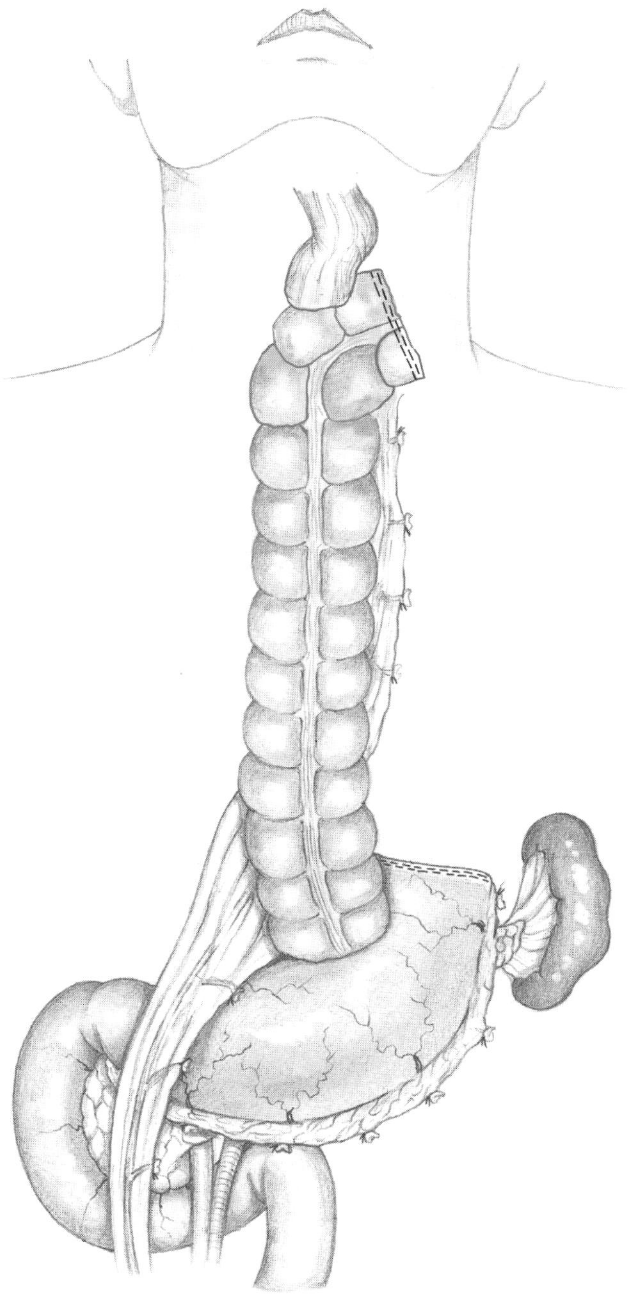

The completed cologastric anastomosis. In this case as shown, a pyloroplasty previously performed is covered by the previously created vascular pedicle of the transverse colon.

Reconstruction of Thoracic Oesophagus

Oesophagectomy, with Thoracic Anastomosis: The Ivor Lewis Procedure

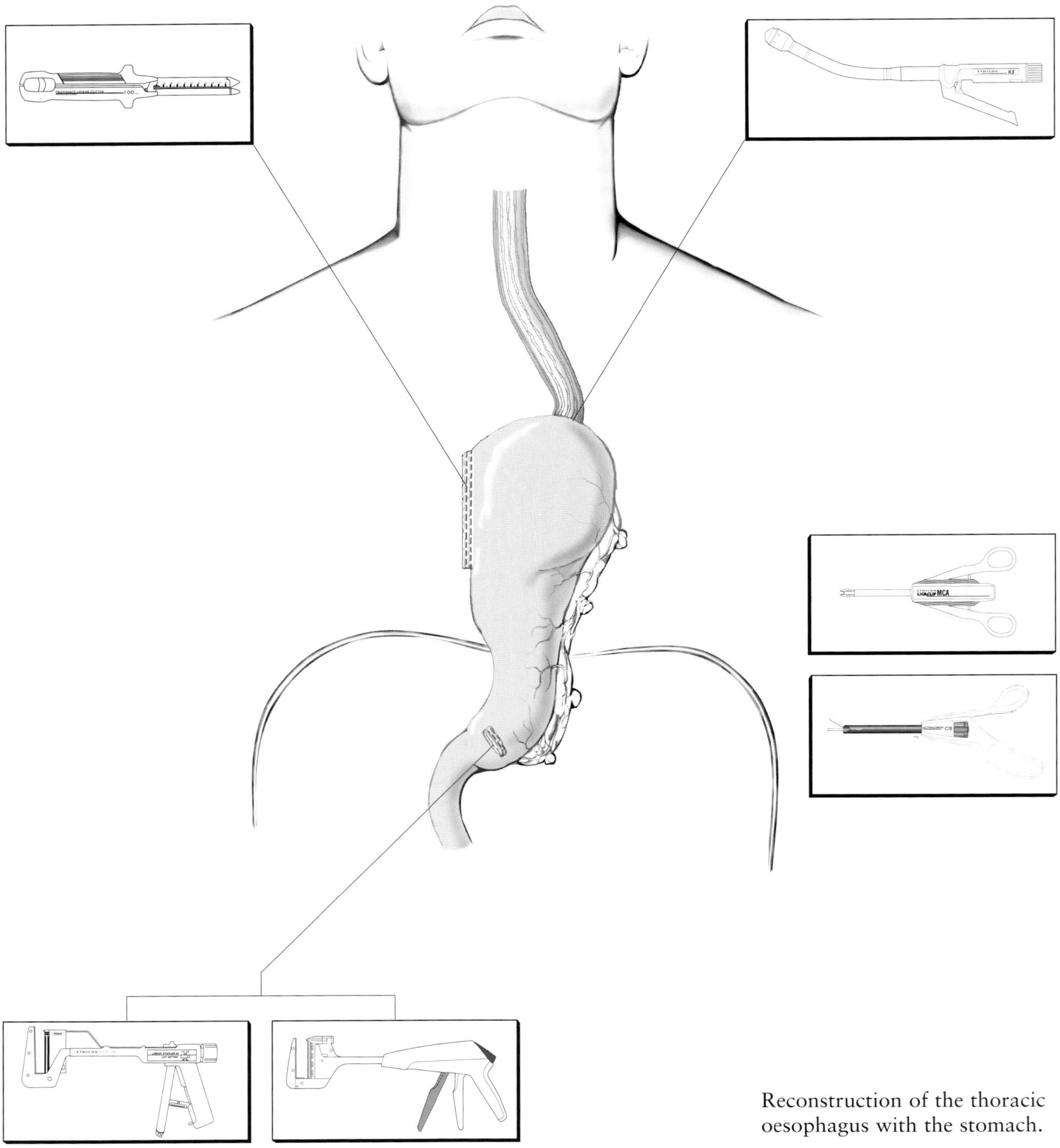

Reconstruction of the thoracic oesophagus with the stomach.

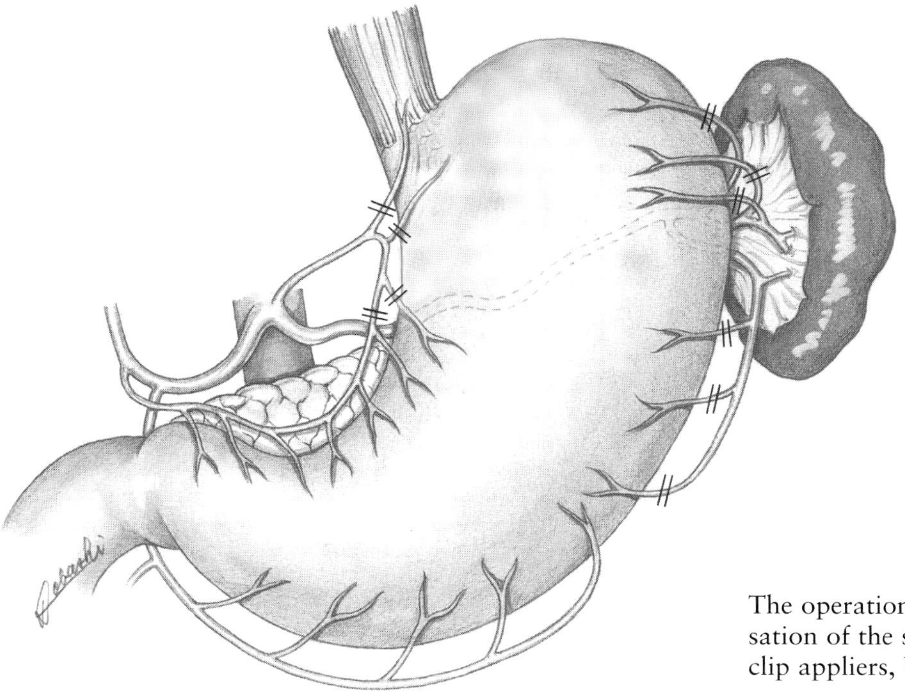

The operation commences with partial mobilisation of the stomach with the aid of multiple clip appliers, Ultracision, or both.

Owing to the transection of the truncal vagus nerve, in a latter step of the procedure a pyloroplasty is performed with a linear stapler thick.

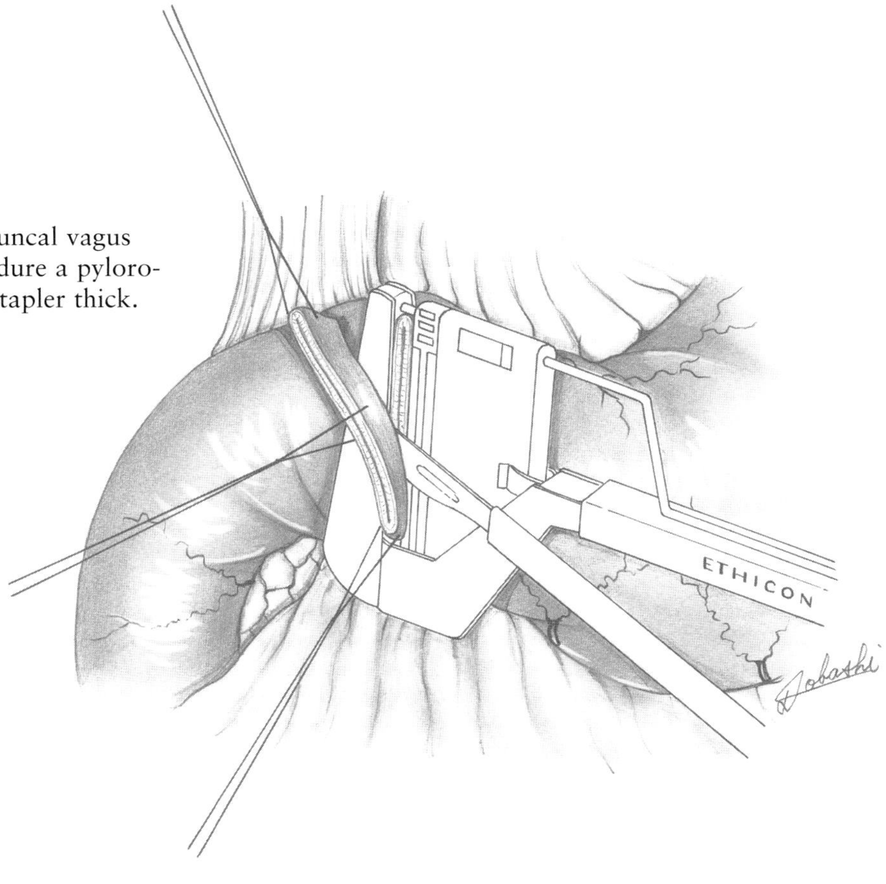

Thoracic part of the procedure. After transecting the oesophagus proximal to the pathological tract, a purse-string suture is performed at its distal end. In order to perform an adequate anastomosis, the mucosa of the oesophagus is exteriorised with four graspers. In fashioning the purse-string, special attention must be paid to the inclusion of all layers, particularly the mucosa, which is the only solid part of the oesophagus at this level, on which the staples will be formed.

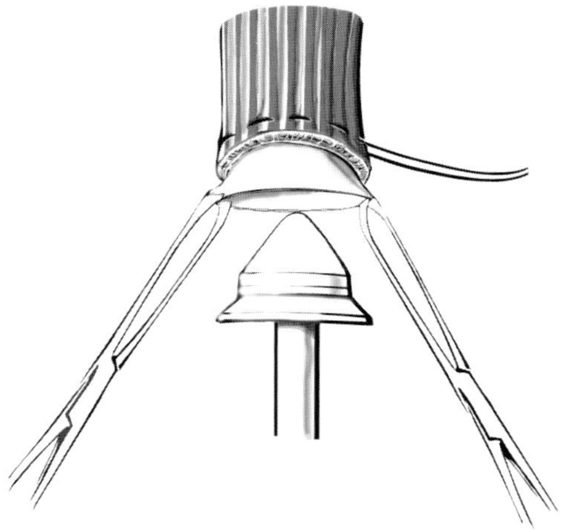

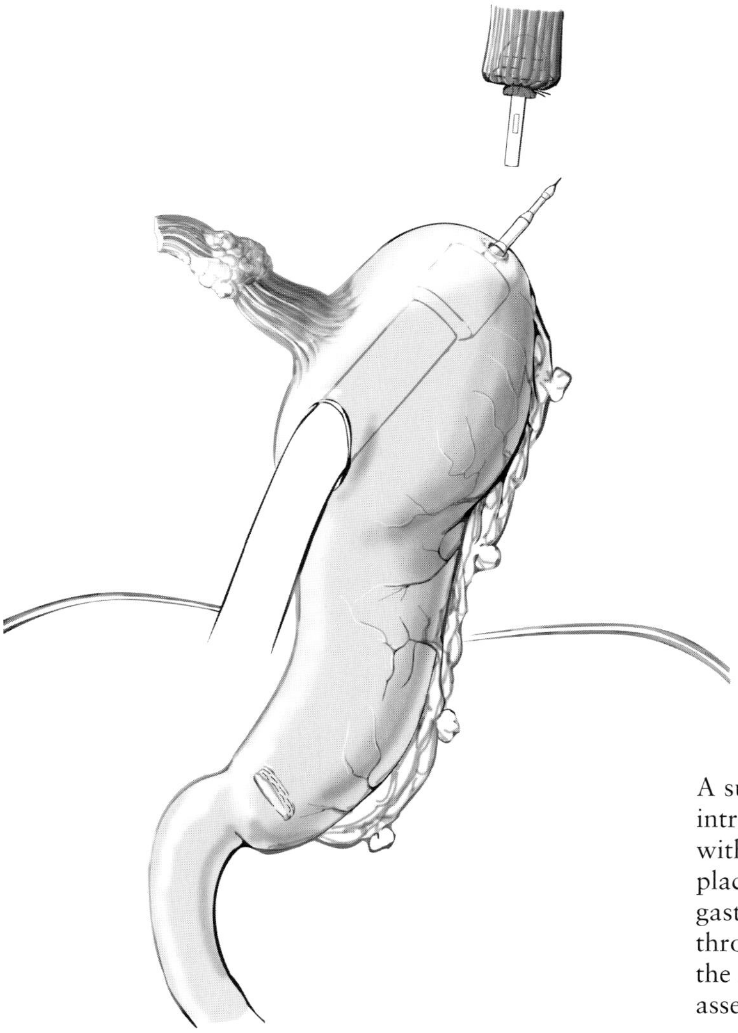

A subcardial gastrotomy is performed in order to introduce the shaft of a circular stapler. Piercing with the trocar of the circular stapler will take place at the level of the termination of the right gastroepiploic artery. The stomach is elevated through the diaphragm into the thoracic cavity with the aid of the circular stapler. The circular stapler is assembled, closed, and fired.

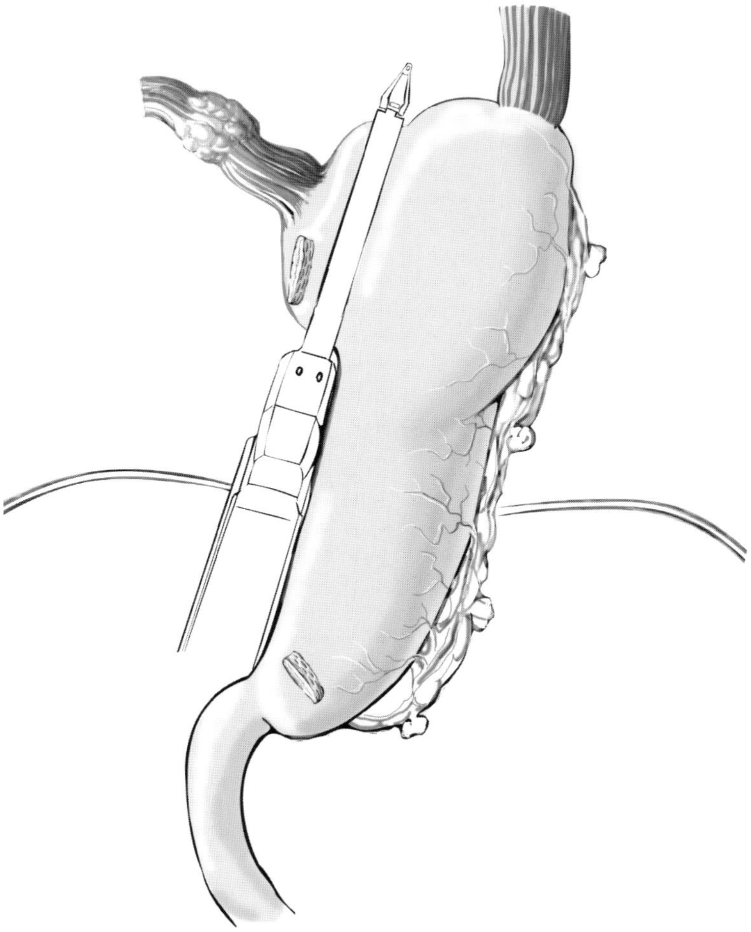

After performing the anastomosis and removing the circular stapler, gastric tubalisation is performed with a linear cutter or linear stapler thick, removing the gastrotomy with the specimen. A tissue bridge of at least 3 cm must be maintained between the two staple lines .

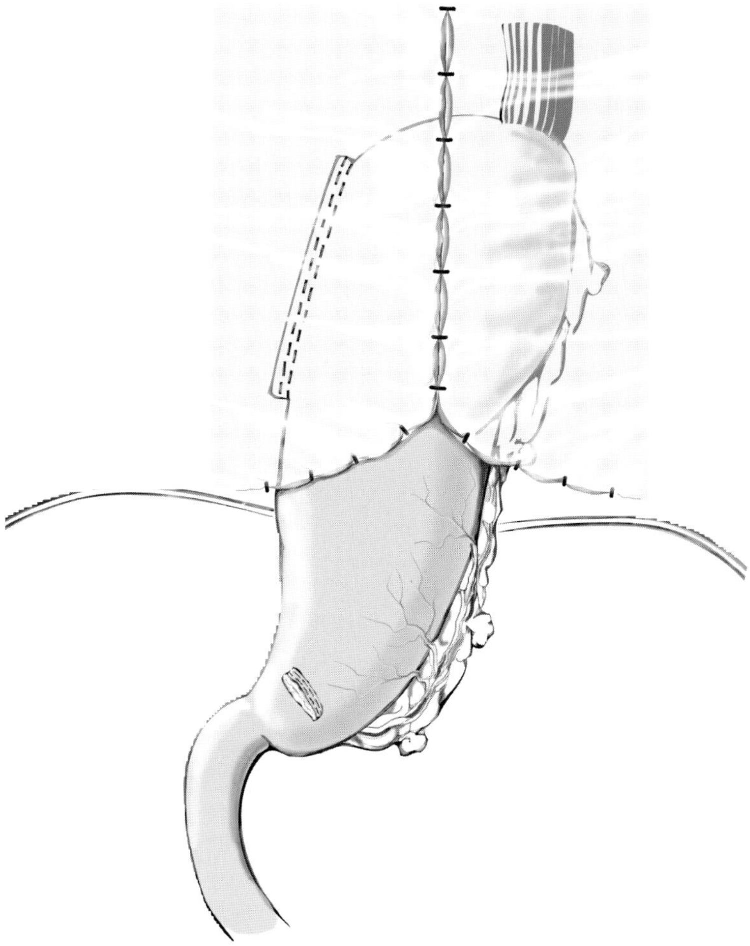

The basic principle in performing a digestive anastomosis, which is to avoid tension between the two segments, is of major importance in oesophagogastric intrathoracic anastomosis. The weight of the stomach, which is suspended only by the staples of the anastomotic device, may lead to high risk of fistula development.

To avoid traction on the staple line, the top of the gastric tube is suspended from the margins of the mediastinal pleura, which were formerly open for oesophageal dissection.

The anastomosis is then buried under a flap of the mediastinal pleura. This will reduce the risk of mediastinal contamination in the case of anastomotic leakage.

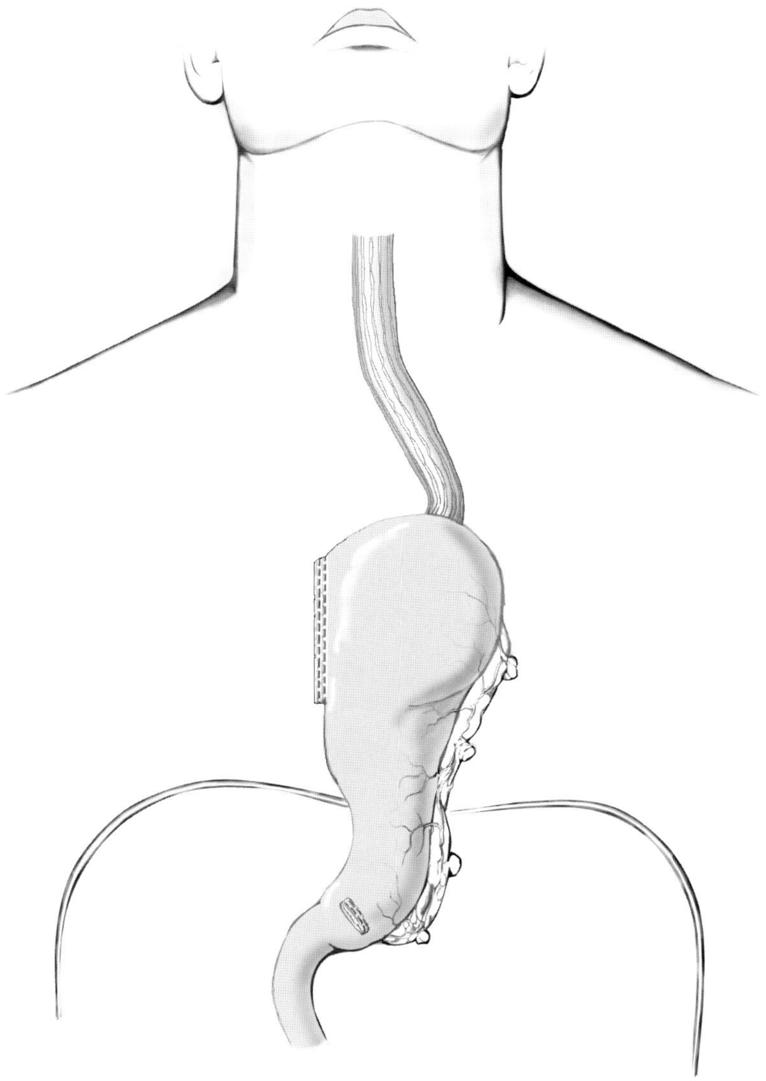

View of the oesophagogastric intrathoracic high anastomosis after completion.

Reconstruction of Thoracic Oesophagus

Oesophagectomy and Total Gastrectomy with Jejunum Replacement and Thoracic Anastomosis

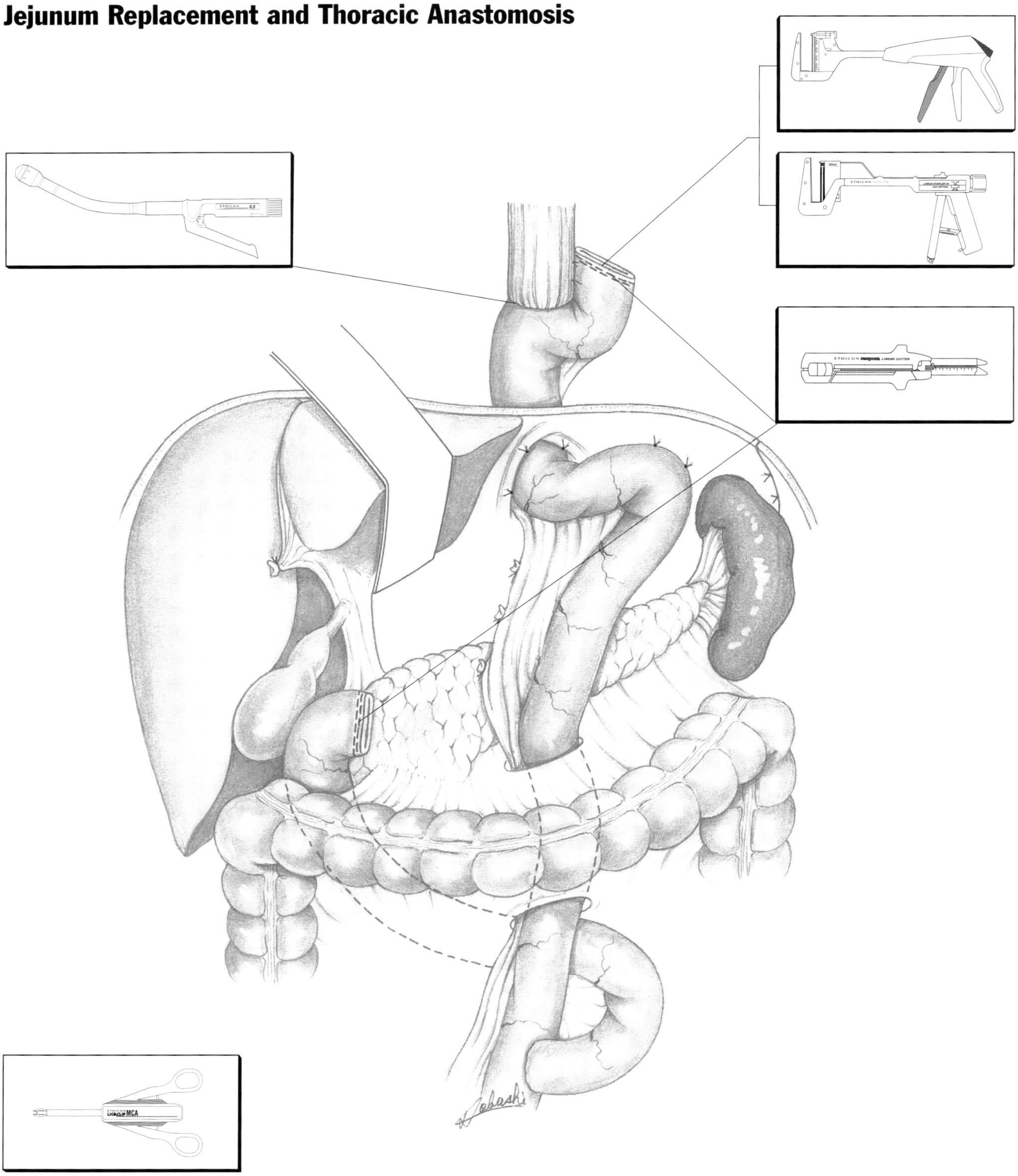

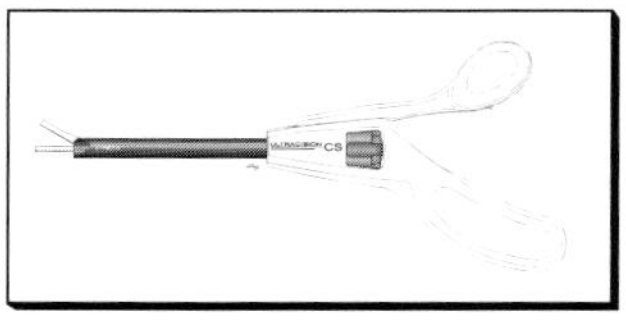

Reconstruction after total gastrectomy and distal oesophageal resection with a Roux-en-Y loop.

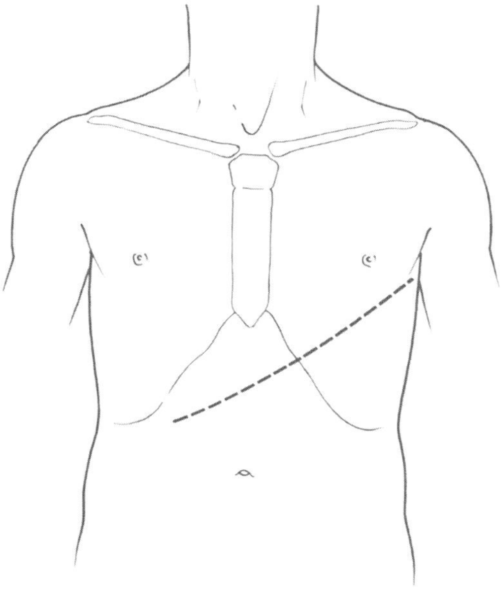

The operation is performed through a left combined thoraco-abdominal incision with the patient's left side elevated about 45 degrees.

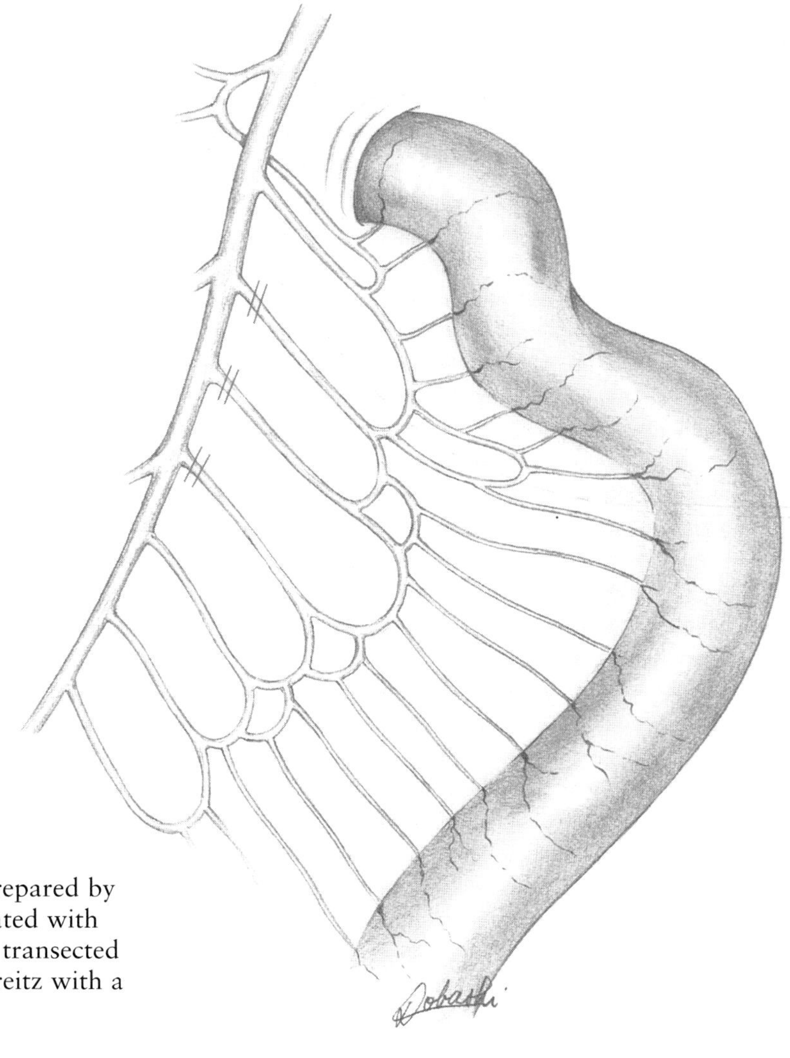

A retrocolic Roux loop of 50 cm length is prepared by taking a portion of at least three arcades ligated with clips, sutures, or Ultracision. The jejunum is transected about 20 cm distally from the ligament of Treitz with a linear cutter standard.

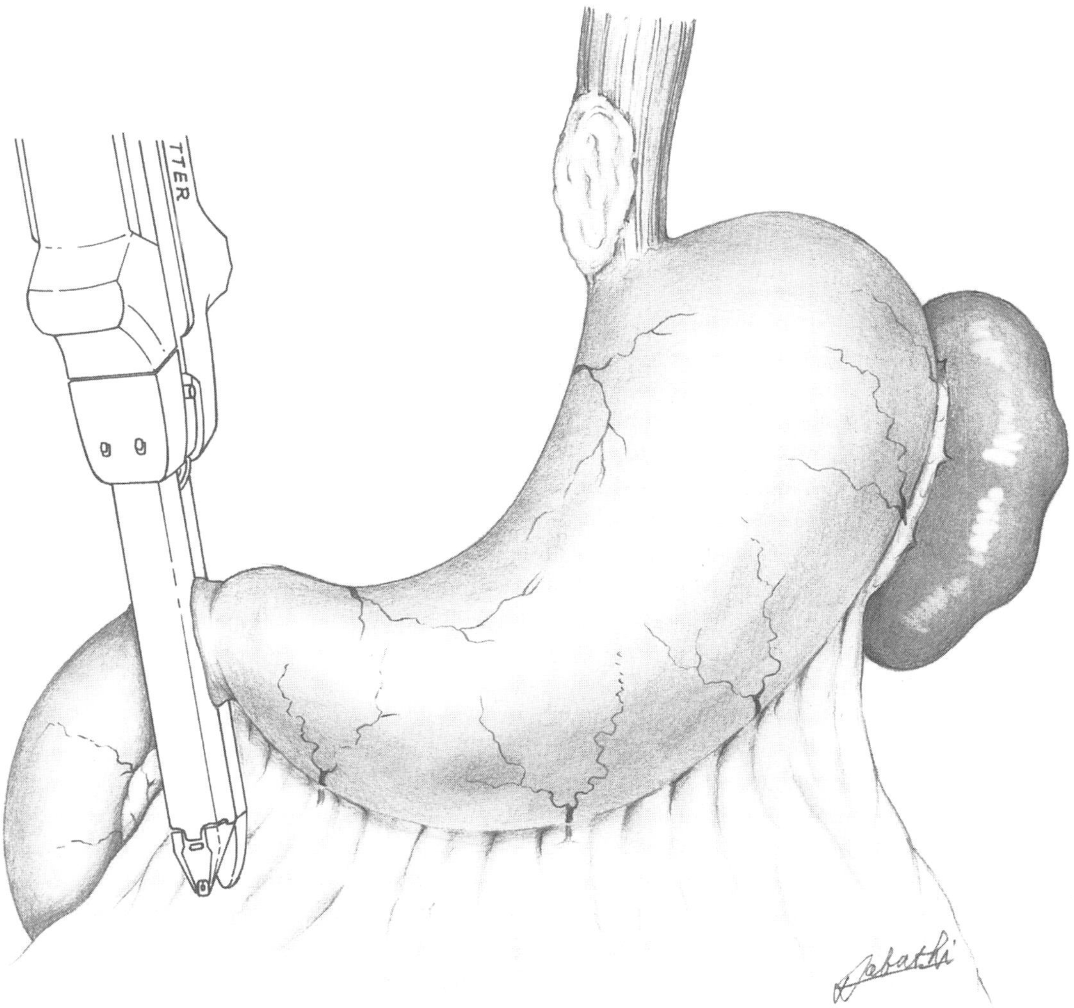

The stomach, including the omentum, is mobilised with the help of multiple clip appliers or Ultracision and transected 2 cm distally to the pylorus with a linear cutter or linear stapler thick. The advantage of the linear cutter is that it simultaneously cuts and sutures the stomach, thus avoiding spillage. The linear stapler, however, is easier to position without tension on the tissue.

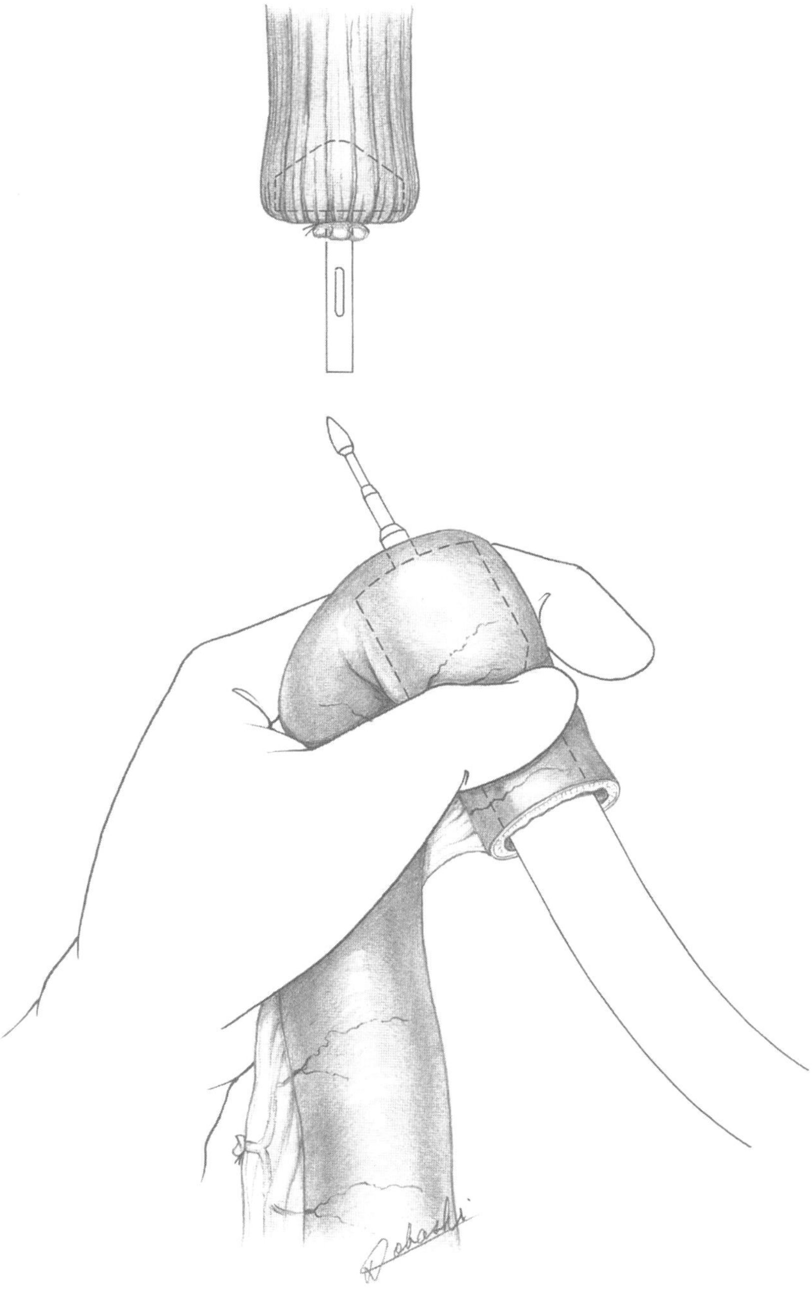

The stomach is removed after transecting the oesophagus. A purse-string suture is placed around the remaining oesophagus. The anvil of the circular stapler is introduced into the oesophagus and the purse-string suture tied. The circular stapler is inserted through the open jejunum end and the trocar emerges through the antimesenteric wall 5 cm from the end. The stapler is assembled, closed, and fired.

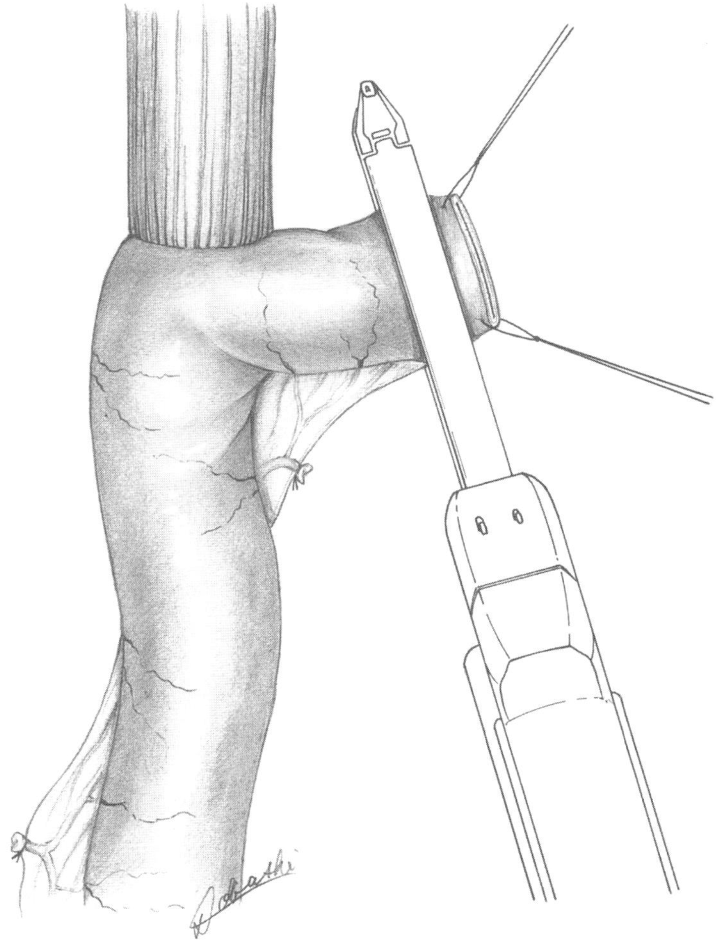

The open end of the jejunal loop is closed with a linear cutter or linear stapler standard.

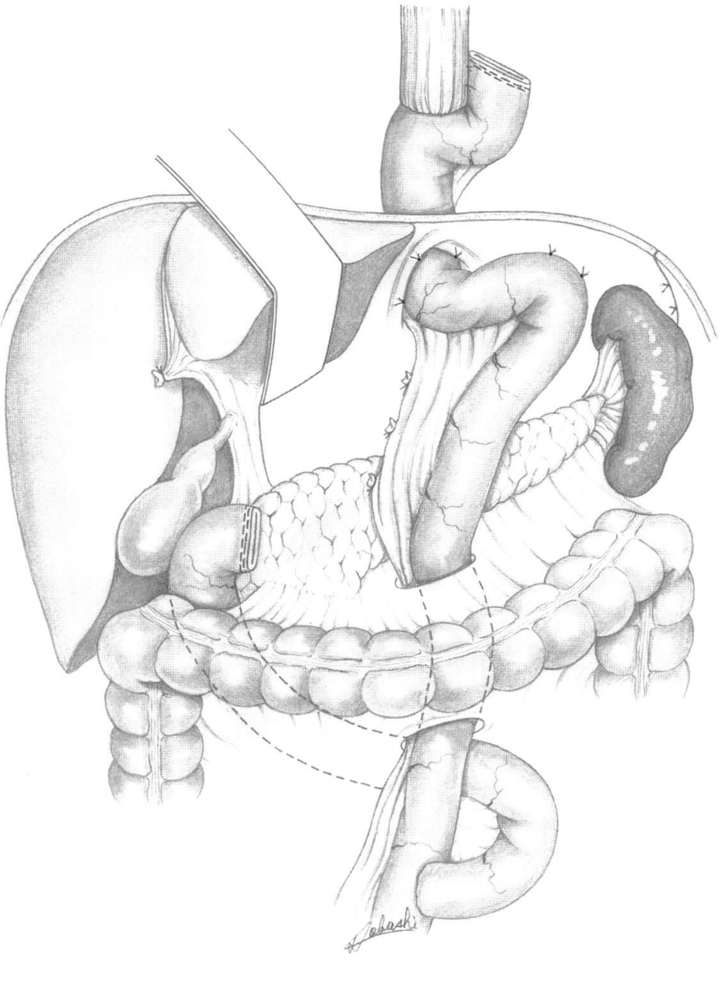

The end-to-side jejuno-jejunostomy is performed by hand suturing. The bowel should be fixed to the diaphragm and hiatus to avoid tension on the proximal anastomosis. The attachment of the blind end of the jejunal loop to the oesophagus is seldom necessary.

Ligation of Oesophageal Varices

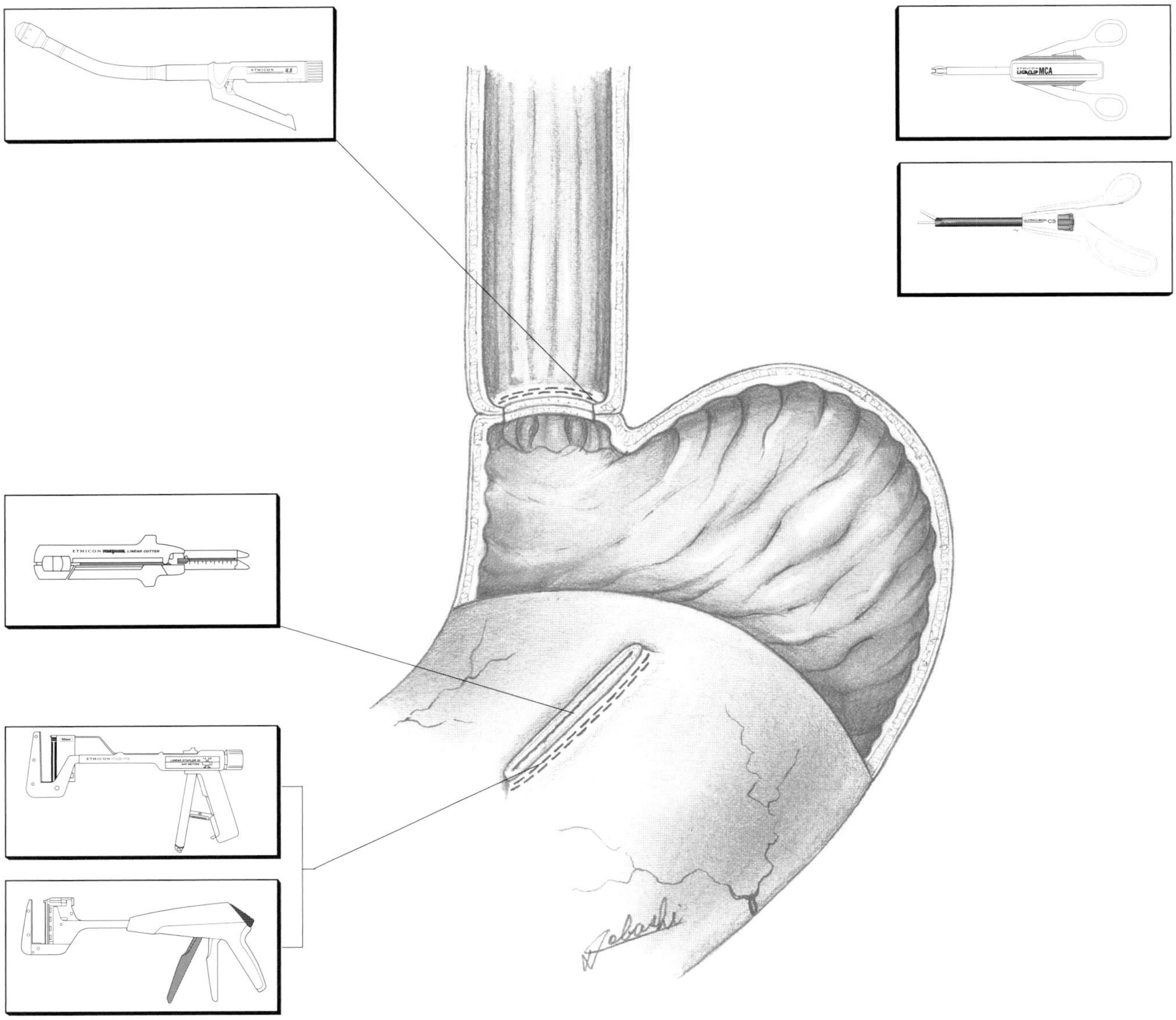

Oesophageal transection with a circular stapling device
for oesophageal varices.

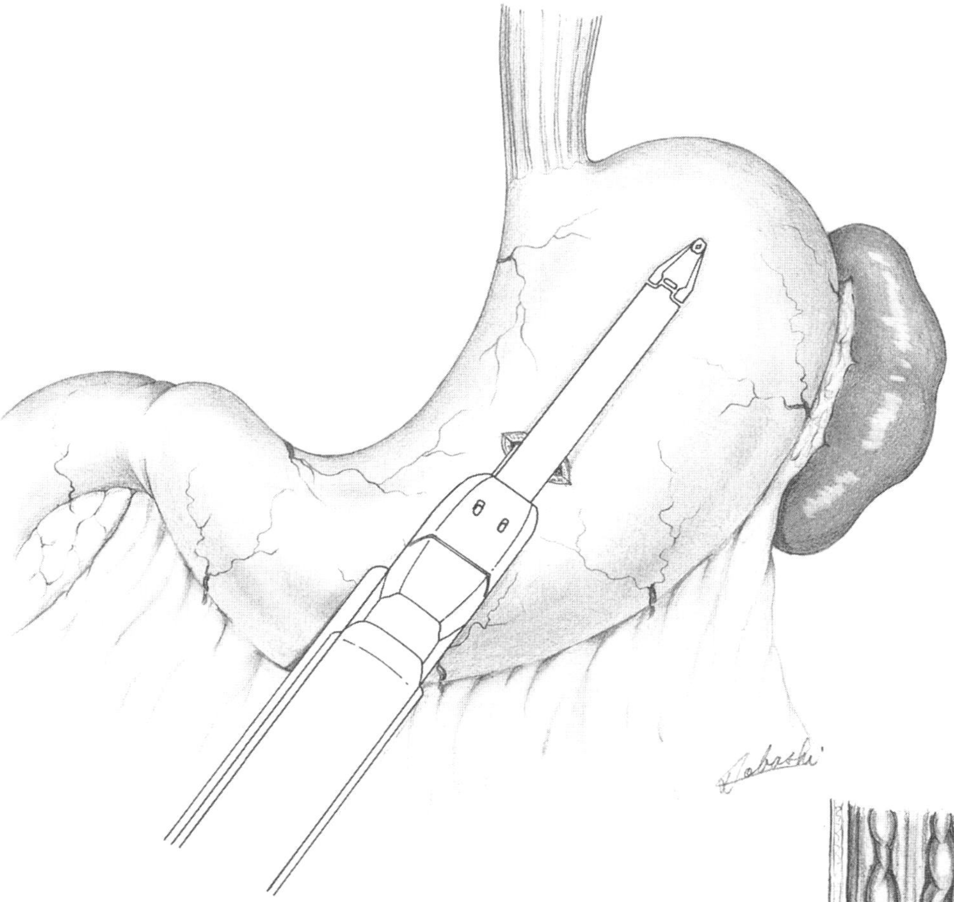

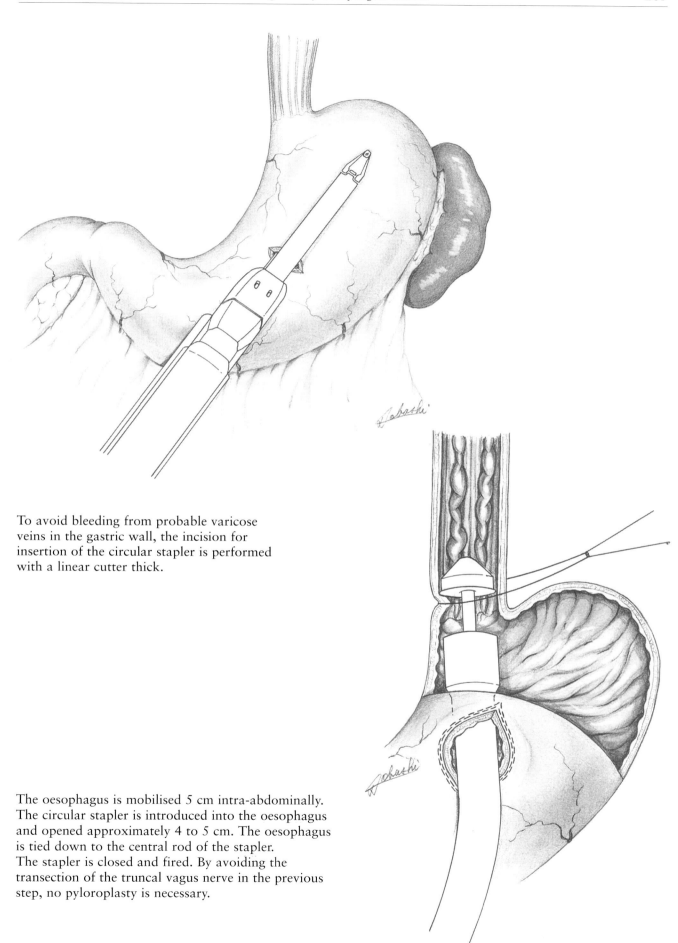

To avoid bleeding from probable varicose veins in the gastric wall, the incision for insertion of the circular stapler is performed with a linear cutter thick.

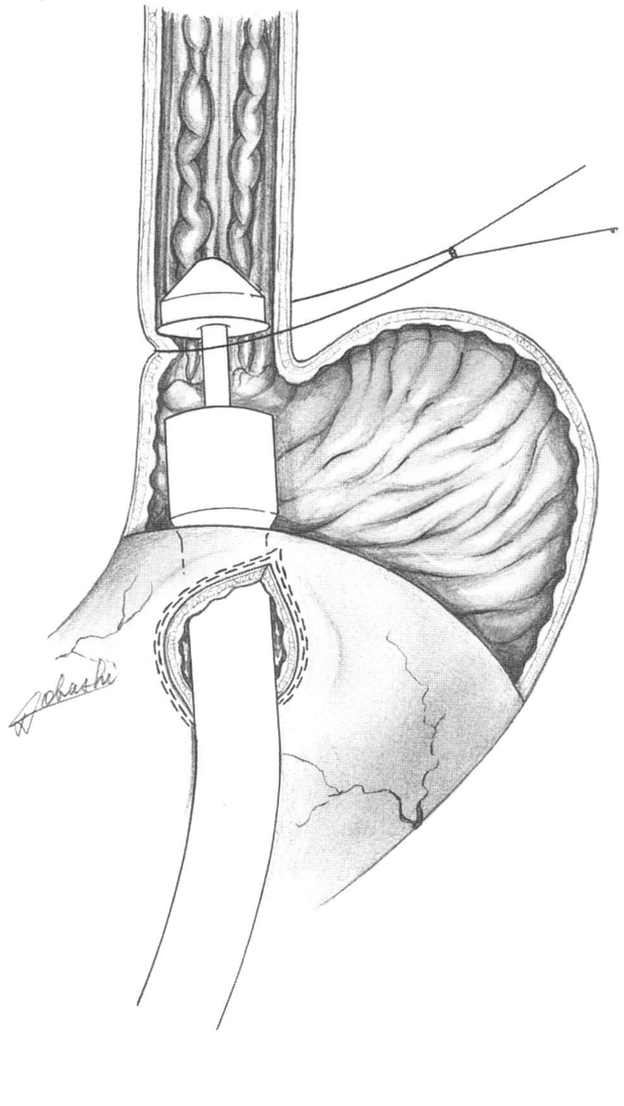

The oesophagus is mobilised 5 cm intra-abdominally. The circular stapler is introduced into the oesophagus and opened approximately 4 to 5 cm. The oesophagus is tied down to the central rod of the stapler. The stapler is closed and fired. By avoiding the transection of the truncal vagus nerve in the previous step, no pyloroplasty is necessary.

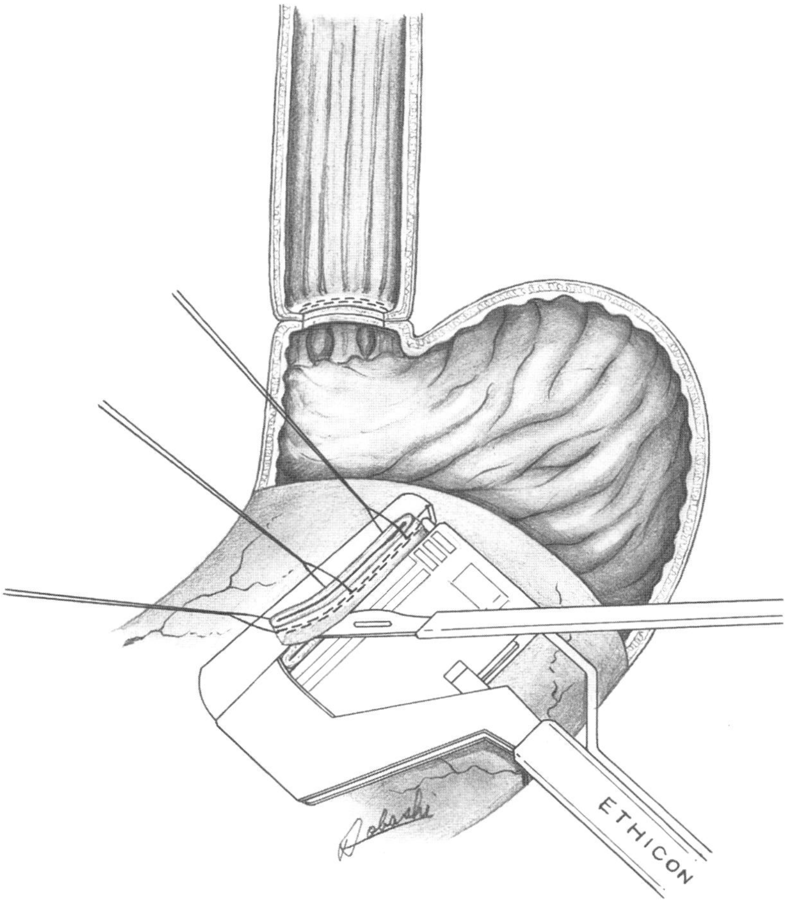

The gastrotomy is closed with a linear stapler thick or hand suturing.

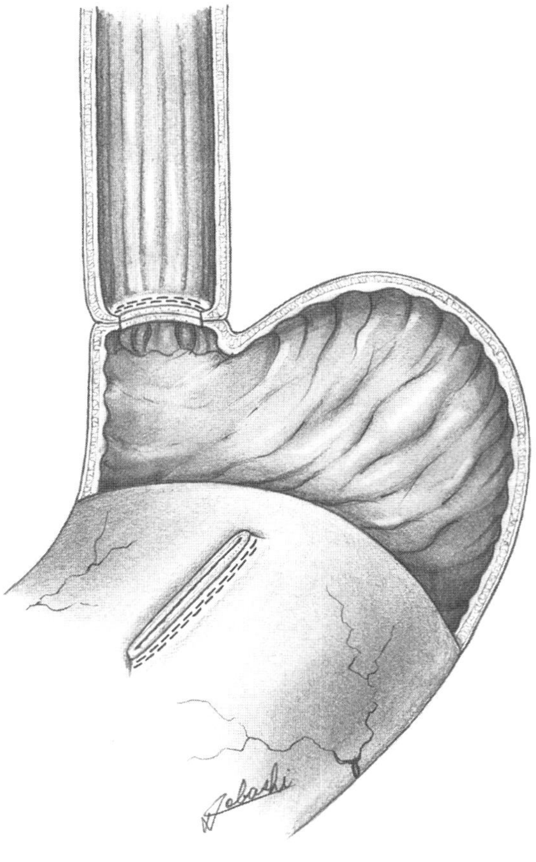

The completed ligation of oesophageal varicose veins.

3 Gastric Surgery

Gastrostomy

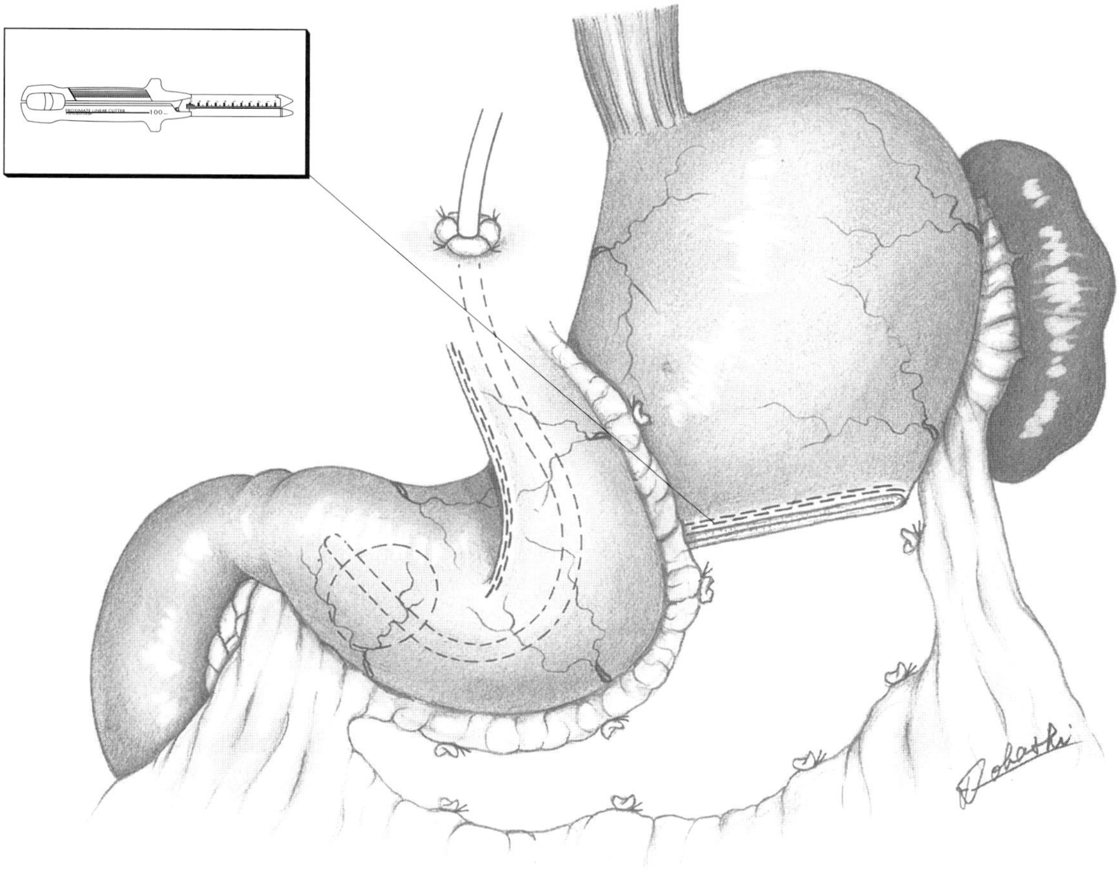

Gastrostomy performed with a linear cutter.

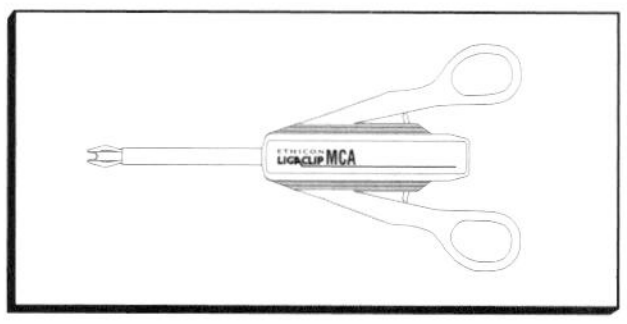

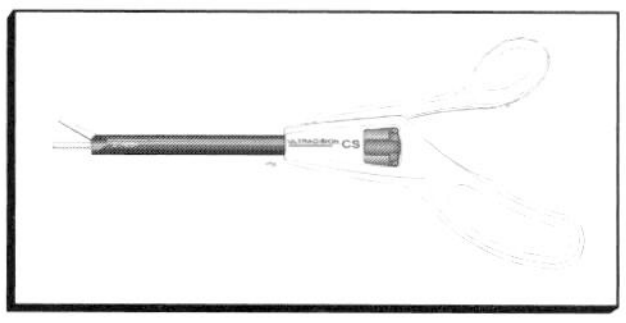

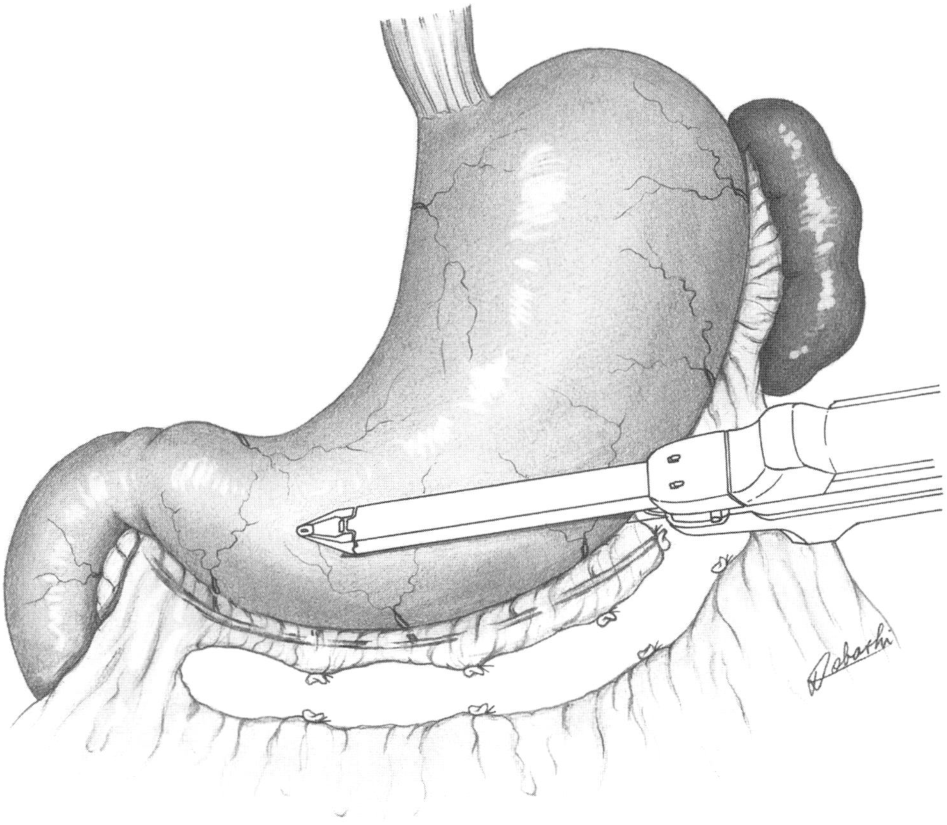

Partial mobilisation of the stomach along the greater curvature by using the multiple clip applier or the Ultracision coagulating shears. Creation of the alimentary tube with the linear cutter thick. After firing the instrument, the staple line should be checked for haemostasis and proper staple closure.

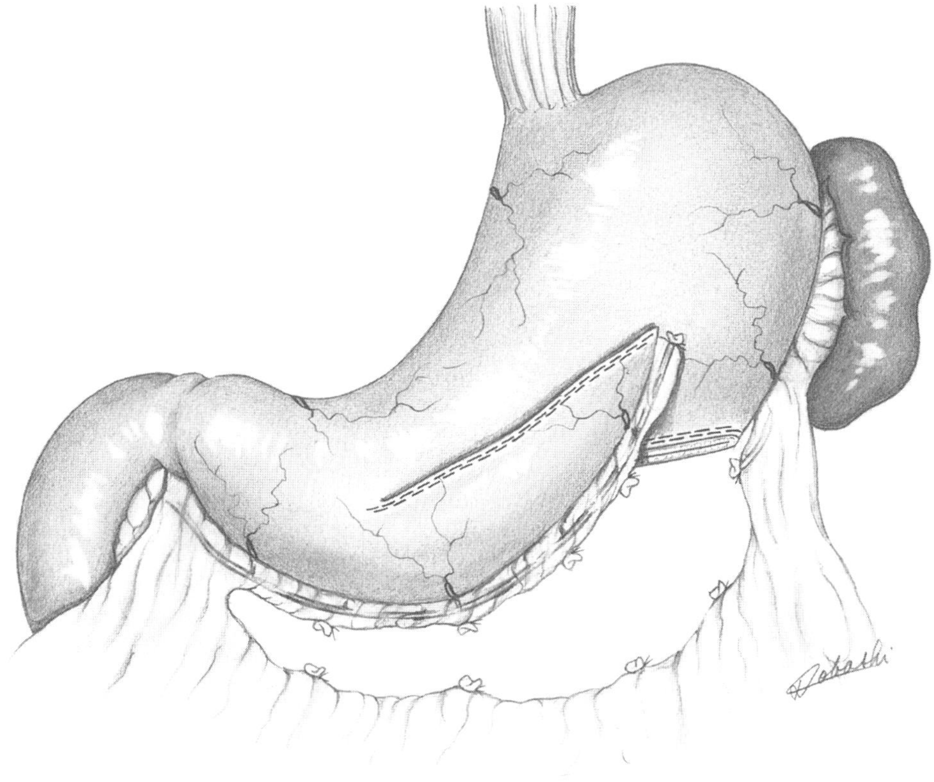

Here are different variations in creating the gastric tube. In making the tube special attention must be paid to its diameter so that a feeding tube may be accommodated.

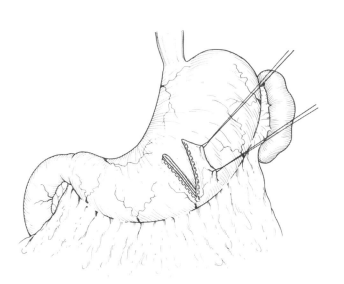

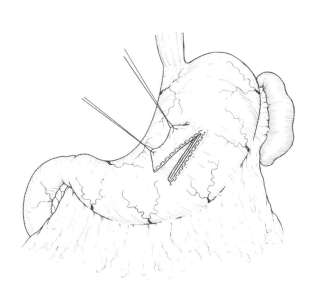

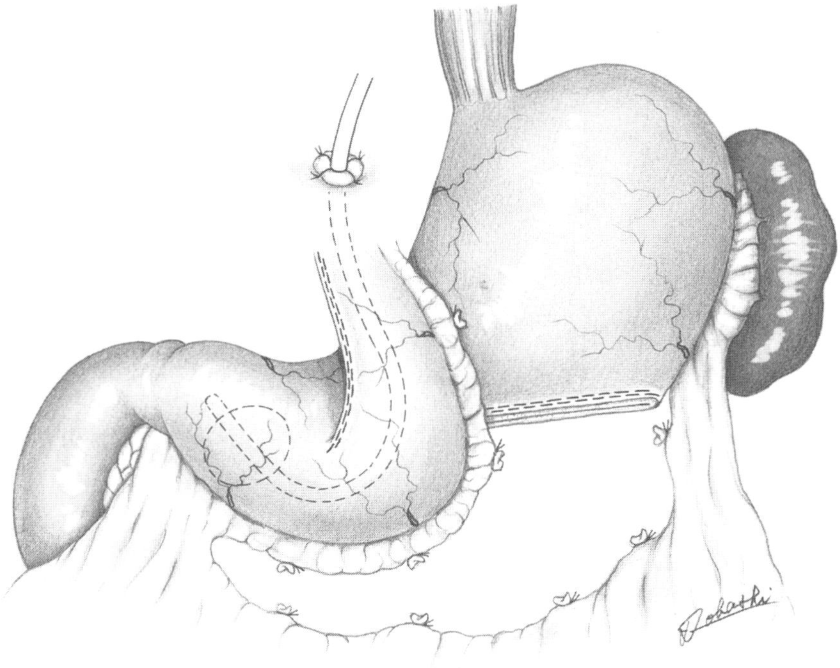

The procedure is completed by creating a small stab incision in the abdominal wall. The newly created gastric tube is secured to the skin with sutures. The tip of the tube is amputated to create the alimentary opening. This opening should be just large enough to accommodate a feeding tube.

Partial Gastrectomy

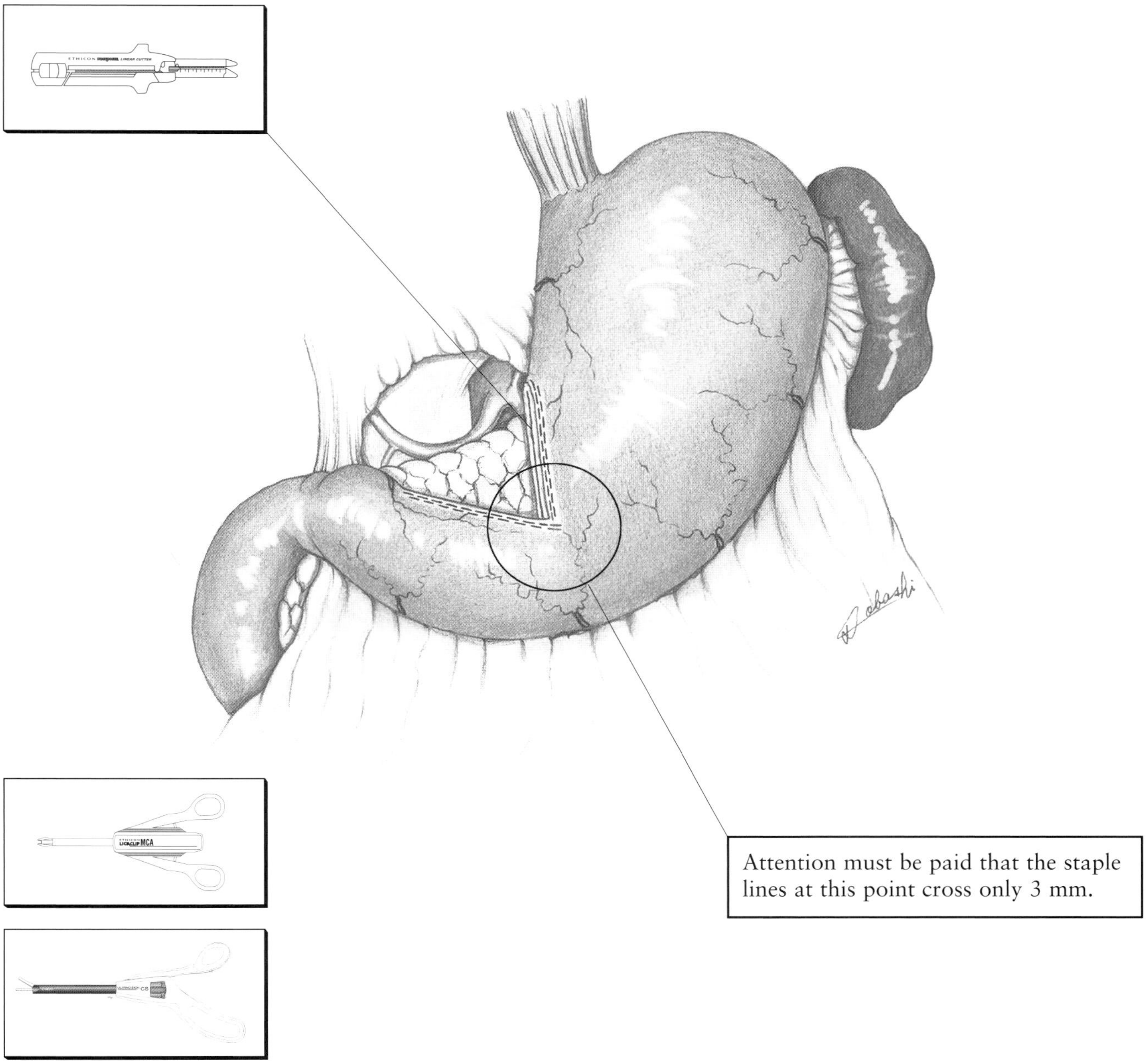
Attention must be paid that the staple lines at this point cross only 3 mm.

The main indication for the so-called wedge resection is found in ulcer surgery.

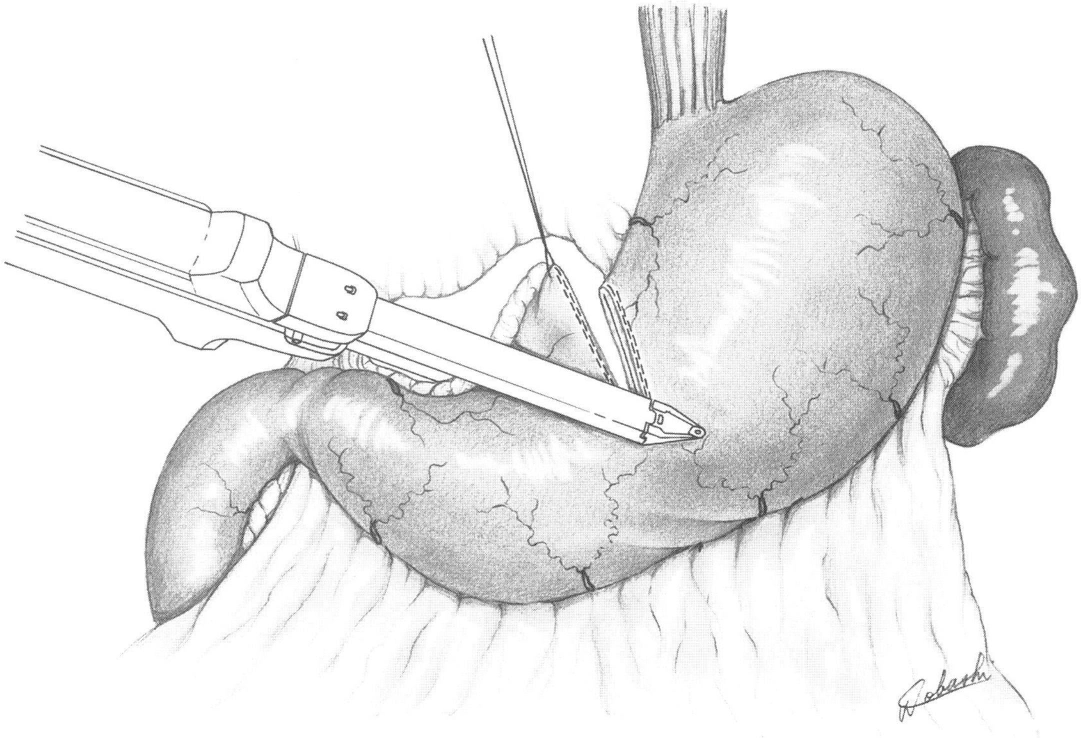

Partial mobilisation of the stomach along the lesser curvature by using the multiple clip applier or the Ultracision coagulating shears.
Partial resection of the stomach by using a linear cutter thick twice. After firing the instrument, the staple lines should be checked for haemostasis and proper staple closure.

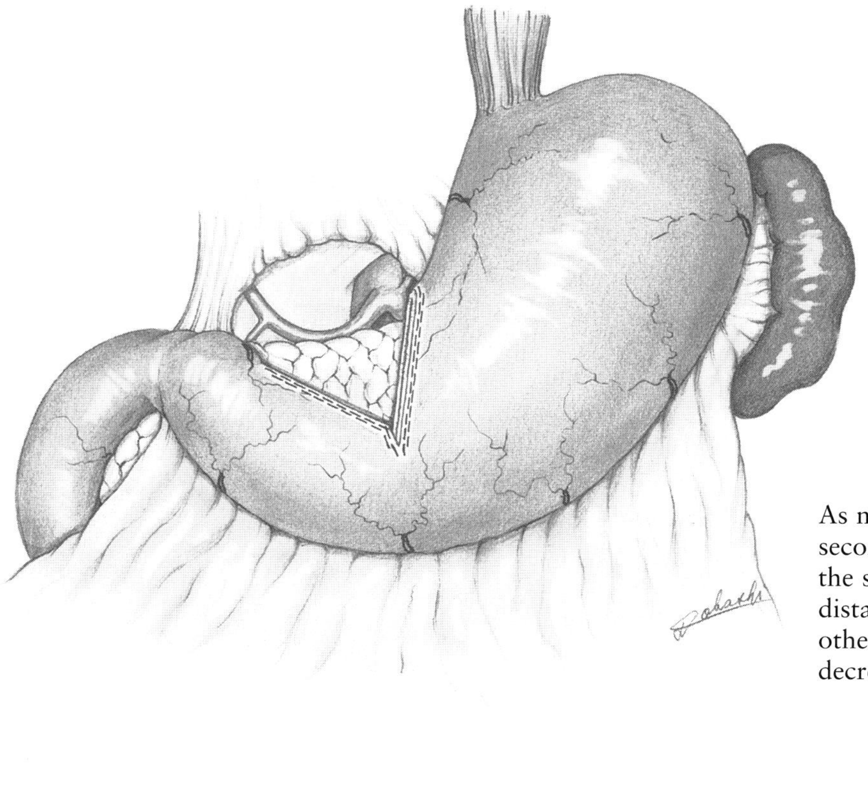

As mentioned above, during the second application of the linear cutter the staple lines must cross at their distal ends, but not more than 3 mm, otherwise the area could be affected by decreased blood supply.

Billroth I

Side-to-end Gastroduodenostomy

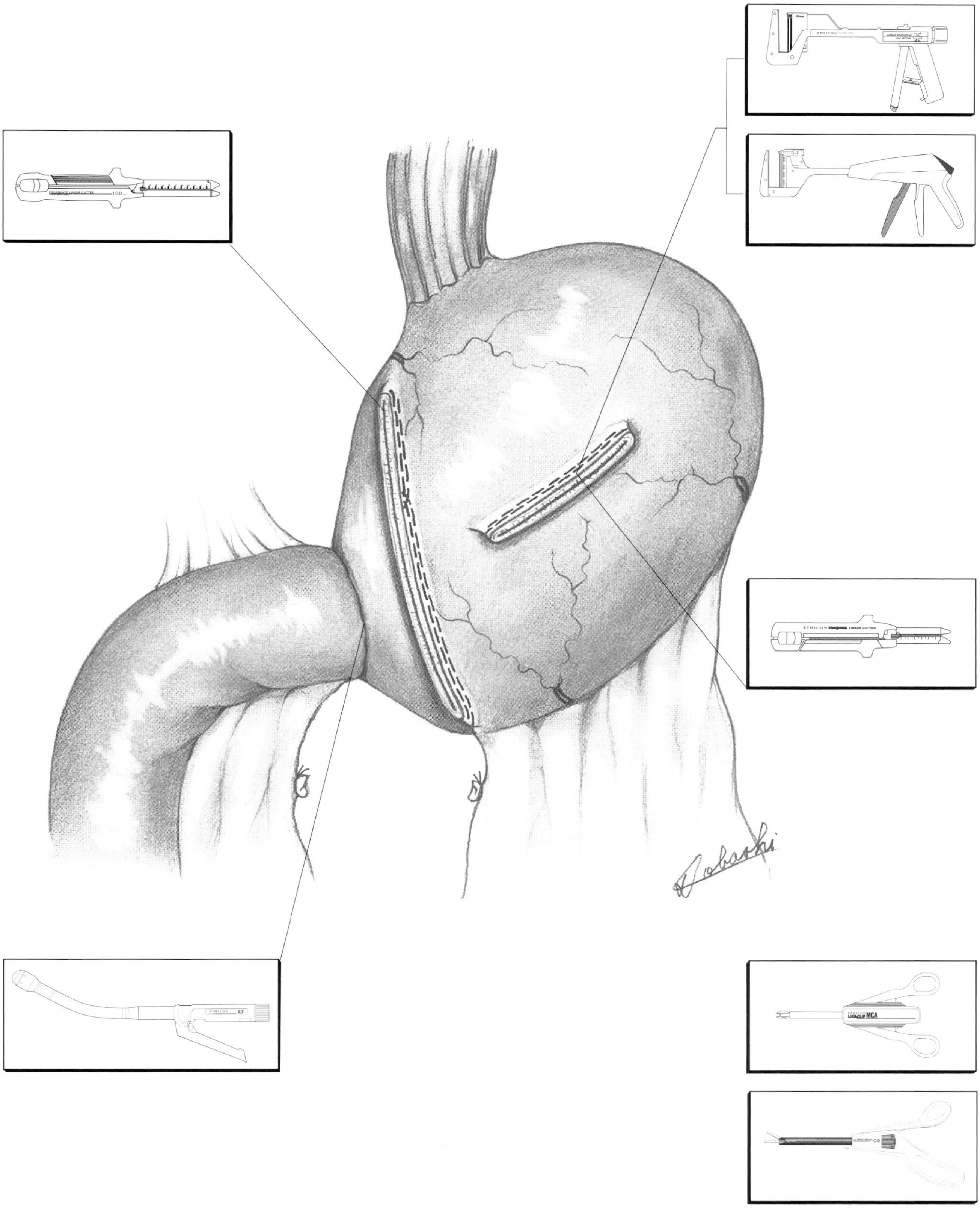

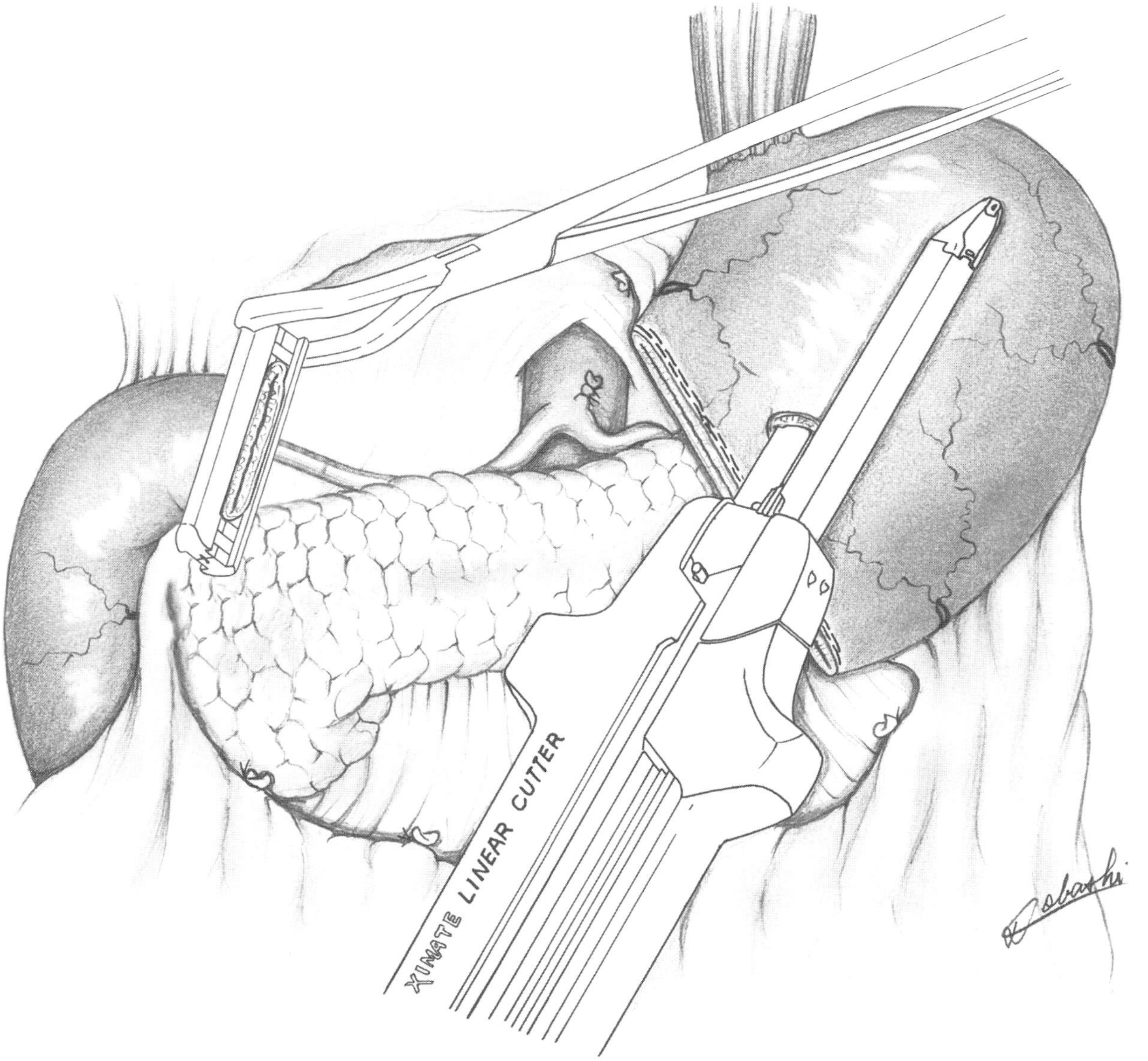

The procedure commences with the mobilisation of the stomach with multiple clip appliers or Ultracision coagulating shears. A subtotal gastrectomy is performed using a linear cutter thick. A purse-string suture is placed at the distal resection line using a purse-string suture clamp. A small gastrotomy is performed, at least 3 cm distant from the proximal staple line, with a scalpel or Ultracision in order to insert the jaw of a linear cutter standard. The linear cutter is fired to make a gastrotomy large enough to allow the introduction of a circular stapler.

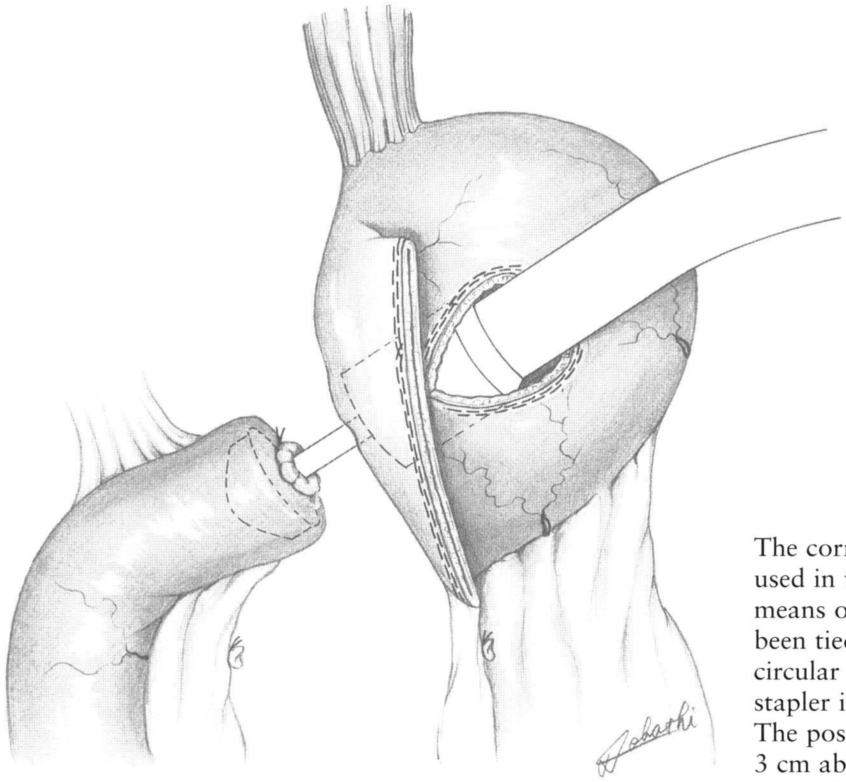

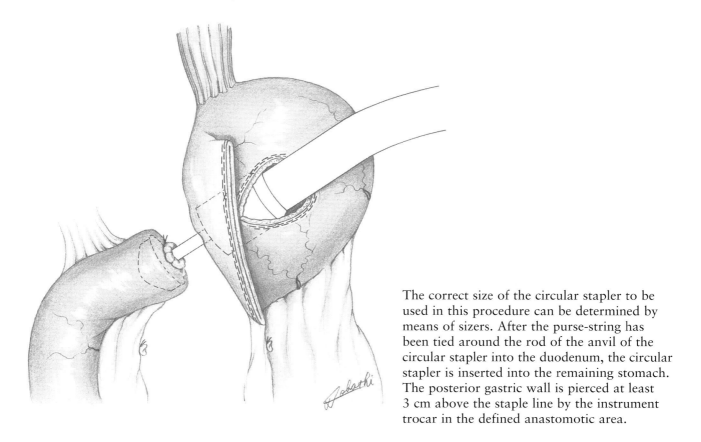

The correct size of the circular stapler to be used in this procedure can be determined by means of sizers. After the purse-string has been tied around the rod of the anvil of the circular stapler into the duodenum, the circular stapler is inserted into the remaining stomach. The posterior gastric wall is pierced at least 3 cm above the staple line by the instrument trocar in the defined anastomotic area.

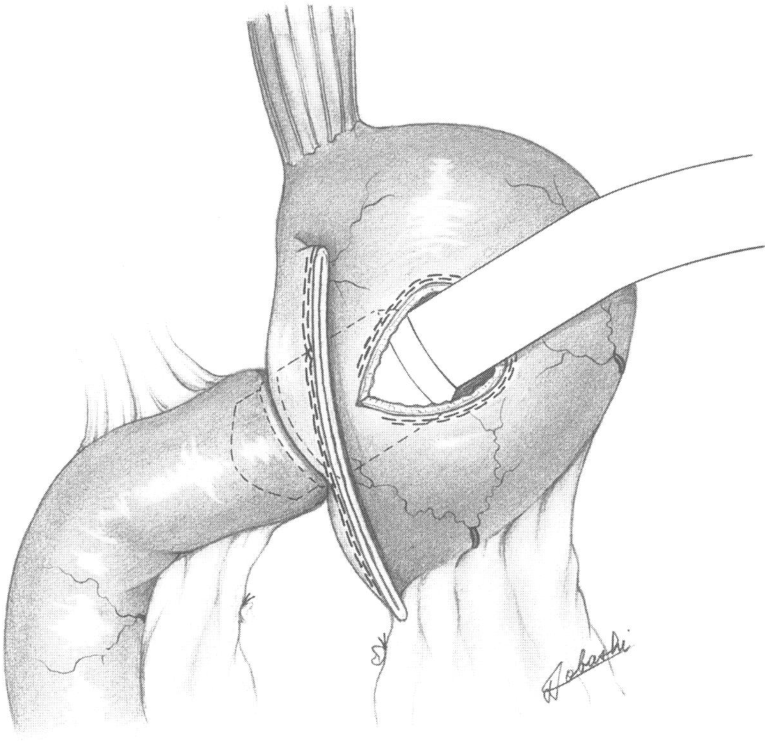

The instrument head and anvil shaft are connected and the side-to-end gastroduodenostomy is created. The staple line is then examined for haemostasis and proper staple closure. After withdrawing the circular stapler, the 'doughnuts' have to be carefully removed from the instrument head and examined for integrity.

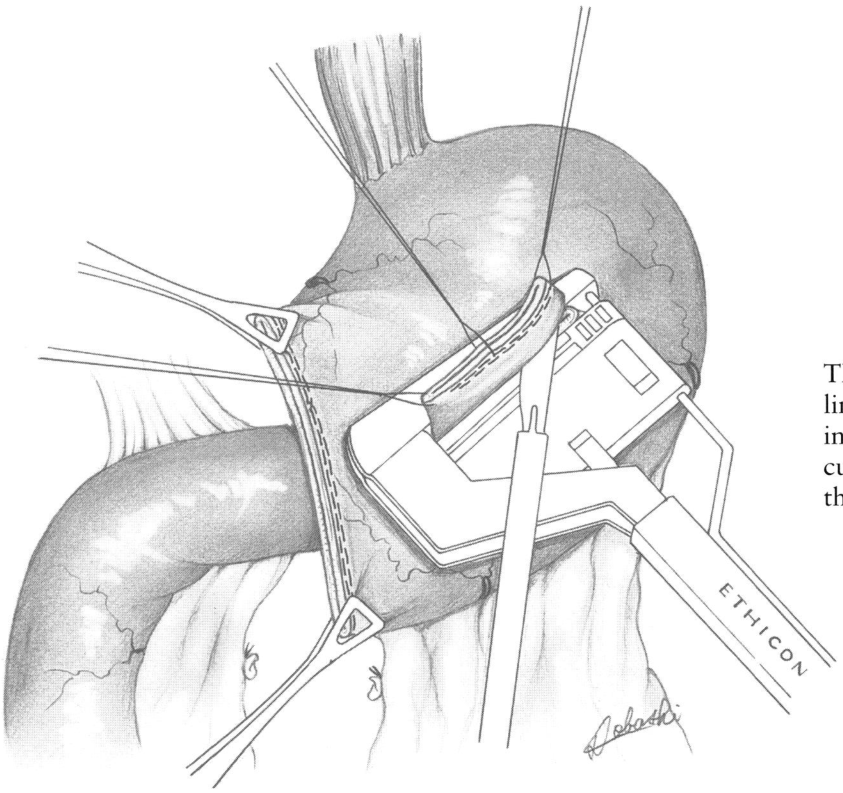

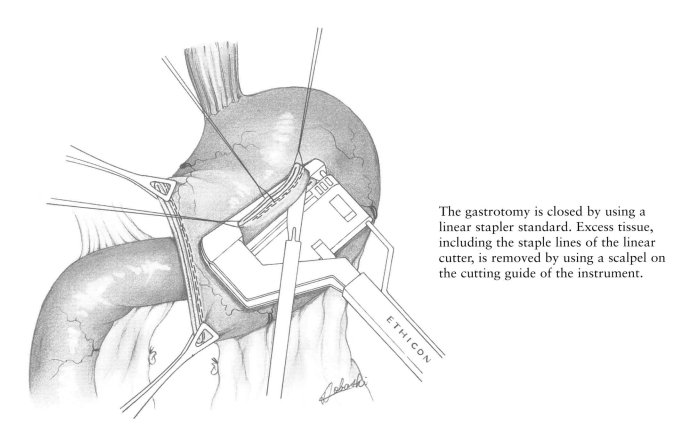

The gastrotomy is closed by using a linear stapler standard. Excess tissue, including the staple lines of the linear cutter, is removed by using a scalpel on the cutting guide of the instrument.

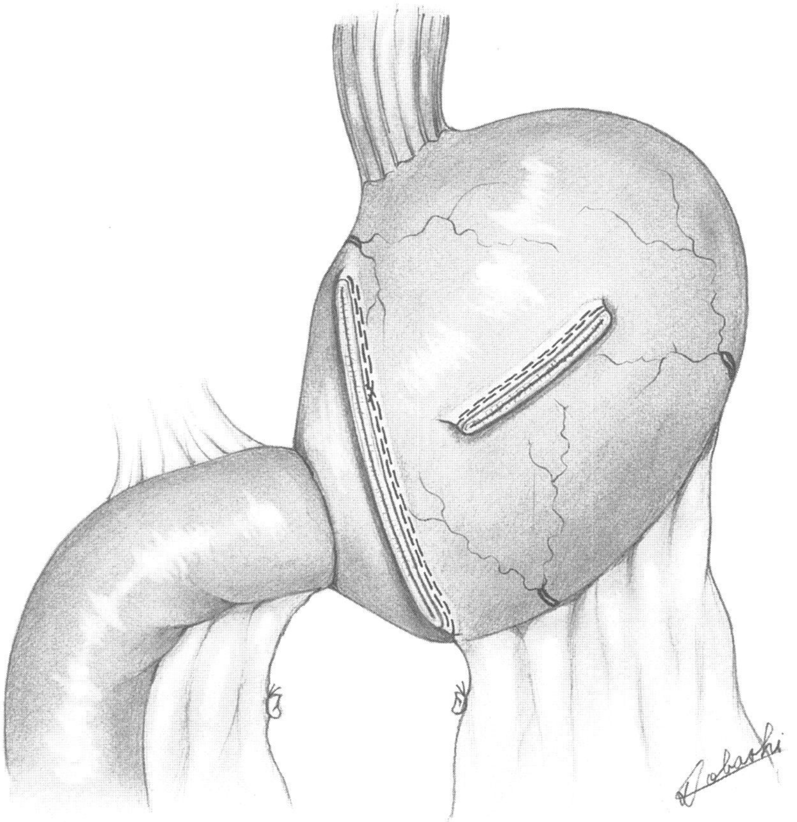

End result of the gastroduodenostomy.

Billroth I

End-to-end Gastroduodenostomy

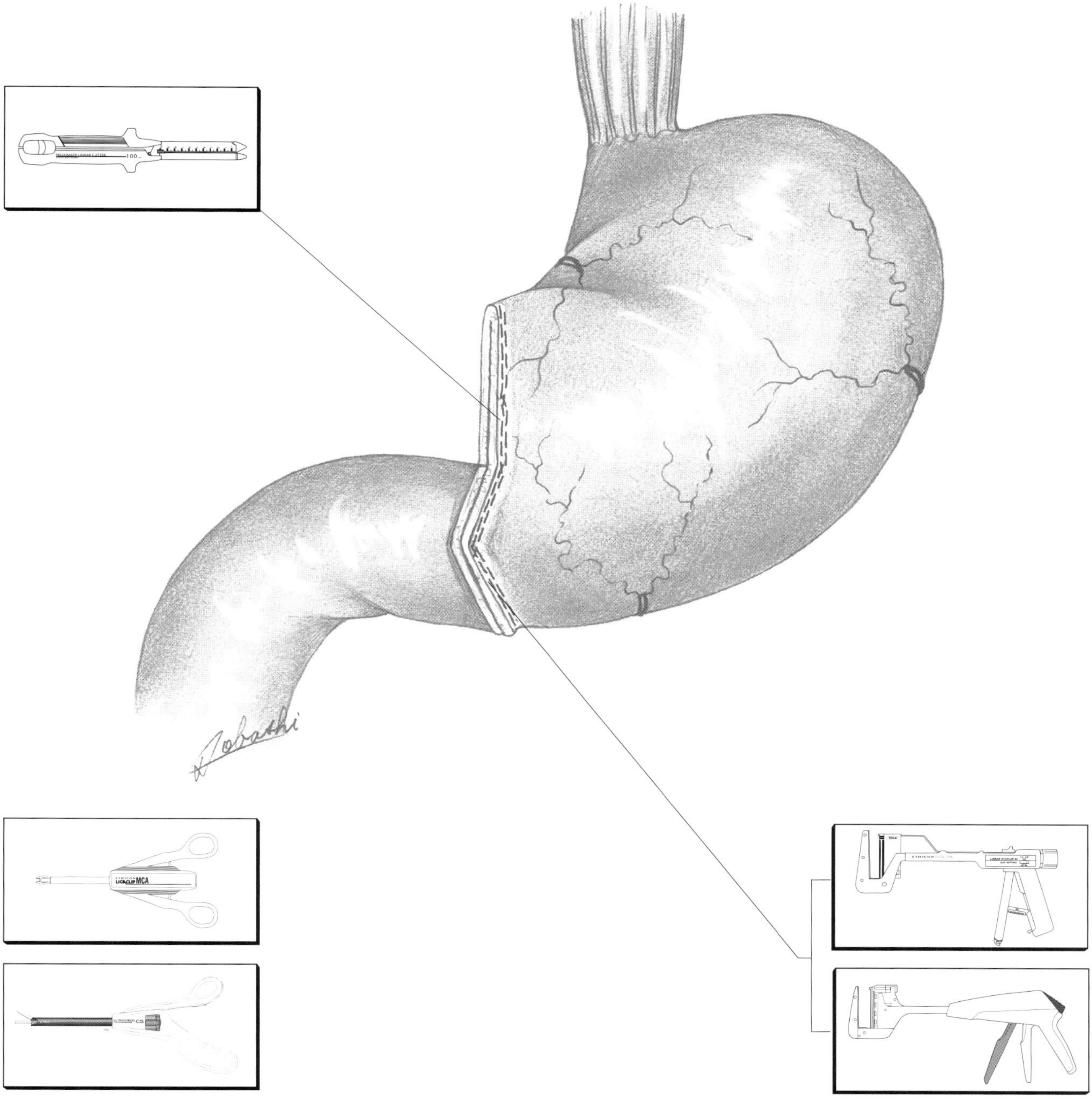

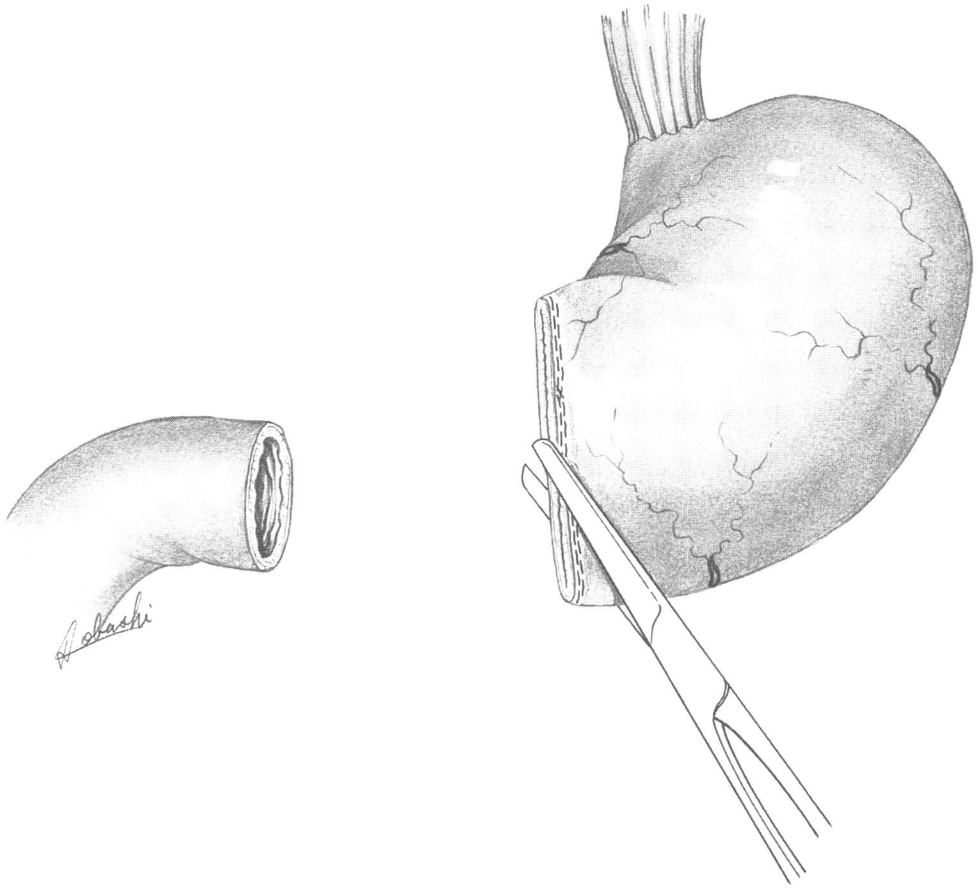

The procedure commences with the mobilisation of the stomach using multiple clip appliers or Ultracision coagulating shears. A subtotal gastrectomy is performed by using a linear cutter thick twice. The staple line of the duodenum is removed. The lower third of the staple line of the remaining stomach is resected with scissors. In doing this care must be taken that the lumen of the gastric opening and the duodenum coincide.

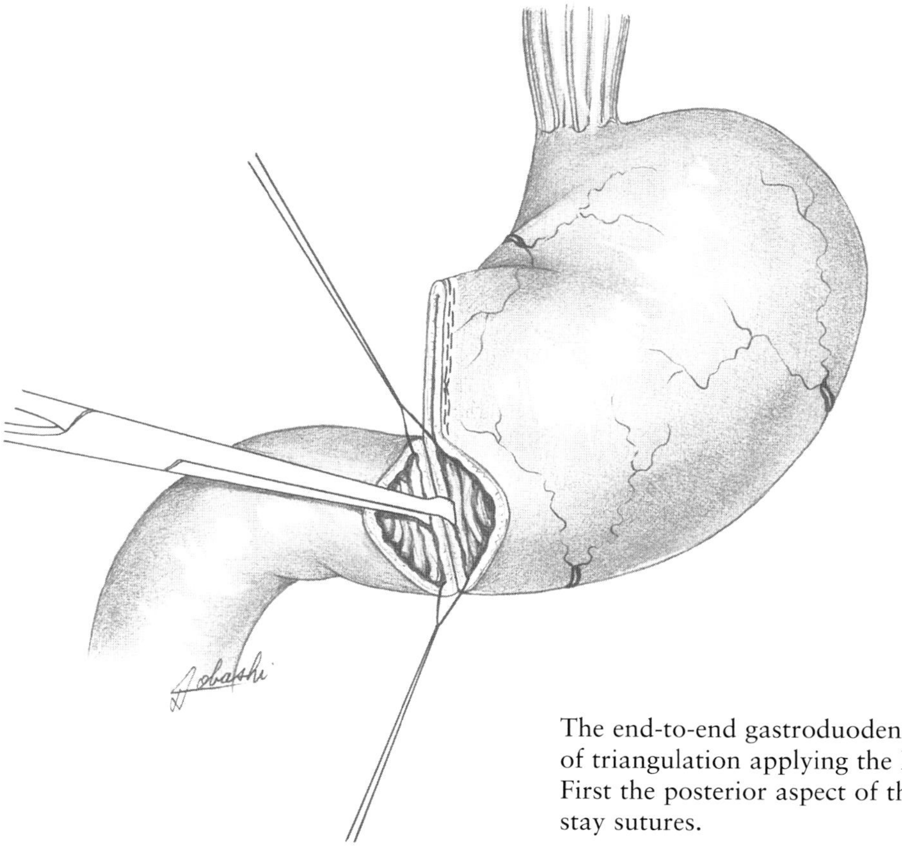

The end-to-end gastroduodenostomy is created by the principle of triangulation applying the linear stapler three times. First the posterior aspect of the anastomosis is everted by using stay sutures.

A linear stapler standard is used to create the posterior aspect of the anastomosis. After firing the instrument, excess tissue should be removed.

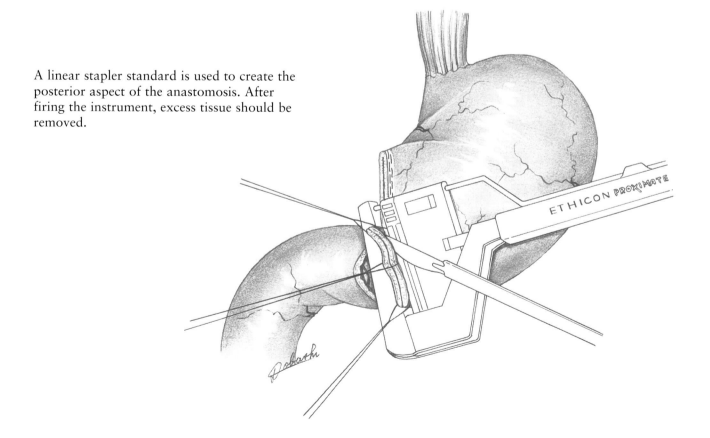

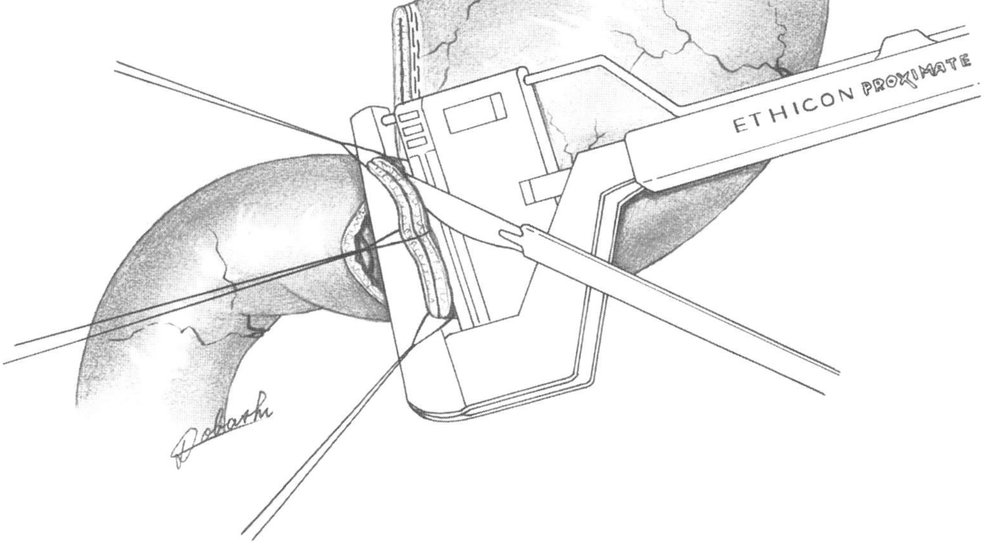

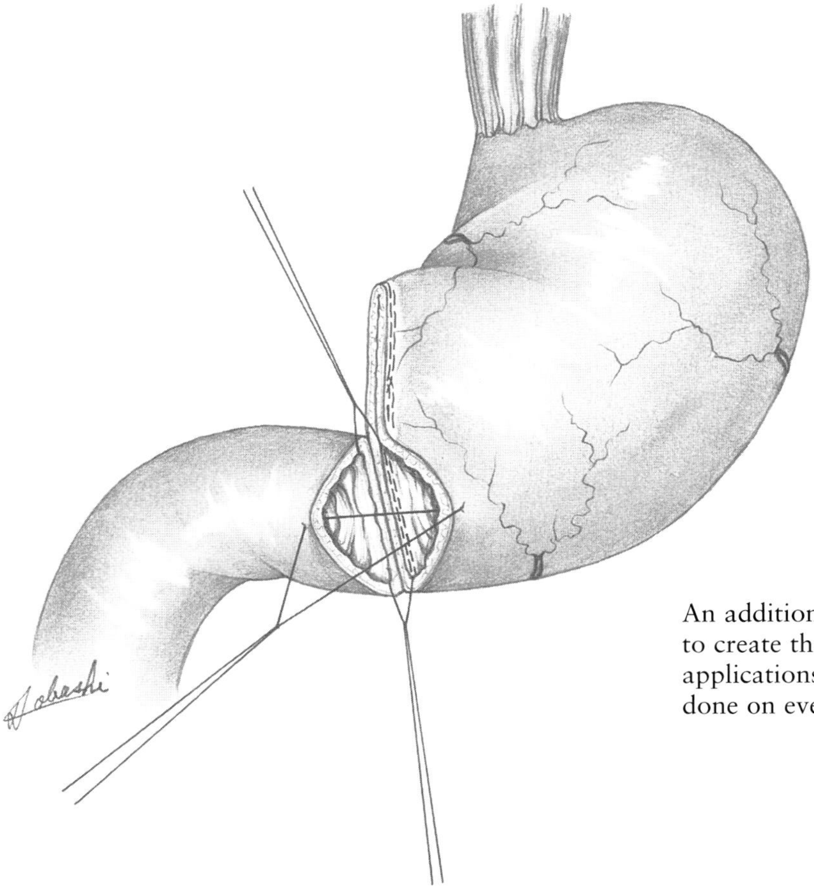

An additional stay suture is put in place in order to create the triangulation. The two remaining applications of the linear stapler standard will be done on everted tissue.

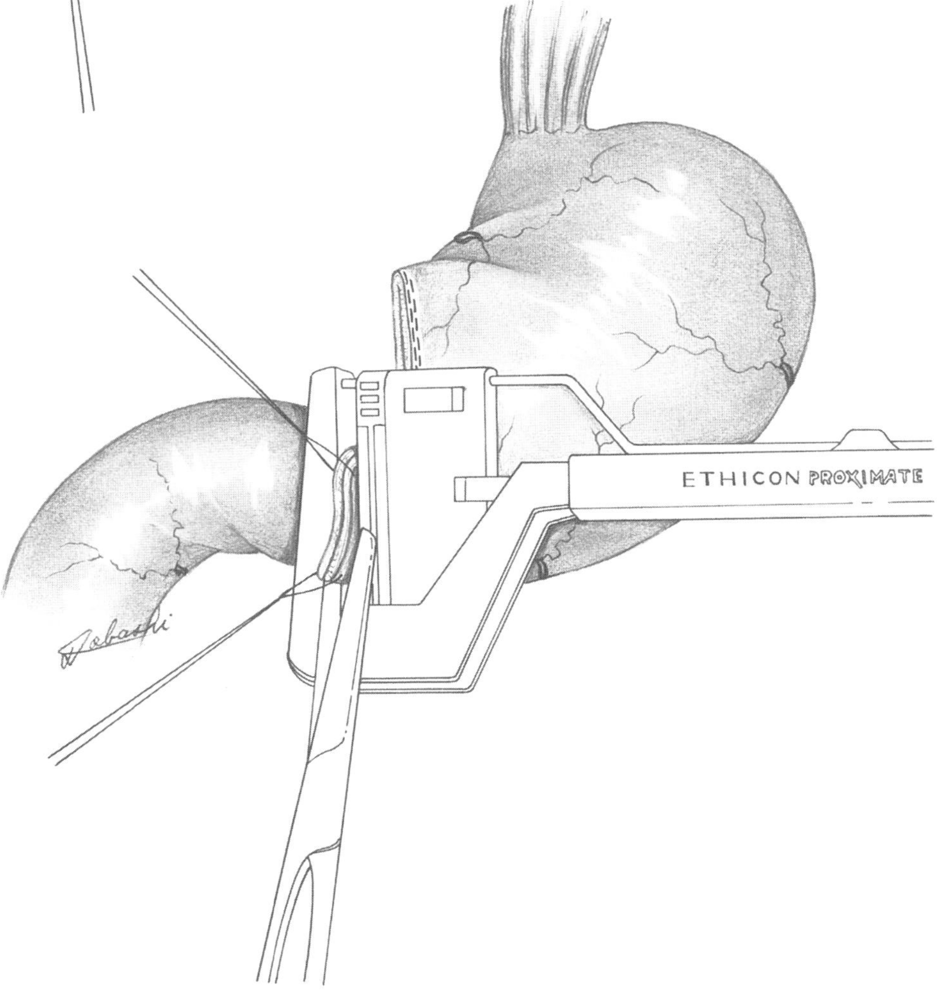

With the second application of the linear stapler standard the first half of the anterior aspect of the gastroduodenostomy is created. It is important that the stay sutures be included in the staple line so that the staple lines intersect. After the stapler has been fired, the excess tissue should be removed with Mayo scissors to facilitate transection through the staple lines.

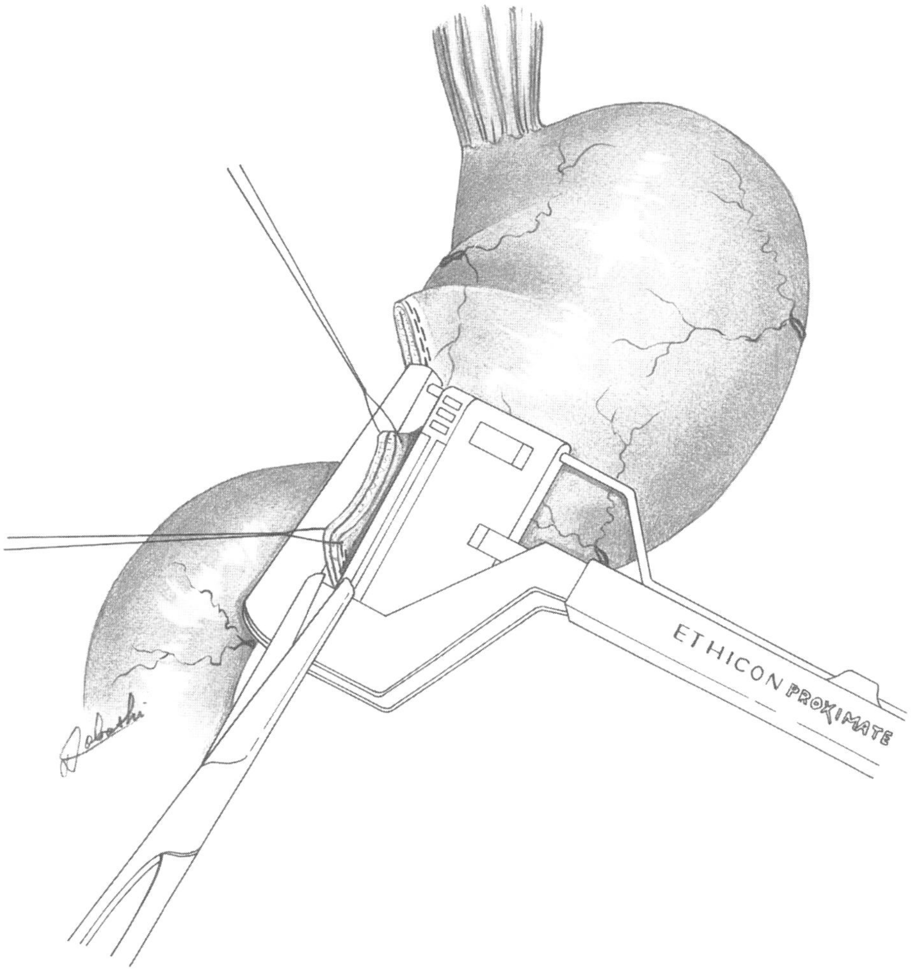

Triangulation is completed by the third application of the linear stapler standard, creating the second half of the anterior aspect of the anastomosis. In doing this, the same principles as above must be adhered to.

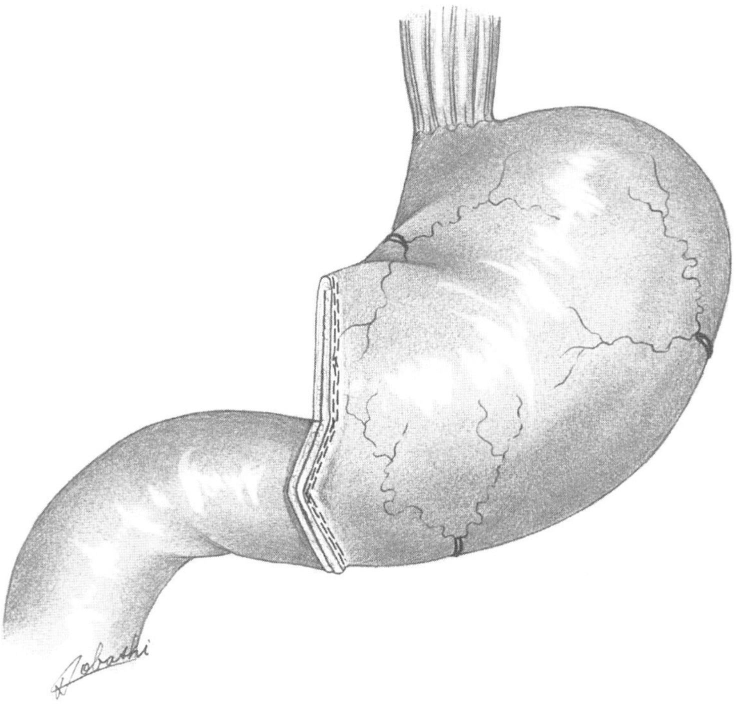

End result.

Billroth II

Subtotal Gastrectomy with a Side-to-side Gastrojejunostomy (with Circular Stapler)

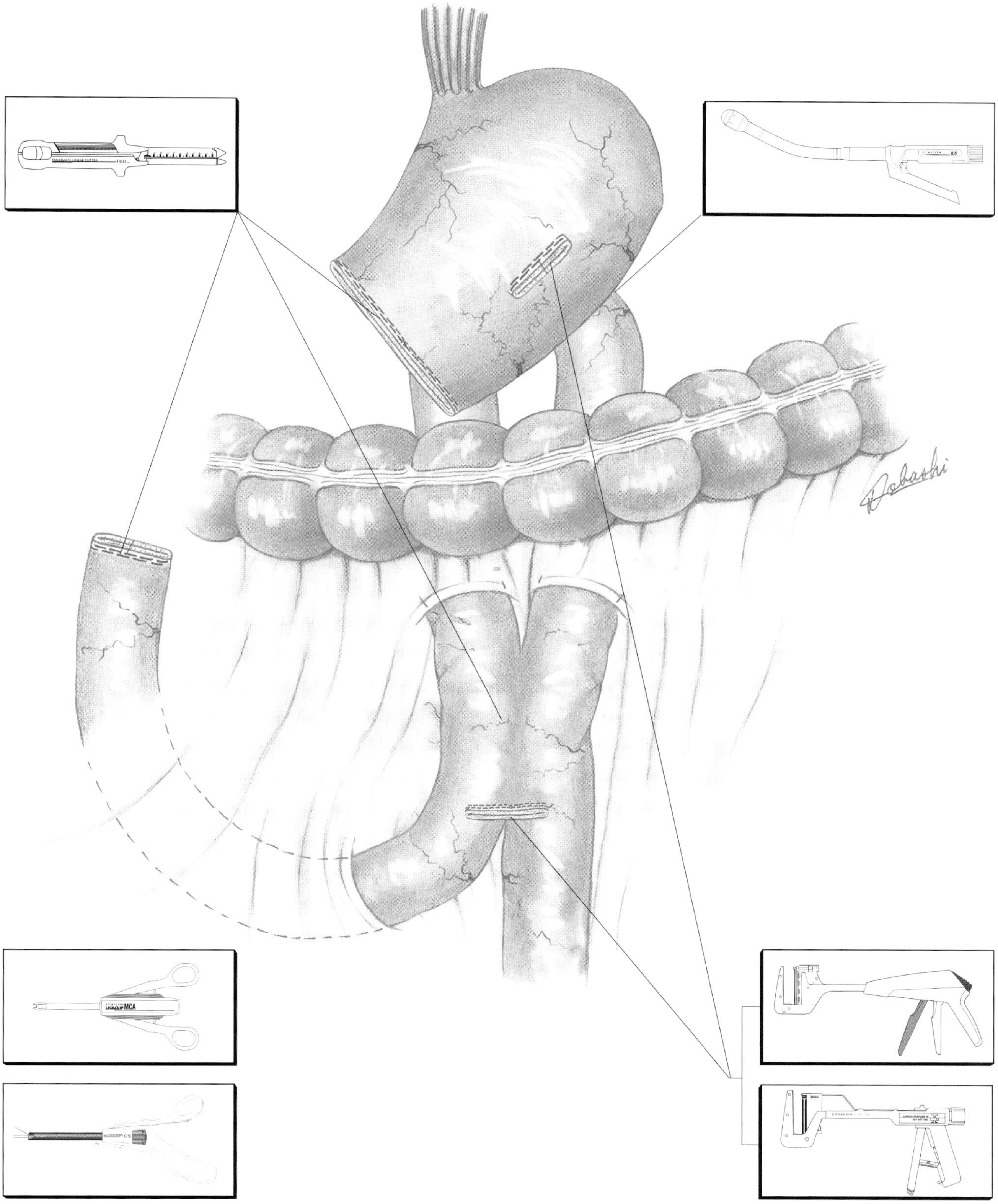

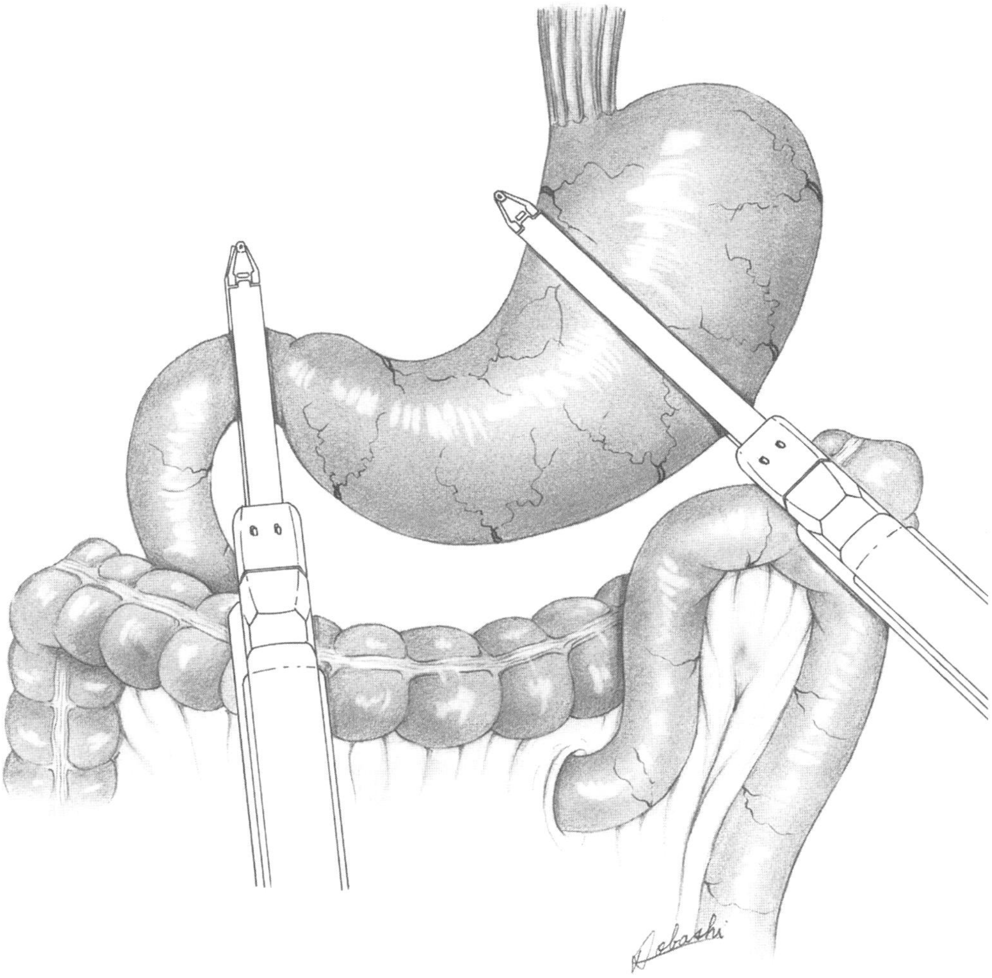

The procedure commences with the mobilisation of the stomach using a multiple clip applier or the Ultracision coagulating shears. A subtotal gastrectomy is performed by using the linear cutter thick twice. After firing, the staple lines should be examined for haemostasis and proper staple closure.

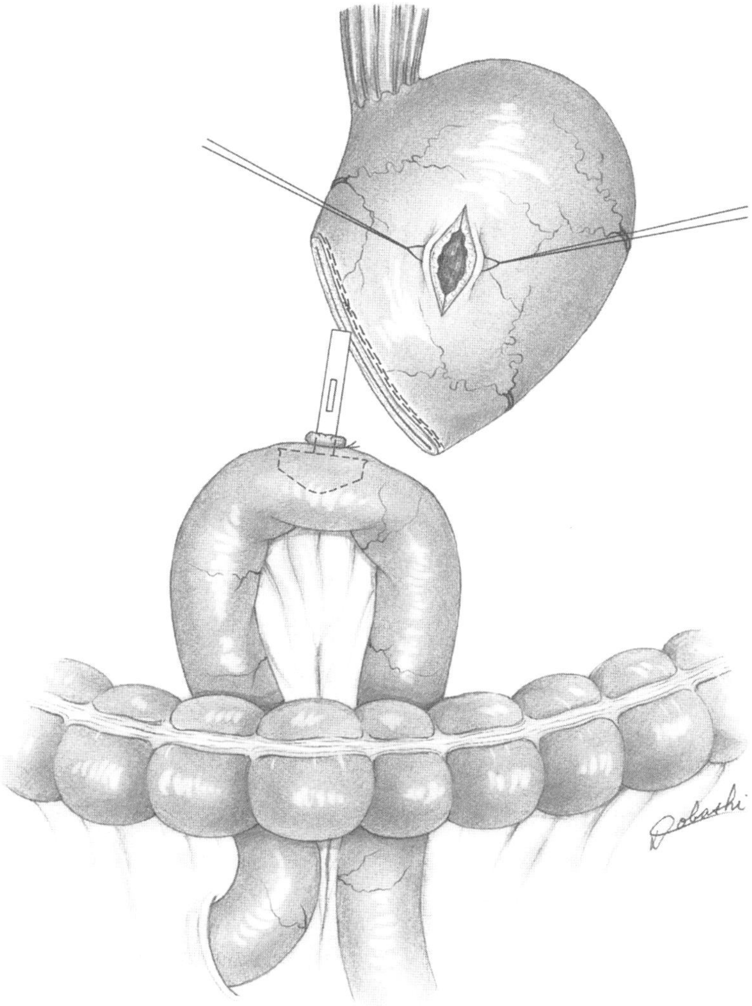

Retrocolic pulling-up of jejunal loop. The jejunal loop is incised antimesenterically in the field of the defined anastomotic area with the Ultracision sharp hook. Then a purse-string suture is put in place.
The size of the circular stapler to be used can be determined by means of sizers. After the instrument anvil of the circular stapler has been tied into the jejunum, the anterior gastric wall is incised at least 3 cm above the staple line at the remaining stomach by using the Ultracision sharp hook.

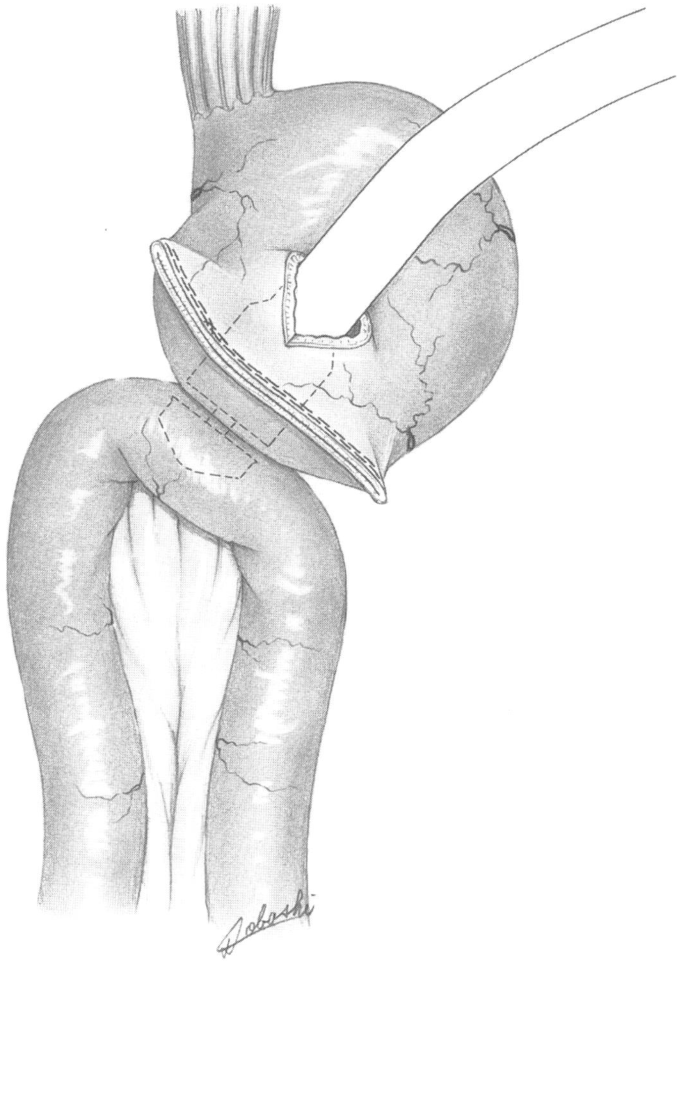

The circular stapler is inserted into the remaining stomach and the posterior wall is pierced with the trocar at the defined anastomotic area at least 3 cm above the staple line. The instrument head and shaft are connected and the side-to-side gastrojejunostomy is created. Then the staple line is examined for haemostasis and proper staple closure. After withdrawal of the circular stapler, the 'doughnuts' have to be carefully removed and examined for integrity.

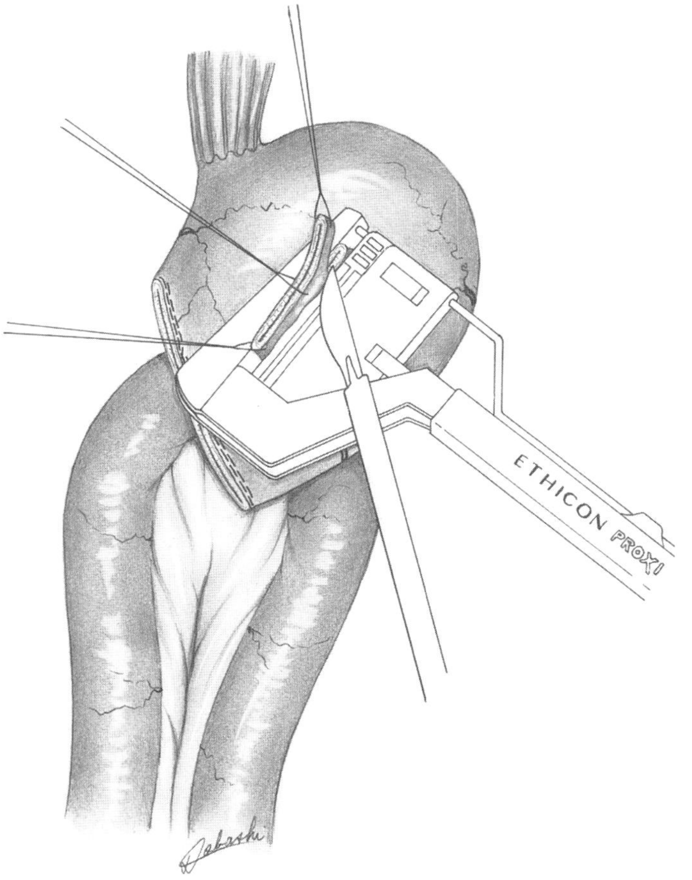

The gastrotomy is closed with a linear stapler standard and any overlapping tissue is resected.

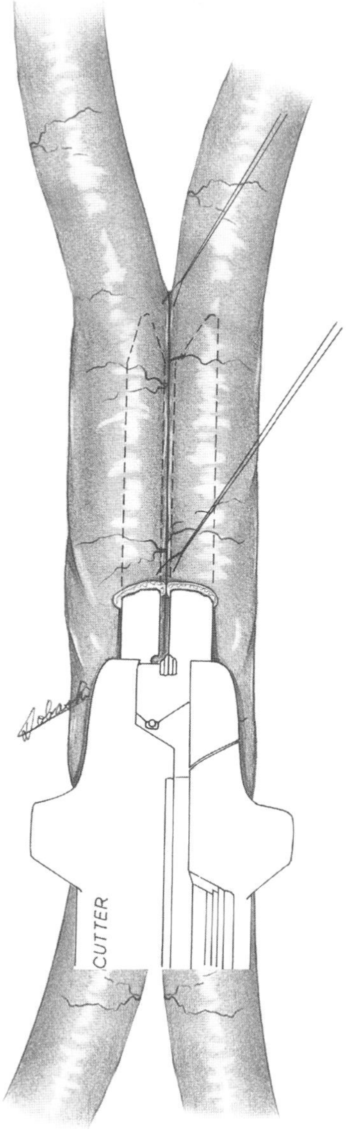

The jejuno-jejunostomy (Braun anastomosis) is carried out by creating enterotomies in the antimesenteric sides of the loops of the jejunum to be anastomosed. The jaws of a linear cutter standard are introduced into the enterotomies, the instrument is closed and fired, and the anastomosis is created.

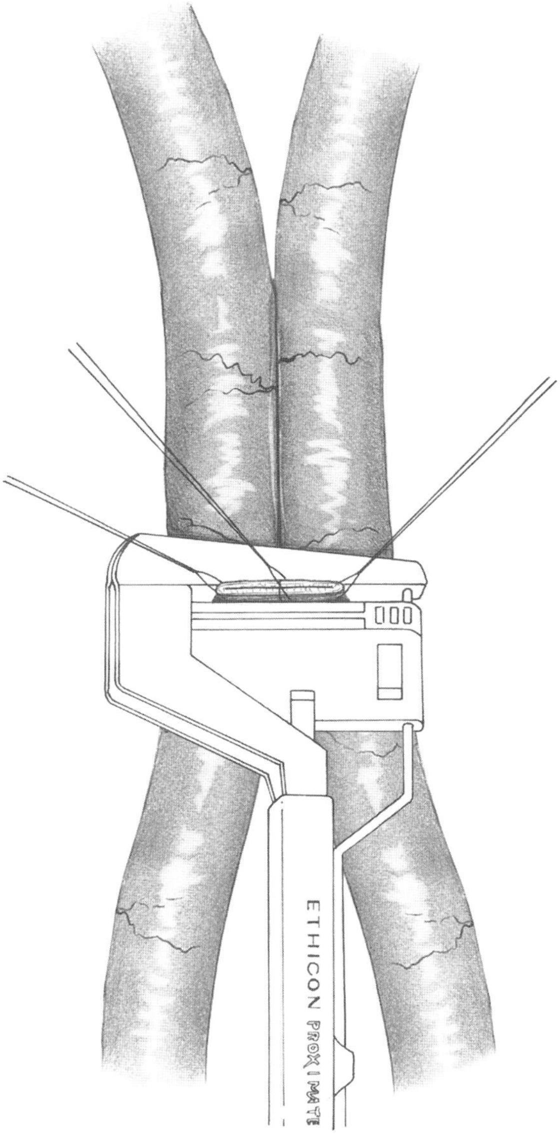

Closure of the enterotomies using a linear stapler standard or hand suture.

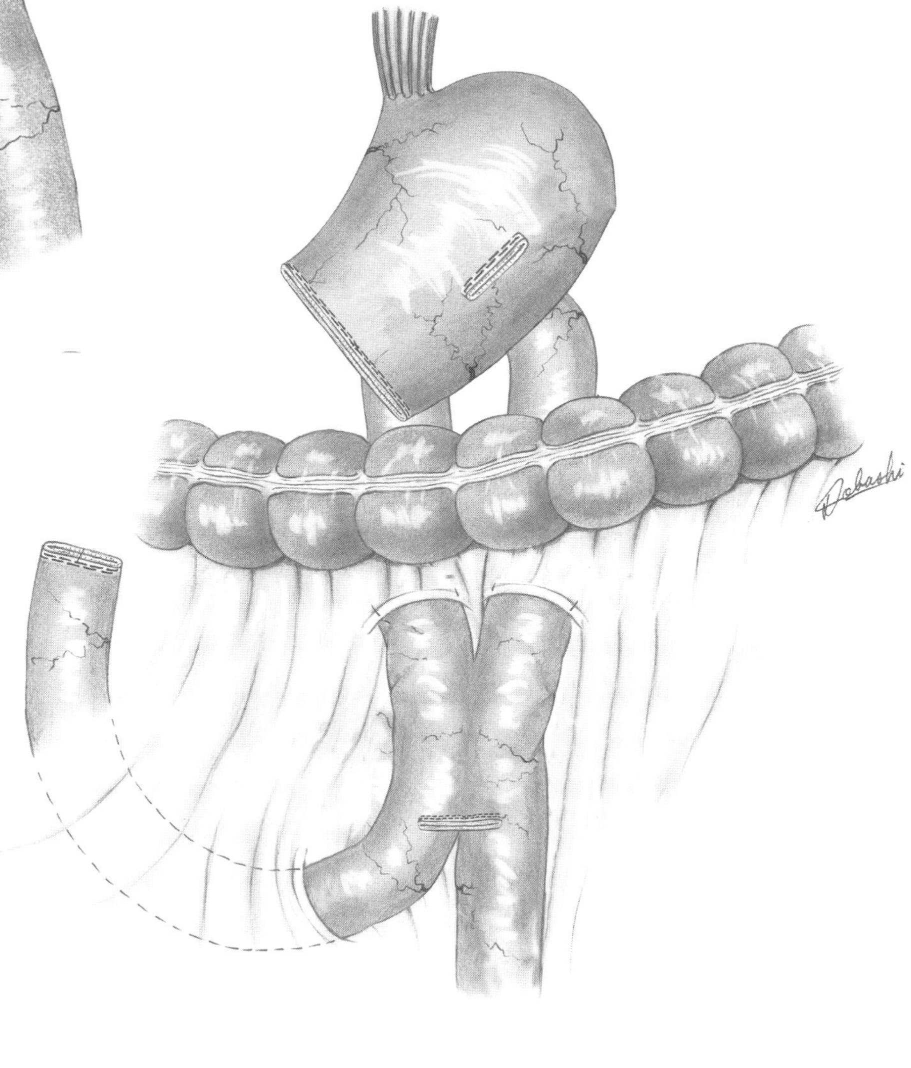

End result.

Billroth II

Subtotal Gastrectomy with a Side-to-side Gastrojejunostomy (with Linear Cutter)

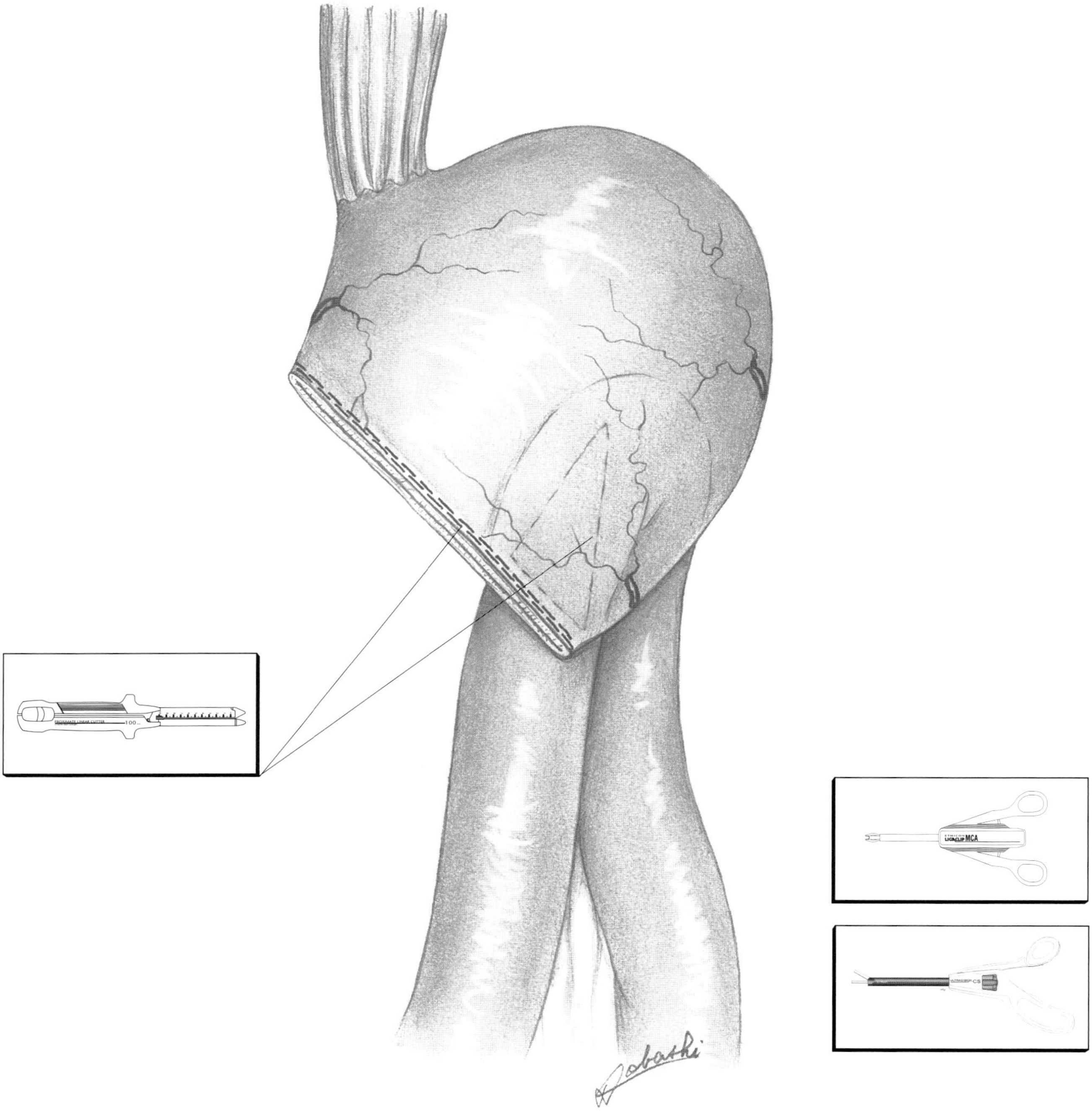

Alternative technique where the gastrojejunostomy is performed with a linear cutter.

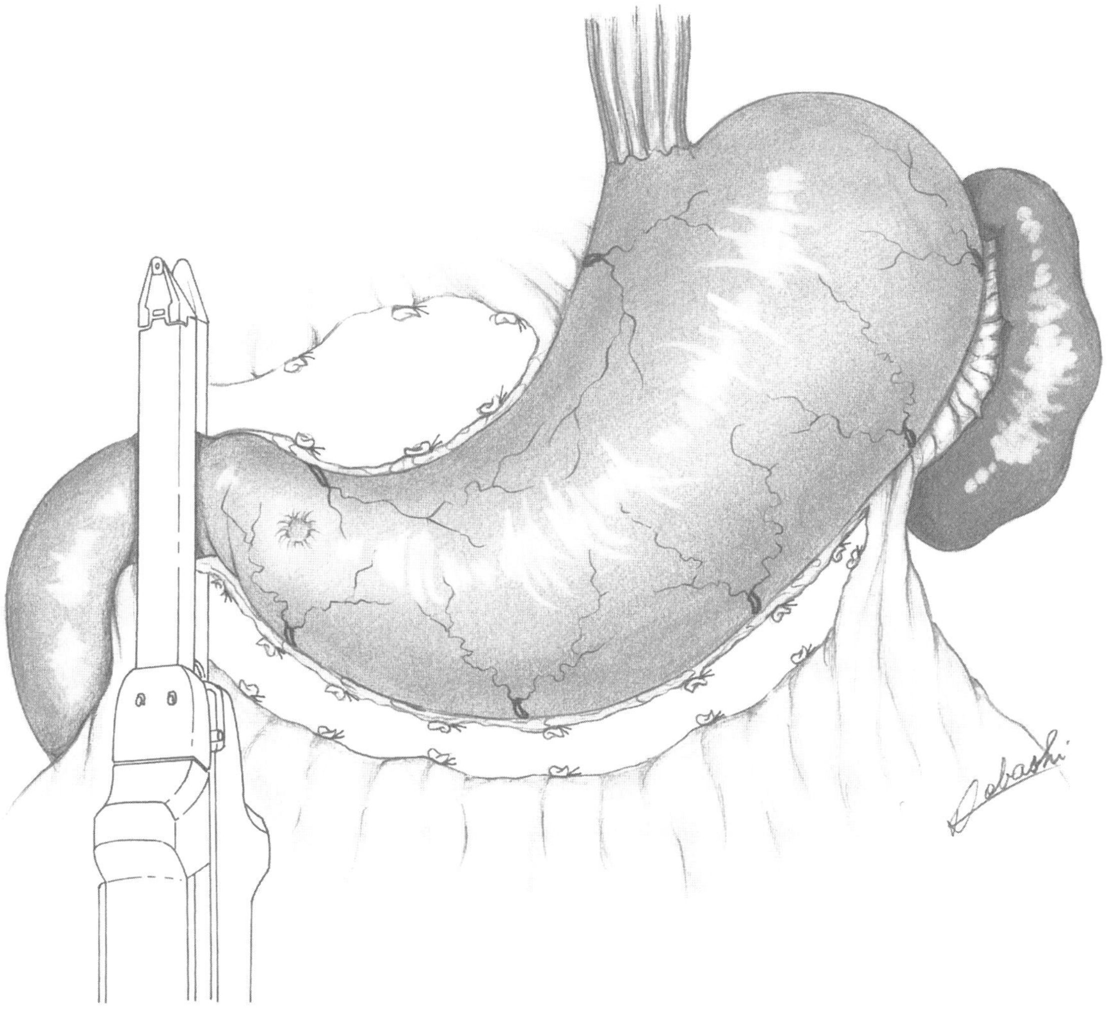

Mobilisation of the stomach with a multiple clip applier or Ultracision coagulating shears. The duodenum is transected with a linear cutter standard, then the staple line is examined for haemostasis and proper staple closure.

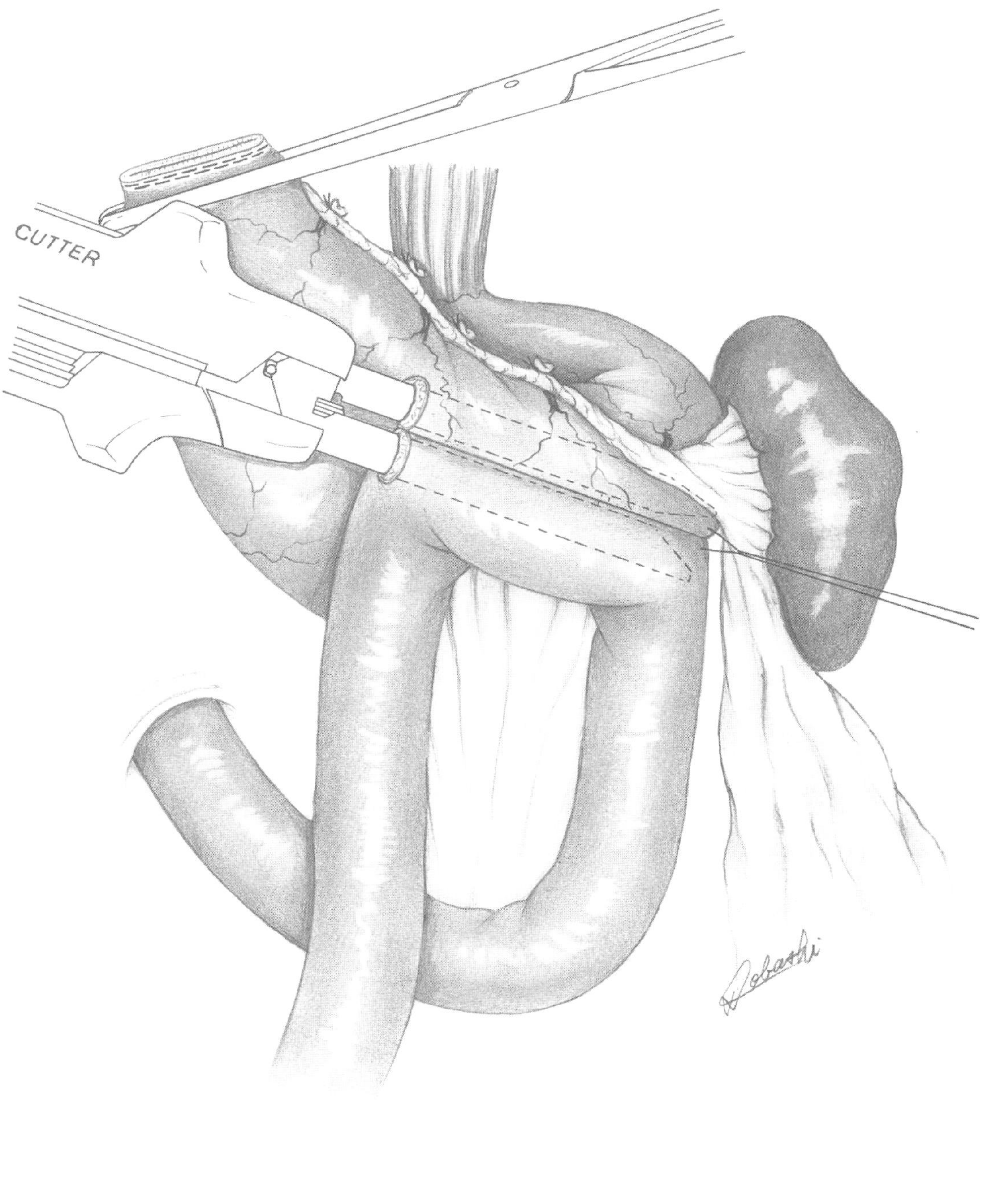

Pulling-up of a jejunal loop. An incision is made with the Ultracision sharp hook in the antimesenteric area of the jejunum and the posterior gastric wall approx. 3 cm from the greater curvature. A side-to-side gastrojejunostomy is then created by using the linear cutter standard. The staple line is examined for haemostasis and proper staple closure. N.B.: the gastrojejunostomy must be parallel to the greater curvature at a distance of approx. 3 cm.

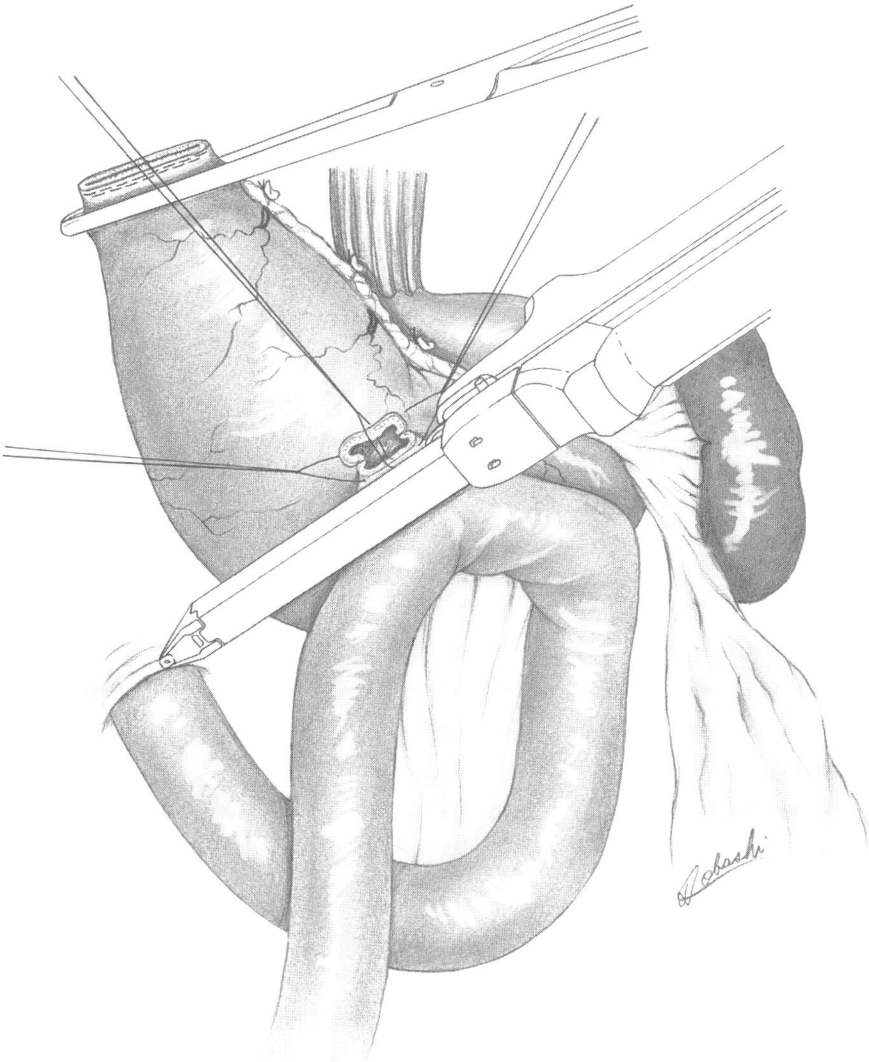

Resection of the stomach and simultaneous closure of the incision with a linear cutter thick. The staple line is then examined for haemostasis and proper closure.

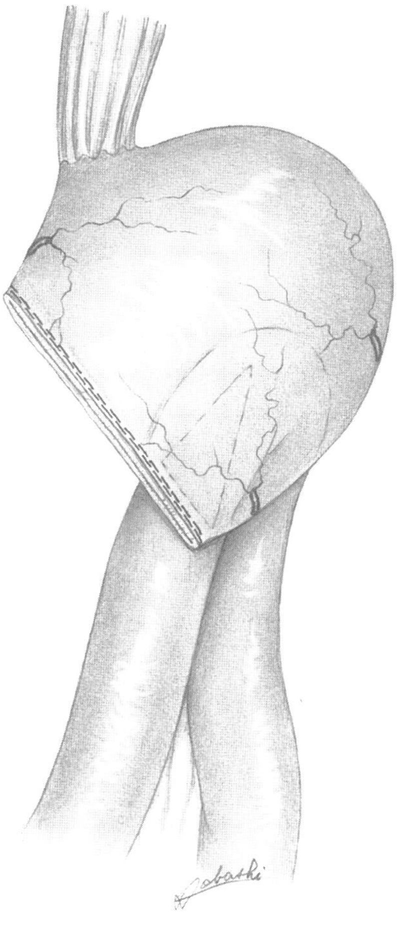

To finish the procedure, a jejunojejunostomy has to be performed following the Braun technique described above.

Billroth II

Subtotal Gastrectomy with a Side-to-side Gastrojejunostomy (with Linear Cutter)

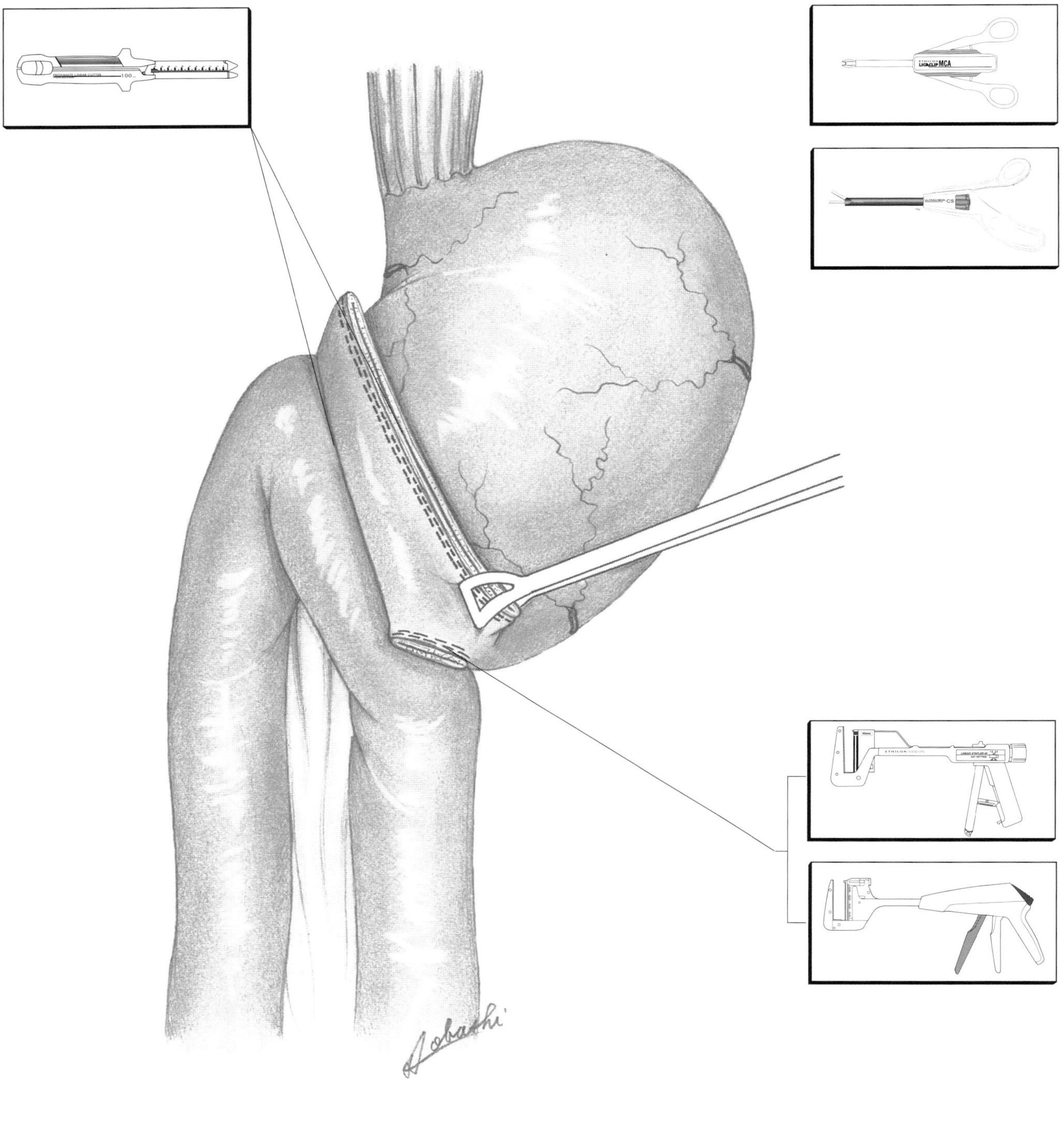

Alternative technique.

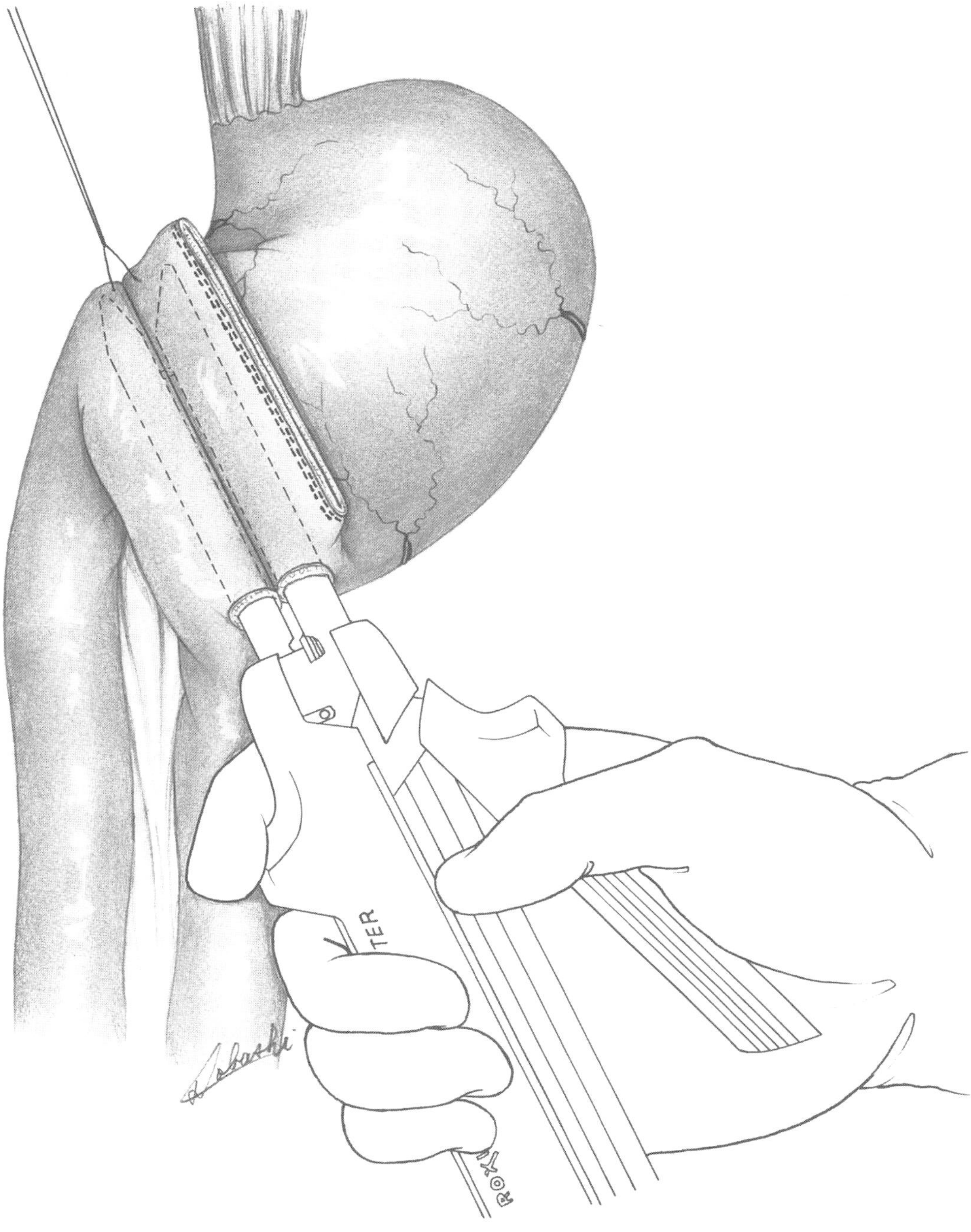

Pulling-up of a second jejunal loop. An incision is made with the Ultracision sharp hook in the antimesenteric area of the jejunum and the posterior gastric wall in the area of the greater curvature approx. 3 cm from the staple line at the gastric stump, in order to introduce the jaws of the linear cutter. A side-to-side gastrojejunostomy is then created parallel to the resection line at the stomach. The staple lines are examined for haemostasis and proper closure.
N.B.: the gastrojejunostomy must be parallel to the resection line at a distance of approx. 3 cm.

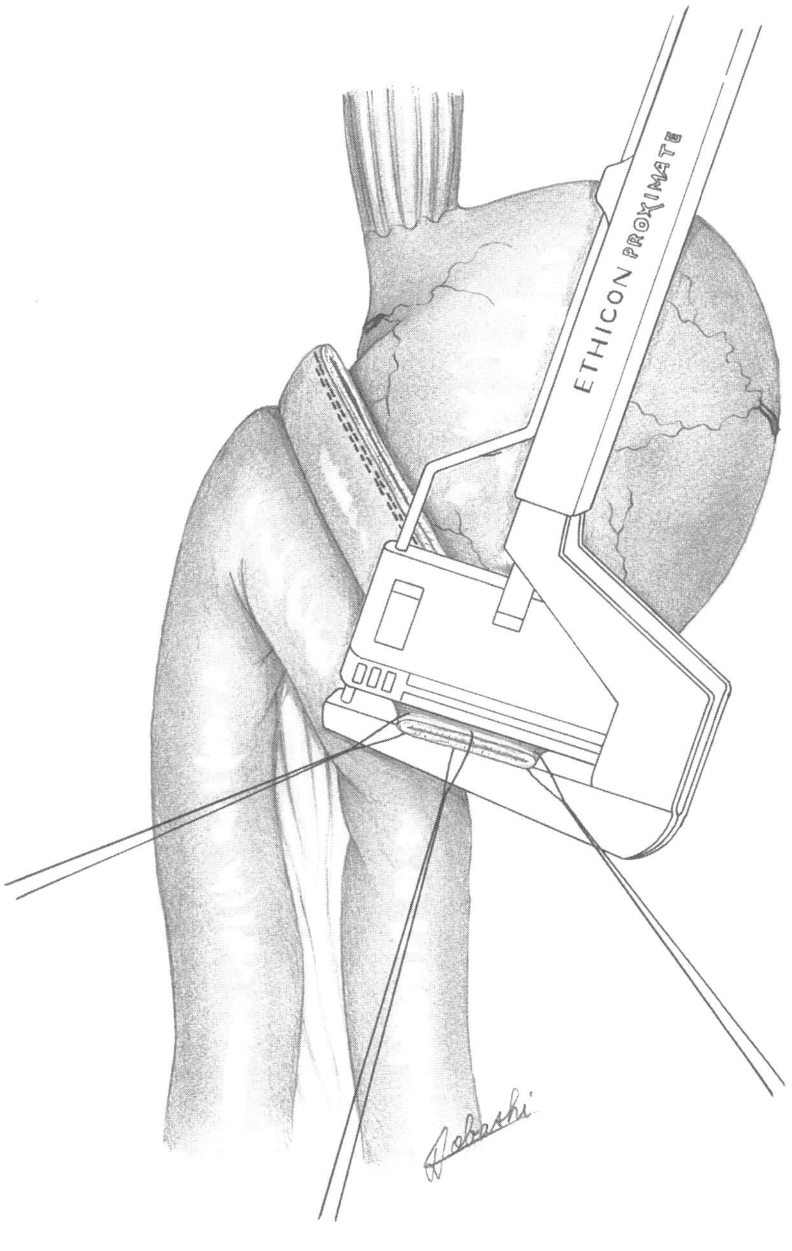

Closure of the incision with the linear stapler standard.

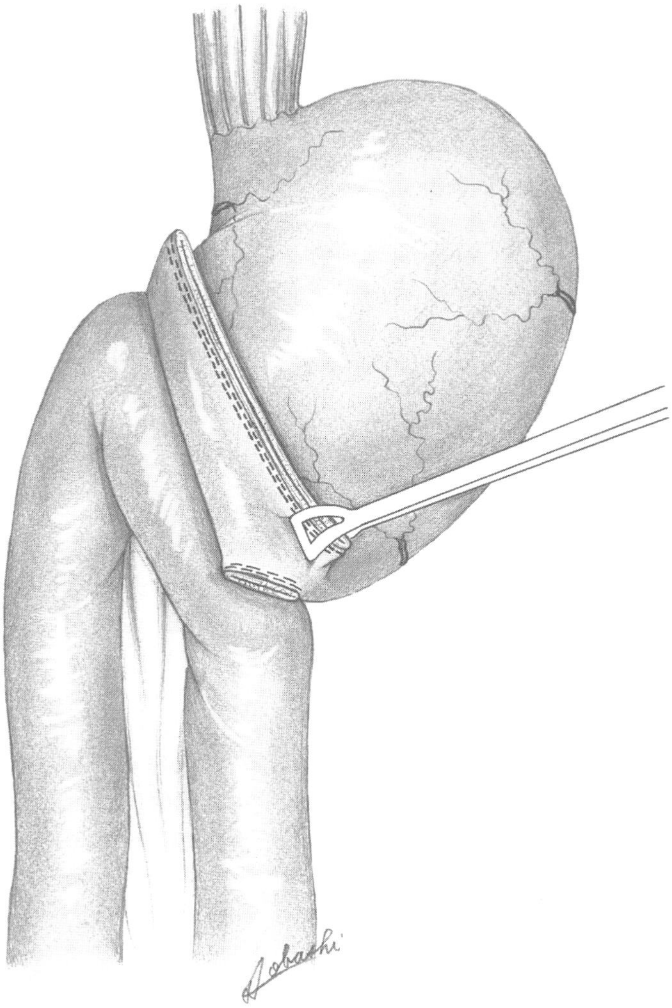

To finish the procedure, a jejunojejunostomy is performed following the Braun technique described above.

Total Gastrectomy

End-to-side Jejunal Interposition (Longmire-Gütgemann)

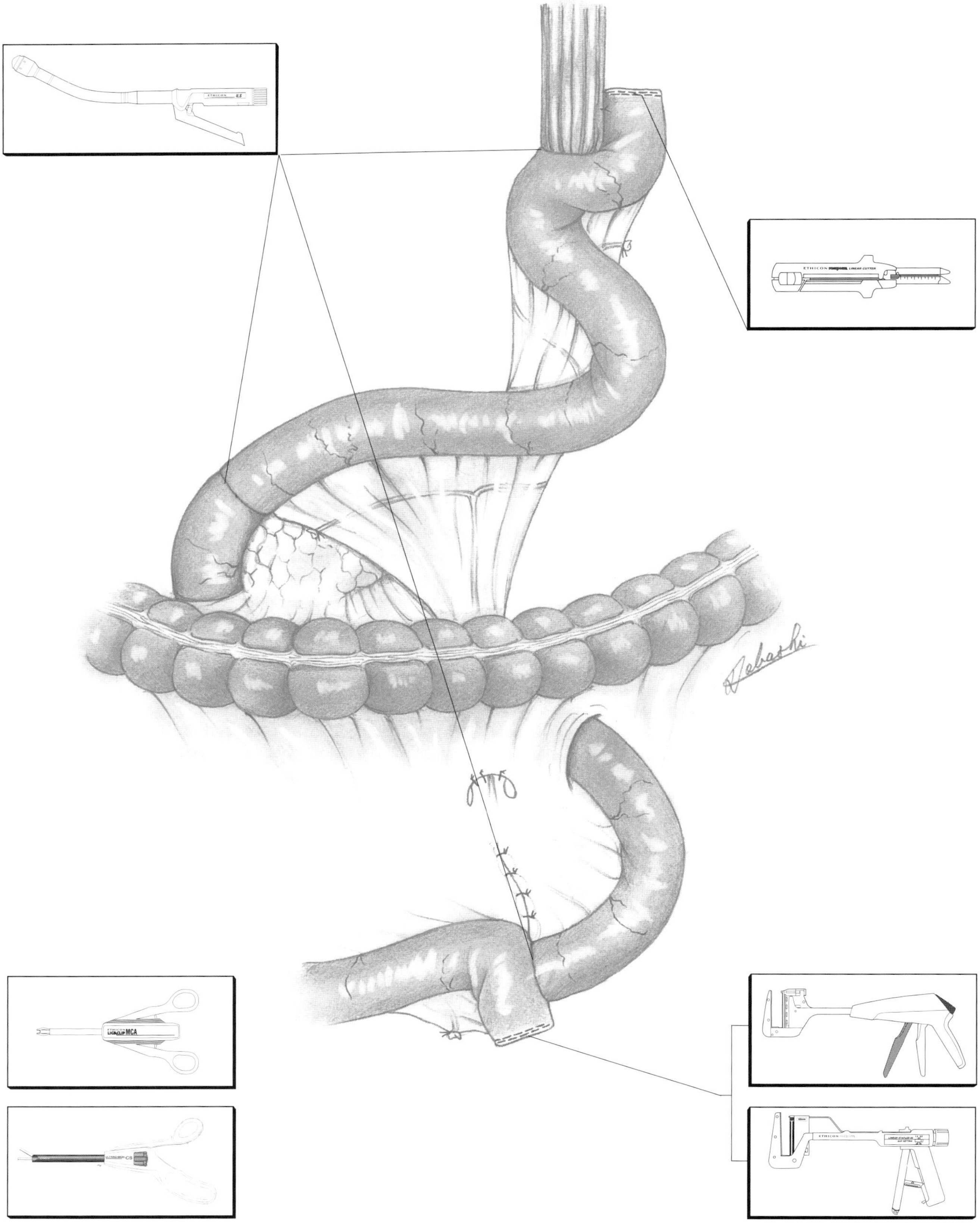

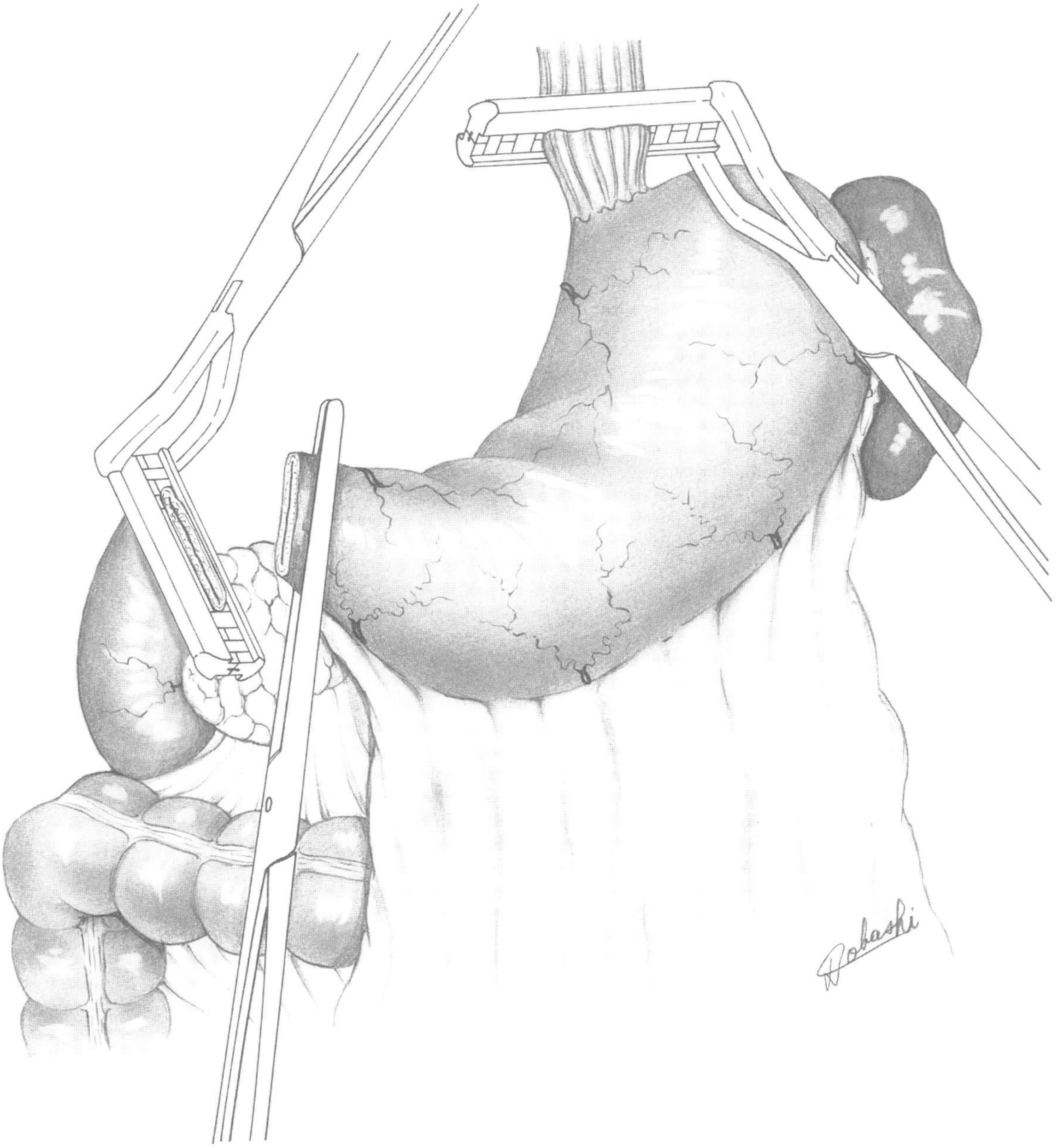

The procedure commences with the mobilisation of the stomach with a multiple clip applier or the Ultracision coagulating shears. A purse-string suture is placed postpylorically with a purse-string suture clamp, transecting the stomach along the cutting guide of the purse-string suture clamp. Another purse-string suture clamp is placed at the distal oesophagus. The stomach can then be completely resected by cutting along the guide of the purse-string suture clamp.

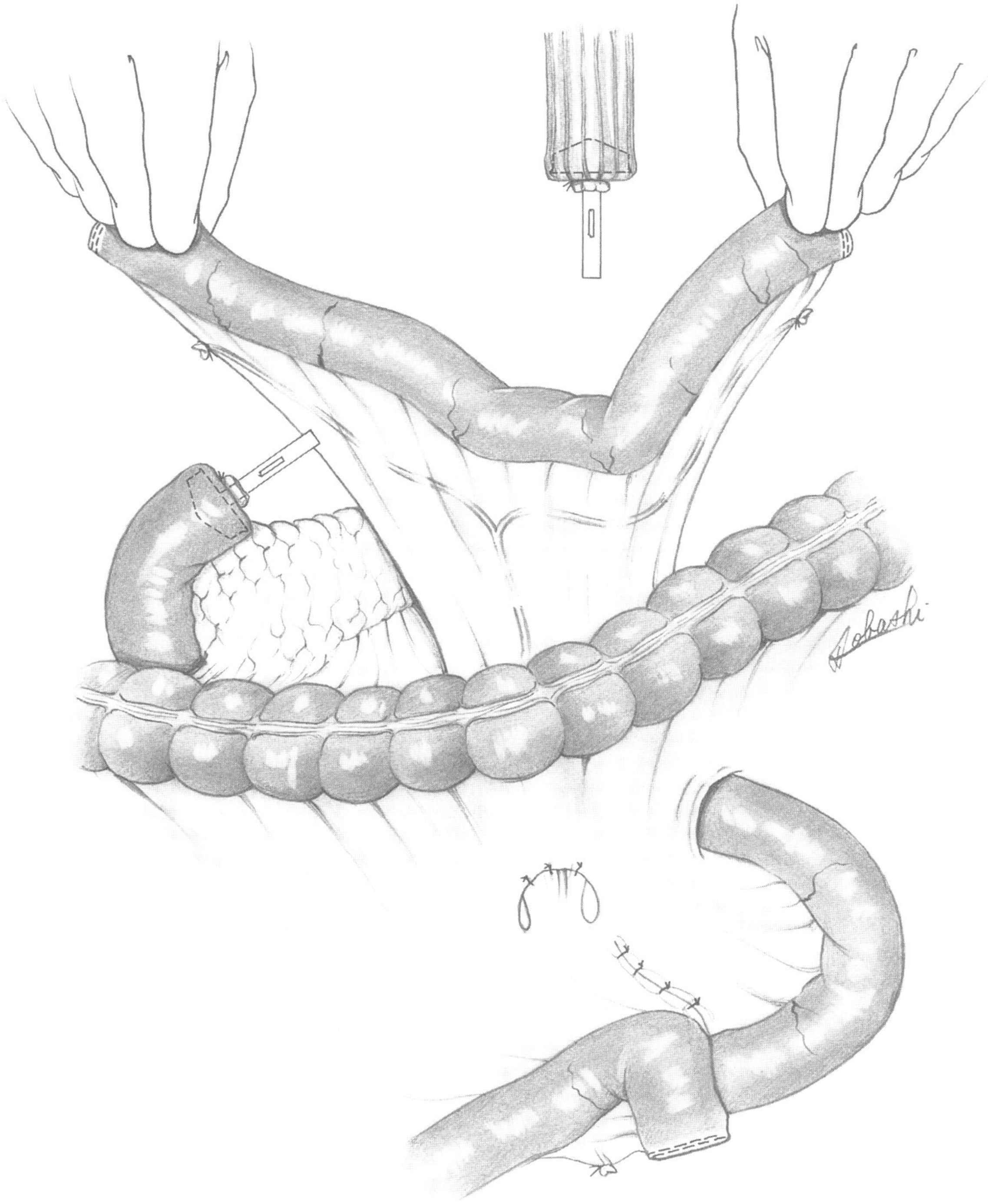

The size of the circular stapler to be used will be determined by means of sizers; the instrument head of the circular stapler can then be inserted into the oesophagus and the duodenum. By using a linear cutter standard twice, a jejunum segment of approximately 40 to 50 cm is transected to replace the stomach. The continuity of the jejunum is re-established by creating an end-to-side jejunojejunostomy with the circular stapler and the linear stapler standard. The staple lines are then examined for haemostasis and proper closure. After withdrawal of the circular stapler, the 'doughnuts' must be carefully removed from the instrument head and examined for integrity.

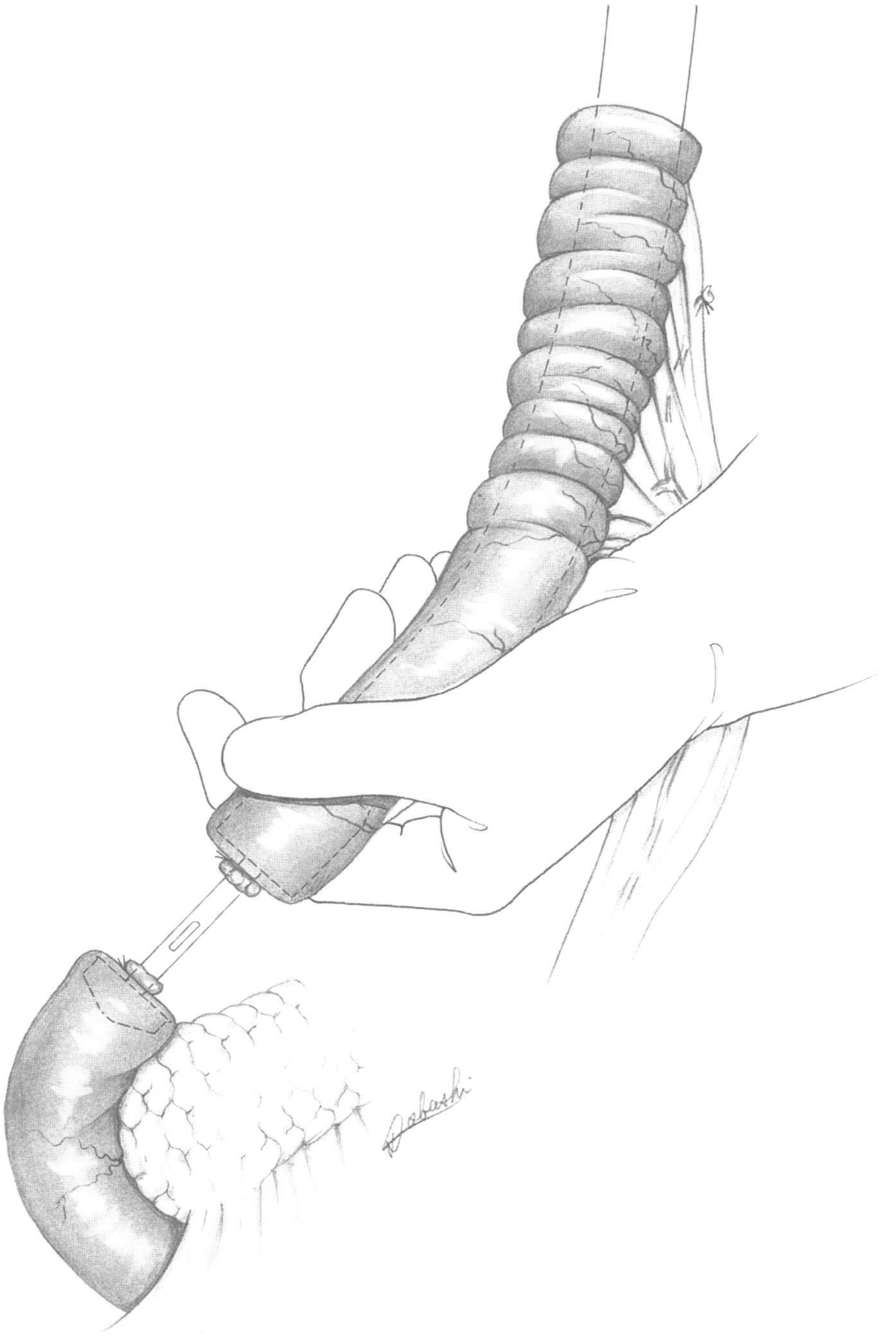

A purse-string suture clamp is placed at the distal end of the interposition to create a purse-string while resecting the staple line. After resecting the proximal staple line, the shaft of the circular stapler is threaded through the interposition and the purse-string is tied around the stapler trocar. This step must be done with extreme care, as otherwise the stapler may damage the bowel, resulting in later fistula development. The instrument shaft and anvil head are assembled and the stapler is closed and fired to create the end-to-end jejunoduodenostomy. After withdrawal of the instrument, the ‘doughnuts’ must be carefully removed to examine their integrity.

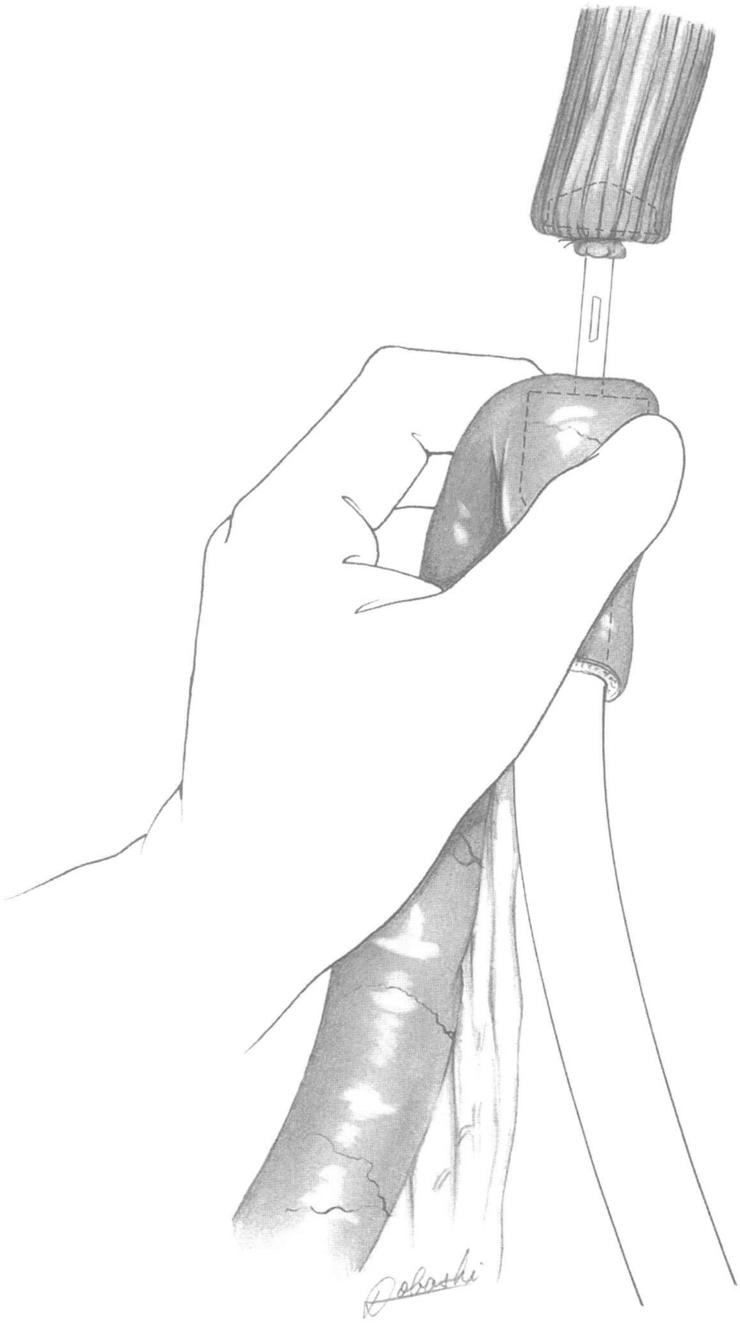

A circular stapler is inserted into the proximal end of the interposition. The bowel wall is pierced by the instrument trocar at the antimesenteric side of the interposition at a distance of approx. 5 cm from the opening. The instrument shaft and anvil head are assembled and the stapler is closed and fired to create the end-to-side oesophagojejunostomy. After withdrawal of the instrument, the 'doughnuts' must be carefully removed to examine their integrity.

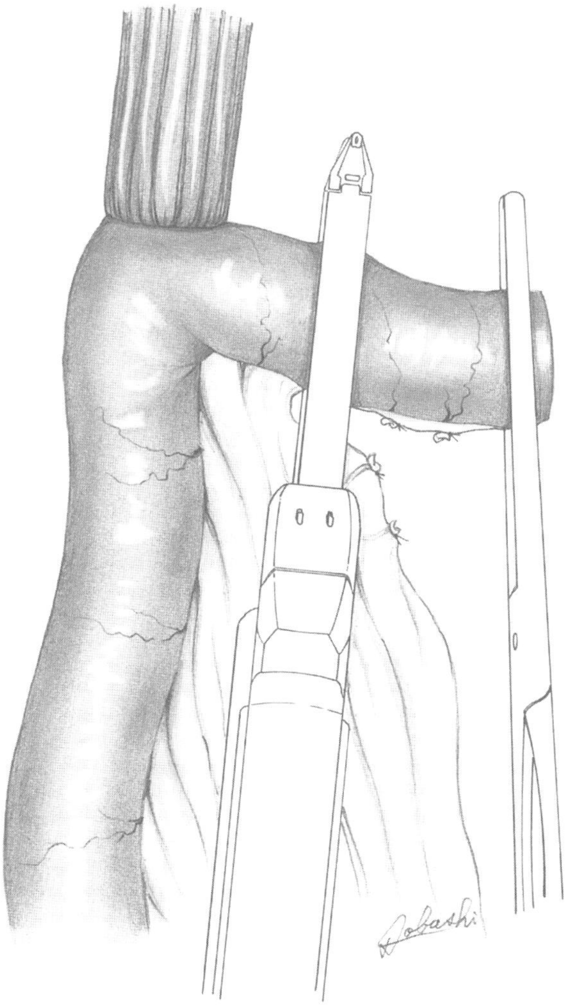

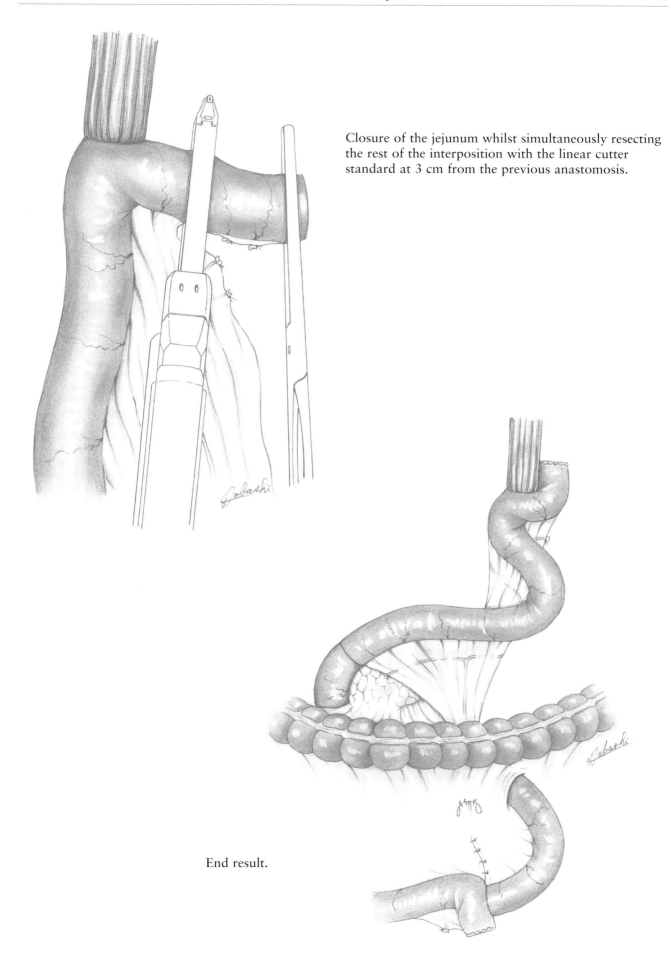

Closure of the jejunum whilst simultaneously resecting the rest of the interposition with the linear cutter standard at 3 cm from the previous anastomosis.

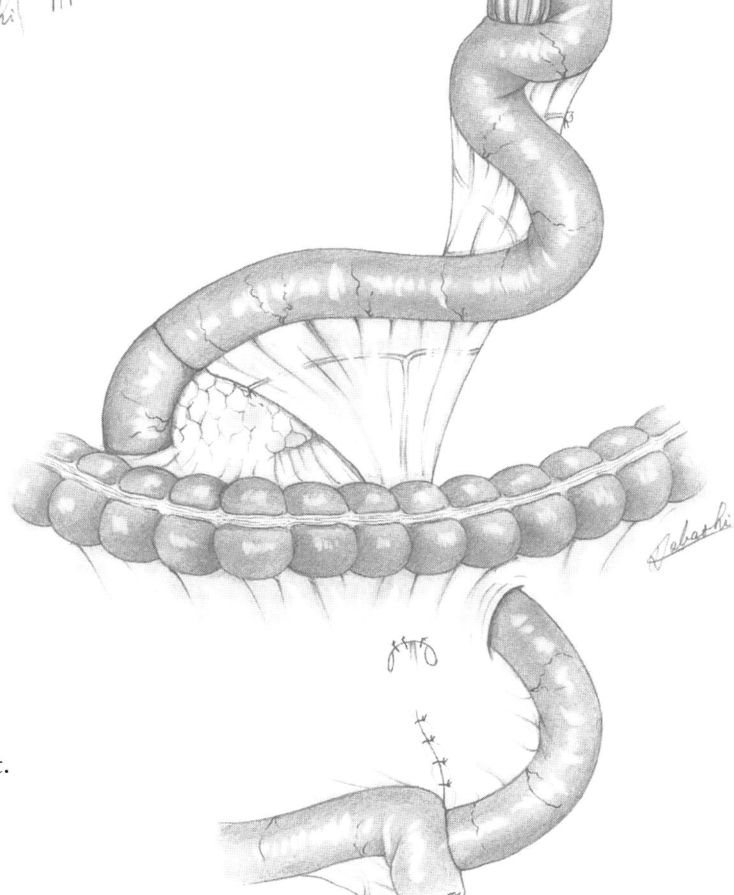

End result.

Total Gastrectomy

End-to-end Jejunal Interposition (Alternative Technique)

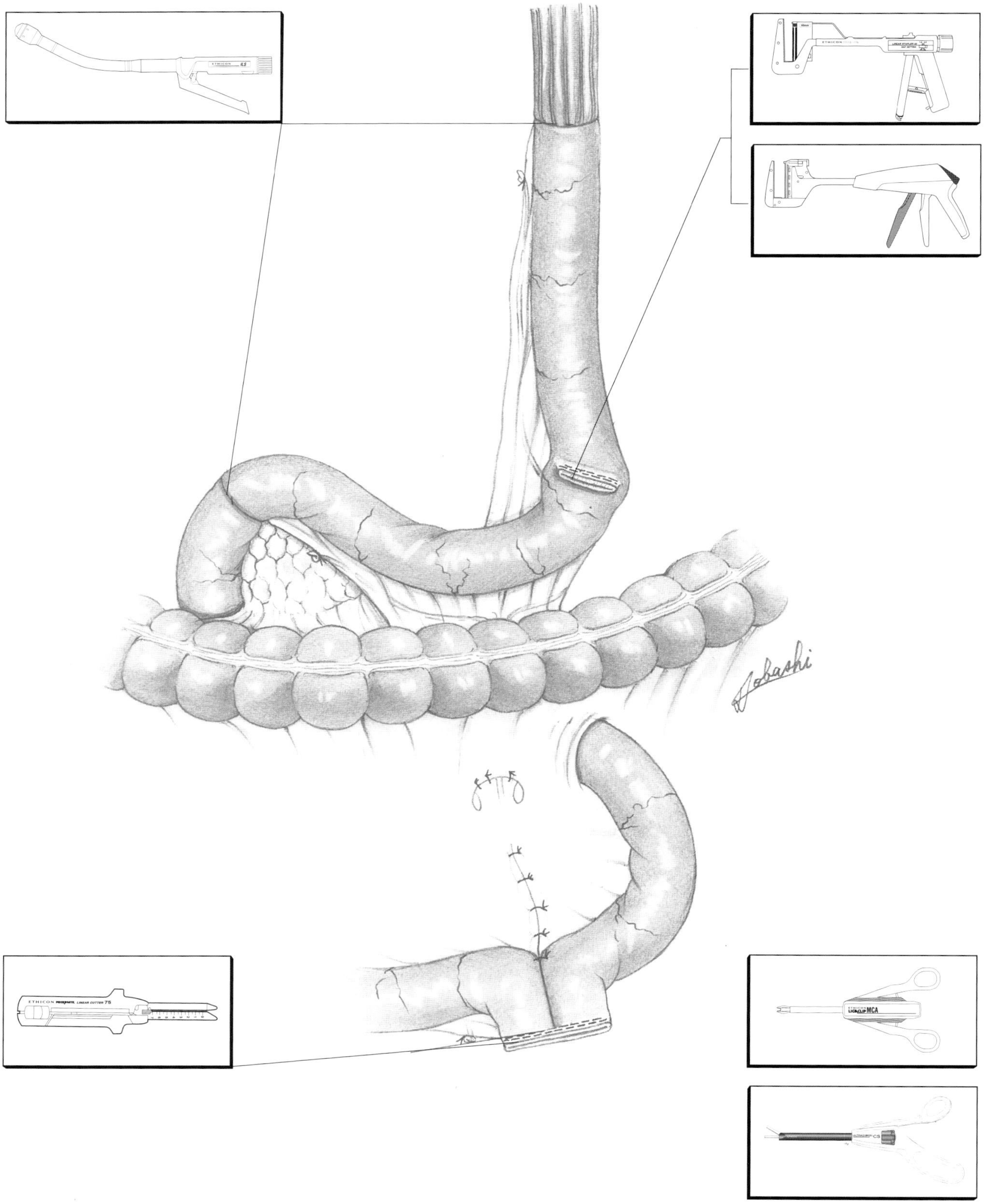

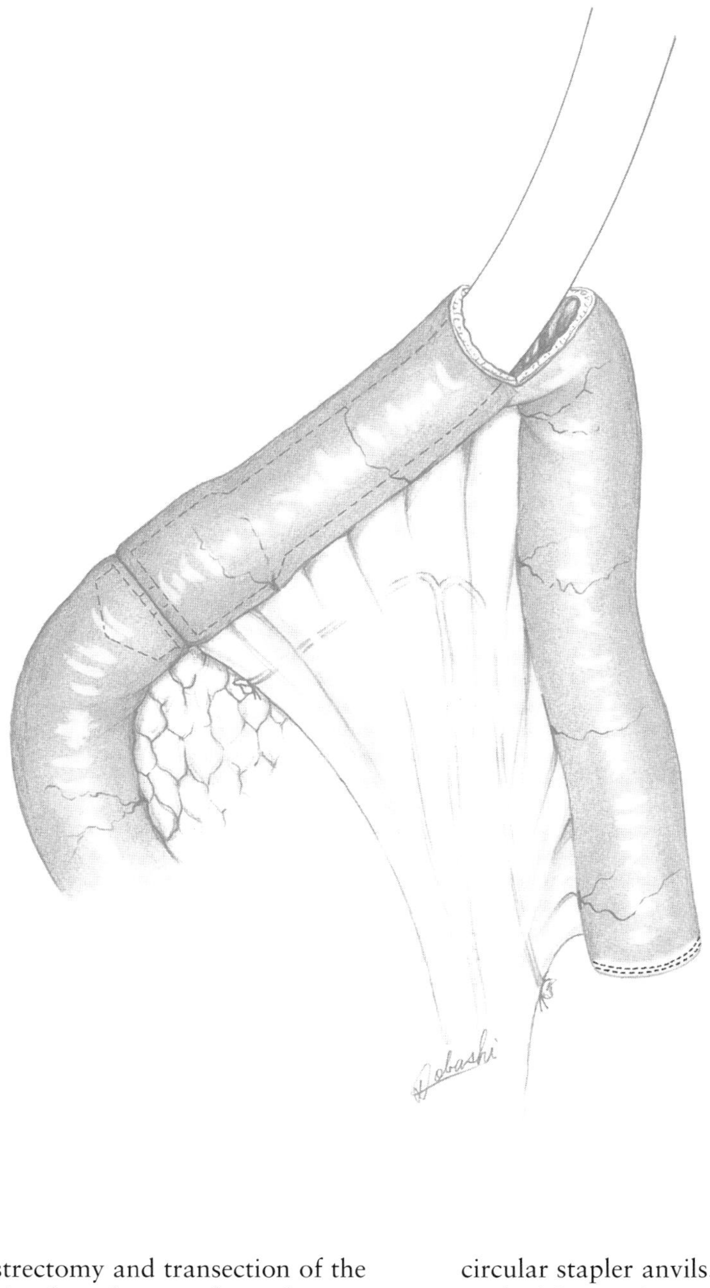

After the total gastrectomy and transection of the jejunum interposition have been performed as described before, the continuity of the jejunum is re-established by a functional side-to-side anastomosis using a linear cutter standard. Three purse-string sutures are created with the aid of a purse-string suture clamp at the duodenum, the oesophagus, and the distal end of the jejunal interposition, whilst excising the staple lines. The purse-string sutures of the oesophagus and duodenum are tied around circular stapler anvils. An enterotomy perpendicular to the jejunum interposition is created with a scalpel or Ultracision sharp hook. The shaft of a circular stapler is introduced into the enterotomy and the purse-string suture is tied around the instrument trocar. The staple is assembled and fired to create the end-to-end jejunoduodenostomy. After withdrawal of the instrument, the 'doughnuts' have to be carefully removed to examine their integrity.

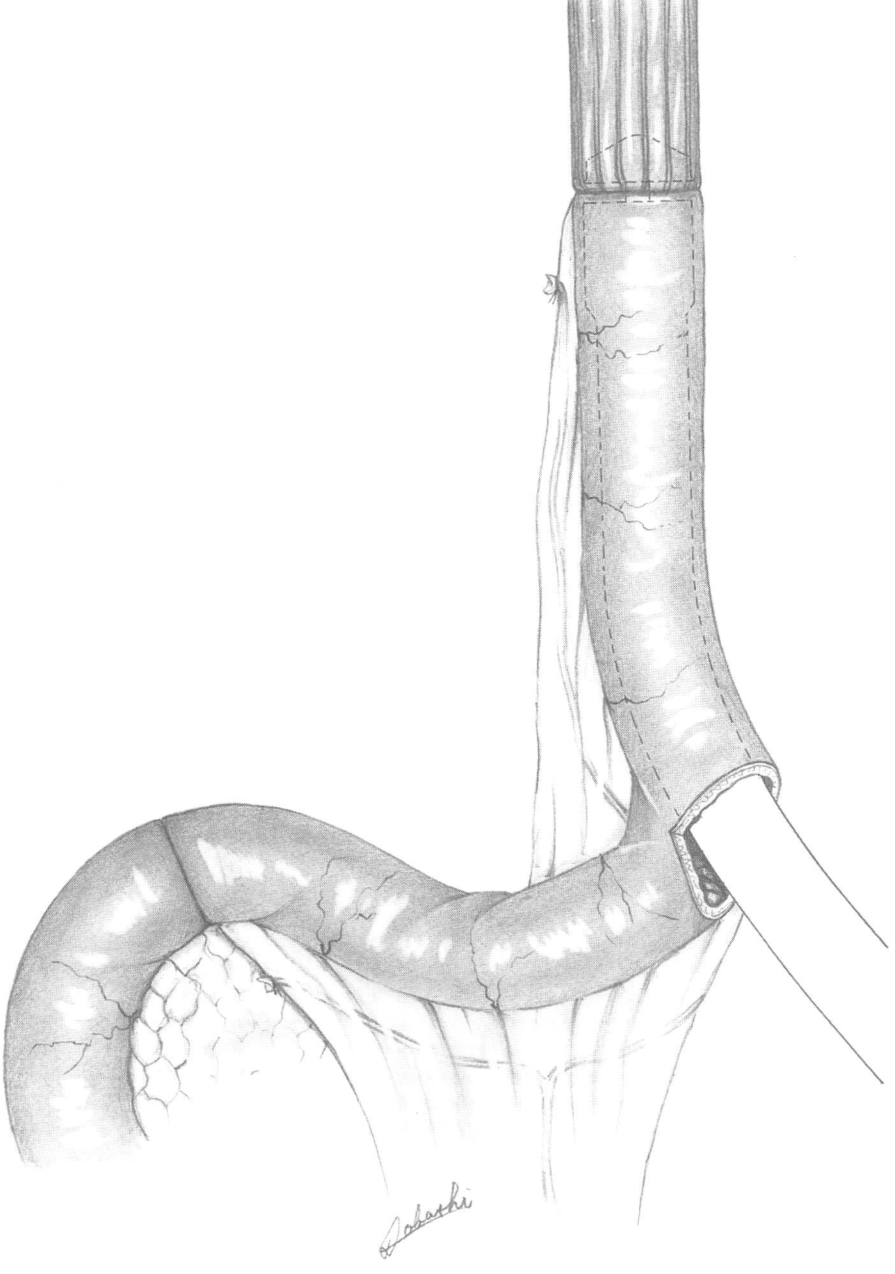

A purse-string is created at the proximal end of the interposition with the aid of a purse-string suture clamp while resecting the staple line. A second circular stapler is introduced through the jejunum enterotomy and the purse-string is tied around the instrument trocar. The staple is assembled and fired to create the end-to-end oesophagojejunostomy.
After withdrawal of the instrument the 'doughnuts' have to be carefully removed to examine their integrity.
N.B.: the preferred technique for the purse-string suture at the oesophagus is the whip stitch.

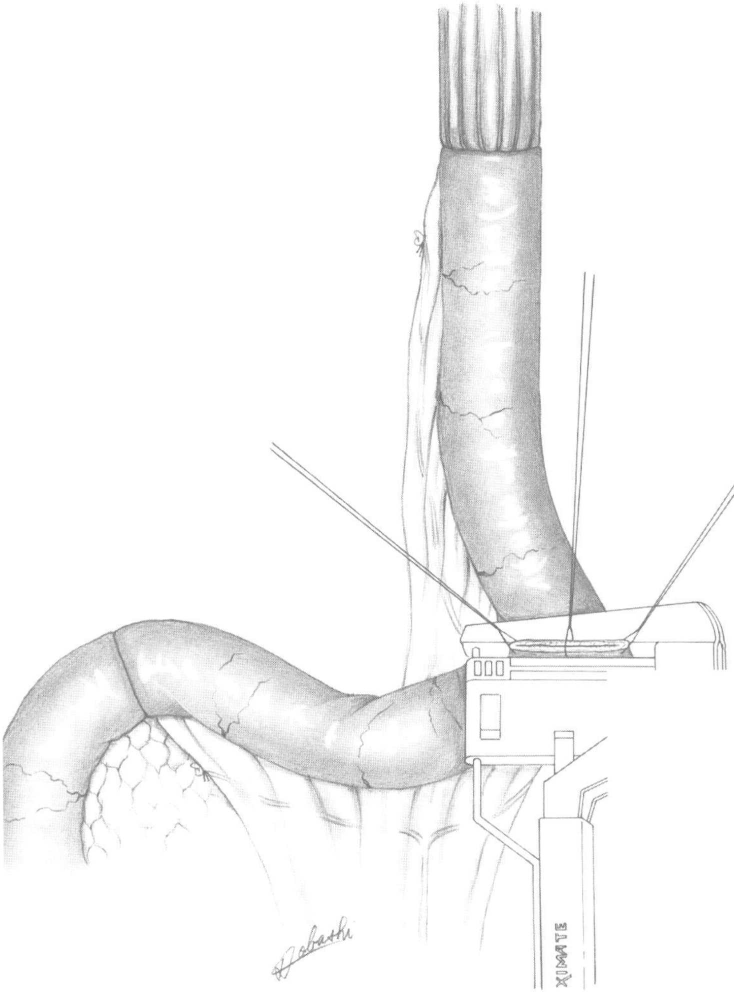

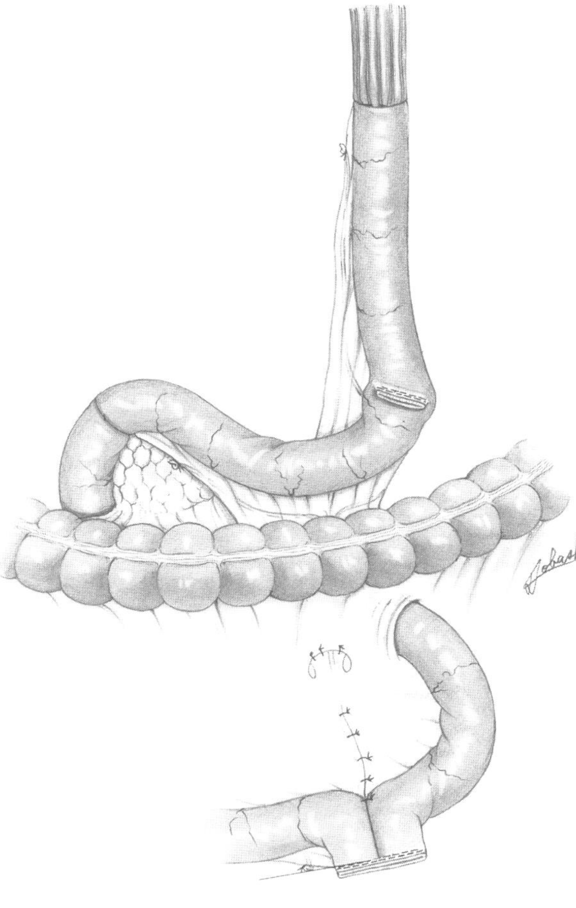

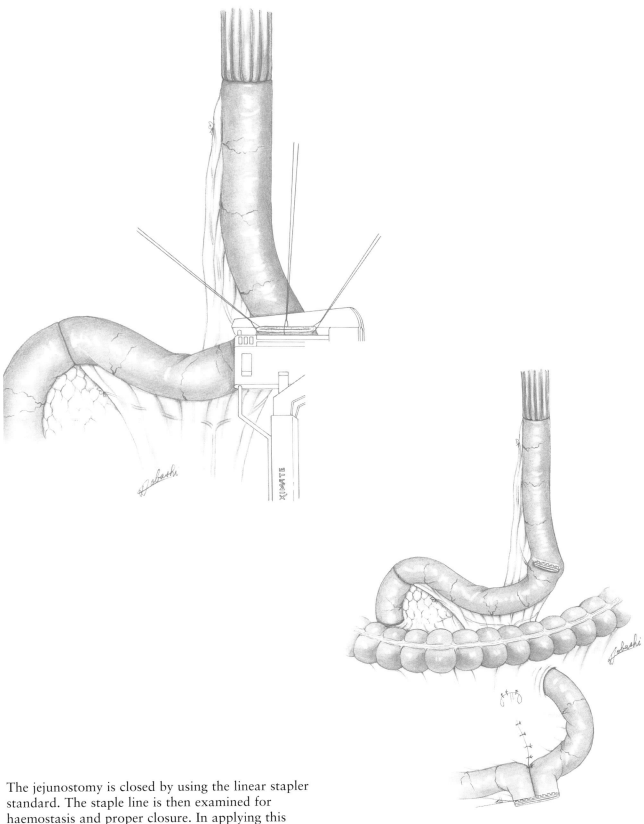

The jejunostomy is closed by using the linear stapler standard. The staple line is then examined for haemostasis and proper closure. In applying this technique, a constriction of the lumen must be avoided to prevent creation of a stenosis.

Total Gastrectomy

Oesophagojejunostomy with End-to-side Roux-en-Y

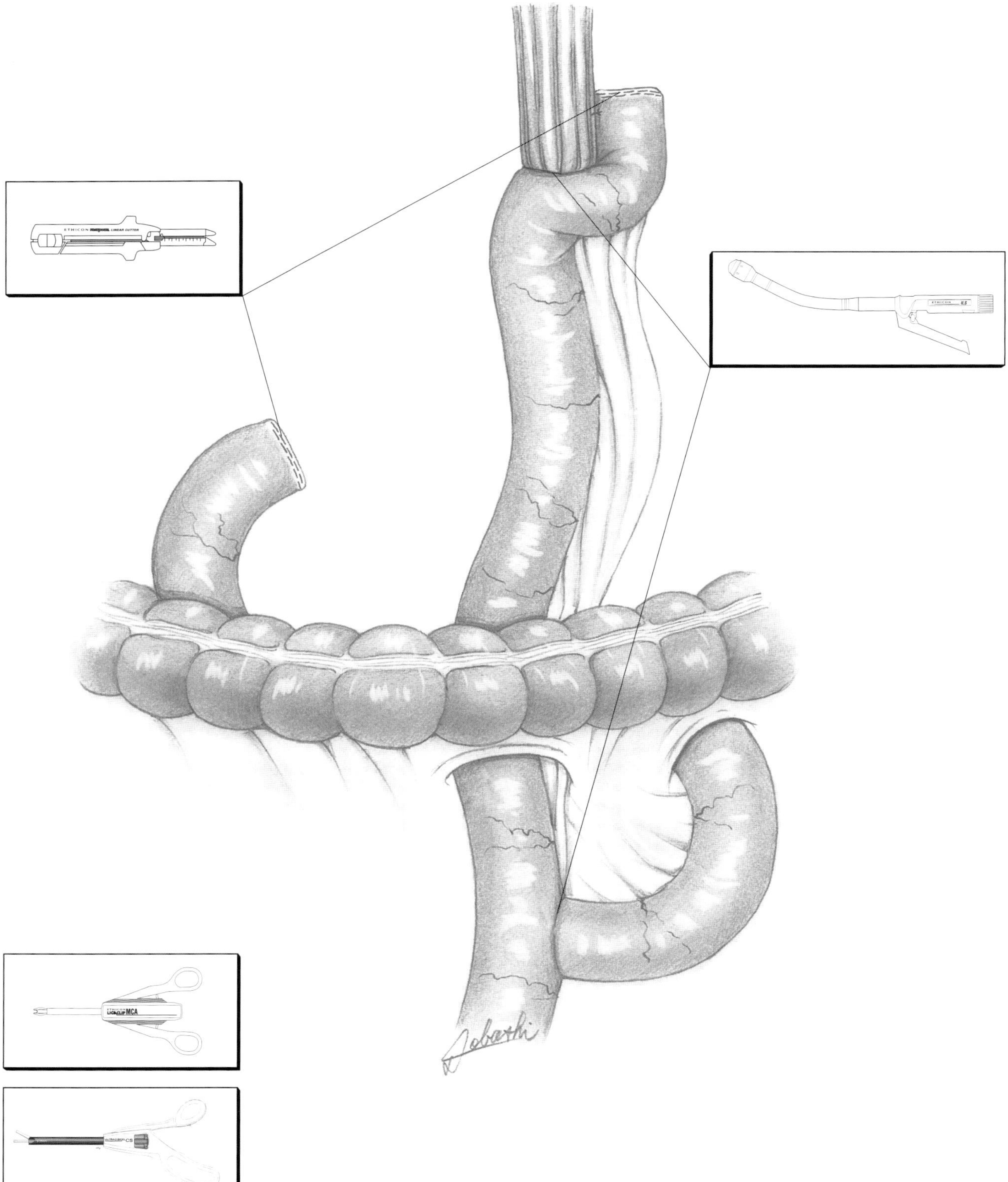

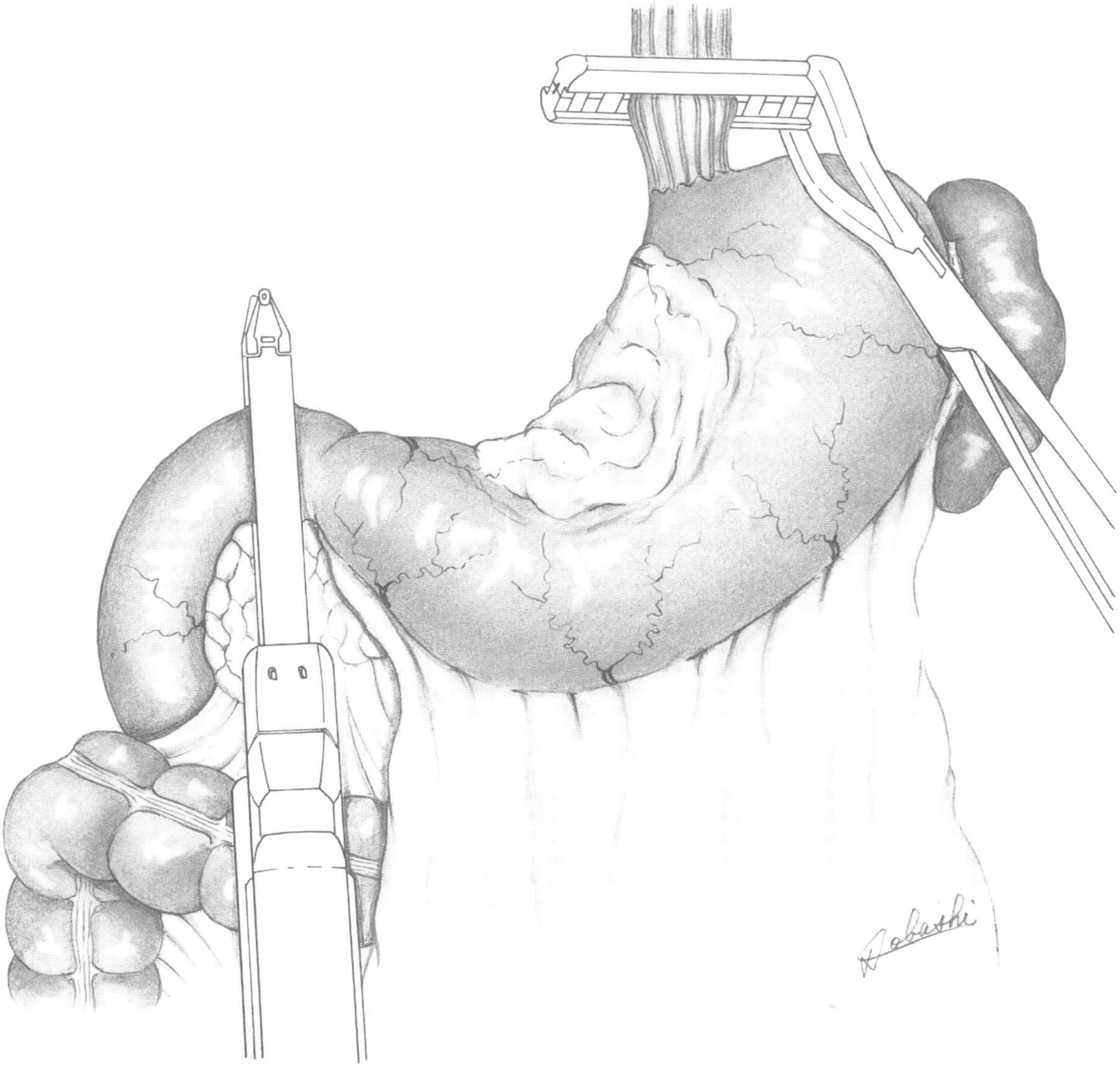

Complete mobilisation of the stomach with the multiple clip applier or the Ultracision coagulating shears. The duodenal stump is closed whilst simultaneously resecting the stomach postpylorically with the linear cutter thick. The staple line is examined for haemostasis and proper closure. At the distal oesophagus a purse-string suture is put in place using the purse-string suture clamp. Resection of the stomach is then performed along the cutting guide of the purse-string suture clamp. N.B.: if the purse-string suture clamp is not used the purse-string technique recommended at the oesophagus is the whip stitch.

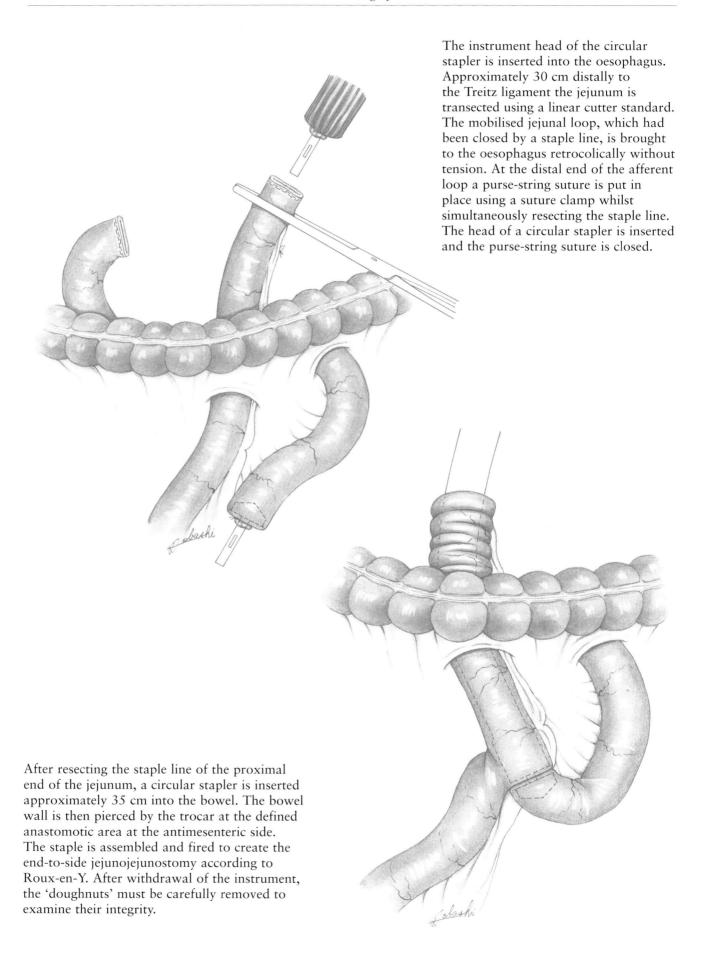

The instrument head of the circular stapler is inserted into the oesophagus. Approximately 30 cm distally to the Treitz ligament the jejunum is transected using a linear cutter standard. The mobilised jejunal loop, which had been closed by a staple line, is brought to the oesophagus retrocolically without tension. At the distal end of the afferent loop a purse-string suture is put in place using a suture clamp whilst simultaneously resecting the staple line. The head of a circular stapler is inserted and the purse-string suture is closed.

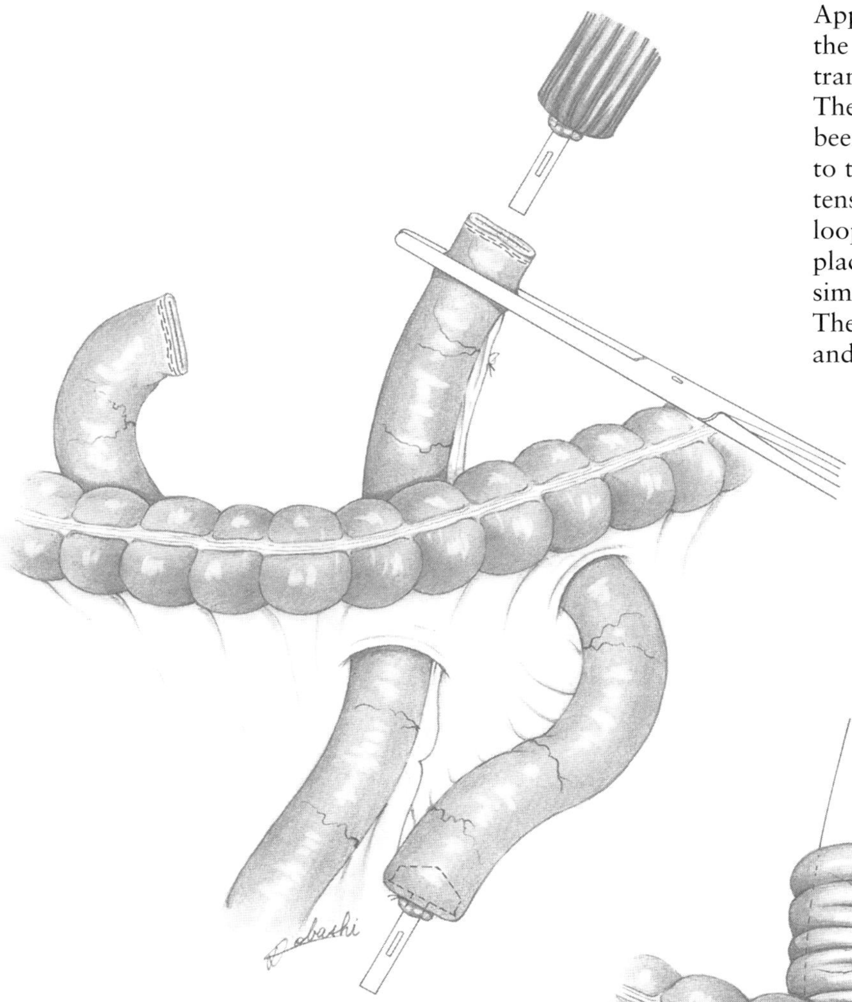

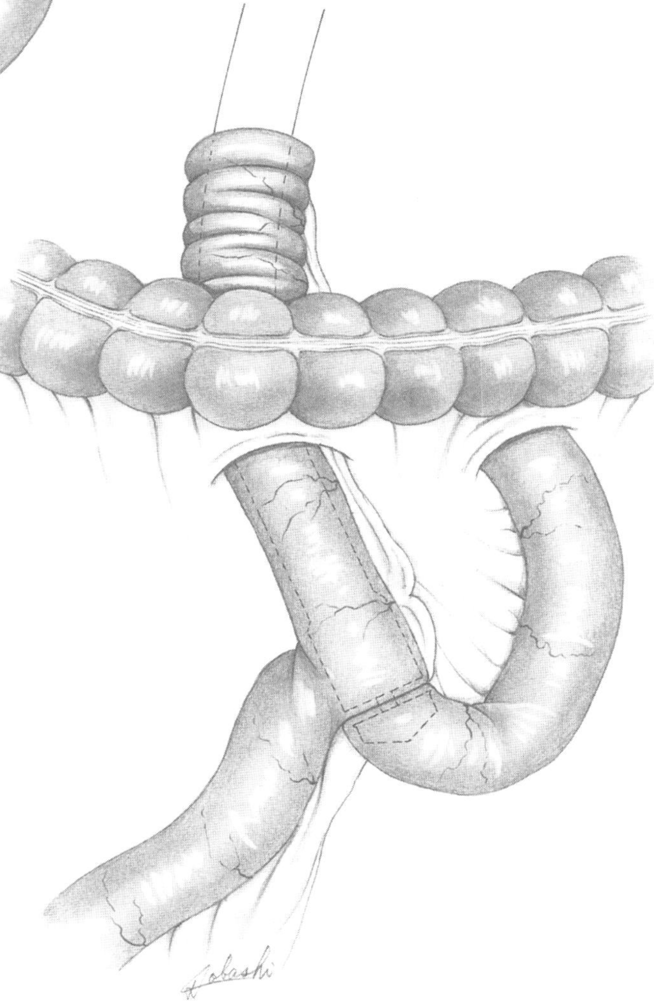

After resecting the staple line of the proximal end of the jejunum, a circular stapler is inserted approximately 35 cm into the bowel. The bowel wall is then pierced by the trocar at the defined anastomotic area at the antimesenteric side. The staple is assembled and fired to create the end-to-side jejunojejunostomy according to Roux-en-Y. After withdrawal of the instrument, the 'doughnuts' must be carefully removed to examine their integrity.

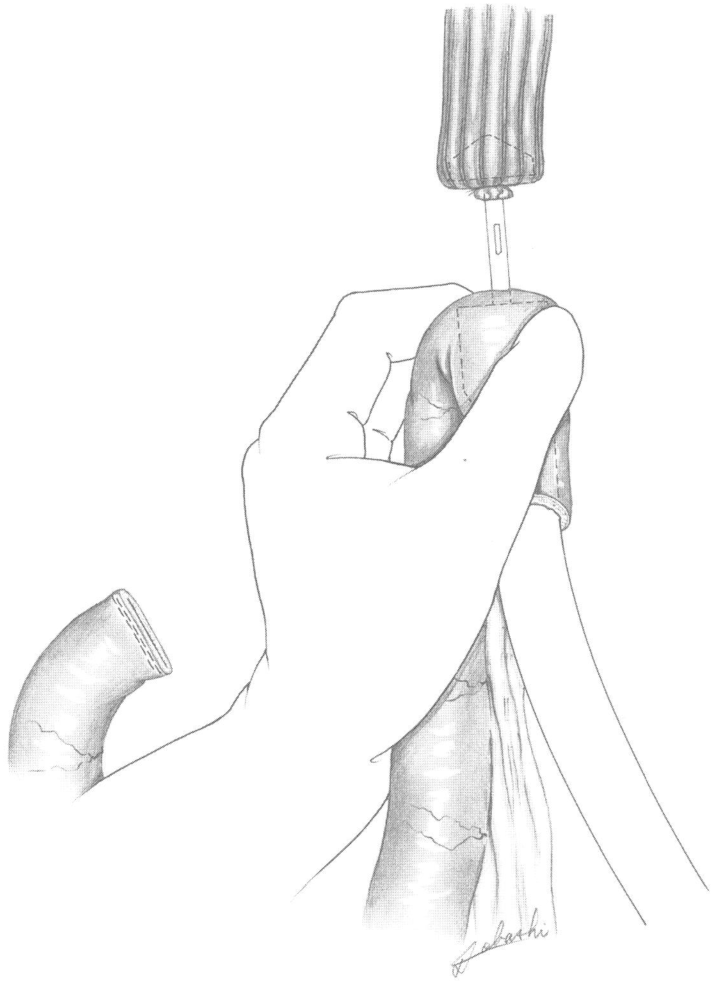

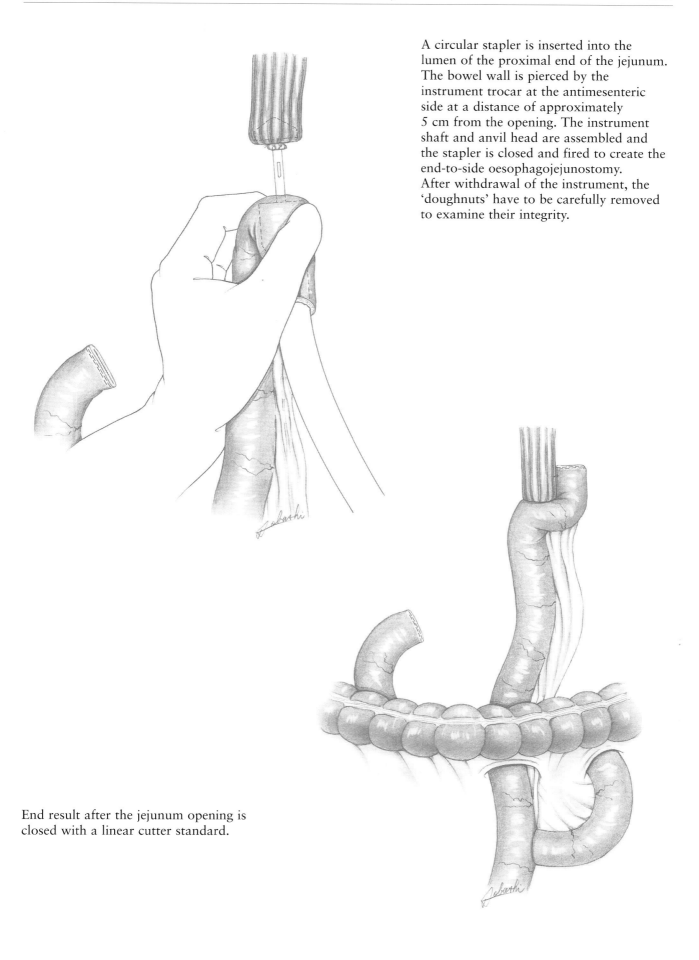

A circular stapler is inserted into the lumen of the proximal end of the jejunum. The bowel wall is pierced by the instrument trocar at the antimesenteric side at a distance of approximately 5 cm from the opening. The instrument shaft and anvil head are assembled and the stapler is closed and fired to create the end-to-side oesophagojejunostomy. After withdrawal of the instrument, the 'doughnuts' have to be carefully removed to examine their integrity.

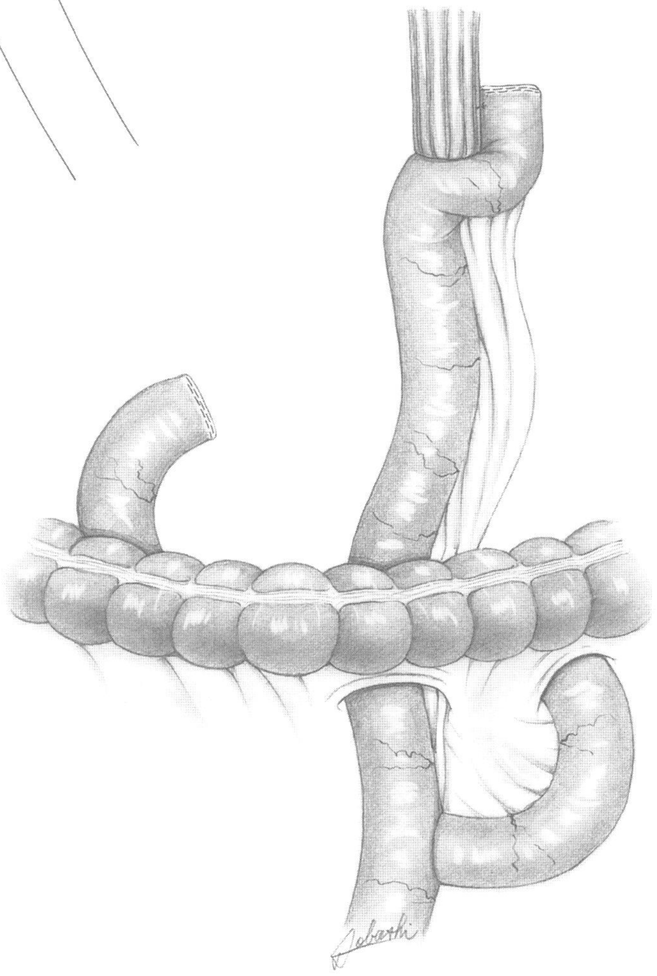

End result after the jejunum opening is closed with a linear cutter standard.

Total Gastrectomy

Oesophagojejunostomy with a Side-to-side Roux-en-Y

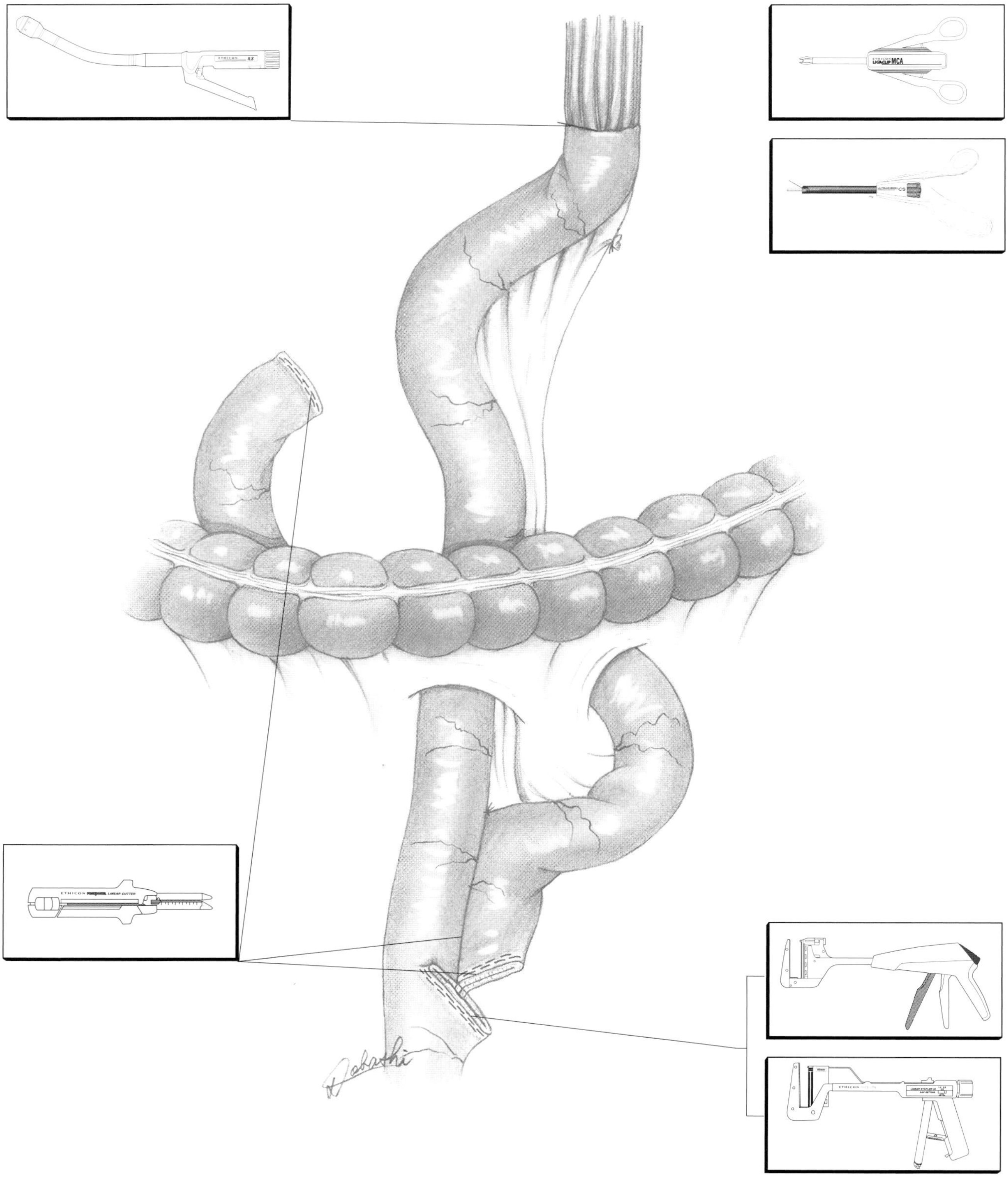

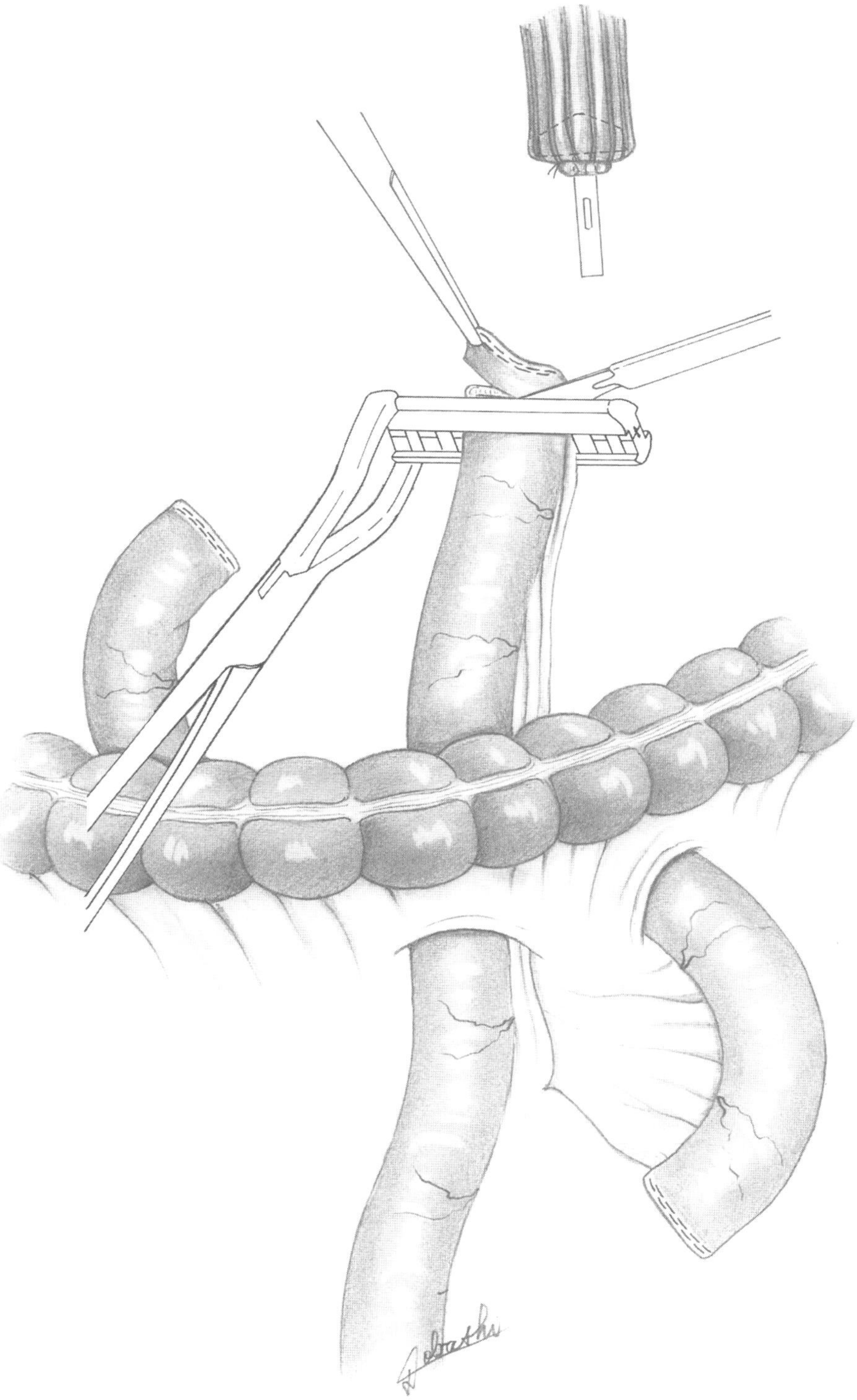

Total gastrectomy and transection of the jejunum are carried out, following the steps previously described. The mobilised jejunal loop, which had been closed by a staple line, is brought to the oesophagus retrocolically without tension. At its proximal end a purse-string suture is put into place using a suture clamp whilst simultaneously resecting the staple line.

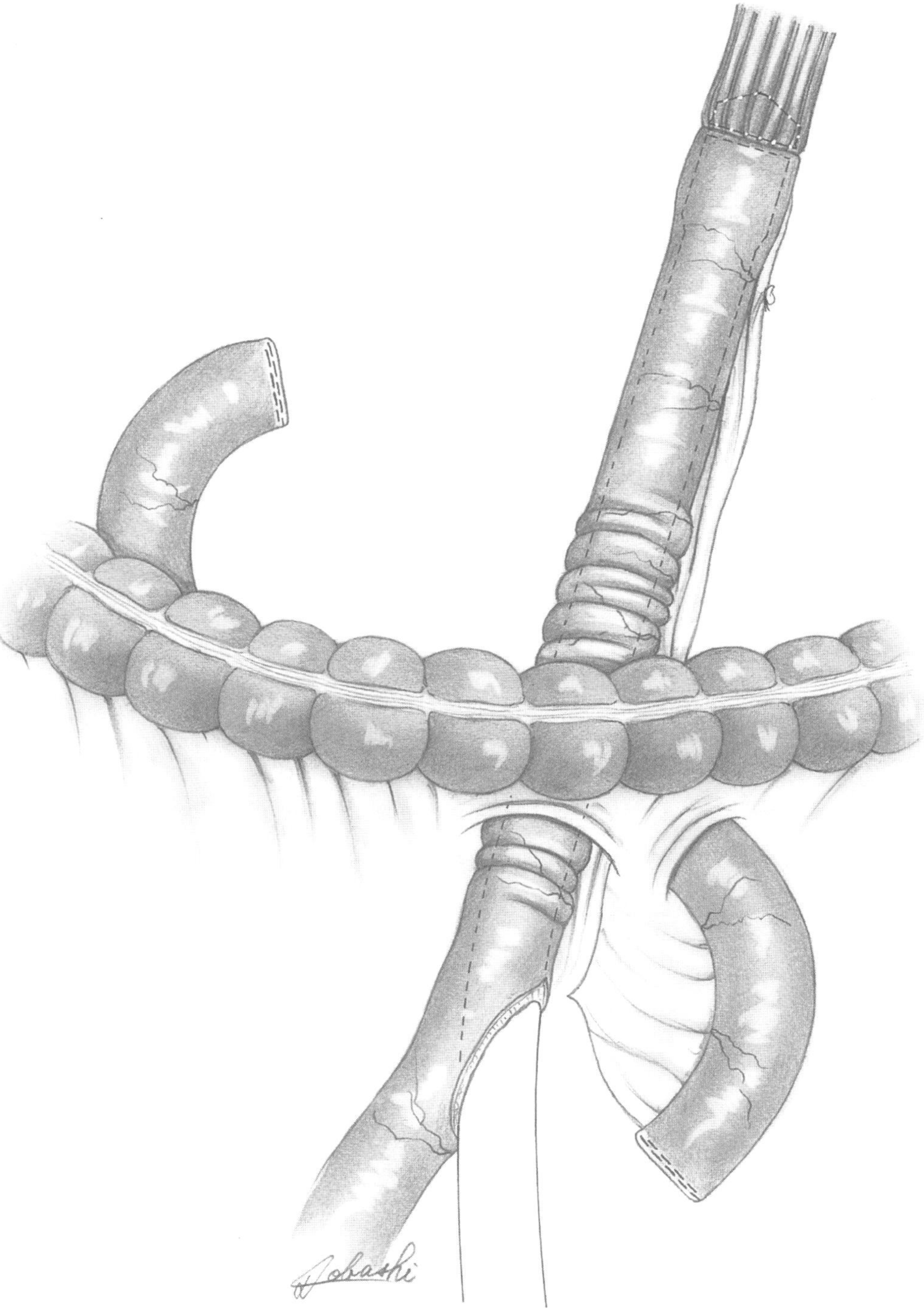

Incision of the antimesenteric area of the jejunum on the same level as the defined Roux-en Y anastomosis (approx. 40 cm distally to the proximal resection line) using a scalpel or Ultracision sharp hook. The circular stapler is inserted into the efferent loop via the incision and threaded to the end. In doing this, extreme care must be taken to avoid damage to the bowel by the stapler, which will lead to later fistula development. The purse-string is tied around the trocar of the instrument. The instrument shaft and anvil head are assembled and the stapler is closed and fired to create the end-to-end oesophagojejunostomy. After withdrawal of the instrument, the 'doughnuts' must be carefully removed to examine their integrity.

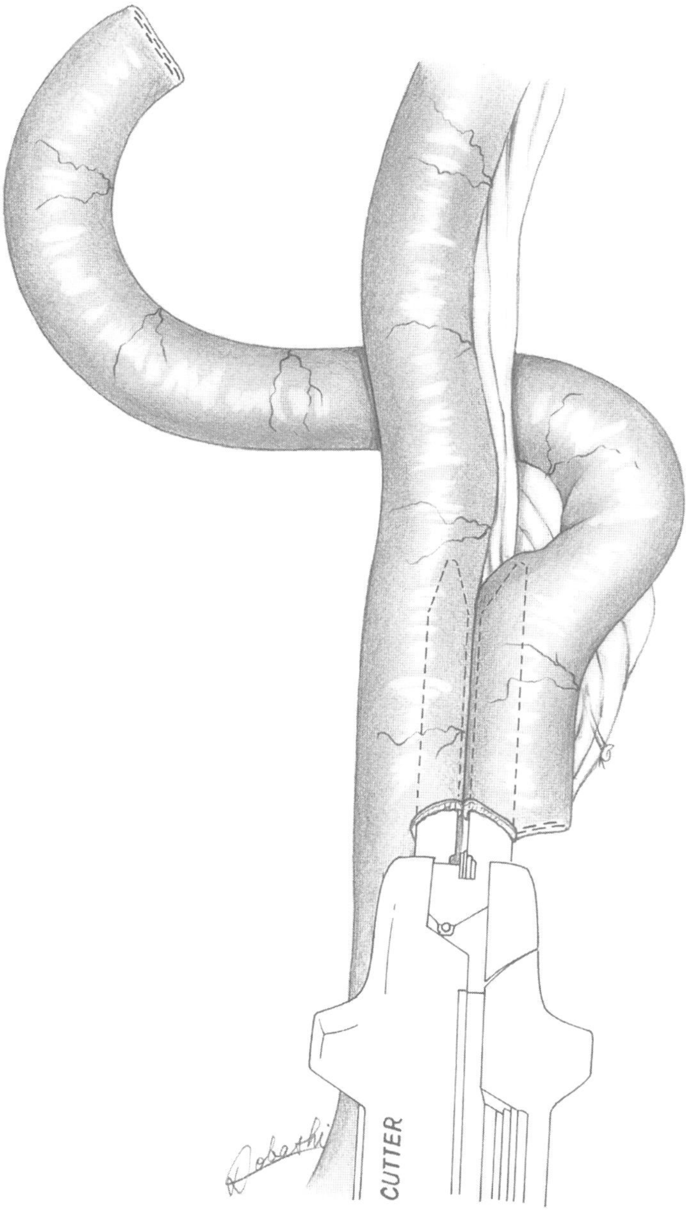

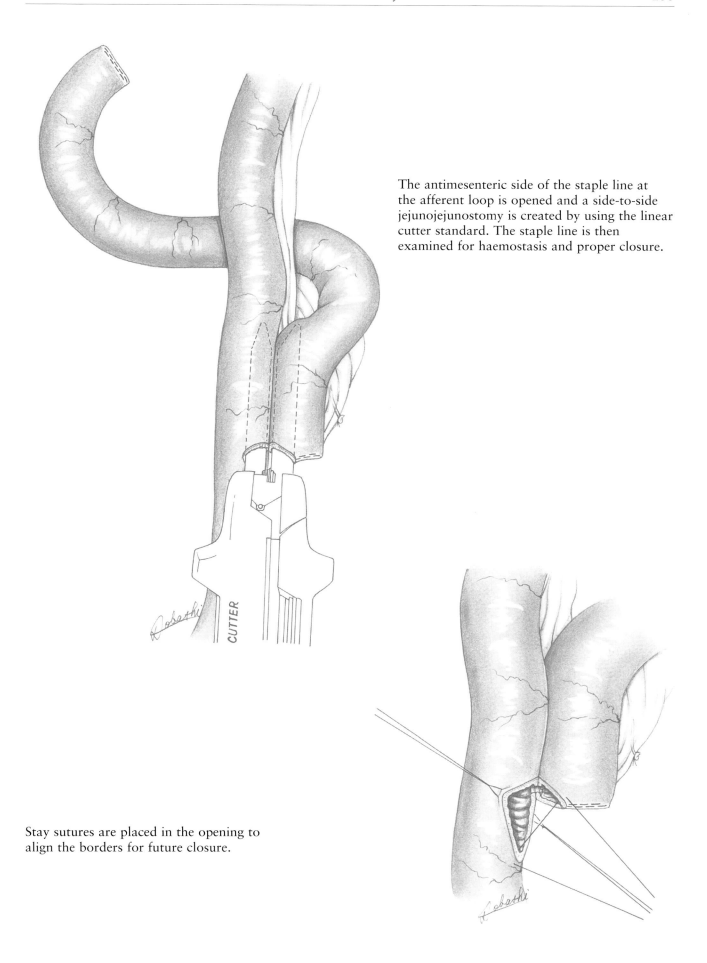

The antimesenteric side of the staple line at the afferent loop is opened and a side-to-side jejunojejunostomy is created by using the linear cutter standard. The staple line is then examined for haemostasis and proper closure.

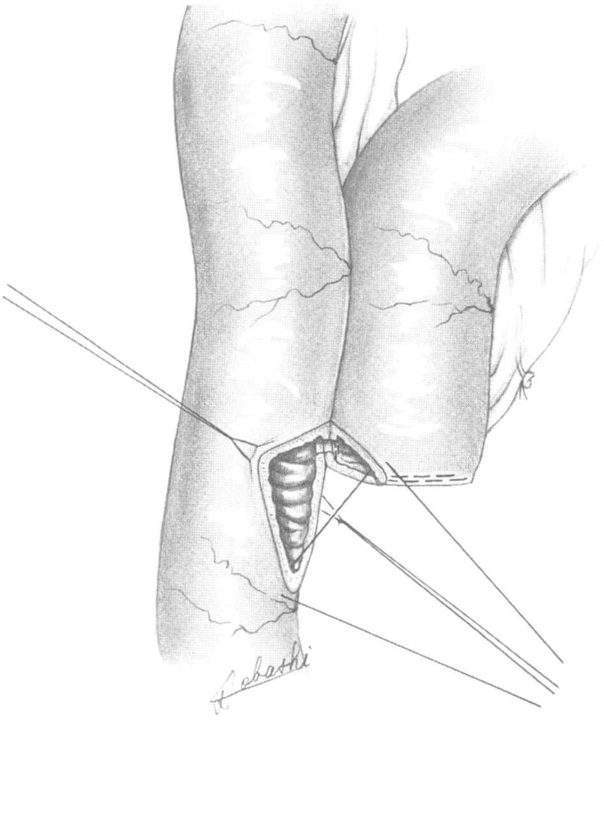

Stay sutures are placed in the opening to align the borders for future closure.

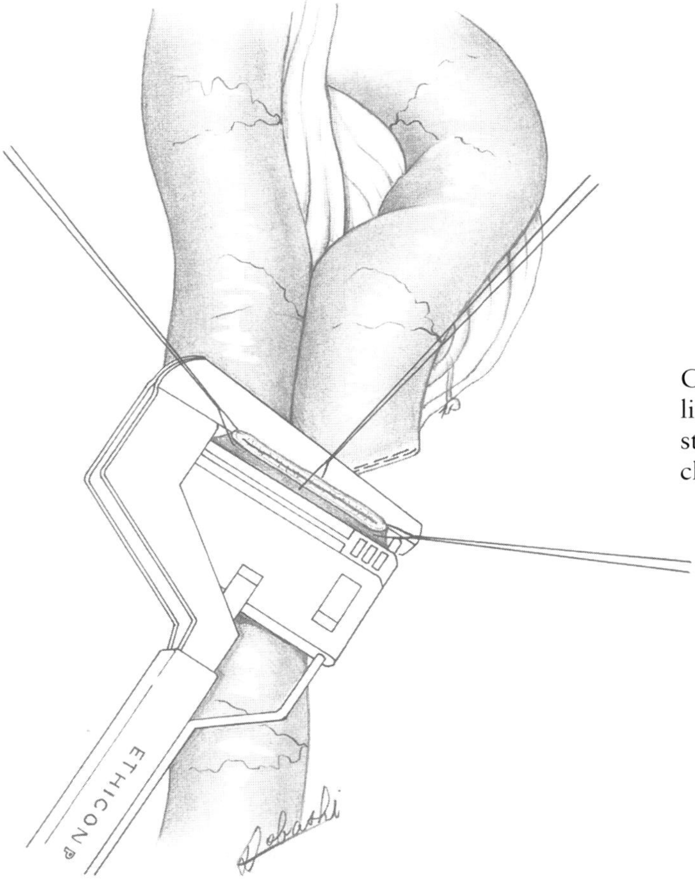

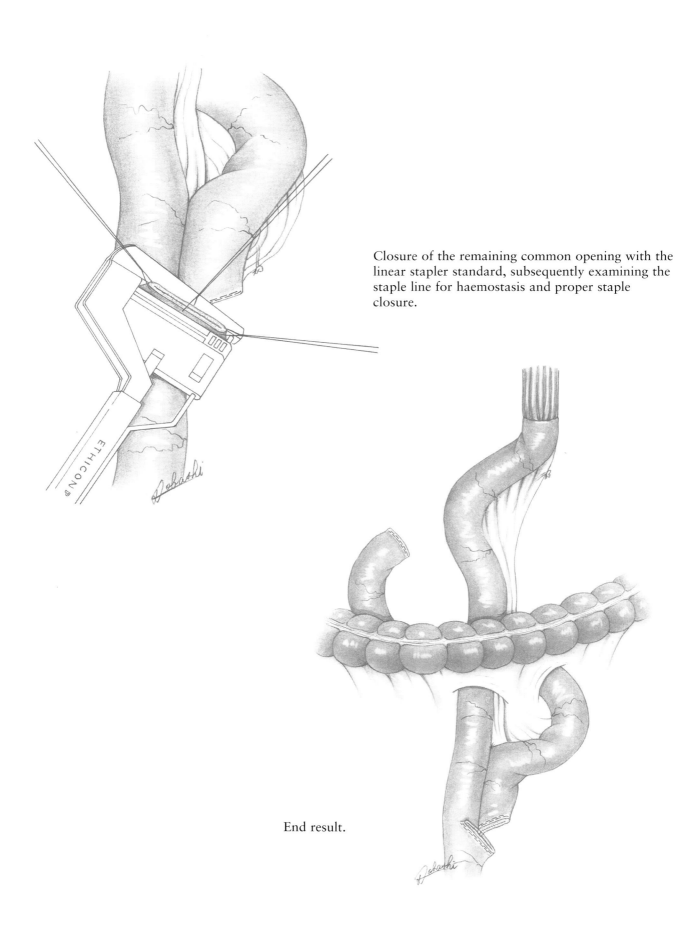

Closure of the remaining common opening with the linear stapler standard, subsequently examining the staple line for haemostasis and proper staple closure.

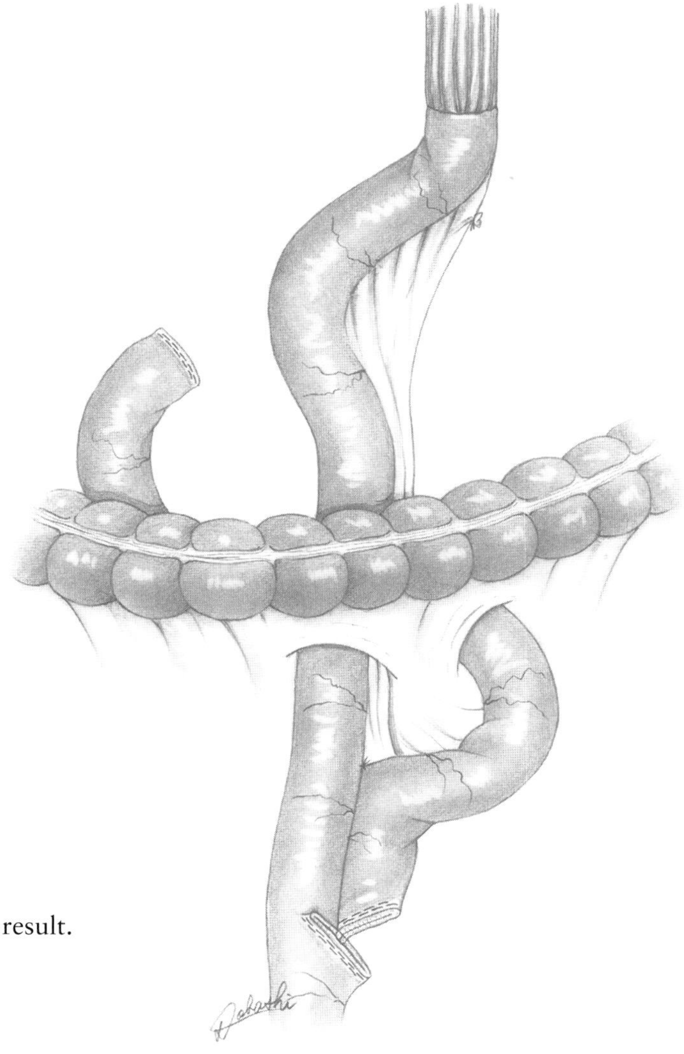

End result.

Total Gastrectomy

Jejunal Interposition with Jejunal Pouch

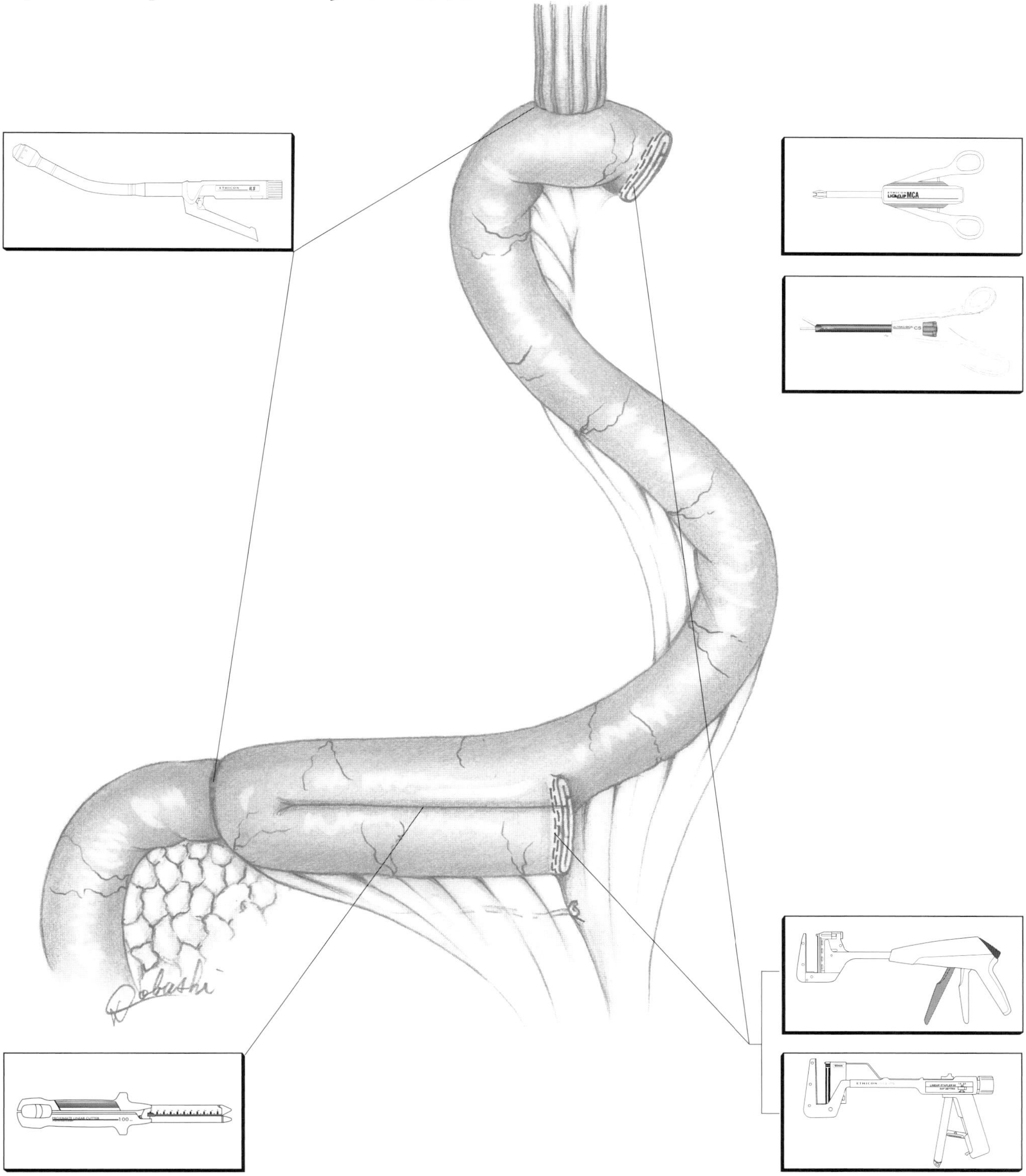

A total gastrectomy and transection of the jejunum interposition are performed as previously described. In doing this, ensure that the length of the interposition loop is long enough (approx. 55 to 60 cm) to later create the jejunal pouch at the distal end of the interposition. An oesophagojejunostomy is performed as described before.

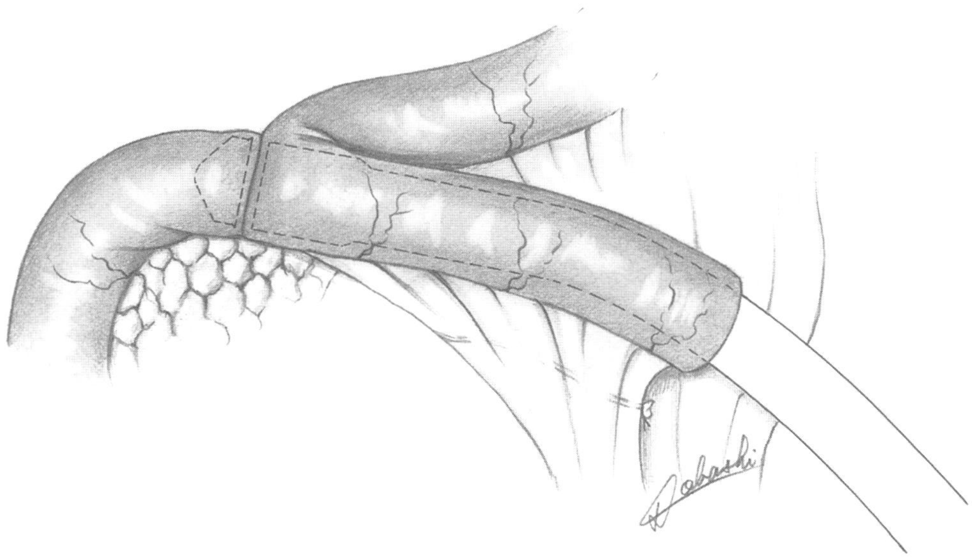

A purse-string suture is then created at the proximal end of the duodenum. The anvil of a circular stapler is inserted and the purse-string suture is closed. A circular stapler is inserted into the lumen of the distal end of the interposition. The bowel wall is pierced by the instrument trocar at the antimesenteric side at a distance of approx. 10 to 15 cm from the opening. The instrument is assembled, closed, and fired to create the end-to-side jejunoduodenostomy. After withdrawal of the instrument, the 'doughnuts' must be carefully removed to examine their integrity.

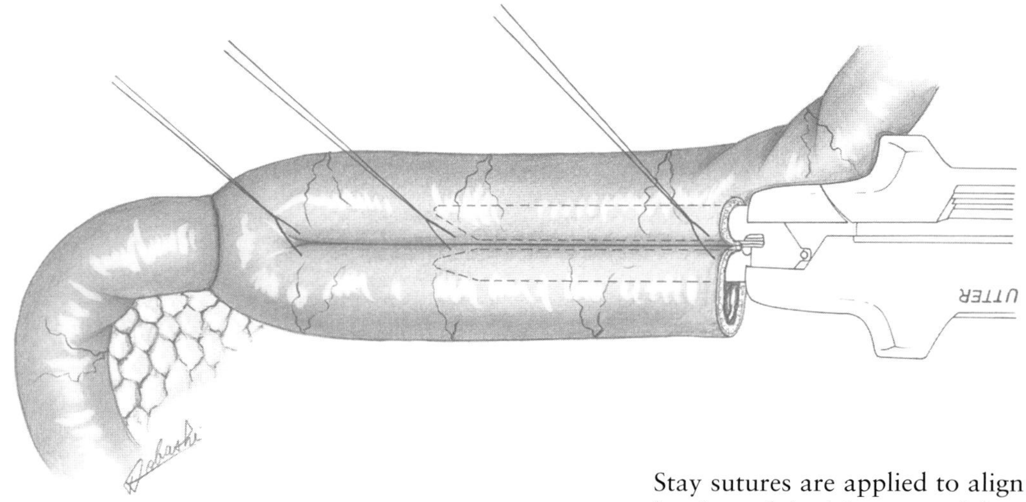

Stay sutures are applied to align the antimesenteric borders of the jejunum and form the pouch. An enterotomy is performed in order to insert the jaw of the linear cutter standard. The instrument is inserted, closed, and fired, constructing the first anastomotic tract. If the length of the linear cutter is sufficiently long, this step can be carried out with only one firing.

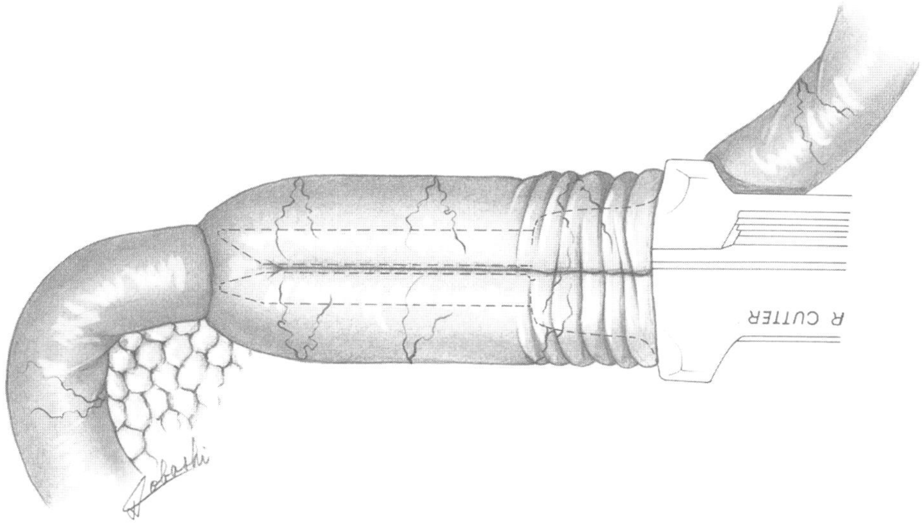

When a second firing is needed to complete the pouch, the anastomosed bowel can be telescoped over the instrument in order to render its distal part accessible.

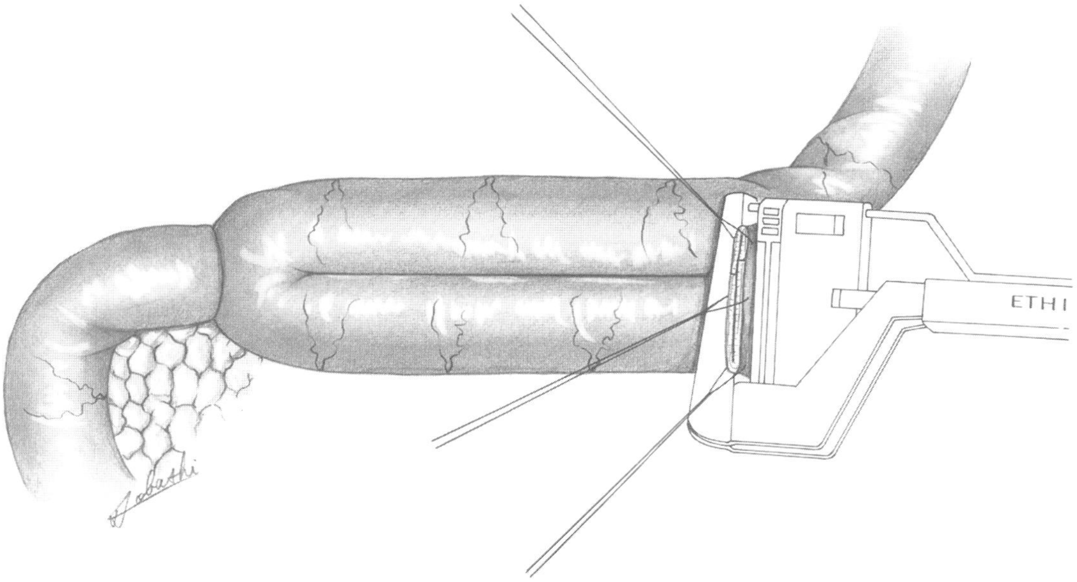

The opening is closed with a linear stapler standard aided by stay sutures.

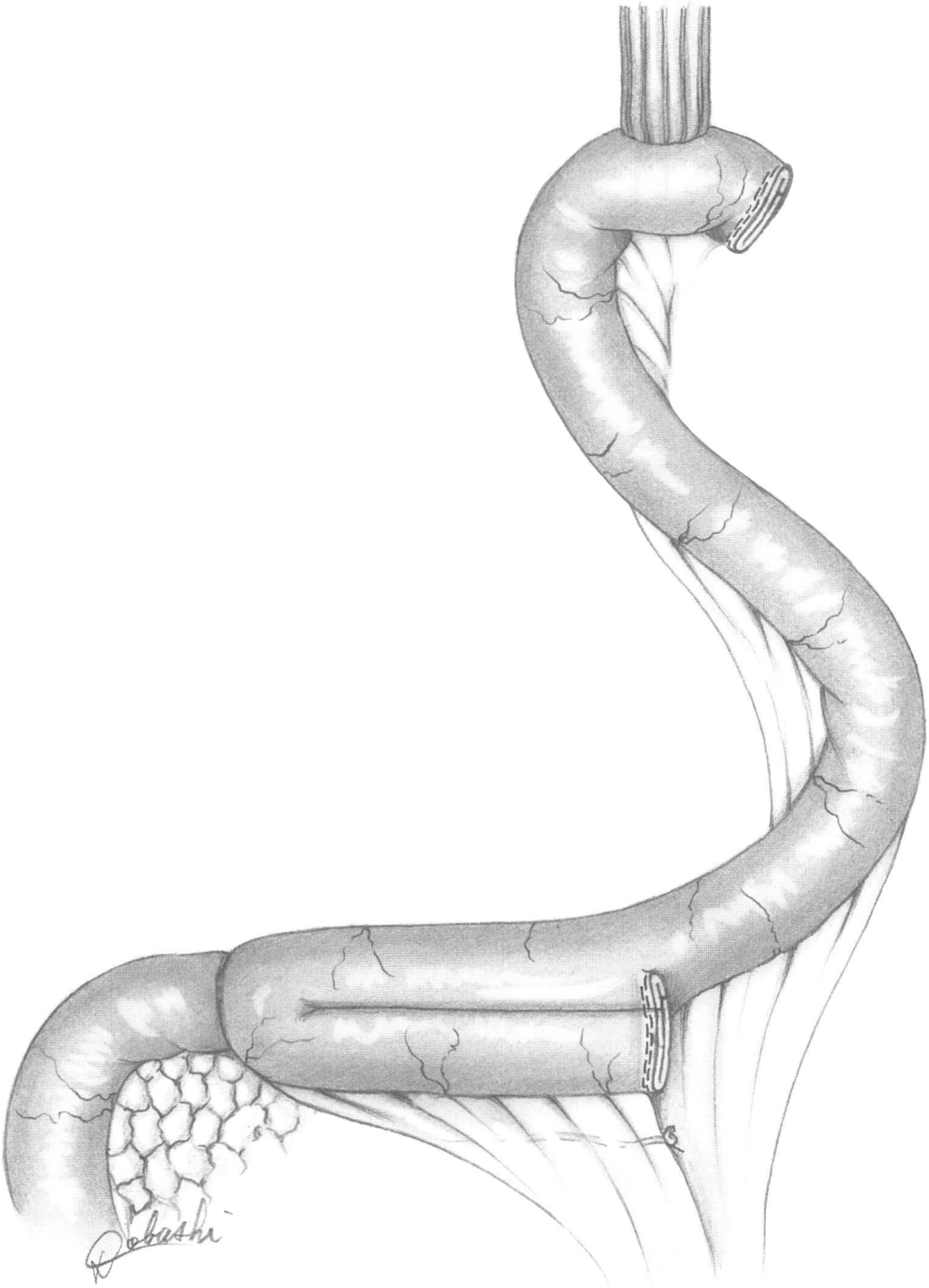

End result.

Total Gastrectomy

Paulino Pouch

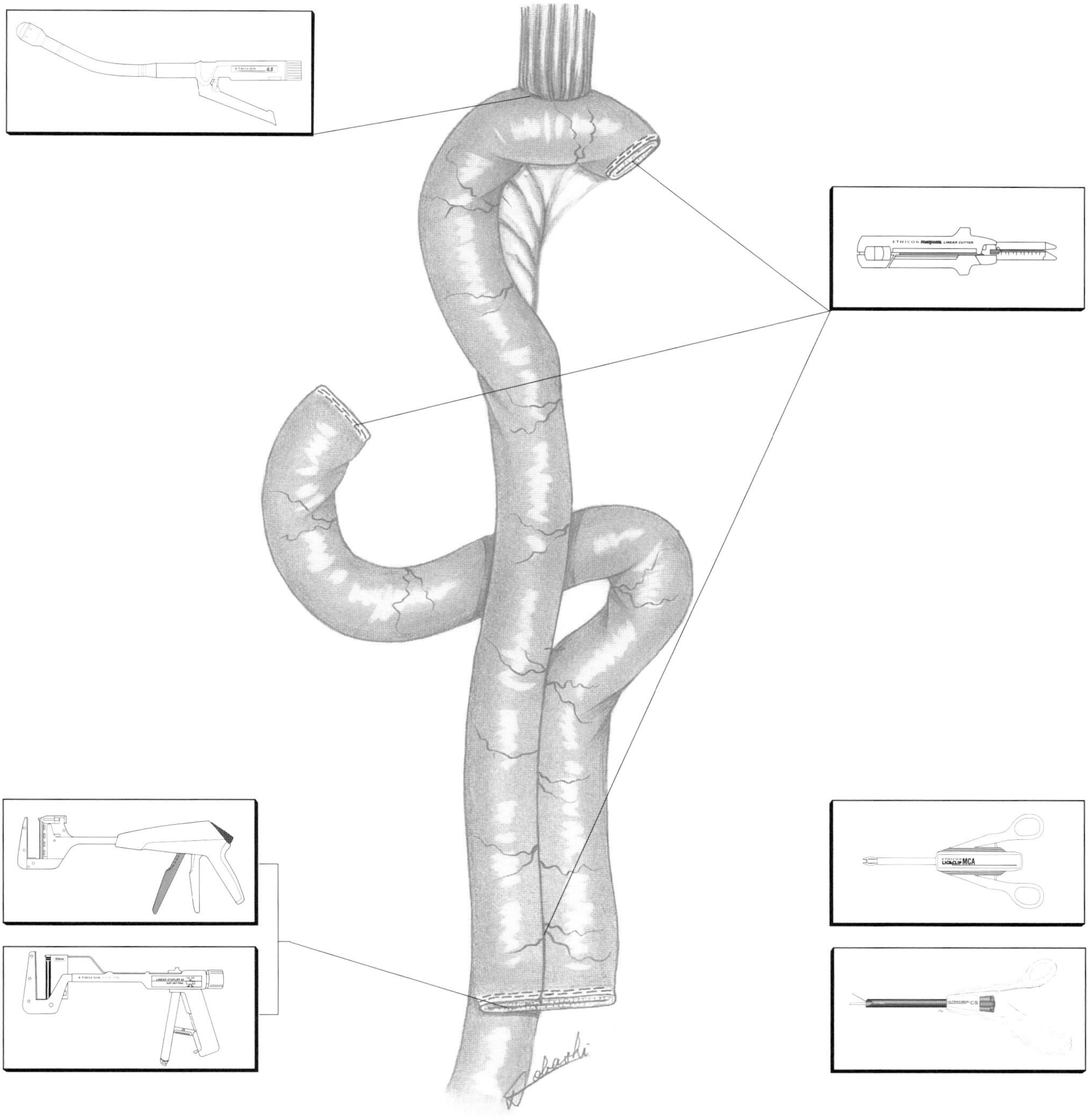

A total gastrectomy and transection of the jejunum
40 to 45 cm distally to the Treitz ligament is performed.
An oesophagojejunostomy is carried out as described before.

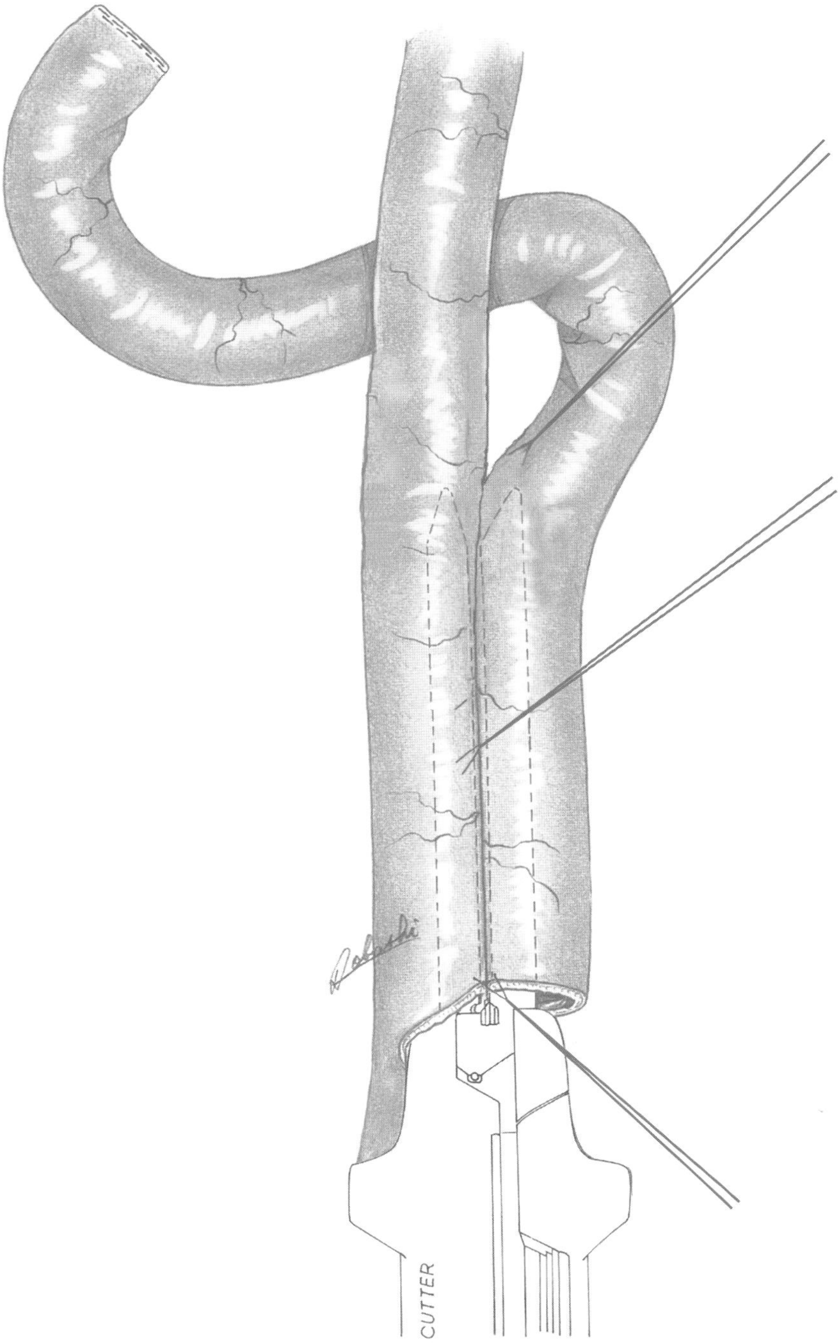

The staple line from the distal end of the afferent jejunum loop is excised. Stay sutures are applied to align the antimesenteric borders of the two portions of the jejunum that will form the pouch. An enterotomy is performed in order to insert the jaw of the linear cutter standard. The instrument is inserted, closed and fired constructing the first anastomotic tract. If the length of the linear cutter is sufficiently long this step can be done with only one firing.

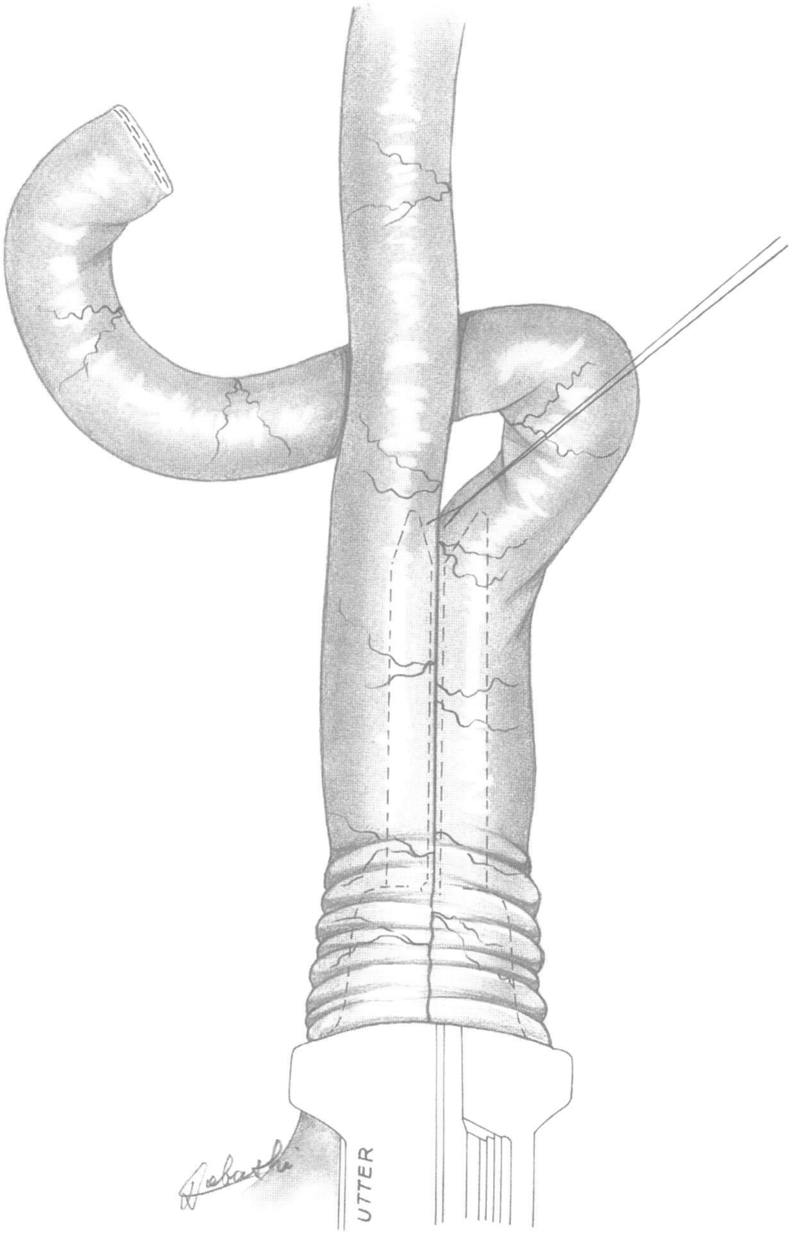

When a second firing is needed to complete the pouch, the anastomosed bowel can be telescoped over the instrument in order to render its distal part accessible.

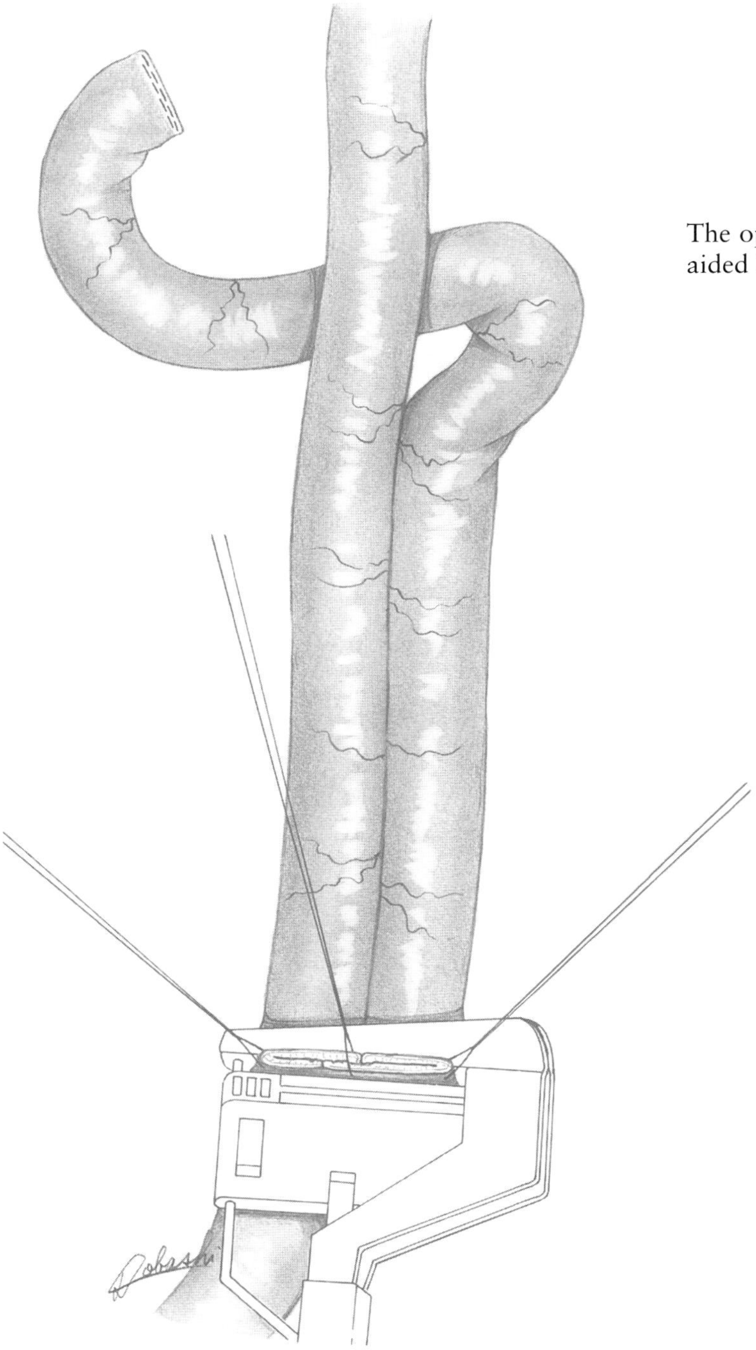

The opening is closed with a linear stapler standard aided by stay sutures.

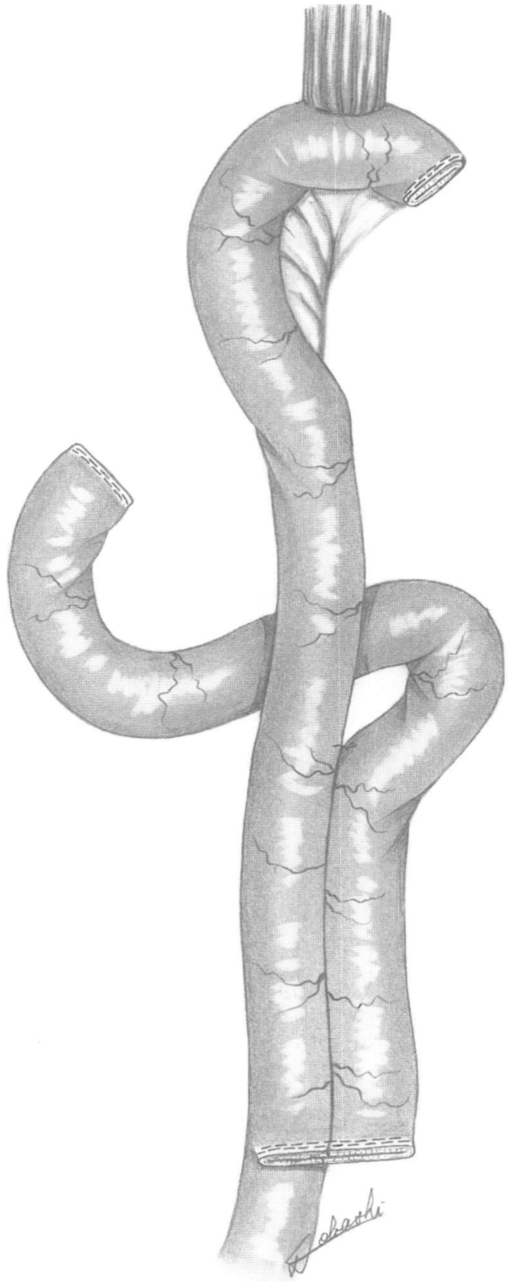

To prevent tension on the anastomosis, a safety suture may be placed at the proximal end of the pouch.

Total Gastrectomy

Lawrence-Pouch

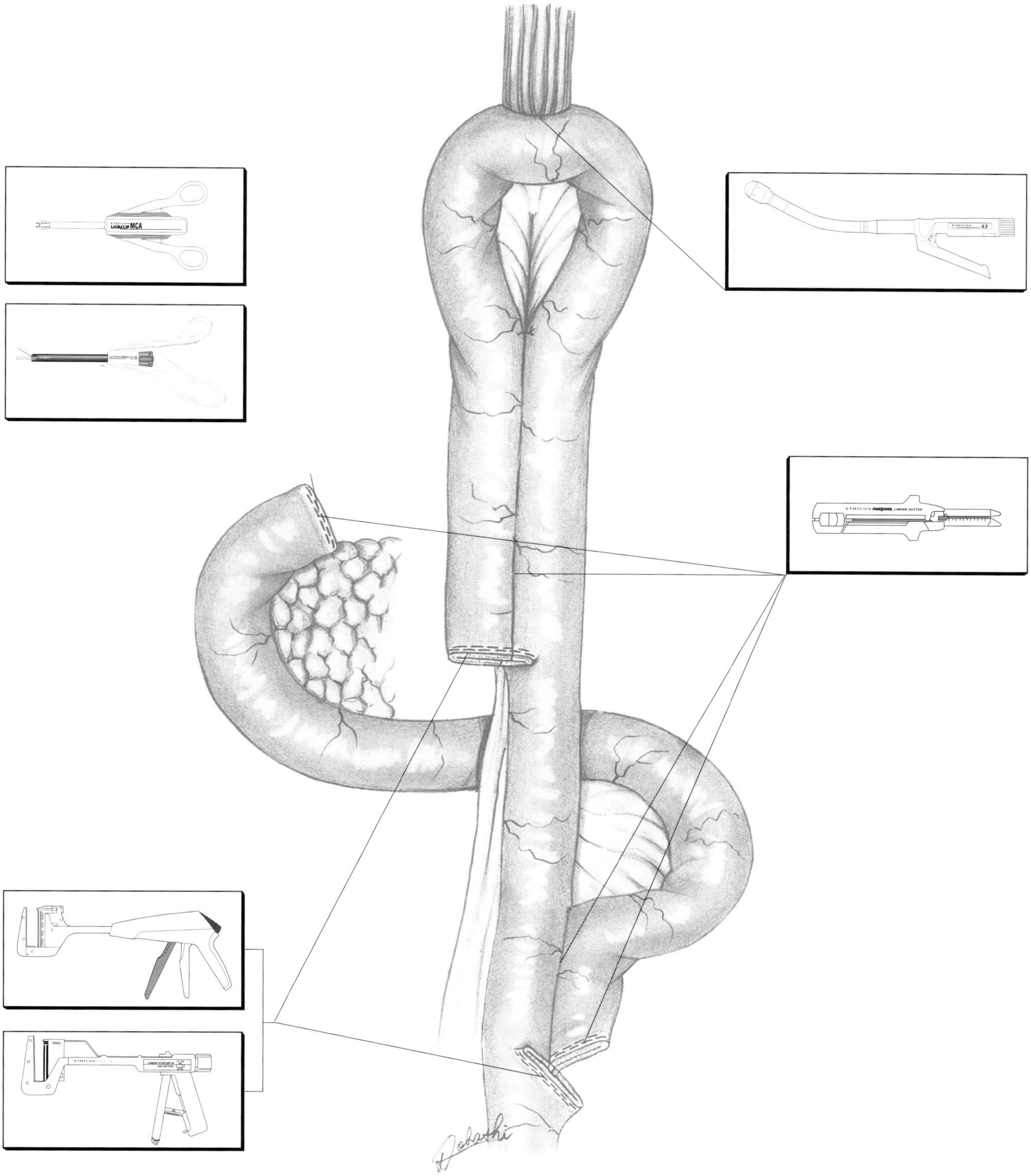

In this drawing the following steps are carried out as described before:
a total gastrectomy, a transection of the jejunum 30 cm distally to the Treitz ligament, and a side-to-side jejunojejunostomy (Roux-en-Y) 60 to 65 cm distally from the distal end of the jejunum.

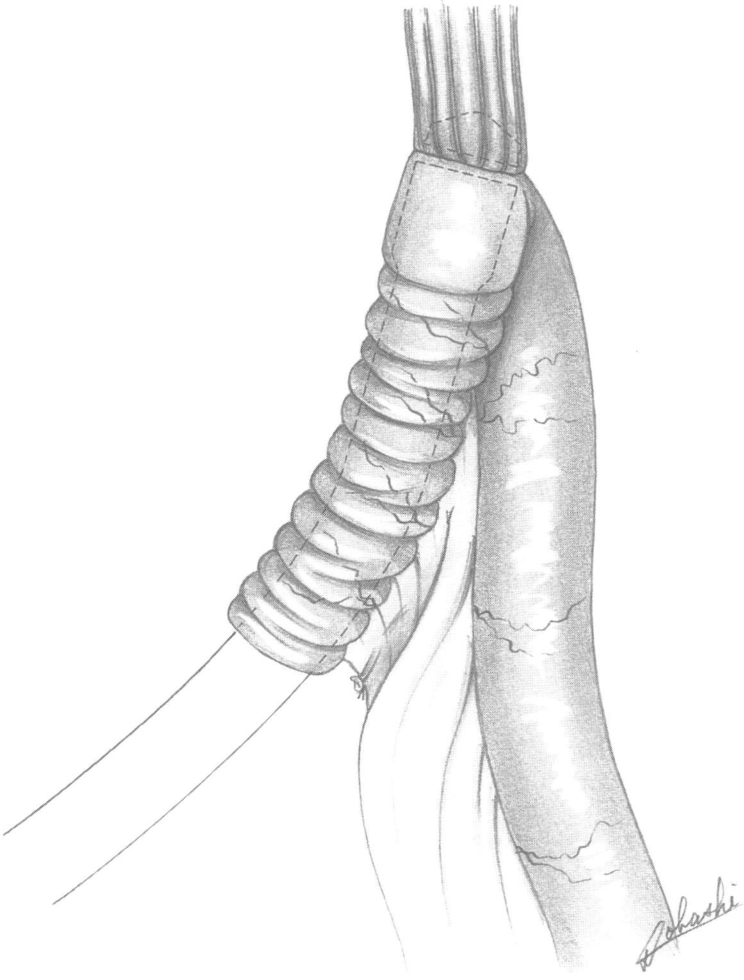

After performing a purse-string suture at the oesophagus, the anvil of the circular stapler is inserted and the purse-string is closed. The shaft of the circular stapler is inserted into the lumen of the proximal end of the jejunum. The bowel wall is pierced by the instrument trocar at the anti-mesenteric side at a distance of approximately 25 cm from its opening. The instrument is assembled, closed, and fired to create the end-to-side oesophagojejunostomy. After withdrawal of the instrument, the 'doughnuts' must be carefully removed to examine their integrity.

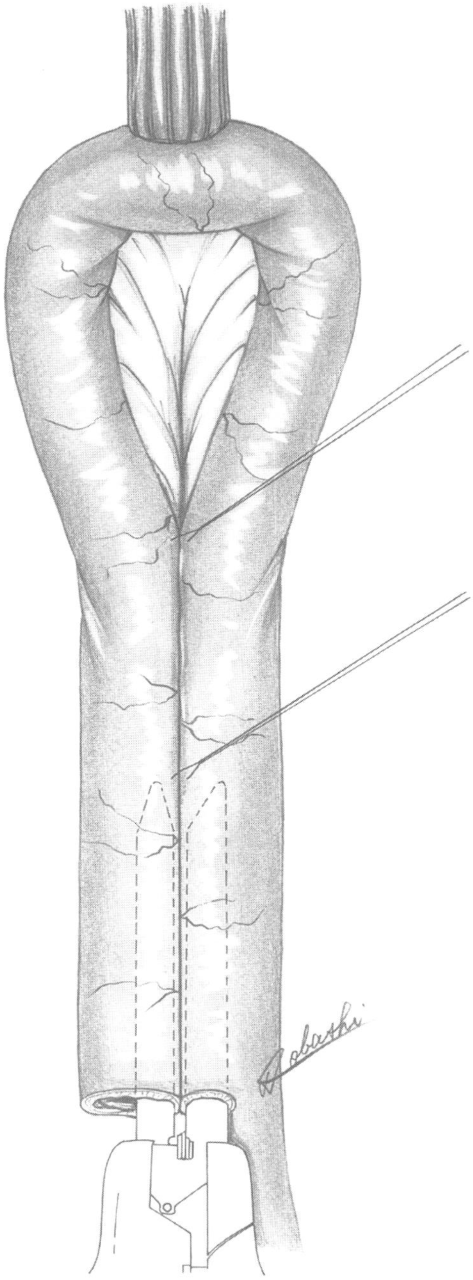

Stay sutures are applied to align the antimesenteric borders of the two portions of the jejunum that will form the pouch. An enterotomy is performed in order to insert the jaw of the linear cutter standard. The instrument is inserted, closed, and fired, constructing the first anastomotic tract.

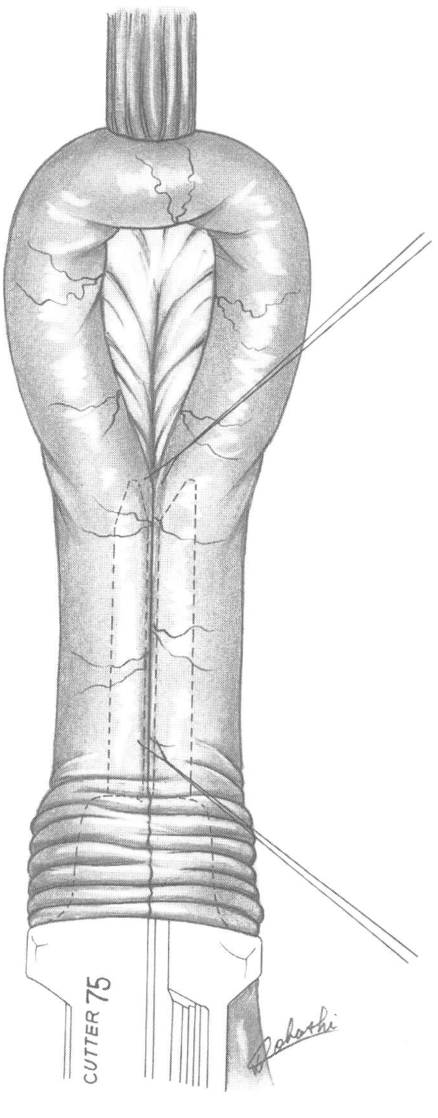

A second firing is needed to complete the pouch. The anastomosed bowel can be telescoped over the instrument in order to render its distal part accessible.

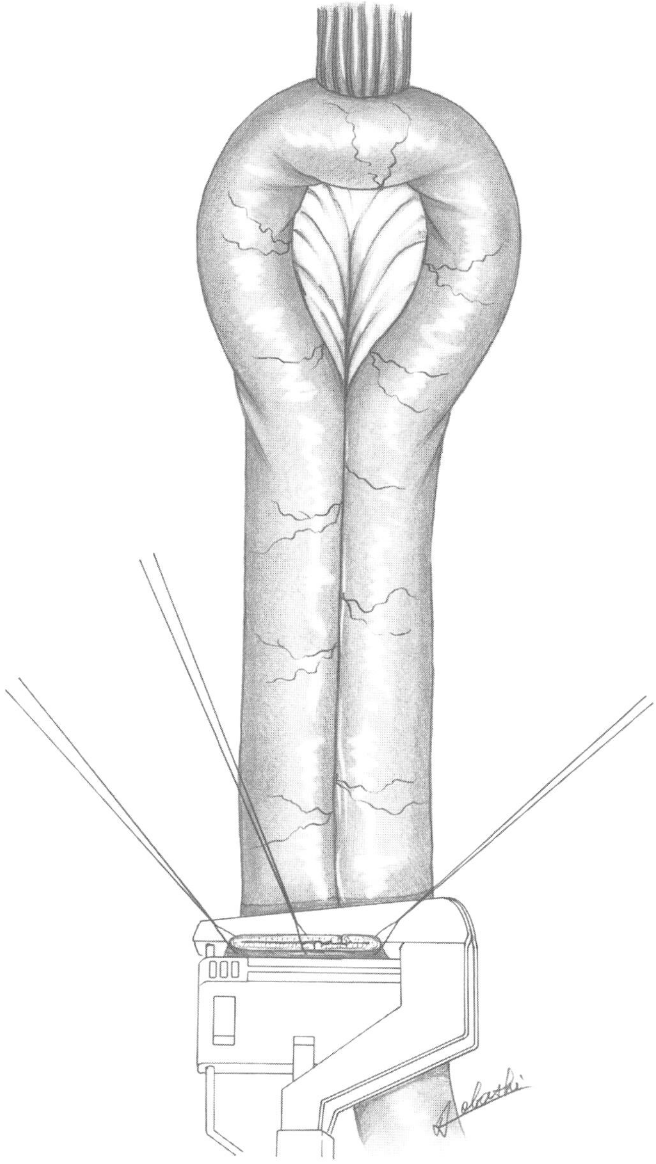

The opening is closed using a linear stapler standard aided by stay sutures.

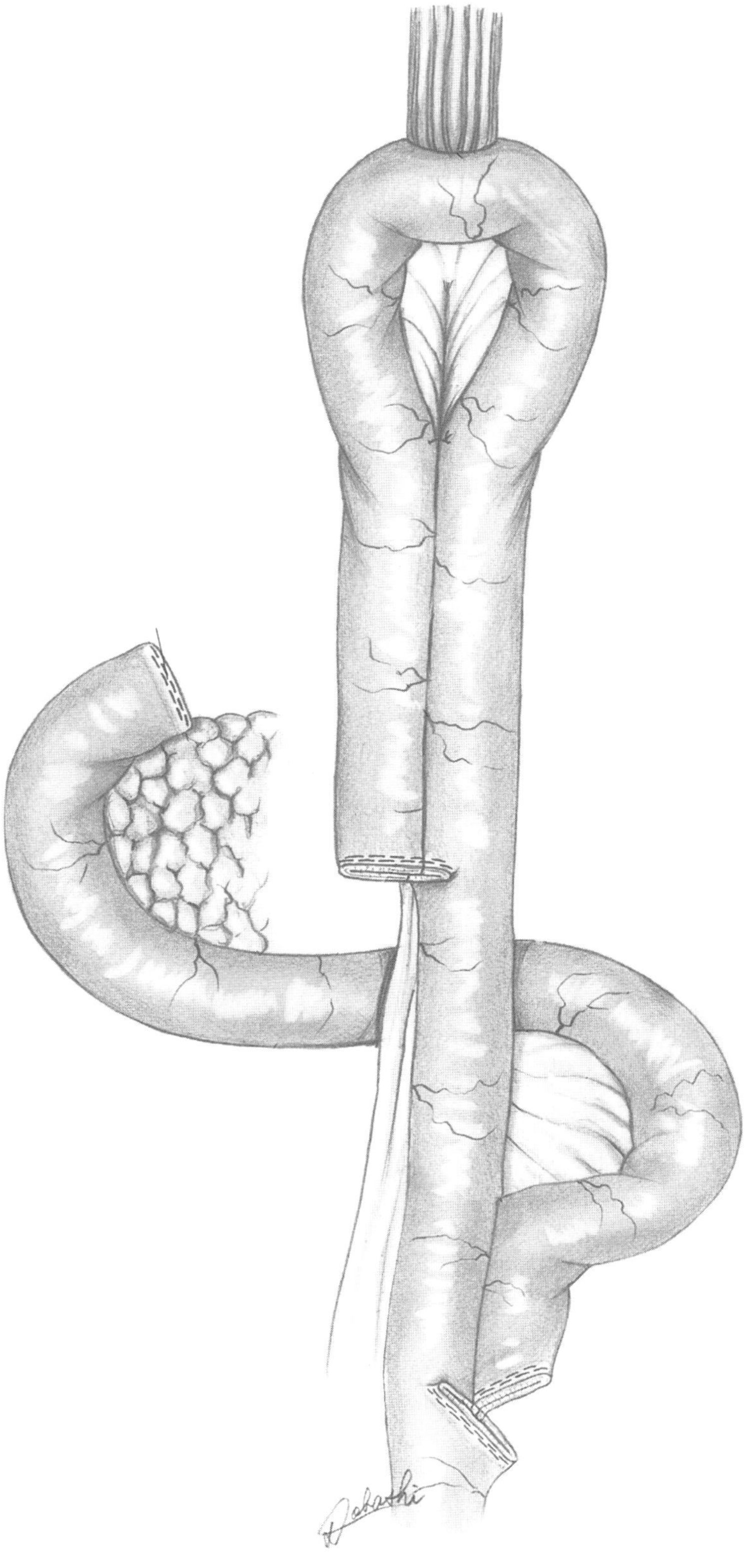

To prevent tension on the anastomosis, a safety suture is placed at the proximal end of the pouch.

Pyloroplasty

According to Heineke-Mikulicz

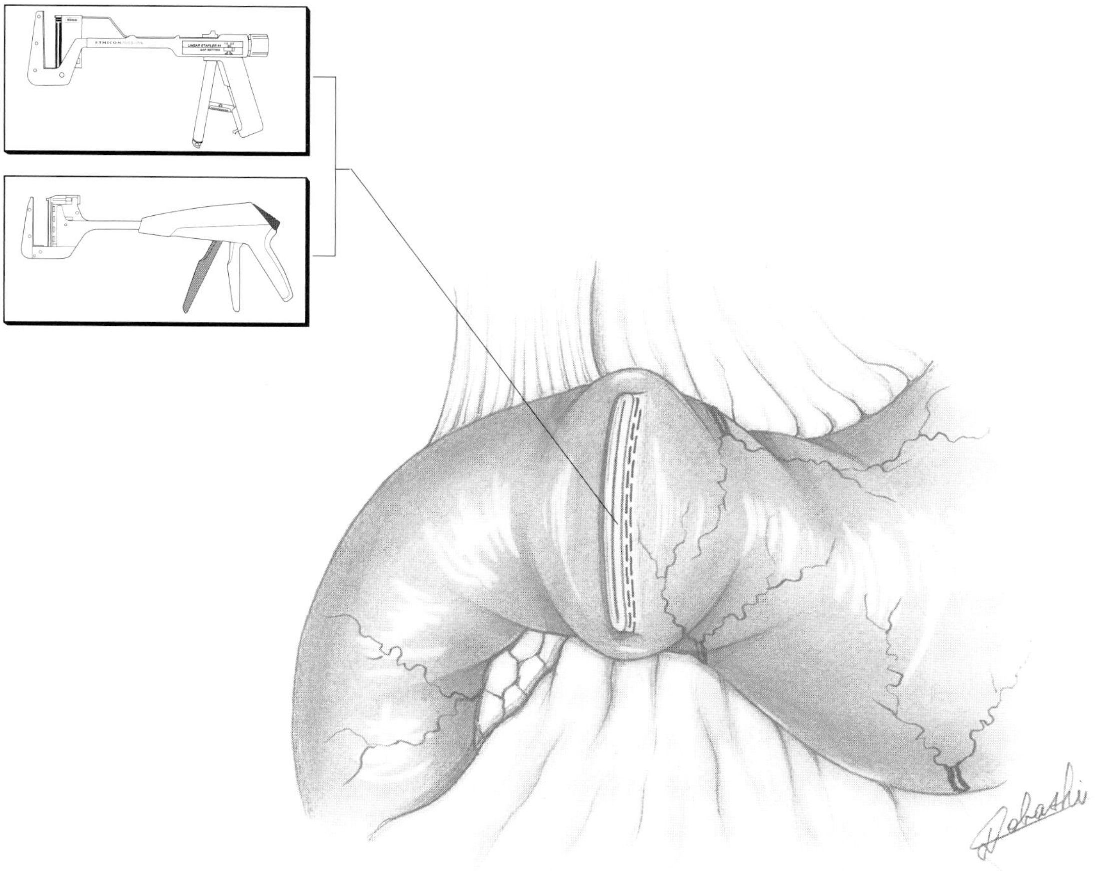

A longitudinal incision is made using a scalpel or Ultracision sharp hook in the anterior aspect of the duodenum in the pyloric and anteropyloric area.

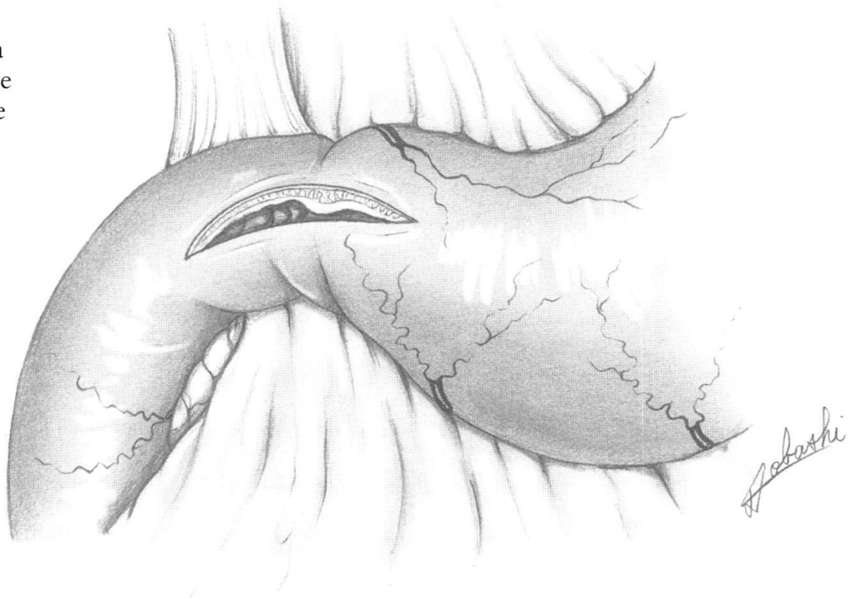

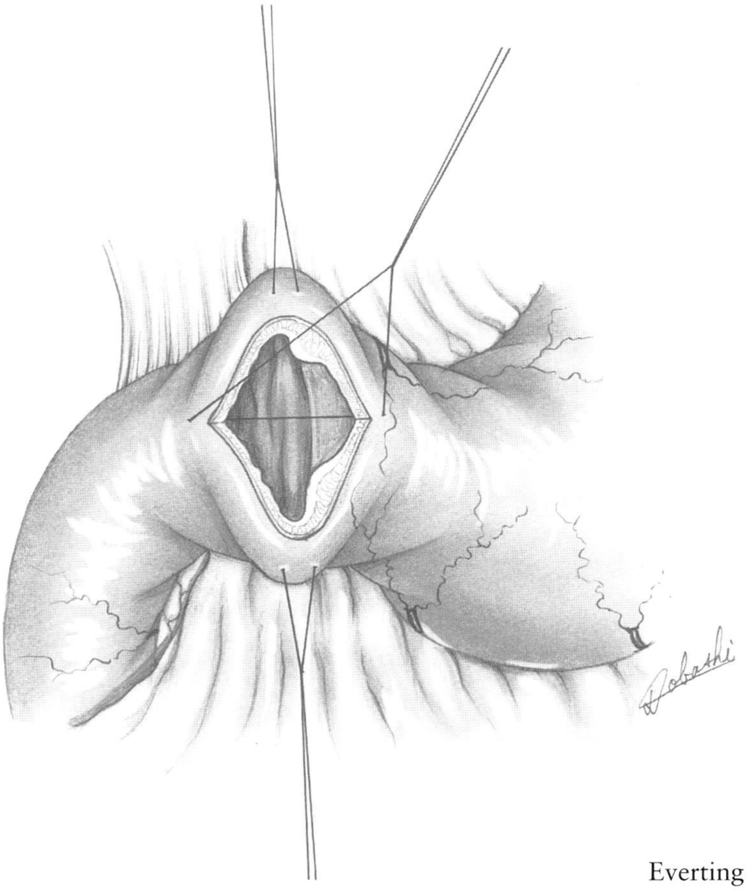

Everting stay sutures are put in place in order to adapt the wound edges perpendicularly.

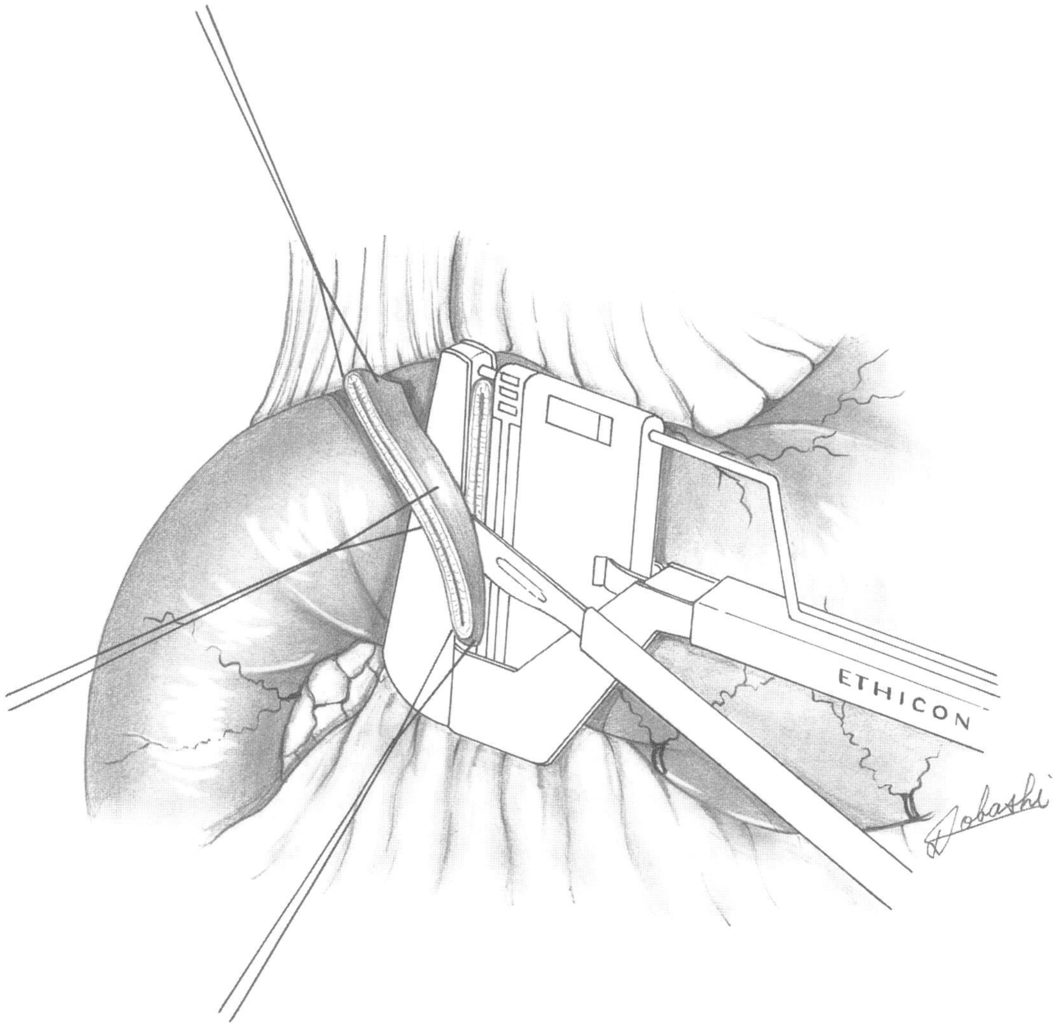

Closure of the incision and resection of the overlapping tissue using the linear stapler standard, subsequently examining the staple line for haemostasis and proper closure.

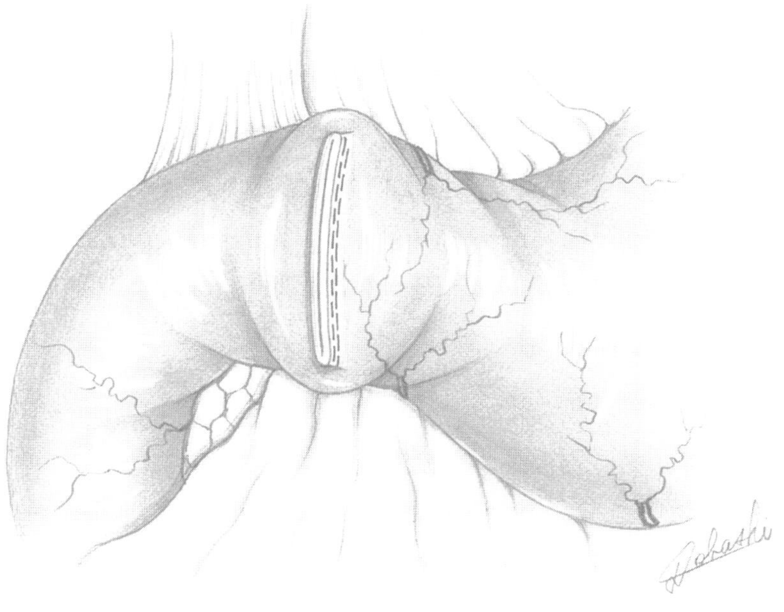

End result.

Pyloroplasty

According to Jaboulay I

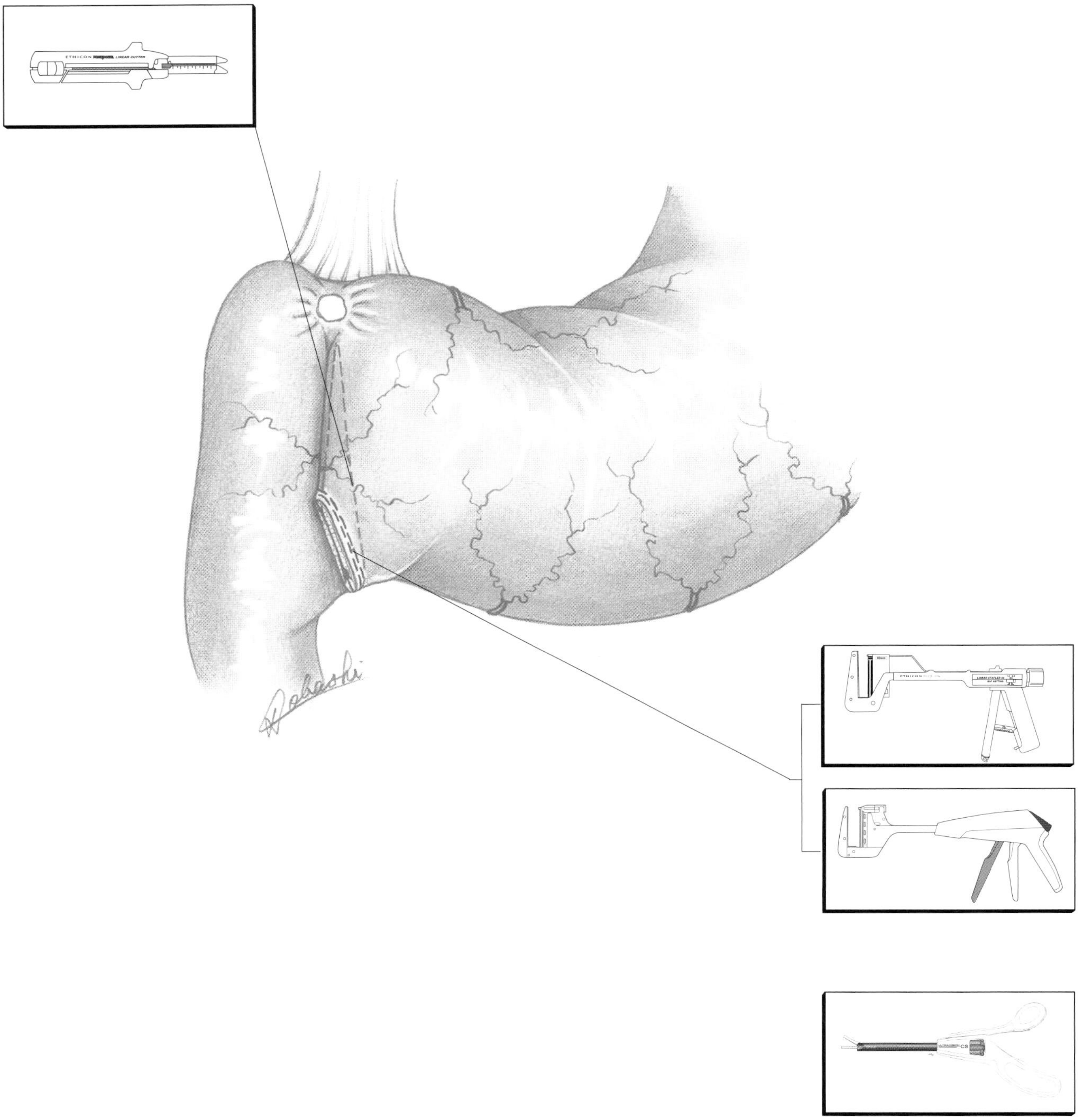

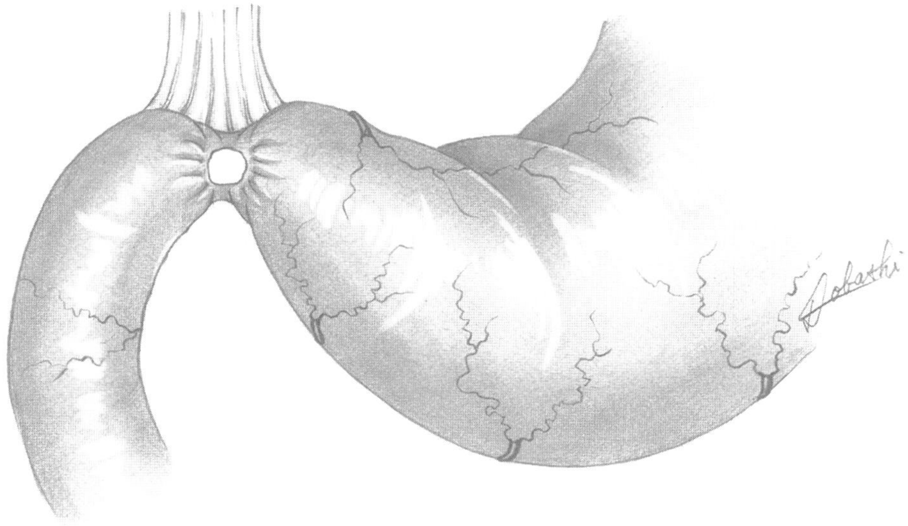

Mobilisation of the duodenum (according to Kocher) using the Ultracision sharp hook or coagulating shears.

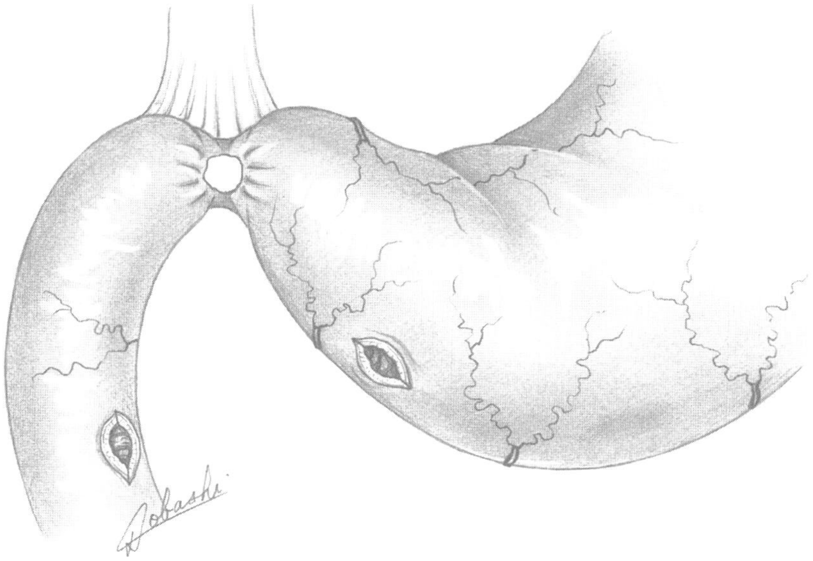

Also with the Ultracision sharp hook, the antrum is incised at the level of the greater curvature, approx. 5 cm proximally to the pylorus and in the duodenum approx. 5 cm distally to the pylorus.

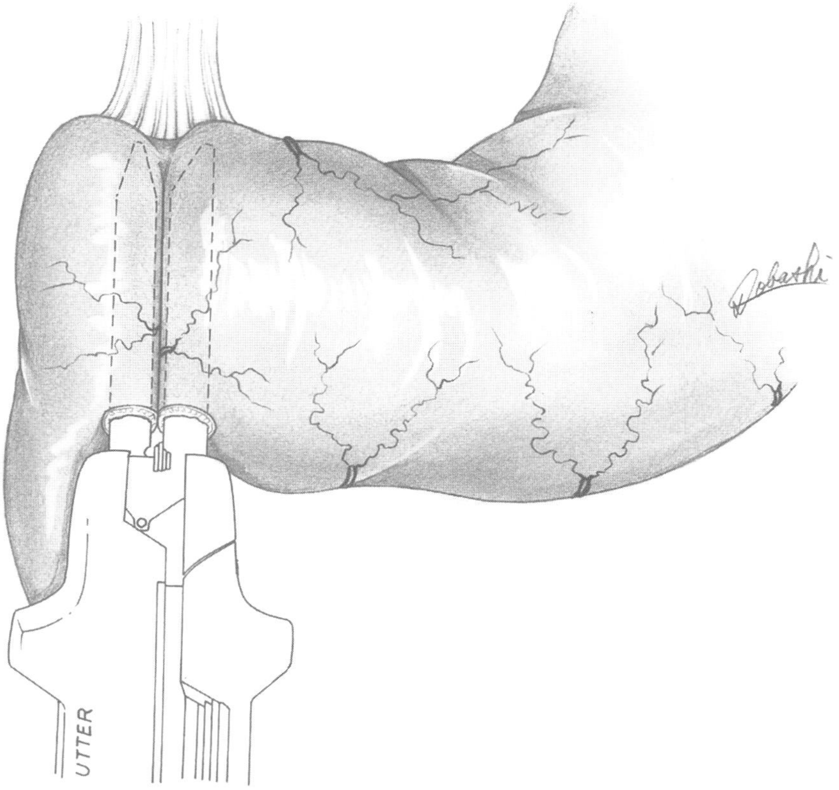

Having inserted the jaws of the linear cutter in the otomies, close and fire the instrument, creating the gastroduodenostomy, and then examine the staple line for haemostasis and proper staple closure.

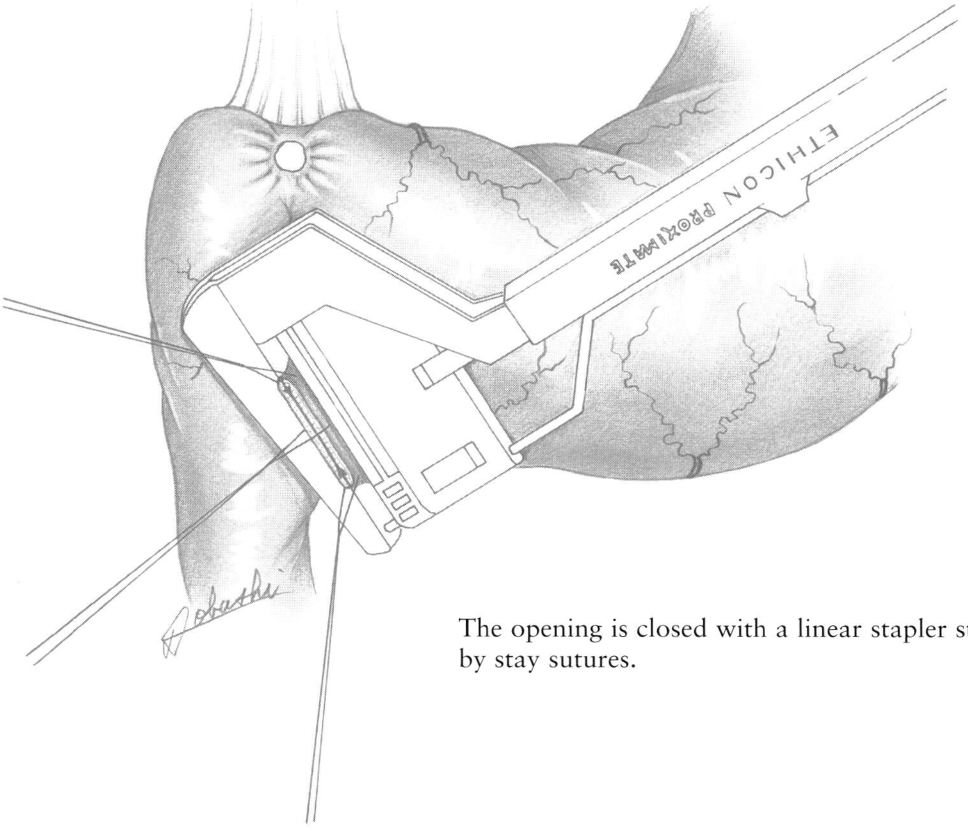

The opening is closed with a linear stapler standard aided by stay sutures.

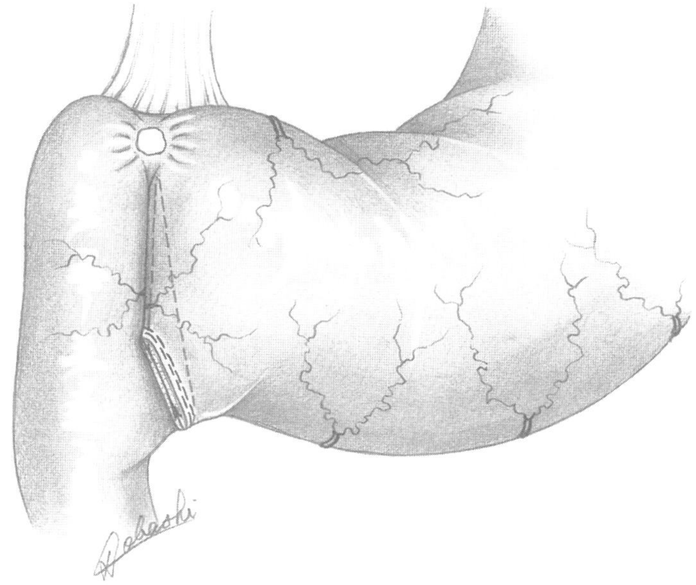

End result.

Pyloroplasty

According to Jaboulay II

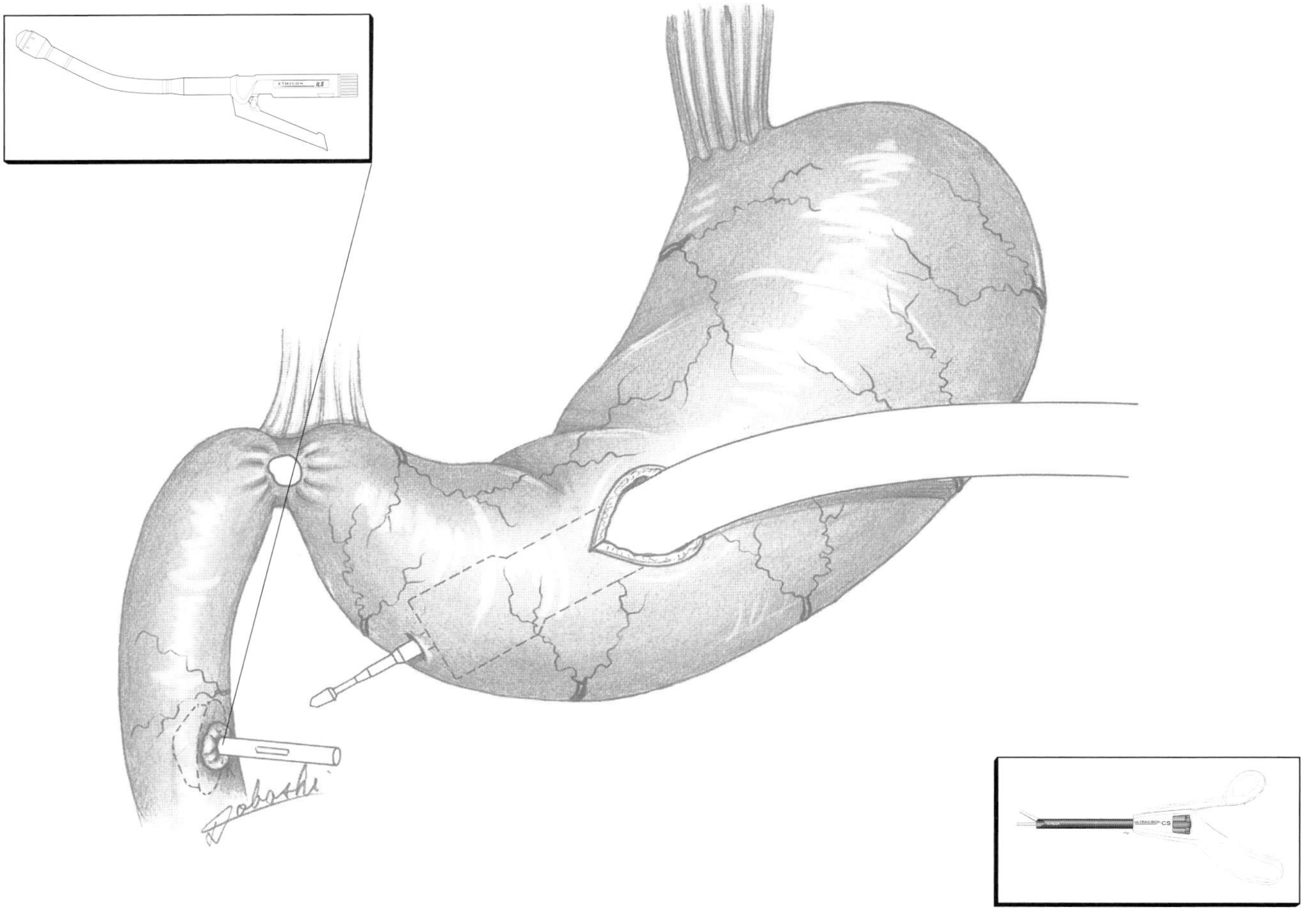

Mobilisation of the duodenum (according to Kocher) using the Ultracision coagulating shears. An enterotomy is performed with Ultracision, 5 cm distally to the pylorus. This incision has to be large enough to allow the insertion of the anvil of a circular stapler. A purse-string is created and the anvil of the circular stapler is inserted.

A gastrotomy is created in the gastric wall using the Ultracision instrument. A circular stapler is inserted into the gastrotomy and the gastric wall is pierced at the greater curvature approx. 5 cm from the pylorus.

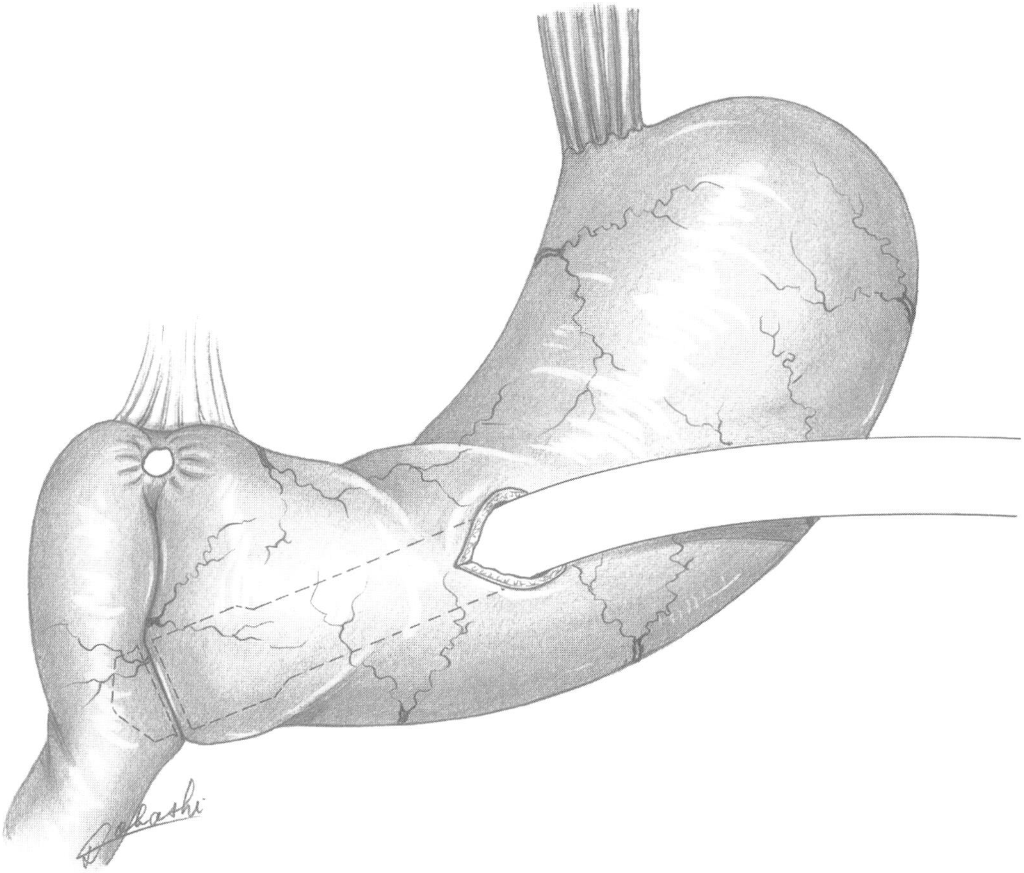

The instrument is assembled, closed, and fired, creating a side-to-side gastroduodenostomy. The remaining gastrotomy will be closed using a linear stapler thick or hand suturing.

4 Pancreatic Surgery

Proximal Pancreaticoduodenectomy and Subtotal Gastrectomy

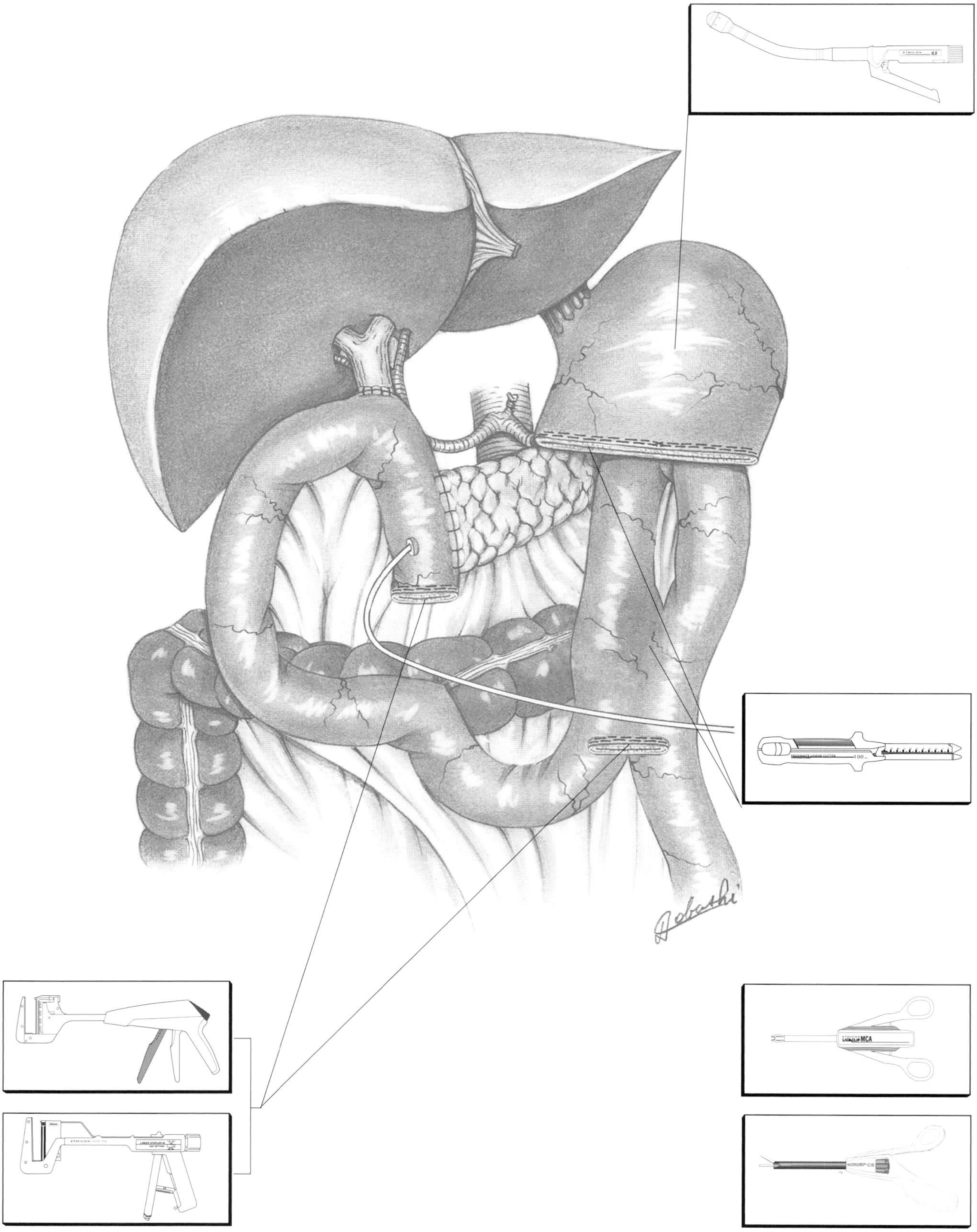

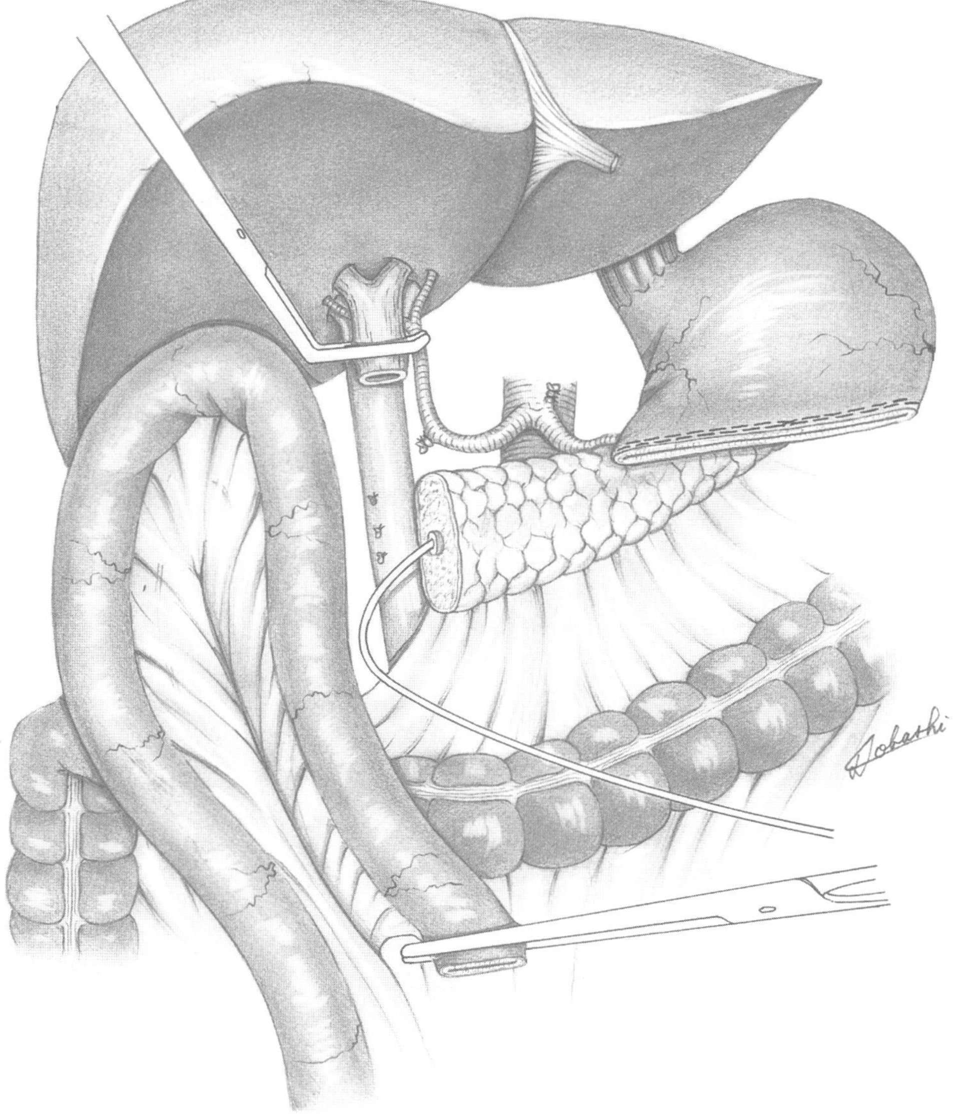

The procedure aims to resect the duodenum and the head of the pancreas.
The first step is the mobilisation of the duodenum and the head of the pancreas with the help of multiple clip appliers or Ultracision, to separate the segment to be resected. A cholecystectomy and a subtotal gastrectomy are then performed following the routine techniques. The gastric resection helps in visualising the pancreatic site to be resected. The head of the pancreas is resected anterior to the portal vein using a linear stapler. A drain may be placed on the pancreas in the Wirsung canal.

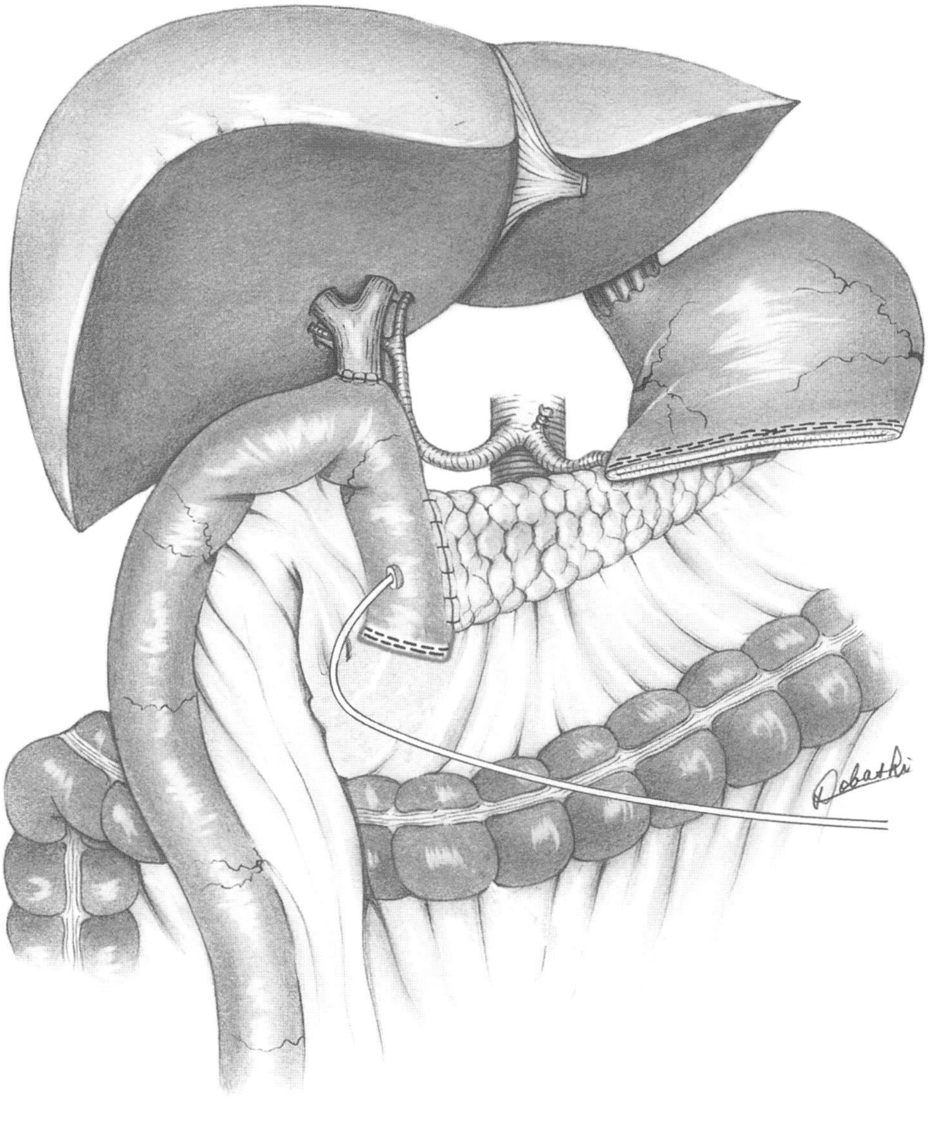

The common bile duct and the remaining pancreas are anastomosed to the proximal end of the jejunum with hand sutures. The opening of the jejunum is closed with a linear stapler standard, and the pancreatic catheter is passed through the jejunum wall.

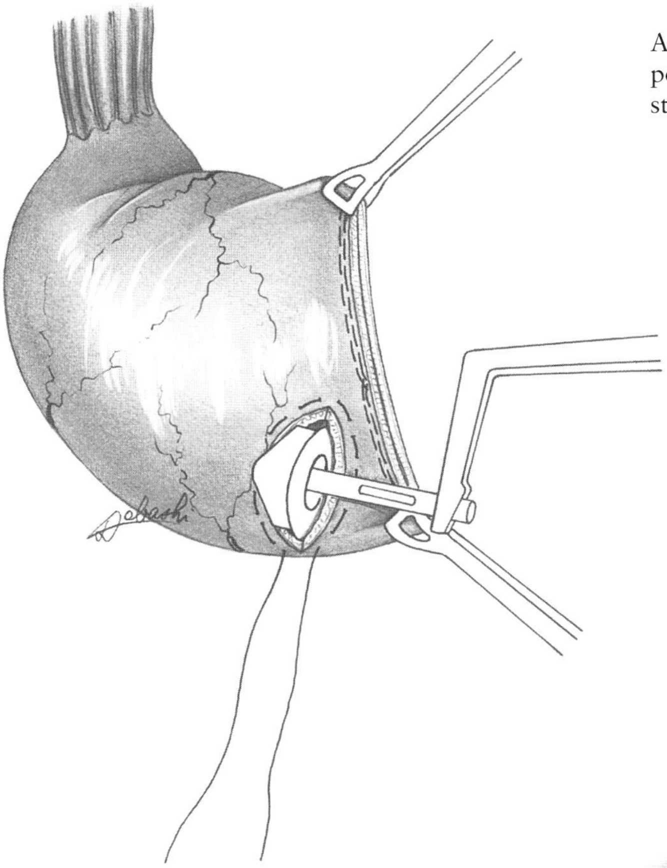

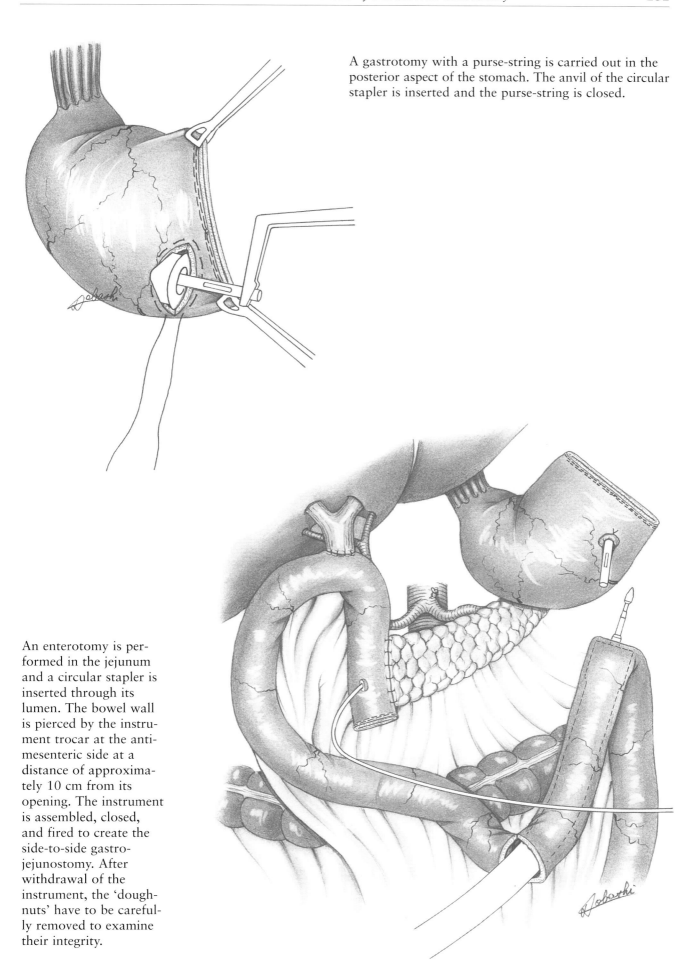

A gastrotomy with a purse-string is carried out in the posterior aspect of the stomach. The anvil of the circular stapler is inserted and the purse-string is closed.

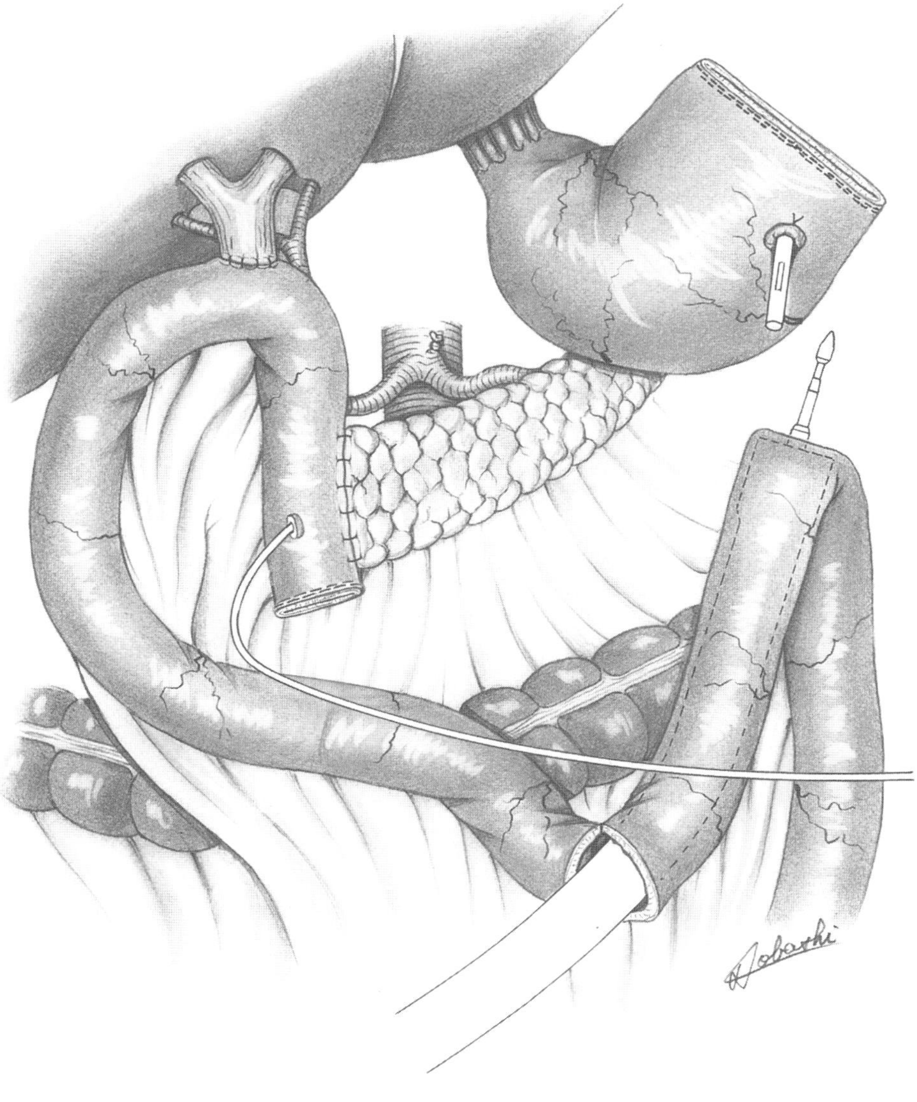

An enterotomy is performed in the jejunum and a circular stapler is inserted through its lumen. The bowel wall is pierced by the instrument trocar at the antimesenteric side at a distance of approximately 10 cm from its opening. The instrument is assembled, closed, and fired to create the side-to-side gastrojejunostomy. After withdrawal of the instrument, the 'doughnuts' have to be carefully removed to examine their integrity.

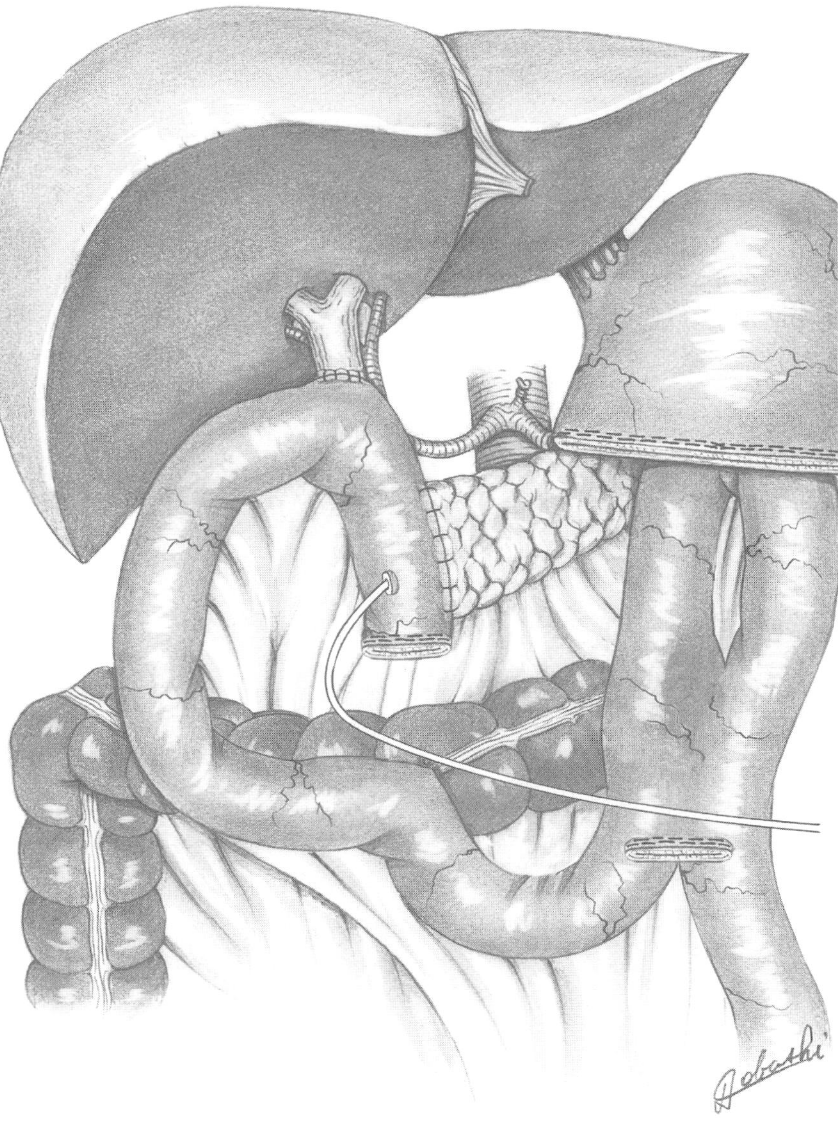

Final result of the procedure after a Braun side-to-side jejunojejostomy is created as described before.

Distal Pancreatectomy with Splenectomy

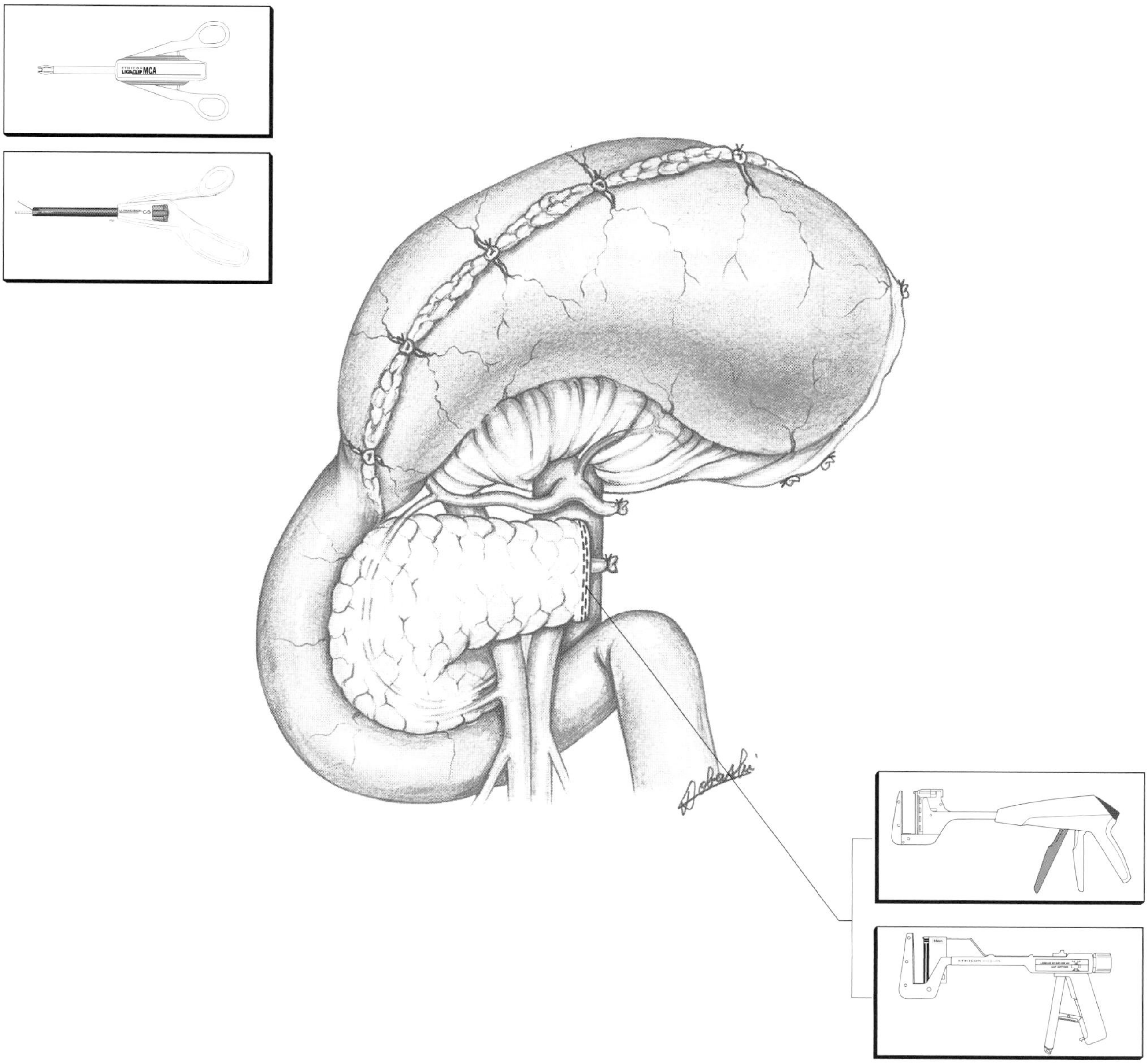

The procedure commences with the mobilisation of the stomach with multiple clip appliers or Ultracision coagulating shears. The spleen is then mobilised using the same instruments and the splenorenal ligament is dissected and both the splenic artery and vein are divided close to the junction with the superior mesenteric vein.

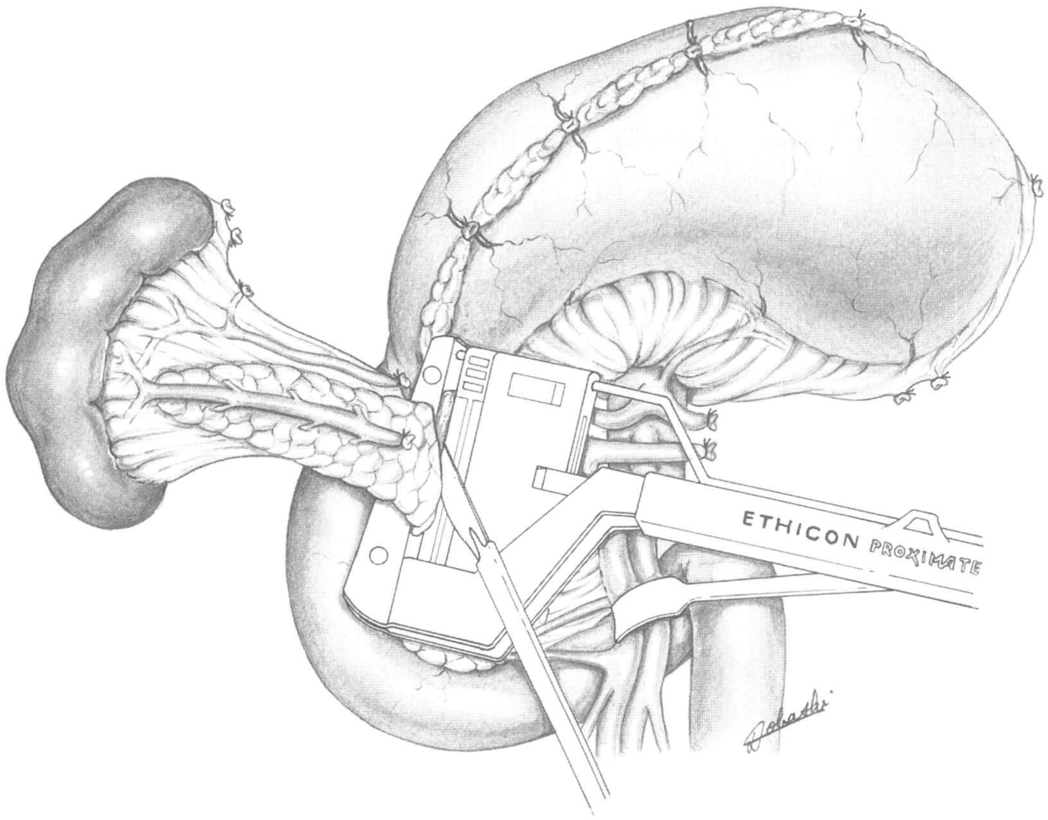

The distal part of the pancreas is resected with a linear stapler and removed along with the spleen.

Pancreaticocystogastrostomy

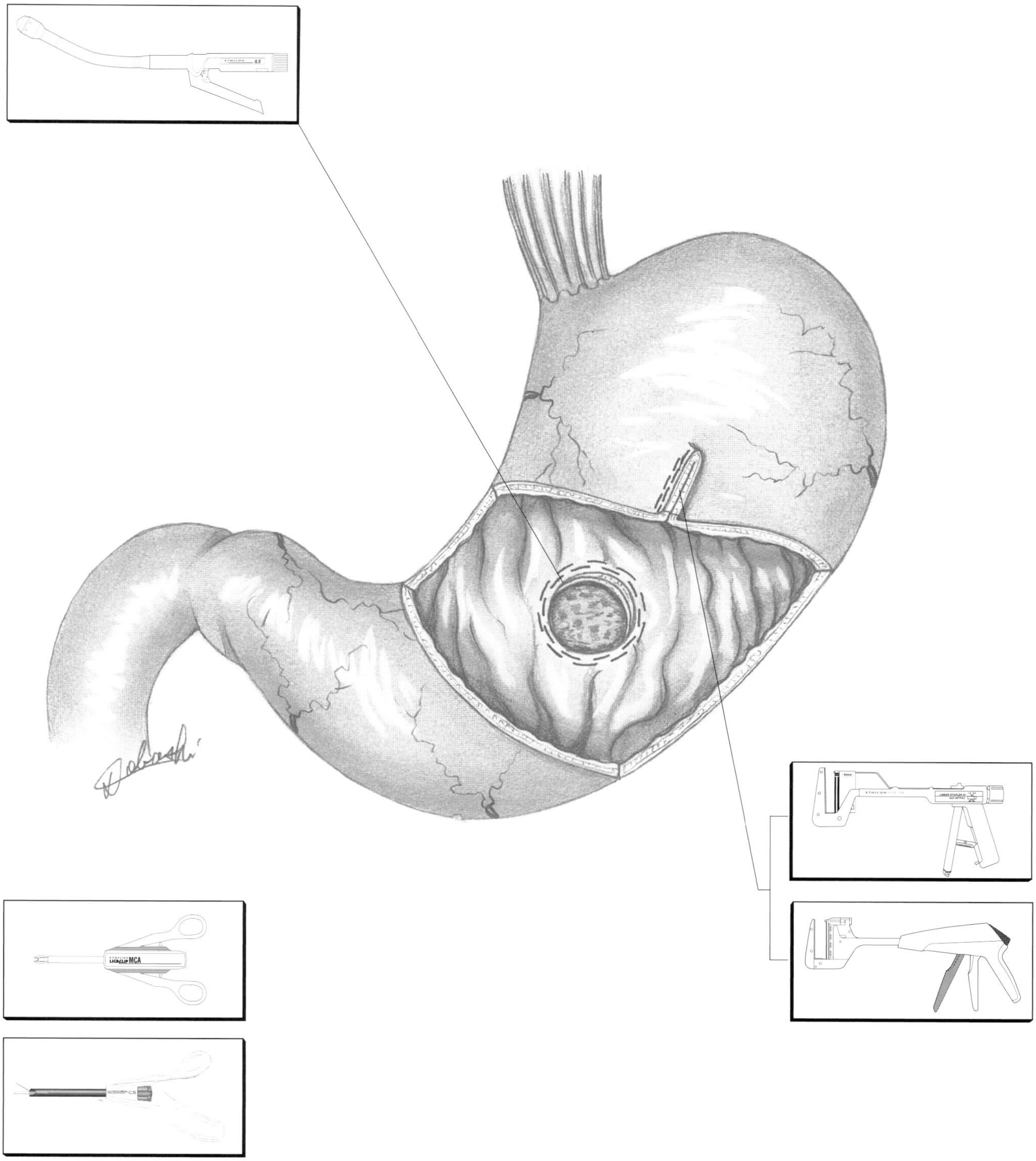

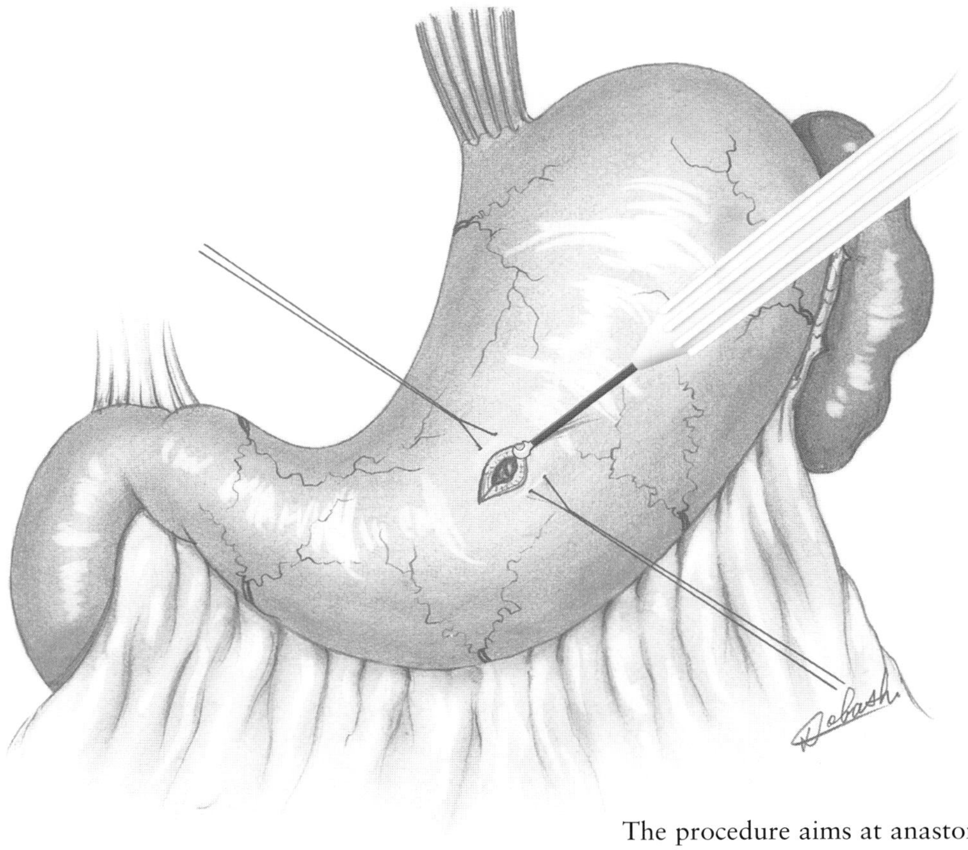

The procedure aims at anastomosis of the pancreatic cyst between the pancreas and the stomach. A gastrostomy is carried out with a scalpel or the Ultracision sharp hook. Traction sutures are used to keep the stomach open.

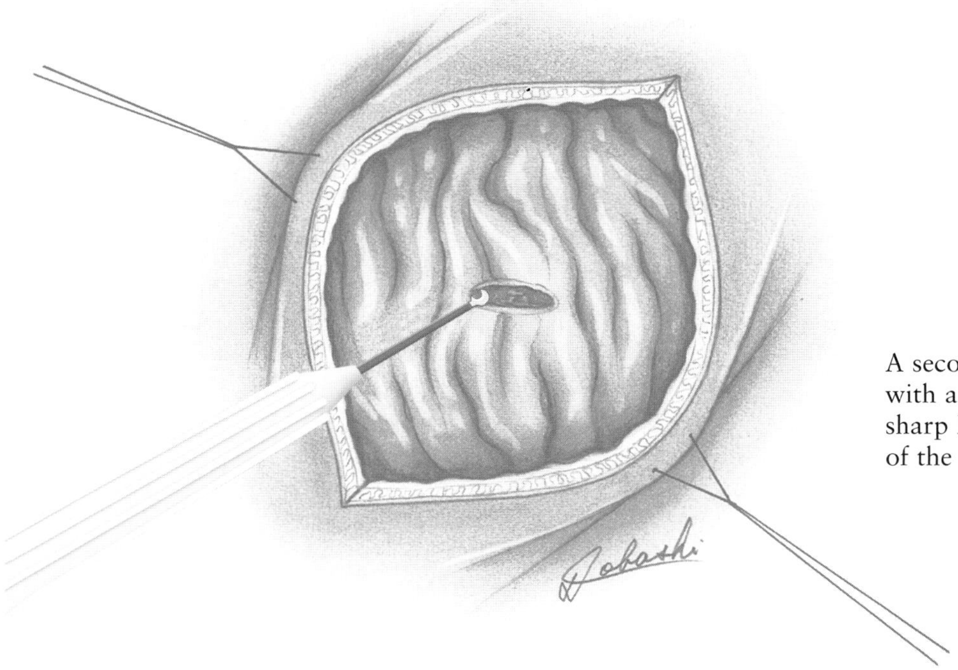

A second gastrotomy is performed with a scalpel or the Ultracision sharp hook on the posterior wall of the stomach.

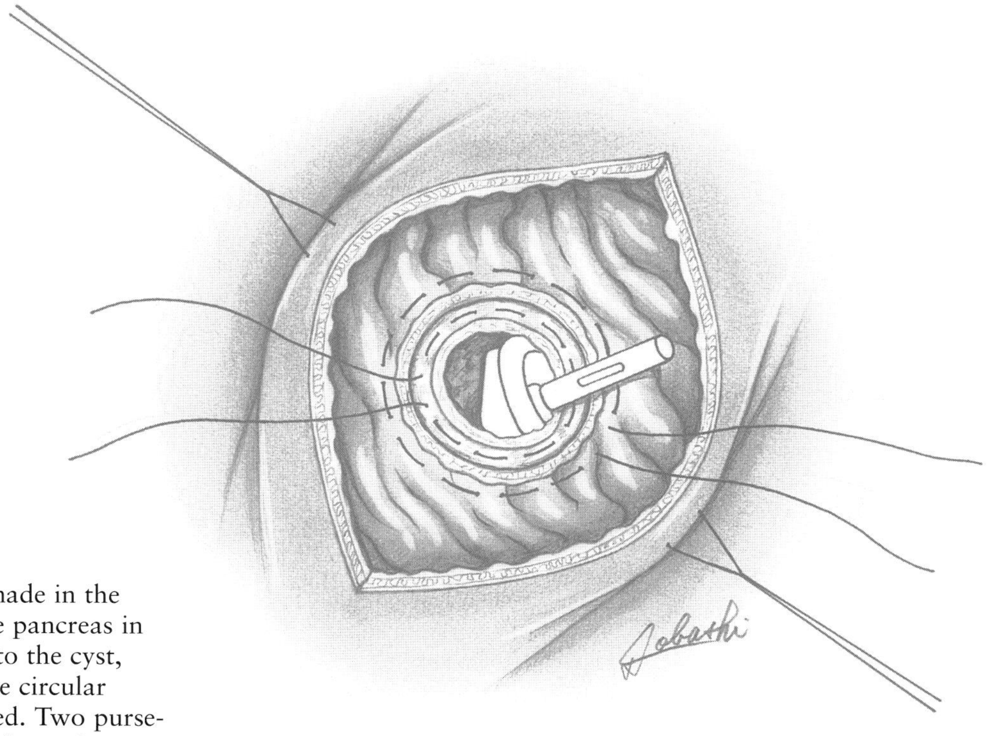

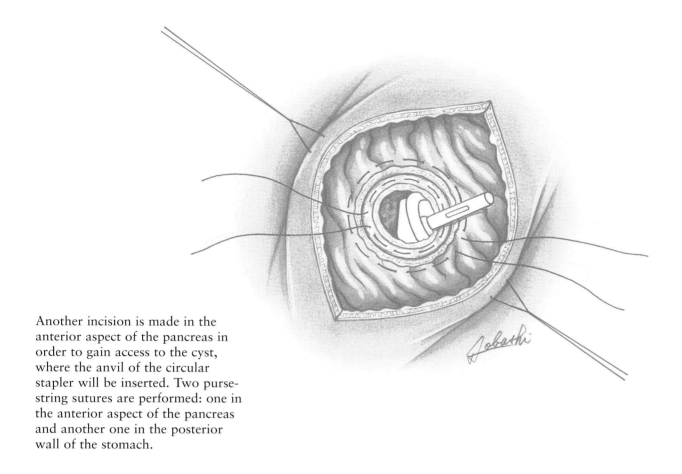

Another incision is made in the anterior aspect of the pancreas in order to gain access to the cyst, where the anvil of the circular stapler will be inserted. Two purse-string sutures are performed: one in the anterior aspect of the pancreas and another one in the posterior wall of the stomach.

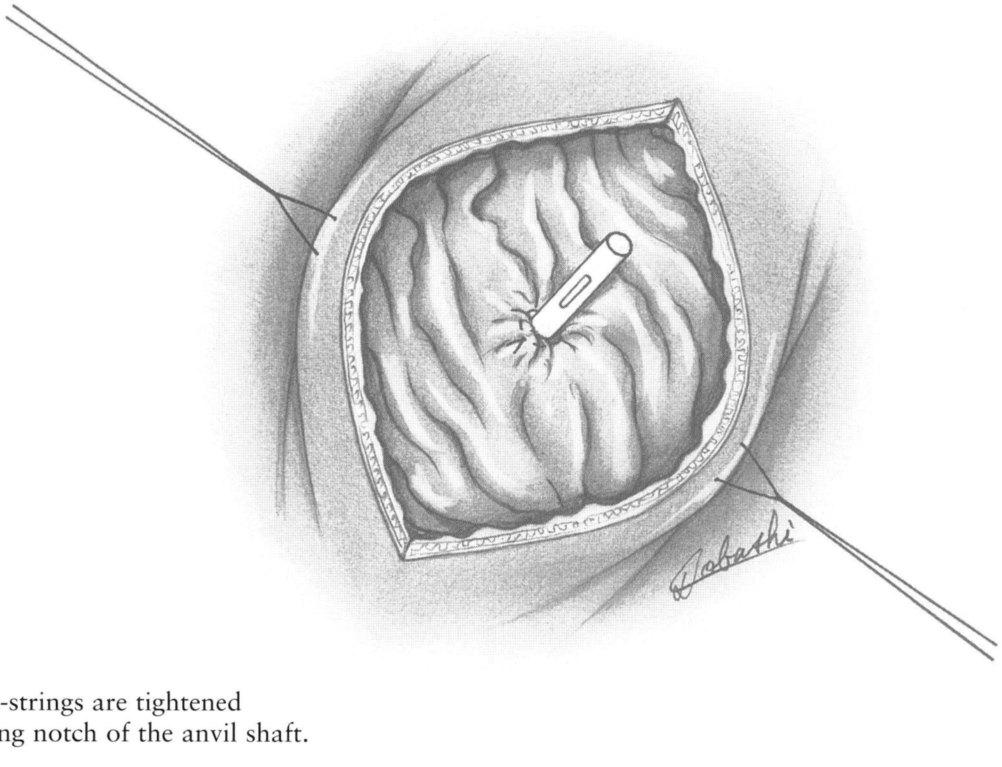

The two purse-strings are tightened around the tying notch of the anvil shaft.

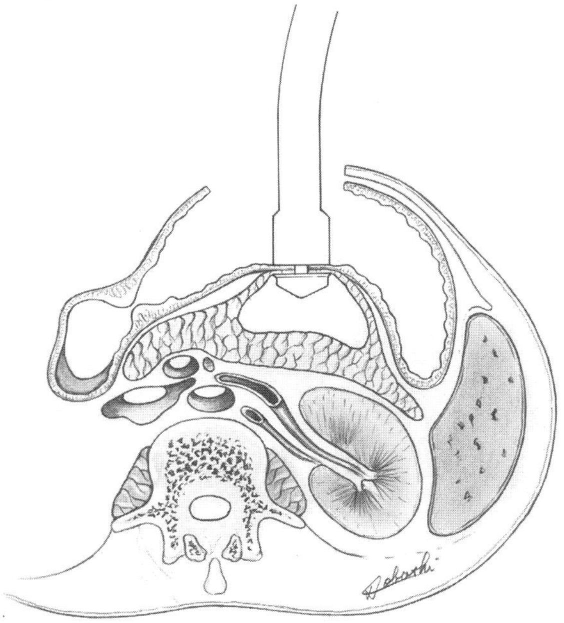

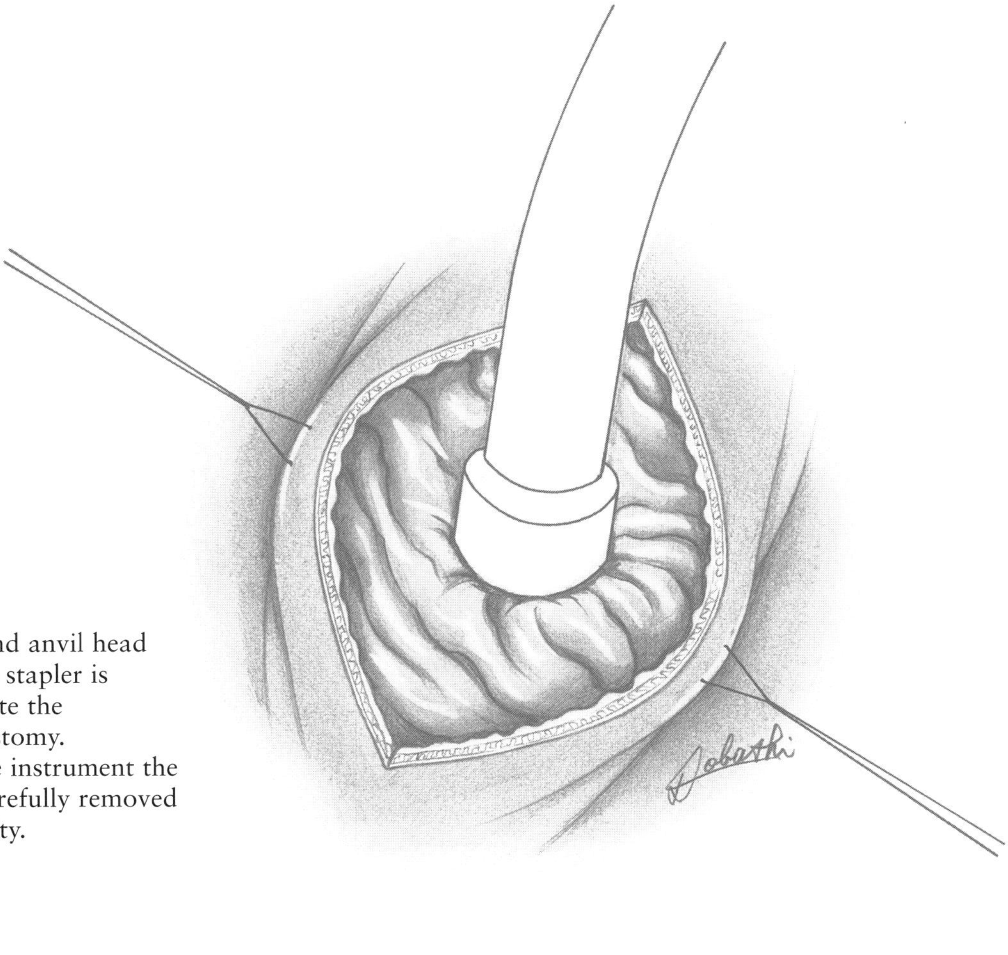

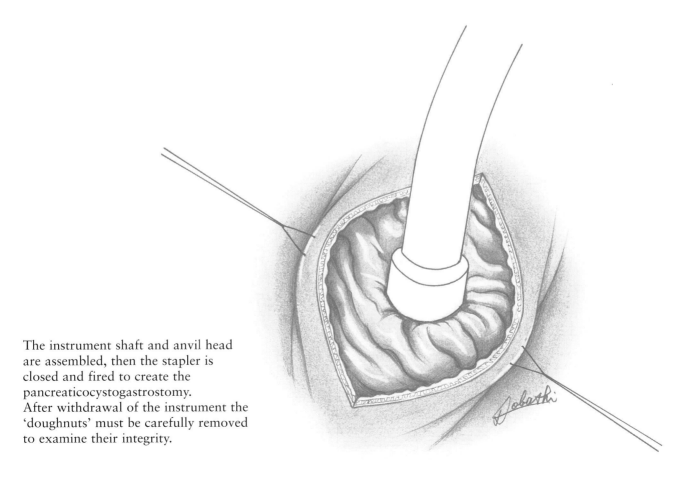

The instrument shaft and anvil head are assembled, then the stapler is closed and fired to create the pancreaticocystogastrostomy.
After withdrawal of the instrument the 'doughnuts' must be carefully removed to examine their integrity.

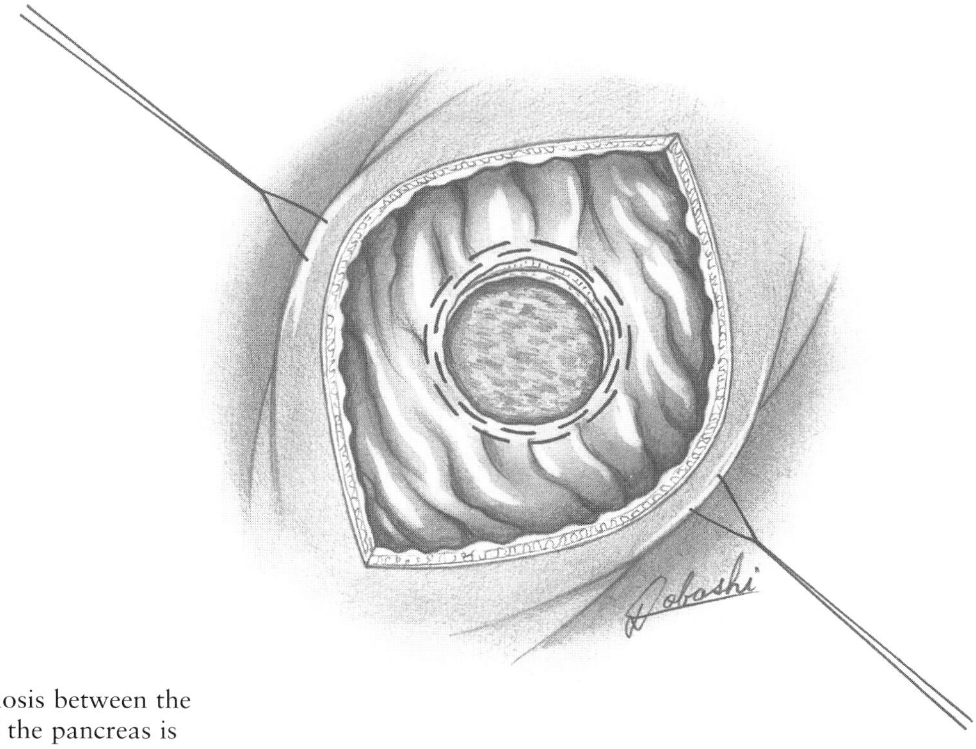

The anastomosis between the stomach and the pancreas is completed. The pancreatic cyst can empty into the stomach.

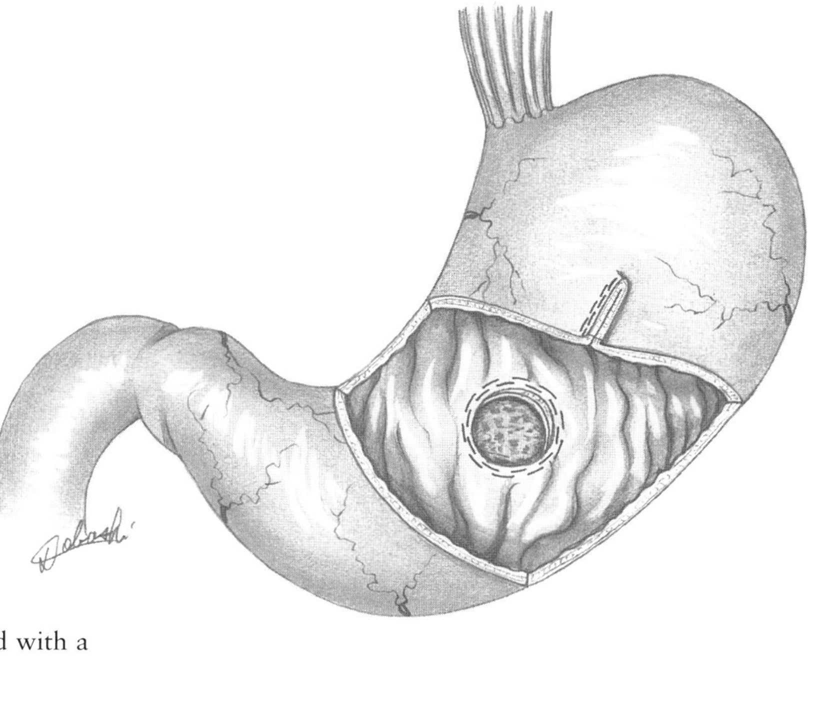

The gastrotomy is closed with a linear stapler thick.

5 Small Bowel Surgery

Partial Resection of Small Bowel with Triangulation Anastomosis

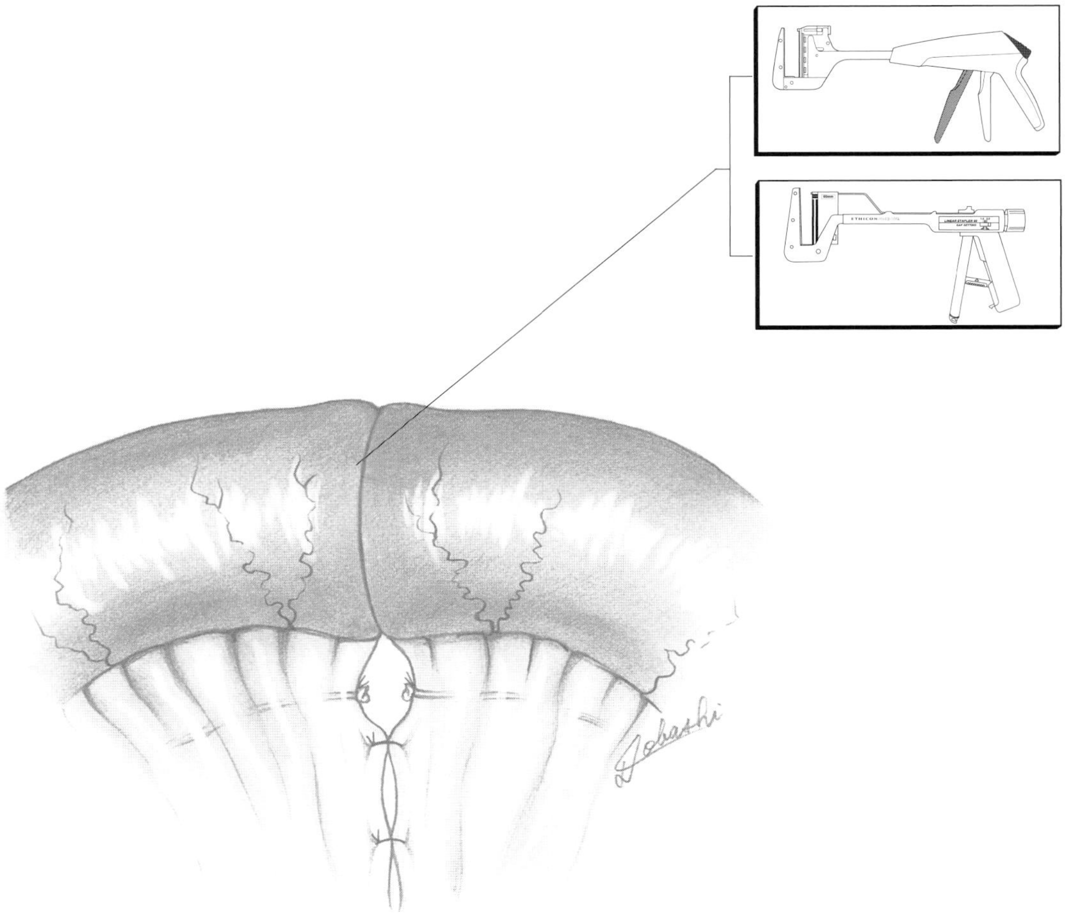

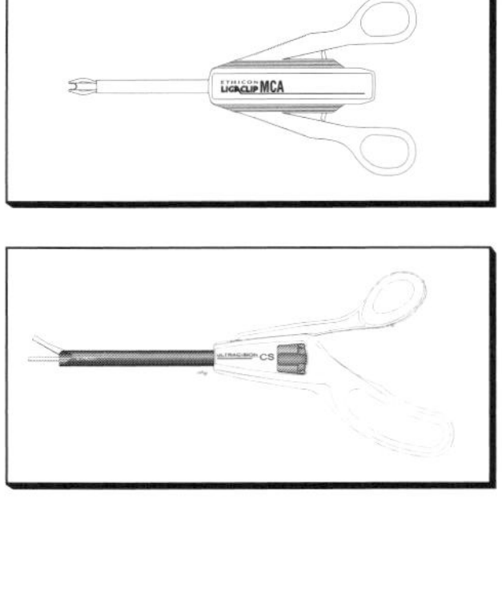

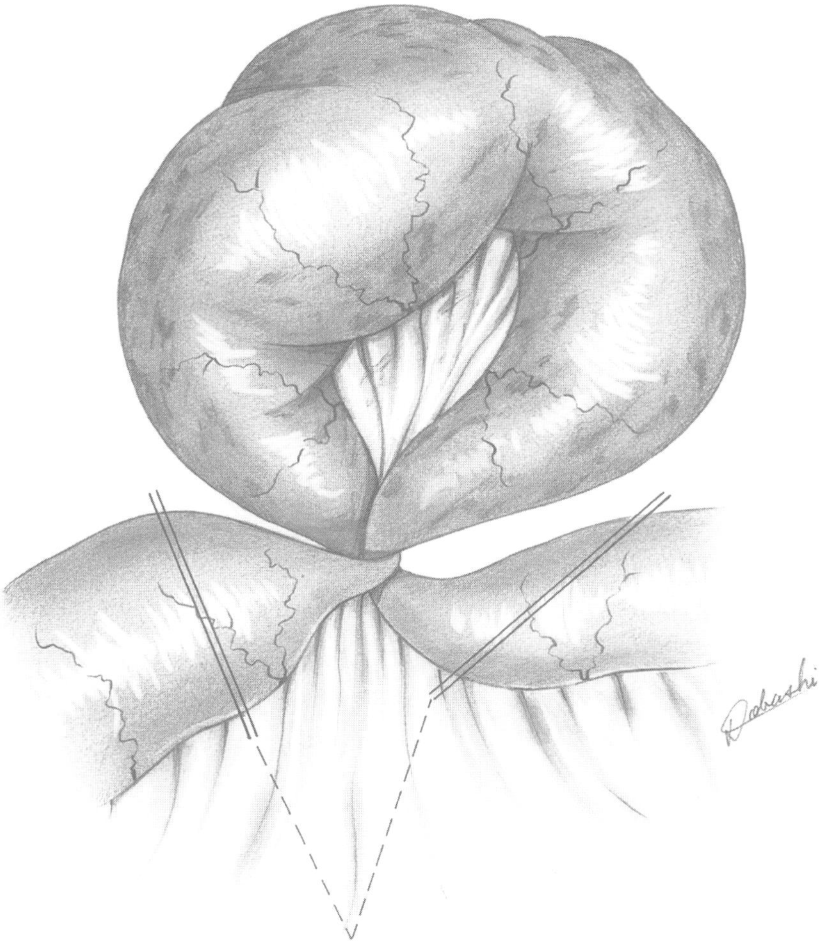

A partial resection of the small bowel can be necessary in the case of an occlusion. The first step is the mobilisation of the segments of the small bowel by using a multiple clip applier or Ultracision coagulating shears.

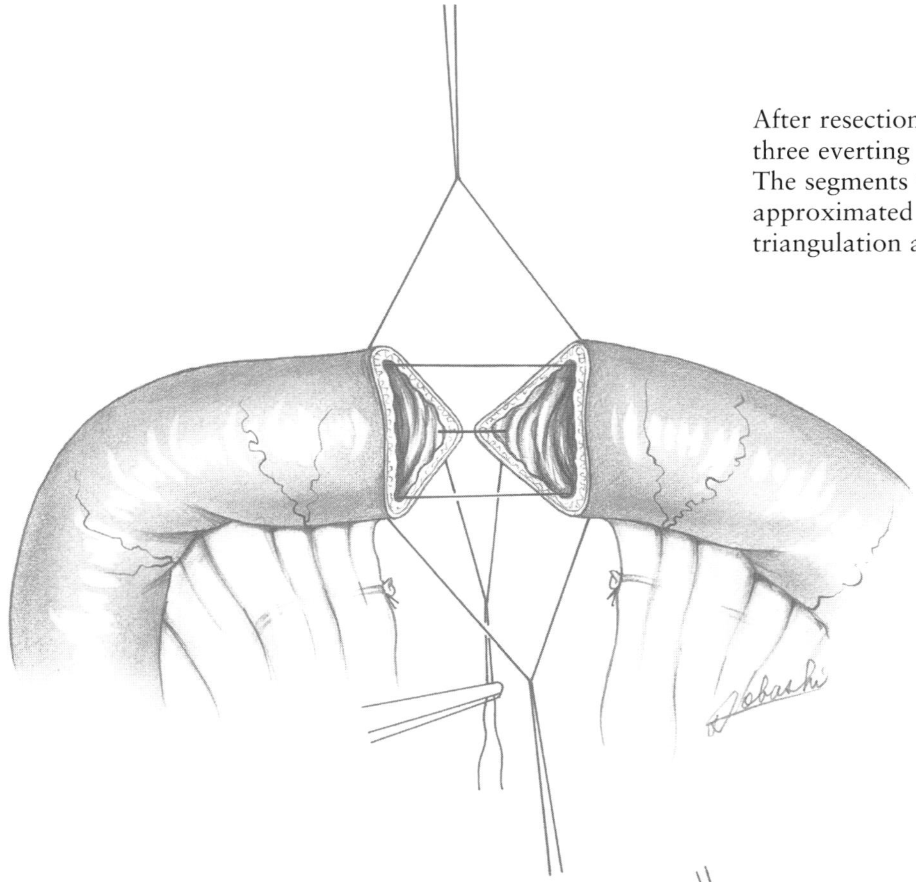

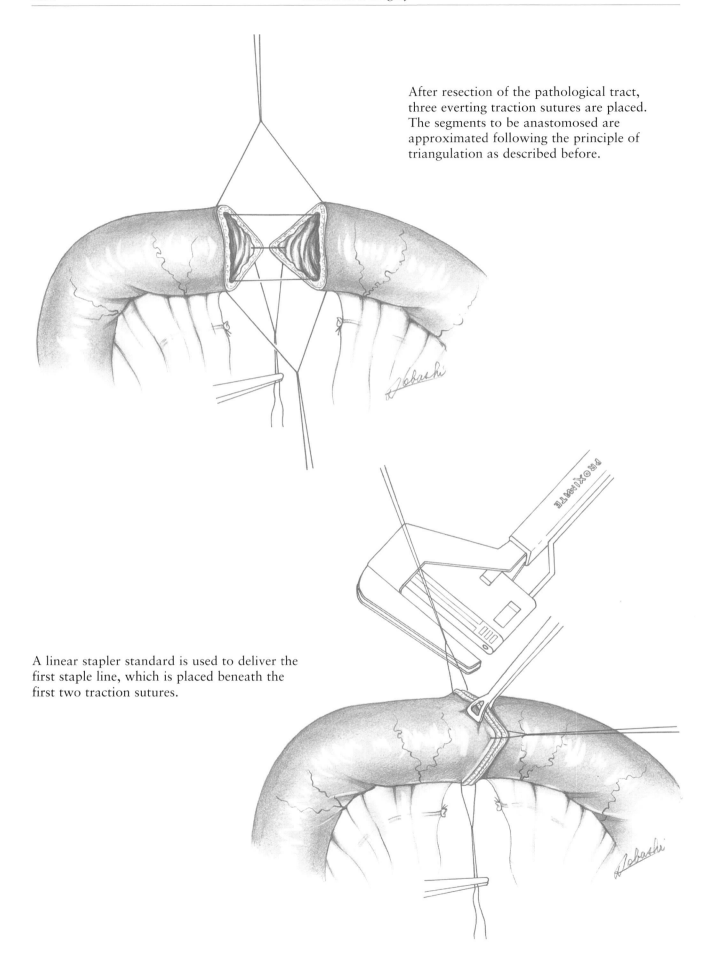

After resection of the pathological tract, three everting traction sutures are placed. The segments to be anastomosed are approximated following the principle of triangulation as described before.

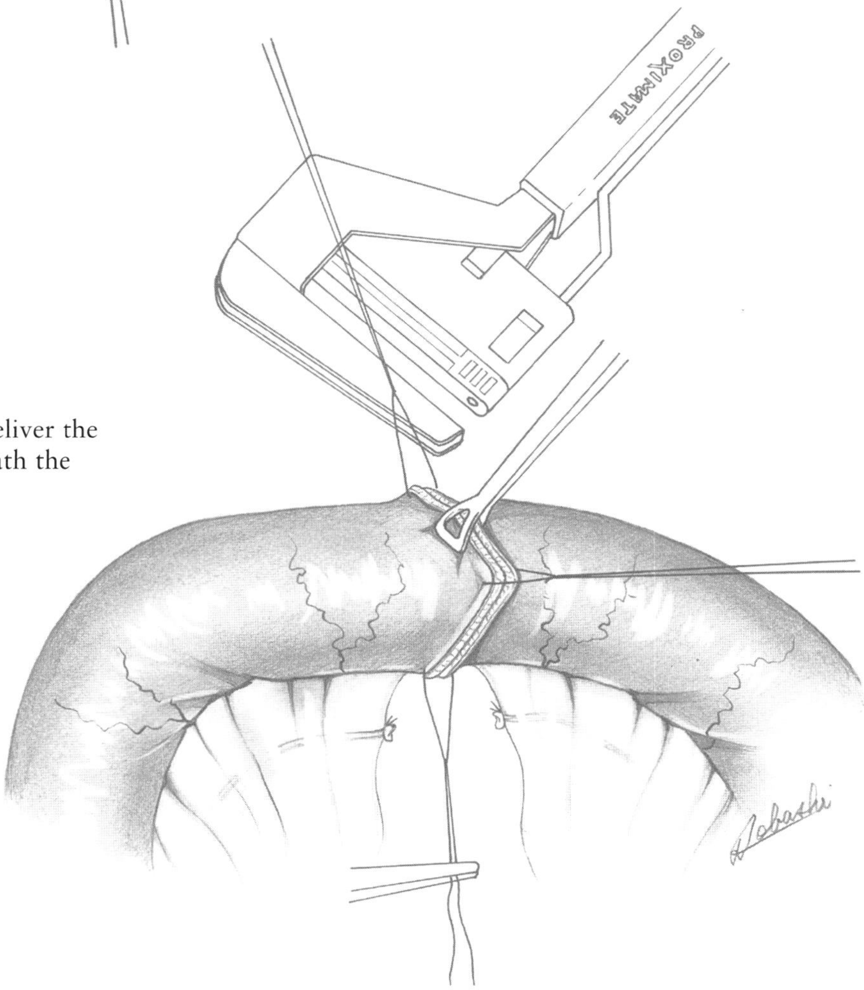

A linear stapler standard is used to deliver the first staple line, which is placed beneath the first two traction sutures.

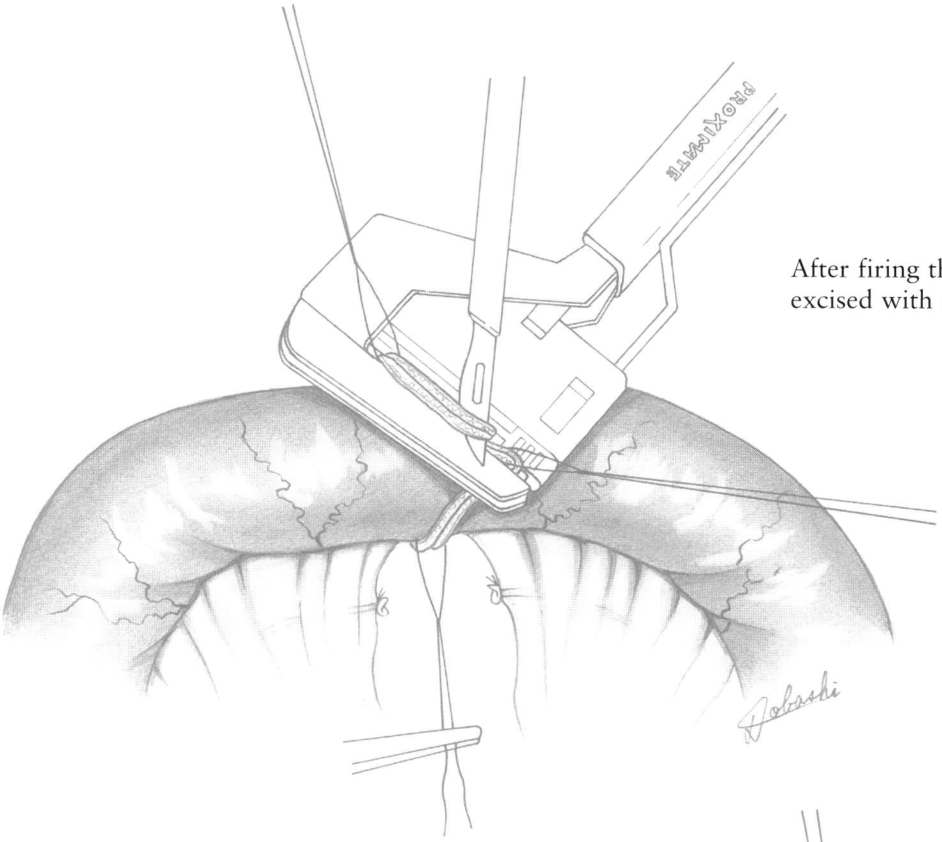

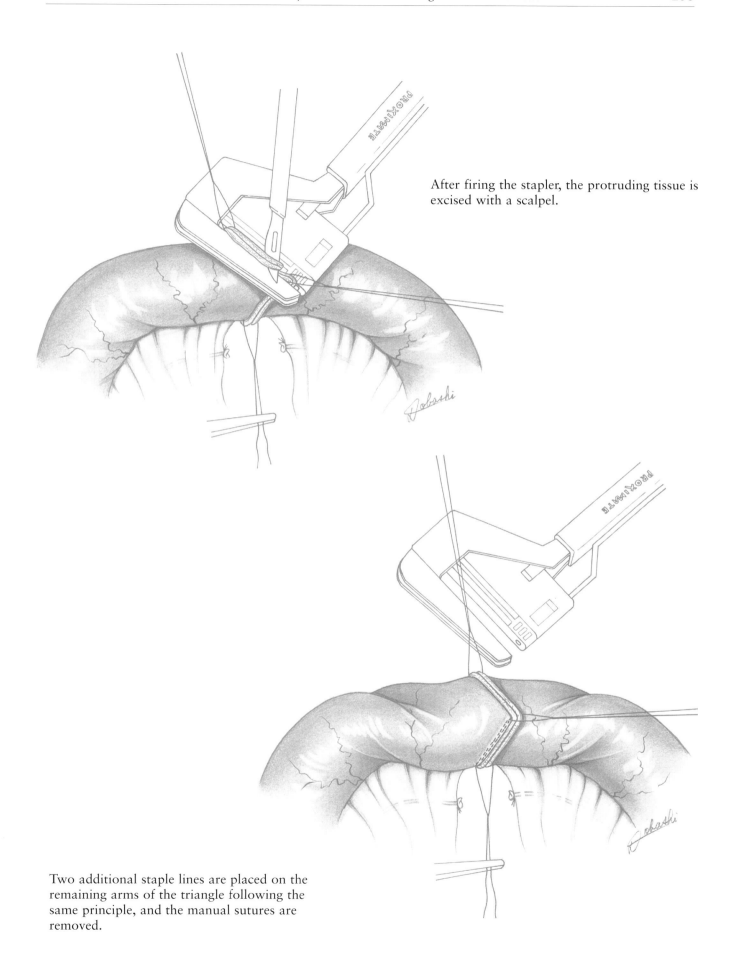

After firing the stapler, the protruding tissue is excised with a scalpel.

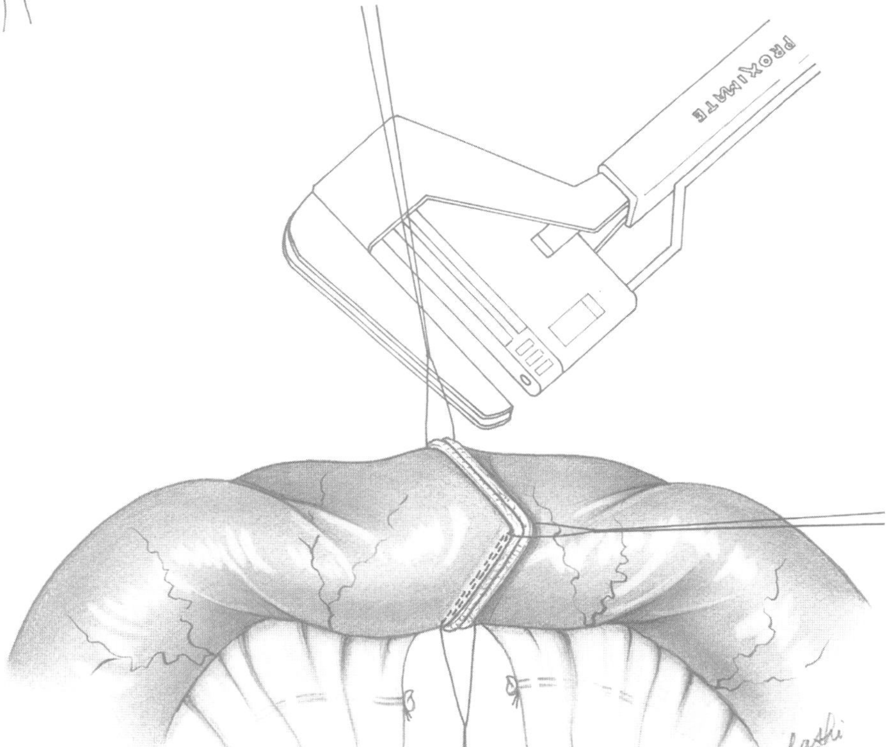

Two additional staple lines are placed on the remaining arms of the triangle following the same principle, and the manual sutures are removed.

Meckel's Diverticulectomy

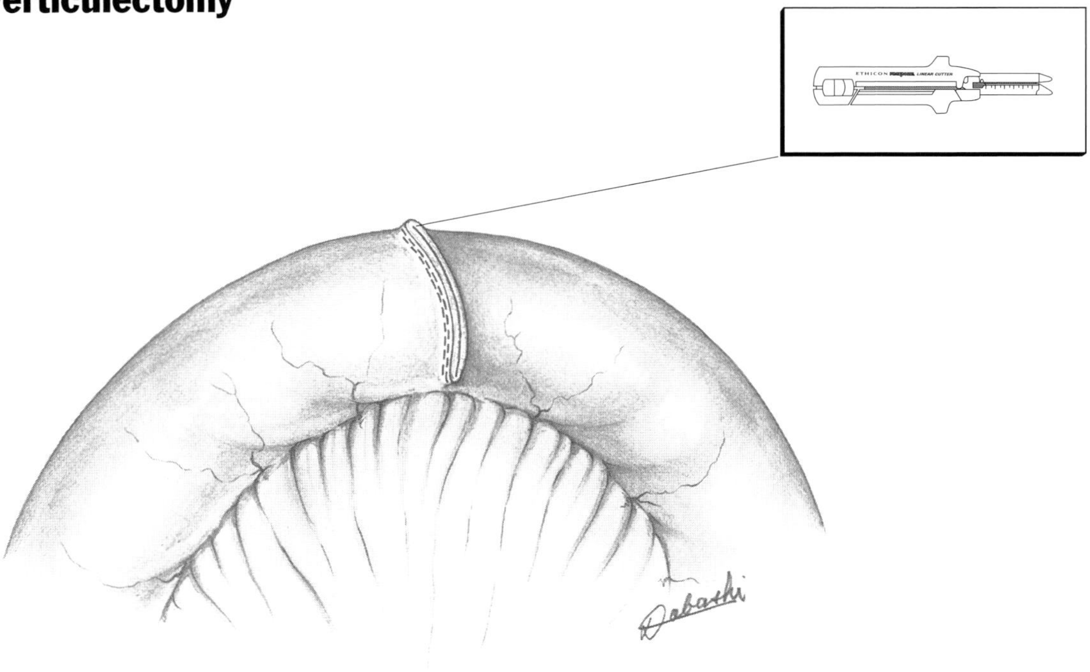

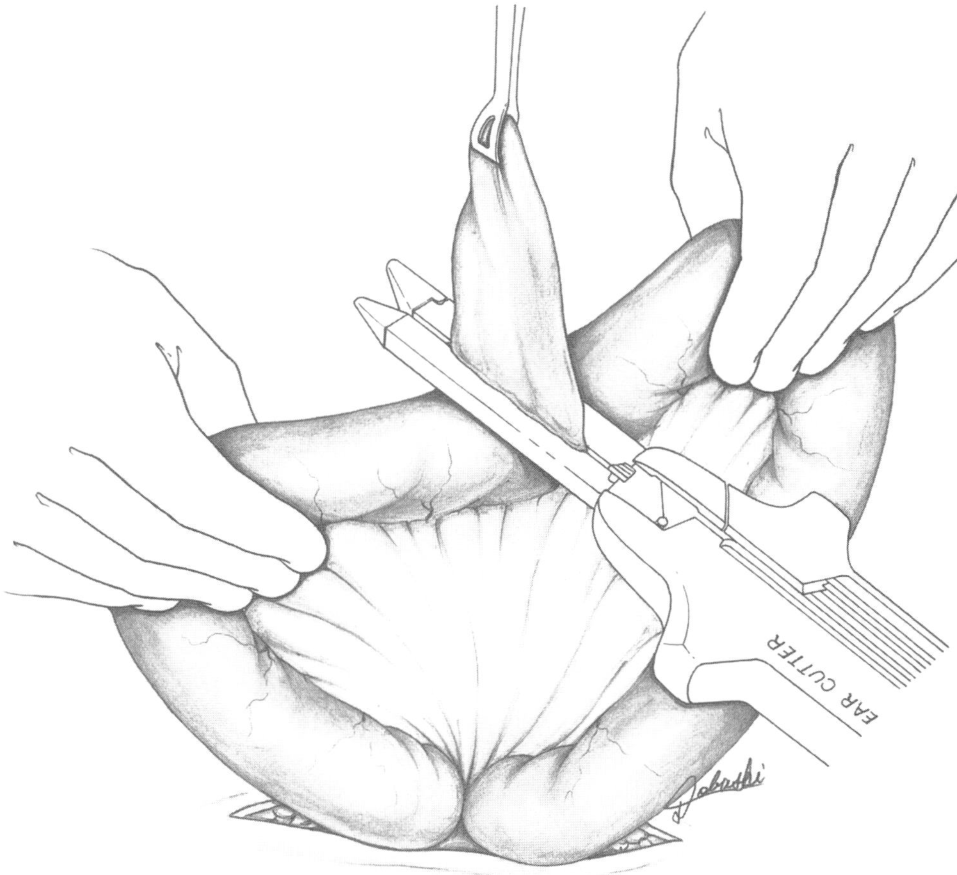

After the diverticulum has been identified a linear cutter standard is used to perform a diverticulectomy. In doing this, care must be taken not to constrict the area, to avoid future stenosis.

6 Large Bowel Surgery

Appendectomy

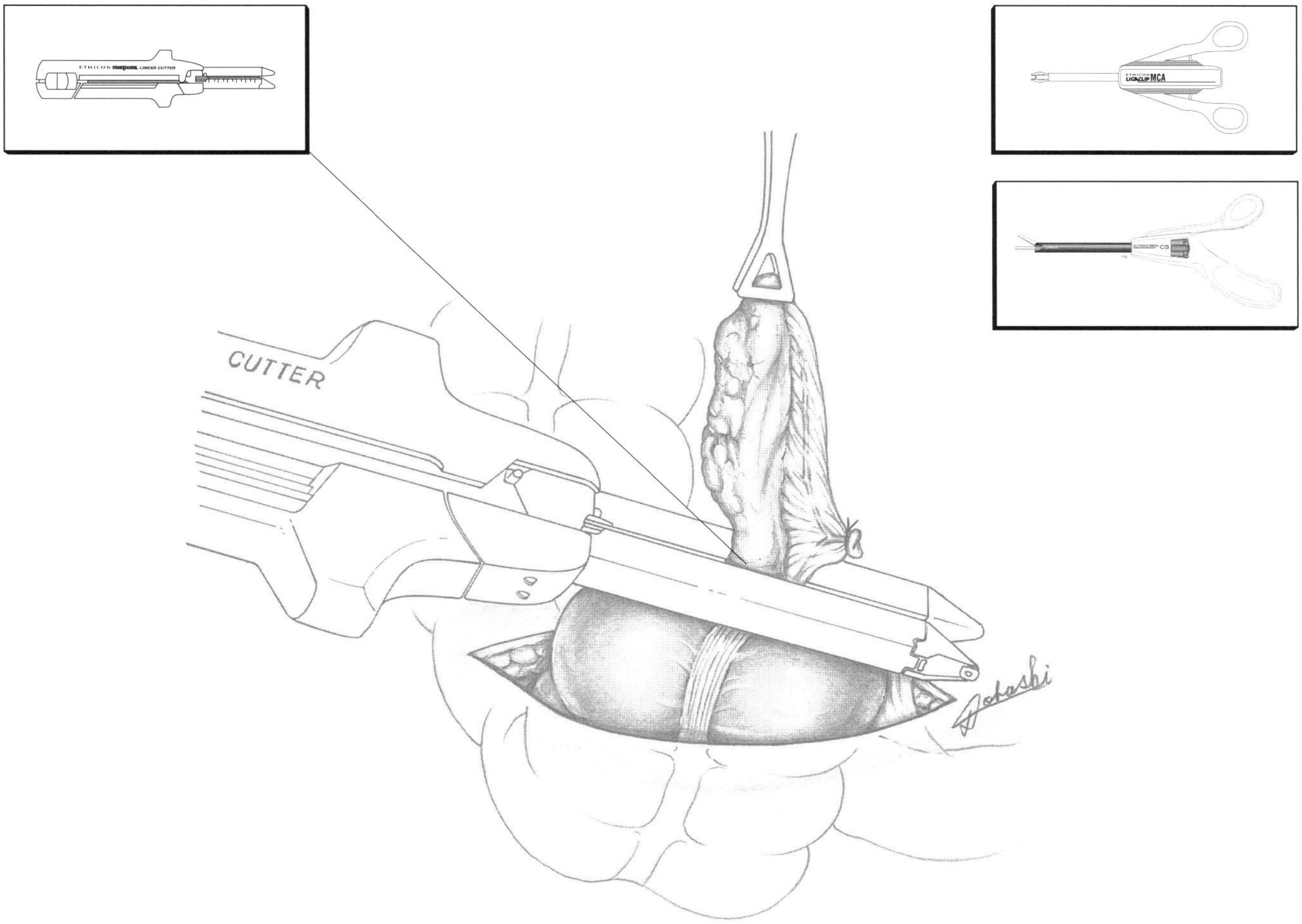

An appendectomy can be carried out by using the linear stapler or the linear cutter standard. The procedure involves ligating the mesentery appendix with sutures, clips, or Ultracision, thereafter transecting the appendix base. By placing the stapler at the base of the appendix, this is stapled, transected, and removed.

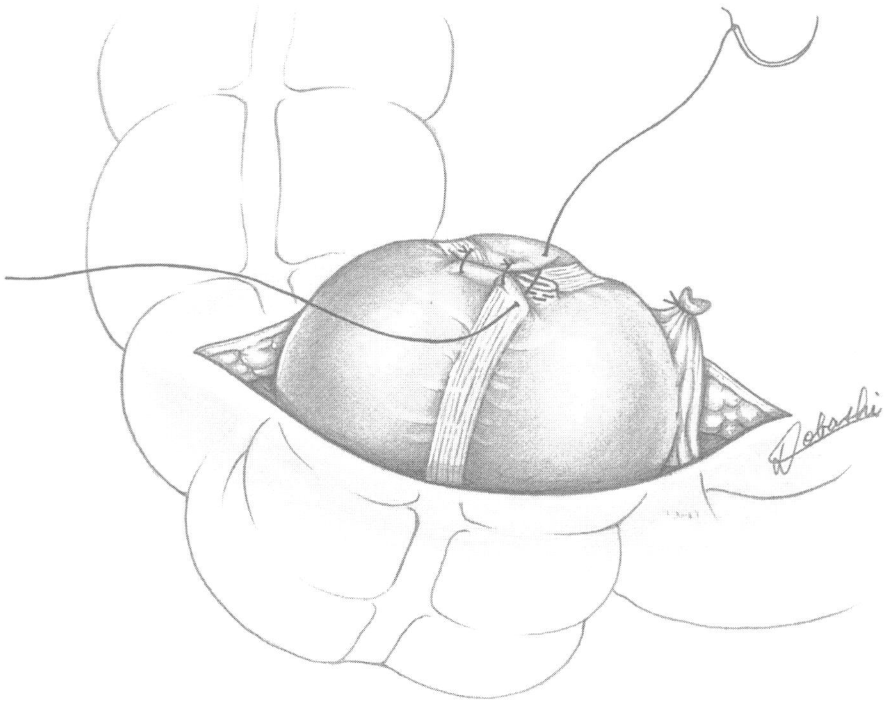

The stump is placed back into position by hand suturing.

By-pass of the Right Colon with Side-to-side Ileocolostomy

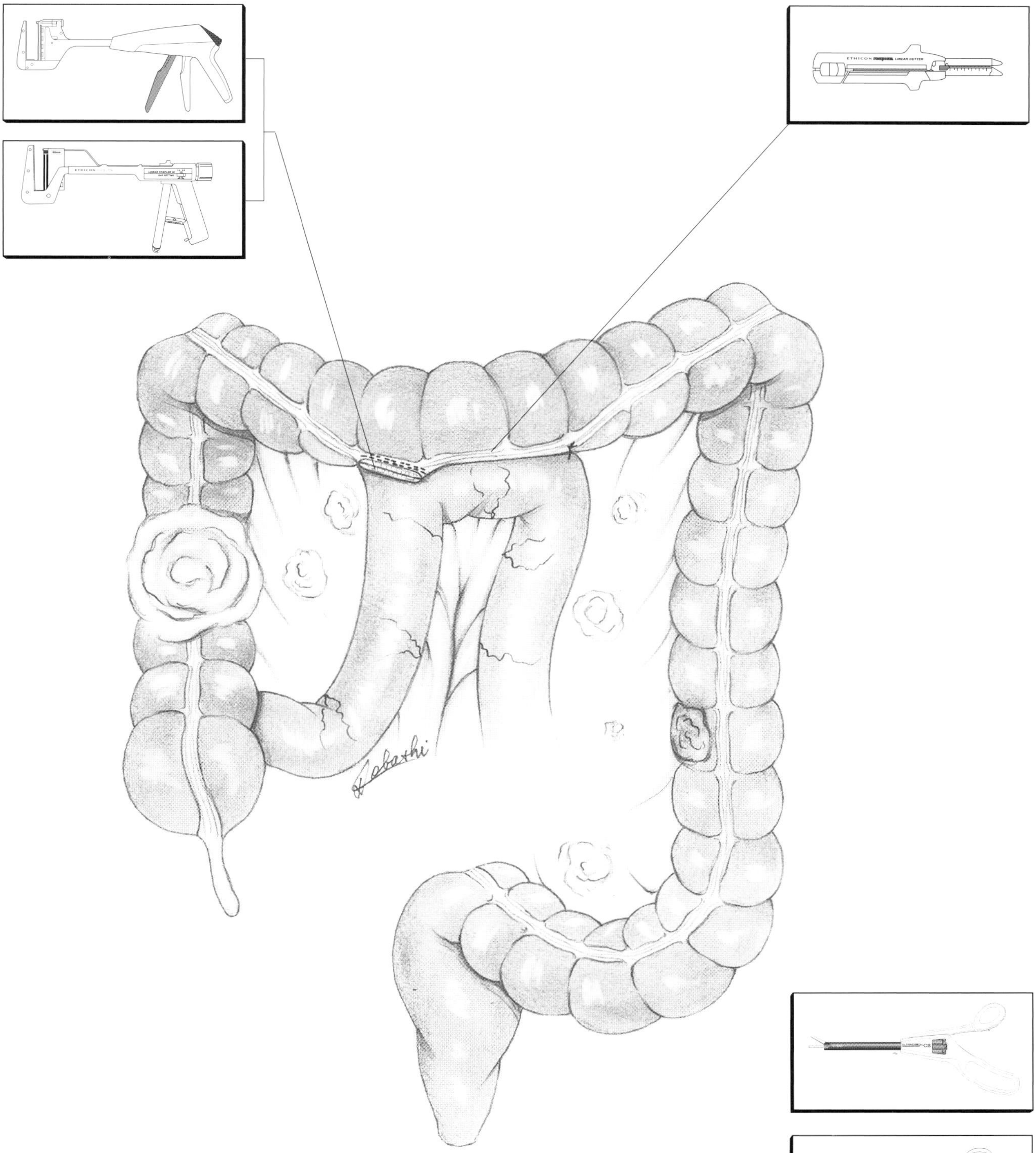

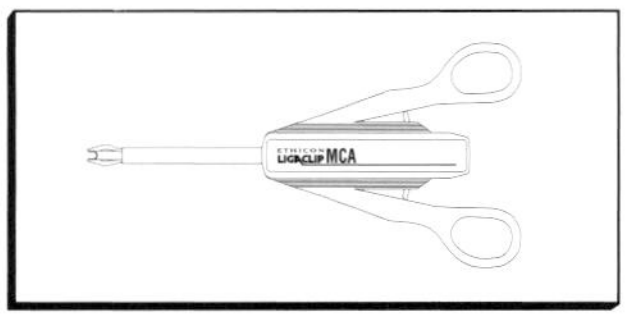

Bypass of the right colon in the case of an inoperable tumour, carried out via a latero-lateral ileostomy on the transverse colon.

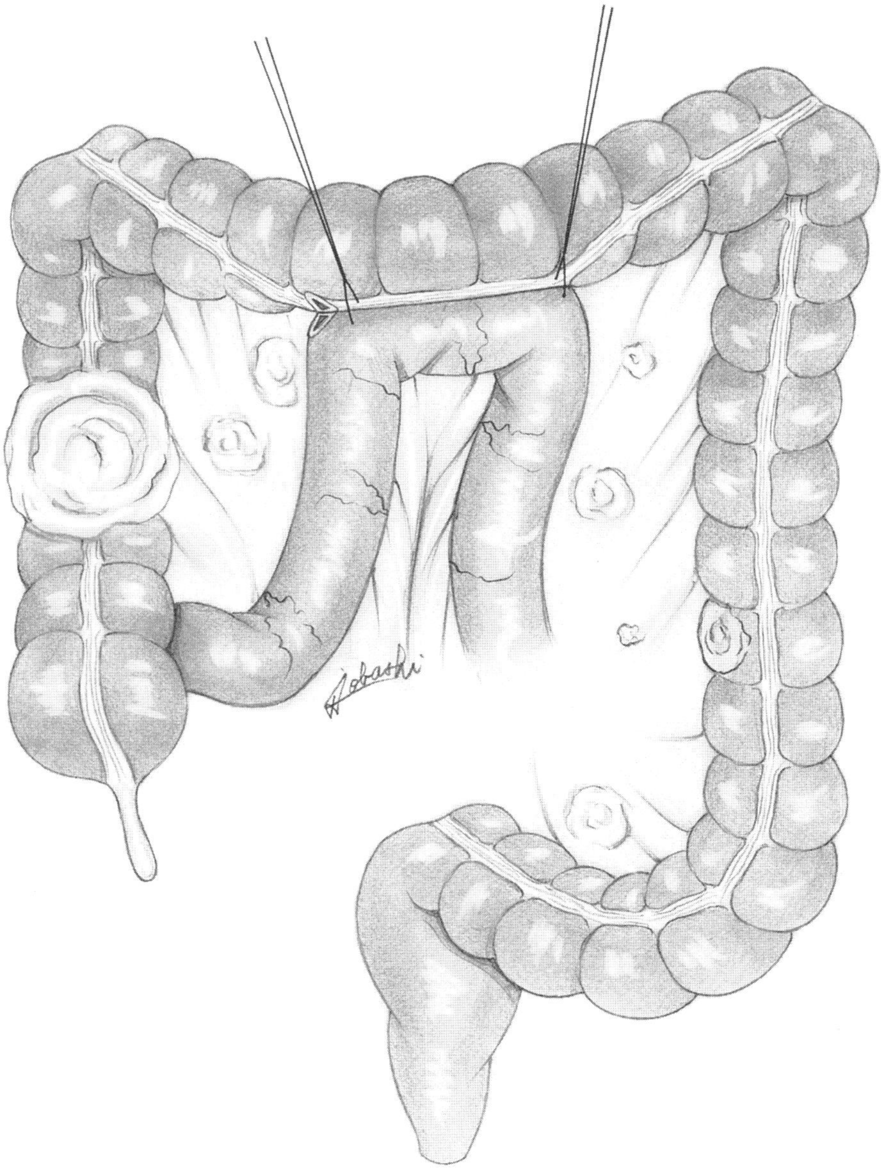

The antimesenteric margins of the transverse colon and the ileal loop chosen for the bypass are brought together. Two enterotomies are carried out in order to perform the mechanical anastomosis.

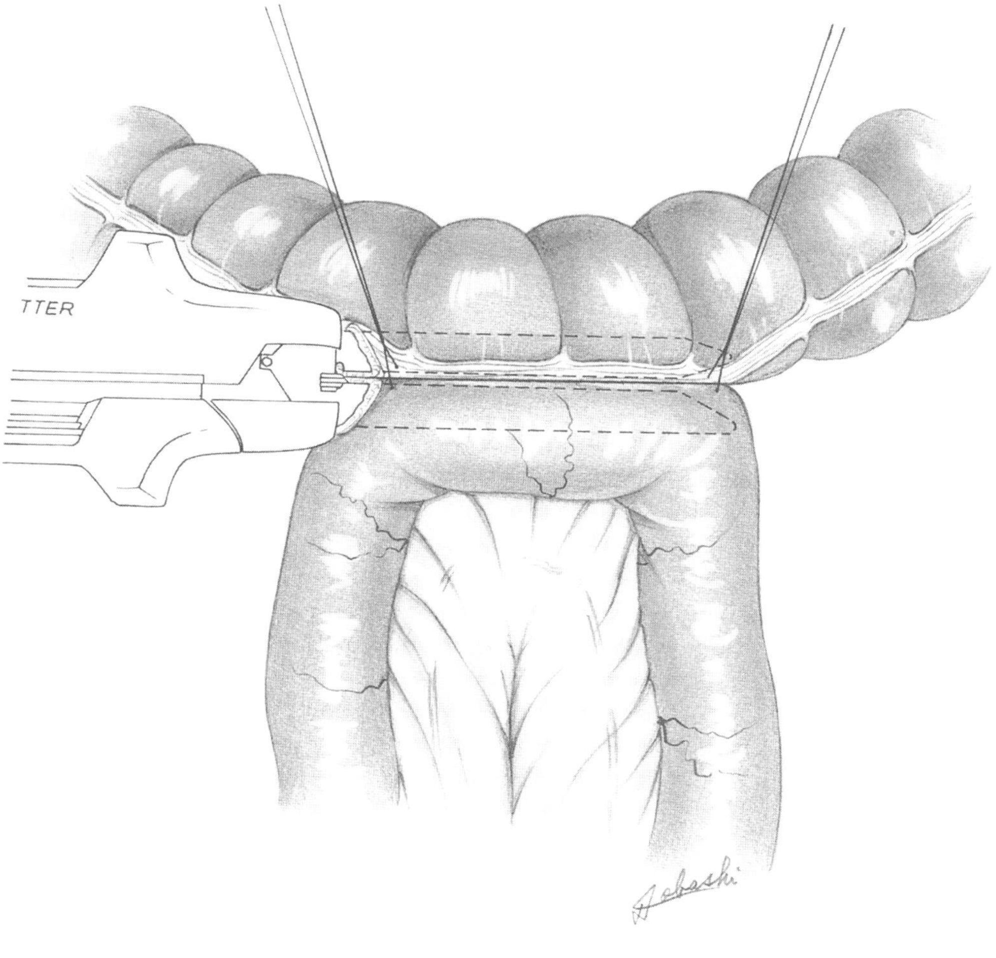

The latero-lateral anastomosis is carried out using a linear cutter standard.

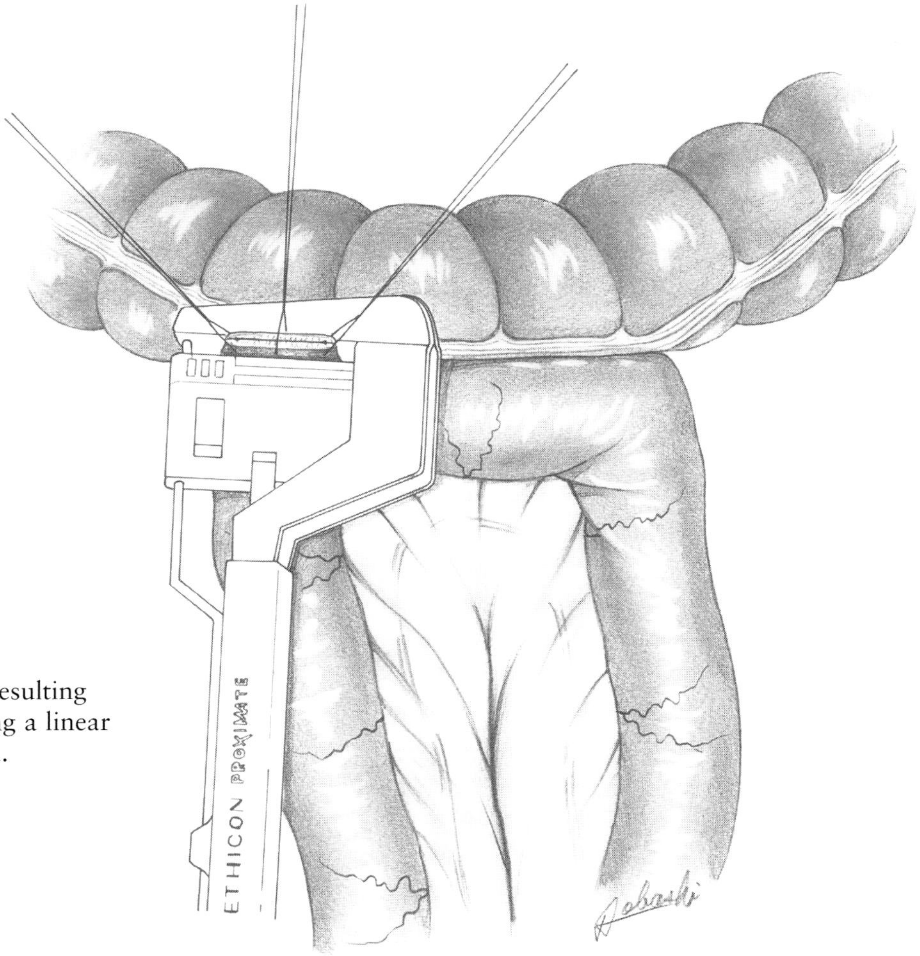

Closure of the resulting enterotomy using a linear stapler standard.

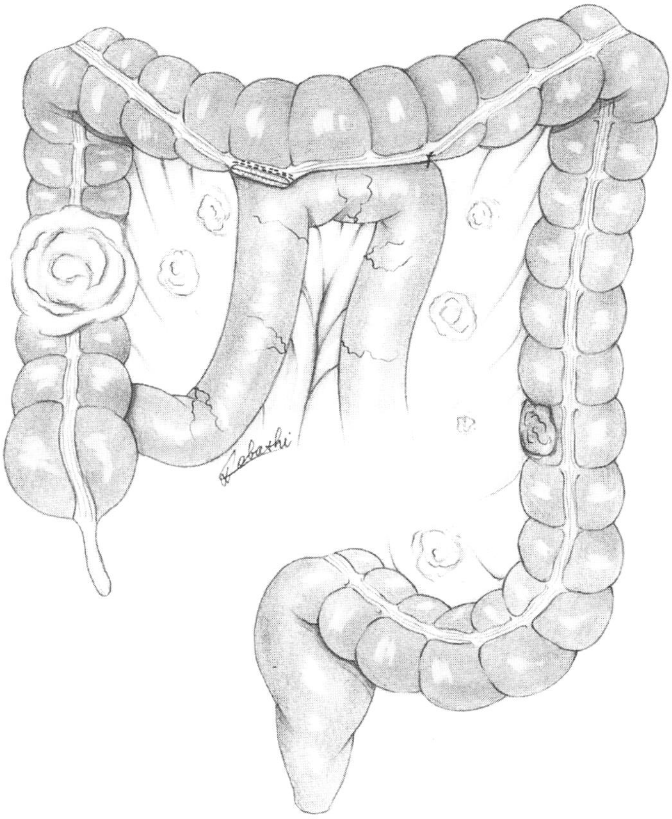

End result.

Right Hemicolectomy with End-to-side Ileocolostomy

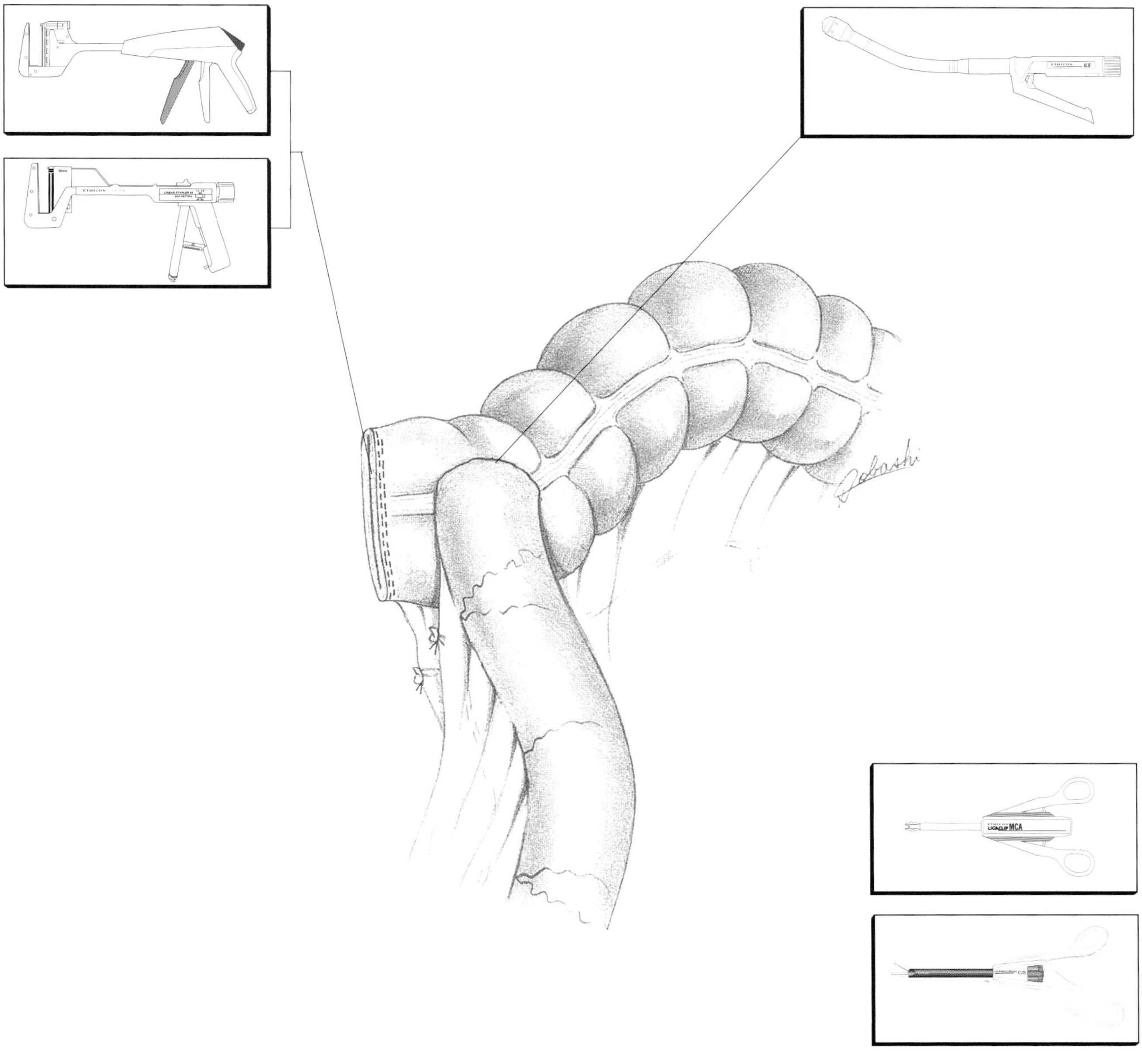

There are several ways of reconstructing the intestinal section after a right hemicolectomy. End-to-side transverse ileostomy and side-to-side transverse ileostomy are the techniques most often used. The former technique uses a circular stapler to perform the anastomosis, inserted at the proximal extreme of the transverse colon, which is left open and is then closed using the linear stapler standard. The anastomosis is carried out, ensuring that it is placed on the antimesenterical colic taenia. The mesocolic breach is then sutured carefully.

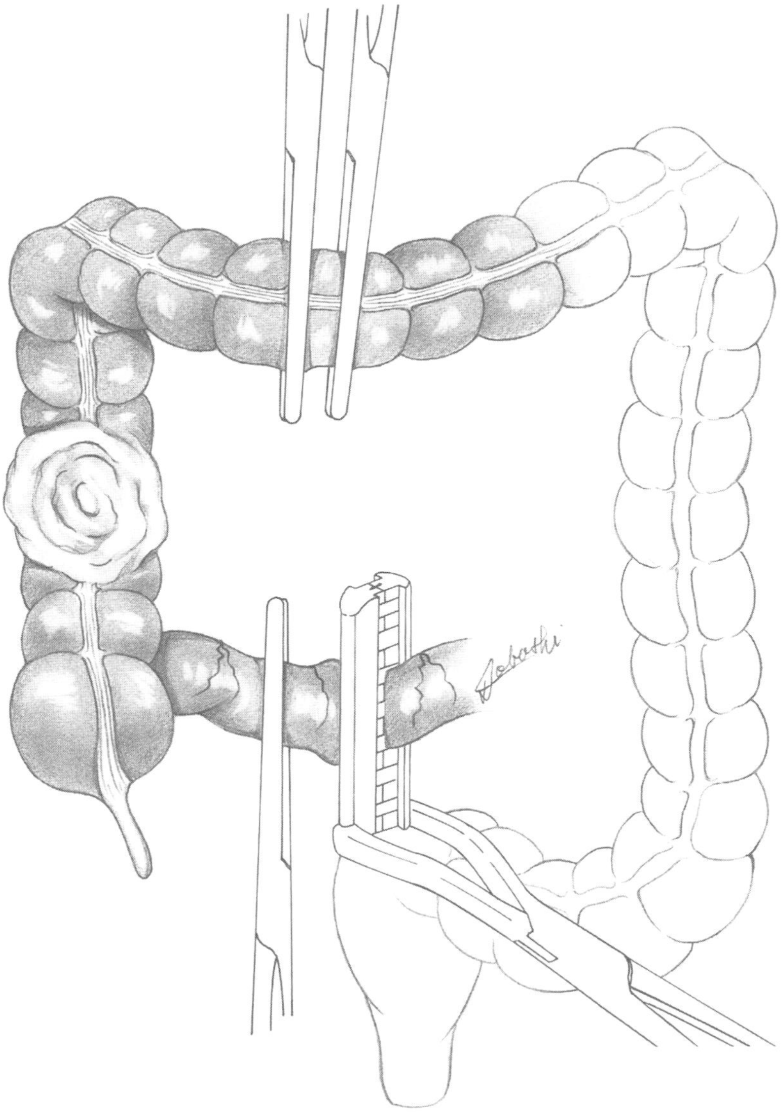

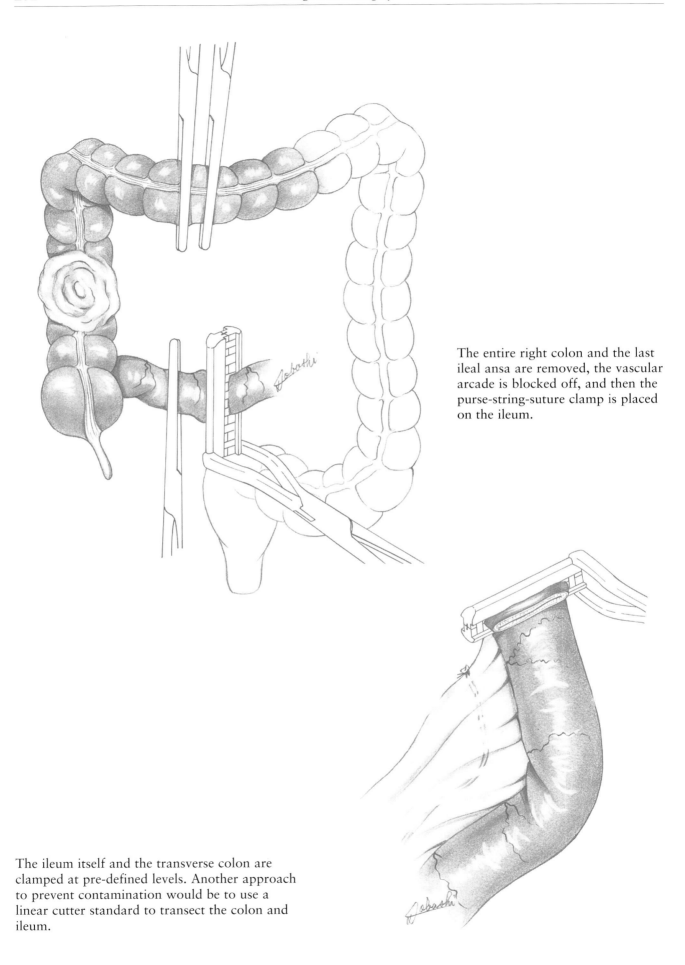

The entire right colon and the last ileal ansa are removed, the vascular arcade is blocked off, and then the purse-string-suture clamp is placed on the ileum.

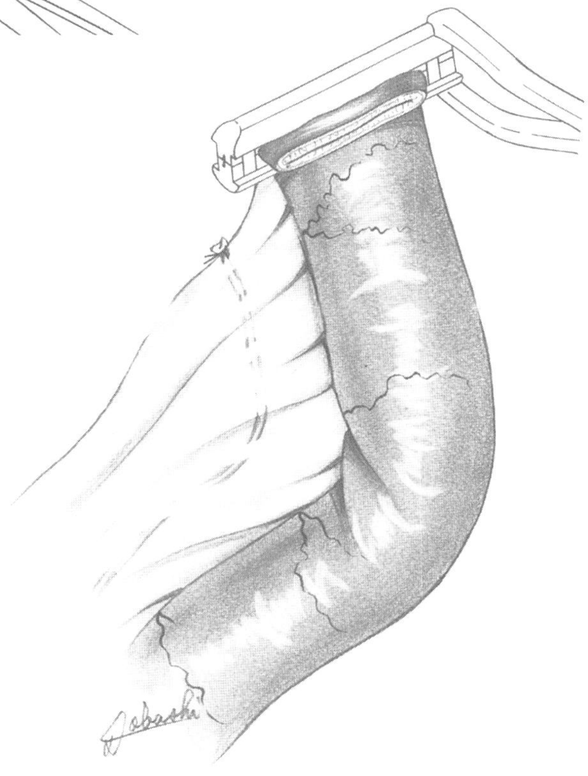

The ileum itself and the transverse colon are clamped at pre-defined levels. Another approach to prevent contamination would be to use a linear cutter standard to transect the colon and ileum.

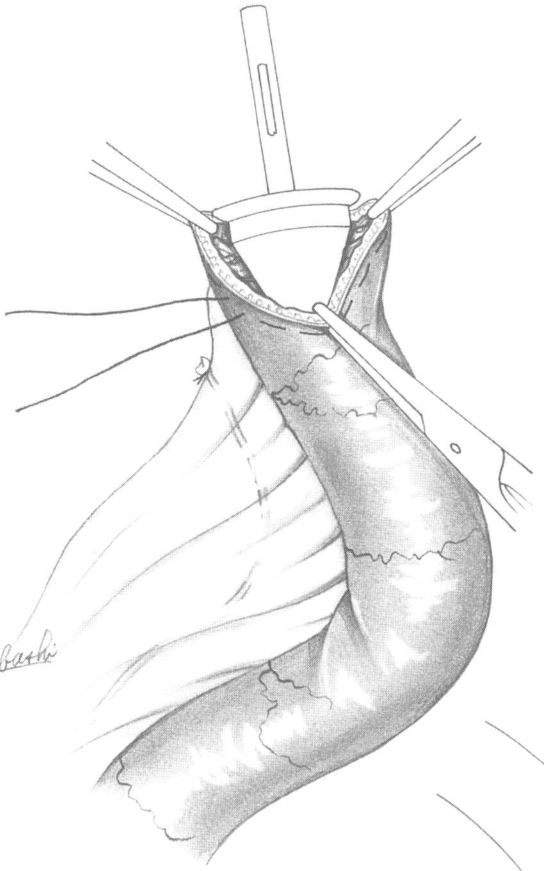

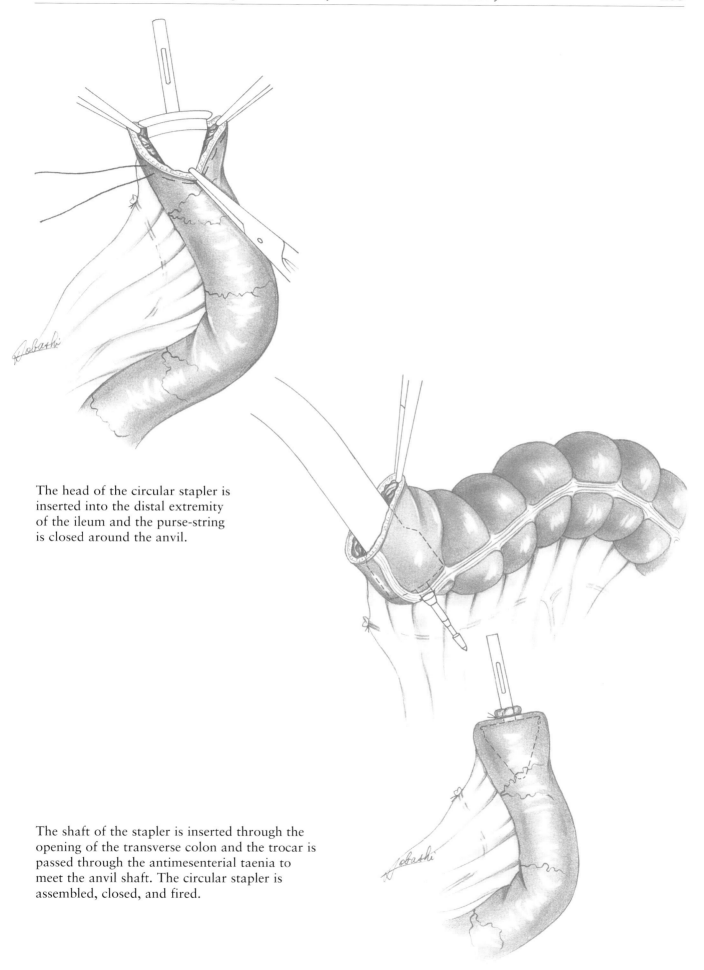

The head of the circular stapler is inserted into the distal extremity of the ileum and the purse-string is closed around the anvil.

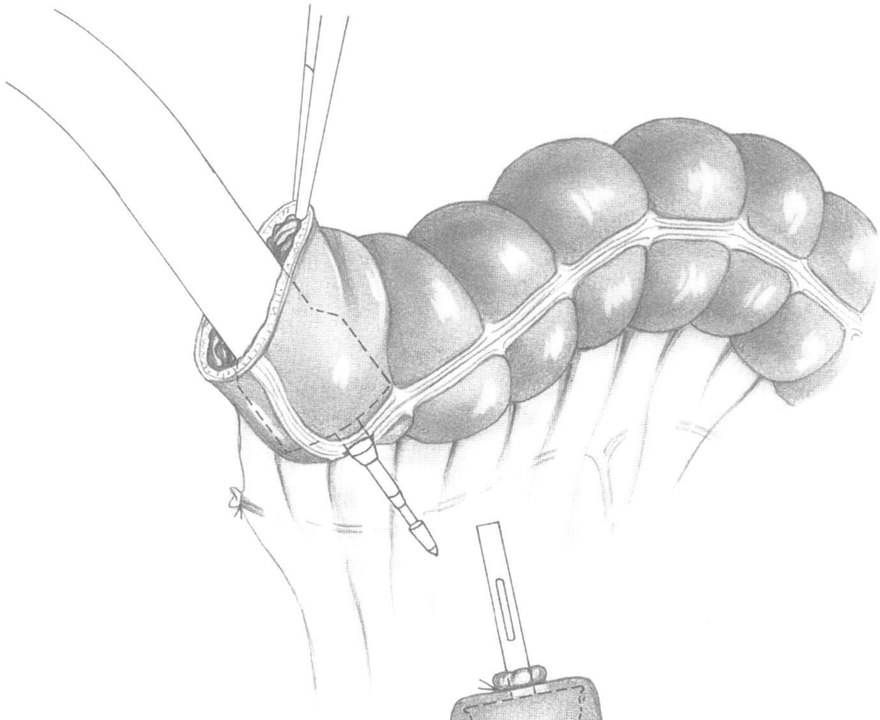

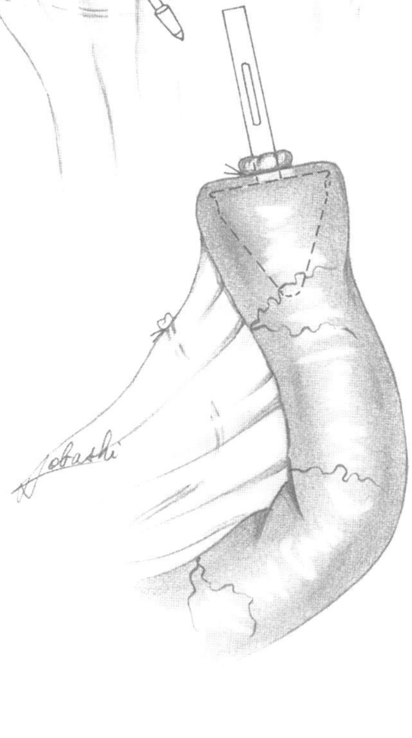

The shaft of the stapler is inserted through the opening of the transverse colon and the trocar is passed through the antimesenterial taenia to meet the anvil shaft. The circular stapler is assembled, closed, and fired.

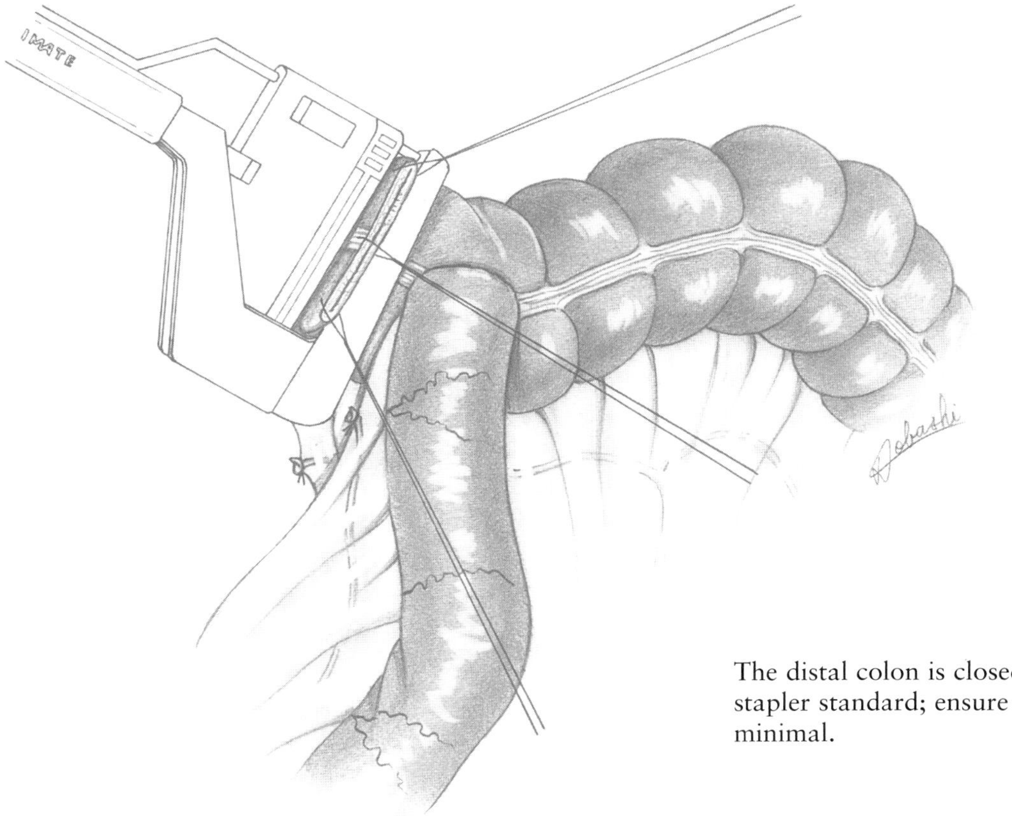

The distal colon is closed using the linear stapler standard; ensure that the cul-de-sac is minimal.

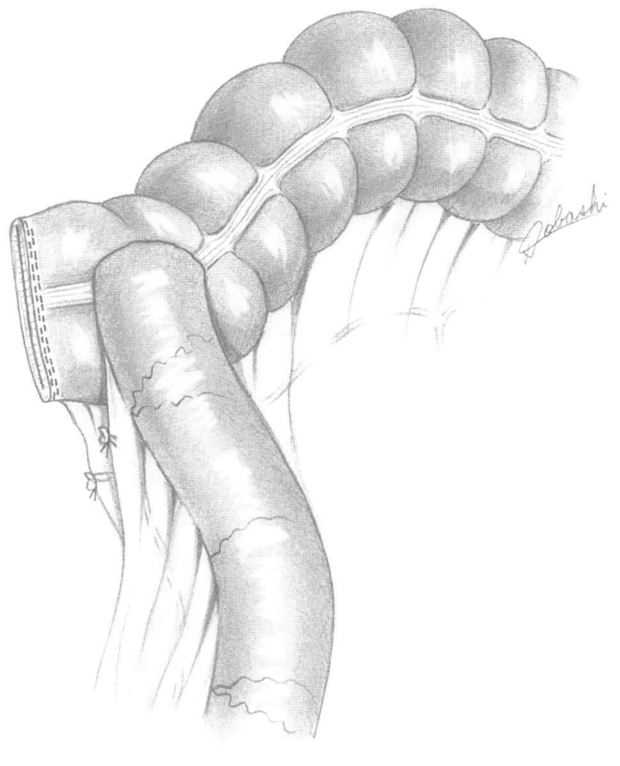

View of the completed anastomosis.
The mesenteries are aligned and sutured to avoid leaving breaches which could lead to potential bowel torsions and hernias.

Right Hemicolectomy with Side-to-side Ileocolostomy

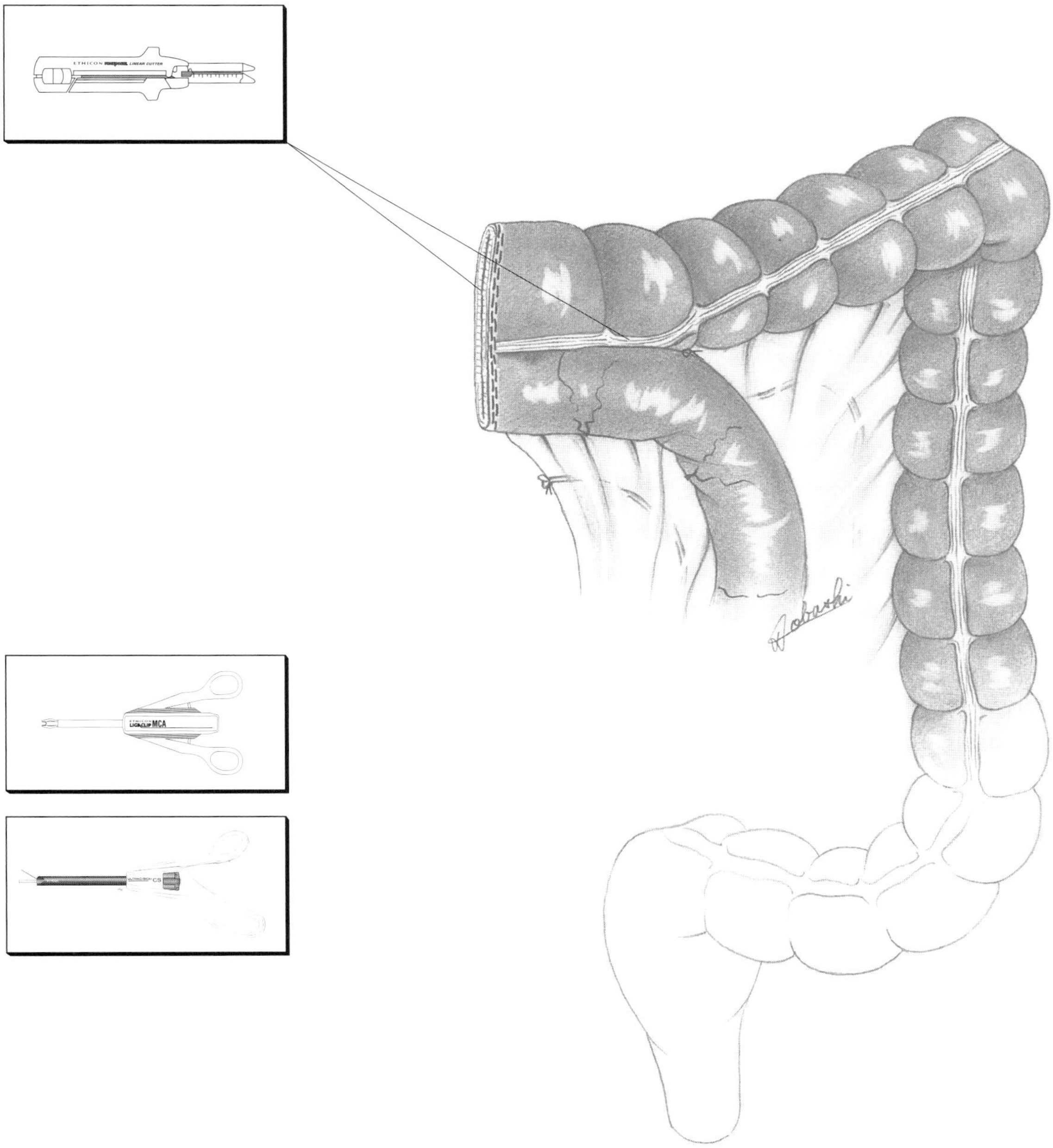

After a right hemicolectomy the digestive tract can be reconstructed by the side-to-side method. This allows the jaws of the linear cutter standard to be inserted directly into the bowel stumps. The operation concludes with the closing of the anastomosed stump using the linear cutter standard.

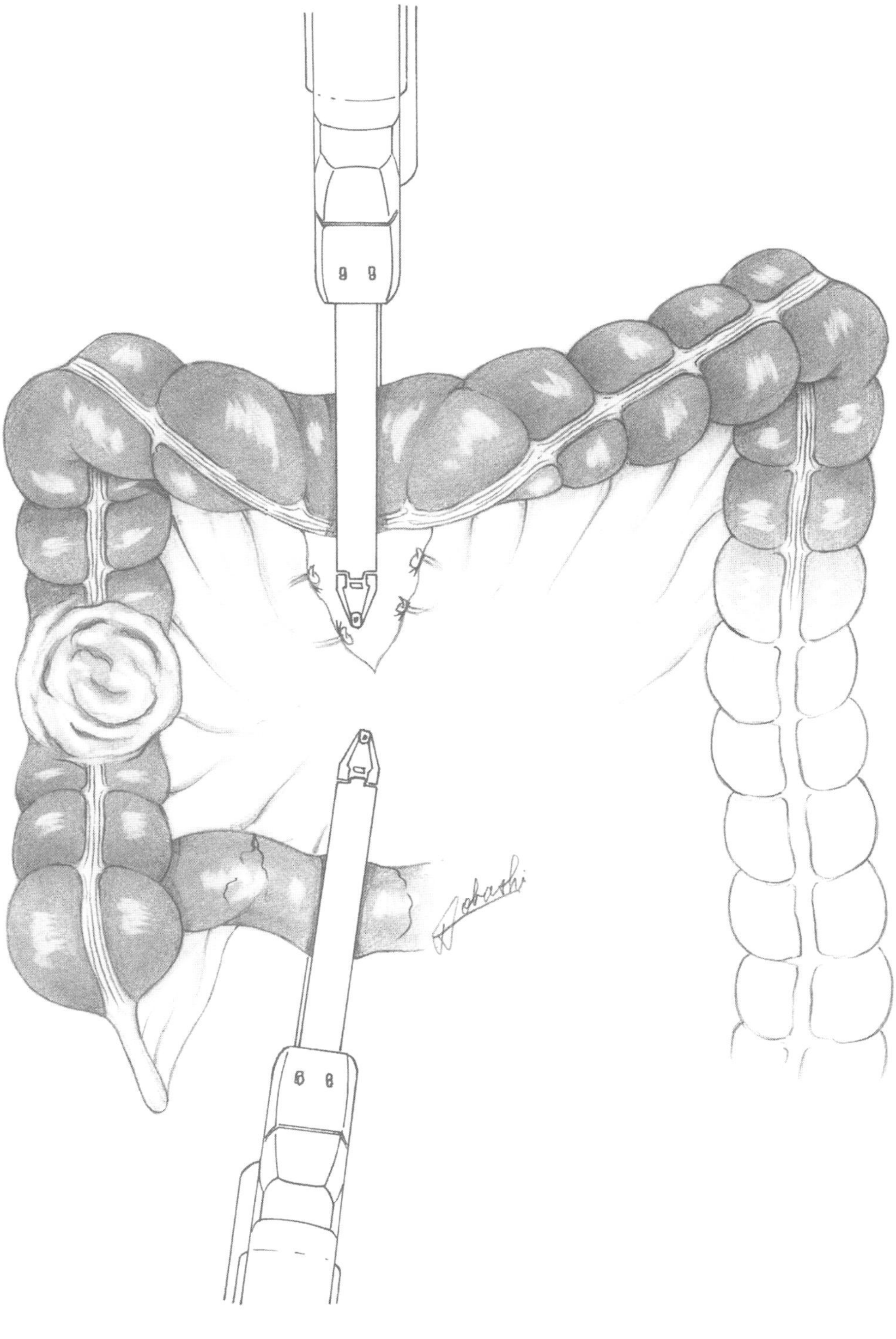

After mobilising the right colon and ligating the vascular arcades with multiple clip appliers or Ultracision, a linear cutter standard is placed at pre-defined points on the ileum and the transverse colon. The pathological tract is then transected and removed.

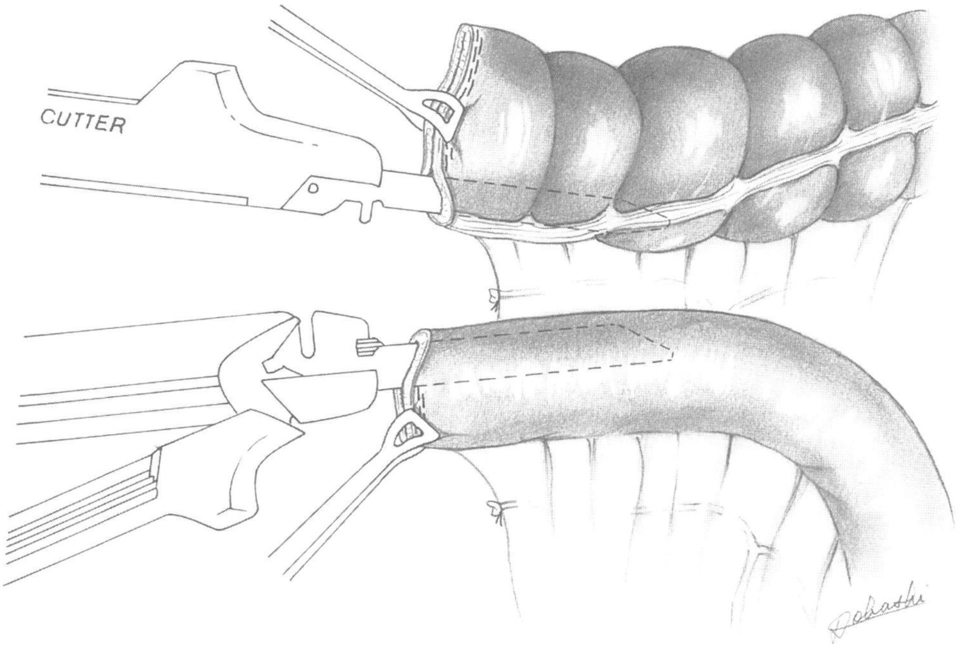

The ansae are aligned and the jaws of the linear cutter are inserted by means of two small incisions in the sutured stumps.

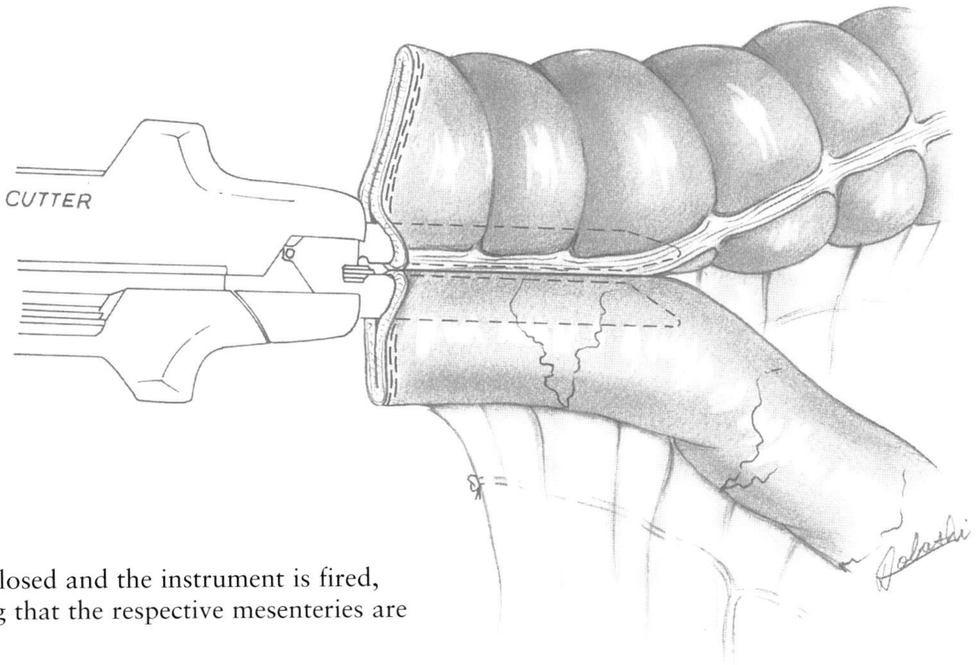

The jaws are closed and the instrument is fired, whilst ensuring that the respective mesenteries are kept free.

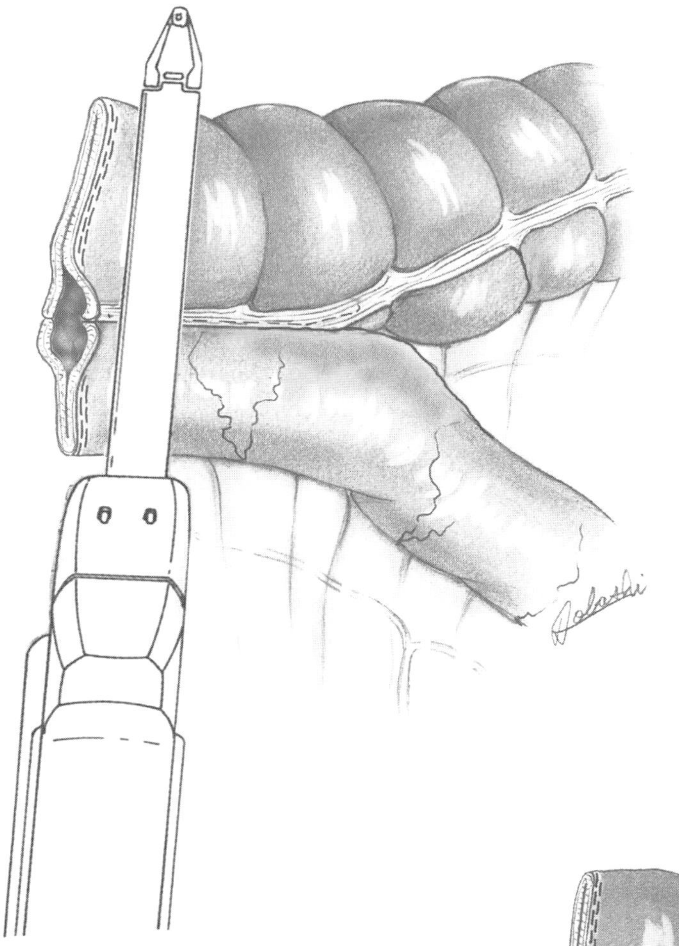

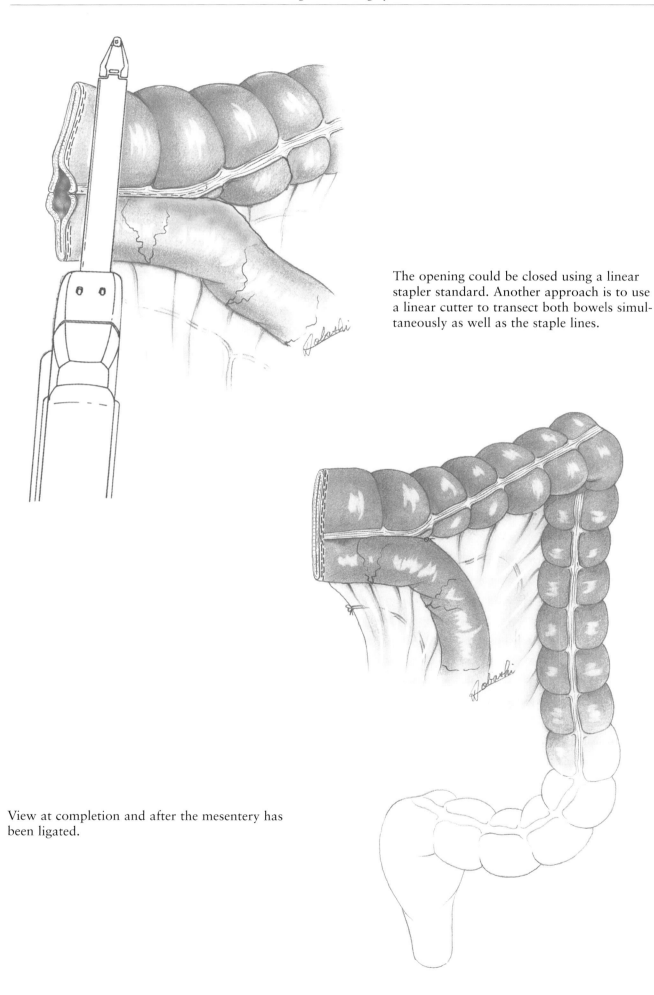

The opening could be closed using a linear stapler standard. Another approach is to use a linear cutter to transect both bowels simultaneously as well as the staple lines.

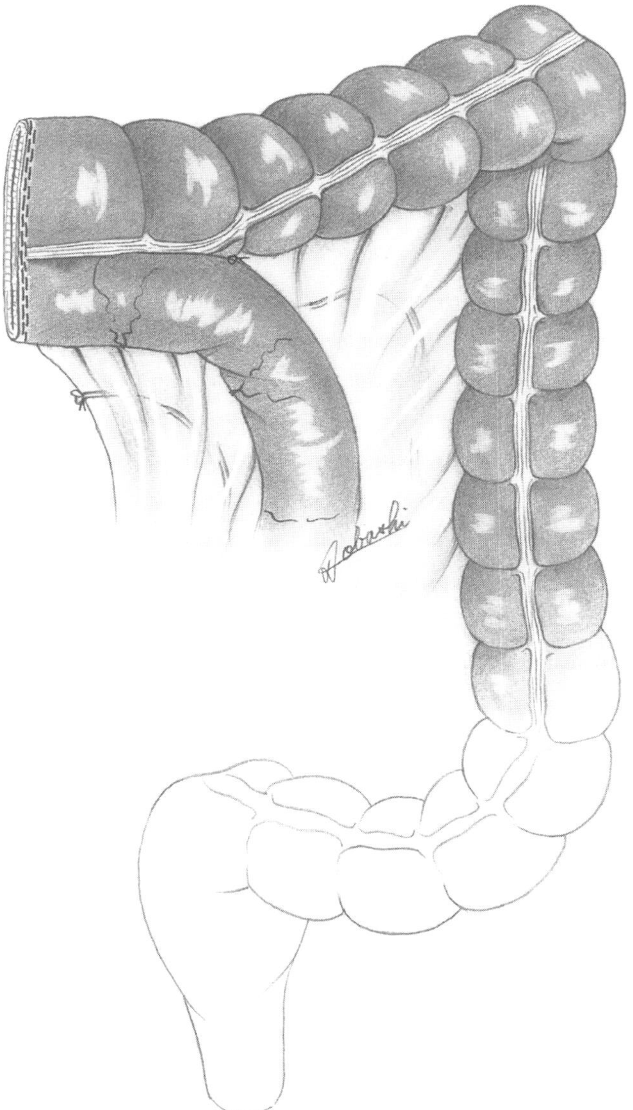

View at completion and after the mesentery has been ligated.

Transverse Colon with End-to-end Anastomosis

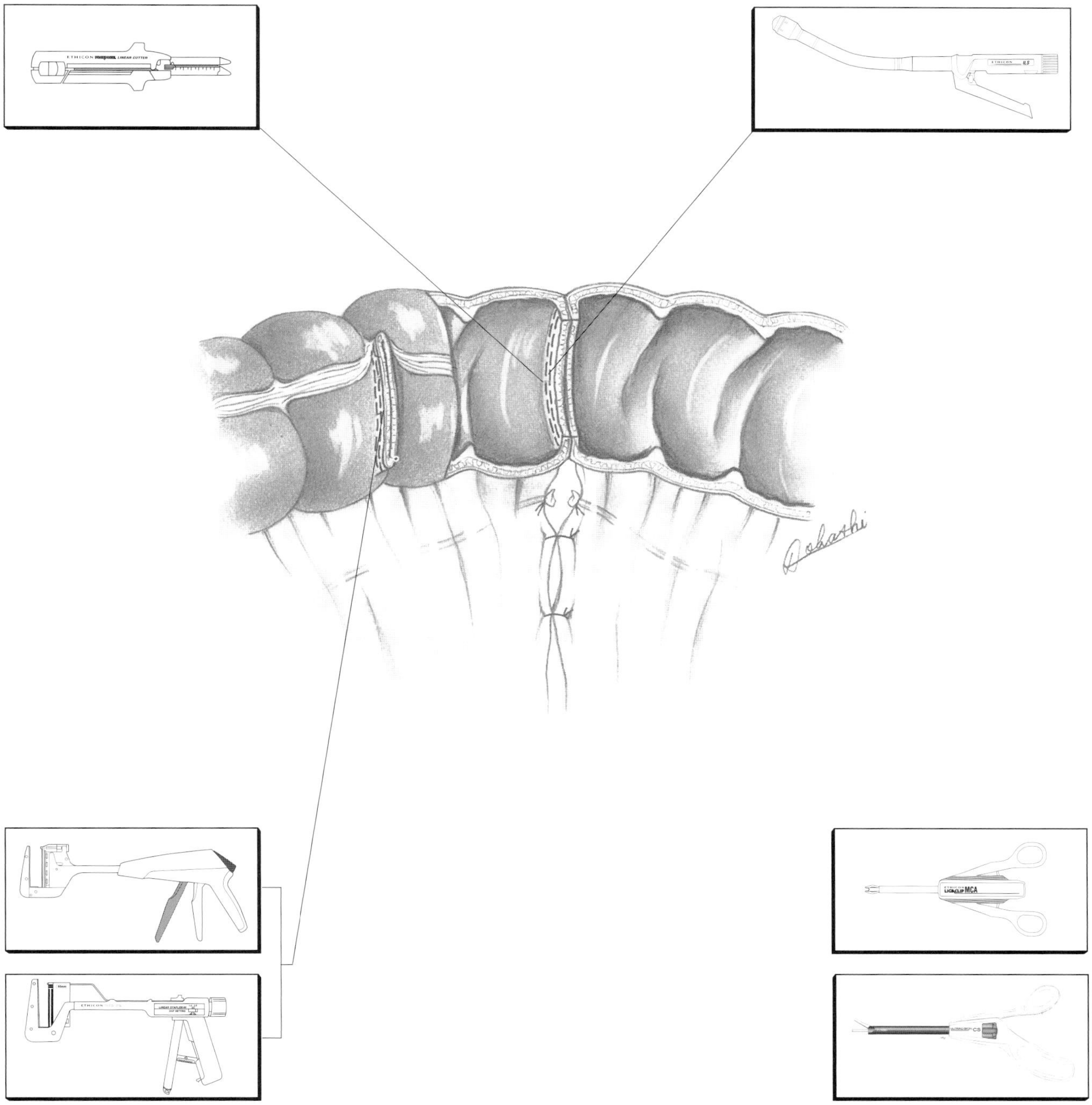

A resection of the transverse colon is carried out. The most frequently used reconstructive methods are end-to-end anastomosis or side-to-end anastomosis. End-to-end colon-colon anastomosis requires an incision to insert the circular stapler.

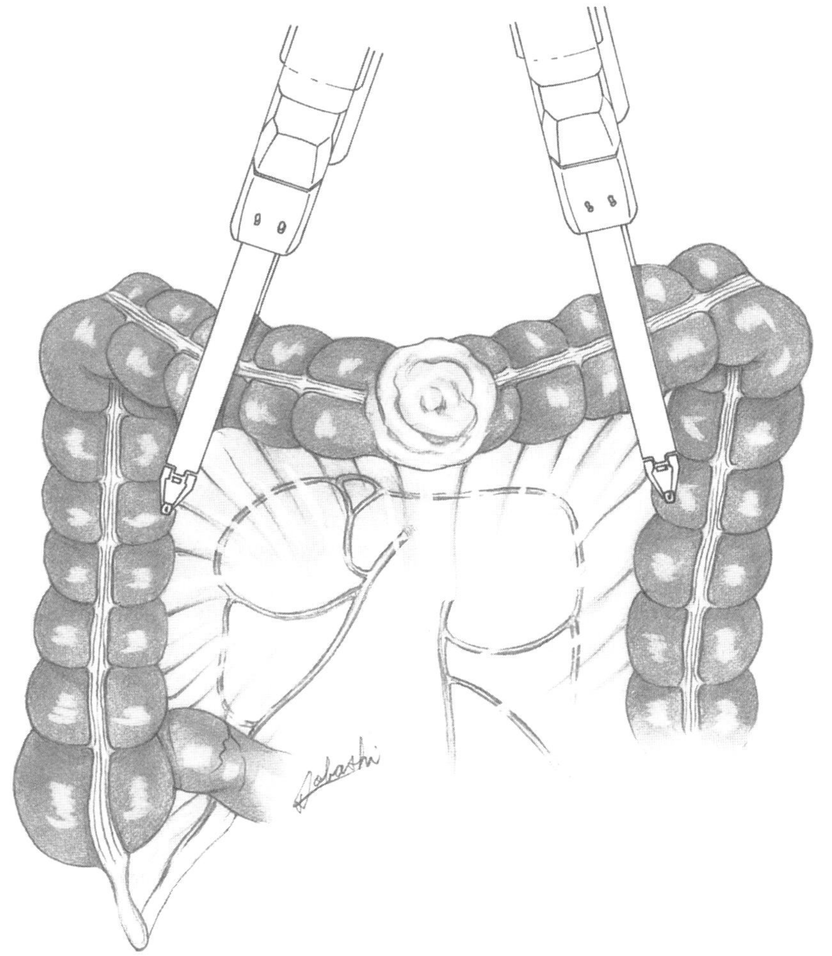

The positioning of the linear cutter standard on the portion of transverse colon to be resected.

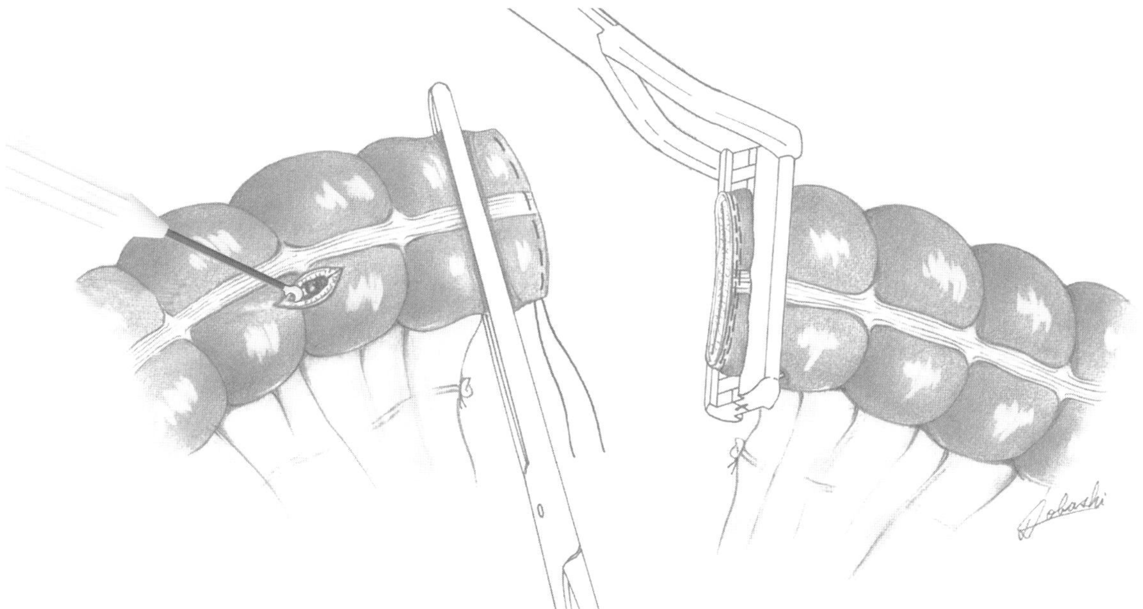

Two purse-string sutures are made for the anastomoses after removal of the colon. An enterotomy is made with Ultracision on the proximal colon.

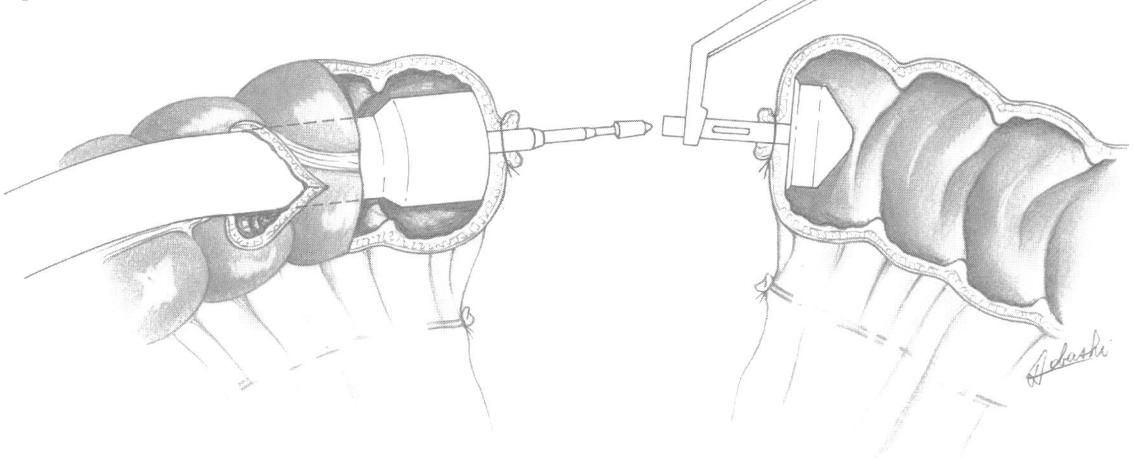

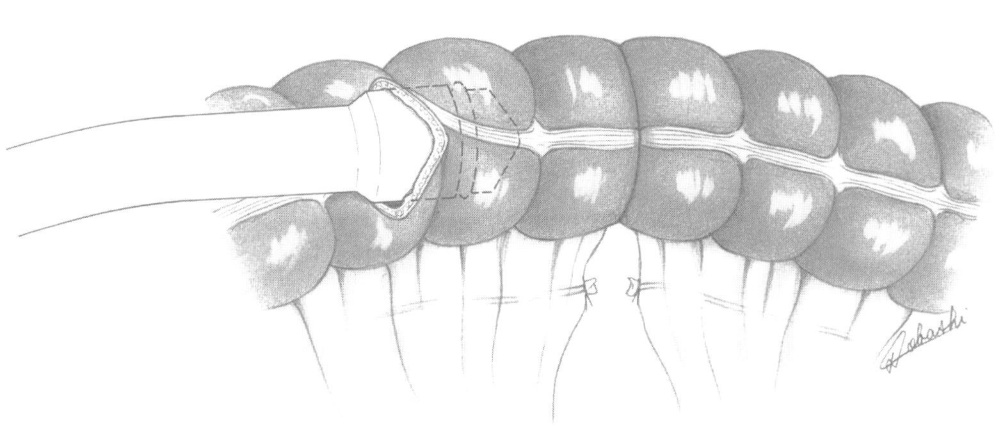

The shaft of the stapler is inserted through the incision and the purse-string is tied around the trocar. The other purse-string suture is tied around the base of the anvil, which has previously been inserted into the distal colon. The stapler is assembled and fired to perform the anastomosis.

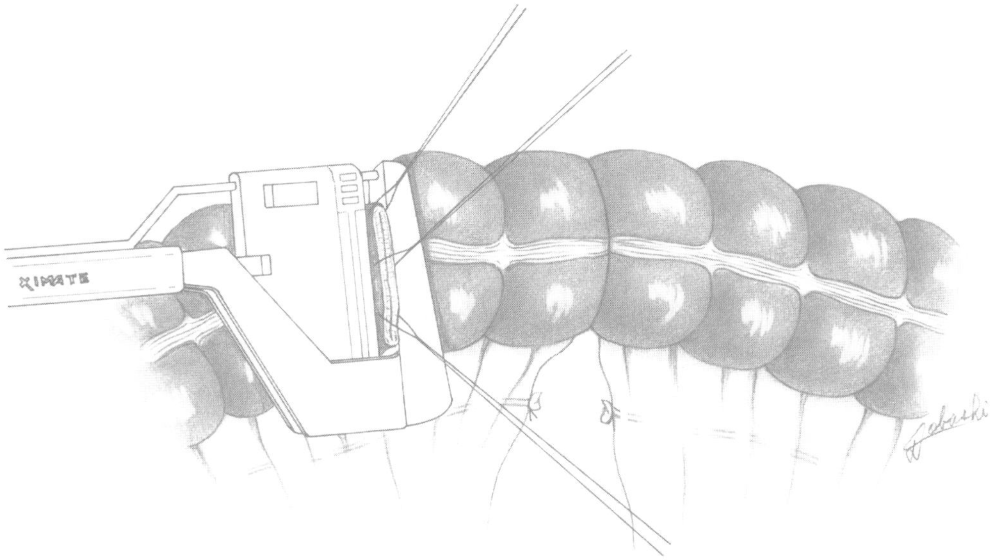

Enterotomy is closed by a linear stapler standard on manual sutures.

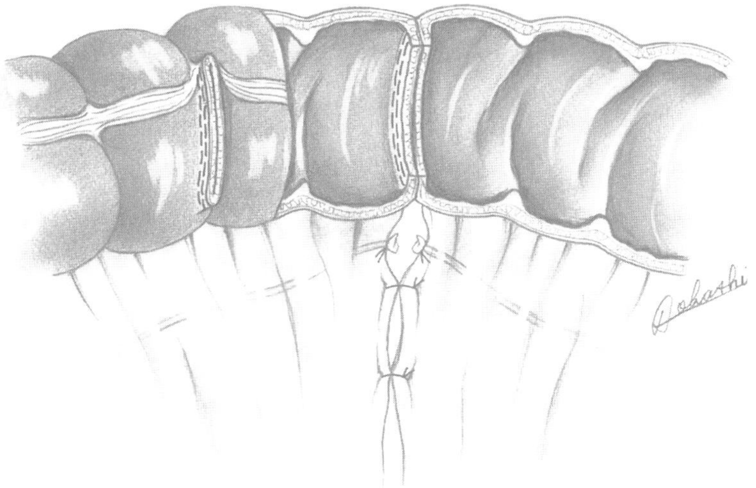

View of the completed anastomosis. The mesentery colon breach is sutured carefully.

Transverse Colon Resection

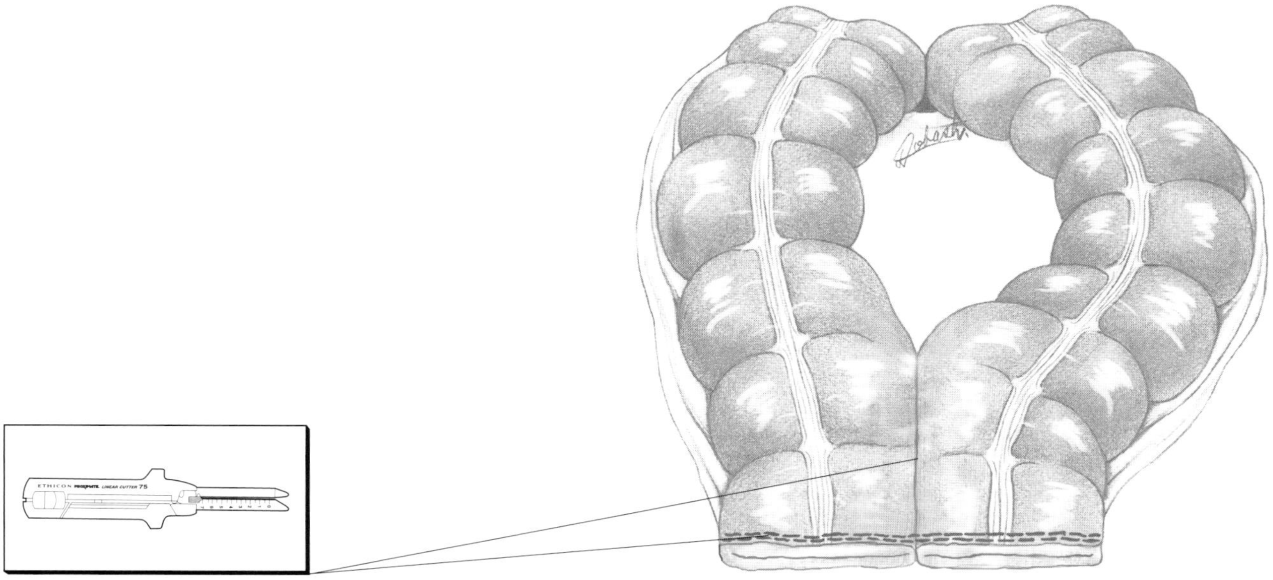

Functional latero-lateral anastomosis carried out by using a linear cutter standard.

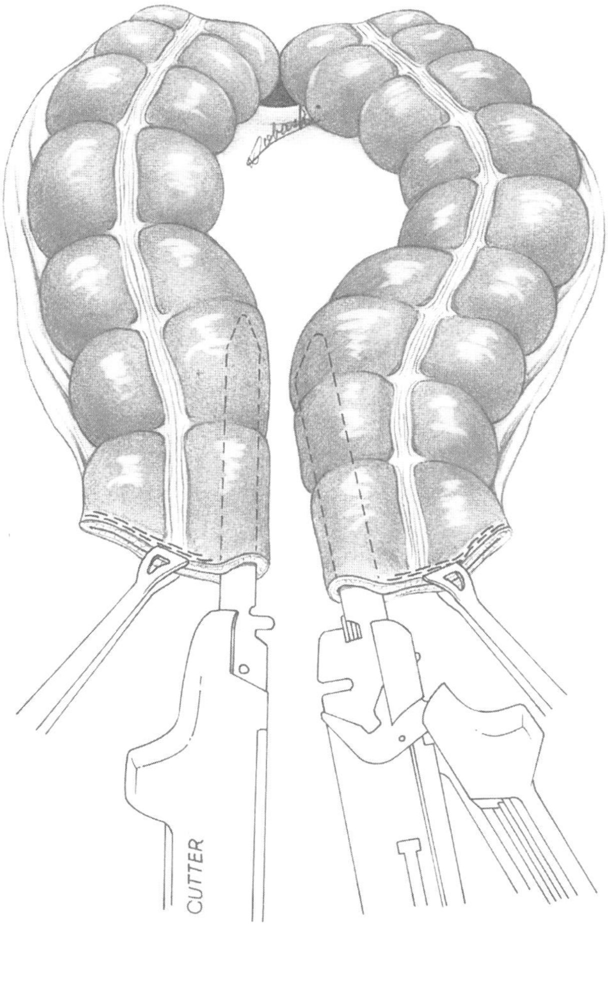

Having resected the transverse colon with two applications of a linear cutter standard, the ansae are aligned and the jaws of the instruments are inserted by means of two small incisions in the antimesenteric edges of the sutured stump.

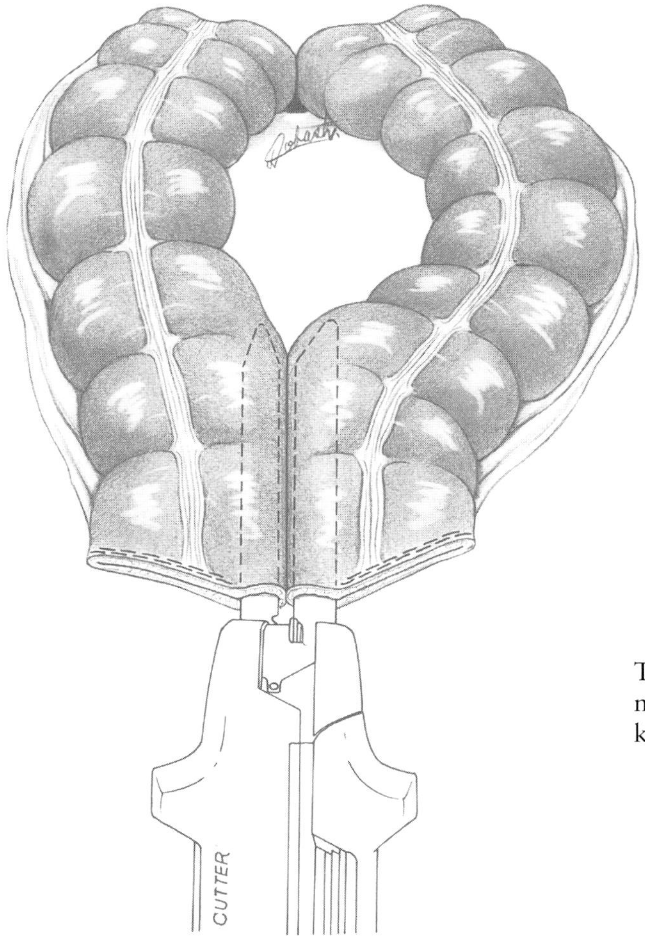

The jaws are closed and the instrument is fired, making sure that the respective mesenteries are kept free.

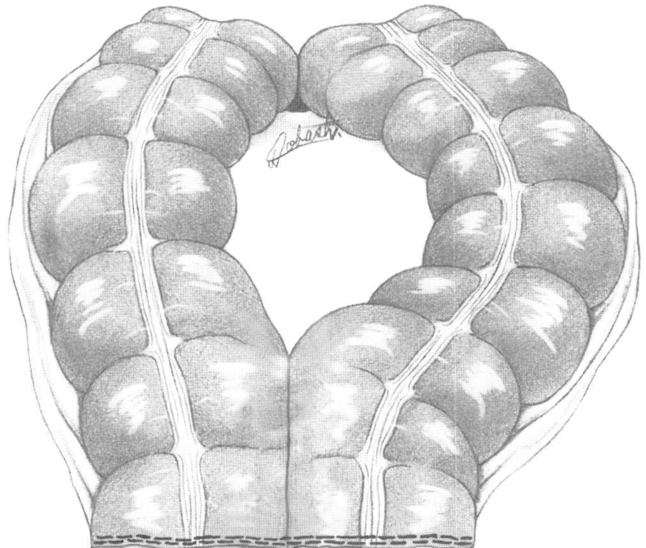

End result of the anastomosis.

Colostomy

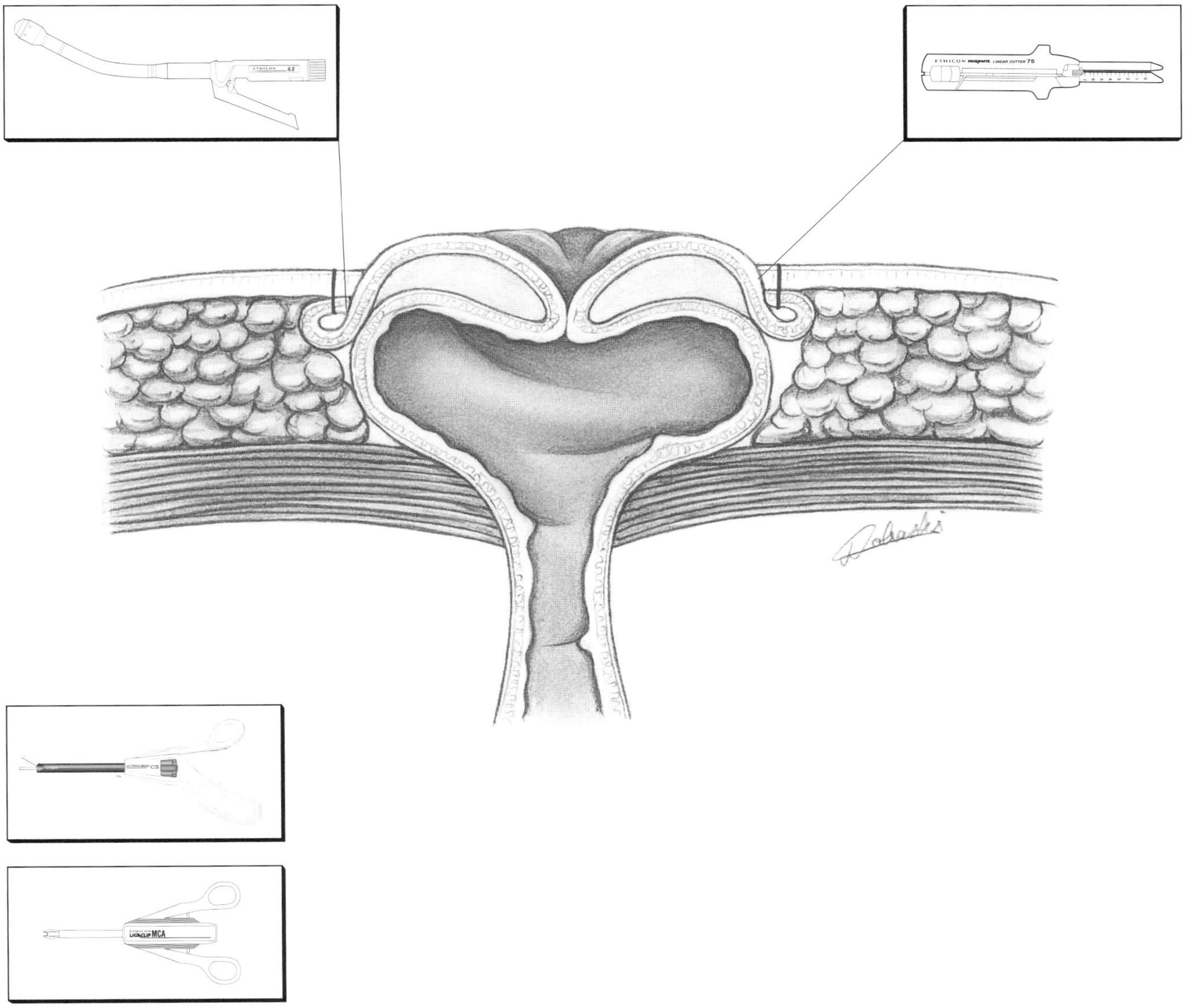

A circular stapler can be used when performing a terminal colostomy. In such cases the pathological tract is resected, externalised, and fixed to the skin, using a wide diameter stapler to avoid stenoses.

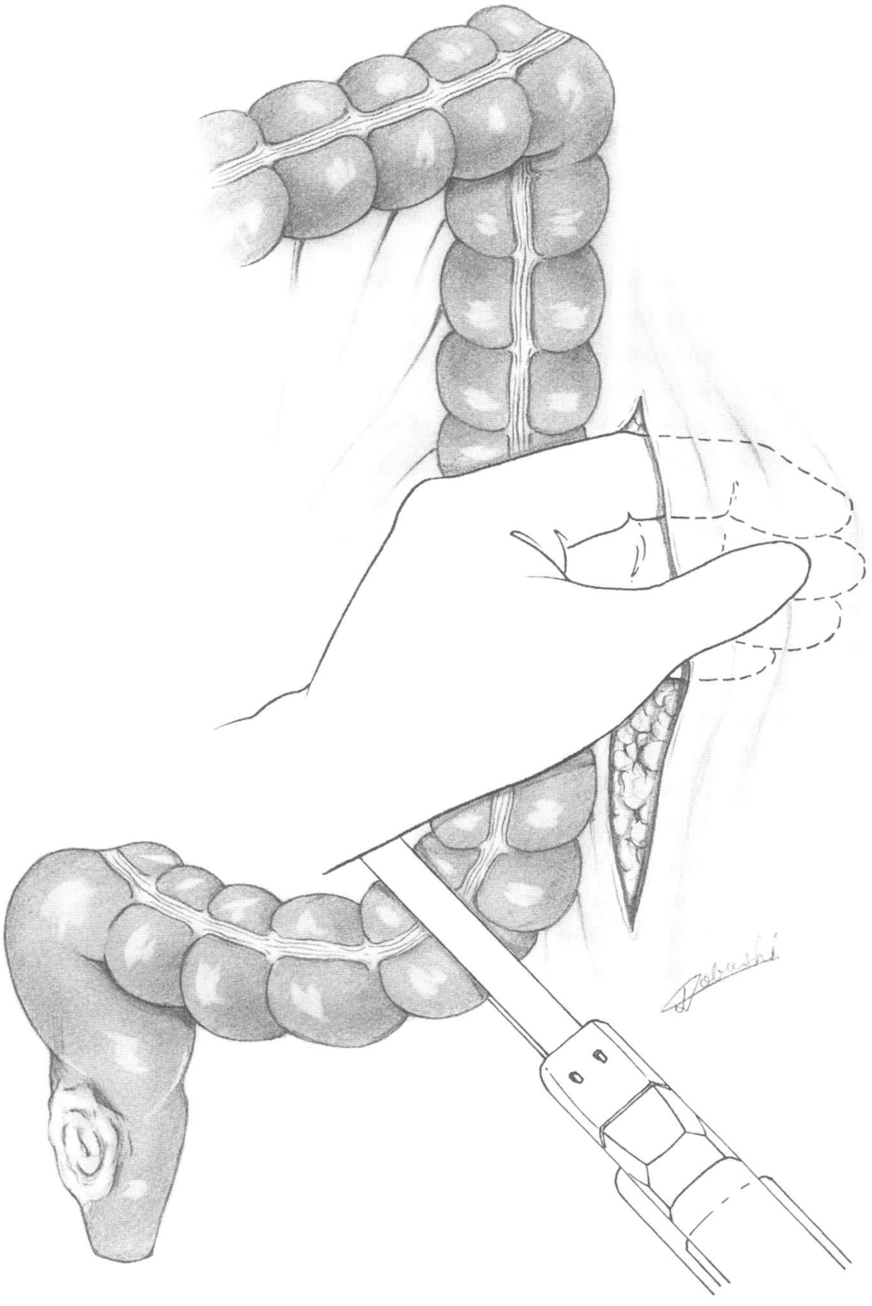

The colon is transected at a pre-defined point by using a linear cutter standard. An opening is made in the abdominal wall to allow the externalisation of the colon.

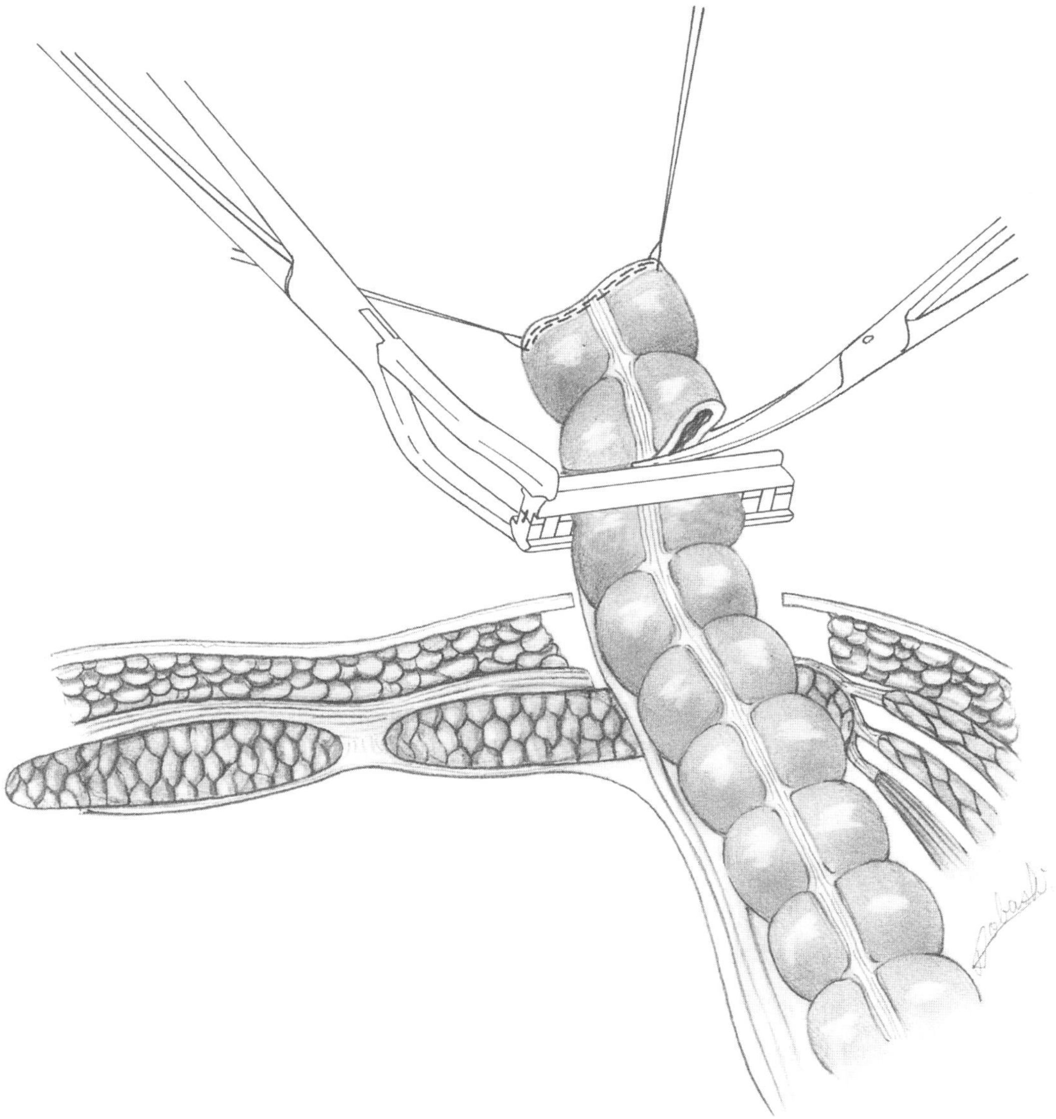

The purse-string device is placed at a pre-defined point in order to perform a purse-string suture for the colostomy. The excess tissue is cut away.

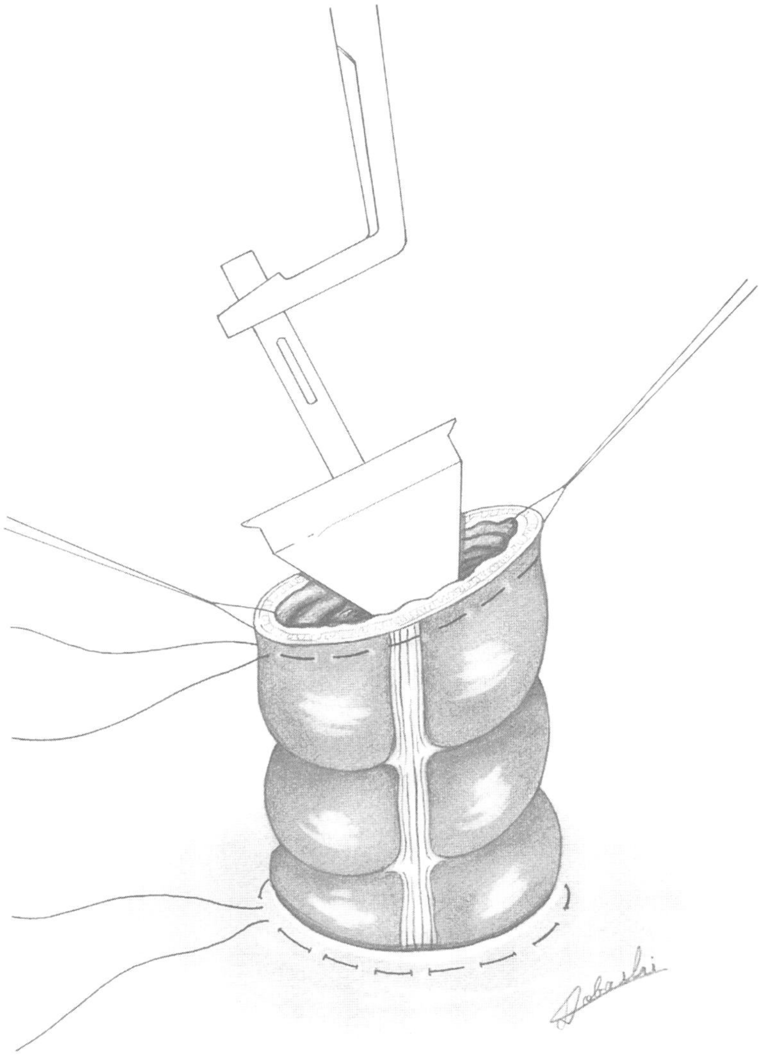

The head of the stapler is inserted into the colon and another purse-string suture is made at the skin.

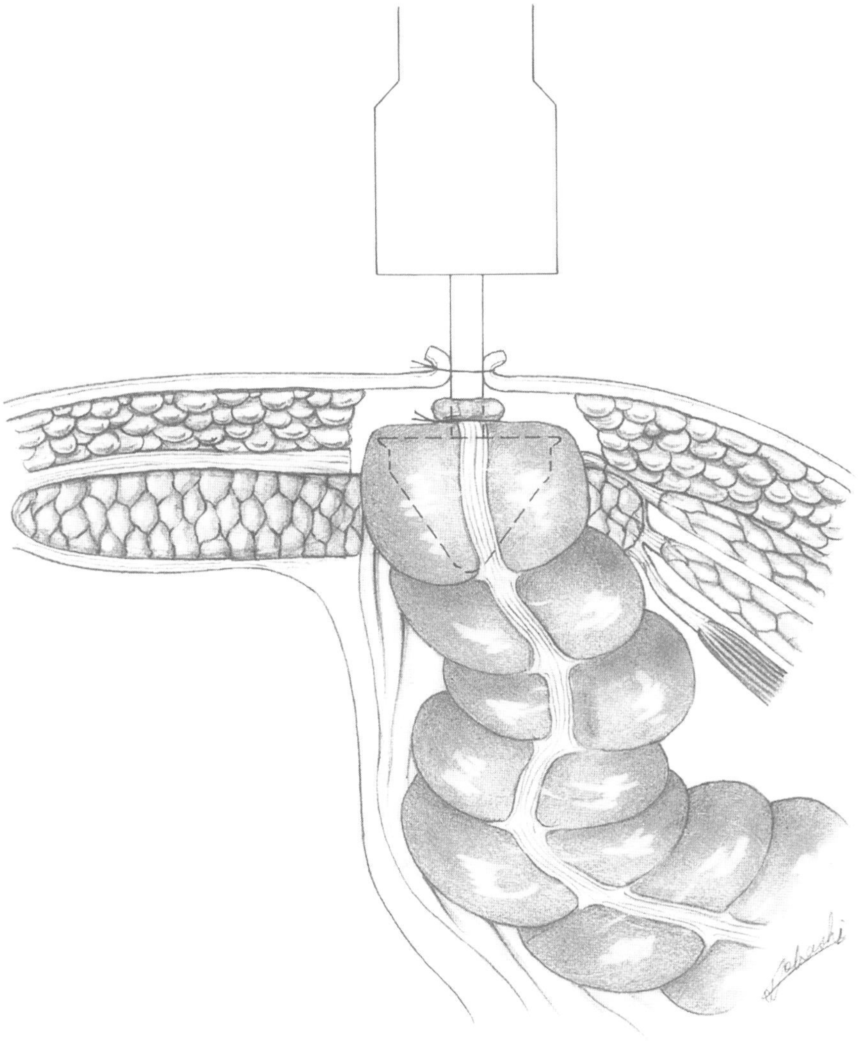

The cutaneous purse-string suture is tied around the rod of the anvil.
The circular stapler is assembled, closed, and fired, creating the ostomy.

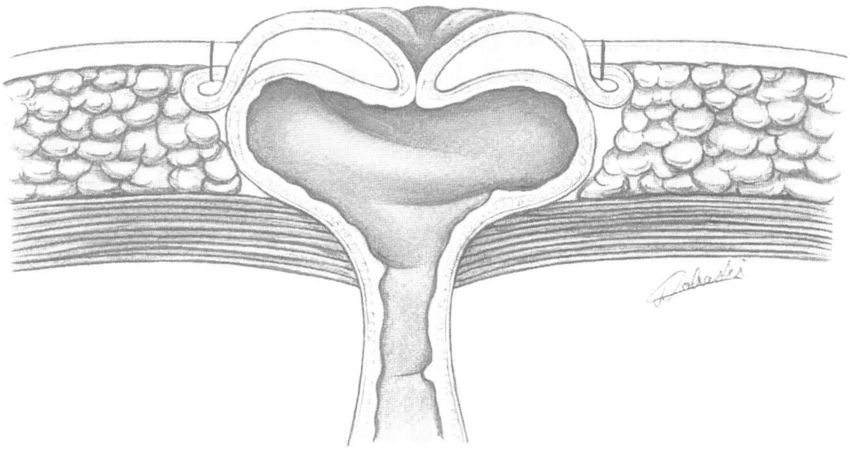

View of the colostomy after the instrument has been fired.

7 Colorectal Surgery

Sigmoidectomy

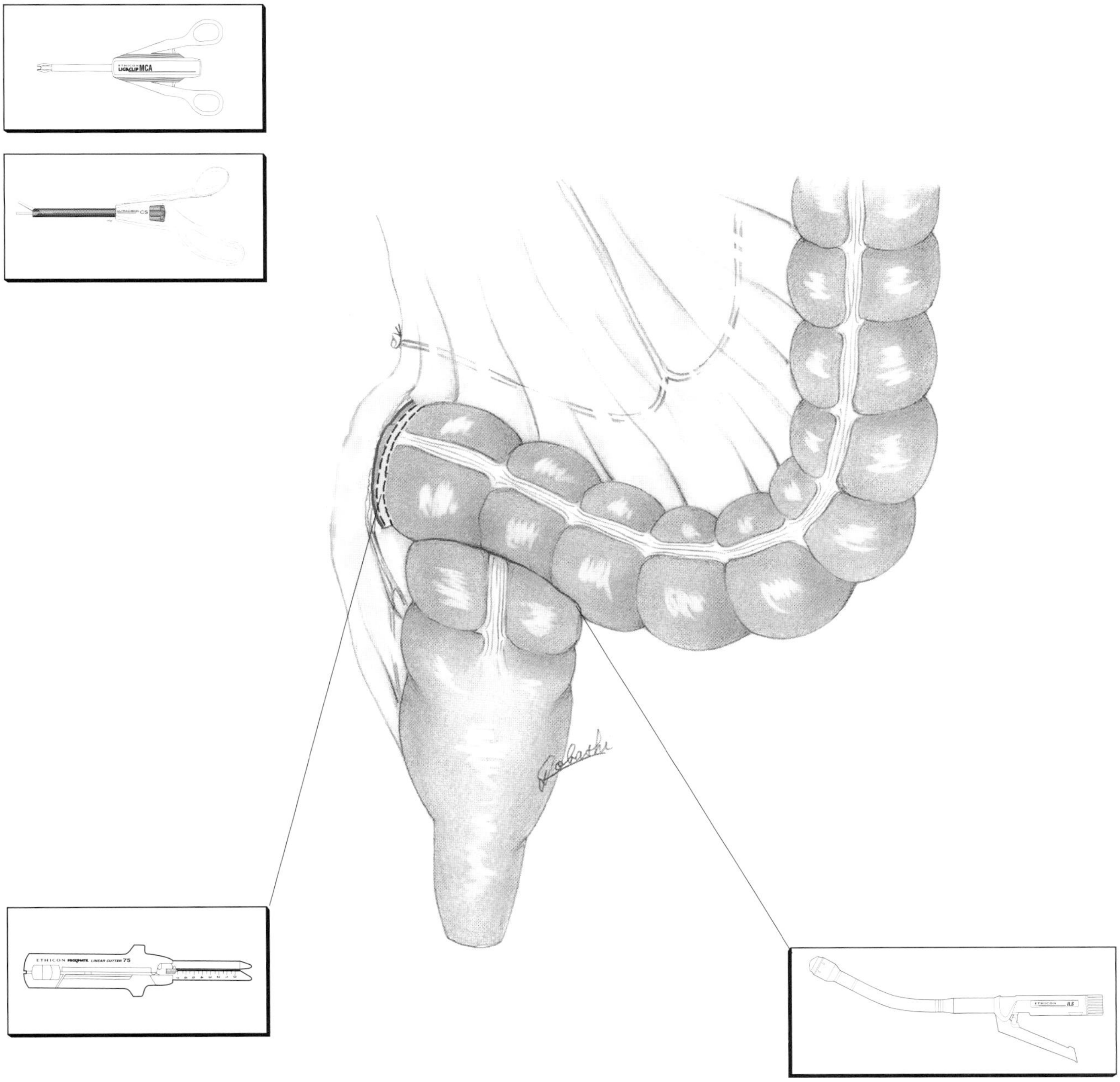

End result after completion of a sigmoidectomy. The following diagrams illustrate a reconstruction technique.

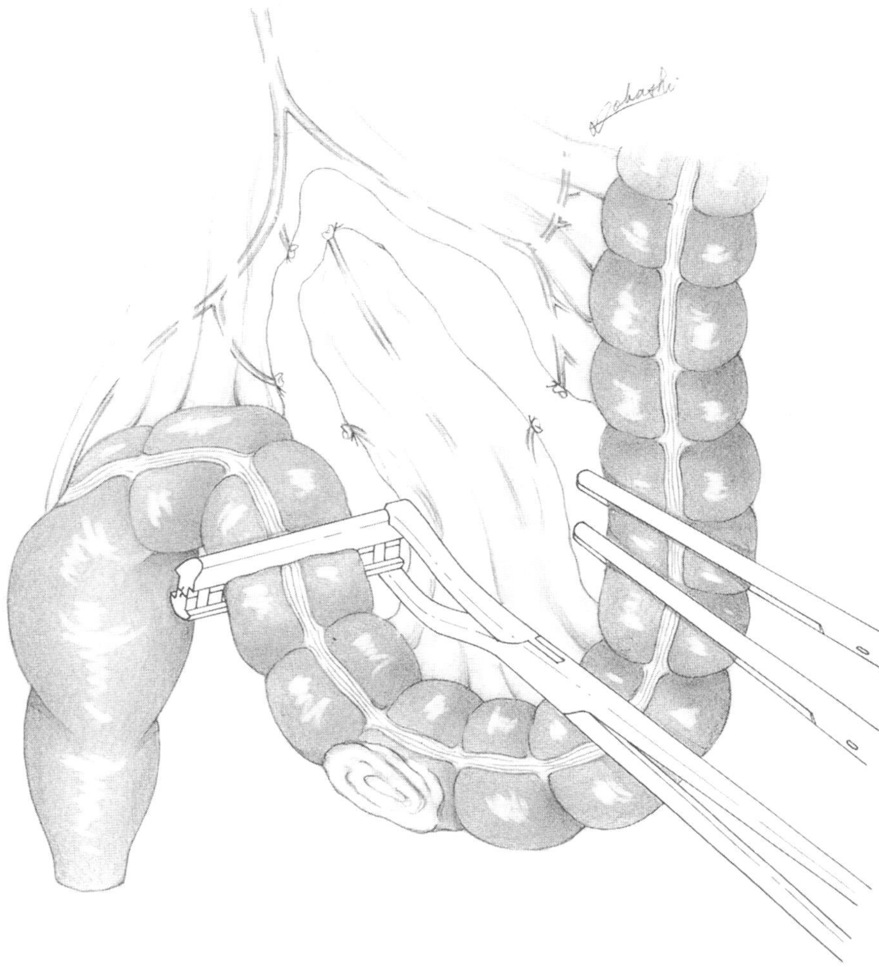

Proximally to the pathological tract, a transection is performed between bowel clamps or by using a linear cutter standard. Distally, a purse-string suture is performed, using a purse-string clamp well below the portion to be resected.

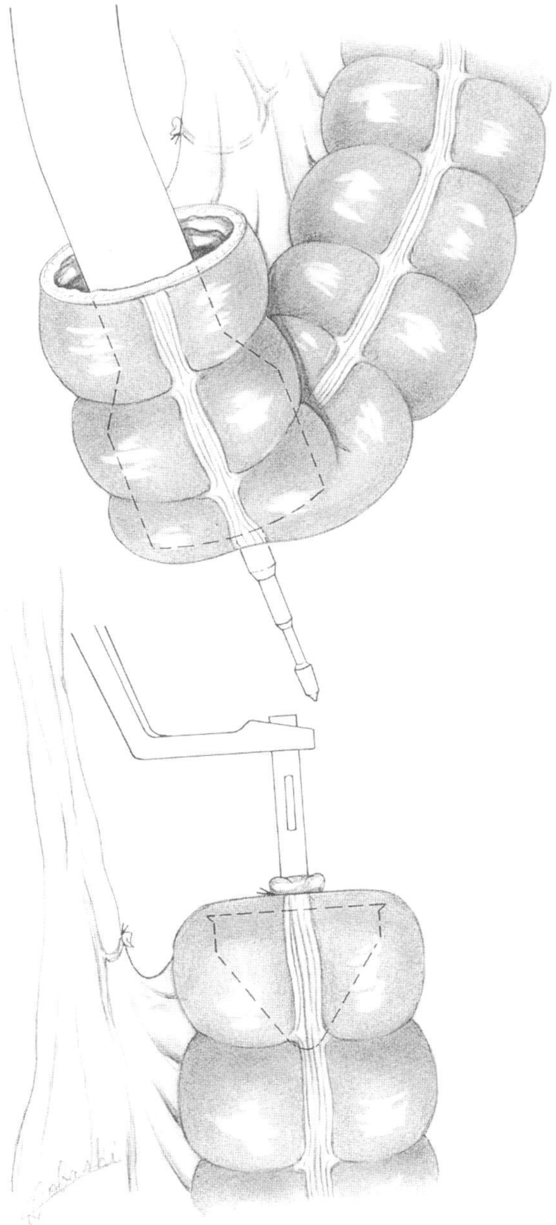

A circular stapler of the right calibre is inserted into the intestinal lumen through the proximal stump. The trocar of the stapler pierces through the wall of the proximal stump, whilst the anvil remains placed in the distal stump, with a purse-string. A side-to-end anastomosis is carried out using the circular stapler.

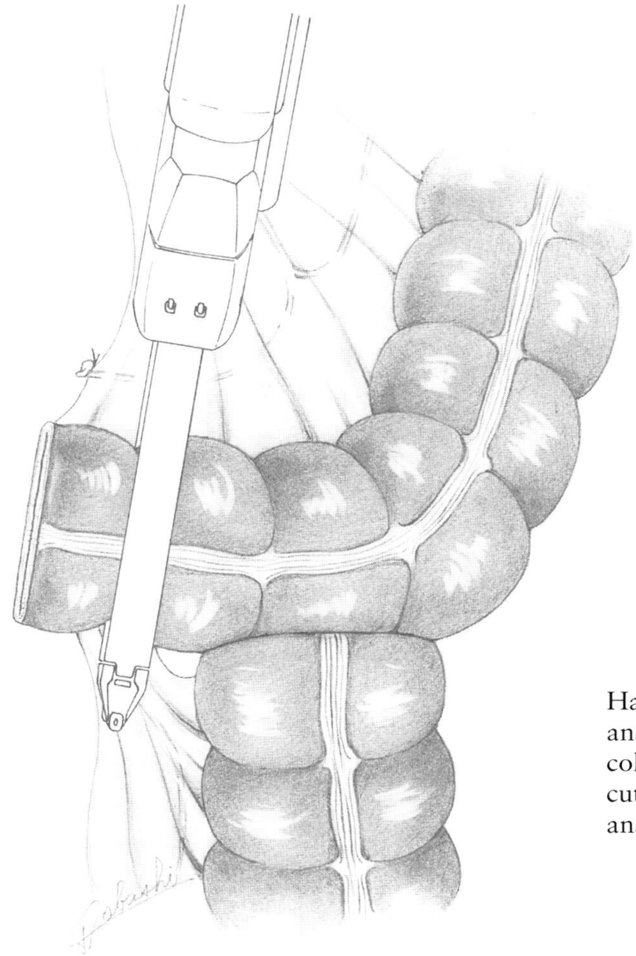

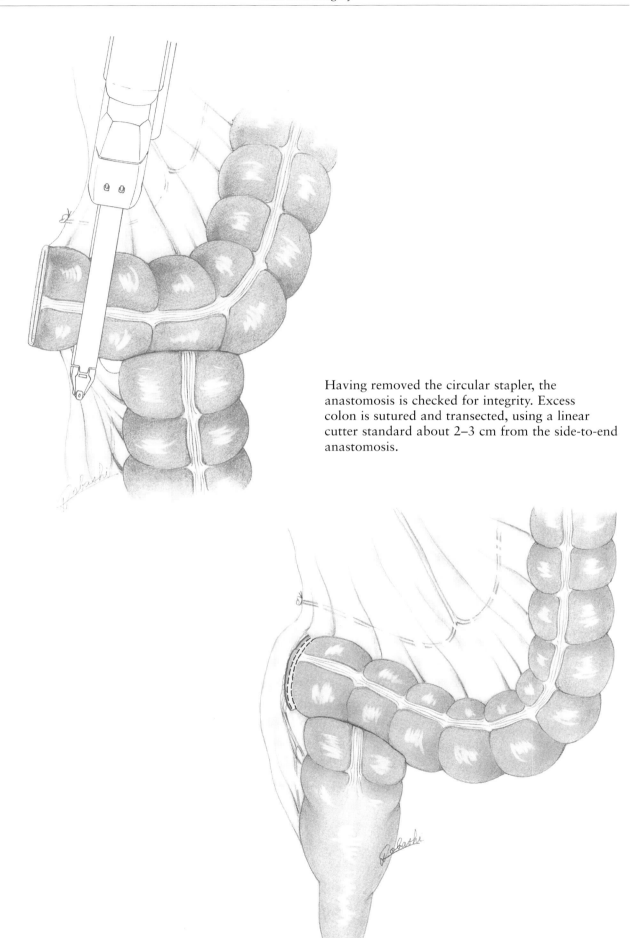

Having removed the circular stapler, the anastomosis is checked for integrity. Excess colon is sutured and transected, using a linear cutter standard about 2–3 cm from the side-to-end anastomosis.

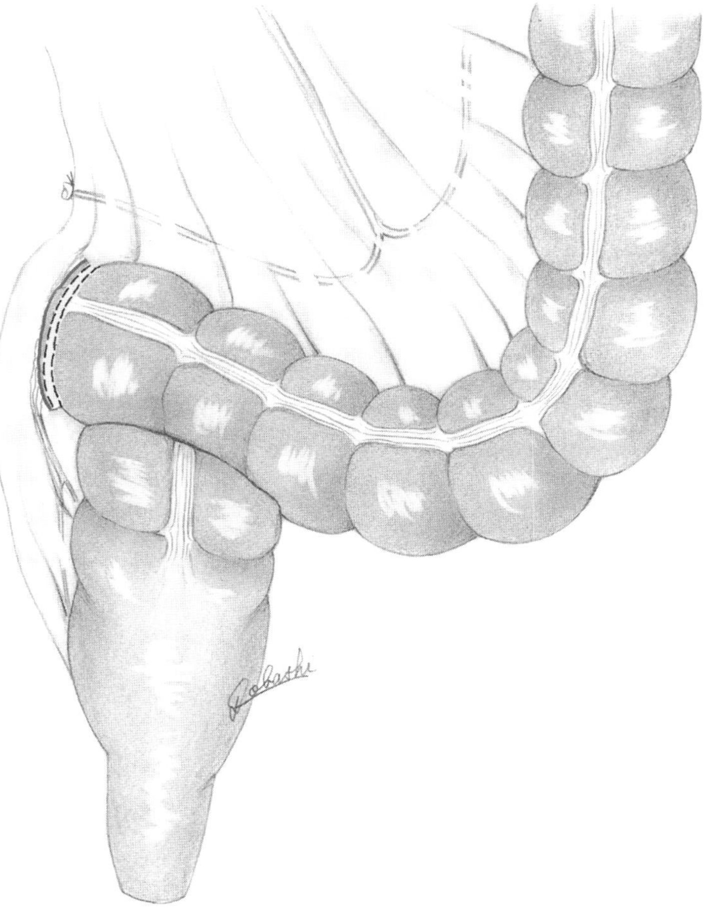

Low Anterior Resection

End-to-end Anastomosis

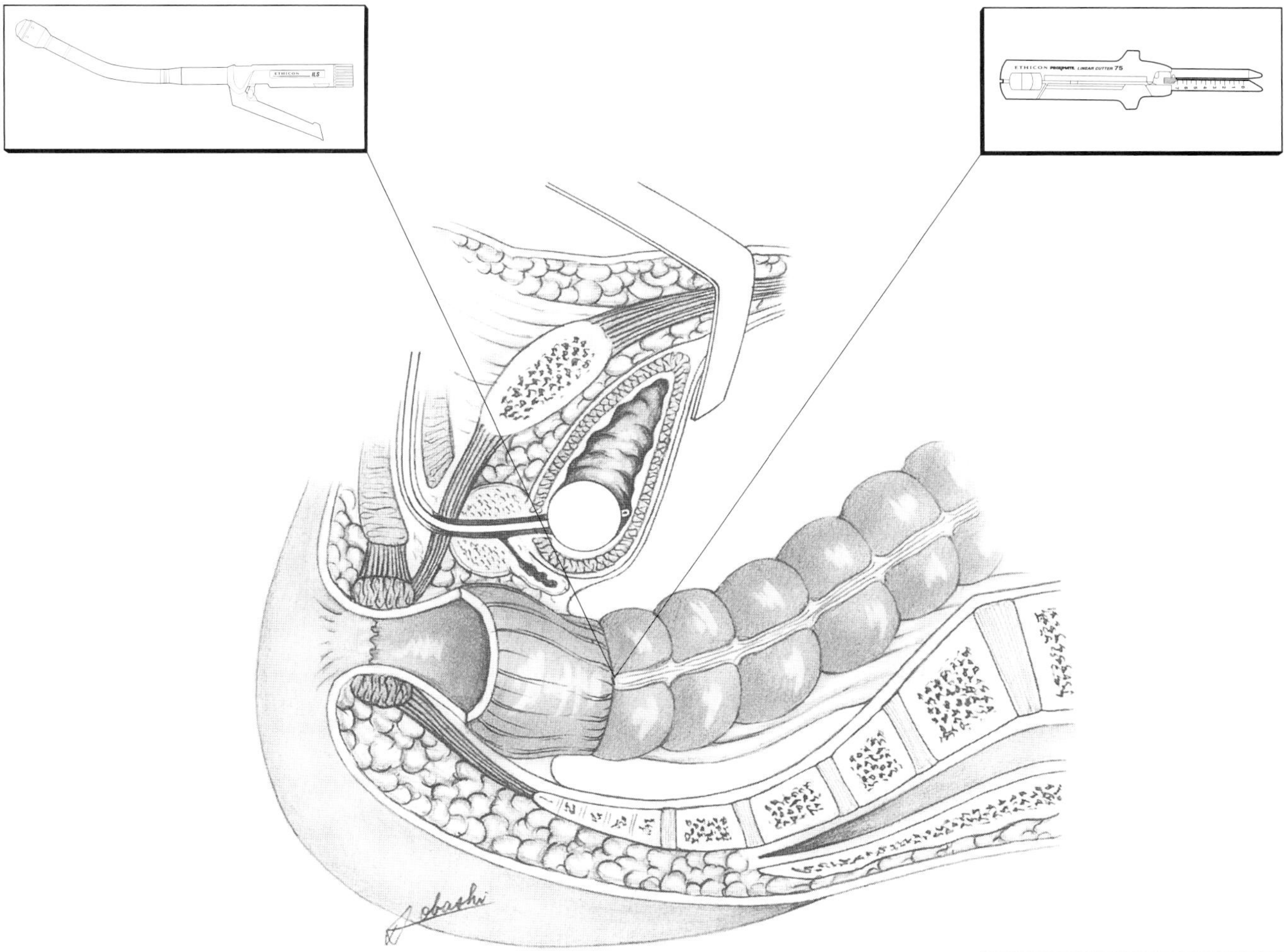

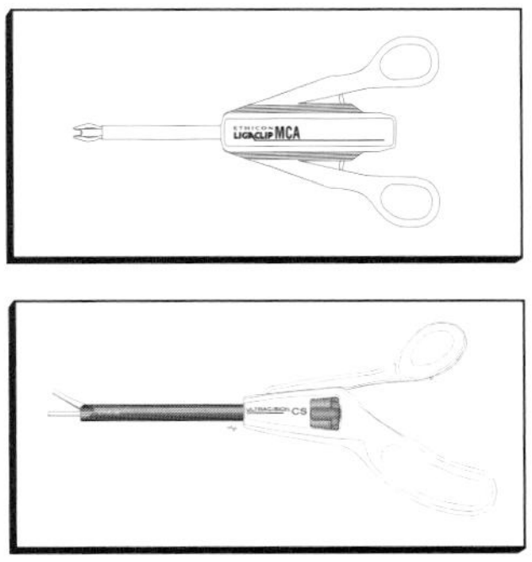

The diagram illustrates the end-to-end reconstruction technique following a lower anterior resection.

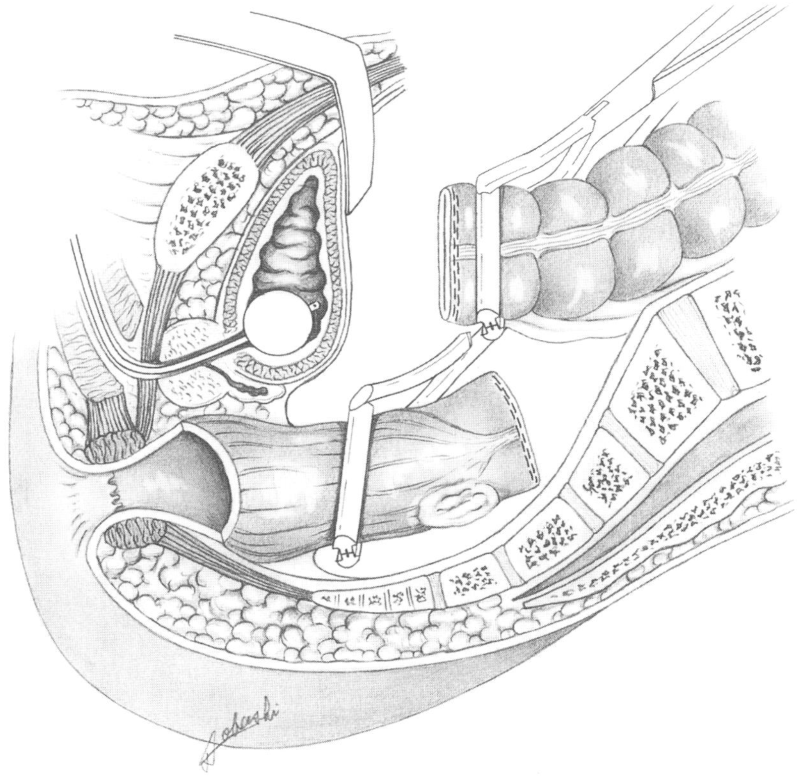

A transection of the bowel is performed using the linear cutter standard. A purse-string clamp is placed on the distal stump below the pathological tract. On the proximal stump another purse-string clamp is placed.

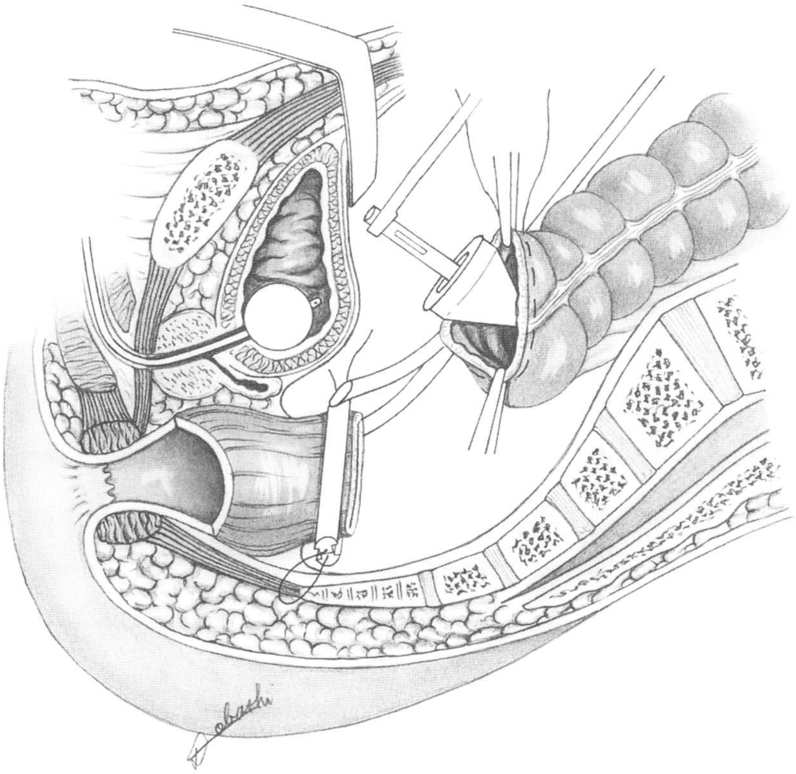

Purse-strings are performed both in the distal and the proximal stumps. After dilating the proximal stump with sizers, the anvil is inserted.

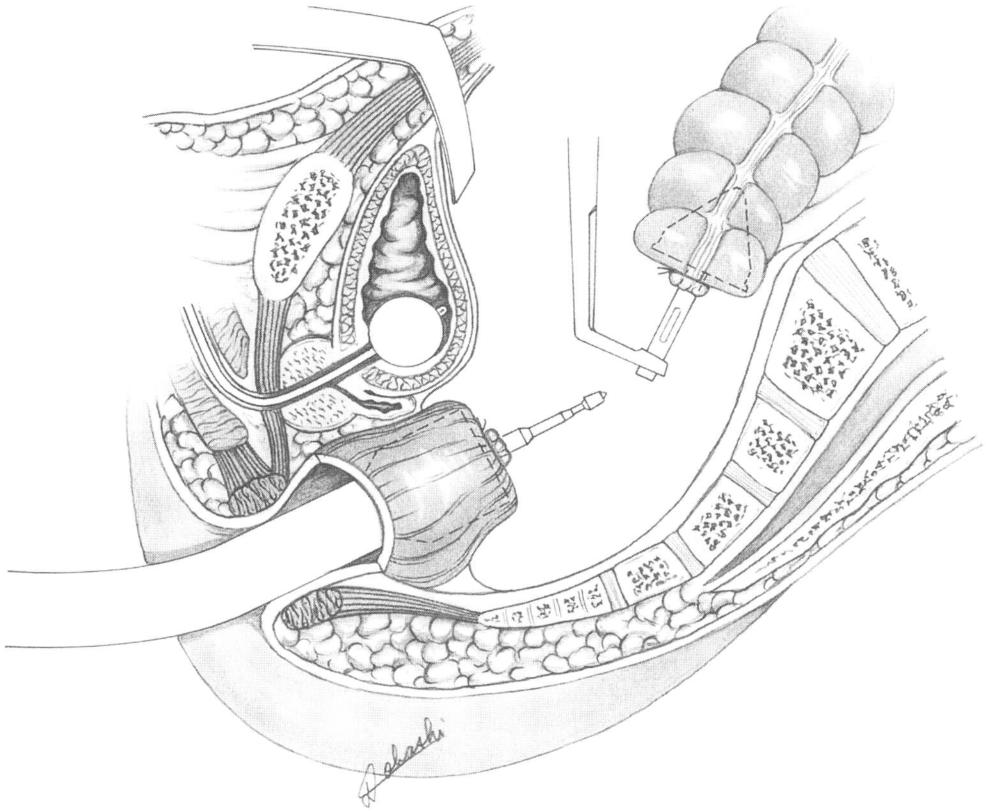

The circular stapler, without its anvil, is inserted transanally. After exteriorising the trocar the purse-string is closed around its base. The instrument is assembled, closed, and fired.

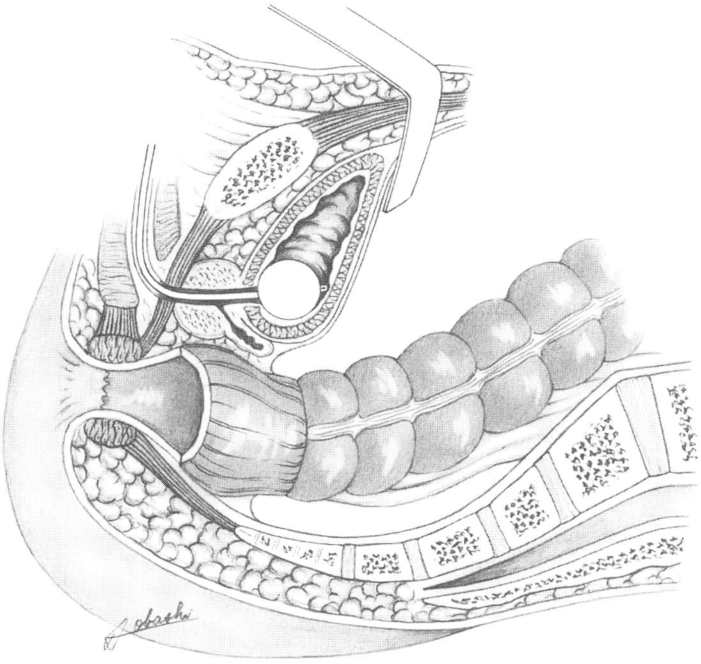

Low Anterior Resection

Double Stapling Technique

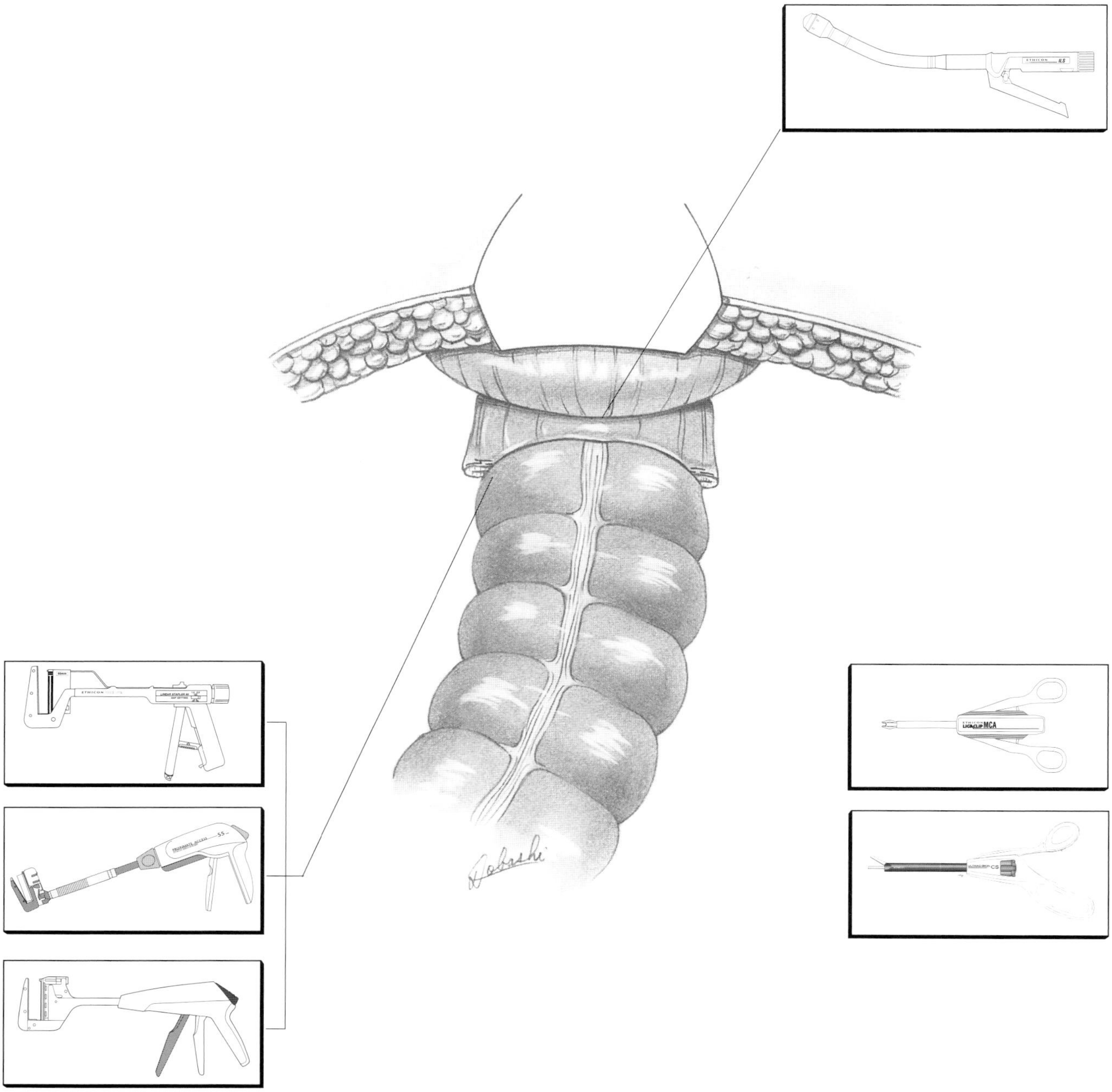

The diagram above illustrates the Knight-Griffen technique, adopted in cases where construction of the distal purse-string presents difficulties, and in cases where the dimensions of the stumps to be anastomosed do not match.

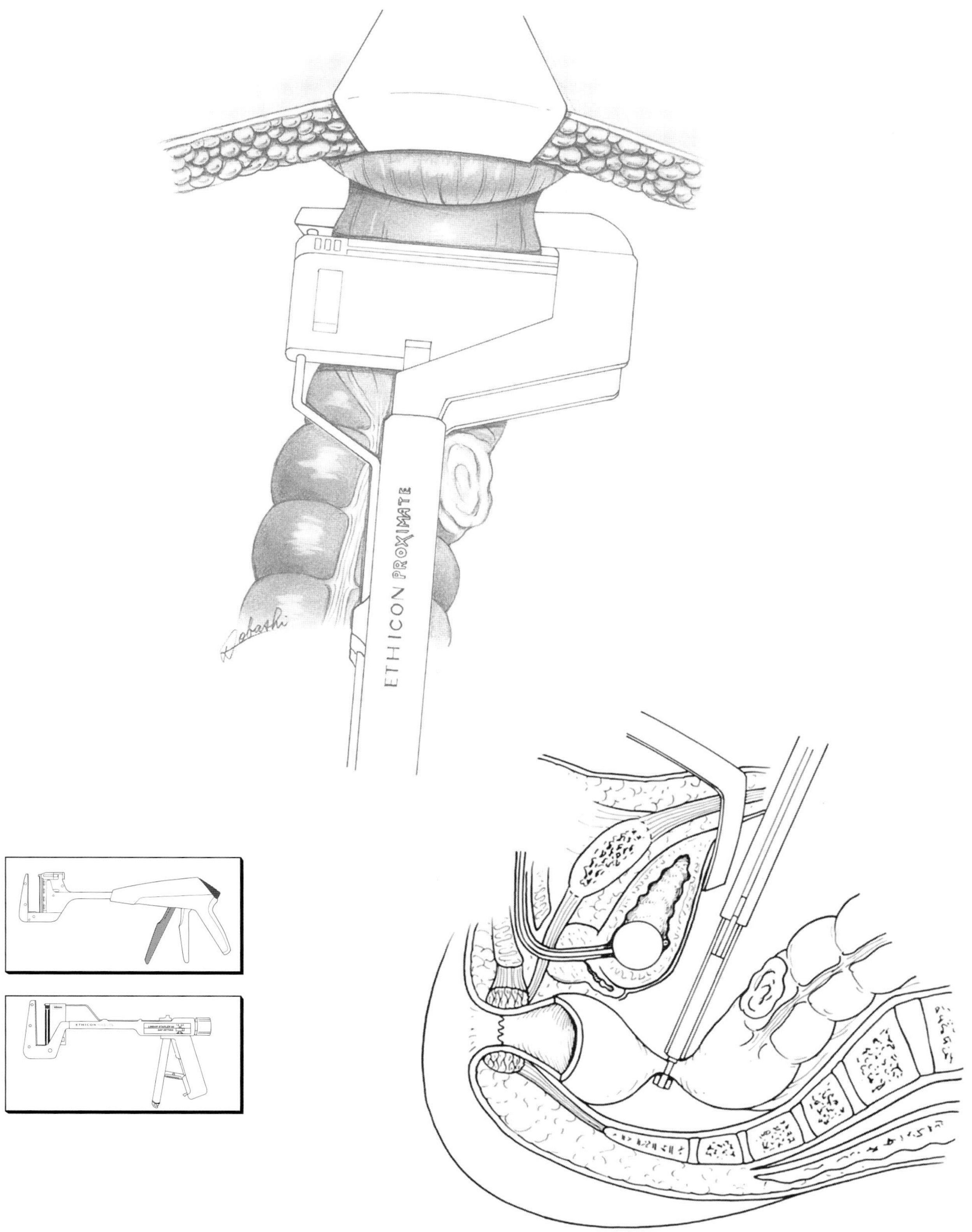

A linear stapler thick is placed below the pathological tract.

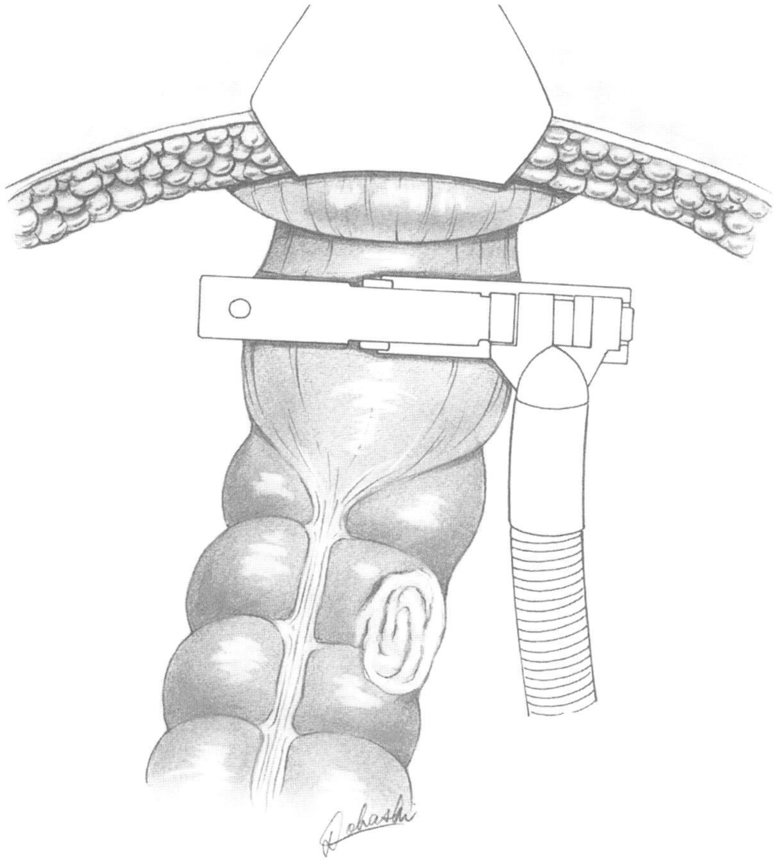

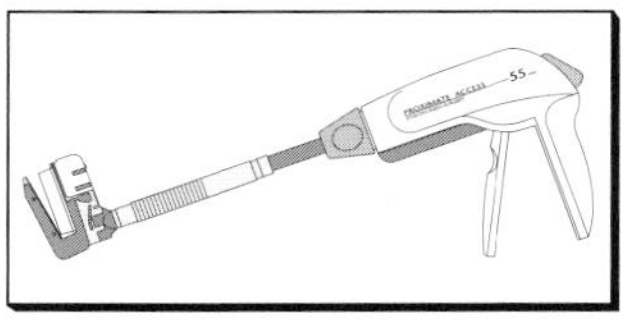

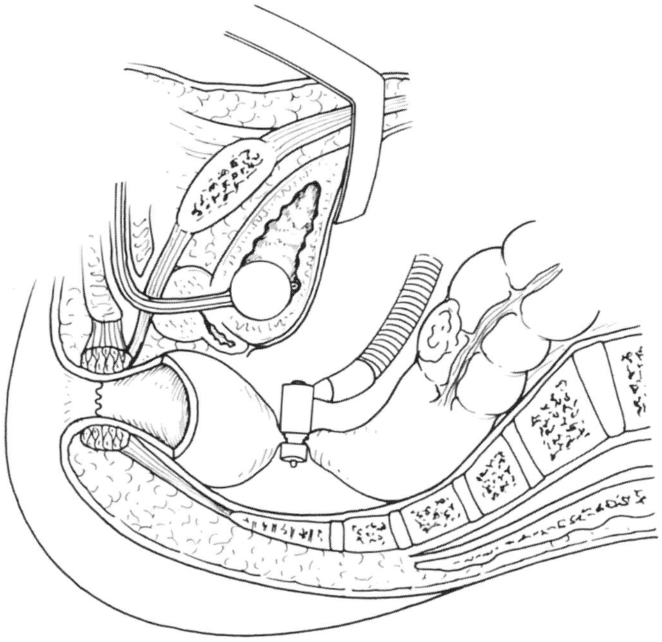

A variation on the previous page – in this case the suture is performed using an articulated linear stapler thick with a flexible shaft.

After firing the linear stapler thick, a transection is performed following the cutting guide of the stapler. On the other side a purse-string clamp is placed proximally to the pathological tract to be resected.

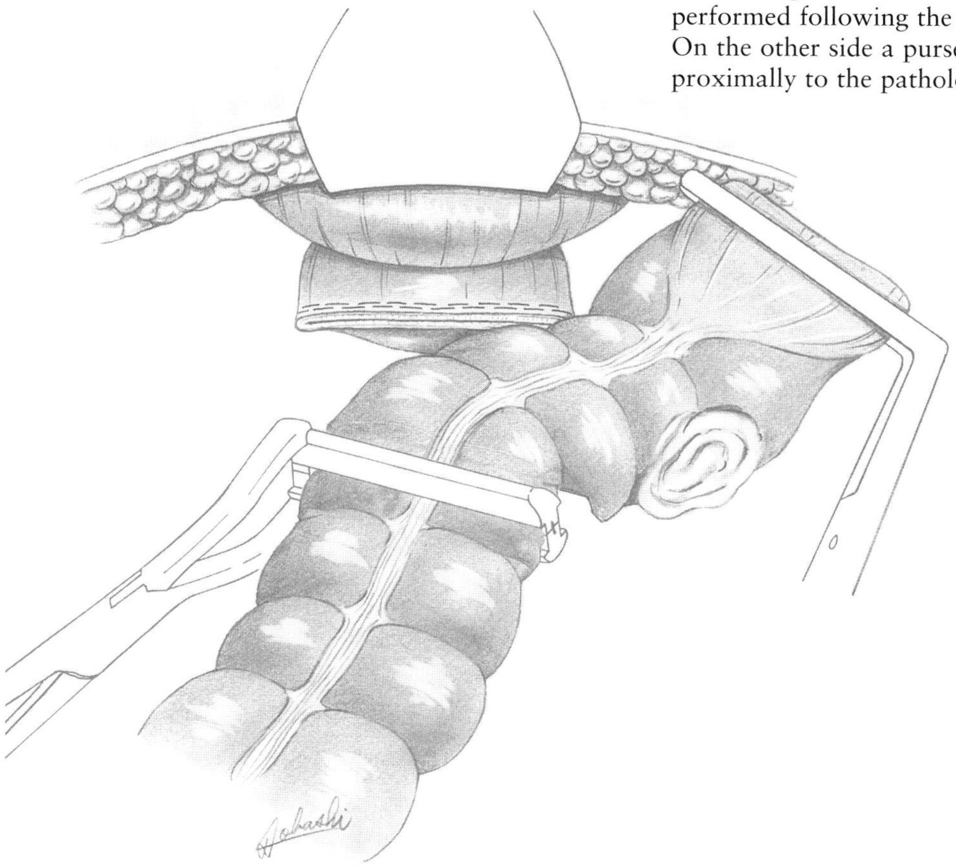

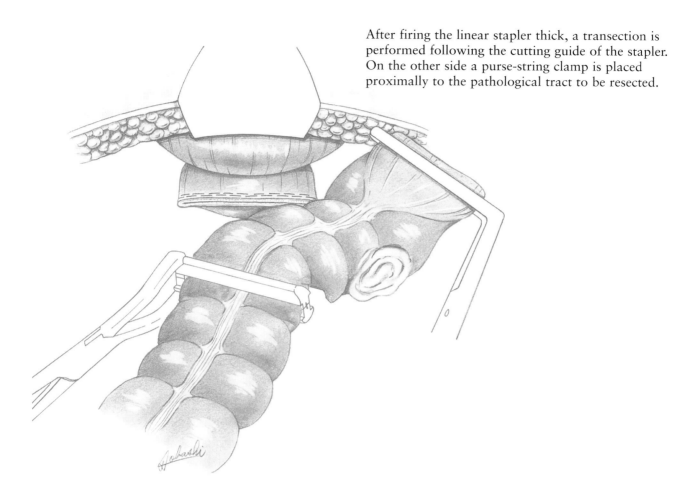

In order to complete the end-to-end anastomosis, the anvil of the circular stapler to be used is inserted in the proximal stump and the purse-string is closed tightly around its rod. The shaft of the circular stapler with the trocar withdrawn into the body is inserted transanally into the distal stump.

It is important, when exteriorising, that the trocar should pierce the anterior wall of the distal stump as close as possible to the staple line.

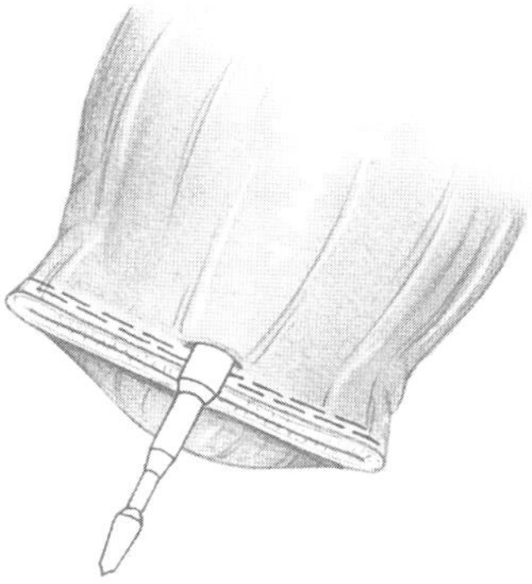

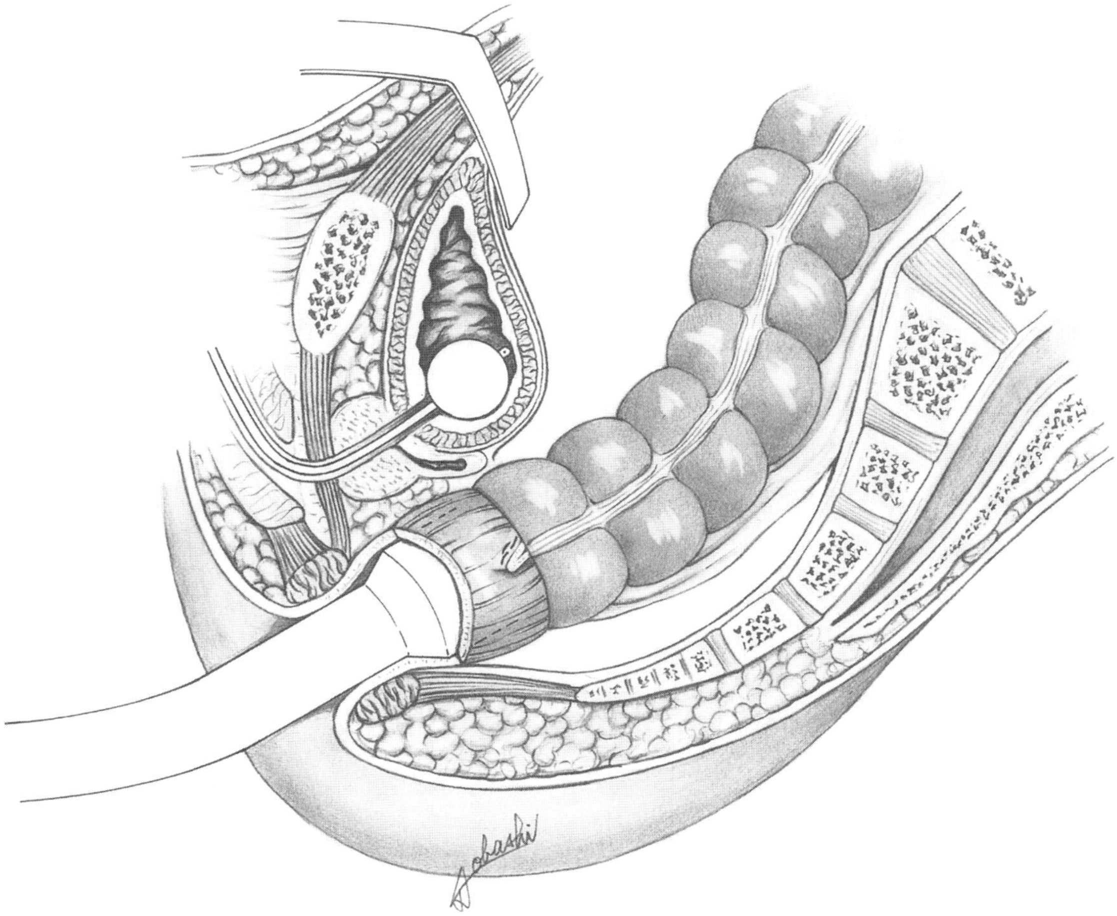

The circular stapler is assembled, closed, and fired, and the end-to-end anastomosis is carried out.

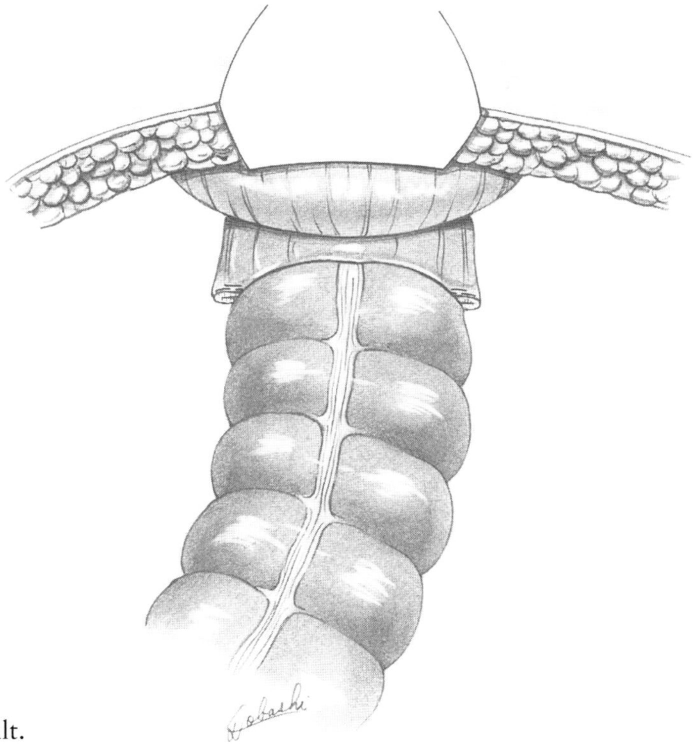

End result.

Low Anterior Resection

Duhamel Procedure

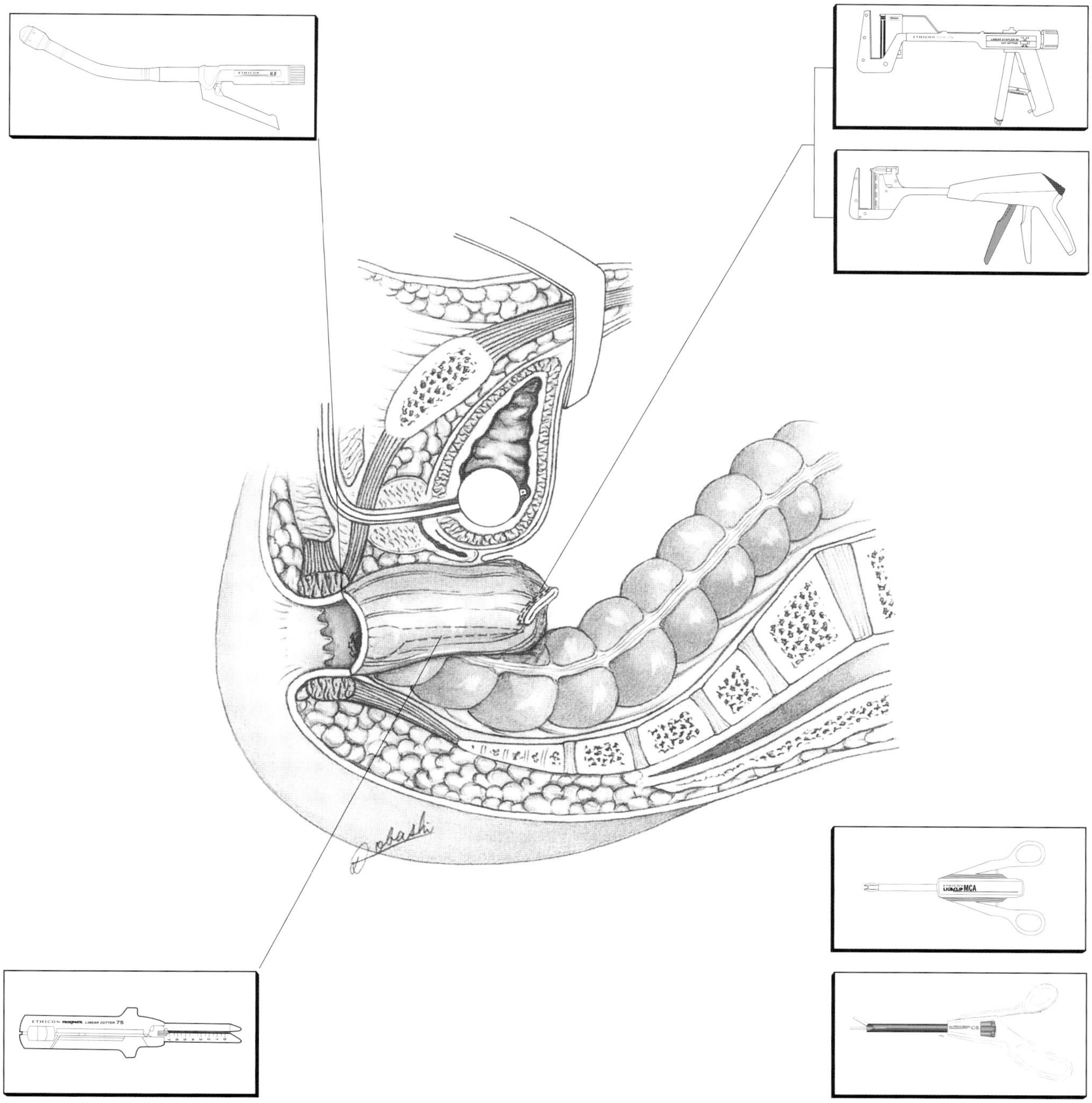

The diagram illustrates the Duhamel procedure, indicated in cases of children suffering from Hirschsprung's disease (congenital toxic megacolon).

A linear stapler thick is placed below the pathological tract. After firing the stapler, a transection is performed following the cutting guide of the stapler. On the other side a purse-string clamp is placed proximally to the pathological tract. The pathological tract is removed; later, a purse-string will be performed in order to insert the anvil of a circular stapler with an ancillary trocar.

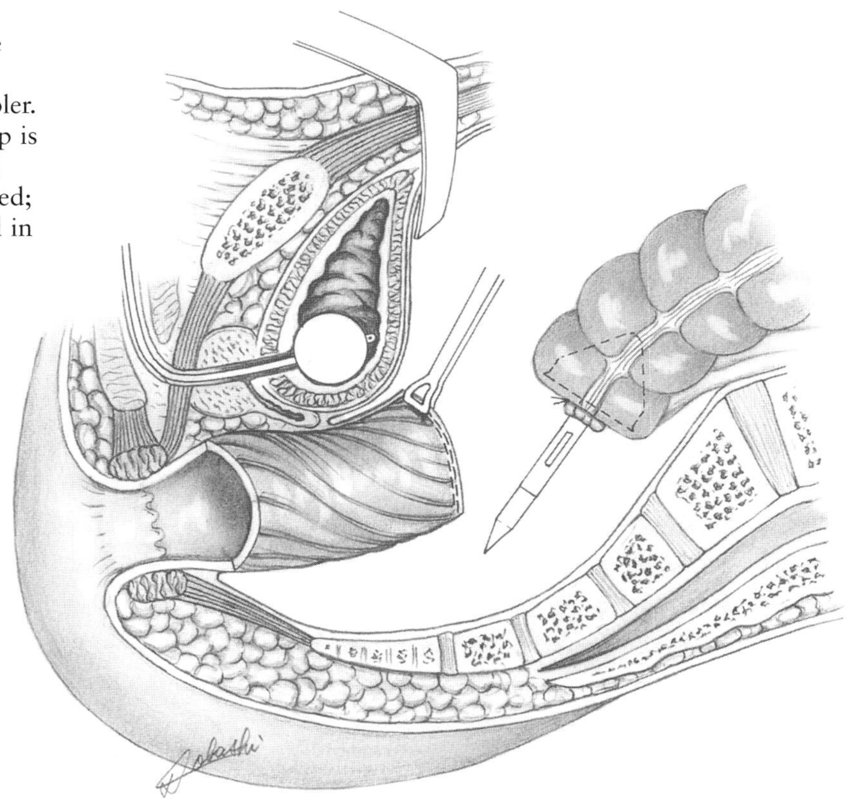

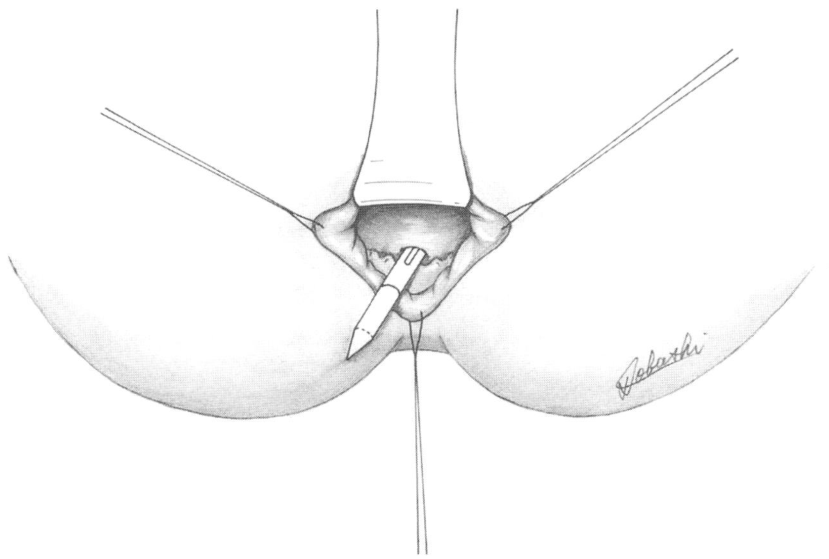

After closing the purse-string around the anvil rod, the tip of the ancillary trocar exits through the posterior wall of the rectum 2 to 2.5 cm above the dentate line.

The circular stapler is assembled, closed, and fired. End-to-side anastomosis between the colon and the rectum is carried out.

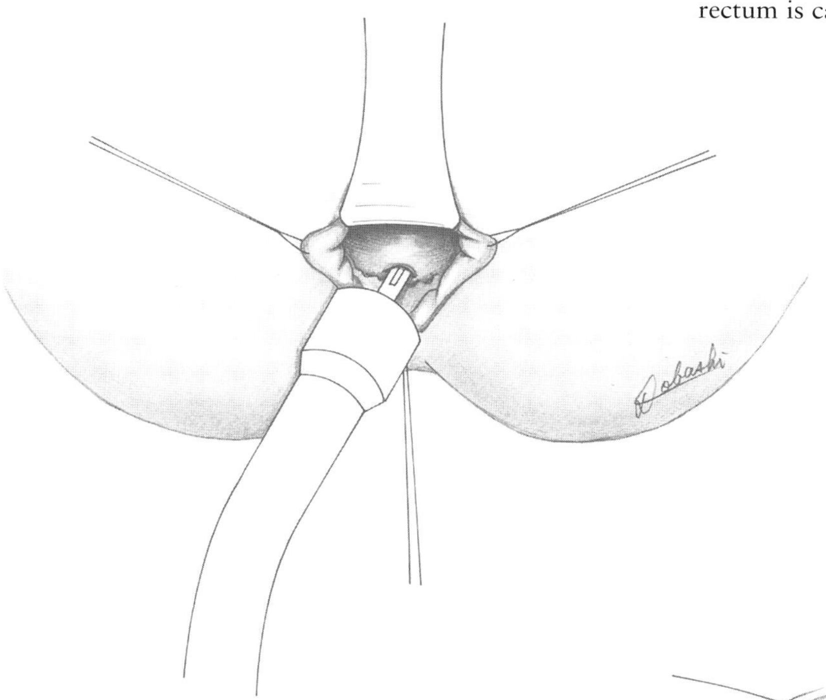

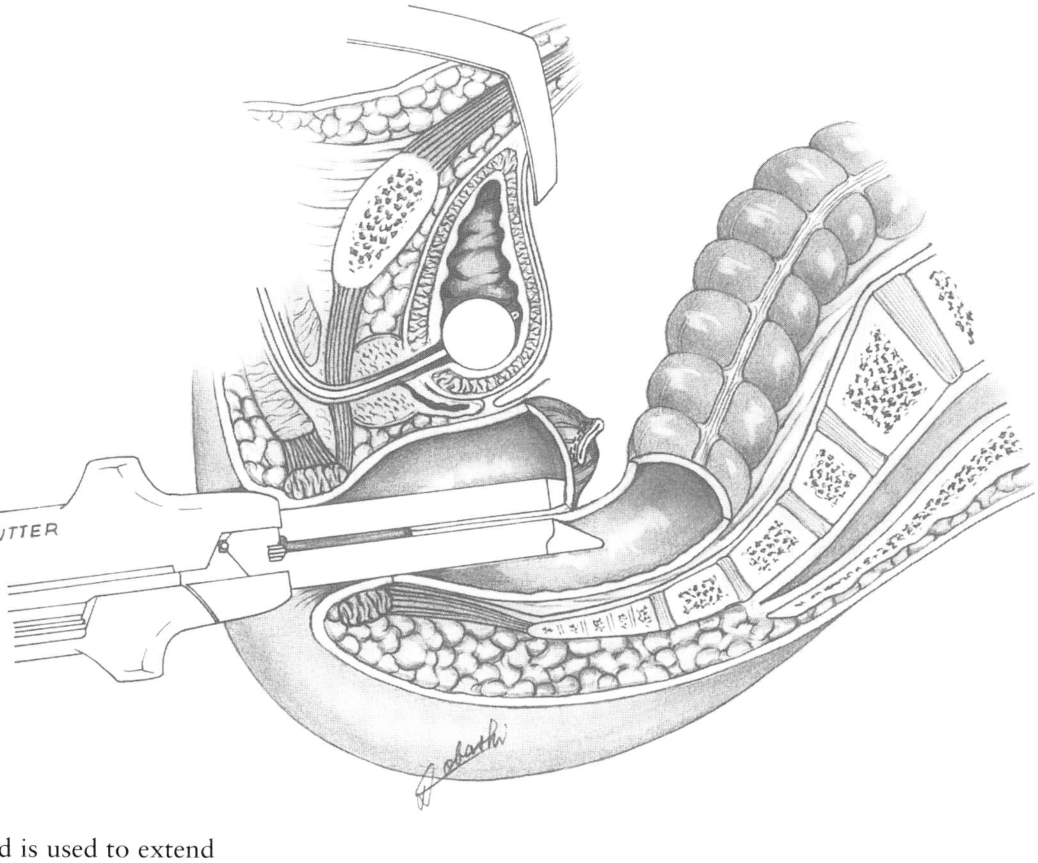

A linear cutter standard is used to extend the anastomosis between the rectum and the colon in order to create a reservoir.

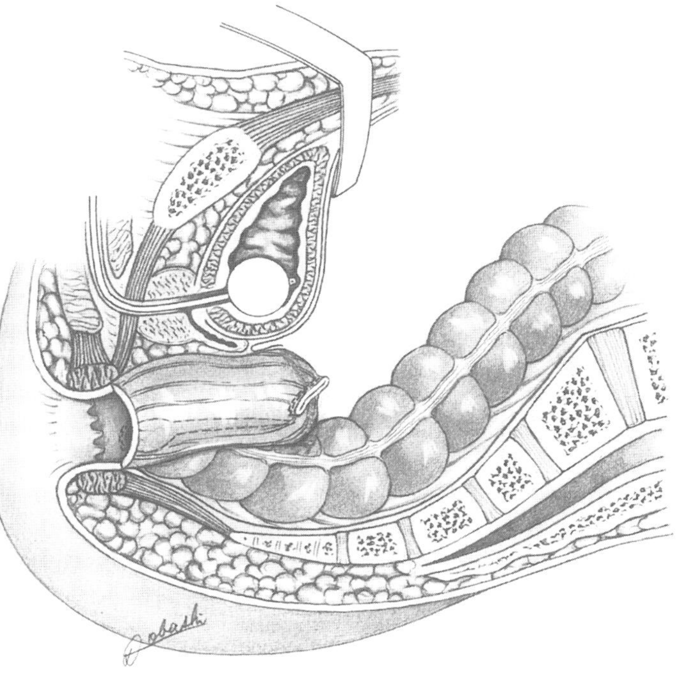

End result.

Colectomy: J-Pouch (1)

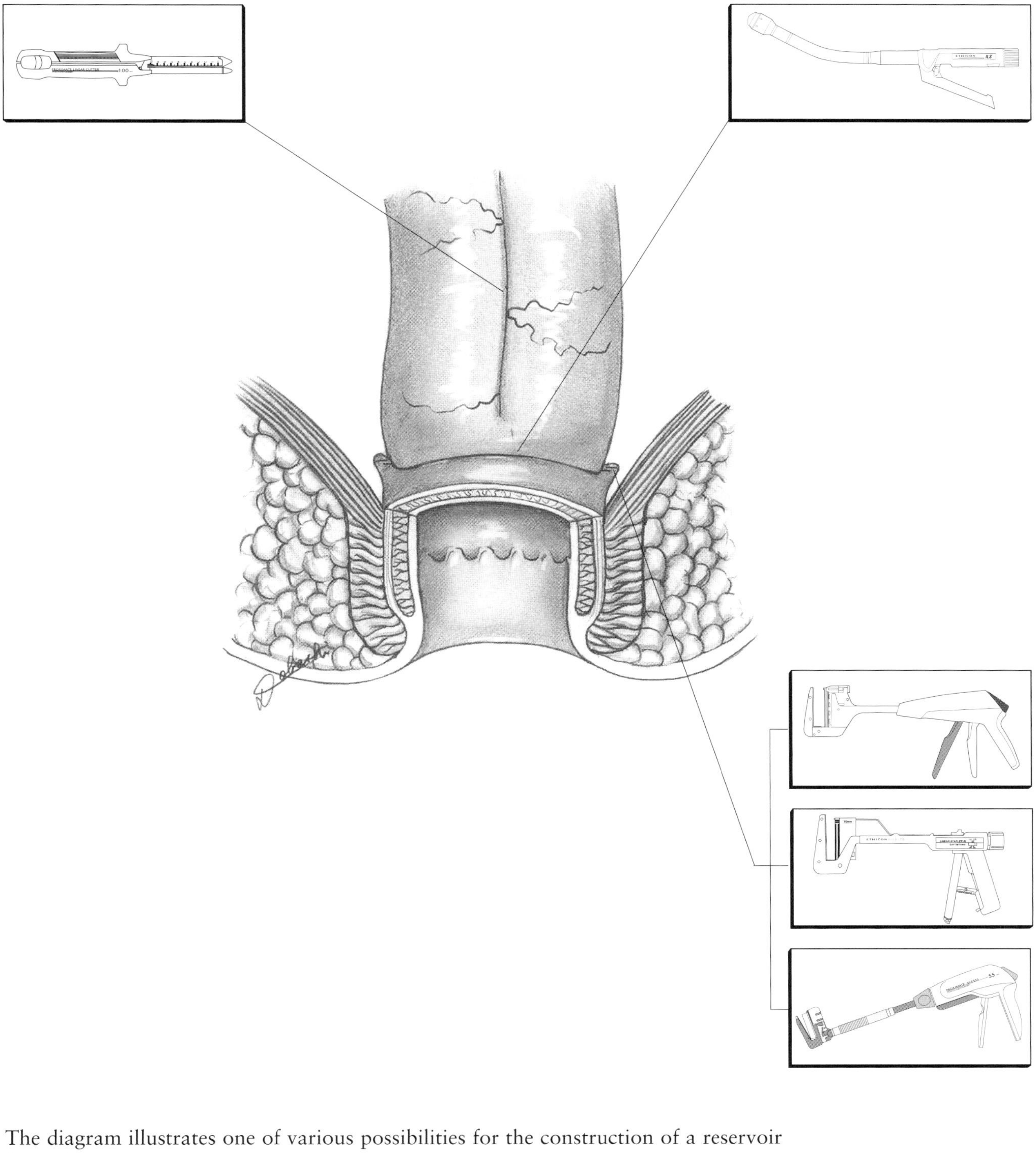

The diagram illustrates one of various possibilities for the construction of a reservoir following a total colectomy.

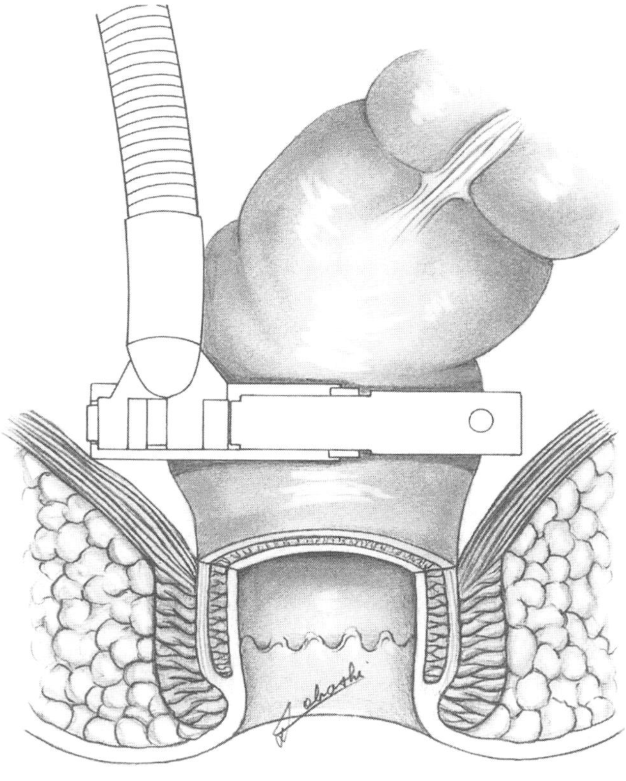

Closure of the rectum using an articulated linear stapler thick with a flexible shaft.

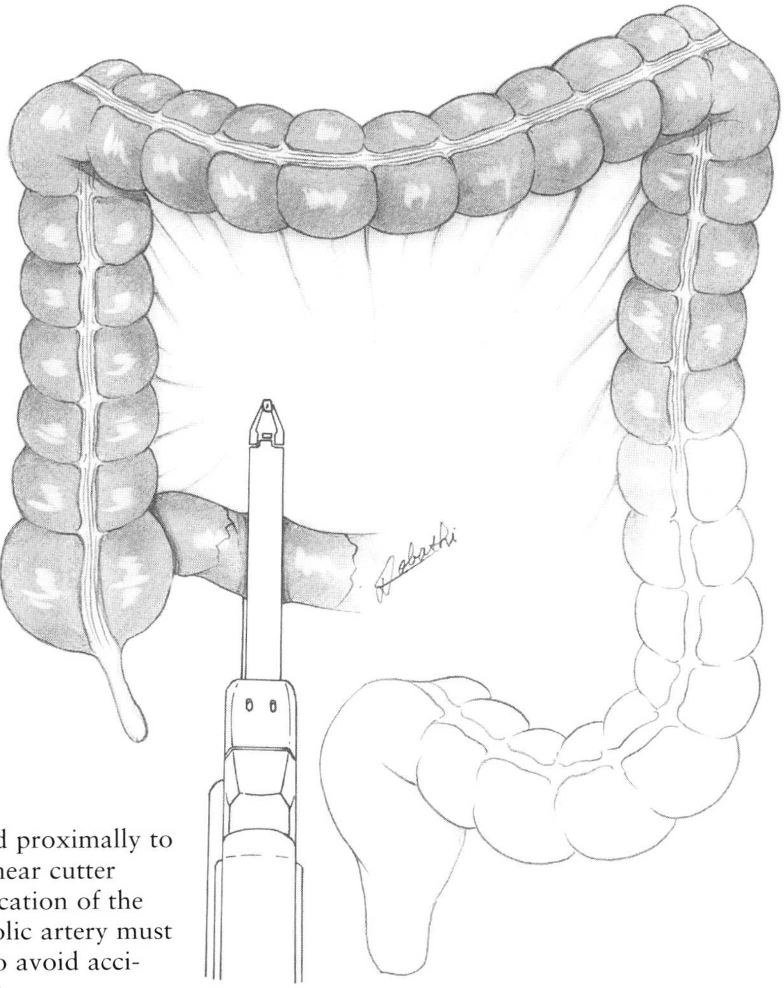

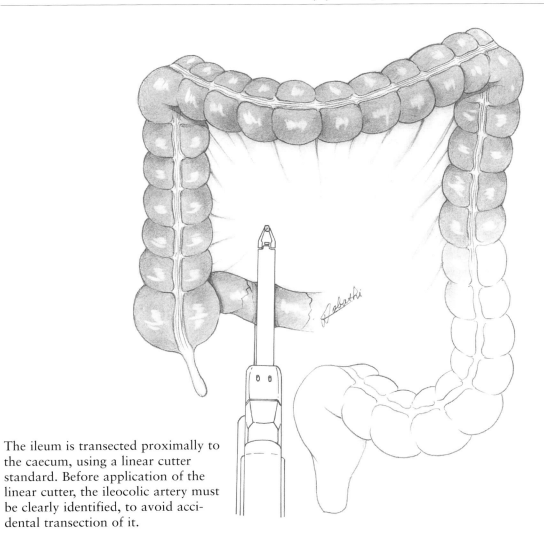

The ileum is transected proximally to the caecum, using a linear cutter standard. Before application of the linear cutter, the ileocolic artery must be clearly identified, to avoid accidental transection of it.

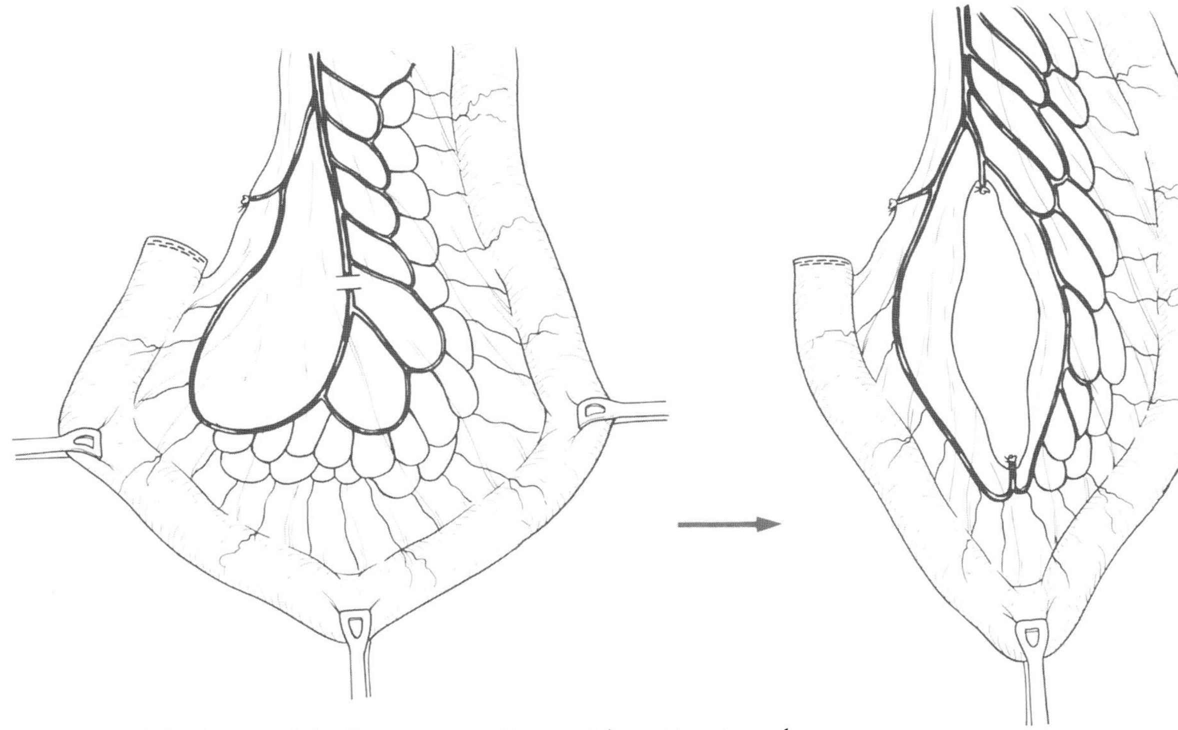

Preparation of the loops of the ileum, using clips or Ultracision in order to create a mesenteric window for posterior construction of the J-pouch.

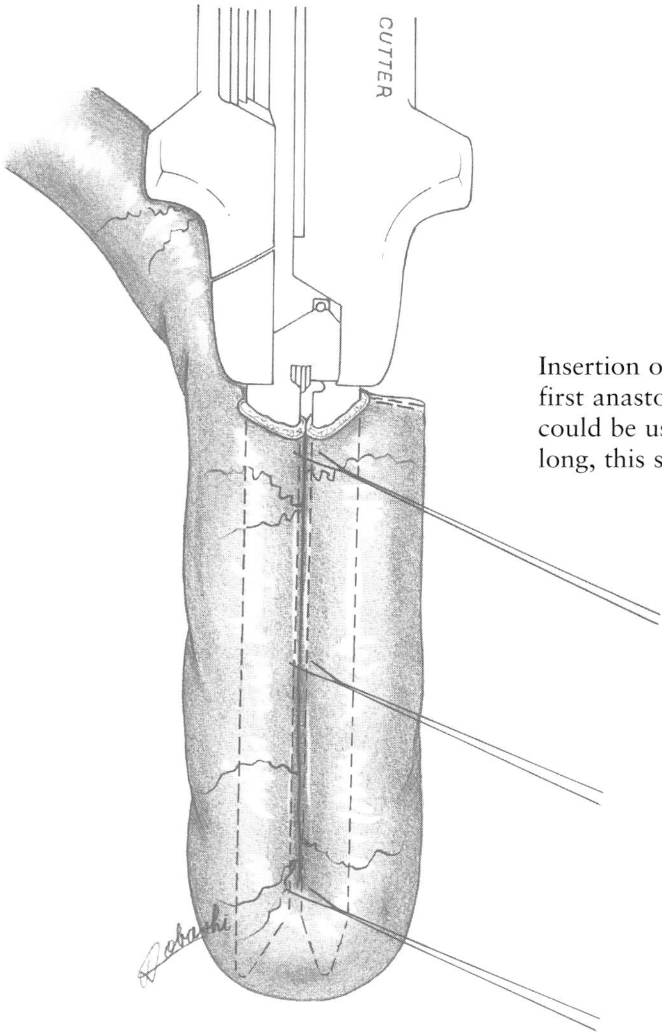

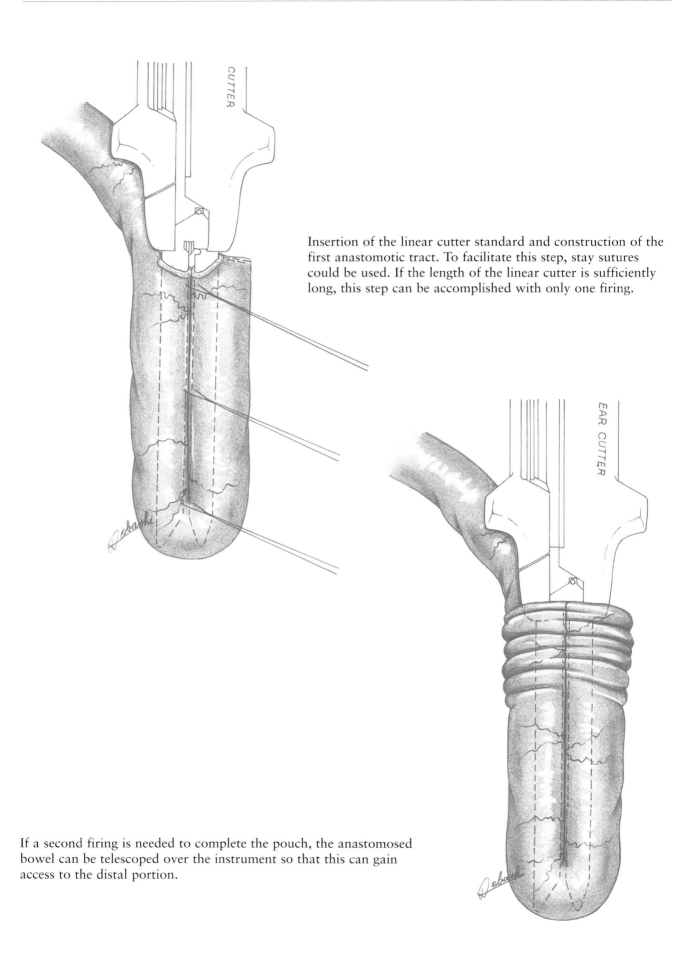

Insertion of the linear cutter standard and construction of the first anastomotic tract. To facilitate this step, stay sutures could be used. If the length of the linear cutter is sufficiently long, this step can be accomplished with only one firing.

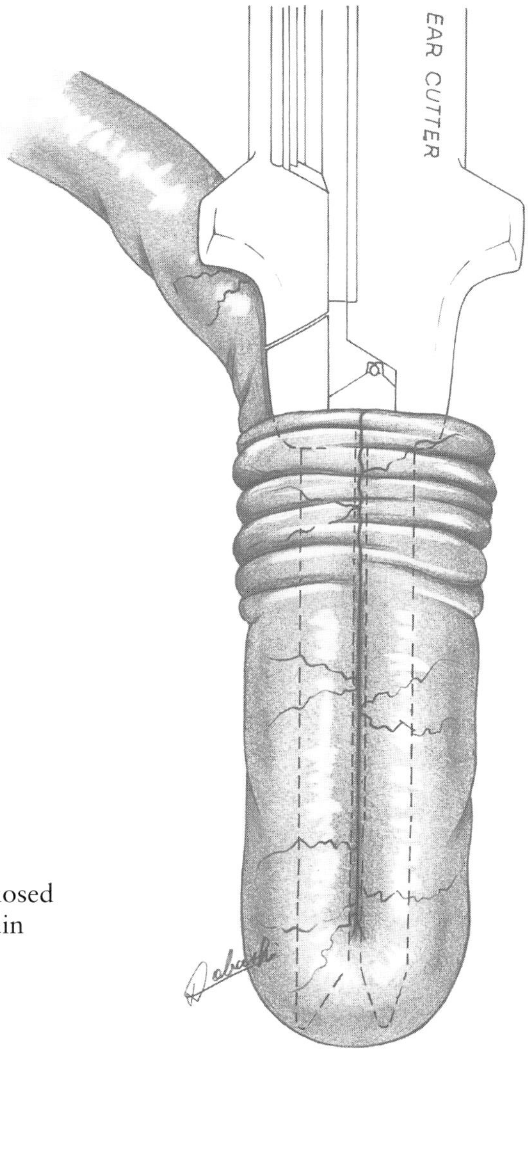

If a second firing is needed to complete the pouch, the anastomosed bowel can be telescoped over the instrument so that this can gain access to the distal portion.

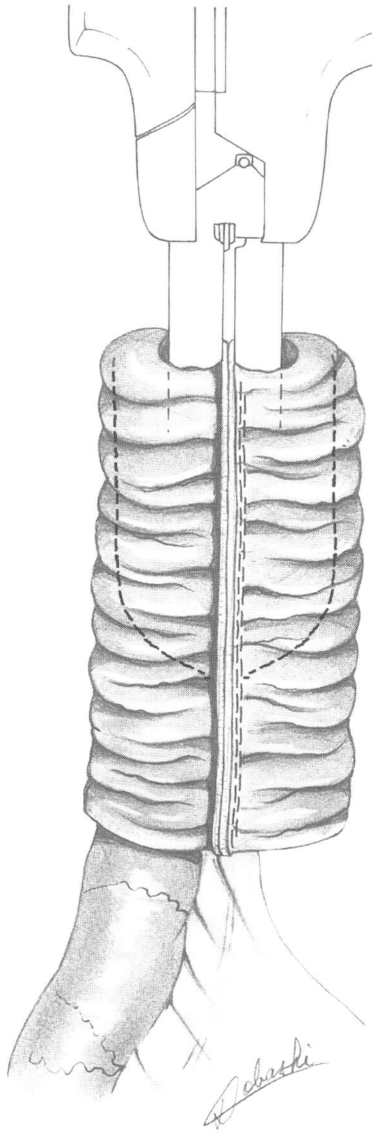

After the last firing, having the linear cutter still closed in place facilitates the eversion of the bowel, needed to control haemostasis.

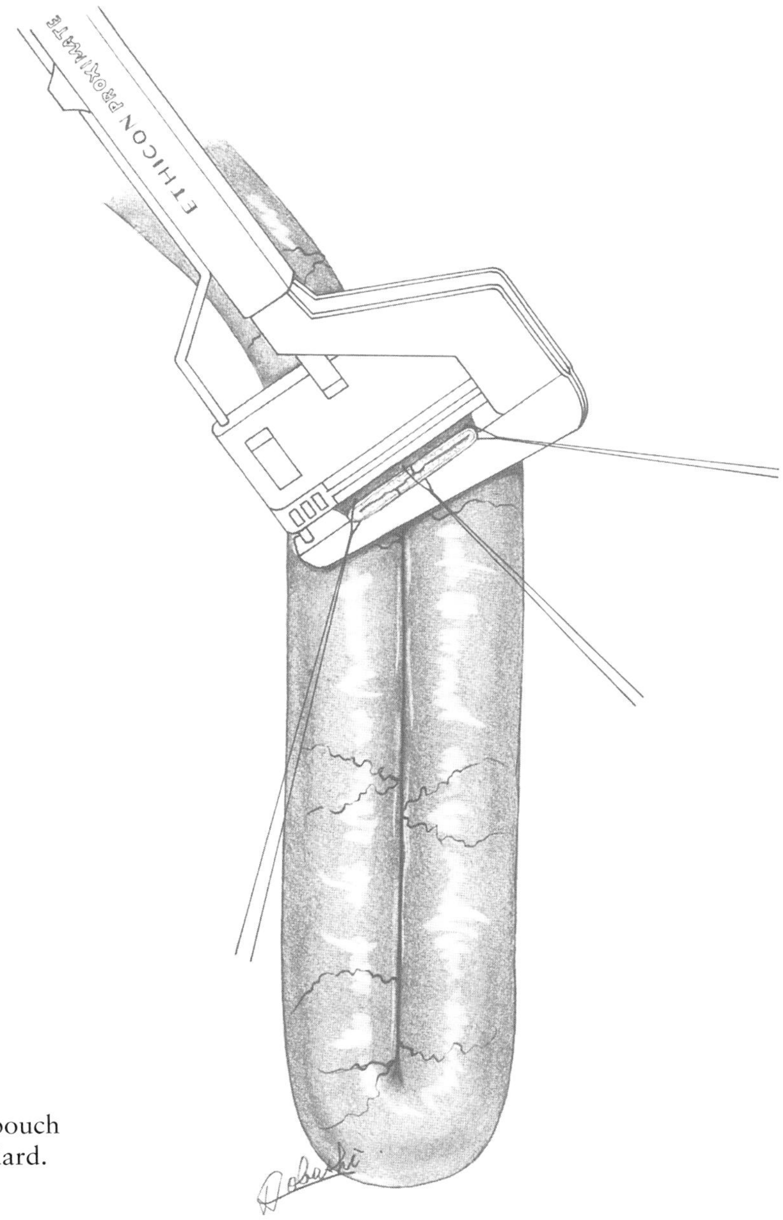

Following construction of the J-pouch, the pouch incision is closed using a linear stapler standard.

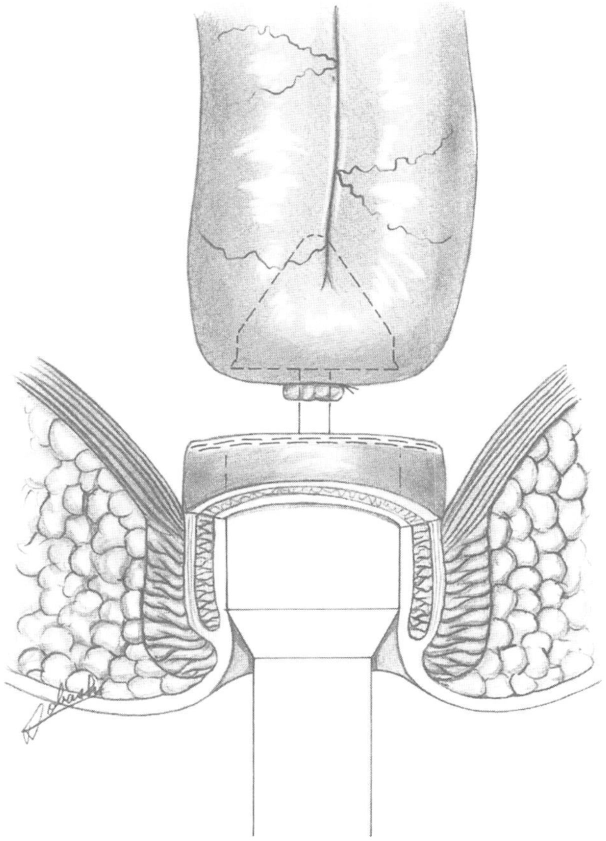

A purse-string is performed in the distal portion of the pouch and the anvil of the circular stapler is inserted. The circular stapler is inserted transanally and the stapler is assembled, closed, and fired, creating the anastomosis.

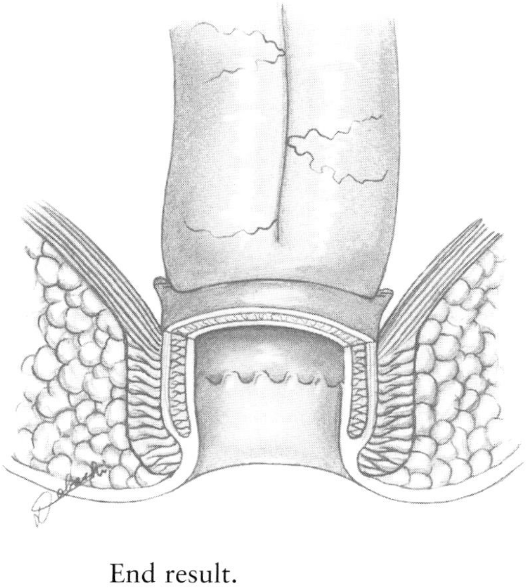

End result.

Colectomy: J-Pouch (2)

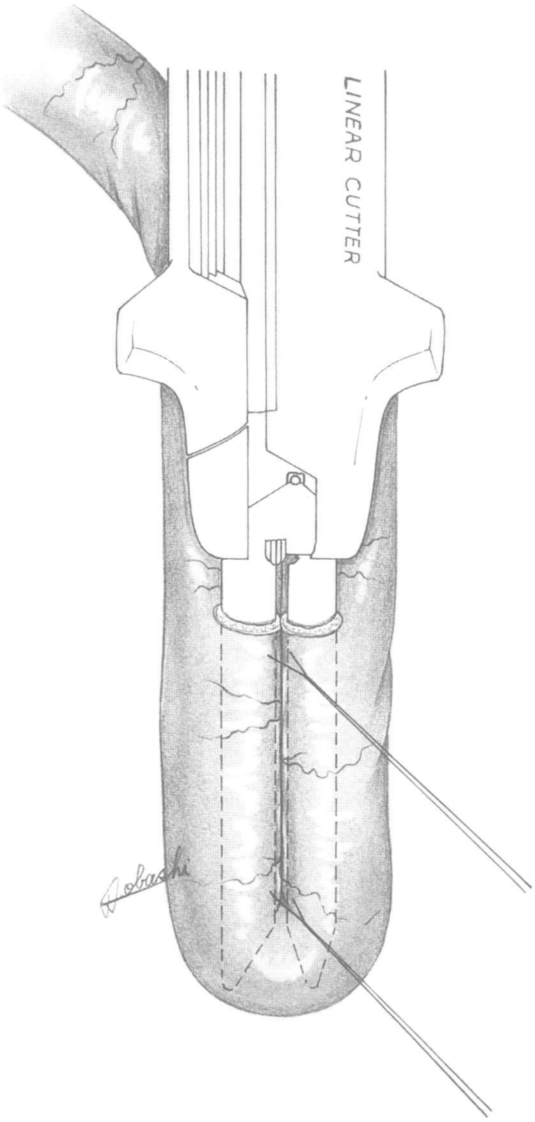

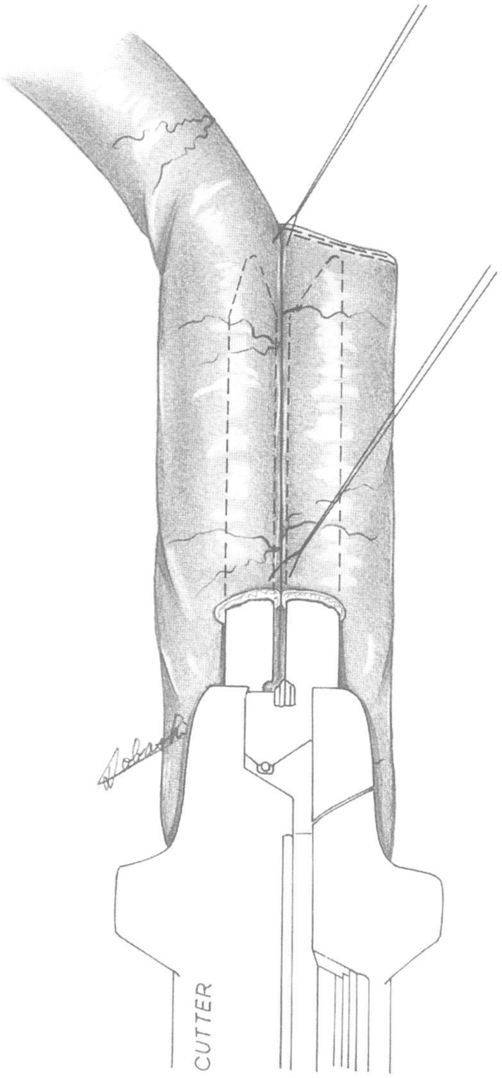

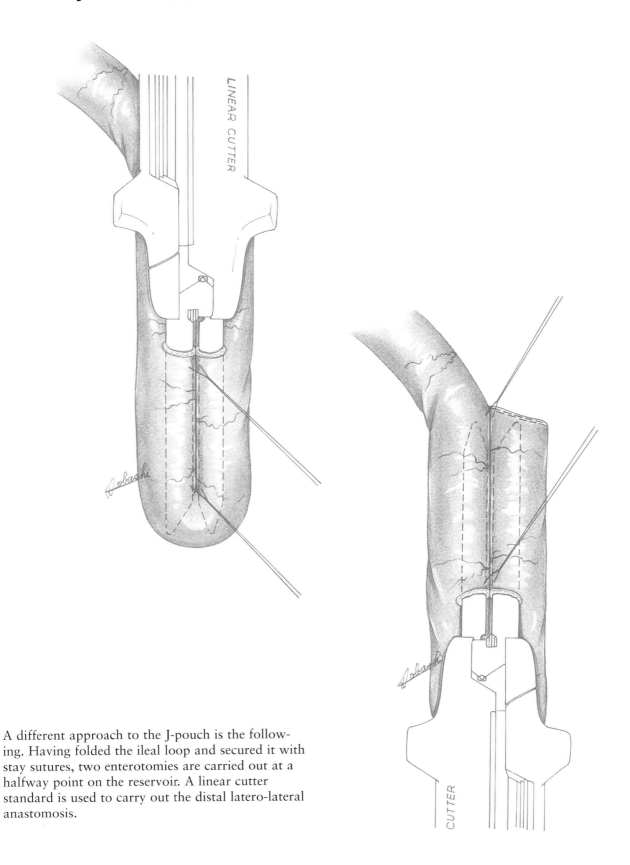

A different approach to the J-pouch is the following. Having folded the ileal loop and secured it with stay sutures, two enterotomies are carried out at a halfway point on the reservoir. A linear cutter standard is used to carry out the distal latero-lateral anastomosis.

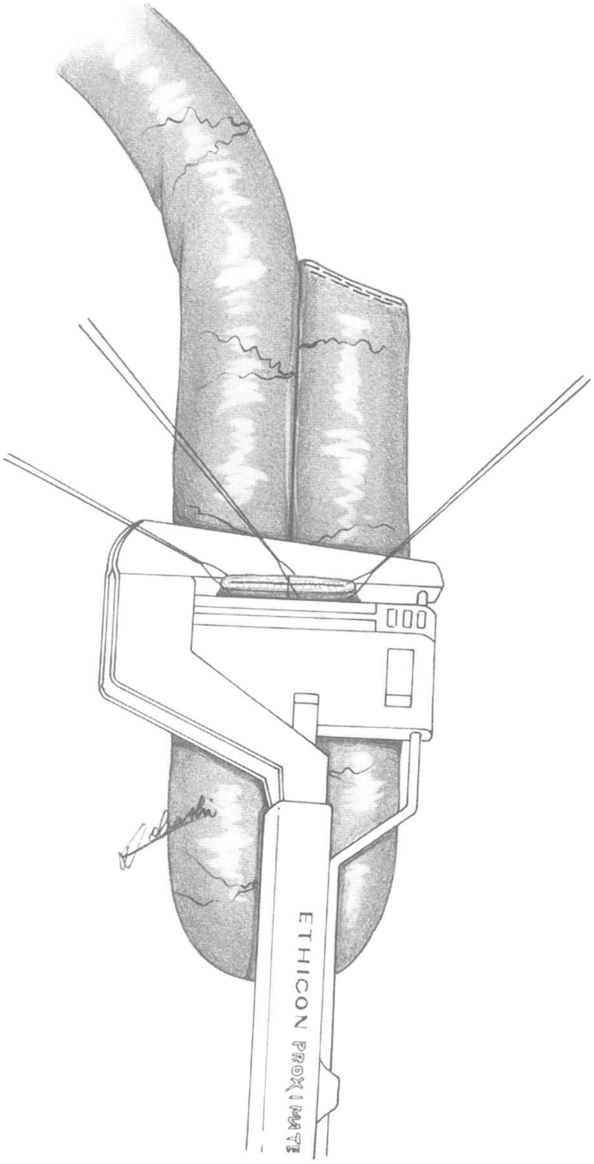

Afterwards, control of haemostasis in the reservoir closure of the enterotomies using a linear stapler standard is obtained with the aid of stay sutures.

Colectomy: J-Pouch (3)

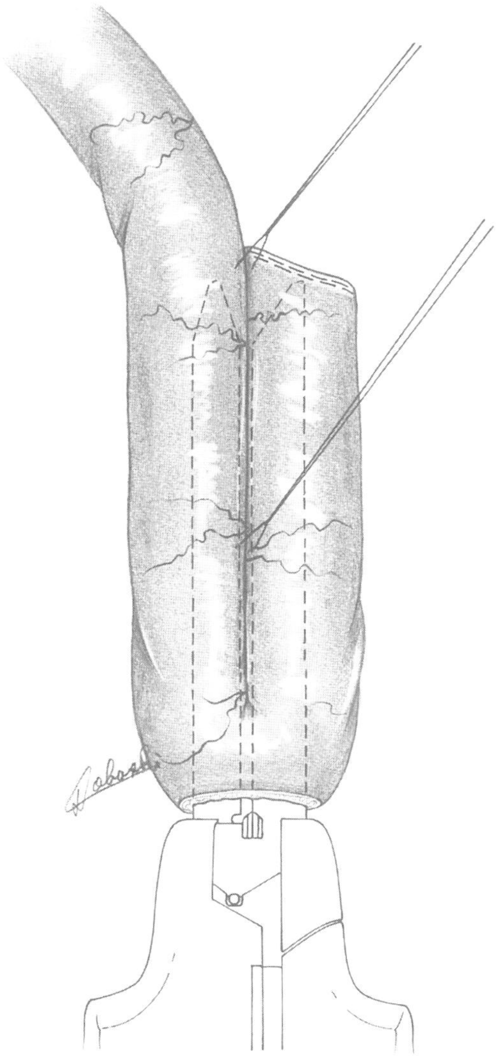

Having folded the ileal loop and secured it with stay sutures, a distal enterotomy is carried out to allow the insertion of a linear cutter standard to perform a latero-lateral anastomosis. If the length of the linear cutter is sufficiently long, this step can be accomplished with only one firing.
The distal enterotomy should be of the appropriate size, as it will later be used for insertion of the anvil of the circular stapler after creation of the pouch.

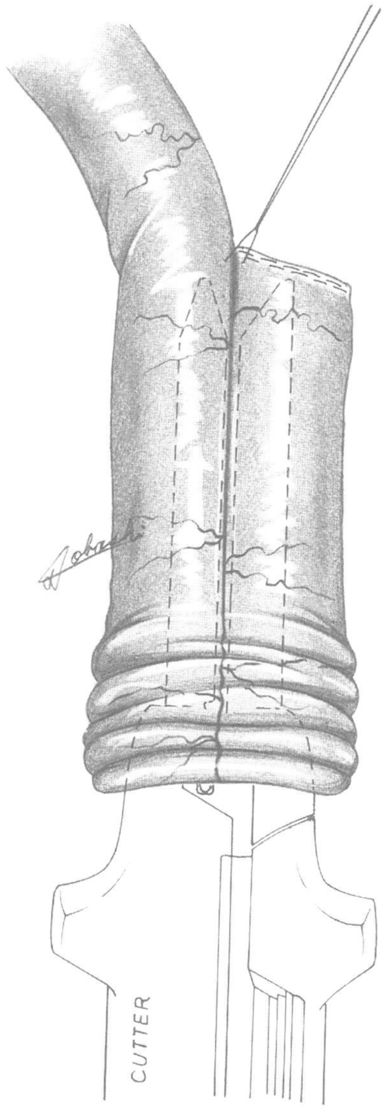

If a second firing is needed to complete the pouch, the anastomosed bowel can be telescoped over the instrument so that this can gain access to the distal portion.

Colectomy: W-Pouch

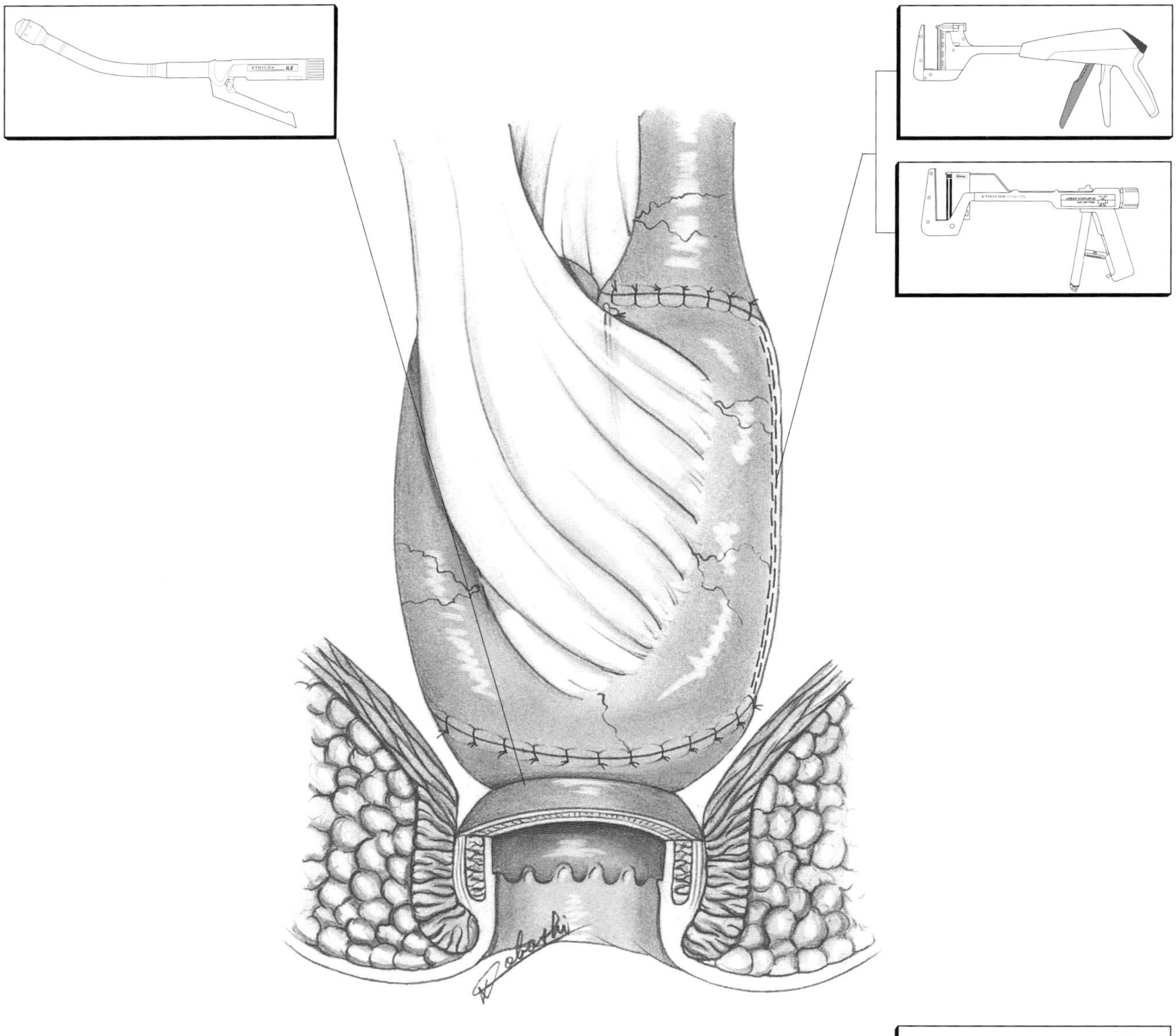

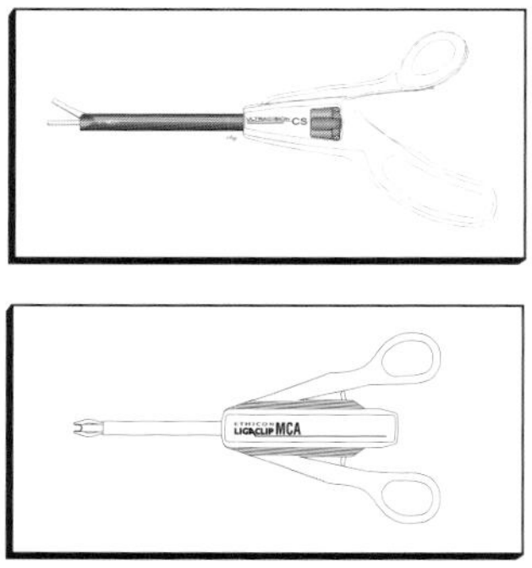

W-pouch performed by using a linear stapler standard and ileo-anal anastomosis with a circular stapler.

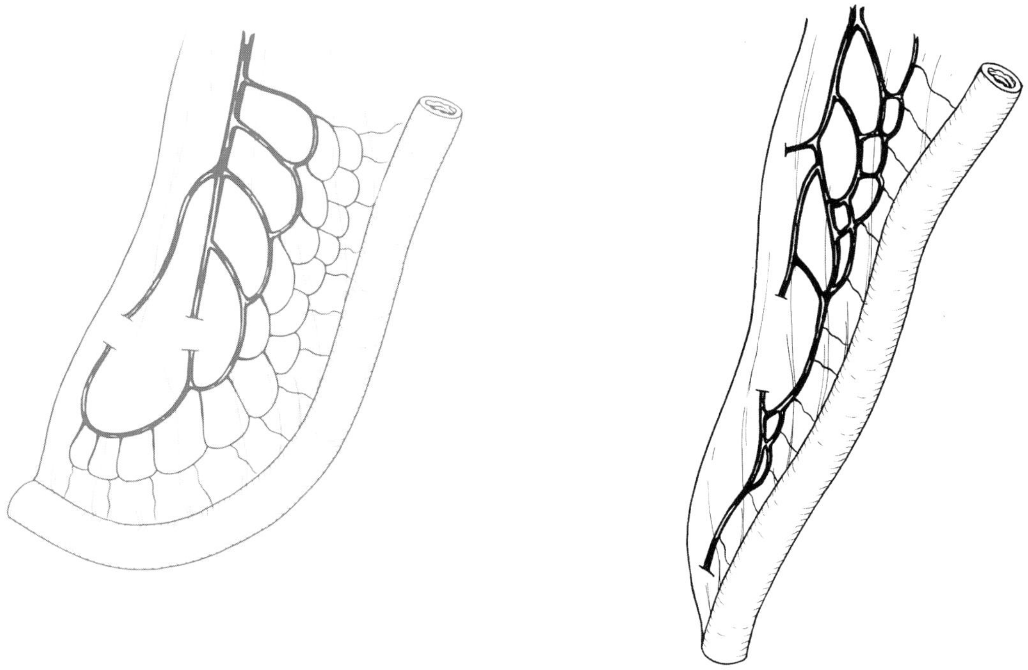

Mobilisation of the terminal ileum by ligating vascular arcades using Ultracision, clips, or sutures. About 50 cm of bowel are required to perform a W-pouch.

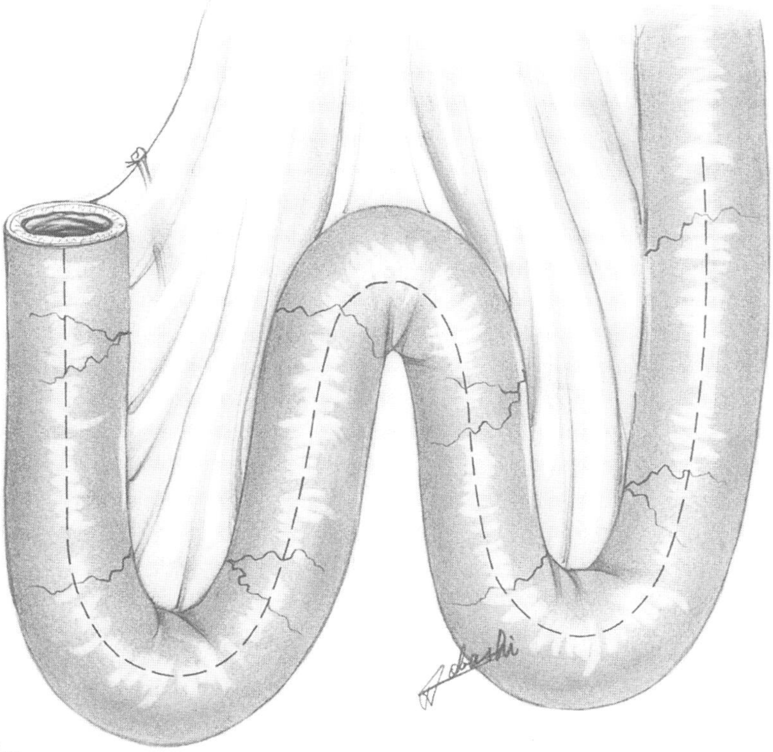

A longitudinal incision must be made on the antimesenteric side of the ileal loop.

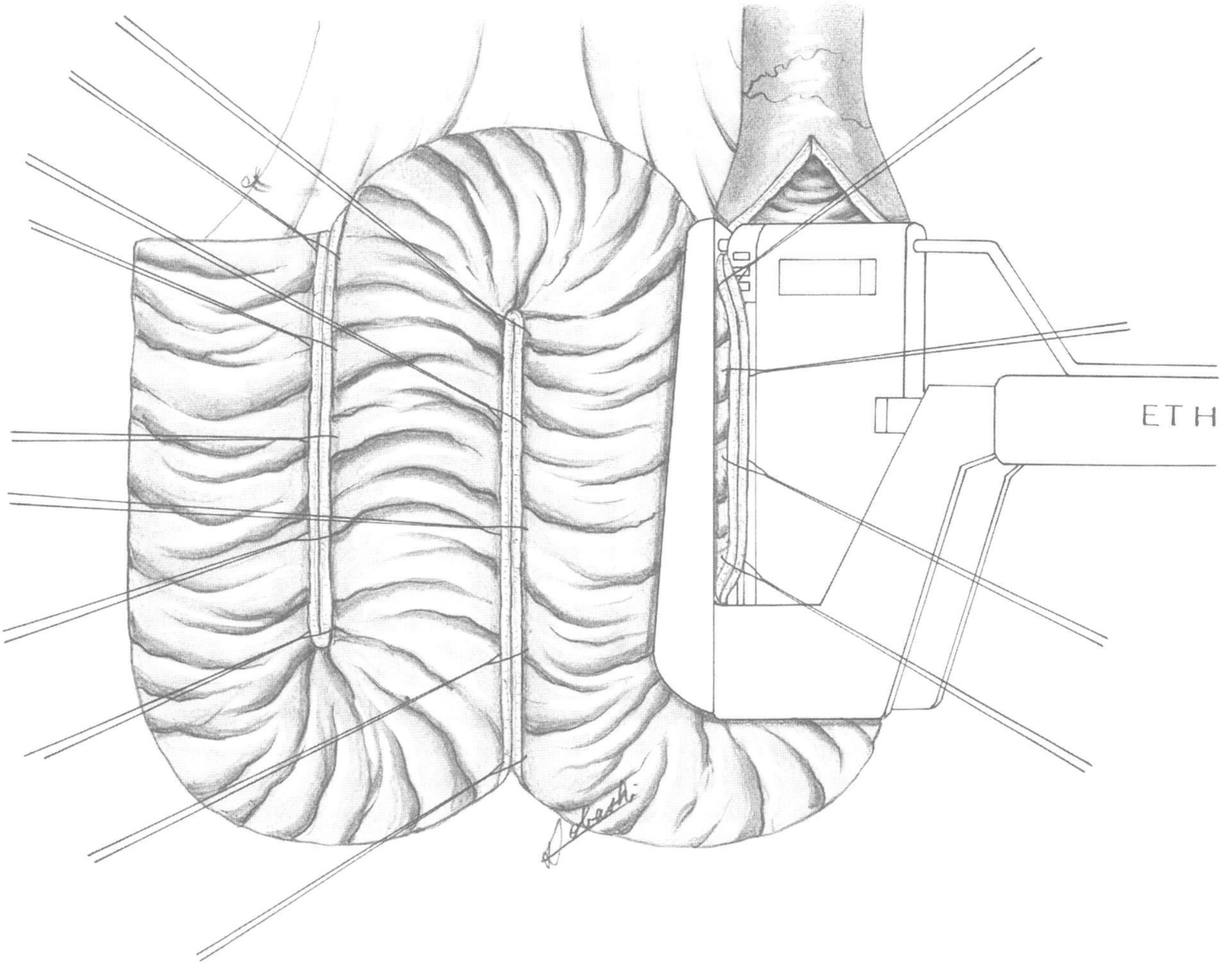

After forming the W, its shape is maintained with stay sutures. The fixed edges are stapled with three applications of a linear stapler standard to create the pouch. The excess tissue, including the stay sutures, is then excised along the cutting guide of the stapler.

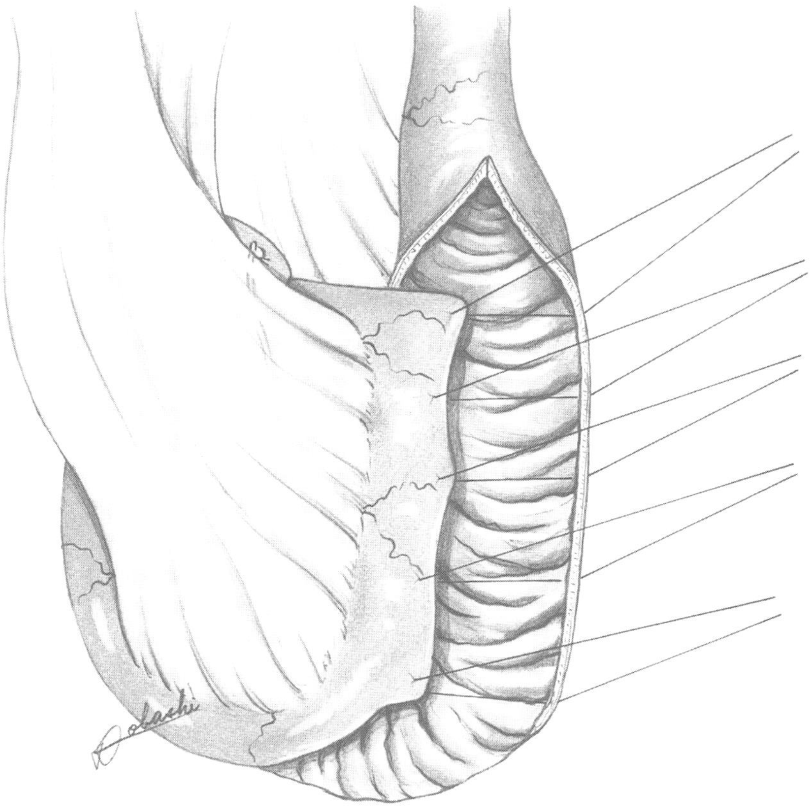

The pouch is finished by approximating the right and left borders with sutures to facilitate closure with a linear stapler standard.

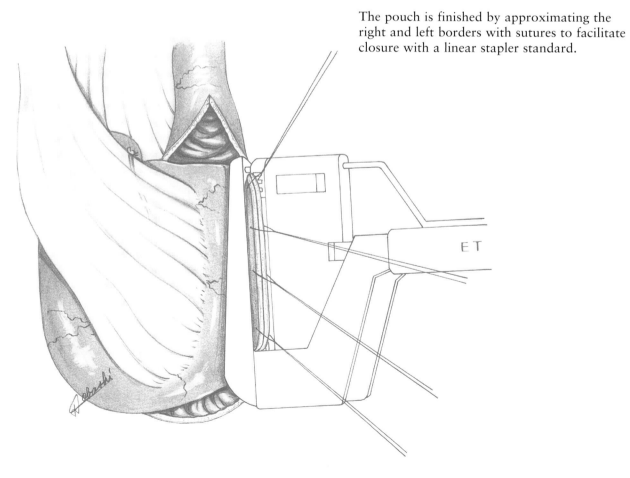

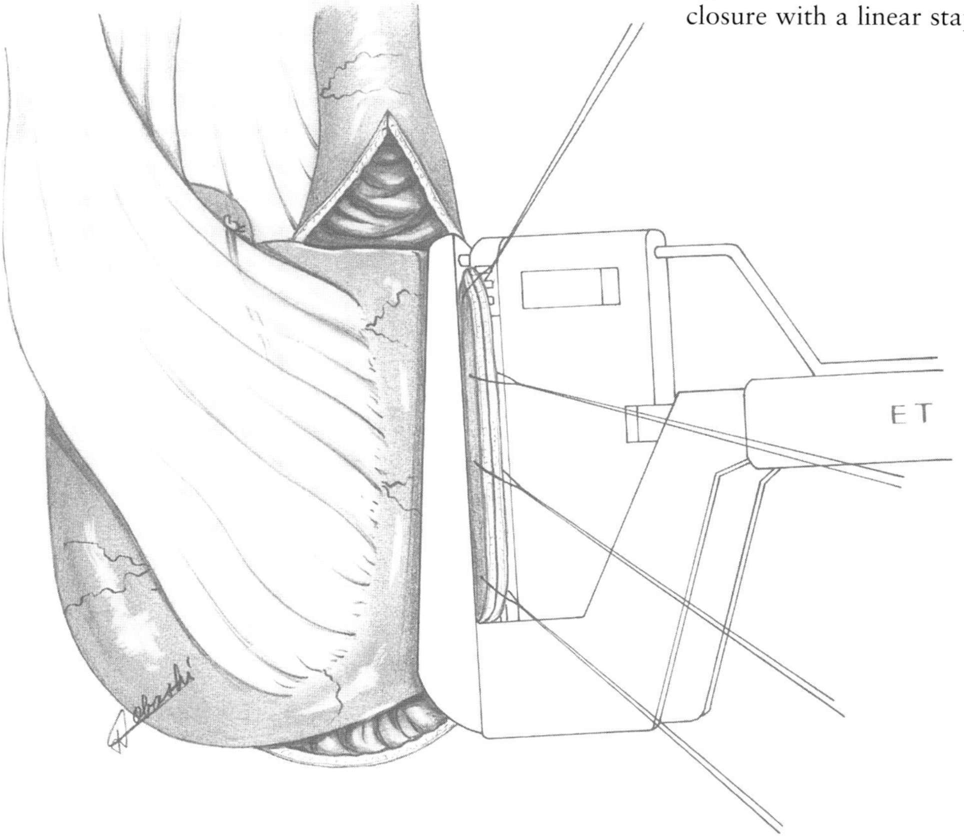

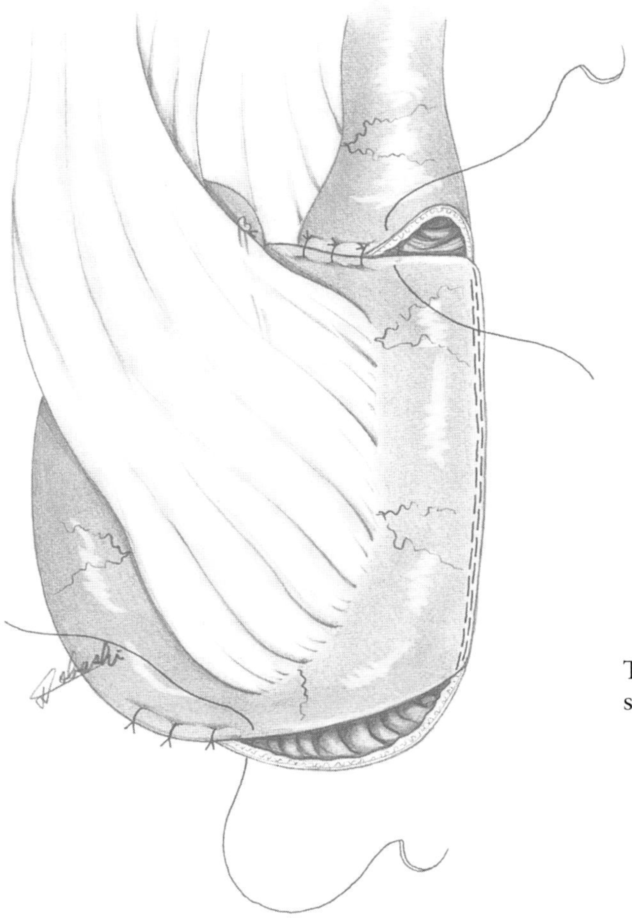

The W-pouch is closed by applying simple suture stitches.

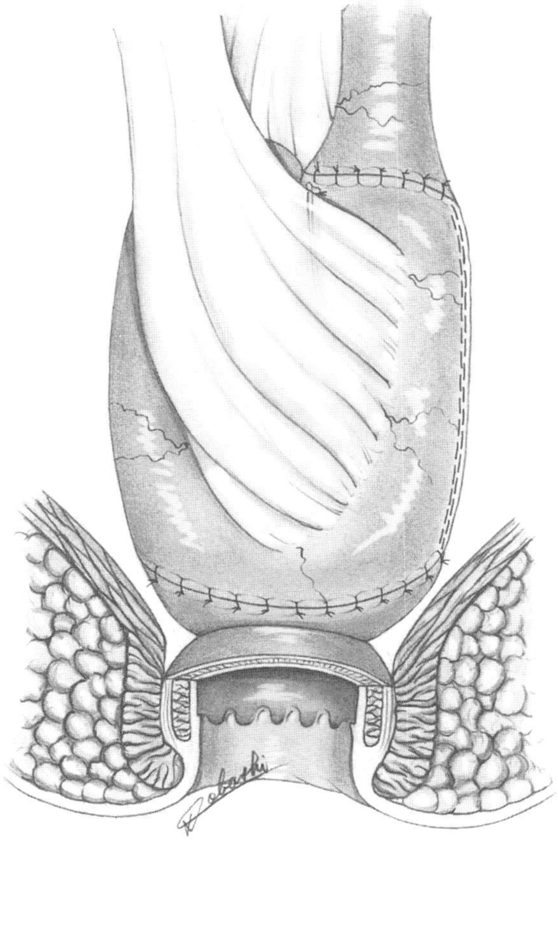

Results of the W-pouch after an ileo-anal anastomosis with circular stapler.

Procedure for Prolapse and Haemorrhoids – PPH

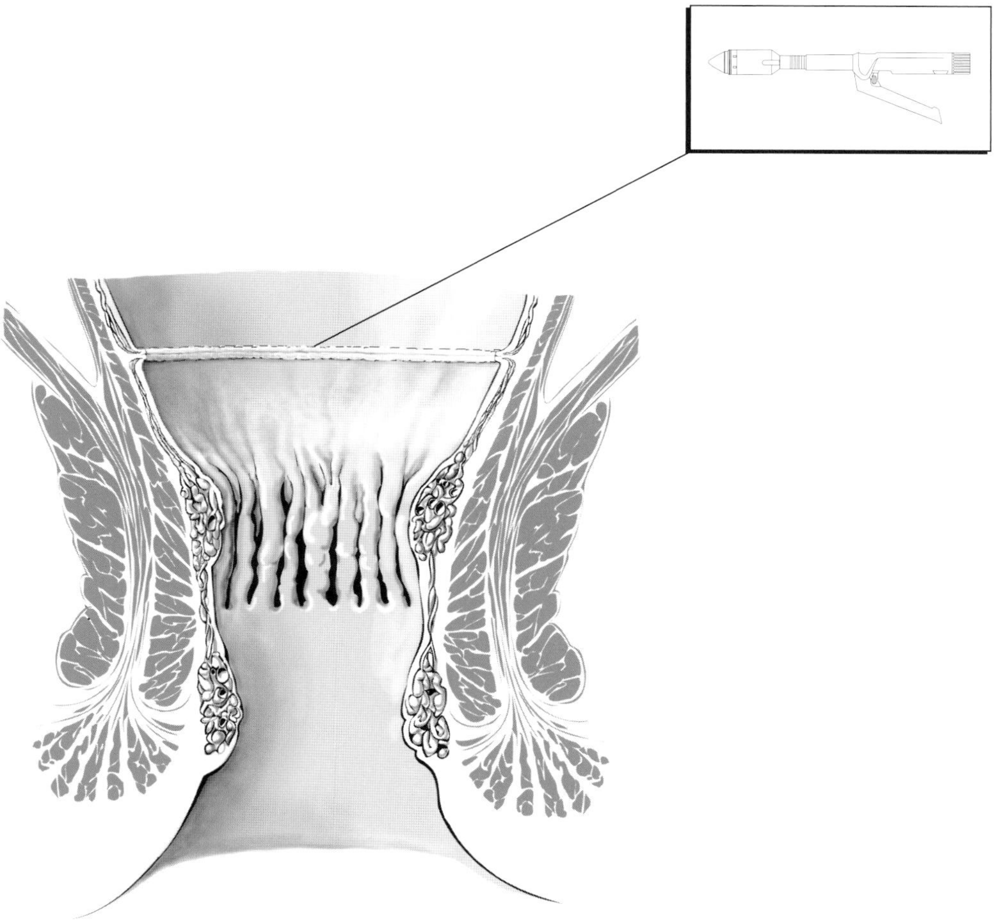

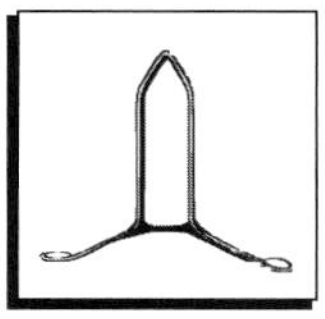

Treatment of haemorrhoidal disease through the circular excision of a band of prolapsed mucosa above the dentate line (anal lifting). A set has been specifically designed for this procedure, containing the following instruments: 33 mm circular stapler with short shaft, circular anal dilator, purse-string suture anoscope, and suture threader.

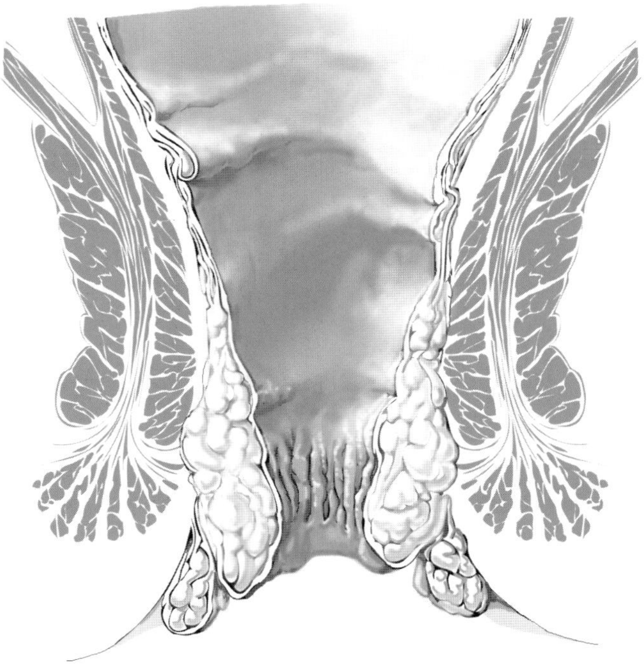

The typical morphological situation of the haemorrhoidal and mucous prolapse is caused by weakening and breakage of the supporting muscular and connective fibres. Prolapse implies the distal dislocation of the internal haemorrhoidal cushions, pushing the external haemorrhoidal sacks in an outward and lateral direction, thus causing the sacks to protrude. The upper haemorrhoidal vessels extend, while the middle and lower haemorrhoidal vessels are subject to the formation of "kinks". The haemorrhoidal volume may remain normal or swell, owing to phlebostasis. It may also regress towards atrophy. In IVth degree prolapse, the dentate line is positioned almost outside the anal canal and the rectal mucous membrane permanently occupies the muscular anal canal.

The introduction of the circular anal dilator causes the reduction of the prolapse of anoderma and parts of the anal mucous membrane. To optimally hold the circular anal dilator in place, it should be sutured to the anoderma at the 4 cardinal points. After removing the obturator, the prolapsed mucous membrane falls into the lumen of the dilator. The transparency of the device allows viewing of the dentate line.

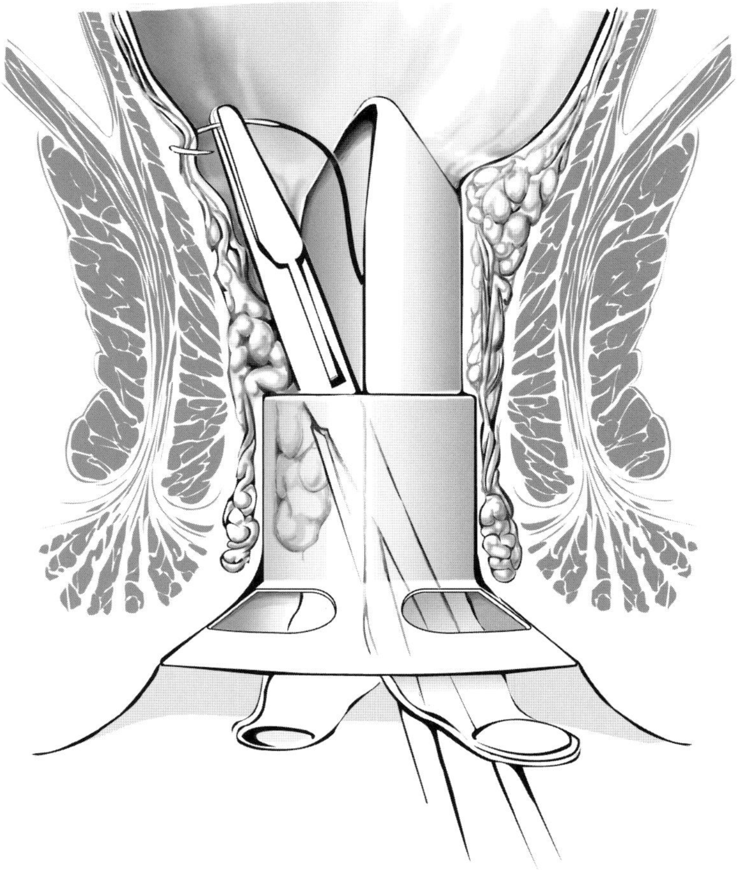

The purse-string suture anoscope is introduced through the anal dilator. This instrument will move the mucous prolapse along the rectal walls along a 270° circumference, while the mucous membrane, which protrudes through the purse-string suture anoscope window, can be easily contained in a monofilament suture which only includes the mucous membrane. This suture has to be carried out at least 5 cm distally from the dentate line, it being necessary to increase the distance in proportion to the degree of the prolapse. Rotating the purse-string suture anoscope enables the execution of a purse-string suture around the entire anal circumference. In the case of asymmetric prolapse it is possible to carry out two "half purse-strings", their distance being established according to need.

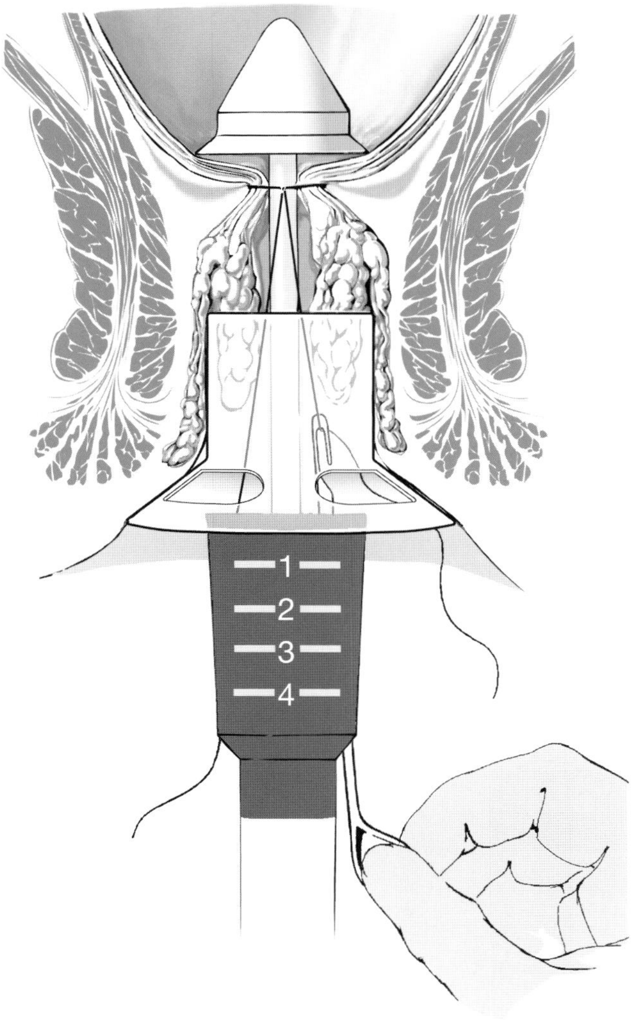

The circular stapler with short shaft is opened to its maximum position. Its head is introduced and positioned proximal to the purse-string, which is then tied with a closing knot. With the help of the suture threader, the ends of the threads are pulled through the lateral holes of the stapler.

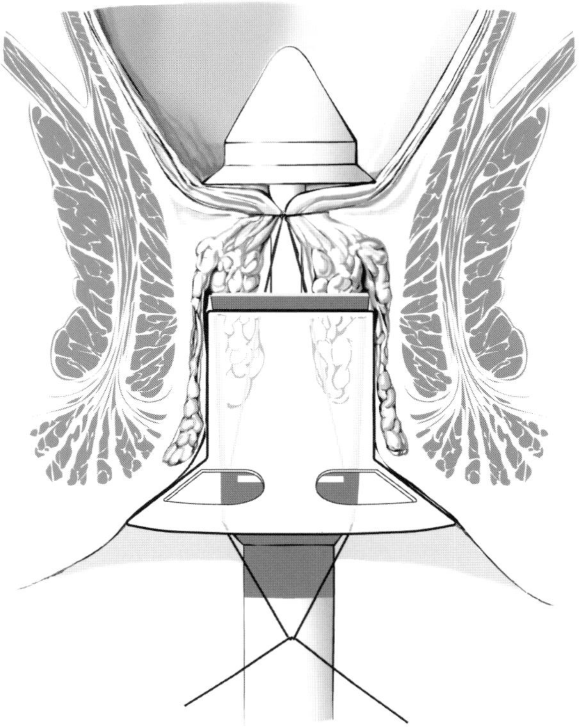

The ends of the threads are knotted externally or fixed using forceps. The entire casing or staple housing of the circular stapler is introduced to the anal canal. During the introduction, it is advisable to partially tighten the stapler.

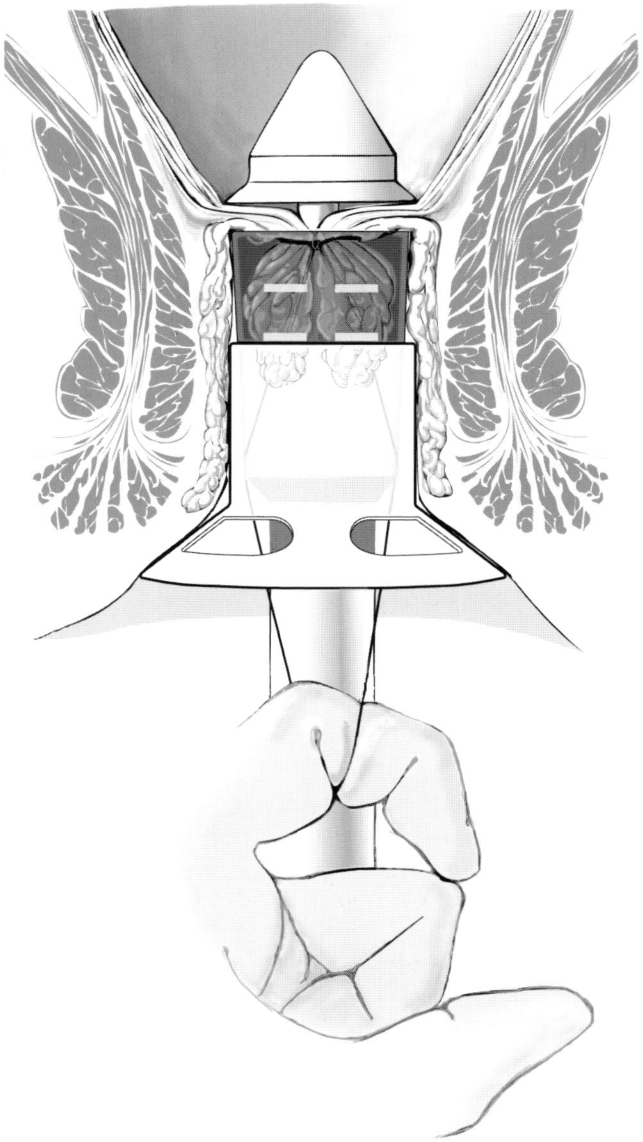

With moderate traction of the purse-string, a simple manoeuvre causes the prolapsed mucous to be drawn into the casing. The tightening of the circular stapler is completed and the stapling of the prolapse is carried out. Allowing the instrument to remain closed in this position for 20 seconds before and after firing acts as a tamponade and may enhance haemostasis. After having completely opened the circular stapler, the extraction of the head should be checked. After the operation, the staple line is examined using the purse-string suture anoscope, which enables the addition of stitches, if needed.

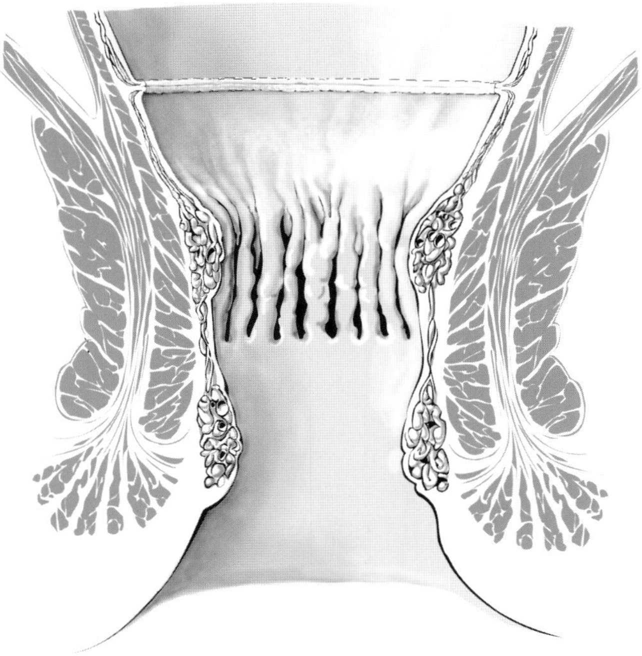

This technique and the set of devices ensure correct placement of the muco-mucous suture above the anorectal ring, at least 2 cm from the dentate line. The circular anal dilator preserves the unstriated sphincter and permits the atraumatic placement of a purse-string. The purse-string suture anoscope assists the measurement of the distance between the purse-string and the dentate line, and simplifies its placement. The circular stapler is very easy to handle, and enables simultaneous resection of larger rectal prolapses. The possibility of standardising the prolapse resection, graduating the traction of the threads and the height of the purse-string, is an important improvement to the technique.

8 Gynaecological Surgery

Salpingectomy

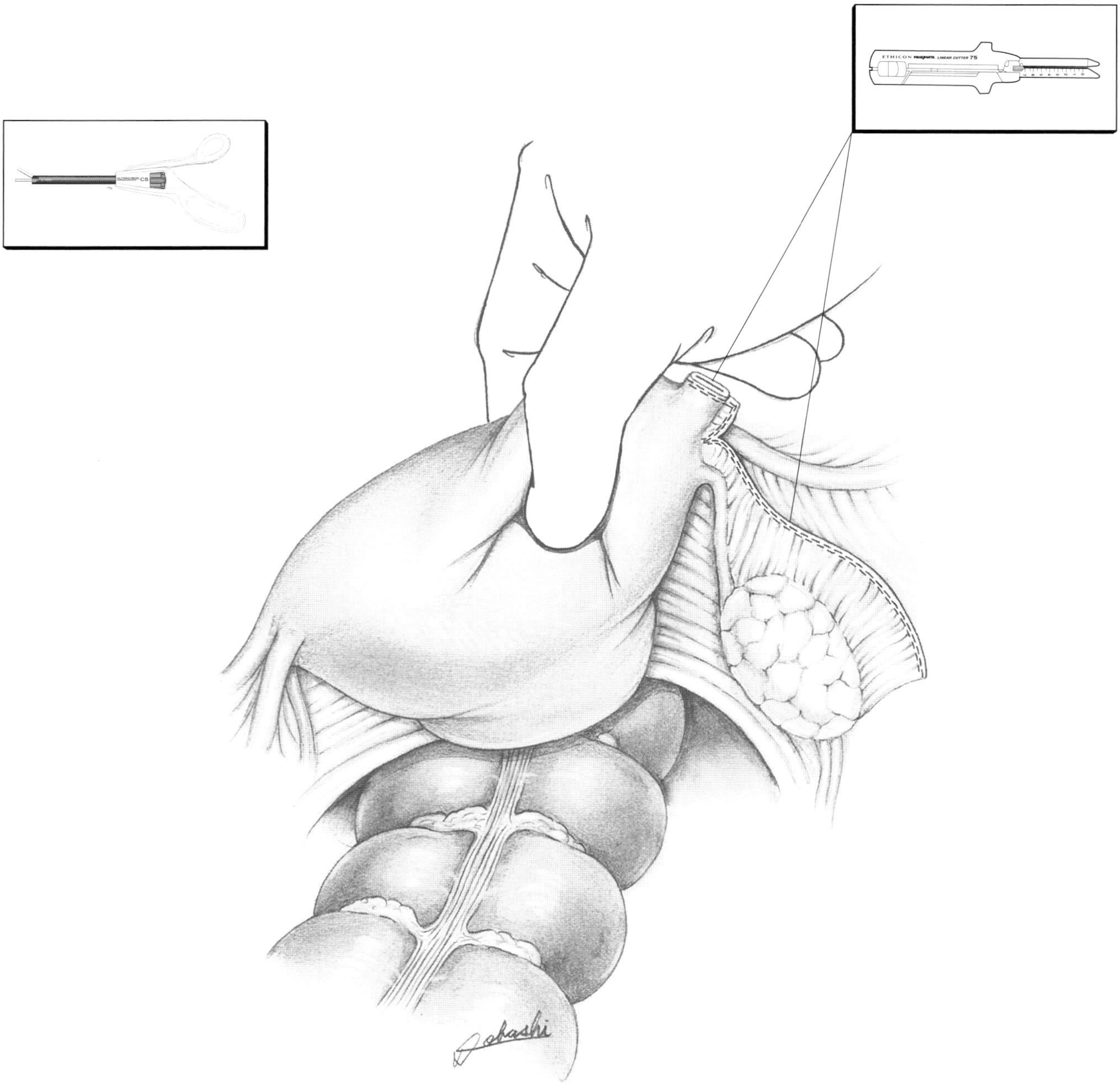

Transection of the mesometrium by using a linear cutter vascular or the Ultracision coagulation shears.

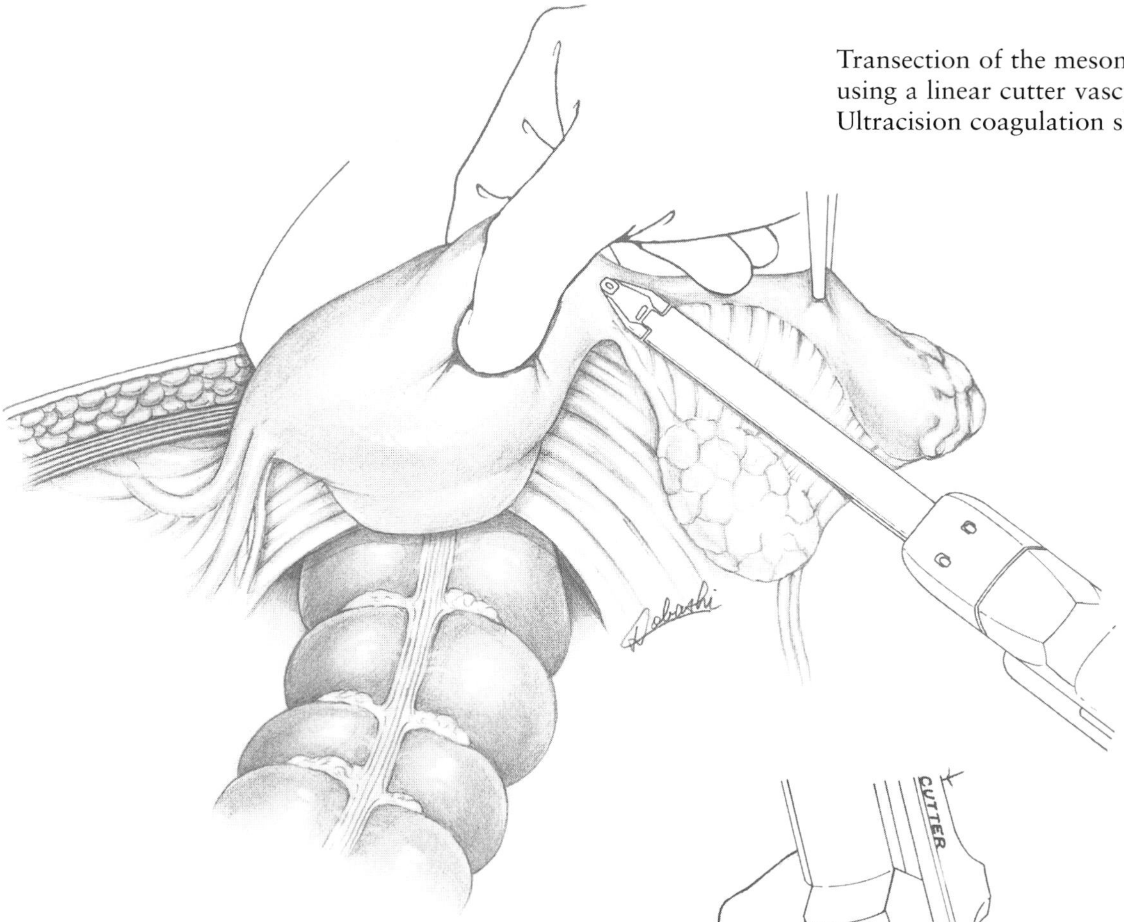

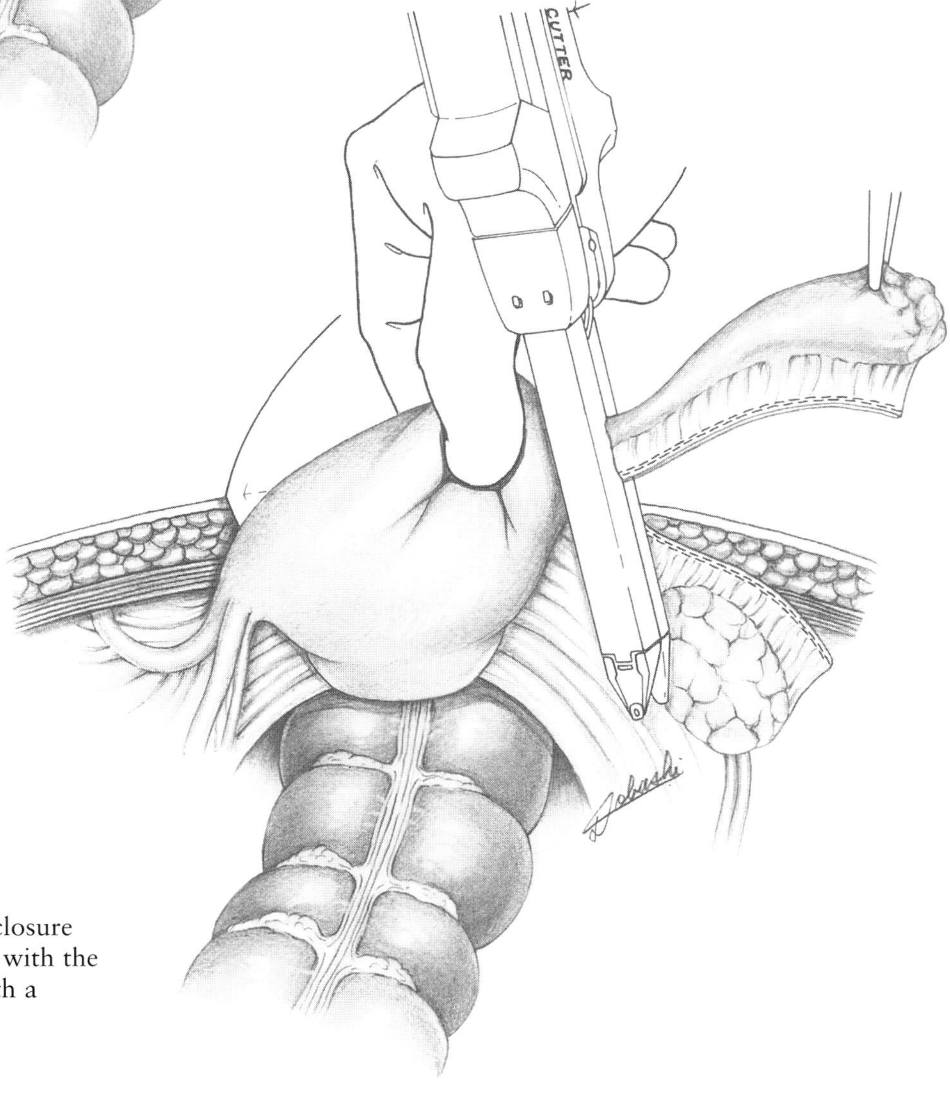

Transection and simultaneous closure of the tube are then performed with the same linear cutter, reloaded with a standard cartridge.

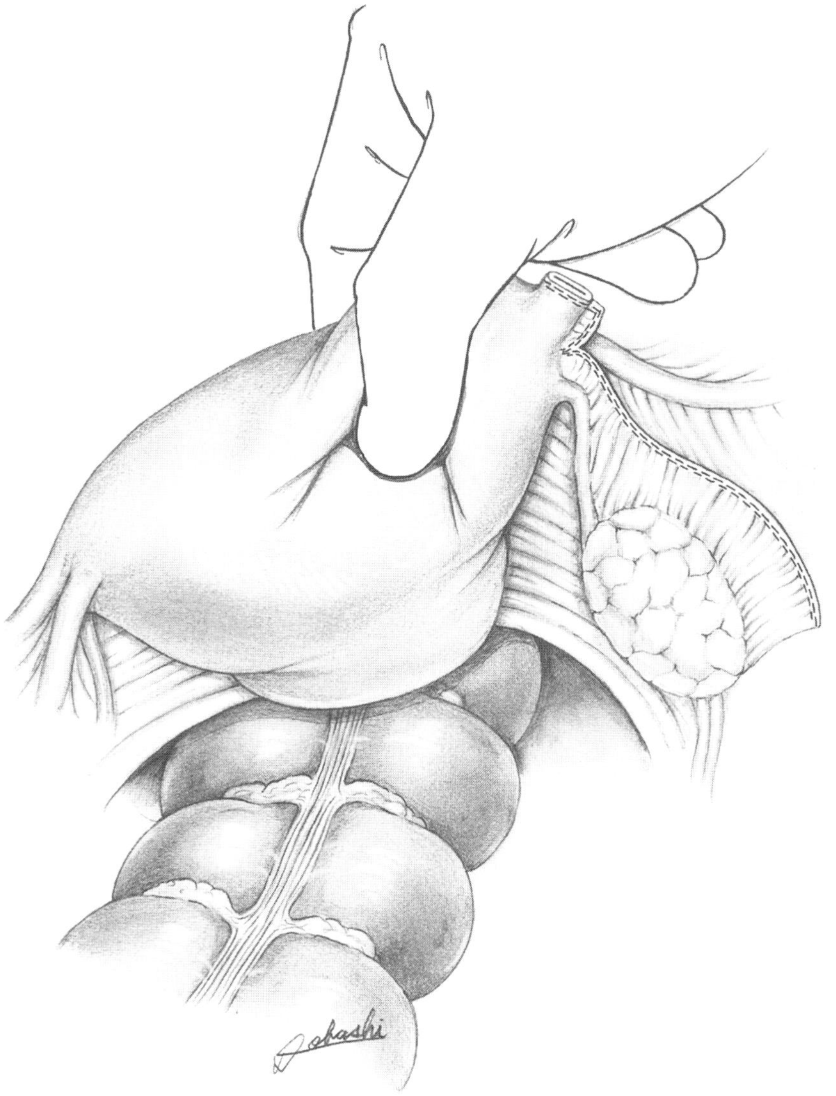

Upon completion the staple lines are examined for haemostasis and proper staple closure.

Salpingo-Oophorectomy

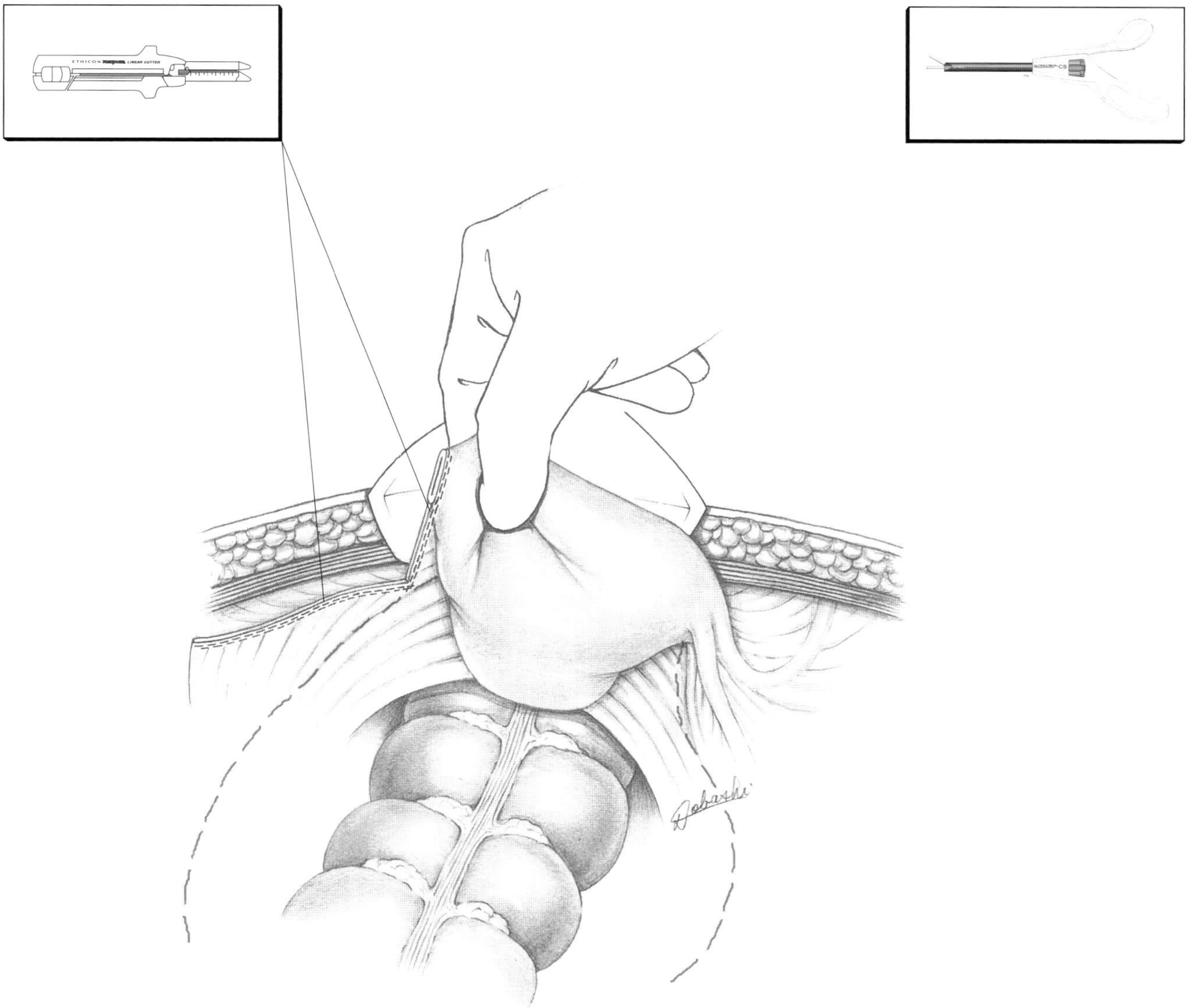

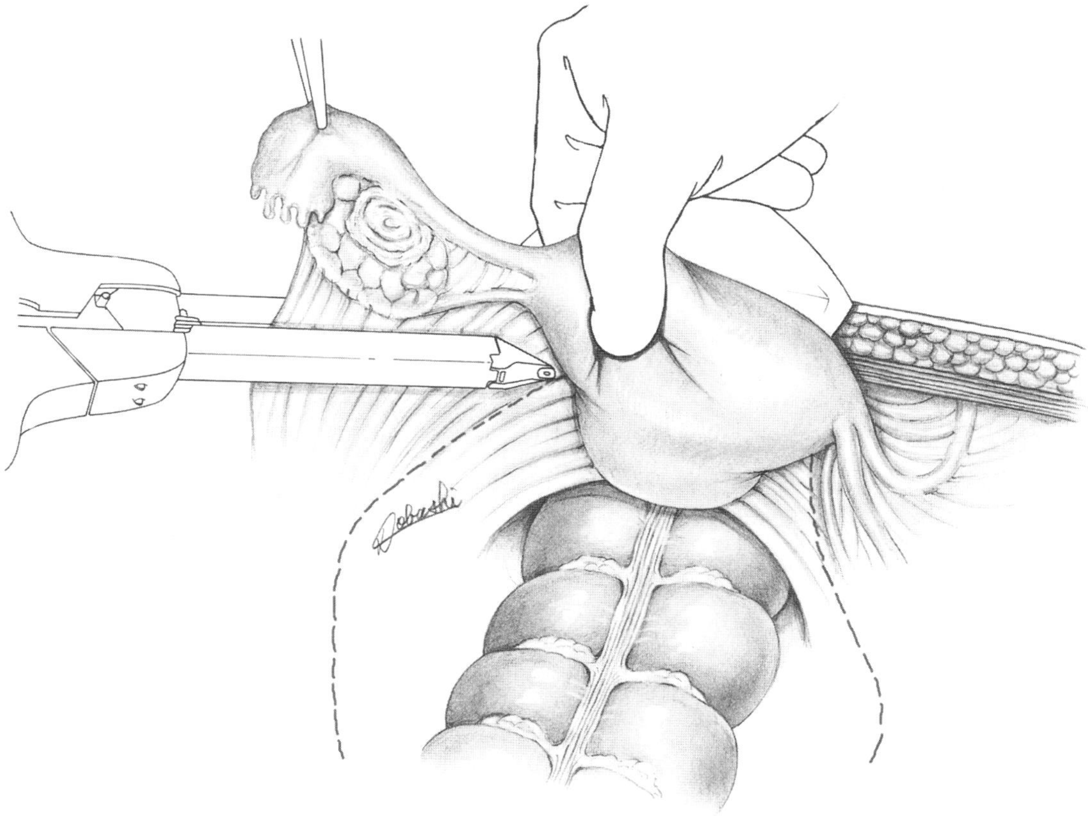

Transection of the mesometrium and the infudivulopelvic ligament using a linear cutter vascular or Ultracision coagulating shears.

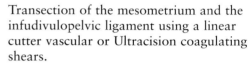

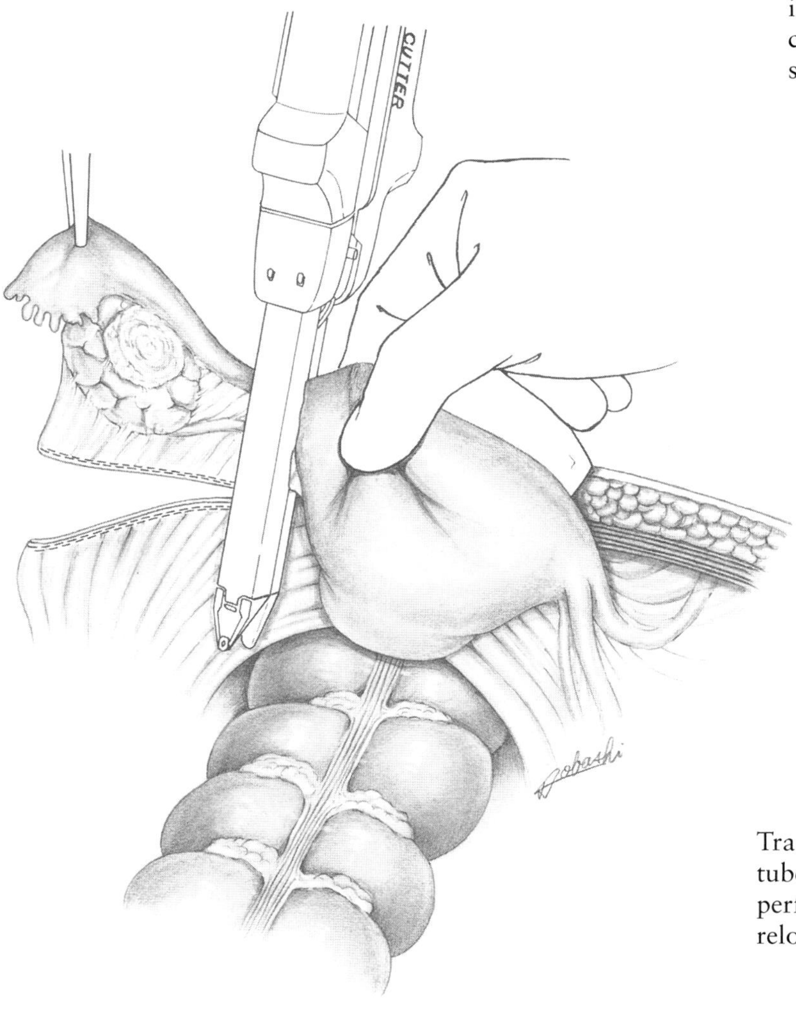

Transection and simultaneous closure of the tube and the utero-ovarian ligament are then performed with the same linear cutter, reloaded with a standard cartridge.

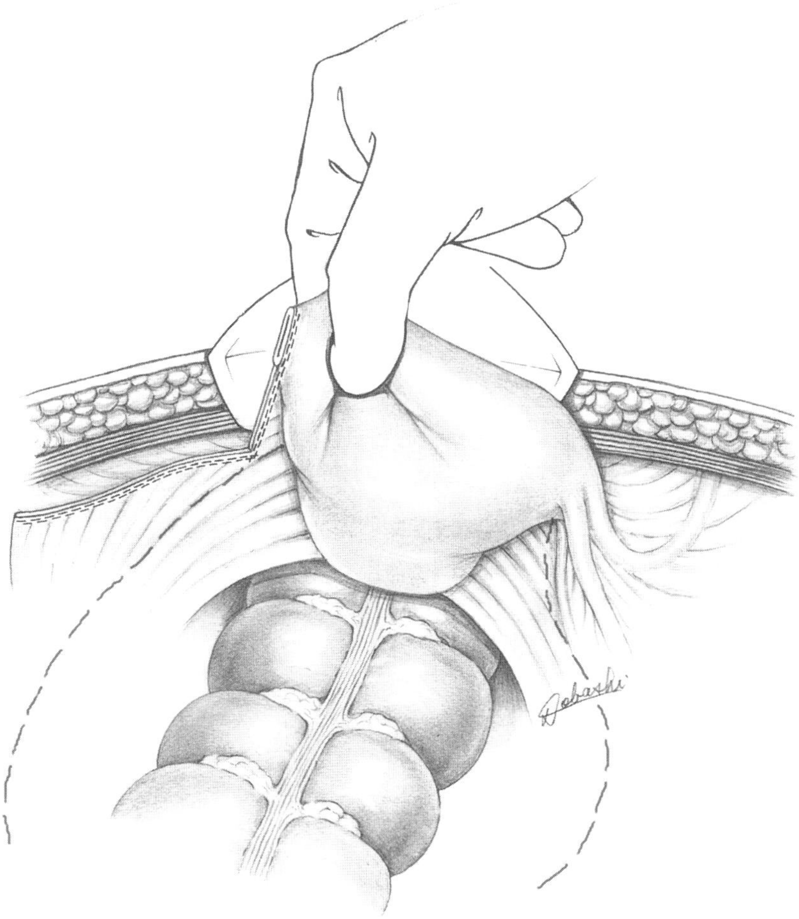

Upon completion the staple lines are examined for haemostasis and proper staple closure.

Complete Hysterectomy

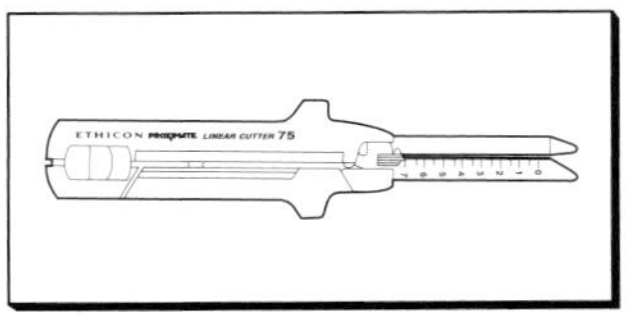

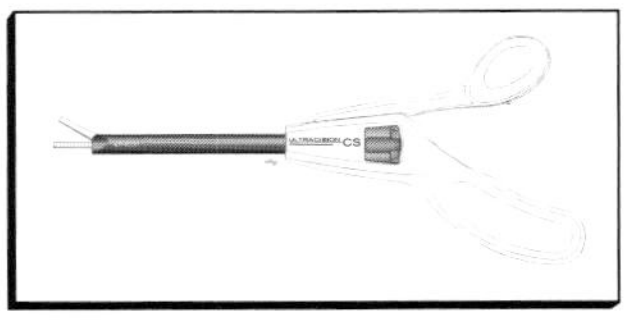

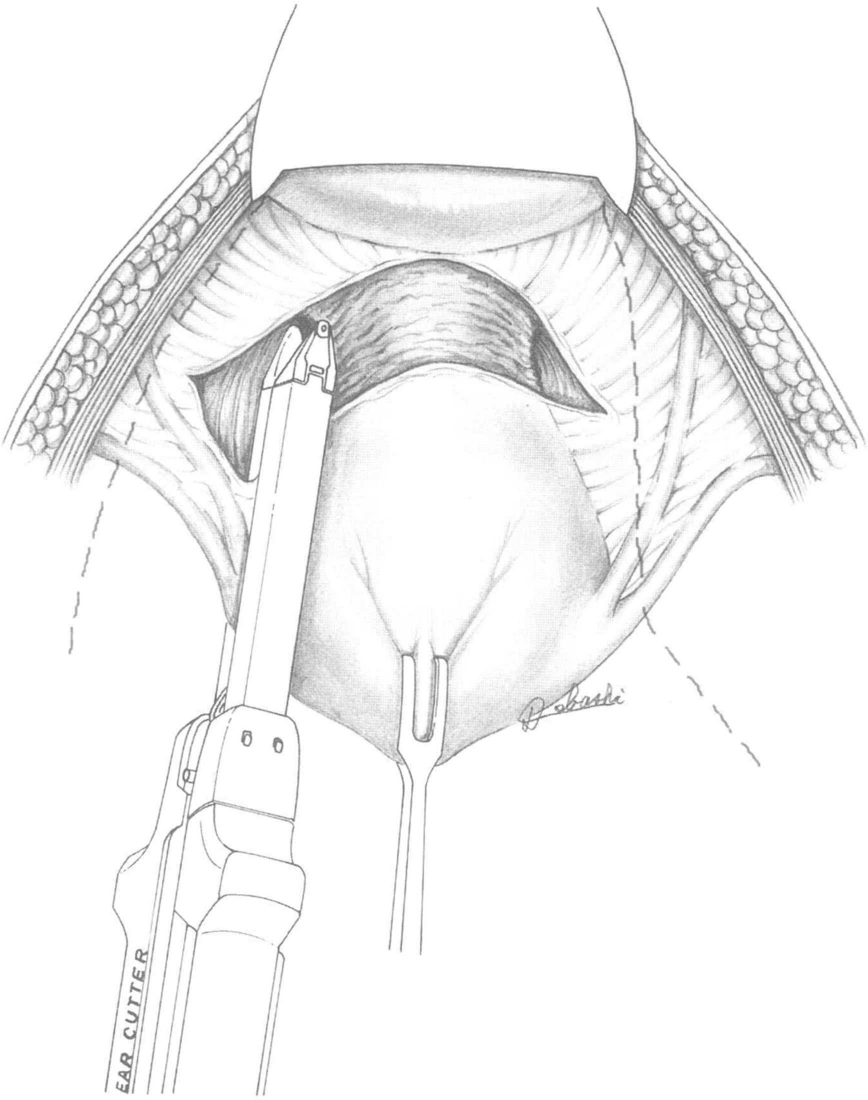

An opening of the peritoneum is created in the area of the defined resection line using a scalpel or the Ultracision sharp hook. Resection of the tube, ovarian ligament, and parts of the mesenterium is then performed close to the uterus, whilst simultaneously closing both sides with a linear cutter vascular. Observe that the ureter may not be grasped when placing the instrument. Upon completion the staple lines are examined for haemostasis and proper staple closure.

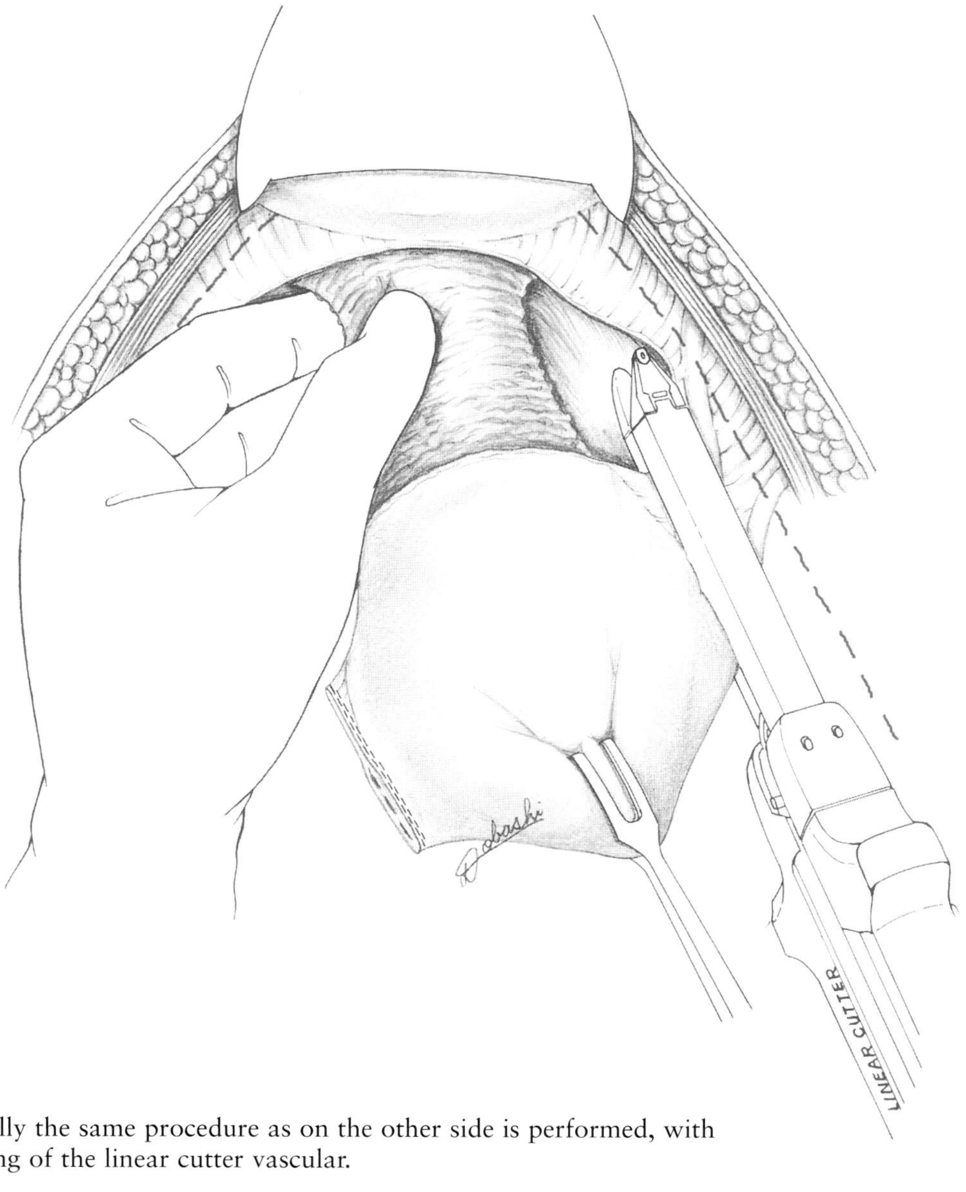

Controlaterally the same procedure as on the other side is performed, with a second firing of the linear cutter vascular.

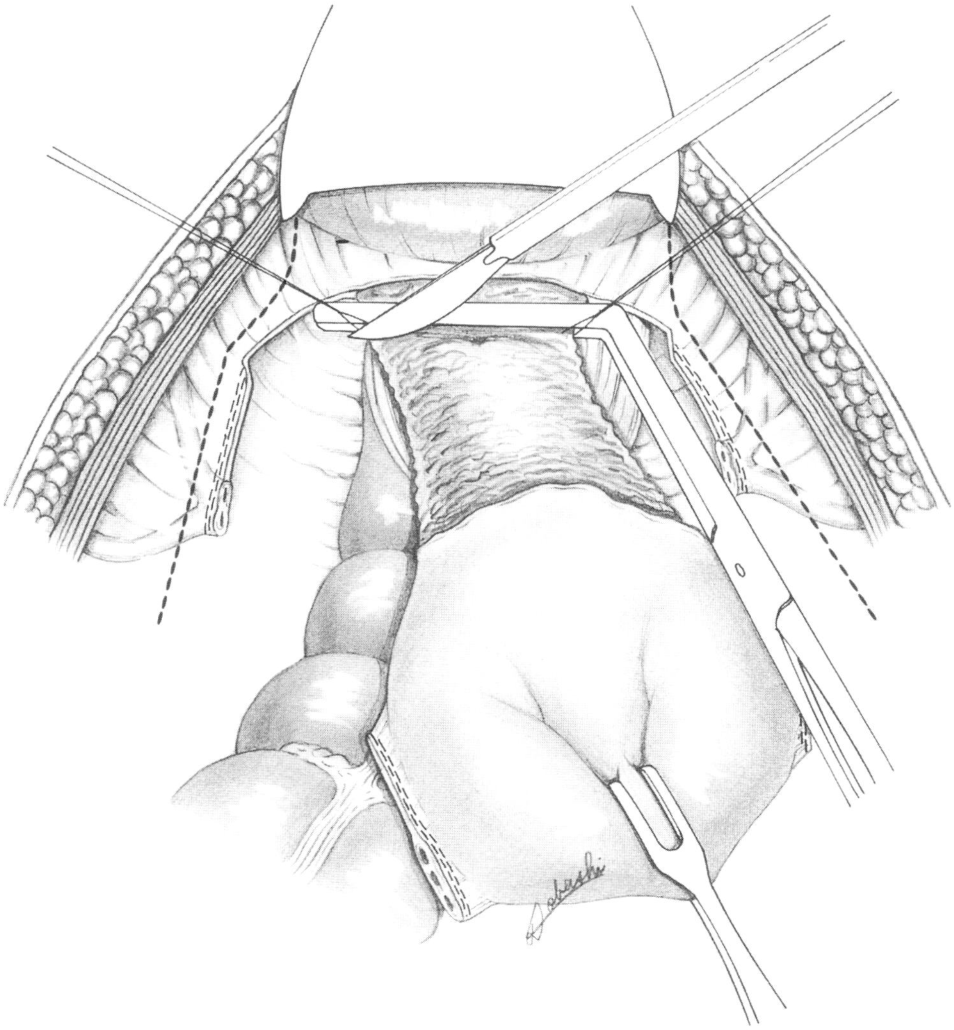

To complete the hysterectomy, a clamp is placed just distally to the uterine cervix, which is then resected with a scalpel. The vaginal cuff is sutured.

9 Urological Surgery

Following a cystectomy the urine must be drained out. In principle we distinguish between two approaches for facilitating this drainage: "Incontinent" urination and "Continent" urination.

"Incontinent" urination

If there is no possibility of creating a continent pouch, urine must be drained directly to the skin and collected by an adhesive bag.

For this kind of procedure different methods can be used:

Ureteral Skin Fistula (Ureterocutaneostomy)

One or both ureters are sewed directly into the skin. If possible, the ureters are brought together internally, rendering only one collecting bag necessary.

Renal Fistula (Nephrostomy)

The urine is drained out into a collecting bag via a renal fistula catheter located in the renal pelvis, where the other ureter will be anastomosed.

Ileal conduit

A segment of the small intestine is excised. One end of this segment is sewed into the skin as performed in an ileostomy whilst the other end is closed. The ureters are then implanted into the conduit. This procedure can also be performed with a segment of the colon. Then it is called colonic conduit.

The following is an example of a procedure using this type of approach:

Ileal Conduit – Bladder According to Bricker

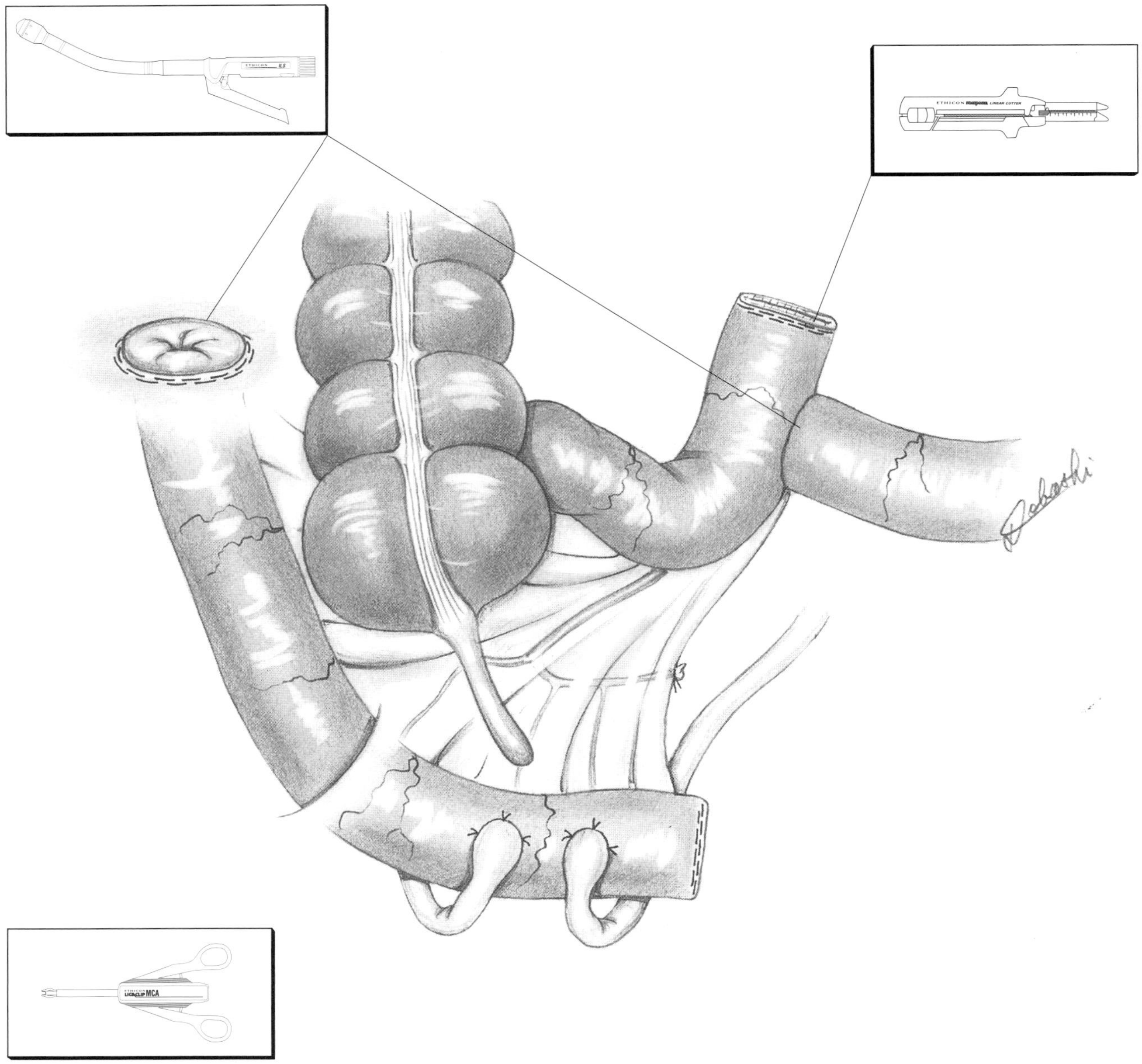

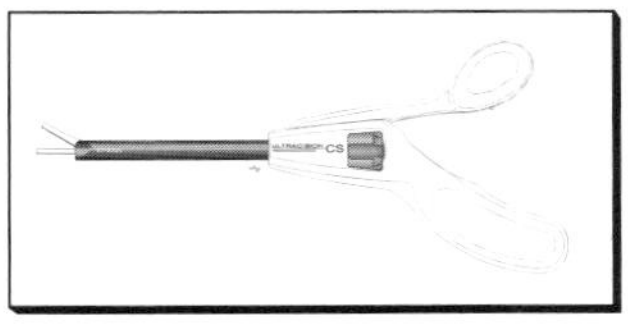

The ileal conduit was developed by Dr. Bricker in 1950 and has been the leading incontinent technique for urinary drainage. Today, however, continent techniques for urinary drainage are preferred. Long-term results of this new type of operation have remained hitherto unknown to a great extent, so that some urologists still use this old operation according to Bricker, which has been tested for over 40 years.

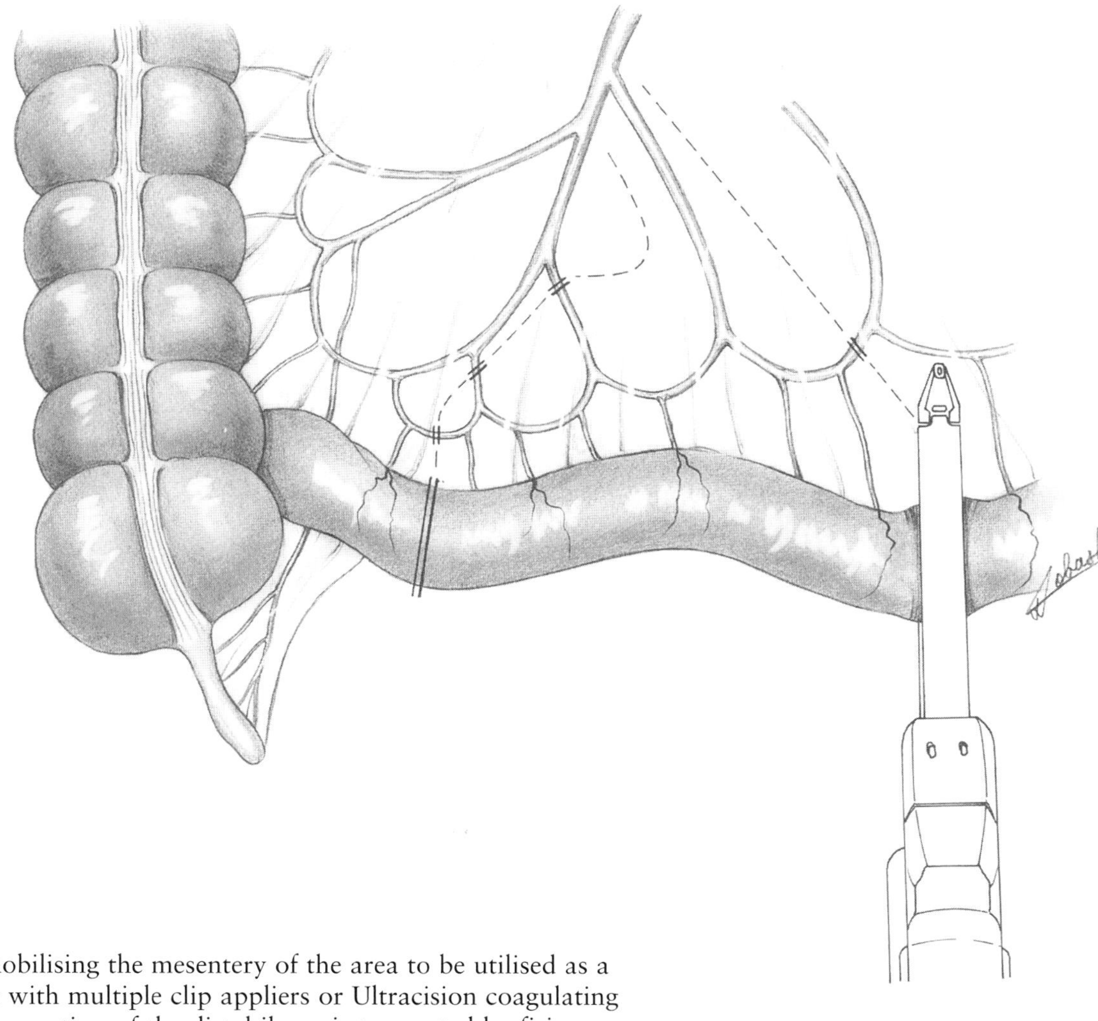

After mobilising the mesentery of the area to be utilised as a conduit with multiple clip appliers or Ultracision coagulating shears, a portion of the distal ileum is transected by firing a linear cutter standard twice.

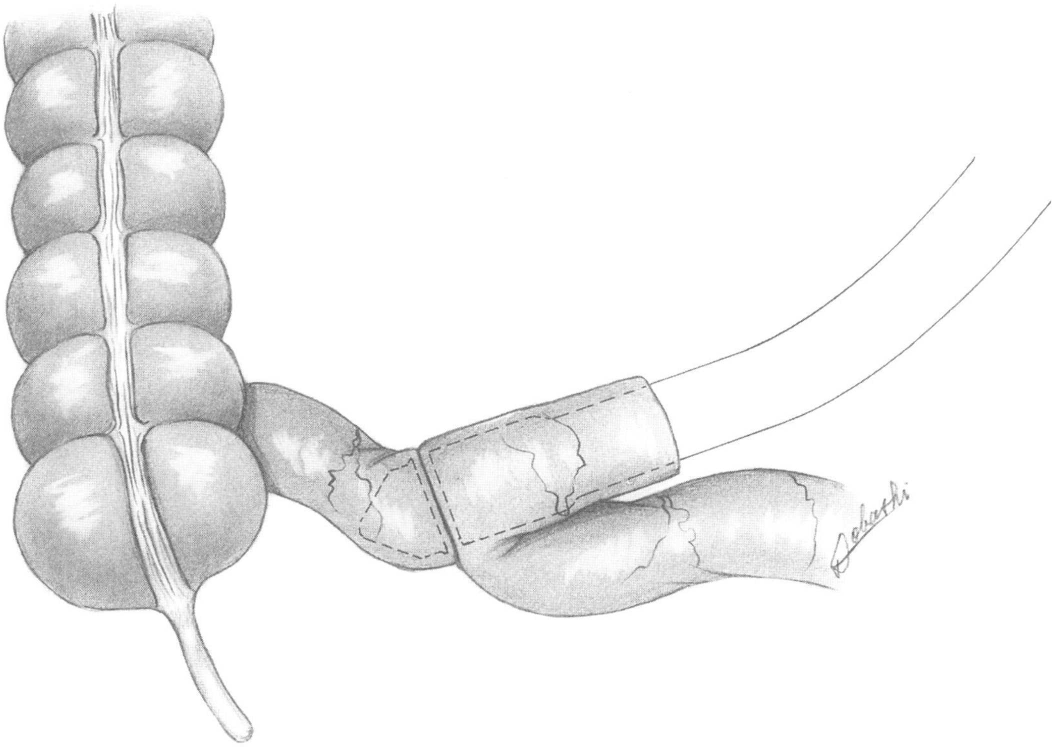

At the distal end of the ileum a purse-string suture is placed by using a suture clamp whilst simultaneously resecting the staple line. The head of a circular stapler is inserted and the purse-string suture is closed.
A circular stapler is inserted into the lumen of the proximal end of the ileum. The bowel wall is pierced by the instrument trocar at the antimesenteric side. The instrument is assembled, and the stapler is closed and fired to create the end-to-side anastomosis. After withdrawal of the instrument, the 'doughnuts' have to be carefully removed to examine their integrity. The remaining open ileum is sutured with a linear cutter standard at 3 cm from the anastomosis.

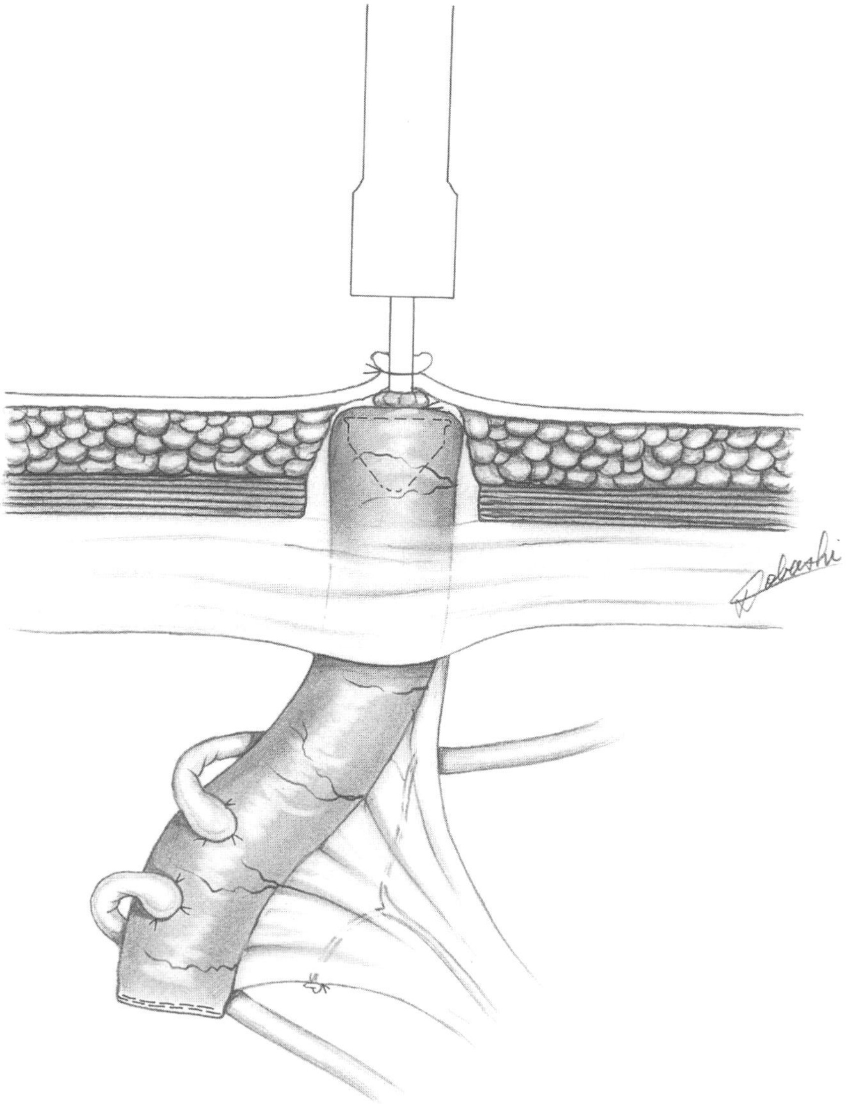

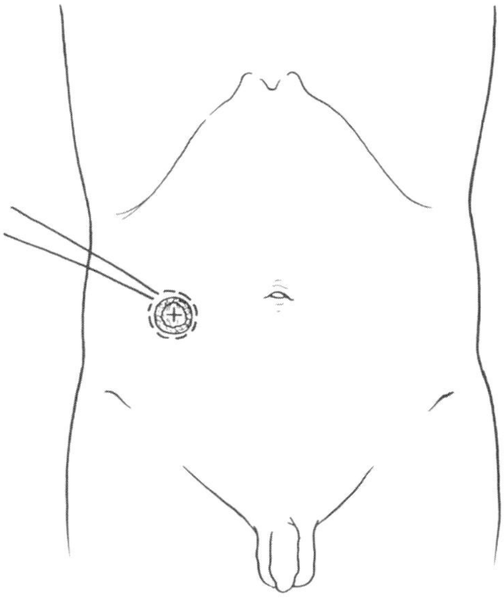

Both ureters are anastomosed to the antimesenteric side of the ileal conduit. The head of the circular stapler is inserted into the purse-string of the ileum. Another purse-string suture is created at the skin. The cutaneous purse-string suture is tied around the anvil of the instrument.
The circular stapler is then assembled, closed, and fired.

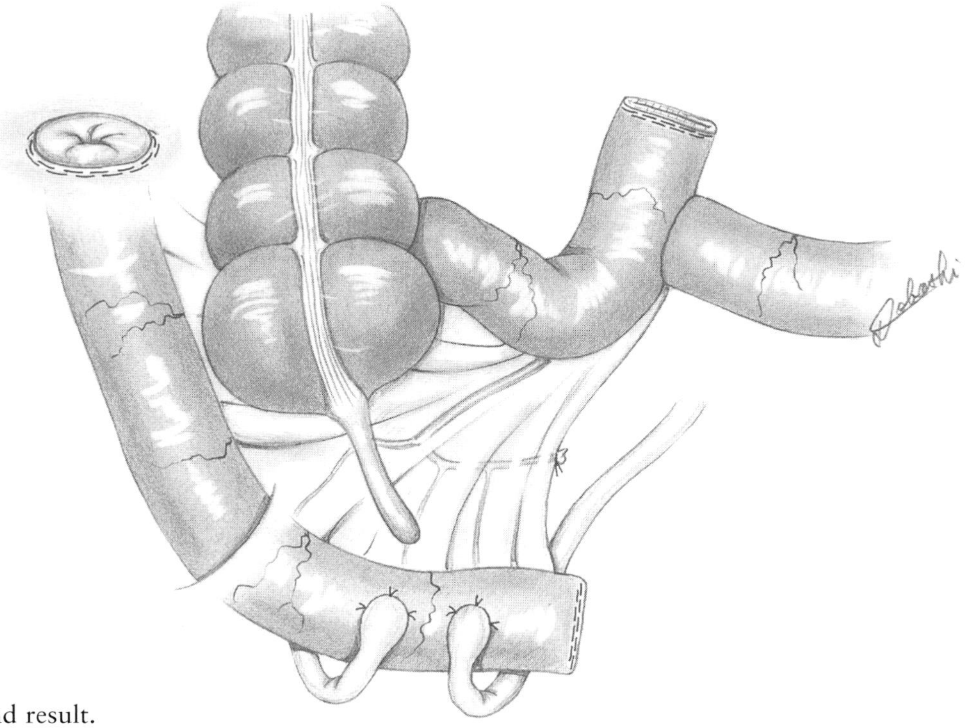

End result.

"Continent" Urination

To perform procedures for continent urination in males, the patient must have a healthy urethra, as well as ureters with healthy distal ends. If this is not the case, then continent stomata or natural orifices must be used in order to attain continence; this approach is most general in the case of females.

Ureterosigmoidostomy

The ureters are inserted into the sigma. Urine and stools are then emptied together. A further approach to this procedure is the Mainz Pouch II (Figure below). This is used to create a larger reservoir.

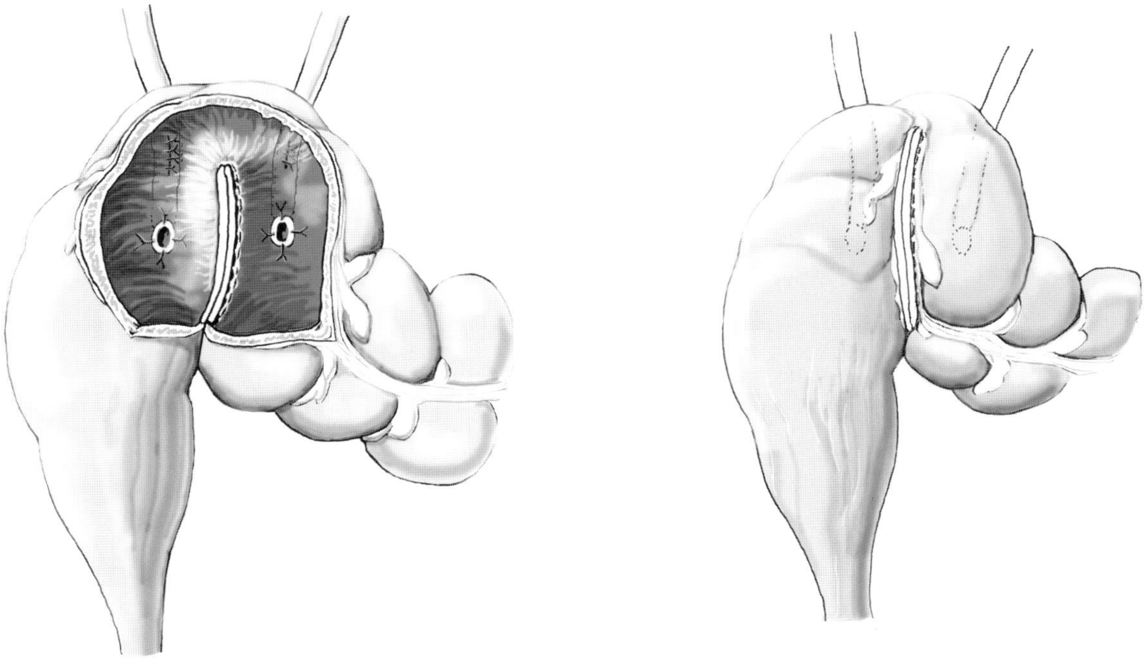

Ileal Neobladder

The ureters can be inserted into a neobladder created with small intestine. A 60 to 70 cm segment of small intestine is transected in order to create a replacement bladder. Both ureters are anastomosed at the upper part of the new bladder so that urine cannot reflux. The urethra is sewed to the lower part of the intestinal bladder. The ileal neobladder permits normal voiding in most cases.

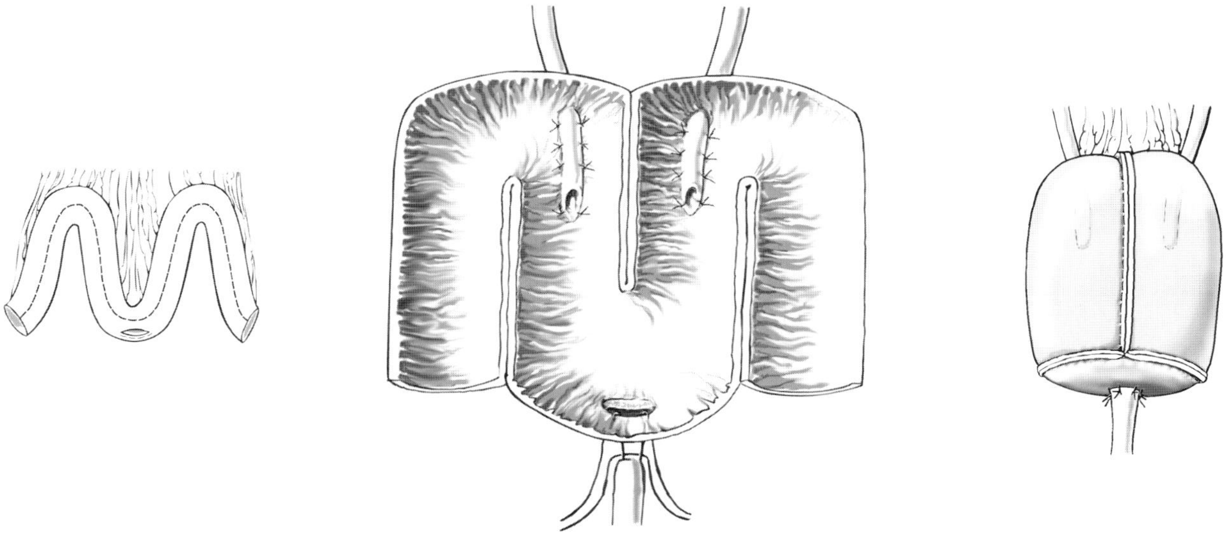

Intestinal Pouch with a Catheterisable Stoma

A reservoir is created out of a small or large intestinal segment or a combination of the two, to which the ureters are then connected. The stoma of the reservoir is exteriorised at a cosmetically favourable place, e.g. in the region of the umbilicus, by means of an intestinal segment or the appendix. As there is no sphincter, the outlet is narrowed surgically to the extent of making the reservoir leak-proof. The patient himself empties the reservoir by using a catheter (three to four times every day, once during the night).

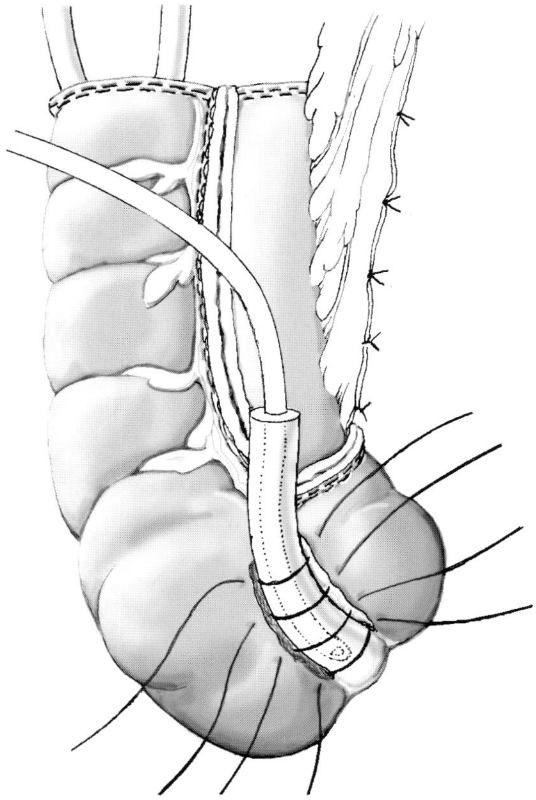

Following are examples of procedures using this type of approach:

Ileal Reservoir – Urological Kock Pouch

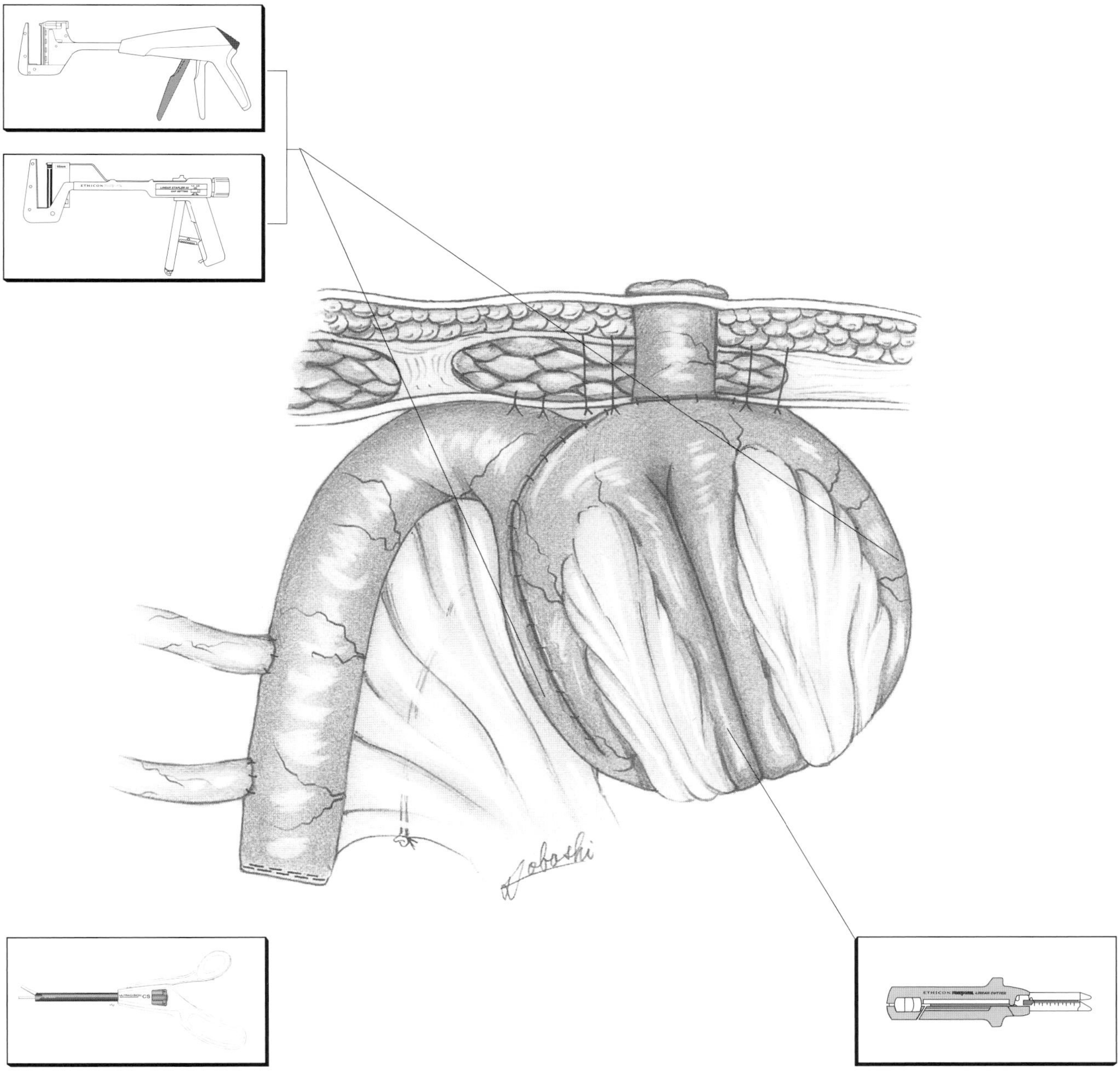

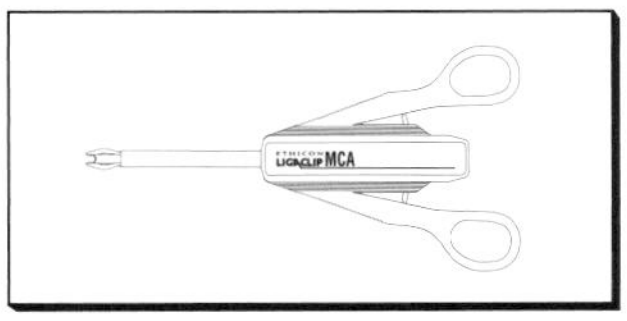

The principle of reservoir construction described by Kock in the sixties ensures urinary storage in large quantities (700 ml and 1500 ml) with low pressure values. The success of the operation depends on the construction and maintenance of the nipple valve mechanism. However, complications occur in over 30 % of cases, and over 18 % of the patients must undergo re-operation to remedy the incontinence. Long-term observations indicate acceptance of this operation on the part of patients, but this technique is used seldom owing to the high rate of complications.

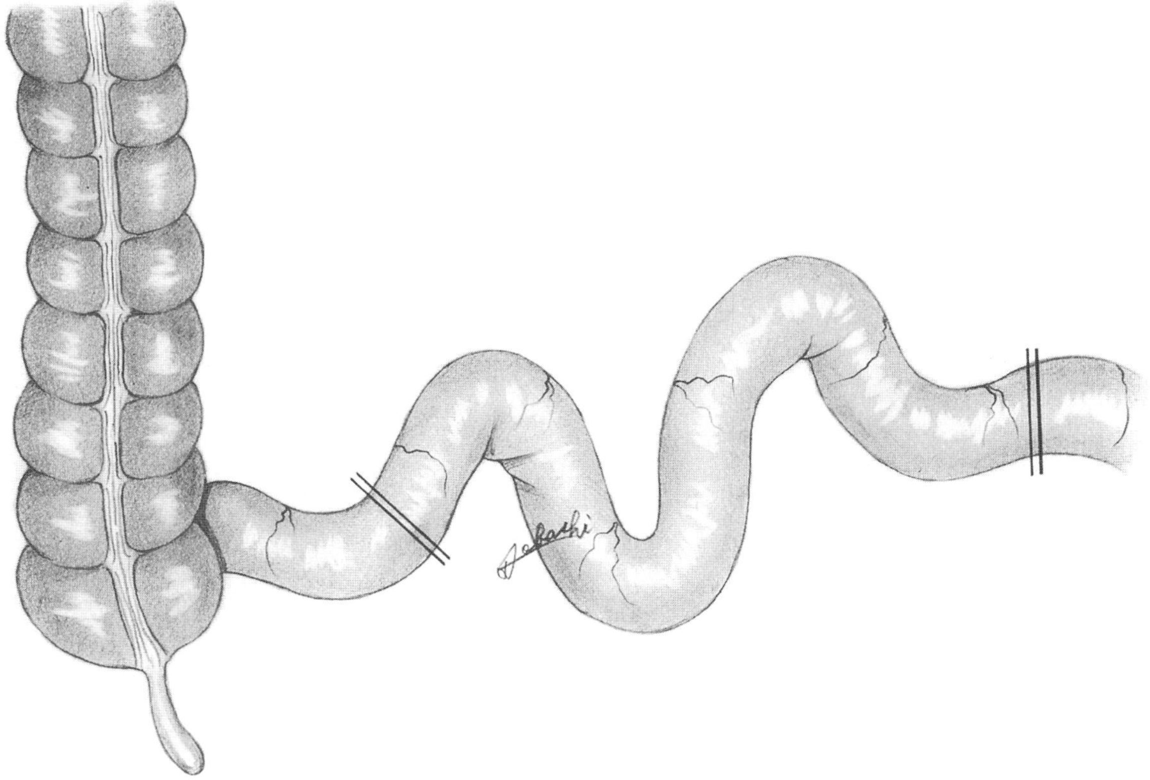

Mobilisation of the terminal ileal loop with multi-clip applier or Ultracision coagulating shears to obtain a 30 cm loop that will later be transected with a linear cutter standard. Subsequently, examination of staple line for haemostasis and proper staple closure.

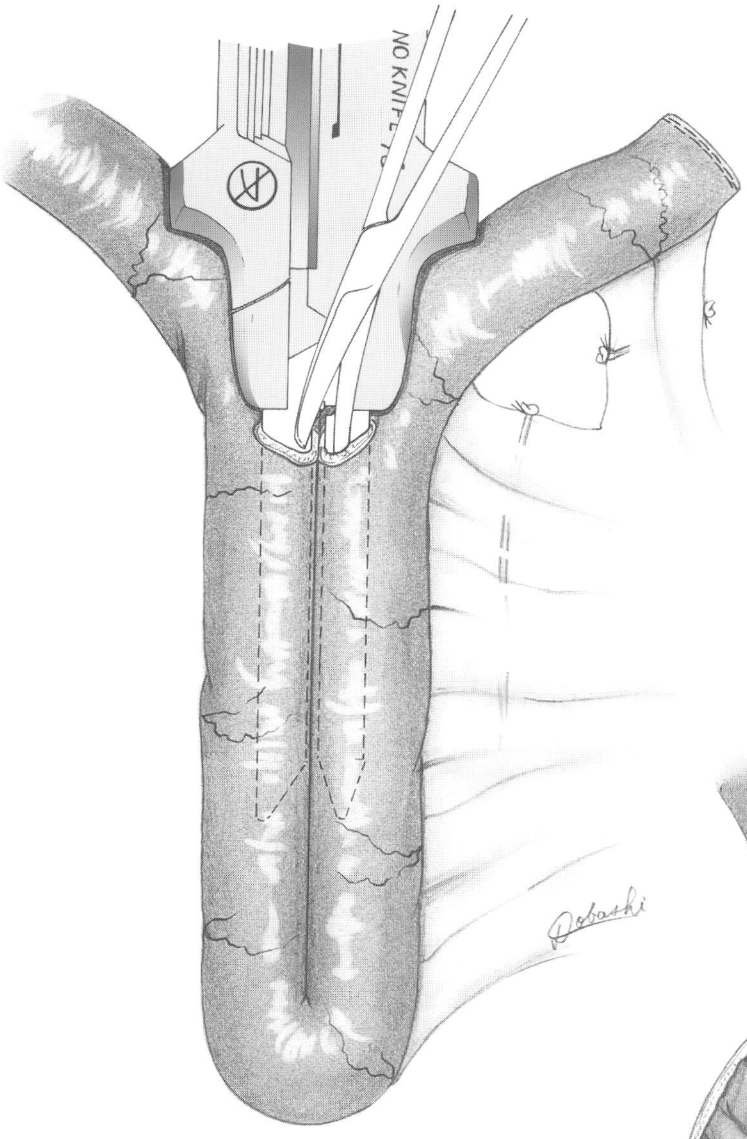

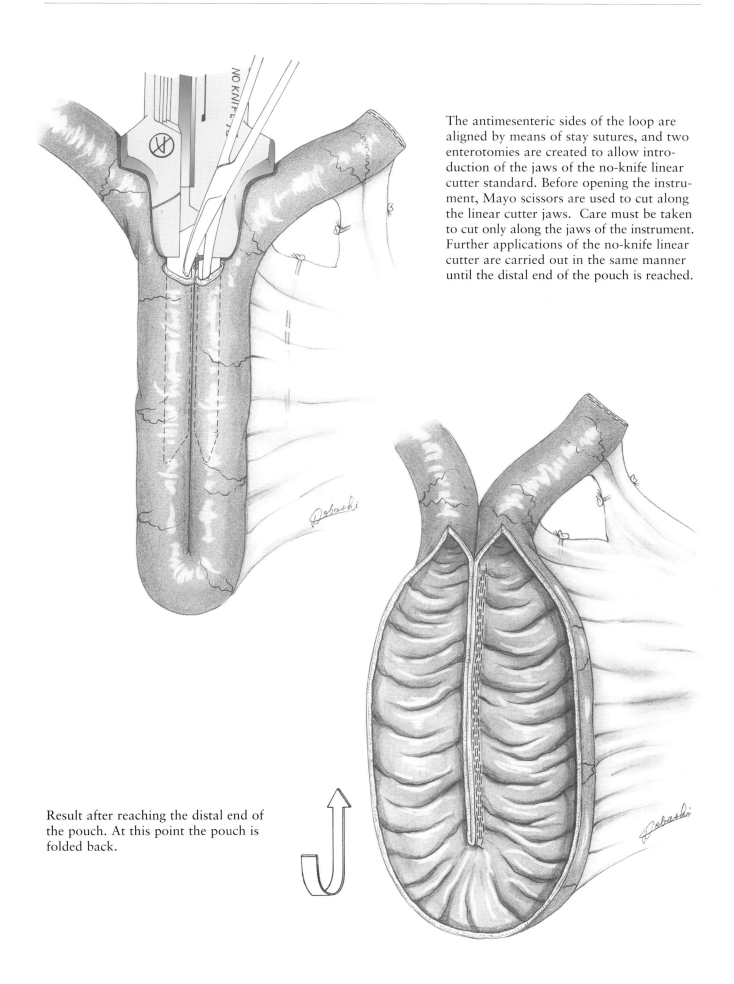

The antimesenteric sides of the loop are aligned by means of stay sutures, and two enterotomies are created to allow introduction of the jaws of the no-knife linear cutter standard. Before opening the instrument, Mayo scissors are used to cut along the linear cutter jaws. Care must be taken to cut only along the jaws of the instrument. Further applications of the no-knife linear cutter are carried out in the same manner until the distal end of the pouch is reached.

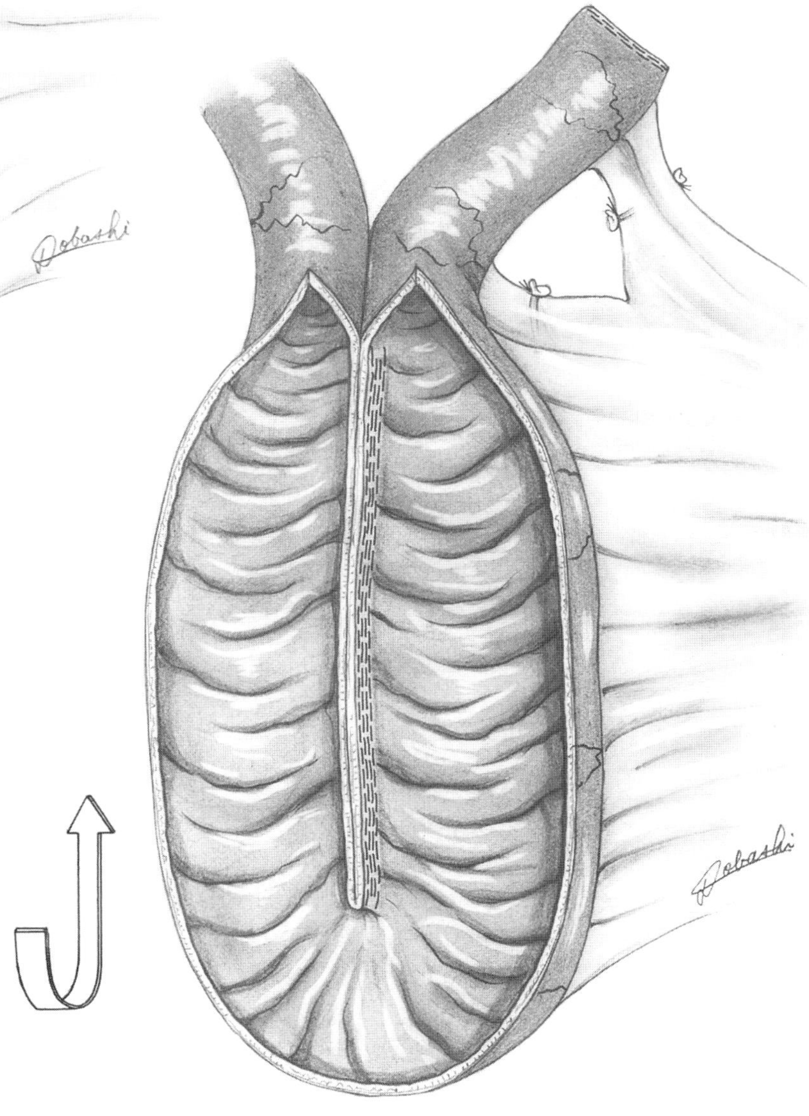

Result after reaching the distal end of the pouch. At this point the pouch is folded back.

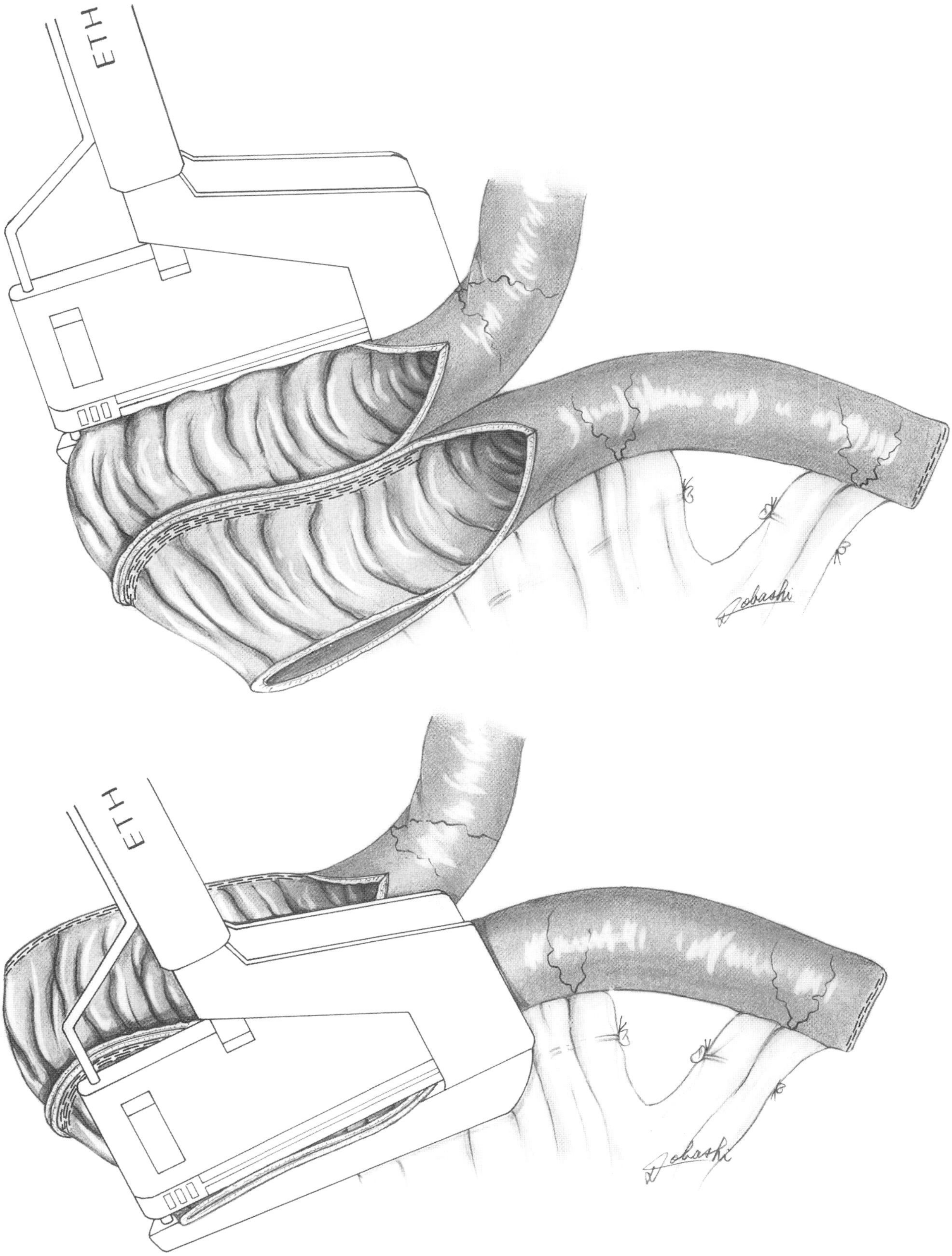

The external edges of the pouch are stapled with a linear stapler standard.

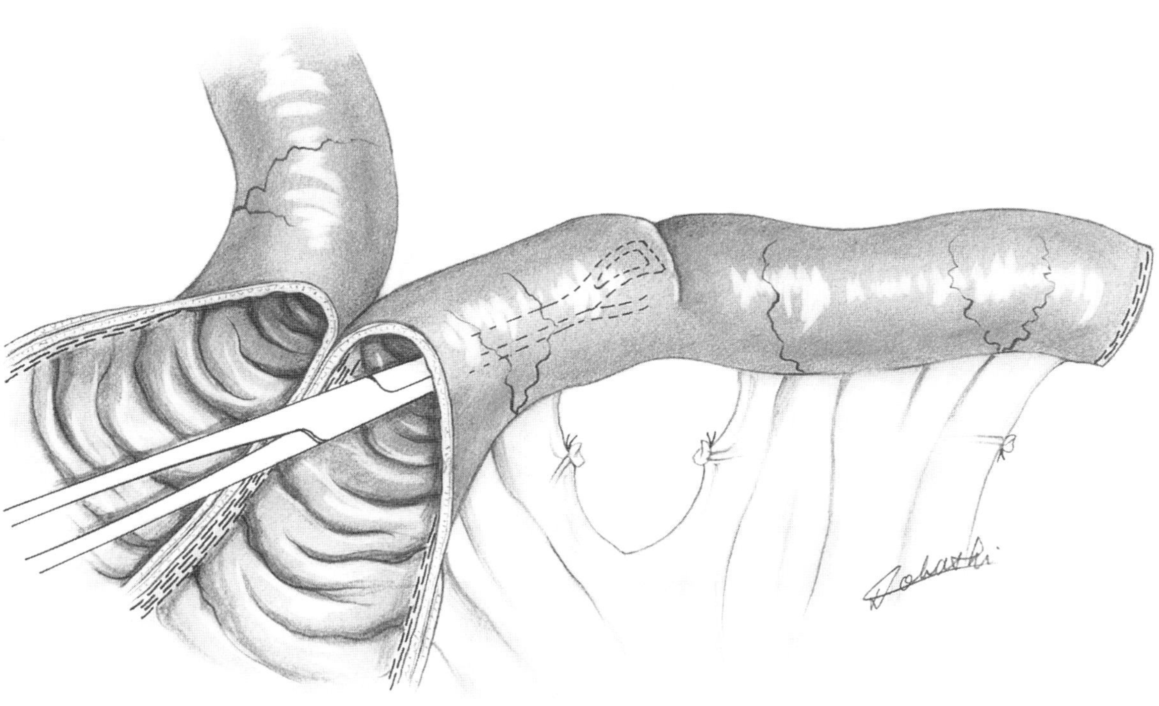

Initial invagination of the ileum to create a nipple valve with the help of atraumatic clamps. Note that a mesenteric window of approximately 10 cm was previously created with Ultracision coagulating shears, but not using any clips in this area.

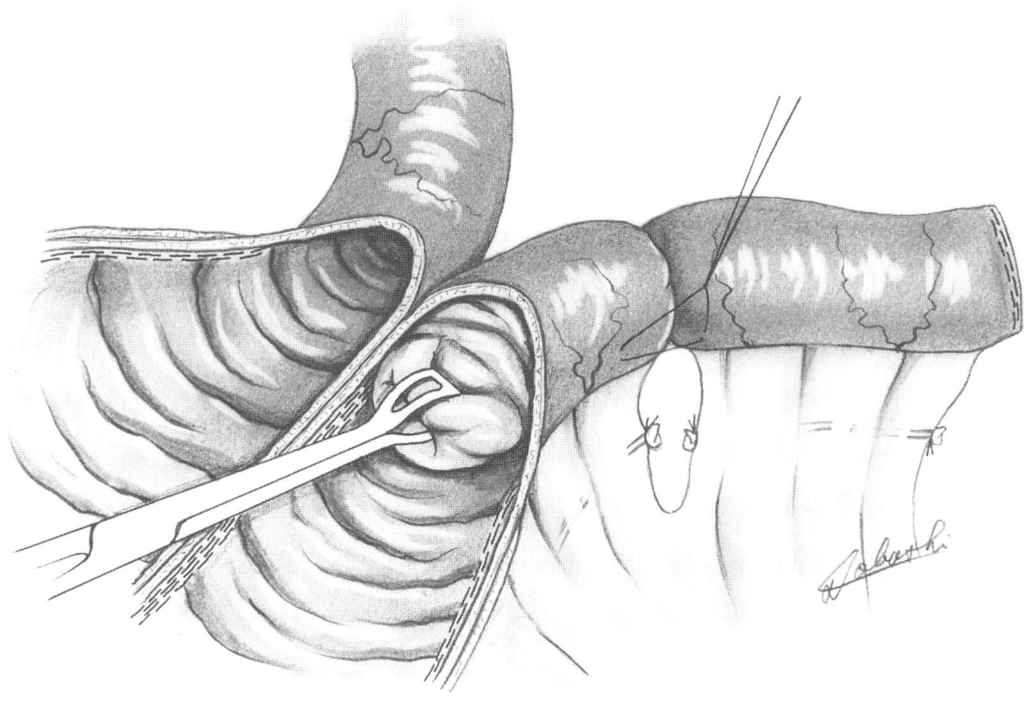

After completion of the invagination manoeuvre (5 cm invagination), stay sutures are applied to aid fixation.

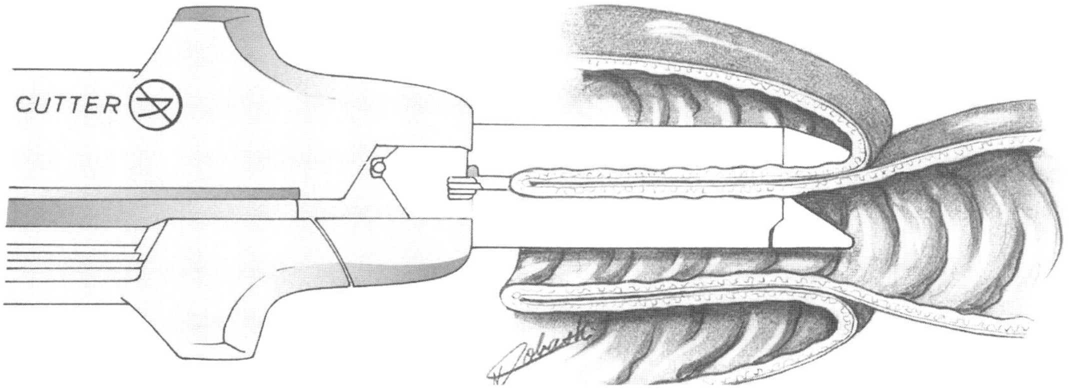

The valve is completed by fixation of the invagination, firing a no-knife linear cutter standard four times.

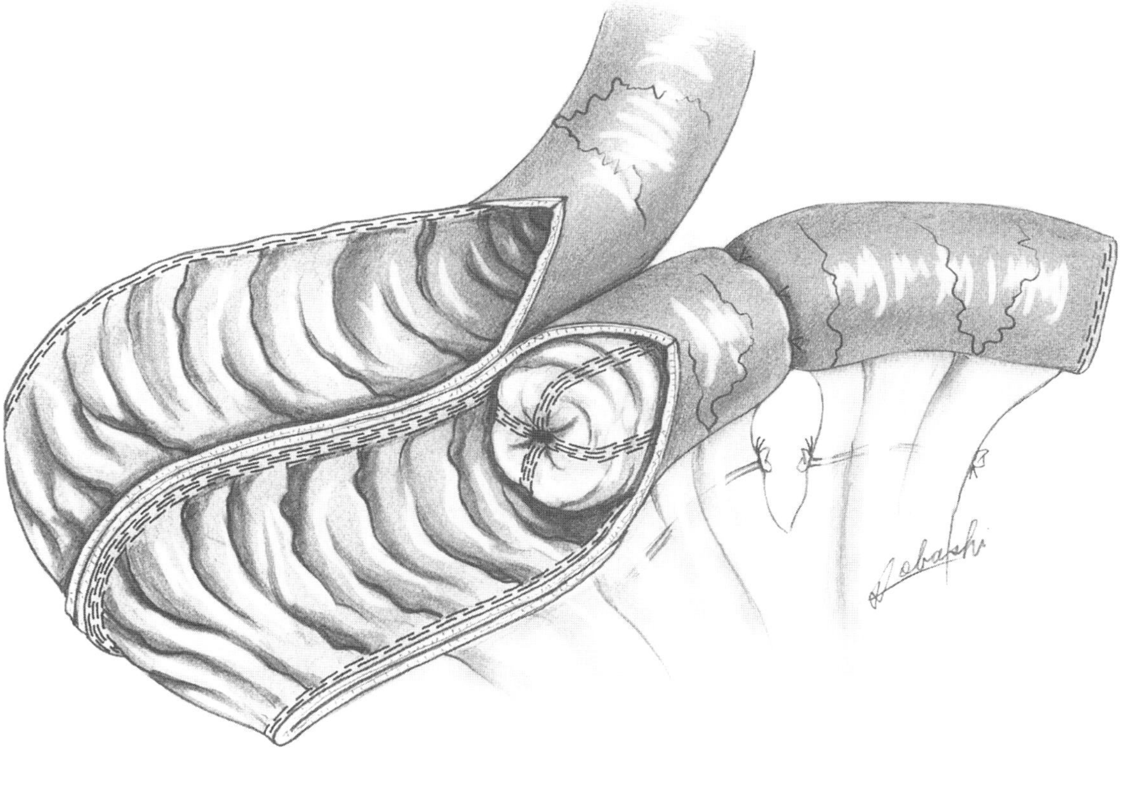

Examination of all staple lines for haemostasis and proper staple closure is critical for the success of this procedure.

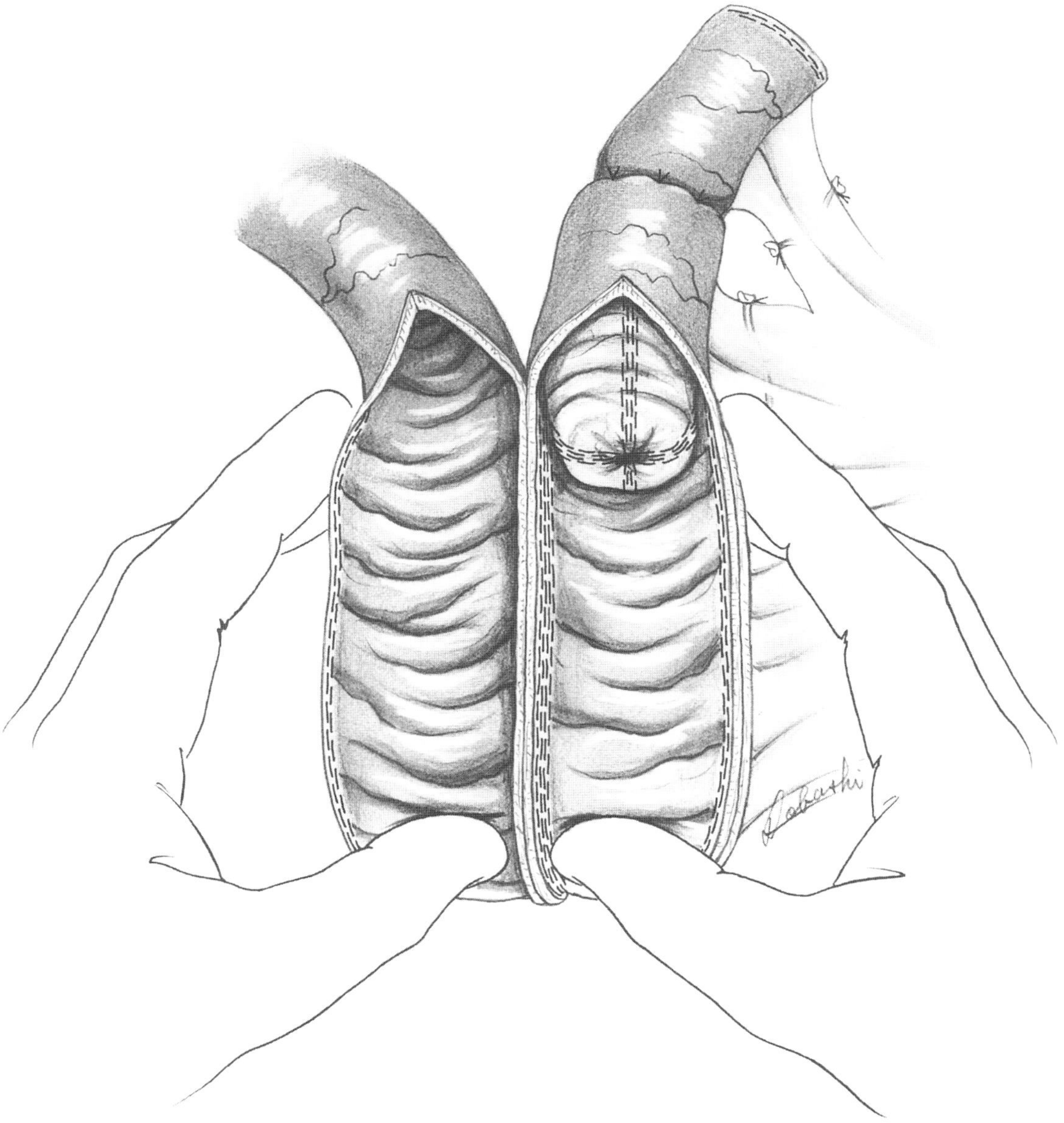

At this point the pouch is turned right side out.

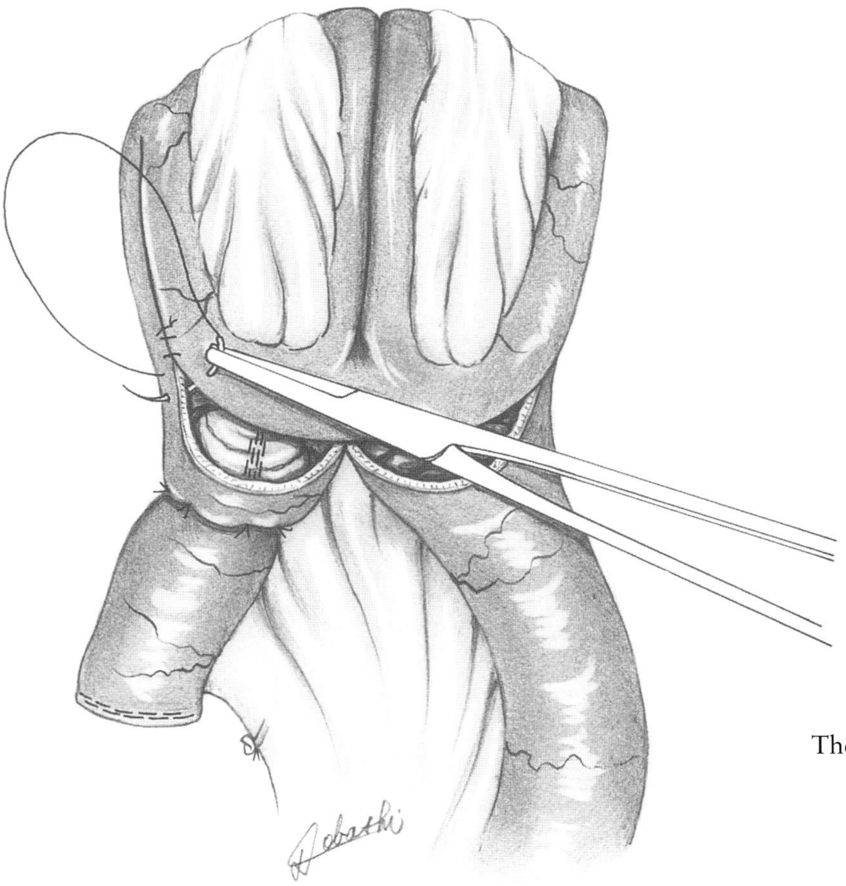

The pouch is closed with manual sutures.

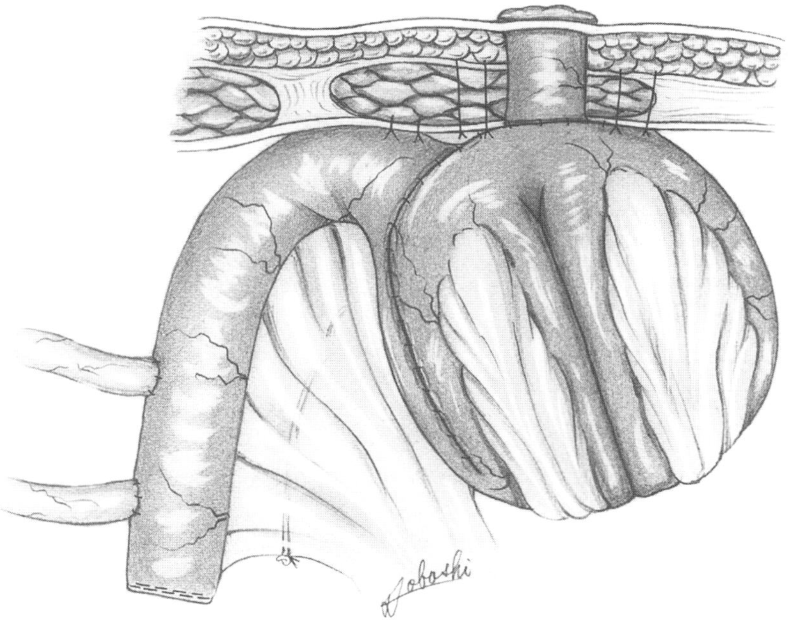

The ureters are anastomosed into the proximal iliac loop and the remaining ileal stump with the valve is exteriorised through the abdominal wall.

Indiana Pouch

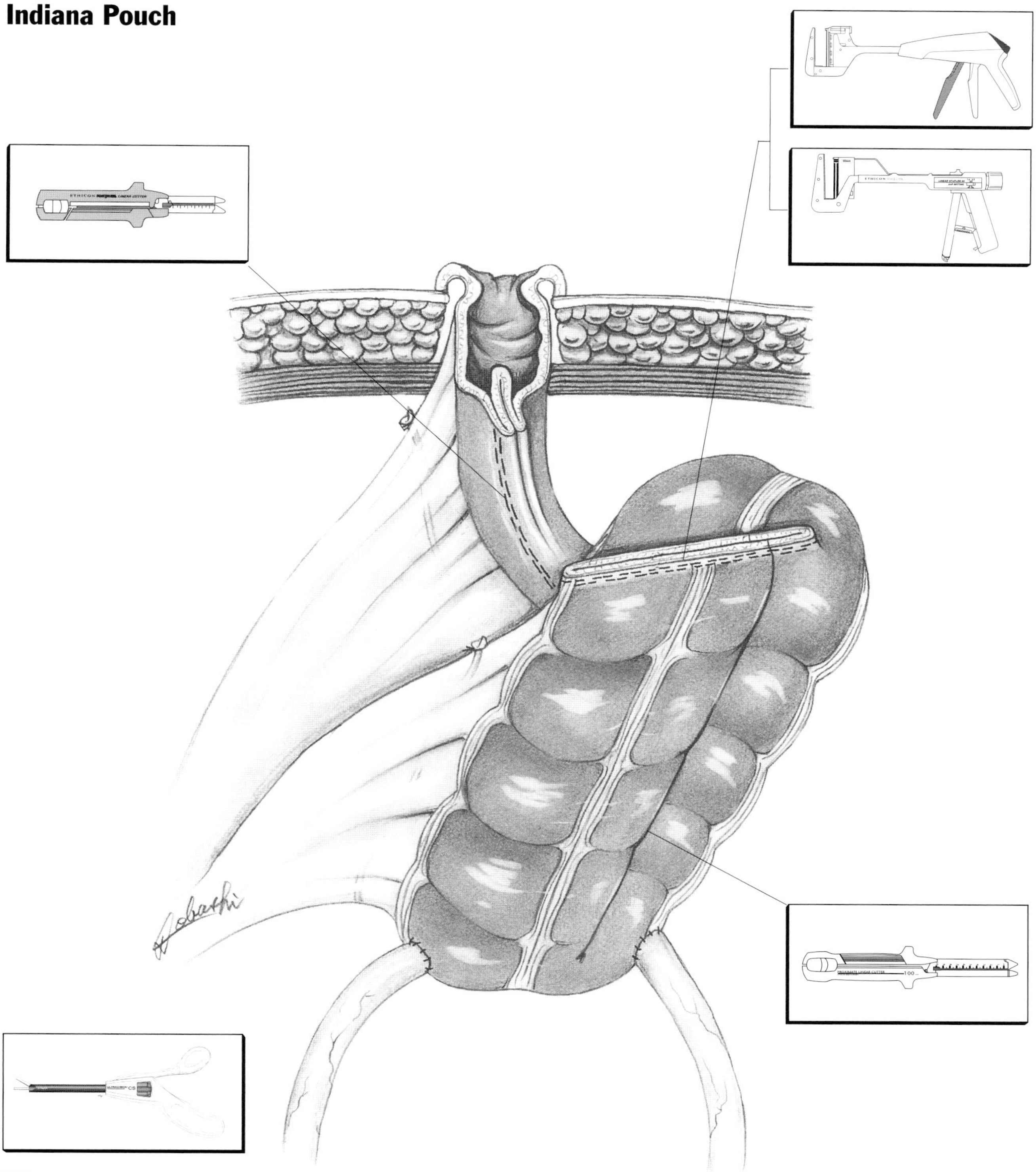

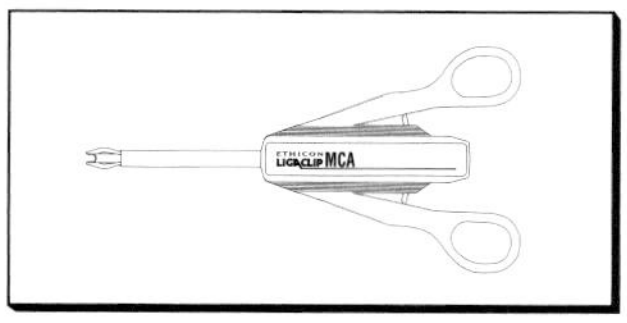

The Indiana Pouch was originally developed in paediatric urology and was later successfully applied in adults. This technique is relatively easy. The reservoir, the anti-reflux-mechanism, and the continence mechanism are reliable. The pouch will remain intact for a longer period if large intestine is used. When modifying the Indiana Pouch, the appendix may be used as a urinary drainage to the umbilicus. The so-called Mainz Pouch I is a variant of the Indiana Pouch principle.

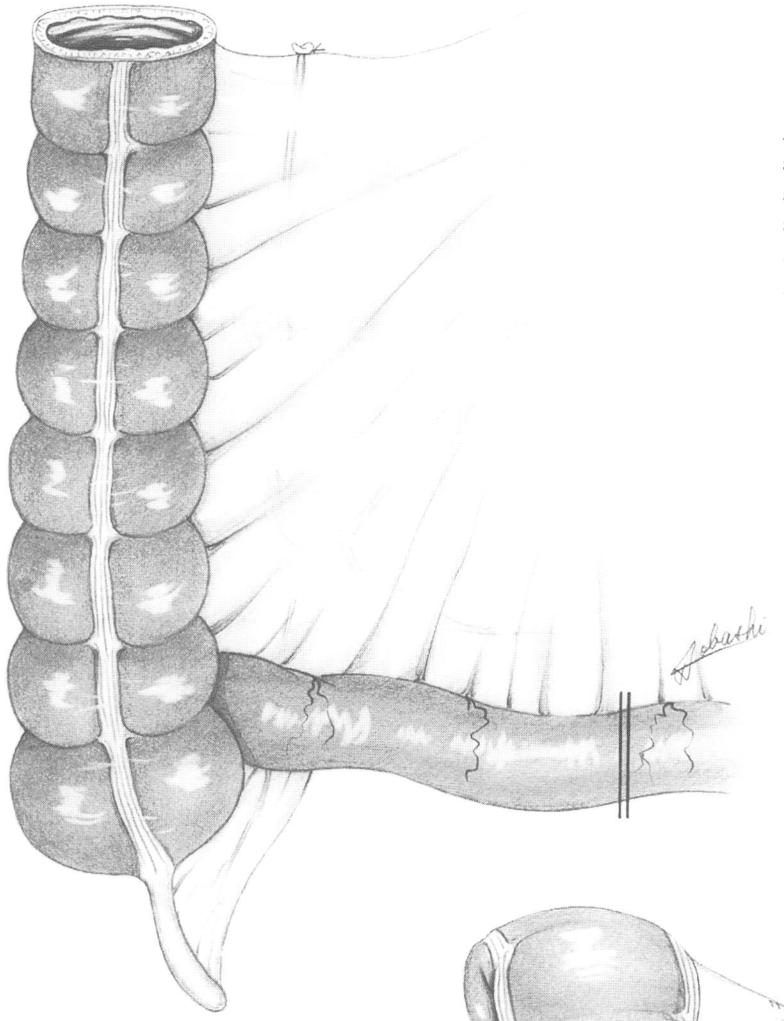

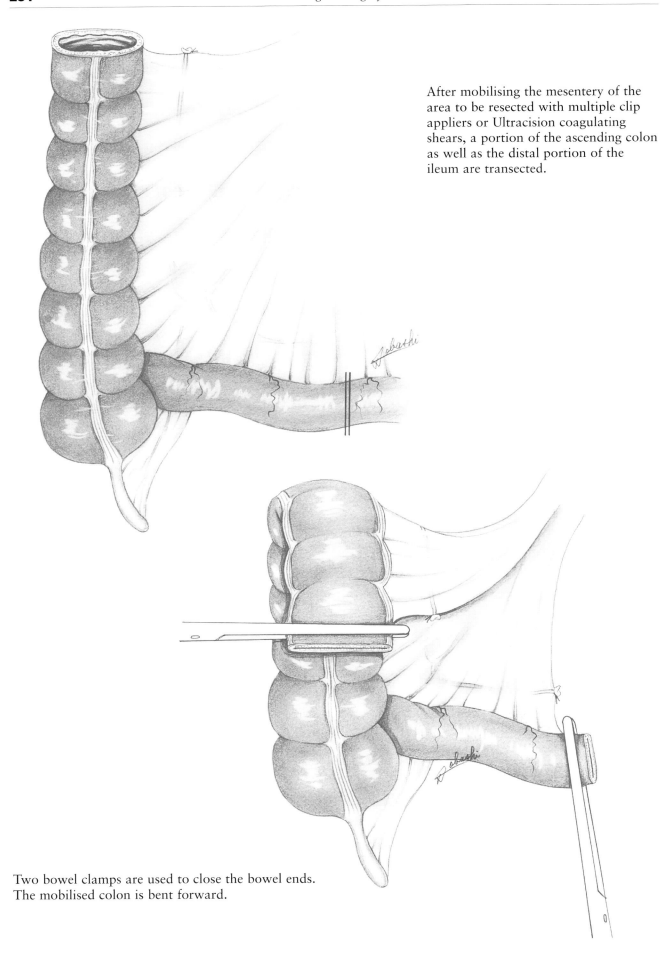

After mobilising the mesentery of the area to be resected with multiple clip appliers or Ultracision coagulating shears, a portion of the ascending colon as well as the distal portion of the ileum are transected.

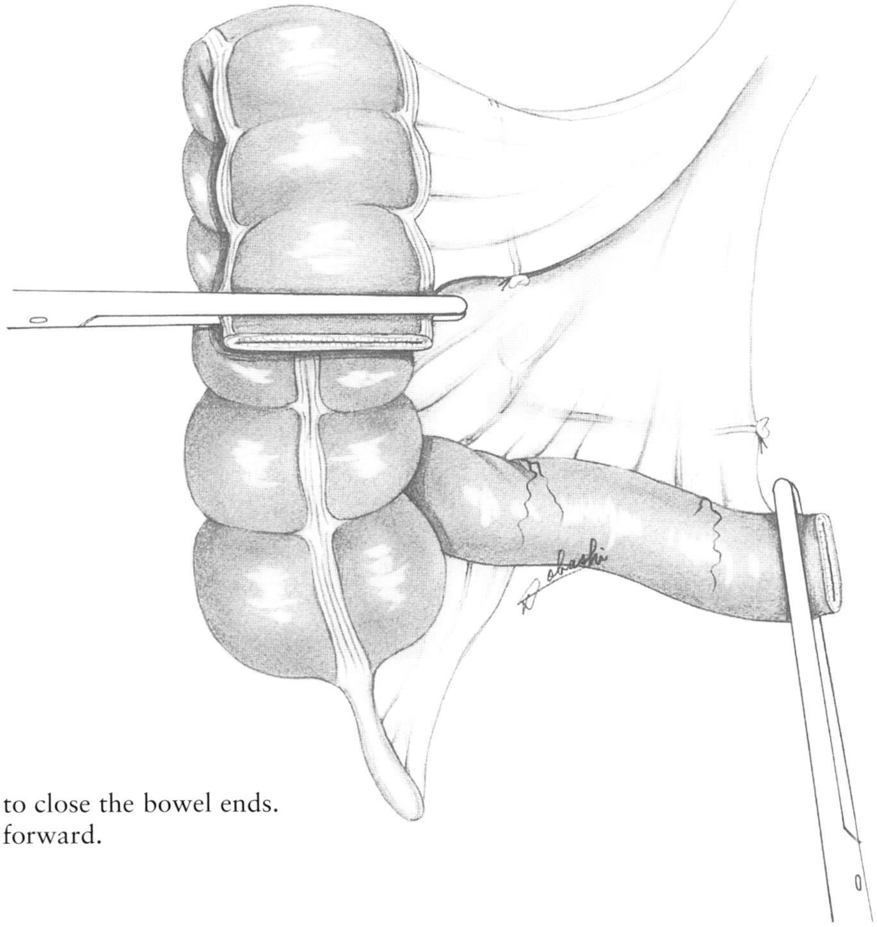

Two bowel clamps are used to close the bowel ends. The mobilised colon is bent forward.

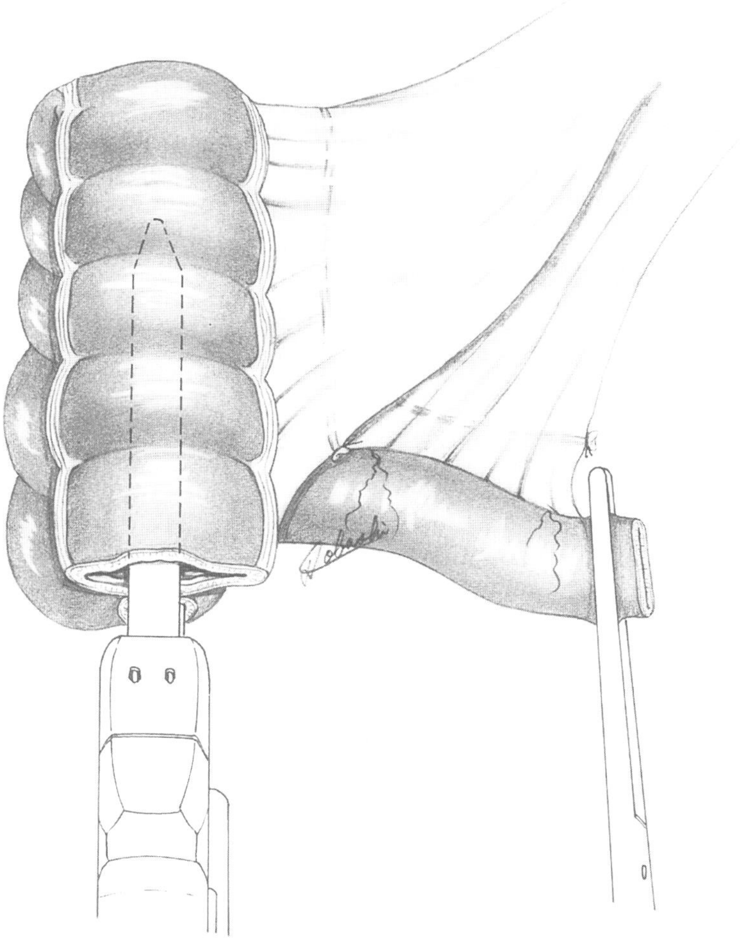

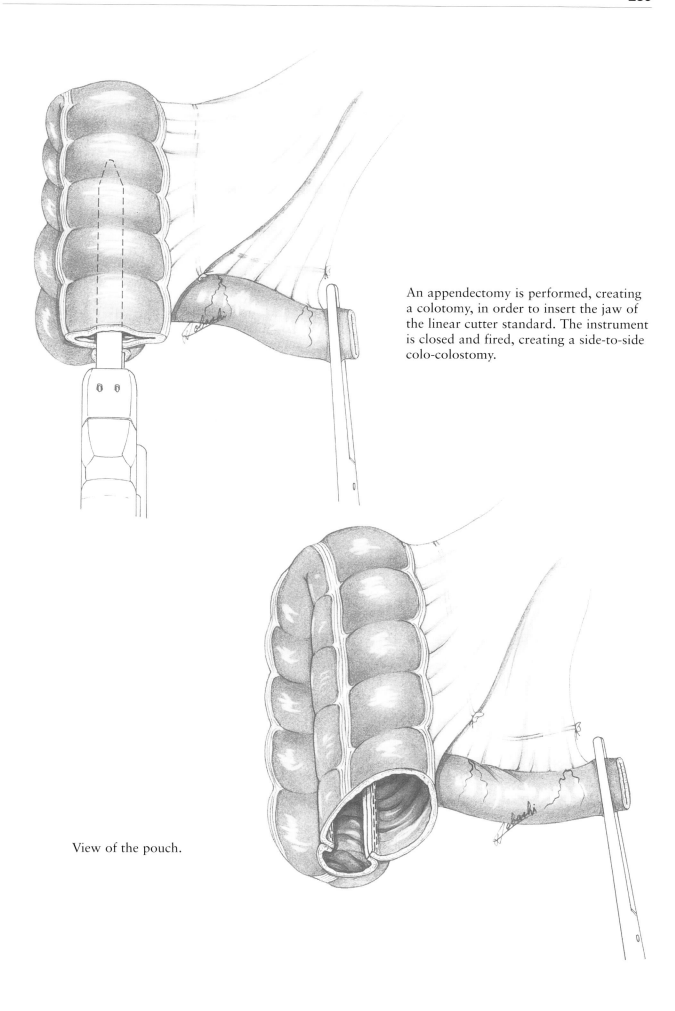

An appendectomy is performed, creating a colotomy, in order to insert the jaw of the linear cutter standard. The instrument is closed and fired, creating a side-to-side colo-colostomy.

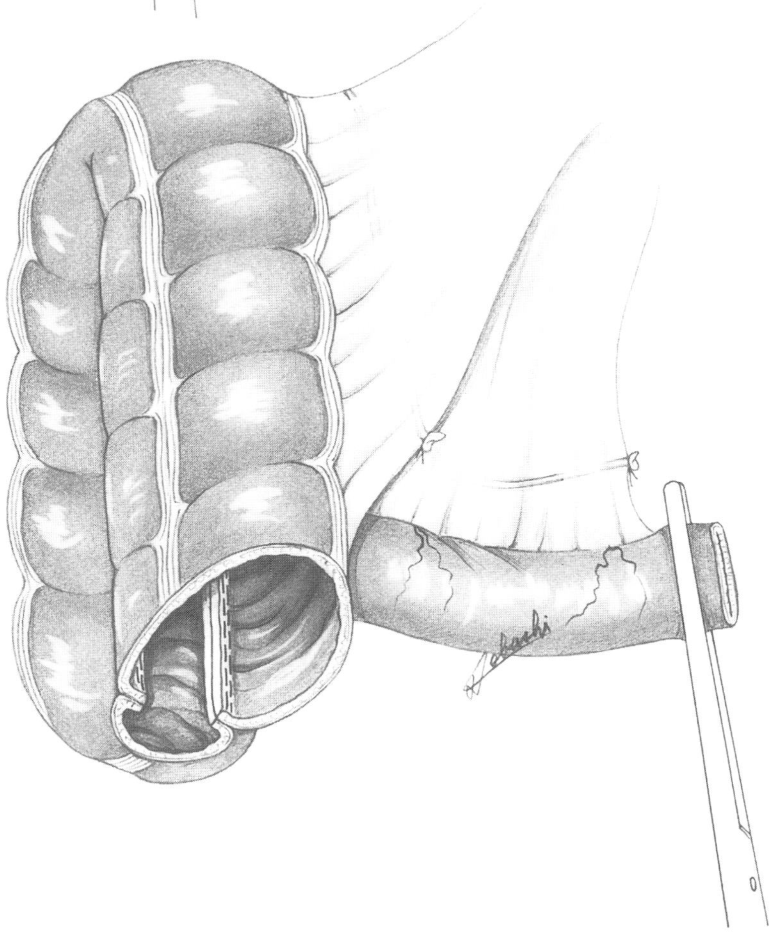

View of the pouch.

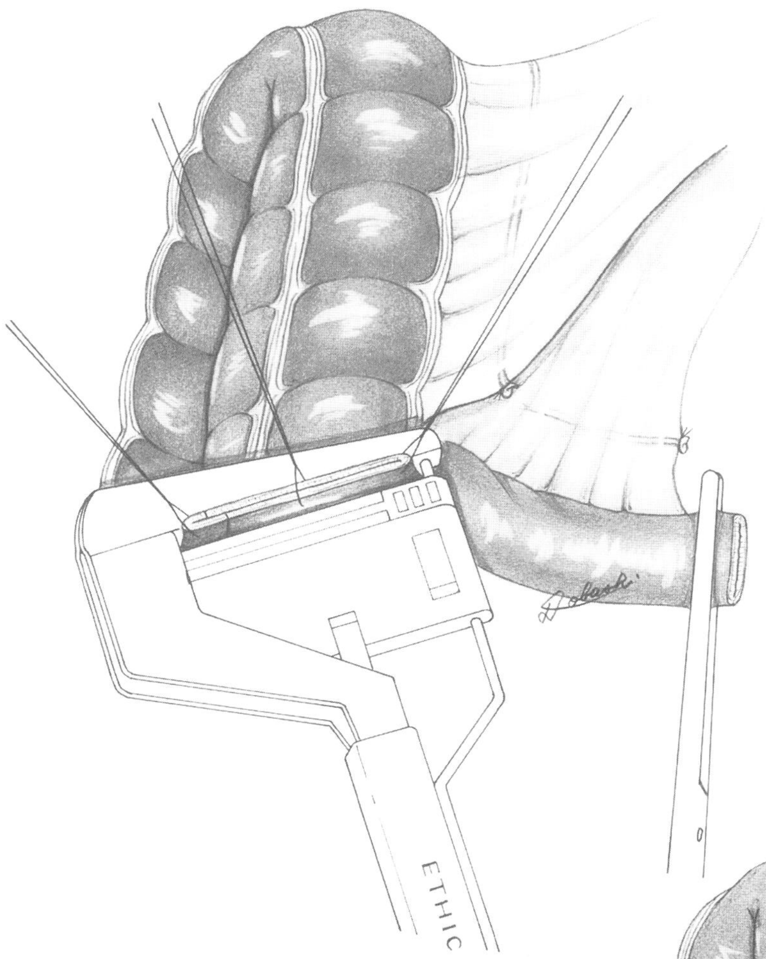

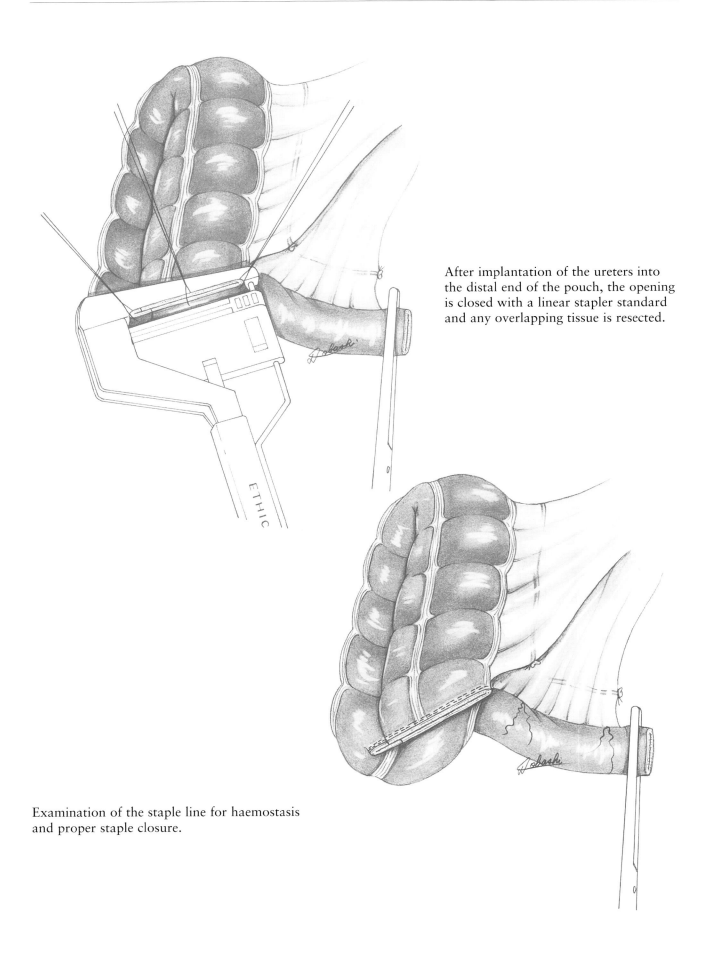

After implantation of the ureters into the distal end of the pouch, the opening is closed with a linear stapler standard and any overlapping tissue is resected.

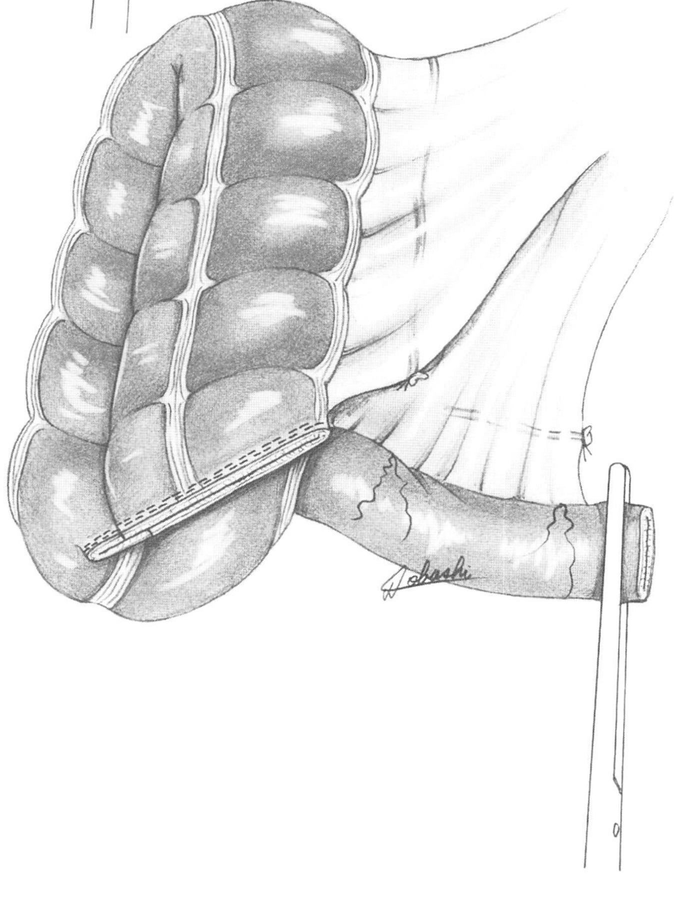

Examination of the staple line for haemostasis and proper staple closure.

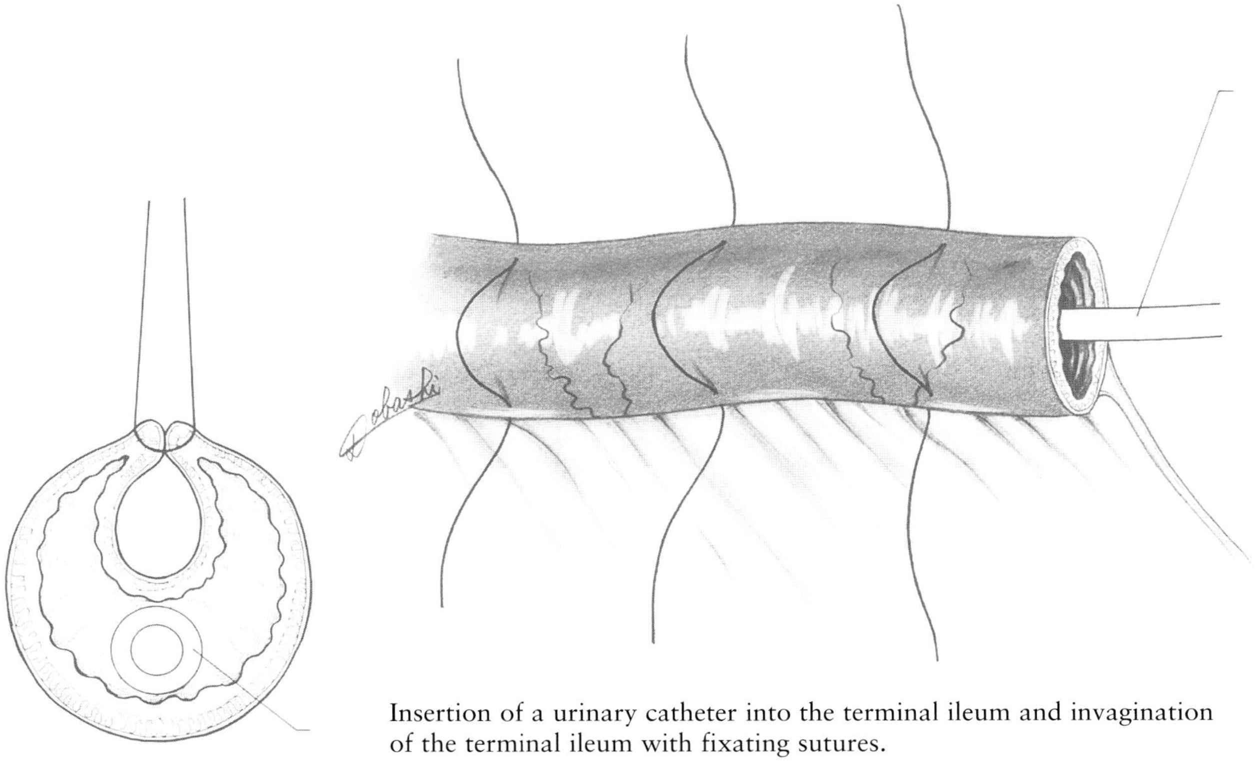

Insertion of a urinary catheter into the terminal ileum and invagination of the terminal ileum with fixating sutures.

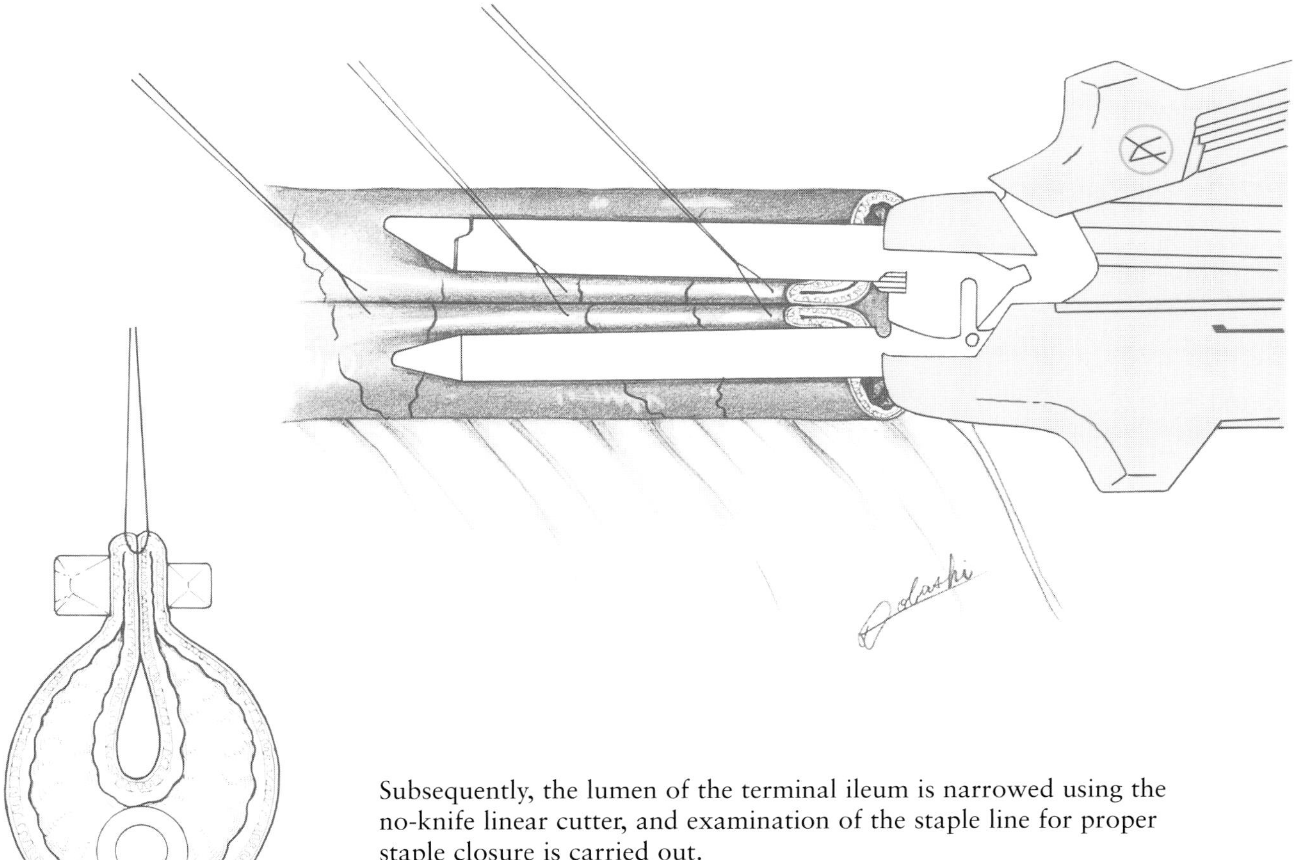

Subsequently, the lumen of the terminal ileum is narrowed using the no-knife linear cutter, and examination of the staple line for proper staple closure is carried out.

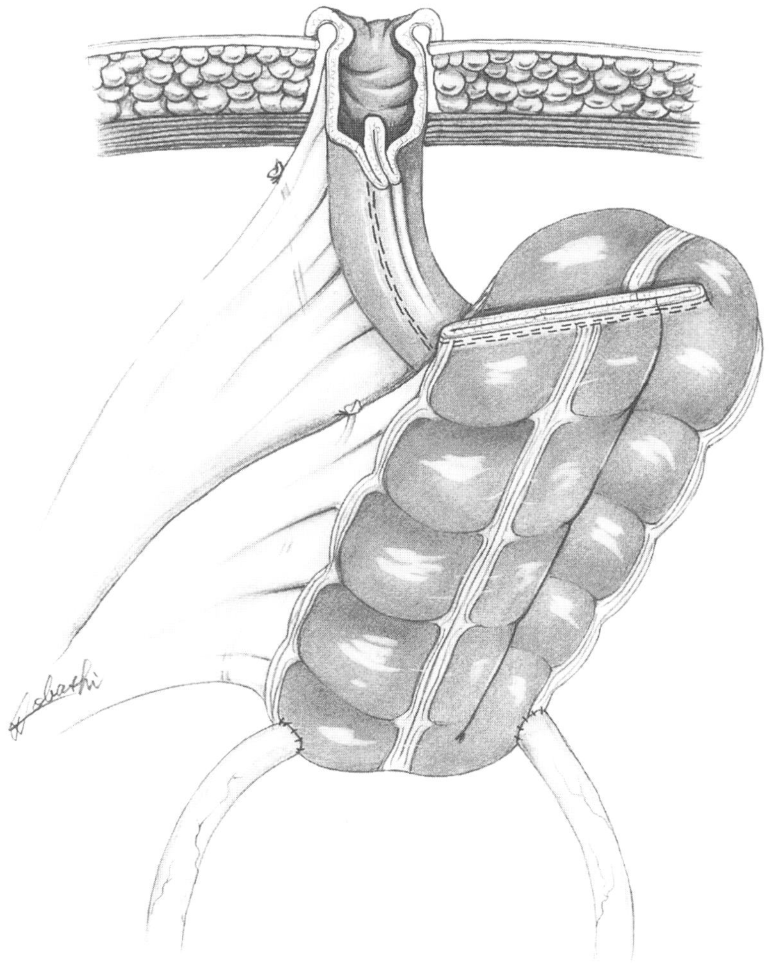

The procedure is completed by exteriorising the terminal ileum into the abdominal wall (ileostomy). The Bauhin valve renders the pouch leak-proof.

Mainz-Pouch I

A modification of the Indiana Pouch is the Mainz Pouch I. In contrast to the Indiana Pouch, where continence is achieved by the ileocaecal valve in conjunction with a constriction of the efferent ileac loop, continence in the Mainz Pouch I is obtained by invagination of the terminal ileum combined with the corresponding creation of a nipple. After completion of the nipple, it is led through the ileocaecal valve and fixed at the caecal portion.

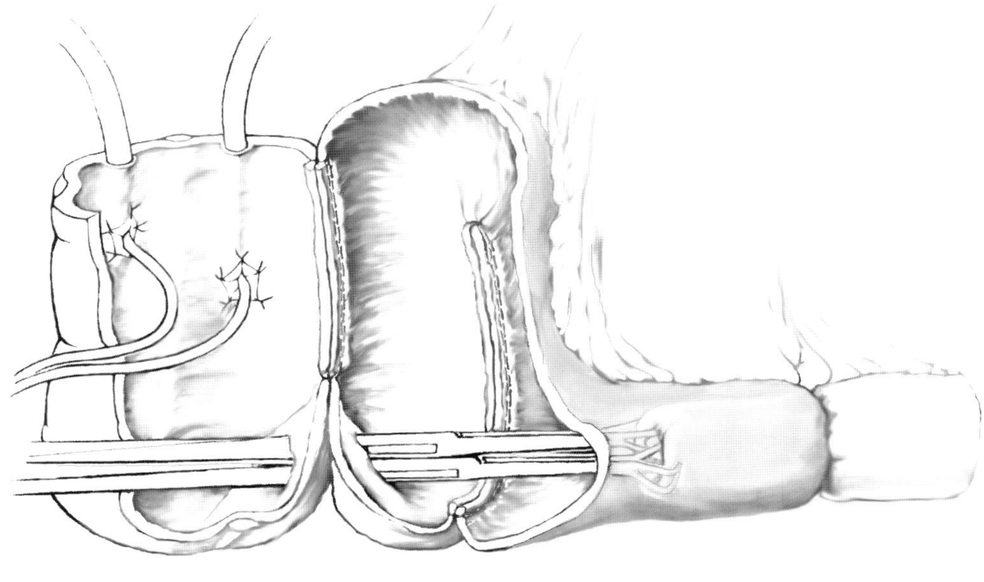

After creating a pouch with part of the proximal ascending colon and the terminal ileum, a mesenteric window of approximately 10 cm in size is made at the distal ileum using Ultracision coagulating shears. Two Allis clamps are inserted through the ileocaecal opening into the lumen of the remaining ileum, up to the middle of the mesenteric window, in order to perform an invagination.

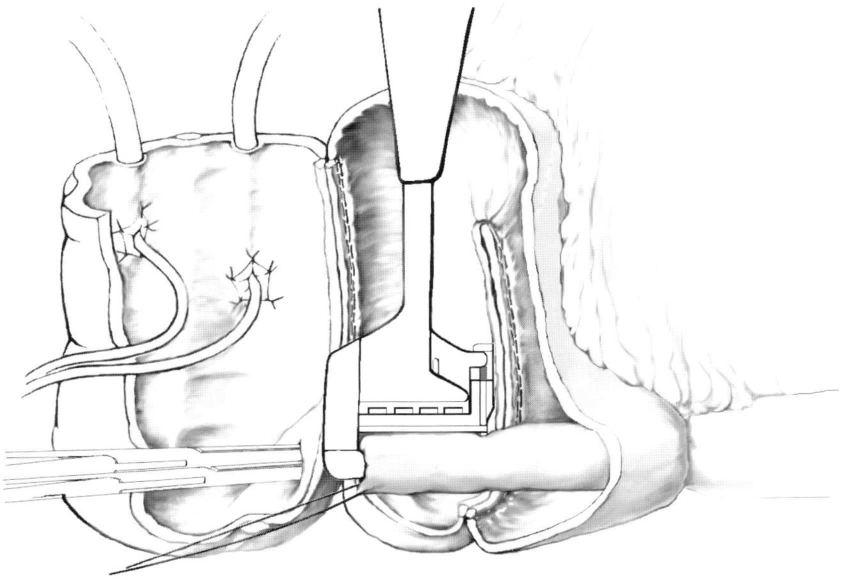

The invagination is fixed at 3 and 9 o'clock respectively, with two staple lines. In order to avoid formation of calculi at the top of the nipple, the last three staples are removed from the cartridge of the linear stapler thick.

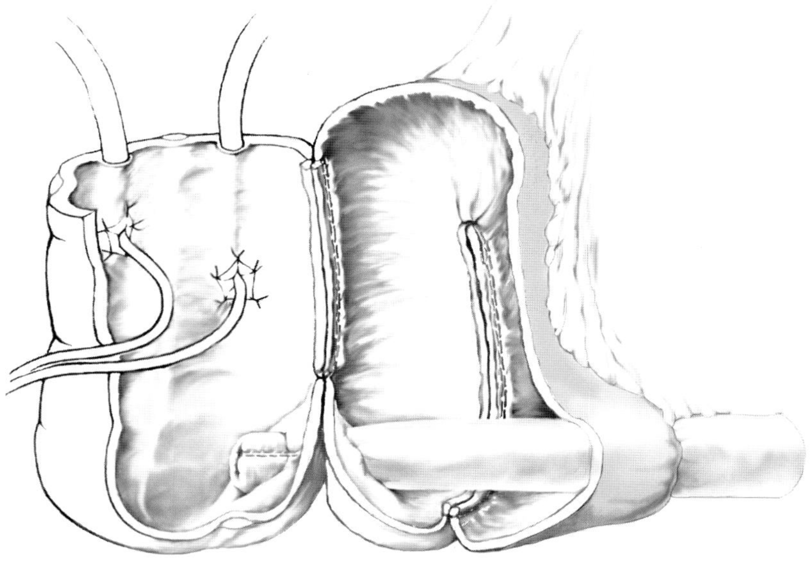

After the nipple has been pulled through the ileocaecal valve, it is stapled onto the anterior aspect for fixation.

III

References

Akiyama H, Tsurumaru M, Kawamura T, Ono Y (1981) Principles of surgical treatment for carcinoma of the oesophagus. Ann Surg 194: 438–446

Amaral JF (1993) Laparoscopic application of an ultrasonic activated scalpel. Gastrointest Endosc Clin North Am 3: 381

Amaral JF (1994) Ultrasonic energy in laparoscopic surgery. Surgical Technology International III: 155

Amaral JF (1995) Depth of thermal injury: ultrasonically activated scalpel vs electrosurgery: Surg Endosc 9: 226

Amaral JF (1995) Laparoscopic cholecystectomy in 200 consecutive patients using an ultrasonically activated scalpel. Surg Laparosc Endosc 5: 255

Ata AA, Bellemore TJ, Meisel JA, Arambulo SM (1993) Distal thermal injury from monopolar electrosurgery. Surg Laparosc Endosc 3: 323

Bazan (1989) La chirurgia del tenue e del colon. Le suturatrici meccaniche in chirurgia. Piccin, Padova

Berrisford RG, Page RD, Donnely RJ (1996) Stapler design and strictures at the oesophagogastric anastomosis. J Thorac Cardiovasc Surg 111: 142–146

Berry SM, Ose KJ, Bell RH, Fink AS (1994) Thermal injury of the posterior duodenum during laparoscopic cholecystectomy. Surg Endosc 8: 197

Bell RCW (1996) Can doing more be faster? An ultrasonic scalpel and speed of fundoplication. Surg Endosc 10: 223

Boltri F (1995) Chirurgia dellostomaco con suturatrici meccaniche. Edizioni Minerva Medica, Bologna

Chassin JL (1994) Operative strategy in general surgery, 2nd ed. Springer, New York Heidelberg

Collard JM, Tinton N, Malaise J, Romagnolis R, Otte JB, Kestens PJ (1995) Oesophageal replacement: Gastric tube or whole stomach? Ann Thorac Surg 60: 261–266

Deschamps C (1995) Use of colon and jejunum as possible oesophageal replacements. Chest Surg Clin North Am 5: 555–569

Dewar L, Gelfand G, Finley RJ, Evans K, Inculet R, Nelems B (1992) Factors affecting cervical anastomotic leak and stricture formation following oesophagogastrectomy and gastric tube interposition. Am J Surg 163: 484–489

Fedele E, Del Prete M, Anselmo A (1996) Stapler. Perché quando come. Appunti sull'uso delle suturatrici meccaniche. Links, Rome

Feil W (1997) Schilddrüsenresektion mit UltraCision. Acta Chir Austr Suppl 130: 23

Feil W (1997) Sphinktererhaltende Rektumresektionen mit UltraCision. Acta Chir Austr Suppl 130: 80

Feil W (1997) UltraCision – Erste Erfahrungen in der offenen Chirurgie. Acta Chir Austr Suppl 130: 128

Feil W (1997) UltraCision – Erste Erfahrungen in der laparoskopischen Chirurgie. Acta Chir Austr Suppl 130: 130

Fok M, Wong J (1995) Cancer of the oesophagus and gastric cardia. Standard oesophagectomy and anastomotic technique. Ann Chir Gynaecol. 84: 179–183

Fowler DL (1996) Laparoscopic gastrectomy: five cases. Surg Laparosc Endosc 6: 98

Gabrelli F, Chiarelli M, Guttadauro A, Puana I, Faini G, Serbelloni M (1998) Considerazioni

preliminari sulla muco-emorroidectomia con "stapler". UCP News Suppl 2: 6–7
Geis WP, Kim HC, McAffee PC, Kang JG, Brennan EJ (1996) Synergistic benefits of combined technologies in complex, minimally invasive surgical procedures. Surg Endosc 10: 1025
Gordon PH, Nivatvongs S (1999) Principles and practice of surgery for the colon, rectum, and anus. Quality Medical Publishing, St Louis
Gritsman JJ (1966) Mechanical suture by Soviet apparatus in gastric resection: use in 4,000 operations. Surgery 59: 663
Hampel N, Bodner DR, Persky L (1986) Ileal and jejunal conduit urinary diversion. Urol Clin North Am 13: 207
Heberer G, Schildberg FW, Sunder-Plassmann L, Vogt-Moykopf I (1991) Lunge und Mediastinum, 2. Aufl. Springer, Berlin Heidelberg New York
Iroatulam AJN, Banducci T, Vernillo R, Lorenzi M (1998) Transanal excision of mucosal rectal prolapse using a circular stapler. Colorectal Disease – Fort Lauderdale, Florida Pre-course Session II February 18, 1998
Kock NG (1969) Intra-abdominal reservoir in patients with permanent ileostomy: Preliminary observations on a procedure resulting in fecal continence in five ileostomy patients. Arch Surg 99: 223
Kock NF, et al (1982) Urinary diversion via a continent ileal reservoir: clinical result in 12 patients. J Urol 128: 469
Kohlstadt CM, Weber J, Prohm P (1999) Die Stapler-Hämorrhoidektomie. Eine neue Alternative zu den konventionellen Methoden. Zentralbl Chir 124: 238–243
Krasna MJ (1995) Left transthoracic oesophagectomy. Chest Surg Clin North Am 5: 543–554
Kremer K, Lierse W, Platzer W, Schreiber HW, Weller S (1989–1999) Chirurgische Operationslehre in 10 Bänden. Thieme, Stuttgart New York
Kremer K, Lierse W, Platzer W, Schreiber HW, Weller S (1995) Chirurgische Operationslehre, Bd. 7/2: Minimal-invasive Chirurgie. Thieme, Stuttgart New York
Lam TC, Fok M, Cheng SW, Wong J (1991) Anastomotic complications after oesophagectomy for cancer. A comparison of neck and chest anastomoses. World J Surg 15: 635–641
Lange V, Millot M, Dahsan H, Eilers D (1996) Das Ultraschallskalpell – erste Erfahrungen beim Einsatz in der laparoskopischen Chirurgie. Chirurg 67: 387
Laycock WS, Trus TL, Hunter JG (1996) New technology for the division of short gastric vessels during laparoscopic Nissen fundoplication. Surg Endosc 10: 71
Lippert H (1998) Praxis der Allgemein- und Viszeralchirurgie. Thieme, Stuttgart New York
Longo A (1998) Treatment of hemorrhoids disease by reduction of mucosa and hemorrhoidal prolapse with a circular suturing device: a new procedure. 6th World Congress of Endoscopic Surgery. Rome 1998, pp 777–784
Lozac'h P (1997) Intrathoracic anastomosis after oesophagectomy for cancer. J Chir Paris 134: 429–431
Lozac'h P, Topart P, Perramant M: Ivor Lewis procedure for epidermoid carcinoma of the oesophagus. A series of 264 patients.
MacKeigan JM, Cataldo PA (1993) Intestinal stomas. Principles, techniques, and management. Quality Medical Publishing, St Louis
Milito G, Cortese F, Casciani CU (1998) Surgical treatment of mucosal prolapse and haemorrhoids by stapler. 6th World Congress of Endoscopic Surgery. Rome 1998, pp 785–789
Moossa AR, Easter DW, Sonnenberg E, Casola G, Agostino H (1992) Laparoscopic injuries to the bilde duct. Ann Surg 215: 203
Orringer MB, Marshall B, Stirling MC (1993) Transhiatal oesophagectomy for benign and malignant disease. J Thorac Cardiovasc Surg 105: 265–276
Palazzini G (1988) Staple sutures in digestive tract surgery. Int Surg
Palazzini G, Tarroni D (1995) Errori di uomini e di macchine nell'uso delle suturatrici meccaniche in chirurgia colorettale. Colanna monografica S.I.C. 261–273
Palazzini G, Tarroni D, Monti M, Lippolis G, Vergine M, De Antoni E (1990) Le complianze delle suturatrici meccaniche nella chirurgia coloretalle: quando e perché. Atti 92° congresso SIC Roma 21–25/10/1990 volume 2: 5–26
Ravitch M, Febiger L (1991) Current practice of Surgical Stapling. Philadelphia
Ravitch MM, et al (1959) Experimental an clinical use of Soviet bronchus stapling instruments. Surgery 46: 97
Ravitch MM, Steichen FM (1972) Techniques od staple suturing in the gastrointestinal tract. Ann Surg 175: 815
Rehner M, Oestern H-J (1996) Chirurgische Facharztweiterbildung, Bd 1. Thieme, Stuttgart New York

Rothenberg SS (1996) Laparoscopic splenectomy using the harmonic scalpel. J Laparoendosc Surg 6: S61

Steichen FM, Ravitch MM (1973) Mechanical sutures in surgery. Br J Surg 70: 191

Steichen FM, Ravitch MM (1984) Stapling in surgery. Year Book Medical Publishing, Chicago

Sugarbaker DJ, Decamp MM (1993) Selecting the surgical approach to cancer of the oesophagus. Chest 103: 410S–414S

Swanstrom LL, Pennings JL (1995) Laparoscopic control of short gastric vessels. J Am Coll Surg 181: 347

Thüroff JW, Alken P, Hohenfellner R (1987) The Mainz pouch (mixed augmentation with ileum and zecum) for bladder augmentation and continent diversion. In: King LR et al (eds) Bladder reconstruction and continent urinary diversion. Year Book Medical Publishing, Chicago, p 252

Tilanus HW, Hop WC, Langenhorst BL, Van Lanschot JJ (1993) Oesophagectomy with or without thoracotomy. Is there any difference? J Thorac Cardiovasc Surg 105: 898–903

Traitment des hemorroides de stade 3 et 4 par la technique de Longo. Ann Chir Lyon (1999) 53: 245

Von Petz A (1924) Zur Technik der Magenresektion. Ein neuer Magen-Darmnähapparat. Zentralbl Chir 51, No. 5: 179–188

Important information on the use of the enclosed CD-ROM

The enclosed CD-ROM "Atlas of Surgical Stapling – Illustrations" contains all the images of the book. The objective is to make the illustrations available for your personal use. You can copy the images into other programmes or print them out via your connected printer.

Technical requirements

For smooth operation the following equipment is recommended: Personal Computer with 133MHz, 32 MB RAM, quadspeed CD-ROM, VGA (640 × 480 pixels) or better and 256 colours or better.

How to start the programme

Insert the CD into your CD-ROM drive.

→ Running the CD-ROM in Windows 95 (or higher):
If the Autostart option is activated, the programme starts automatically. If this is not the case, please proceed as follows:
Double-click the following icons successively: My computer, CD-ROM and finally Atlas32.

→ Running the CD-ROM in Windows 3.11:
Select File Manager, double click CD-ROM and finally double click Atlas16.

How to use the programme

When using this product for the first time, click the Help tab to display the help menu. Here you find the description of all buttons and tabs. The system is very intuitive and simple to use.

Selection of illustrations. There are two options:

→ Selection of illustrations via entry of page number: Enter the respective book page number in the field Enter page number. Press Enter and the image appears on the screen. If there are more than one figure on one book page, the figures come in alphabetical order.

→ Selection of illustrations via index pages. Click the Index tab. A selection of 20 successive images will be displayed. Select the desired image by positioning the cursor on it and click. If the desired image is not offered on the selected index page go to the next or previous index page by clicking the buttons previous / next page and repeat the procedure.

There is a Contents list tab that will display the full contents of the atlas with the respective page numbers. By entering the appropriate page number this will provide you direct access to the images of the chapter you are interested in.

Printing and exporting illustrations.
In order to print or export an image to another programme, use the Print image and Export image buttons respectively.

Clicking the button Publication data activates publication details.

To close the programme press the Quit button.